OXFORD HISTORY OF
THE CHRISTIAN CHURCH

Edited by

HENRY AND OWEN CHADWICK

THE
FRANKISH
CHURCH

J. M. WALLACE-HADRILL

CLARENDON PRESS · OXFORD
1983

Oxford University Press, Walton Street, Oxford OX2 6DP

London Glasgow New York Toronto
Delhi Bombay Calcutta Madras Karachi
Kuala Lumpur Singapore Hong Kong Tokyo
Nairobi Dar es Salaam Cape Town
Melbourne Auckland

and associated companies in
Beirut Berlin Ibadan Mexico City Nicosia

Oxford is a trade mark of Oxford University Press

Published in the United States
by Oxford University Press, New York

British Library Cataloguing in Publication Data
Wallace-Hadrill, J.M.
    The Frankish church. – (Oxford history of the
    Christian church)
    1. France – Church history – 6th century
    2. France – Church history – Middle Ages, 600–1500
    I. Title
    274.4'01   BR844
    ISBN 0-19-826906-4

Library of Congress Cataloging in Publication Data
Wallace-Hadrill, J. M. (John Michael)
    The Frankish Church.
    (Oxford history of the Christian Church)
    Bibliography: p.
    Includes index.
    1. Church history – Primitive and early church, ca.
30–600.   2. Church history – Middle Ages, 600–1500.
I. Title.   II. Series.
BR162.2.W27 1983   274.4'02   83-13051
ISBN 0-19-826906-4

Typeset by Oxford Verbatim Limited
Printed in Great Britain
at the University Press, Oxford

TO
MERTON COLLEGE
OXFORD

PREFACE

HE who seeks a measured account of the Frankish Church in all its manifestations – in a word, a textbook account – must continue to look elsewhere. I have attempted no more than a consideration of those aspects of it that have most interested me over the years. Like a Carolingian thinker I much admire, *scripsi quod sensi*. I must assume moreover that the reader has a general political background against which to place the history of the Frankish Church.

Obeying the recommendation of the general editors, I have kept footnotes to an absolute minimum; to no more in fact than references to essential sources. Secondary literature, of which I provide no more than a tiny fraction that could easily have been swollen to a volume on its own, is confined to the bibliographies.

The Merovingian chapters are based on some Birkbeck Lectures delivered in Trinity College, Cambridge in 1973–4, and I take this opportunity of thanking the Master and Fellows for the honour they did me as well as for their hospitality.

Some chapters were read in draft, and to their lasting benefit, by friends whom I warmly thank; namely, Professor Peter Ganz (chap. XV, vi) and Mr Karl Leyser (chap. XVI, iii). No less warmly do I thank my wife, my daughter-in-law and Anne Farquharson for typing the book and never once 'correcting' medieval into classical Latin, Richard Gerberding for help with my map, and Mrs H. Chadwick for help with proof-reading. In dedicating the book to Merton College, Oxford, where for many years I read and thought about the Frankish Church, I attempt to express what I owe to the College and what I feel about it.

CONTENTS

ABBREVIATIONS

AA	SS Acta Sanctorum (Antwerp, 1643–)
BEC	Bibliothèque de l'École des Chartes (Paris, 1839–)
CC	Corpus Christianorum, Series Latina (Turnhout)
CLA	Codices Latini Antiquiores, ed. E. A. Lowe (Oxford, 12 vols).
CSEL	Corpus Scriptorum Ecclesiasticorum Latinorum (Vienna, 1866–)
DA	Deutsches Archiv (Weimar, 1936–)
FMSt	Frühmittelalterliche Studien (Berlin, 1967–)
MGH	Monumenta Germaniae Historica
	AA Auctores Antiquissimi (Berlin, 1877–)
	Capit. Capitularia Regum Francorum, Legum Sectio ii (1883)
	Conc. Concilia, Legum Sectio iii (1893–)
	Epist. Epistolae Merovingici et Karolini Aevi (1892–)
	Form. Formulae Merovingici et Karolini Aevi, Leges Sectio v (1886)
	Leges Legum Sectio I (Hanover, 1888–)
	Poet. Poetae Latini Karolini Aevi (1881–)
	SRG Scriptores Rerum Germanicarum (Hanover, 1840–)
	SRM Scriptores Rerum Merovingicarum (Hanover, 1884–)
	SS Scriptores (Hanover-Leipzig, 1826–)
NA	Neues Archiv (Hanover, 1876–)
PL	Patrologiae cursus completus, series latina, ed. J. P. Migne (Paris, 1844–)
SC	Sources Chrétiennes (Paris, 1942–)
Spoleto	Settimane di Studio del Centro Italiano di Studi sull' Alto Medioevo (Spoleto, 1954–)

I

GALLO-ROMAN PRELUDE

THE Merovingian Church was a luxuriant overgrowth. Beneath it, and not far beneath it, lay the rich soil of Gallo-Roman religious experience. But while it would not be imprecise to speak of a Gallo-Roman Church, as distinguished broadly from, say, the African Church, the term is best seen as one of convenience. Had it been more clearly identifiable, more than one pope of the fifth century would have been a happier man. In the earlier fifth century we meet in Hilary, metropolitan of Arles, the type of the great Gallic bishop; a man eager to exercise authority outside his own ecclesiastical province, whether through councils or by word of mouth; a man ready to do battle with so formidable a pope as Leo I and to face resistance from other metropolitans. It is a type that looks forward to Hincmar of Reims and beyond. The reality, however, is Gallo-Roman churches; Christian communities, social nuclei embedded in the cities, aware of their separate histories and their separate identities. When they spoke, they betrayed a tendency to diffraction; and this long before the Germanic invasions. Some had ancient beginnings in the days of persecution – Lyon, for example, with St Irenaeus – while others, younger, owed more to a good start under imperial encouragement, like Arles and Trier. Some were very rich, others pathetically poor. In occasional councils they could be induced to speak regionally on a limited number of subjects of common interest. That they influenced each other is certain; but no more than they were influenced, as chance afforded, by Rome or Milan or by churches much further afield in Egypt, Syria, or Constantinople. We start with churches of the Gallo-Roman cities, each under its bishop and all grouped in provinces that bore close, if not invariably close, relationship to the structure of late-imperial administration.

Churches, then, rather than a Church, all confronted in the fourth and fifth centuries with a common problem; how, namely, to come to terms with the fact of absence of persecution, whether as reality or threat. Constantine and his successors had not made all men Christians; there were plenty of good pagans in fourth-century Gaul, as elsewhere, and not a few in the fifth. But though it was now safe and right to be a Christian, some difficult questions still required an agreed answer: what was a Christian community, and was every city with a bishop a Christian community? St. Augustine had looked at these problems in a rather liberal way, but still there lurked the suspicion that Tertullian had been right: Christian communities might, after all, have no better destiny than to be persecuted minorities, reserved for salvation in a lost world. It was one thing to conform, to lapse, as it were, into the imperial Christian cultus; but another to recognize that baptism made a new man, cut off from his secular past. It was precisely this negation of the past that tempted others to over-value it, not merely for public and private virtues glimpsed through the golden-age haze that was never far from Roman thought at any time, but for the very literature that was its vehicle. This made straight for two characteristic strands in early medieval thinking: anthologizing and archaism, both dominant in the East but neither absent in the West. Radical Christianity must take its share of blame for this, if blame there is.

The fifth century was also the age of barbarian invasion and settlement in Gaul. Salvian was there to witness something of the initial destruction,[1] and Sidonius Apollinaris to describe to his correspondents what it was like to live under barbarians.[2] Archaeology lends some confirmation to their pictures of disruption. Cities and villas did indeed suffer, though not all, nor all at the same time or for the same reason. The political and social effects of the invasions were deep and lasting. But whereas destruction could sometimes be remedied quite quickly, disruption bit more slowly and deeper into the Romanity of the Gauls. A process long evident was given dramatic impetus: the cities closed in on themselves, the local gaining at the expense of the provincial and the regional. The inhabitants of the city, within the walls and in the *territorium* without, were now the social unit that could identify itself and be said to have a purpose. What part could Christians as a community play in this process of self-identification? The bishops, by and large, stood firm. Sometimes they led resistance to the barbarians where secular authority failed; and they remained to lead, to negotiate for favourable terms and to administer relief on a substantial scale. Thus they passed into the period of barbarian settlements with a name for staying put, identified in trial with their communities, and their communities identified with them. They had taken the place of secular Roman officialdom as local protectors, and in doing so had accepted the burden of a Roman tradition. Salvian, who liked to think of the barbarians as children of nature rich in virtue, was really focusing attention upon lost Roman virtues. He seemed to want his countrymen to recapture, through adversity, what they had once had – the stern virtues of Latinity; and to believe that the Church was the

---

[1] *De Gubernatione Dei*, ed. Schanz, CSEL viii (1883), and ed. Halm, MGH AA i, I, i; trans. by Eva Sanford, Columbia Records of Civilization, xii (1966).
[2] Ed. P. Mohr (Teubner, 1895), carmen xii.

instrument to help them achieve it. Such at least he seemed to say, though he strangely lacked Augustine's firm episcopal sense of the continuing threat of paganism. Indeed, *De Gubernatione Dei* reads more as if Salvian felt that the time for a return to the status quo through repentance was almost past beyond recall. No bishop, he was a free agent without a mission to a flock. He could afford to be wild. The real significance of Salvian was negative: he was virtually on his own, and no bishop with any sense of responsibility took up his cry. Less equivocally to others, the invasions offered a direct challenge to the Church to take up the Roman burden, and to prove that victory and prosperity depended on God's favour. And God was not unfavourable, to judge from the donations, particularly of land (impossible, now, to evaluate), that came the way of many Gallic churches in the fifth century; for donations and legacies, not regular offerings, were the source of their slowly-won stability. The greater the church, perhaps the greater its chance of attracting gifts from any, great or small, who had something to give or to leave in expiation for sin. It was a question whether a man's first duty was to his family or to his church. Opinions differed. Donations plainly created a problem for the giver as well as for the recipient. Salvian held that charity on a heroic scale, the returning to God of what was his own, could alone save Gallic souls. But charity in its turn presented the churches with new and often unwelcome problems of how to deal with wealth. Generally they may be said to have acquitted themselves well. The way they tackled the problem of the relief of distress, their reasons for doing it, and the view they took of themselves as landed proprietors, were inherited by their Frankish successors.

We come thus to the bishops. Though leaders of an official cultus closely controlled by imperial legislation, they were not secular administrators, as to some extent their Merovingian successors were to become. Yet they were representatives of *Romanitas* in a world that feared barbarization. The office of bishop was thus attractive to the man of assured social standing, well provided-for, conscious of his family's past and proud to be lettered; attractive, too, to the civil servant faced with redundancy in troubled times. There were many such bishops in fifth-century Gaul: as a rule, not men from the highest senatorial families, though men with whom such would associate. Sidonius was atypical in this as in other respects. As a group, they give the impression of being conservative, and so can be seen (and have been seen) as Christians only in so far as Christianity tended to preserve the social values dear to their class. Was Sidonius a Christian in the sense that Augustine was a Christian? Certainly he would have held, with Augustine, that the whole community of his see belonged to his spiritual charge: there were no outsiders. The *civitas* was a Christian unit, personified in its bishop, lord of its church. The conservative bishop was no mere half-Christian because he had expensive tastes and knew the rules of composition. Indeed, it was because he believed in holy men that Sidonius could indulge his taste for composition. Their prayers were an umbrella under which secular culture could be pursued by a bishop. Repeatedly his letters betray his confidence in them, the experts, because of whom he could permit himself a few liberties. It was under such that Gaul ceased to be a country of little cemetery-churches gathered round the martyrs' shrines outside the city-walls and became instead a country of city-cathedrals, the remains or foundations of some of which can still be seen. To put it no higher, the conservative bishop was ready to stake his name and his wealth on the permanence of the city-community. Bishop Patiens of Lyon astonished contemporaries by his munificence to the Rhône-landers in times of famine; no less he astonished them by his building.[3] No better proof could be had of the continuity of Roman aristocratic ideals in the Gallic episcopate – to the seventh century, indeed – than what is to be read on bishops' epitaphs; ideals of public service, often running in families that had made the transition from *comes* to *episcopus* easy and acceptable. The family see was the proper and expected culmination of a successsful career. The virtues that were fitting to a bishop – *pietas* for example – were not unlike those fitting to his secular forebears; at least they invited the same words when it came to the composition of their epitaphs. One can watch this happening with the noble succession of bishops of Lyon buried in the church of St Nizier, where the cosy proximity of one epitaphed grave to another seems to argue a family connection. A strain of ascetic idealism runs through from imperial days. Cassian had not introduced asceticism to Gaul, nor were monasteries its exclusive home. However, though the bishop might look back with pride to his family's practice of public, as of private, virtues, he knew he was something more: the dispenser of sacraments, the master of liturgy and the teacher of his flock. So Irenaeus of Lyon, in the second century, had taught from his chair behind the altar, preaching the faith as unalterable and one.

The radical or reforming bishops, like the conservatives, were mostly men of birth and substance; there is no social distinction between them. What does distinguish the radicals is their asceticism. It was a tradition as old as the Church. The ascetic bishops cannot, however, be equated with those who opted altogether out of social responsibilities; with Paulinus of Nola, for example. Whatever their

---

[3] His construction and embellishment of his cathedral at Lyon is described by Sidonius, *Epist.* II, 10.

inclination, they did not retire to their estates to pursue their austere ideals in isolation; they belonged to the world of the cities. The ascetic Eutropius, bishop of the wretched see of Orange, said that after death he would continue to pray for his Orangemen ('pro Arausicis meis')[4]; his responsibility for them would not end with his life. On the other hand, some of them did show signs of believing that Christianity as they understood it – the Christianity of personal renunciation – was not for everyone. The real thing was for élites, small groups and families for whom baptism meant new life. It was something private by its nature, a preserve of the elect, a treasure for aristocrats. Herein, rather than in any substantial point of doctrine, may have lain the attraction to some of them of the example of Pelagius and his followers. It was an exclusive way of looking at Christianity. Such is the tone of ascetic correspondence. Moreover, the asceticism was of a special kind, nurtured in the Gallic tradition of St Martin and of the fathers of Lérins and Marseille.

St Martin was a great man in his own day, the latter end of the fourth century; a heroic left-over from the Prophets. He had had singleness of mind and soldierly energy, whether as missionary in the Celtic country-side, father of monks (some well-born) or bishop. These qualities stand out from every page of the splendid biography composed by his disciple, Sulpicius Severus;[5] a tribute (and this is something new) rather to his life than to his death. Most of all, he was a spiritual force, an embodiment of the ideals of personal asceticism and active involve-ment finding expression in the working of miracles. What was remark-able about him was the combination of recluse with man of action. At no time was he shut away like some Eastern contemporary to browse at will in the approaches to heresy. A *vir apostolicus* with his feet on the ground, he was up to his ears in work – healing, exorcising, arbitrating and so on. The familiar scene of his labours was the crowded basilica. But the paganism of the countryside did not escape him: the paganism of temples, sacred trees and springs. But in labour of this kind he certainly did not stand alone. Archaeologists are showing that the later fourth century was precisely the time of wholesale destruction of pagan cult-sites throughout Gaul. He was not an intellectual in the sense that his disciple was; and though it is hard to see behind the pages of Sulpicius, we can feel fairly certain that Sulpicius has cast his hero in a mould suited to a new generation. The Martin of Sulpicius, drawn with delicate sophistication, was an ideal for the aristocratic circle at his home, Primuliacum, and soon for others further afield. He was a challenge to the aristocrat to be a bishop, to be up and doing, to live a

---

[4] *Vita Eutropii* (Gallia Christiana, Nov., VI, col. 17).
[5] Ed. J. Fontaine, SC 133–5.

life of renunciation, perhaps to earn, at the end, his own literary monument. The biography set a standard in a new literary genre; and it set a standard for bishops, not all of whom liked this powerful, unorthodox figure. They feared him not for his reported miracles but for himself. Unlike them, he was a foreigner, an ex-soldier and at one and the same time a bishop and a monk with hazy ideas about diocesan boundaries. He had his following, particularly among laymen of all ranks; and this too was unlikely to placate the more old-fashioned clergy. But despite the stir he undoubtedly made, he was to owe his vast reputation to Sulpicius. The success both of hero and of biographer is witnessed by many church-dedications of the fifth century to St Martin and by the spread from Tours of his cultus as Gaul's principal miracle-worker. A reflection of this success is the career of Germanus, bishop of Auxerre in the mid-fifth century, and in his biography composed by Constantius of Lyon.[6] Germanus was not Martin; and their biographies do not conceal their differences. But they spoke the same language. Constantius wrote for his bishop and disseminated what he wrote at the request of another bishop. His rhetorical training did not prevent him from writing simply and vividly for a new public avid for hagiography. The Germanus he presents is, like Martin, the witness of Christ, the model of virtues, the man of action elevated above ordinary men and proved to be so through the God-given gift of miracle-working. But man of action in a particular field. He, too, was a bishop, though his life was a sort of martyrdom. And we are still with the aristocrats. Constantius was a friend of Sidonius – indeed, caused Sidonius to publish his letters – and he wrote for bishops and their cultivated circles. He is giving them (what might otherwise, he fears, be lost) a portrait of a man like themselves in essentials; a man who stood for the old things they liked: rigid dependence on orthodox doctrine, a proper relationship to secular authority, paternalism wrapped up as patriotism, good education. More than that, Germanus' austerities after he became a bishop, and God's evident acceptance of him, were not the slow growth of dawning involvement but something radical and sudden that made a new man of him.

It may be that Germanus was touched by another great ascetic experience, the life of Lérins and Marseille. Here, as with St Martin, it is something from the East that the Gallo-Romans accepted and made their own as part of their thinking about Christianity. The ascetic fathers of Lérins did not live as monks in the later, Benedictine, sense; their organization was looser and their objectives different. They lived the ascetic life, each for himself, in a loose-knit society without communal objectives. Theirs was a school of asceticism, and to a lesser

[6] Ed. R. Borius, SC 112.

extent of theology. Some of them refugees from the North, they were aristocrats seeking perfection the hard way, making their religion something private – the religion of the closed shop – yet ready to accept office in the Church as bishops, when they must. Eucher of Lyon was one of them, and may have been typical. His little book, *De Laude Heremi*,[7] affords a glimpse into their view of life. He wants the asceticism of the desert fathers, and therefore to the desert he must turn. Most of the book is devoted to the biblical desert of the Chosen People, the desert of Moses and the prophets and finally of Christ. It is the secret place where God may be heard and the Devil conquered, the silent place where not merely the desire to sin but opportunity itself is absent. So he praises the desert for what it does not produce; and it is a real enough place. Then he turns to the desert he knows from experience, the *veneranda tellus* of the island of Lérins. This is a desert that blooms, where nothing is lacking; a place where spiritual peace is inseparable from natural beauty; and a very private place. He lists his friends, who have enjoyed it with him, and he takes it in his heart to the great bishopric of Lyon. There, he remembers nostalgically the quiet times they had once enjoyed together. Cassian's ascetic community in nearby Marseille was essentially different from Lérins in one main respect: here were monks who sought no physical isolation from the secular world but made their own spiritual isolation in the middle of a busy port. They came within the *castrum* like the bishops of the post-invasion time, because that was where life was. And because they did so, and chose to live with the world about them, they lived by a Rule. Cassian offered them security and continuity – for death binds them just as effectively as does life. They could persevere with their Christianity as a professional business, held together in a new social and economic pattern. They had the opportunity, denied to them outside, of seeking perfection as a community under the guidance of a legislator who knew exactly what he was doing. Obedience alone ensured their solitude. So guarded, they remained an élite. Cassian went further. It seemed best to him to encapsulate the ascetic teachings of the past, known to him from experience, in writing. Thus we have his *Institutes*[8] and *Conferences*.[9] Asceticism could now be read about and no longer depended on oral transmission. It could be taught by an abbot, the monks' intermediary with God, himself the supreme abbot of the elect. Gallic monks were hereby encouraged to read books; and they could write them.

The fifth century thus welcomed both the monks within and the

[7] Ed. K. Wotke, CSEL xxxi, i (1894).
[8] Ed. J. C. Guy, SC 109.
[9] Ed. E. Pichery, SC 42, 54, 64, 109.

monks without; and perhaps the most remarkable group of all, the fathers of the Jura, flourished at this time in a nearer approach to a real desert than anything Eucher had known. Monks of the mountain and forest, they were the outermost of those without. In fact, the austerities of the three Jura communities – Condat, Laucone and the nunnery of La Balme – were imposed not so much by a Rule (though they lived by a Rule) as by nature. The founder, Romanus, and soon afterwards his brother Lupicinus, abandoned their family domain to live as hermits in a mountain-valley north-west of the lake of Geneva, far from any normal route. Only spasmodically were they in touch with the monks of that other Alpine fastness of Agaune, perched on a narrow spit in a gorge, away to the south-east of the Lake. The pages of the excellent biography[10] – the earliest hagiographical triptych – of the first three abbots, written soon after the death of the last, are full of foul weather and its perils, only less trying to the monks – because more foreseeable – than the moral perils of the occasional good crop. Thus they lived, in the pine-forests of the Jura, for the ninety years between the arrival of Romanus at Condat about 435 and the composition of the *Vita Patrum Iurensium*. They were not merely opting out of the life of civilization (a point their biographer insists on); they were actively hostile to it. The repulsive clothing of Lupicinus was meant as an affront to civilized ways. So, too, I interpret the extraordinary tale told of Lupicinus on his visit to the court of the Burgundian king, Chilperic, where he had to defend himself against the charges of a courtier who is best seen as a Gallo-Roman landowner.[11] 'Aren't you the impostor', says the courtier, 'who for the last ten years has been disparaging the power of the Roman Empire and proclaiming that our ancestral land is threatened with imminent ruin? . . . Why haven't these frightful auguries been fulfilled?' 'But', replies Lupicinus, 'they *have* been fulfilled!' Had not the rapacity of aristocrats been punished by expropriation at Burgundian hands? This hostile reflection on the landlords, so much in the style of Salvian himself, seems to have amused the Burgundian king. He granted the request that Lupicinus had come to make and paid him further honour.

What was the effect of so uncompromising an outlook on contemporaries? A large increase in the number of monks in the Jura, and frequent pilgrimages to their retreat. The first necessitated the imposition of a Rule; and this one can suppose to have been an amalgam of the practices of St Martin, Cassian, Lérins, and the primitive Church. For men wedded to contemplation and the winning of a livelihood from a hard soil, there seems to have been unexpected attention paid to

[10] Ed. F. Martine, SC 142.
[11] Ibid., pp. 336–40.

reading, notably of the records of St Martin and St Antony, The anonymous author of the *Vita* was not the only monk who could command a good literary style. But pilgrims were drawn rather by the skill of the abbots as healers of disease. The author of the *Vita* lays less stress on the miraculous than do others – for example, Sulpicius. He thinks people were suspicious of the written word. His discretion in this respect was rather due to good literary sense than to any short-fall in miracles, especially of healing. A magic could, when called for, be worked. The abbot Eugendus writes a letter of exorcism addressed to the Devil, to be sent to a patient and worn by her. We have its text, short and to the point.[12] And it worked, even before delivery. Nor was this the only occasion. 'These letters', says the biographer, 'to be worn by the sick, went to the most distant provinces and, with faith, brought the same relief to them as if they had been presented themselves to the saint in his monastery.'[13] Renunciation of society thus had its attractions to the society renounced. It could ensure the benevolence of the new barbarian kings of Arian faith. If we knew more of the pagan ethos of the bulk of Germanic settlers, on which Christianity cannot yet have made any deep impression, this might seem less surprising. It could draw the sick. The entire town of Geneva reacted to the cure of two lepers: 'all the citizens wept as one man'.[14] But the Jura monks were still exceptional. An authentic manifestation of the fifth-century Gallic Church, they were not characteristic of it. Possibly the Church was already too complex to be characterized at all. In some ways it is perhaps true that, with its estates and servants and communities of monks, it was economically a burden upon a hard-pressed society; certainly it can be represented as such; but society wanted it just the same for its moral witness, its spiritual protection, and its reassuring semblance of continuity of Roman ideals.

The striking new feature of the fifth-century Church, in Gaul quite notably, was the cultus of relics. Its roots lay in Antiquity and in pagan practice, but its flowering owed more to specifically Christian developments than to traditional paganism. It, too, is characteristically aristocratic, though not only aristocratic, in its appeal; as characteristic as the pursuit of *belles-lettres*. What is taken from the East and elsewhere is subsumed into the culture of Gaul and grafted upon the tradition of St Martin. One has only to read the account by Bishop Victricius of Rouen of the arrival of relics in his city in about the year 396,[15] or the inscription of 473 on the Church of St Martin at Tours,[16] to appreciate

[12] Ibid., pp. 392–5.   [13] Ibid., p. 398.   [14] Ibid., p. 294.
[15] PL 20, col. 443. This and the following item are translated by J. N. Hillgarth, *The Conversion of Western Europe* (Englewood Cliffs, N.J., 1969).
[16] Paulinus of Périgueux, *De orantibus*, ed. M. Petschenig, CSEL xvi (1888), 165.

the flavour of the national preoccupation. Saints' biographies and martyrologies had become, in the intervening time, an essential part of the equipment of the well-found Church. Oriental saints were significantly popular. The bishop had to take steps to provide himself with the tools of the expected cultus. Not merely the relics of local saints but those of others more distant were to be revealed, collected, housed and commemorated on the proper anniversaries.

But who were the saints? In the first place, they were the martyrs to whom the Church accorded public cultus, and by extension the confessors – those whose lives had been a conquest of human nature, white martyrdom at a time when red martyrdom was scarcely ever available. By further extension the class could include any whose heroic virtues had seemed to witness the evident approval of God; and ascetic bishops were natural candidates. The martyrs of Lyon are a classic instance of what amounts to popular canonization from an early date; a spontaneous product; but, though classic, rare. The cultus of most Gallic saints, however popular, does not go back so far and it is not necessarily popular in origin. A cultus may equally have its beginning in the deliberate action of a Church. To take an example: the spread of St Martin's cult, as revealed in church dedications in the Parisian region, may look like the result of popular affection but is just as likely to have been due to well-considered episcopal choice. Similarly, the dedication of the cathedral church of Paris to St Stephen (soon after 415) and thereafter of several other churches in the surrounding *vici*, was the bishop's doing. At least it is clear that the evidence of sanctity that most appealed to the fifth century was asceticism and its fruits. The ability to work miracles, before and after death, was often taken as proof of sanctity. The power of relics over the demon-world, the cure of the possessed and others, were matters constantly in the forefront of the bishops' minds. The impression is left that the faithful of Gaul were moved, frequently and in large crowds, to seek the assistance of miracle-working relics, to invoke the local saints and martyrs and in death to lie as near them as possible. Rogation-days suggest the same, and so too, sometimes, inscriptions. The priest Vigilantius, distressed by the cult of St Saturninus at Toulouse, would not have raised his lone voice against the whole business if it had not been a living issue.[17] The spirituality of the age demanded active proof of divine favour, not dogma. But there is a hint of something less spontaneous in the occasional objection that a saint was not being adequately honoured, or that the memory of a saint's deeds was in danger of being forgotten. St Augustine had made this

---

[17] His attack is known only from the reply of St. Jerome, *Contra Vigilantium*, PL 33, cols. 339–52.

point; and it is interesting, as Peter Brown pointed out, that what annoyed him was that a *clarissima femina* should have kept quiet;[18] one who should have known better, and who was in a position to influence people. Why, then, was it a duty to publicize miraculous cures? Could it have been that relics worked cures because they were popular, and were not popular in the first place because they worked cures? The community as a whole had to be persuaded of the importance of the relics in their midst, and of the dependence of their *fortuna* upon these collective sources of supernatural intervention. Their acclamations were the essential witness that the city, the community, formally acknowledged a miracle at home. Sidonius shows how this happened.[19] It may be that this is the reason why so many biographies of saints insist on the presence of large crowds, as representative of whole communities.

A word more as to Rogation-days. Avitus describes the inauguration of Rogations by his predecessor, Bishop Mamertus of Vienne, probably in the 460s.[20] They were devised as a city's confession of guilt, a means of escape from divine wrath in the shape of earthquakes; in short, as a ritual for an emergency. Avitus' account breathes the intense emotion of the occasion; all were involved, of whatever rank or age. It was a communal profession, the bishop taking the lead. But the matter did not rest there; emergencies justifying Rogations cropped up elsewhere, and frequently. Sidonius, the contemporary of Mamertus, quickly grasped their value: they marked a total commitment of his flock. To Caesarius, too, if in a different way, Rogations were vital: how better to integrate personal remorse with public penance? The man who stayed away, he said, was like a deserter from an army – surely a very revealing image.[21] In short, Rogations demonstrated in a dramatic way how the Church could identify local disaster with local sin and provide the remedy in a communal act of propitiation that involved everyone. It was Nineveh all over again: today's citizens, like yesterday's, could earn salvation through repentance. When Sidonius wrote to the expert, Mamertus, about the plight of his city of Clermont beleaguered by Goths, he made two further points that are worth noting. First, that the inaugural Rogation had been preceded by a miracle; the mere presence of Mamertus had stopped the spread of fire in Vienne. And secondly, Clermont was specially exposed at the present time because Mamertus himself had transferred the relics of two saints – 'all the holy body of Ferreolus and the head of our martyr

[18] *De civitate Dei*, xxii, 8.
[19] *Epist*. IV, 18.
[20] *Hom.* VI (*Sermo de primo Rogationum*), *Œuvres Complètes*, ed. U. Chevalier (Lyon, 1890).
[21] *Sermo* 133, on a verse of Psalm 49, ed. G. Morin, CC 103.

Julian' – to Vienne. He concludes: 'It is only fair, then, in compensation for the loss of this hallowed relic' – he means the head – 'that some part of your patronage should come to us from Vienne, since a part of our patronal saint has migrated thither.'[22] It is unclear what *patrocinium* is being asked for, but at least we can see that we are back again with local saints, their patronage and their relics. Saints were the patrons of communities and agents of integration. They were also the patrons of bishops. A martyr's evident patronage could reinforce a bishop's personal claims to leadership in his community. The martyr was his personal guarantor. Such liaison mattered more now than skill with hendecasyllables; through it, and through deeds, came the sanctity the bishop himself sought. Most of what is known of the startling advance in the cultus of saints and their relics in fifth-century Gaul comes from literary sources composed with one aim: to further a cultus. All this was to have a great future with the Merovingians.

However one looks at it, the heritage of the Merovingian Church from the fifth century was a rich one. We may call it a heritage of saints, bishops, and books. The bishops had indeed identified themselves with their city-communities. They had learnt to speak for them in adversity and, what was just as difficult, in prosperity. And in prosperity they had taken decisions that were irreversible. The churches of Gaul were now great landlords, recipients of legacies, distributors of charity on a large scale, builders of fabrics that were meant to last. Their bishops were powerful administrators controlling a hierarchy of diocesan clergy. They were also controllers of an impressive literary tradition. In the end, the Church needs to record what happens to it and in it: the evidence is before us in the shape of saints' Lives, martyrologies, inscriptions, council acts, sermons and correspondence; and the evidence is in Latin, not in the Celtic that was widely spoken in the still only partly-converted countryside. The great book, the Bible, was in Latin: a book for rulers. It was a victory for the Roman tradition. Thus Gennadius of Marseille could without incongruity sit down to the task of continuing St Jerome's *De Viris Inlustribus* in the Gallic interest.[23] He reveals that many books, especially of fifth-century apologetic and commentary, were available to him in the libraries of Marseille; and he provides what is at once a useful bibliography and a tribute to what the century since St Jerome had achieved. One might almost say that the time had come to issue a class-list; and this was it. Those he mentions who were of special interest to Gaul included Sulpicius, Sabbatius, Paulinus of Nola, Victorinus, Cassian, Eucher, Vincent, Syagrius, Salvian, Hilary,

[22] *Epist.* VII, i.
[23] Ed. E. Richardson, *Texte und Untersuchungen*, xiv, i (Leipzig, 1896).

Musaeus, Claudian, Prosper, Faustus, Victor, Sidonius – and himself. These were the men whose salvation had depended on active doing in the interest of the communities they had been associated with. In so far as semi–Pelagianism meant self-help, the active spirit of a chosen few, it was certainly evident in the careers of some of these. But Gennadius believed in doctrinal orthodoxy; indeed, in orthodoxies generally. Heresy, differentiation, was an enemy the bishops had encountered in several shapes. Some of them had worked among the Arian barbarians of the south and east of Gaul and others had met the challenge nearer home. The differentiation they accepted was not in belief but in pastoral care; the right of every church to have a past, to rule itself and be itself, the duty of every church to identify itself as the whole community of a city. From this there was no turning back.

One man above all others has left us the means to penetrate to some depth into the significance of the identification of a secular with a Christian community. This was Caesarius, bishop and metropolitan of Arles from 503 to 543. His ministry was mostly exercised under Arian Gothic kings in a city and countryside where Catholics, Arians, Jews and pagans daily rubbed shoulders. His influence was large on several counts: as monastic legislator, writer of treatises, moving spirit of councils and as possible author (if it were not Gennadius) of the *Statuta Ecclesiae Antiqua*, a systematic collection of over a hundred canons.[24] He was, too, a specialist in sermons as literature. In his scriptorium he edited, composed and disseminated a famous collection of over 200 sermons, manuscripts of which were widespread from the sixth century onwards. Many of the sermons he edited were written by St Augustine and others; but it is the total effect that counts. Caesarius made all of them his own, and they are our best way into the meaning of a Gallic community.[25]

In his popular sermons, Caesarius addresses, simply but also subtly, a community that knows the extremes of wealth and poverty, but which, on the whole, is more preoccupied with the good things of life than with their absence: men of business, tradesmen, farmers and women with plenty of time for talk and not too much inclination to read. He pictures to them the society they are and the society they might be; and nothing that they do or think is safe from him. He is, he says, their *superinspector*.[26] The bishop's involvement with them is total. As Christians, he tells them, they belong to a community whose continuous existence goes back to biblical times. Both Testaments of

---

[24] See C. Munier, *Les Statuta Ecclesiae Antiqua* (Paris, 1960).
[25] Full edn. by G. Morin, CC 103, 4, and in part by M.-J. Delage, SC 175, 243. It is possible that Caesarius was also responsible for the collection of sermons known as Eusebius Gallicanus (see CC 101, 101A). [26] Sermon I, 19.

the Bible are their family-books which he expounds to them and which they must read and memorize and propagate. If, he says, a farmer can memorize a love-song he can also memorize a little of the Bible, and illiteracy is no excuse. The scriptures are letters from heaven, an invitation to the kingdom – to God's Jerusalem as opposed to the Devil's Babylon. 'These truths', he insists, 'were not written for us for purposes of history.'[27] The Old Testament was written for us as a type of the moral life we enter at baptism. For Caesarius, as for all his contemporaries, the Devil is a real Christian Devil, firmly conceived within the Christian framework of good and evil, and no mere name for the negative residuum of what is not Christian. He goes on: 'But someone says, "I do not want the kingdom of God, I only want eternal rest". Let no one deceive himself, brothers: there are two places but not a third. You reign with Christ or you perish with the Devil.'[28] The Devil is a father, and a king with an army always ready to attack and claim his own. One should not underestimate the cumulative effect, week after week, of this persistent typological approach to Scripture, with its message that things are not what they seem and that events and words should not be taken at their face value. Such, then, is the community that his people of Arles constitute. Each man and woman is required to consider his or her actions and thoughts in relation to it.

The Devil will, of course, worm his way into the faithful heart by routes familiar to any generation – for example, through attitudes to charity and prayer. But he can also make use of what is special to their own time and place. He can use paganism. Caesarius is more pre-occupied with present solvents of Christianity than with classical paganism. Hence his obsession with the small change of popular paganism. There is still, he laments, ritual bathing on St John's day; bacchanalian orgies among country folk; vows to trees, prayers at fountains; pagan altars and idols are still to be found; there are women in Arles who refuse to spin or weave on a Thursday out of deference to Jove; and above all there is consultation with soothsayers and healers about omens and symptoms. This last is specially worrying because sometimes, as he admits, soothsayers are right and healers do heal. His flock is to recognize these as the Devil's temptations, and resist them. To resist is to be a martyr. In a way, sickness is the crux of control over the mind, and for this reason Caesarius greatly fears the traditional influences that pull his people out of his grasp whenever sickness touches them. He can associate with these specific relics of popular paganism the seasonal feastings and drunkenness and debauchery that the Church had to put up with and to some extent subsume. Even priests, he allows, find that getting drunk is a social asset. All this,

[27] Sermon 94.   [28] Sermon 47.

whether rooted in paganism or merely in the past, can be seen as the Devil's work. He casts his net even wider. The taking of drugs to have, or not to have, children is no concern of the Christian. All in all, the self-restraint that must be practised in daily life is indeed what the bishop calls it, a kind of martyrdom, because it cuts into the life of family and neighbourhood and market-place at every turn. The mere buffoonery (*scurrilitas*) of daily life is a menace in its own right. There is thus no longer any moral privacy for a man who takes seriously his membership of the community. He must naturally not expect to dispose of his money as he wishes. Almsgiving is the great palliative for sin, the act of love *par excellence*, of which remedy clergy as much as people stand in need. But it is the motive as much as the act that counts. The poor are plainly an essential part of Caesarius' community, a means of grace that must be present. (In one sermon on widows, orphans and the poor he gives a vivid example of how the Bible could be reinterpreted by a preacher to suit present needs.)[29] The poor, then, are built into the structure of the local Church. But it has another structure that needs constant attention. There are buildings to keep up and properties to administer; and their demands are severe on time as well as on money. In fact, Caesarius, excellent administrator as he was, believes that his colleagues give overmuch time to administration. It is an excuse for not preaching. The soul comes before the soil, and there are usually good substitutes for bishops as administrators, even of charity. Christ said, 'feed my sheep', not 'look after my estates'.[30] In a word, bishops and priests are up against the perils of affluence. They had not become civil administrators but something worse, ecclesiastical administrators.

From Caesarius, then, we have a picture of what it was like to be a Christian in fifth- and early sixth-century Arles. The Arlésiens behave and react much as one would have expected. The significance of the sermons lies in the preacher himself and his assumptions. He expects to have total control over the thoughts and lives of his community. He has not, but he behaves and speaks as if he had. Other bishops had spoken, and were speaking, in much the same vein. But Caesarius does it for Arles at a particular moment. It makes it easier for us to understand why the incoming Franks saw so quickly that only the bishops spoke to and for the people, and that without their goodwill nothing much could be done with Gaul.

By such means, then, by preaching, by ascetic example and careful administration and by loving observance of local tradition, Gallic bishops forged Christian communities. Their preoccupation with social *mores* is some indication of what they understood by conversion.

---

[29] Sermon 49.　　　　[30] Sermon 1.

It had a long future. But in the last resort a Church stands or falls by its administration of the sacraments and its observance of the annual liturgical cycle (this last an area in which local experimentation might always be expected; nor do the Gallo-Romans disappoint us). We can tell from conciliar legislation that Caesarius was not alone in proclaiming that the mass, on Sundays and feast-days, was, as it had always been, obligatory for all the faithful because it was their principal means of access to salvation. From canons, sermons, and *Lives* (that of Caesarius himself is admirable) some picture can be formed of the faithful at mass: their participation and comportment, and the preparation required of them. Here, at the central rite, willingly and unwillingly, they showed themselves to be one. This, too, they taught to their Frankish heirs.

FROM PAGANISM TO CHRISTIANITY

THE time has gone, if it ever existed, when we could think of the Franks, or any other Germanic people, as pagan one day and Christian the next. So heroically simple a solution does no justice to the texts and is quite overthrown by archaeology. We must move more cautiously, as did the Germans themselves.

Fifth-century Gaul was Christian and mostly Catholic in a formal sense. But behind the forms lay a scarcely-converted countryside where Celtic and other pagan beliefs still worried the clergy. These beliefs remained active in the sixth and seventh centuries, and not only among the indigenous populations; they affected the way the Franks accepted Christianity, as indeed they had already affected the way the Gallo-Romans themselves accepted it.

This is one side of the picture. The other is the nature of Germanic paganism. No sense can be made of Frankish Christianity, when it comes, unless allowance is first made for the fact that all Germans were religious people. Their lives, as individuals and as members of communities, were conditioned by the sense they had of good and evil, life and death, gods and demons. This can best be seen in the archaeological evidence from their remote homeland in a yet more distant time. Much, too, can be inferred from later literary evidence. Recent work has shown what can be done for the religion of the continental Saxons by collating the evidence of Scandinavian and Germanic literature with that of the gold bracteates – medallions, once worn as amulets, that have been found in Scandinavia and on the German mainland. From it emerges a picture of sixth-century paganism that has subsumed late Roman coin-material to make its own iconography of a conquering cult of Woden. Not nearly so much can be attempted for the Franks, for the sources scarcely lend themselves to this treatment. It is the rarity rather than the abundance of gold bracteates on Frankish soil that needs explaining. There are very few of them, notably fewer than in Anglo-Saxon England, from which indeed those few may have come. However, the archaeological field in which Frankish paganism may be studied is not confined to bracteates.

In an archaeological sense one must be content to speak loosely of Franks. Roman Gaul, basically Celtic, found room for other peoples – Germanic Burgundians and Goths, notably, but also for smaller enclaves of settlers, such as Huns, Taifali, and Sarmatians, who were not German. Their grave-gods can easily be confused. The cultural zone that can reasonably be called Frankish covers northern Gaul, the centre as far south as, and a little beyond, the Loire, and the east as far as the Middle Rhine. Here have been found the bulk of grave-goods, covering the approximate period 500–700 or rather earlier, from which we must find such clues as we can to Frankish paganism.

There is little evidence of Frankish interest in the cult of specific gods, and indeed little direct religious evidence of any formal kind from the earliest Frankish remains; though where we find any it is right to assume that we have not found all. The Scandinavian cult of the gods developed after the Franks had lost continuous contact with the Baltic. They may only have learnt of them from neighbouring Germans, such as the Frisians, the continental Saxons and the Anglo-Saxons, and, apart from that, have had to content themselves with worship and sacrifice of a more primitive type. The Frankish royal dynasty, still feeling its way towards pan-Frankish over-lordship in 500, did not, so far as we know, attach special importance to any one god, as did the East Saxon kings to Saxnot (or Tiwaz) and other Anglo-Saxon dynasties to Woden – though precisely when they began to do so is unclear. There is nothing in Frankish sources corresponding to Adam of Bremen's vivid picture[1] of Scandinavian worship of Thor, Woden and Frey, written in the late eleventh century. We know from Gregory of Tours that the name of the eldest son of Clovis and Chrotechildis was Ingomer, which may betray the father's adherence to the cult of Ingvi-Frey. But it was not from these gods that Gregory says the queen endeavoured to win her husband, but rather from the cults of Saturn, Jupiter, Mars and Mercury.[2] The king resisted on the ground that the Christian god could not be shown to be descended from the race of the gods. The story is commonly seen as no more than Gregory's version of early Christian demonology, and it may be so. There seems to be no reason why he should not have named the Germanic gods if he had meant them. It is just possible, on the other hand, that some Franks had found the Romano-Celtic gods so like their own that they had accepted Roman-Celtic names for their own gods while keeping their attributes. It could have been as easy for the Franks to absorb Celtic gods as it had undoubtedly been for the Celts to absorb Roman gods. The Franks must have found many a Celtic *fanum* or temple-shrine in the forests, such as have been identified near Rouen and Trier. As late as the seventh century paganism had a strong hold in the dioceses of Rouen, Beauvais, Amiens, Noyon and Cambrai.

[1] *Gesta Hammaburgensis ecclesiae pontificum*, iv, ch. 26 (MGH SRG in usum schol., ed. G. Waitz, 1876).
[2] *Libri Historiarum*, ii, ch. 29 (MGH SRM 1, i, ed. B. Krusch and W. Levison, 1951).

Many Franks married Celtic women, and in primitive village-communities it is often the woman who calls the tune in religion; for it is she who is the guardian of the sanctity of the home, and the one on whom religious ritual mostly falls. Women, more than men, are still the target of ninth-century bishops on the hunt for village-magicians. This coming-together of Celt and German would explain much, as, for instance, why a huge statue of Diana should have been worshipped by the Franks on the hill of Yvois,[3] and why Eligius, bishop of the very Frankish diocese of Noyon, should have forbidden his flock to address the sun and moon as 'lord' or to invoke Neptune, Diana, Orcus, Minerva or other *genii*.[4] It might also explain why Frankish place-names betray no attachment to the gods of the Germanic pantheon. The position is quite different from that of the Anglo-Saxons. However, the Antique gods and heroes had a more illustrious destiny that cannot concern us here. From, among others, Eusebius, St Jerome, Orosius and especially Isidore, medieval men learnt how the gods could be saved and utilized by seeing them as men and women with a place in history and with lessons to teach as benefactors of humanity. Thus they were to emerge, euhemerized, as a force to be reckoned with in art and literature. One of Charlemagne's seals displayed, not incongruously, the bust of Jupiter Serapis; and Flodoard in the tenth century believed that his city of Reims had been founded by Remus. Gregory of Tours observed that he had had enough of Saturn, Juno and Jupiter; others clearly had not.

One pagan god to whom the Merovingians certainly attached importance as their dynastic patron was a sea or river god, apparently represented with horns, as was customary among both Romans and Germans. This was the sea-beast, part man, part bull, and therefore like a Minotaur, from which Merovech was descended, as Fredegar reported in the seventh century.[5] Gregory of Tours, more squeamish, omitted any mention of this background, though he betrayed knowledge of the legend by remarking that 'some hold that Merovech was of the race of Clodio'.[6] He would not commit himself as to whether Merovech was the son of Clodio or of the Minotaur. It may well be, also, that he was confused, as we still are, about the identity of Merovech, who could have been either the eponymous founder of the family or the historical Merovech, son of Clodio. The likelihood is that the story had become attached to the wrong Merovech by Gregory's time. But in any case we are left with a legend commonly

---

[3] Ibid. viii, ch. 15.
[4] *Vita Eligii*, ii, ch. 16 (MGH SRM iv, pp. 706–7).
[5] *Chron.* iii, ch. 9 (MGH SRM ii, ed. B. Krusch, 1888).
[6] *Hist.*, ii, ch. 9.

accepted by the Franks of the sixth and seventh centuries, and perhaps earlier, that their conquering dynasty had a respectable progenitor in a sea god. This does not mean that the Frankish people worshipped such a god nor that the Merovingians had no other god. He was rather a private acquisition for the Merovingian pantheon, an ancestor peculiar to them. He does not help us to understand in what sense the Franks as a whole were a religious people. For this we must look at their grave-gods.

There is always a temptation to interpret any scene depicting warriors, birds and animals as representing specific Germanic heroes, gods or myths. This can be taken too far. On the other hand, when we look at such an object as the Franks Casket (Northumbrian work of about 700) we are reminded that quite elaborate stories could be depicted that contemporaries could interpret without difficulty, though we cannot. In the present state of knowledge, nothing is lost if we see Germanic gods depicted in plausible situations so long as we acknowledge that this is only a working hypothesis. For example, Woden may be intended by the naked figure armed with a spear on a seventh-century gravestone from Niederdollendorf.[7] On his breast is a ring (as it might be, the ring Draupnir of the Eddas), a nimbus of rays surrounds his head and a snake or dragon lies beneath his feet. On the other side of the stone is a representation of the dead man, a singular pantalooned figure with a comb in his hair and a huge scramasax in his hand. Over his head is a two-headed bird-snake, while a third monster grips the hilt of the scramasax in its beak. Beneath it is an unidentified object rather like a plump money-bag with a symbolic coin in it that could signify booty, a wergild or an offering. It might be a cult-object. Altogether the impression is thoroughly pagan.[8] Woden more certainly appears armed with a spear and mounted on his horse, Sleipnir, on a metal ring from Bräunlingen.[9] And again we have him, accompanied by his ravens, Hugin and Munin, on a metal ring from Soest, and conceivably also in the bearded head between two birds on sword-chapes from Krefeld-Gellep and from the district of Namur. These witnesses to the cult come from the borders of Frankish settlement. But we have, plausibly, a Frankish Woden-like god nearer the centre of things Frankish on a late belt-buckle from a cemetery at Rouen, where he appears in an ecstatic pose, encircled by a great bird; and again, we may have a Germanic god in profile, facing a swastika, on a buckle from Monceau-le-Neuf.[10] All this is little enough. But we must bear in mind that the Germans

[7] E. Salin, *La Civilisation mérovingienne*, vol. 2 (Paris, 1952), plate 1, i.
[8] Salin, vol. 1, plate 1.   [9] Salin, vol. 4, fig. 100.
[10] Ibid., fig. 91.

generally seem to have been unwilling to portray the human figure.[11] A god may be represented by some token specially associated with him; as, for example, a swastika (often the sign on Thor), a bear (associated with Thor and Woden), a stag, a horse, an eagle, a serpent or, in the case of Frey, a boar. All these appear on Frankish grave-goods, on which scenes and symbols proliferate in hundreds. What, for example, should be made of the extraordinary representation on a buckle from Picardy[12] of two mounted men whose horses drink from an urn? Or of a series of buckles showing horses covered with eyes and accompanied by birds?[13] Or of the backward-looking monster on a buckle from Arnay-le-Duc?[14] Or the naked figures on another Picard buckle?[15] Or the face and inscription on a silver brooch from Liverdun?[16] Or the two-headed dragon holding a magic ball on a buckle from Mont-sur-Lausanne?[17] It is easy to be misled into a misreading; for instance, where we think we see an animal or bird attacking a man, the craftsman may have seen them communicating quite amicably with each other. To take an example, the two monstrous birds or griffins, whose beaks rest on the head of a man on a plaque from Combles, near Péronne,[18] may be attacking the man, or they may not; and this is only one of a class of which the iconography remains to be interpreted. At present, at least, it would be unwarranted to assume that worship of the gods was not implied. And there is yet another way in which the gods may be present in a burial. A severed head in a grave (and there are not a few) may be a tribute to a god; drinking vessels buried with the dead may be not only for the use of the dead but also for ritual drinking; the looped or writhing dragons or snakes so common in Frankish iconography, whether singly or in groups, may hark back to serpents of northern myth; gods, the magicians *par excellence*, may be present in a number of guises we do not yet recognize; and they may also be present in the magic of runes. A runic message may be direct, such as that on a brooch from Kärlich, near Koblenz. It reads: 'I am consecrated to Woden: I have the power of good luck'. Or again, on a Scandinavian bracteate: 'I write runes', which signifies that the wearer is charmed and should be given a wide berth. But the message may be unintelligible, as with the runic inscription on the Charnay brooch.[19] Secrecy could be the essence of runic protection to the illiterate. It was certainly so in the ninth century. In

---

[11] So Tacitus, *Germania*, ix, writing of course of an earlier period.
[12] Salin, vol. 4, fig. 97.
[13] Ibid., table A, figs. 1, 3; table B, figs. 1–4.
[14] Ibid., fig. 62. [15] Ibid. 67.
[16] Salin, vol. 2, table B, 17.
[17] Salin, vol. 4, fig. 14.
[18] Ibid., fig. 126. [19] Ibid., fig. 35.

any case, runes are rare enough in Francia proper. There are only a few
on metal and any on wood have long since perished. Two points need
emphasis. The first – again – is that much of this must of necessity be
conjecture. We have at present some, but very little, hard evidence of
the worship of Woden, most powerful of the gods exported from
Scandinavia; but there is this to add: he was not a god to travel in the
baggage of an isolated warrior here or there. By the sixth century he
was central to Germanic religion. Secondly, Woden was more than
the spear god, the god of battle, though he was that to bands of young
warriors advancing into fresh territory. Success in battle was a kind of
magic. He was also the god of inspiration, regeneration and healing,
the magician who could protect a kindred or a family just as well as a
warband. This was how the continental Saxons regarded him. The
Franks were physically and spiritually further from the seat of Woden's
cult at Odense in Denmark than were the Saxons. But we are learning
more of the ties, cultural and economic, that held these peoples
together in the early middle ages. At present we can go so far as to say
that by the sixth century Woden was worshipped by some Franks; and
if Woden, then his colleagues; and if not Woden, then a god remarkably
like him.

    Frankish grave-goods witness in a more general way to the Germanic
pagan view of the after-life and of the relationship of the dead to their
surviving kindred. Religious feeling seems to have played some part in
the choice of burial-sites. There was a preference for the slopes of hills,
the proximity of running water and, as occasion afforded, old tumuli.
More obviously suggestive is the filling-in of graves with soil brought
from elsewhere; the evidence of ritual fires at the time of burial and
later; the burying of three arrowheads with the body or of the remains
of animals and birds not meant for consumption hereafter by the dead
– and of this a famous instance is the presence at the cemetery of
Noiron-sous-Gevrey of massive *sacrificia mortuorum*, sacrifices for the
dead, a practice that continued to worry the Carolingians – placed in
separate excavations; libations on a generous scale; human hair worn
in belt-buckles, as at St Quentin; the presence of boars' tusks and
bears' teeth. And to all this may be added, for good measure, the
burying of parts of, or symbolic representations of, animals and birds
of special religious significance, such as the stag (the conductor of the
dead) and the horse, at once a means of travel and a source of strength.
Of course it is easy to see symbolism where contemporaries would
have seen none, or a different symbolism. Moreover, much of the
symbolism that we associate with the Germanic peoples was common
to the Celts and the peoples of the Steppe. Ideas and artefacts spread
from East to West. However, we are left in the end with certain

practices and beliefs of the Franks exemplified in a formidable number of graves. They were complex and deep-rooted and by no means suggestive of a people looking for a new religion.

But a new religion they found, and found it under their conqueror of northern Gaul, Clovis (or Chlodovech, to give him his right name). His father, Childeric, had been buried at Tournai, presumably by Clovis himself. Fragments of his grave-furniture can still be inspected in Paris and a valuable contemporary account of the discovery of his grave in 1653 can be read.[20] The contents have often been described. They constitute much what one might expect for a well-established federate chieftain with wide contacts. The war-gear and jewellery and other paraphernalia (some of it, possibly, like the bull's head, symbolic of belief) betray a good pagan, to whom the gods have been kind. Under the same gods, one supposes, his son advanced south in force to take over control of northern Gaul and to establish his authority, as and when he could, over neighbouring Frankish chieftains.[21] But he did more than this. He overcame neighbours who were not Franks; powerful neighbours, like the Rhenish Thuringians, the Alamans and the Visigoths. Whether he did so as a pagan or a Christian is keenly debated to this day. Much turns on whether one accepts the chronology established by Gregory of Tours, the historian of the Franks.[22] It may well be that Gregory sometimes got his dates wrong but yet put events in the right order; which means that Clovis won his early victories as a pagan but the last at least as a Christian. Moreover, there was an intermediate stage between his decision to seek baptism and baptism itself. To Gregory of Tours, at least, what the victories as a whole proved was that Clovis belonged to the original, noblest, long-haired race of the royal Franks; and there was nothing Christian about that. Three aspects of the process are relevant here and call for comment: the nature of his conversion, the immediate implications of his baptism, and the effect of his baptism on his subsequent actions.

First, as to conversion. It was certainly not implied by his first foray into Gaul. The hard-headed bishop of Reims, Remigius, made no such assumption when he wrote to Clovis soon after his advance into Gaul, but merely congratulated him on taking over the administration of

---

[20] J. J. Chiflet, *Anastasis Childerici I Francorum Regis sive Thesaurus sepulchralis Tornaci Nerviorum effossus* (Antwerp, 1655). Modern studies of Childeric's grave-goods are extensive. Reference may be made to my 'The grave of kings', *Early Medieval History* (Oxford, 1975), ch. 3.

[21] One of these gods may have been Hludana to judge from the 'Hlud' element common in Merovingian names. See S. Gutenbrunner, *Die germanischen Götternamen der antiken Inschriften* (Halle, 1936), pp. 83 ff.

[22] I have discussed this controversial matter in *The Long-Haired Kings* (London, 1962), ch. 7, with special reference to the arguments of A. van de Vyver in *Revue belge de philol. et d'hist.*, xv (1936), xvi (1937), and xvii (1938).

Belgica Secunda and loftily advised collaboration with the bishops. There is no word about conversion.[23] In fact, the tradition recorded in some detail by Gregory of Tours suggests that the process was slow and difficult. For Gregory, it began with the marriage of Clovis to a Catholic Burgundian princess, Chrotechildis, and with her wish to have her two sons baptized. In the death of the first, just after baptism, the king saw the natural consequence of denying the pagan gods. It was a set-back. But the queen kept up the pressure until, at Tolbiac, Clovis faced defeat at the hands of the Alamans. Caught out, he tried the patronage of a new war god, Christ, and saw defeat turned into victory. It was his Milvian bridge. The Constantinian parallel struck Gregory too. But for all his writing-up of the incident there is no reason to reject the factual basis of Tolbiac. Clovis was not converted but he was impressed and readier to listen. At this stage the queen's efforts were supplemented by those of Bishop Remigius of Reims. The final stumbling-block for Clovis was how the Franks would take the news. But those whom the king consulted accepted his lead, and he was finally baptized with his following in arms – for this is the best interpretation of Gregory's statement that he was baptized with more than three thousand *de exercito*.[24] In the end, it was not the Frankish people that was converted but the king and a warband that presumably recalled the story that got around after Tolbiac. The upper crust, or part of it, had accepted a new, perhaps an additional, war god, on approval, though some may have remained loyal to the old gods. The three thousand warriors (or whatever the number may really have been) comprised a high proportion of Clovis's leading men. It was to such, duly ensconced on their estates, that the earliest missionaries – often from Aquitaine – must have turned. Nor did they turn in vain.

The Frankish notables, and they were counts before they were bishops and abbots, had become Christian long before their humbler followers. From them, as well as from kings, came the earliest endowments of churches and monasteries. This is most clearly observable in the north-east. The earliest non-royal charter of foundation of a monastery dates from 543; but others, earlier still, may have perished. From Hordain,[25] near Valenciennes, comes tantalizing evidence of what a recently converted Frankish community of the sixth or seventh century may have looked like: a cemetery containing some 300 early burials in association with a little chapel and altar and signs of a settlement. In the chapel lay a chieftain, perhaps the founder and

[23] MGH *Epist.* i, p. 113.
[24] *Hist.* ii, ch. 31.
[25] See P. Demolon, 'L'implantation du christianisme dans le bassin supérieur de l'Escaut', *Francia*, 7 (1979), p. 533.

builder, though two horse-burials outside suggest a different background. The chapel seems to have been abandoned or destroyed in the
seventh or eighth century though burials in the cemetery were later
resumed. A comparable settlement at Brebières,[26] near Douai, yielded
no evidence of conversion; but it is difficult to believe that a seventh-
century community of farm-workers raising stock for the nearby
royal villa of Vitry had never heard of Christianity.

One need not underestimate the practical advantages of conversion
to the king. By it he gained not merely the more active collaboration of
the Gallo-Roman bishops, with all that that meant administratively,
but direct control over them; that is to say over the Gallo-Romans
who really ran Gaul. This he was to exercise in a manner that was new.
Also, he entered into the select company of the barbarian *filii* of the
Eastern Emperor, becoming an imperial ally in the task of containing
Gothic Arianism. To the Eastern emperor, who accorded him an
honorific title, he seemed a God-sent champion against Arianism;
and that Clovis took the point is suggested by his following imperial
example in dedicating his Parisian Church to the Apostles. It equally
suggests some deference to Rome. He would probably have attacked
the Visigoths of southern Gaul in any event, but he could do it with
more colour as the Catholic ally of the emperor. On the other side was
still the risk of Frankish disapproval. This is made quite clear in a letter
written to him by the Catholic Bishop Avitus of Vienne, a subject of
the part-Arian Burgundians.[27] The bishop considers that it takes
courage to break with your ancestors' faith. Clovis will lose his
heathen *fortuna*, for which a Christian counterpart is substituted at
baptism; *sanctitas* is added to his armoury. Baptism is a rite that will
take the place of sacrifice in assuring victory in battle. The break with a
cherished ancestral past is what worries Avitus – and Clovis. Avitus
glances anxiously at that past but hopefully at the future. Something of
ancestral charisma might be saved, certainly, but its principal use as
the mainspring of present *fortuna* will be compromised. Avitus ex-
poses, as no one else, the true nature of the risk of conversion for a
king, which is not primarily how many of his subjects will accept
baptism for themselves, but how his good luck will be affected by
mortal insult to pagan gods sacred to his house, from whom in
addition he may have claimed descent. The dynastic basis of Clovis's
kingship was threatened.

How could the Church deal with this enduring risk, once royal
conversion had been obtained by opportune victory in the field? One
is not baptized twice, let alone every time one feels the need of divine

[26] P. Demolon, *Le Village mérovingien de Brebières* (Arras, 1972).
[27] Letter 38 (ed. Chevalier) or 46 (ed. Peiper).

reassurance. Will *sanctitas* replace *fortuna*? Are offerings at a Christian shrine really as efficacious as sacrifices? Is missionary work, such as Avitus advises, really a way of extending power? Clovis accepts the risk when he accepts the patronage of the miracle-working holy men of Gaul. Like others of his kind, he casts his net wide. The Apostles by themselves are not enough. He needs St Martin of Tours, St Hilary of Poitiers and perhaps more. Though baptized by Remigius at Reims, Clovis becomes first and foremost the man of St Martin of Tours. The shrines of holy men, and especially of martyrs, will be the homes of Frankish piety, the substitute for pagan *fana*. It was to Tours that Clovis turned before his assault on the Visigoths, and to Tours that he came back after his victory at Vouillé to give thanks and gifts and to receive the marks of imperial approbation. We do not have to treat sceptically the report of Gregory[28] that he ordered his warriors to take nothing but water and hay as they passed through the *territorium* of St Martin, out of reverence for the saint. He issued an *edictum* to this effect, and Gregory knew what an *edictum* was. Moreover, the king had sent to the basilica for an omen of victory, which was forthcoming. Pagan sacrificers had normally expected a sign from the gods in answer to the question that accompanied their sacrifice. Clovis offered his sacrifice: he gave gifts. In brief, he did not defeat the Visigoths, as he did the Alamans, on the off-chance of a prayer to the Christian god but as the man of St Martin, the miracle-worker *par excellence* of Gaul. He had acquired for his house the greatest of the Gallo-Roman patrons, to whose relics he could turn at any time. He also acquired other Gallic patrons of significant standing, like St Hilary of Poitiers. It was the kind of ghostly patronage a barbarian could understand. Even so, the centre of the king's interests lay north of the Loire. It was not in Tours or Poitiers that he arranged to be buried but in Paris, in the church dedicated to the Apostles that he himself built. Church-building of this period, both royal and aristocratic, was inspired above all by the need to provide a place of burial. The body of the Catholic Clovis was not to lie in a mound, like his ancestors' bodies, not in a stone mausoleum, like Theodoric's at Ravenna, but in a Catholic basilica, probably surrounded with a good deal of splendour. He may well have hoped that his successors would join him there, so that the church would become a dynastic burial-place, as St Augustine's at Canterbury was to become for Æthelberht's family. If so, he was to be disappointed. His successors showed a strong tendency to lay their bones near the holy man that each in his turn found most efficacious. It is very difficult to see behind the idealized picture of the successful Christian warrior that Gregory of Tours made out of the traditions

---

[28] *Hist.* ii, ch. 37.

available to him nearly a century later. It was a very skilful picture. But the real Clovis was more complex than he looks in the pages of Gregory. In his last years, for example, he exercised a controlling interest in the doings of the council of Orléans and yet at the same time sanctioned a barbarian law-book, *Lex Salica*, in which little if any Christian influence can be detected.[29] He might no longer on his own account sacrifice to the gods but *Lex Salica* implies that he protects the sacrificial pigs of his still-unconverted subjects.[30] He upholds the pagan practice of name-giving on the tenth day after birth; imposes a heavy fine on plunderers of corpses, buried or not; and makes a special case of the plundering of a body in a *tumba*, or the destruction of a *tumba*.[31] *Tumba* has the sense of *tumulum*, which indeed is the reading preferred in two manuscripts of *Lex Salica*. The fact that the crime, glossed with a Frankish word, *tornechale*, is distinguished from similar sacrilege committed against a body laid in a Christian basilica or against a mere gravestone, indicates that the king meant to protect those who had been buried as pagans just as much as those buried as Christians. Perhaps this is why the grave of his father, Childeric, remained undisturbed at Tournai. Conversion, therefore, was a lengthy business.

The seventh century marks a big change in what is known of Frankish graves and grave-goods. There are more of them, and the iconography is more distinctively Christian. Rural cemeteries continue in use even though the big men now lie in churches, often of their own foundation and dedicated to the holy men whose relics protect them and their kindred. The *locus classicus* is the monastery of St Denis, near Paris, where the saint's tomb was embellished in the late sixth century in the reign of Sigebert I,[32] and still further embellished by Dagobert I a few years later. This ancient burying-place was above all others sacred to the Merovingian house. The graves of several of its members have been excavated. The church of Jouarre, east of Paris, is a good example of the burying-place of a non-royal family that rose to prominence in the seventh century. In its crypt can still be seen the sarcophagi of some of them. At this social level and to some extent lower we can expect to find a grave-iconography that is no longer explicitly pagan. But it is from a pagan root that it has grown; a root that, like other strong roots, continues to send up suckers. Thus we

---

[29] Ed. K. A. Eckhardt, MGH Leges, iv, parts 1 and 2. *Lex Salica* 55, 5 is cited as a possible exception. The same prohibition is found in the council of Mâcon of 585, canon 17 (MGH Conc. i, p. 171).   [30] *Lex Salica* 2, 16.

[31] Ibid. 55 1–3, 6. Note in this context the burial of a fifth-century Frankish mercenary at Vermand, surrounded by a ditch and covered by a tumulus (Vera I. Evison, *The Fifth-Century invasions south of the Thames,* London, 1965, p. 11).

[32] Gregory of Tours, *Liber in gloria martyrum,* ch. 71 (MGH SRM I, ii, p. 535).

find grave-goods and monuments incised with motifs that are Christian
in intent though derived from pagan models, or are part-Christian,
part-pagan, in such a way that the dominant factor is sometimes in
doubt. Old habits persist, in religious iconography as in all else. There
will be times when the maker of a brooch or the sculptor of a stone will
be ignorant of the original meaning of a motif he adapts to a new
purpose; and this may equally apply to the owner and to those who lay
the object in his grave. In the early sixth century a Frankish chieftain
was buried at Lavoye (Meuse) in an extensive cemetery.[33] His grave-
goods (largely weapons) included a liturgical jug, presumably booty
from a church. Its presence in the grave must suggest that those who
buried him were either ignorant of its proper function or indifferent to
it. Whether or not formally Christian, the warrior was not to be
deprived of his loot because he was dead. We must also allow that the
pagan tutelary intention persists in a general way. There are many
examples.[34] What are we to make of human masks, often of great
ferocity and quite numerous in the seventh century, above which
Christian crosses have been cut? Or how should one interpret a buckle
from Marchélepot, on which two human heads seem to face a praying
figure, the whole surmounted by a swastika? Even so commonplace a
Christian scene as Daniel between his lions is not as straightforward as
it appears, for reminiscence of a pagan solar cult is possible, if not
probable. A pagan background is much more likely in the case of such
a brooch as that from Précy-sur-Vrin. Extremely barbarized, it seems
to portray Christ between St Peter and St Paul. At least it can be said in
favour of the identification of Christ that he holds a cross of sorts, if
nothing else can. Other brooches show a mixture of human figures,
crosses and animals that cannot be understood at all, at least at present.
If any of them were meant to be Christian, the pagan imagery is
dominant enough to swamp the message. The prize exhibit is a
funerary plaque of terracotta from Grésin in the Puy-de-Dôme.[35] It
shows Christ armed as a soldier, scramasax in belt and lance in hand,
with other curious accoutrements. He has a long phallus, there are
beasts round him and a snake under his feet; and he wears a head-dress
not unworthy of a pagan god. Were it not for the presence of the
Christian monogram with alpha and omega it would never occur to
anyone to detect Christ here, and the figure could pass for that of a
perfectly good pagan god. It has points of resemblance to the figure on
a brooch from Finglesham in Kent, which is now thought to be
Woden.[36] What was made of it by those who nailed it as a phylactery

---

[33] See R. Joffroy, *Le Cimetière de Lavoye* (Paris, 1974), p. 99.
[34] All illustrated in Salin.   [35] Salin, vol. 4, plate 11, i.
[36] See Ellis Davidson, *Antiquity*, 39 (1965), pp. 23–7.

inside a tomb? If they believed in Christ they had not got very far. Nor is the Grésin plaque unique. The same questions arise when one looks at the god on the Niederdollendorf gravestone.[37] If he is Christian, as some hold, because of the nimbus, we have a parody of Christianity by and for men still essentially pagan. Iconographically at least, one must conclude that examples of this sort from the seventh century betray a Christianity that is largely an adaptation of paganism, and one would not care to say that the symbolic content of that paganism had disappeared from the minds of makers or users.

This view is reinforced by literary sources, which also leave a clear impression that there was a religion of the countryside that was not that of the cities. It was outside the city-walls that Germanic paganism met the still-active paganism of the Celts and to an undetermined extent fused with it. The official pagan cultus of Rome, as practised in the cities, had long since yielded to Christianity; but the countryside was another matter. Indeed, there may have been some resurgence of Celtic paganism once the grip of Rome had slackened upon Gaul. The *dii patrii* of the Celts, gods of rivers, springs, woods and hills, were certainly worshipped at rural cult-centres in the earlier fifth century; and it was with such, whether Celtic or Frankish, that the first missionaries had to wrestle. How they set about it is vividly illustrated in an incident related by Gregory of Tours in his *Liber in gloria confessorum*.[38] It seems that a peasant community in the diocese of Javols, in the Lozère, observed a ceremony of throwing libations into a lake (probably the Lake of Saint-Andéol). These took the form of clothing, wool, cheeses, wax, bread and so on. The peasants came by carts, bringing picnics. They also sacrificed animals and then feasted for three days at a stretch. When the party was broken up by thunder and downpour, these were taken as omens – perhaps of the displeasure of a thunder-god like Thor. In due course the local bishop came to preach there, and got no reaction from the rustics. Learning of their ceremony, he dealt with the problem by building a church near the lake, which he dedicated to St Hilary of Poitiers and equipped with relics of the saint; and he admonished them to venerate the relics rather than the spirits of the lake: 'there is no religion in a pond!' This satisfied the rustics to the extent that thereafter they laid some offerings before the saint's relics; but almost within living memory they had not entirely abandoned their lake. Their conversion was neither from the purpose nor (sacrifice excepted) from the ritual of their former religion. They simply changed their patron and their venue. The line of demarcation between magic and prayer, an offering to a spirit of the countryside

[37] Salin, vol. 2, plate 1, i.
[38] MGH SRM 1, pp. 749–50.

and to a local saint, remained sufficiently vague to haunt generations of clerics. The *Passio* of St Vincent of Agen betrays another peasant-community – that of Vernemet – up to its pranks in the sixth century.[39] Annually, we are told, the peasants met on their hilltop under the leadership of their *praeses* to indulge in a specifically pagan ceremony. They rolled a flaming wheel downhill into the river, from which it emerged still flaming to make its ascent into the temple at the top. St Vincent put a stop to the practice by making the sign of the cross, whereupon the flames were extinguished and the wheel vanished. Vernemet was in southern Gaul, not in the Frankish north to which pagan practices were by no means confined. It was Caesarius, address-ing his people of Arles and not the Franks, whose writings were to prove specially useful to missionaries of a later time; and no bishop of the ninth century was more worried about widespread belief in signs and other magic than Agobard of Lyon. There had to be a source of magic, some god to propitiate. 'A shadowy conception of power that by much persuasion can be induced to refrain from inflicting harm is the shape most easily taken by the sense of the Invisible in the minds of men who have always been pressed close by primitive wants.' A missionary who proved rather less accommodating, after his Irish fashion, was St Columbanus. When he found some Alemannic peasants near Bregenz assembled round a great cauldron of beer intended as a sacrifice to Woden, he smashed their cauldron and released the devil who he had no doubt was hidden therein the better to seize the souls of the sacrificers.[40] In the worship of St Julian on the hill of Brioude there remained strong traces of the preceding pagan cult. Nor was it only the rustics who believed in devils. Columbanus saw them as Christian devils and dealt with them accordingly. He is not said to have built a church at Bregenz though the stupefied barbarians were suitably impressed and converted. Another missionary, Eligius, met with a more overtly hostile reception when he interrupted a pagan ceremony near Noyon. The pious natives, and Franks more powerful behind them, were so enraged that they almost killed him, remarking that they were not going to have their solemnities upset by a *Romanus*.[41] He further objected, as had Caesarius and others, to the wearing of amulets of any kind, even if made by a cleric or said to be holy or to contain biblical phrases; such things were not to be seen as tutelary gifts of Christ.[42] Grave-goods would hardly bear out that amulets

[39] See B. de Gaiffier, *Recueil d'hagiographie* (Brussels, 1977), ch. xi.
[40] *Vita* I, 27 (MGH SRM iv, 102). Columbanus had more to say about eating and drinking at pagan temples in his Penitential (ed. G. S. M. Walker, *Sancti Columbani Opera*, Dublin, 1957, p. 178).   [41] *Vita* I, 20 (MGH SRM iv, pp. 711–12).
[42] Ibid. 16, pp. 706–7.

became any less popular as a result of such teaching. Eligius escaped with his life. A bishop of Soissons was less lucky: he was thrown into a well.[43] St Boniface, later, saw danger in the placing of pagan motifs on clothing, such as a fringe of snakes, which he considered a presage of Antichrist.[44]

If missionaries found the going hard, so too did the Merovingian kings on whose protection they counted. According to Gregory of Tours, Theuderic I had to pacify a crowd of enraged peasants at Cologne, whose temple and idols had been burnt by a missionary. It had been an elaborate shrine, where offerings were made and feasts celebrated. Wooden images of injured human parts were suspended round it. The king took the best way out: 'he calmed them with smooth words and thus quenched their fury.'[45] Not very far to the west was Nivelles – Niuwiala, the new place of sacrifice – in due course to be the site of a famous nunnery. It was a strongly pagan region. Yet further north, Frankish missionaries under Merovingian protection suffered serious set-backs in an area that has rightly been described as vibrantly pagan. The see of Tournai had to be moved south to Noyon in 577, while that of Arras was combined with Cambrai. The bishop of Tongres took refuge in the *castellum* of Maastricht and for a while his see was combined with Cologne. This retreat of the Church, even when backed by Frankish forces, may be connected with some renewal of pagan cremation in the Low Countries and western Germany in the sixth and seventh centuries. Theuderic's son, Theudebert I, while at a safe distance from his bishops, sacrificed Ostrogothic women and children to celebrate the winning of control by his army over a bridge at Pavia. 'These barbarians,' commented the Greek historian Procopius, 'though they have become Christians, preserve the greater part of their ancient religion, for they still make human sacrifices of an unholy nature, and it is in connection with these that they make their prophecies.'[46] This same Theudebert was the recipient of the first known (but no longer extant) papal letter to a Frankish king; it came from Pope Vigilius and faced the issue of a barbarian's marriage with a sister-in-law. The popes were by no means to remain indifferent to the Merovingians, nor the Merovingians to them. Both Theuderic and Theudebert found themselves drawn into the affairs of pagan Germania as overlords of the southward-moving Saxons, and, with them, as implacable enemies of Thuringian power. It was not a

[43] *Gallia Christiana* ix, col. 339, art. 25.
[44] Letter to Archbishop Cuthbert (*Die Briefe des heiligen Bonifatius und Lullus*, MGH Epistolae Selectae i, Berlin 1955, ed. M. Tangl, no. 78, p. 170).
[45] *Vitae Patrum Liber* vi, 2 (MGH SRM I, ii, p. 681). There are further accounts of temple destruction in saints' Lives.
[46] *History of the Wars*, Bk. vi, xxv, 7–10 (ed. H. B. Dewing, Loeb 1924).

propitious field for Christian missionaries and one must suppose that at this early stage the Merovingians were content to leave these important pagans to their own beliefs.

But whatever the risk to themselves or to the charisma of their house, the Merovingians did try to suppress paganism within Francia proper. There survives a fragment of a *carta* or *praeceptum* of Childebert I, issued probably in 533 or soon after.[47] (We can date it so because the contents seem to be consequential upon canon 20 of the Council of Orléans of that year, which was attended by the bishops of Childebert's kingdom as well as of the kingdoms of his two brothers.) He starts off by stating his belief that it will be to his personal advantage as well as to his peoples' if they now serve God properly by abandoning the worship of idols. They have not, he goes on, listened to their bishops and so he proposes to correct them himself. All who have idols or images are to destroy them forthwith. He is thinking not of rustics throwing objects into lakes but of men of property on whose lands cult-idols stand. Only when he has made this clear does he proceed to consider the simpler manifestations of paganism, such as drunken wakes and scurrilous songs and dancing, through which God is injured and sinful men find death. Equally significant are the personal reasons he advances for this active intervention. His words suggest that the Franks he rules have only recently been converted. They had not yet grasped that the destruction of idols is a consequence of their accepting the Christian god 'to whom I have pledged my entire loyalty'. He speaks for himself and undertakes to compel his whole people to abandon paganism in every shape. So far, his bishops have failed to bring this about. He therefore intervenes to back them with his personal authority because his salvation depends on it. He is going much further than his father, Clovis, ever did. We have reached a new stage in national conversion and have no reason to think that Childebert is acting under episcopal compulsion, unwillingly, or in the hope of gaining short-term material advantage only. He accepts the Christian god as a complete substitute for the pagan gods, in war and peace, for himself, his family and his people. What he understood by the Christian god is a matter on which we have no direct information. He ends by imposing a penalty of one hundred lashes for any servile person who persists in sacrilege. If the culprit were a free man or one of higher rank, he too would have his punishment, but the manuscript that alone records the *praeceptum* is mutilated at this point. At least we know that Childebert envisaged no exceptions. All his Franks were to give up paganism. His brother, Chlotar I, whose bishops were also present at the Orléans council of 533, seems to have been more

[47] MGH Capit. 1, pp. 2, 3.

equivocal in coping with his pagans. According to the Life of St Vaast of Arras, one of Chlotar's courtiers gave a party at which a cauldron of beer, following pagan custom, figured in a prominent place. The excuse that some of those present were Christians but others pagan did not stop the holy man from marking it with a cross, and thus breaking it. The incident is said to have led to the conversion of many who were there. Chlotar had not been very active up to that point.[48] We are now a full generation from the baptism of Clovis. Subsequent evidence points to a steady move away from paganism among the men of property and position, though pagan practices among the rustics (or such practices disguised as Christian) were stamped out neither by royal edicts nor by busy bishops. Indeed, some last to this day.

In conclusion, what can be said of the nature of Frankish paganism? In the first place, the evidence is thinner for all the West Germans than it is for the East Germans; and the Franks were West Germans. Much of it is late sixth or early seventh century and some of it that we call Frankish may not be Frankish in the strict sense. Nevertheless, a people ruled by a dynasty that they accepted as divine, inasmuch as it claimed to be sprung from a Minotaur, fits well into the general pattern of Germanic paganism as it is nowadays understood. To look no further, we are in the same thought-world as the Goths with their *semi-dei* or *Anses* for ancestors of the royal line.[49] Kings who were divinely descended were mediators between their people and the gods, ensuring good luck in war and peace. It is not out of the question that *Lex Salica* was Clovis's way of reassuring his people that conversion had not divorced him from their traditional interests and pursuits. He still cared about their daily life and took its moral guide-lines under his protection. He was still their father; indeed, would look after them more. Their trust in his charisma is such that they do accept him as the servant of a new god, without for the most part abandoning their old gods. They were on the way to seeing the new Merovingian god as successful in war and active for their protection through the shrines of holy men. Miracles at local shrines were a substitute for local pagan cultus. Holy men and their servants cared for the kindred, living and dead. This is another way of saying that the Christianity they slowly came to accept must have been presented to them, as far as was possible, as a religion essentially aimed at the same objects as the paganism they were asked to abjure. A good source of information about Frankish paganism is therefore Frankish Christianity. We should, then, see that paganism as the religion of a social people, a people living and thinking in terms of kindreds and families. It gave them a

---

[48] *Vita Vedastis*, ch. 7 (MGH SRM iii, pp. 314–16).
[49] Jordanes, *Getica*, xiii (ed. Mommsen, MGH AA v, i, p. 76).

past and a future, uniting them as kindreds with their ancestors. Their gods, too, had a history that will have been closely associated with their occupation of new lands. It is precisely this historical web that was precious to them and that could unwisely have been discarded in the process of conversion. There is virtually no place-name evidence in France, as there is in England, of the identity of the gods who saw them to victory and new lands. Why this should have been so is a matter still requiring investigation. The Parisian Mercury's hill, so named by the Romans, remained Mercury's hill. The Celtic equivalent would have been the hill of Teutates or Esus. But the Celts had been satisfied with the Roman name, and so were the Franks. Mons Mercurius it remained until comparatively recent times, when the martyrs took it over, to give us Montmartre.

It is hard to tell if the Franks attached any religious significance to the names of the days of the week commonly used by the Gallo-Romans. Most of these names were taken from the stars or planets and so were associated with the gods whose names they bore. Some Germans, but not the Franks, substituted equivalent Germanic gods for the gods of Rome. It could be that the Latin words had long lost their original religious sense; yet this seems not always to have been the case. The fifth-century church was worried about the blasphemous usage. St Augustine instanced 'Mercurii dies' as a regrettable usage, which many Christians adopted; Caesarius considered them 'disgusting names'; and Isidore echoed this in his reference to the fourth day of the week 'which pagans call Mercury's day'. Experts say that it is not merely the name but the form that is revealing;[50] for those people who said 'Mercurii dies', 'Martis dies', etc. (and this includes the French with their 'Mardi') remained longer aware of the religious content of the word than did those who said 'dies Mercurii', dies Martis', etc. Gregory reports that the Franks in his day still preferred *dies solis* to *dies dominicus*;[51] and Gregory's contemporary, Martin of Braga, considered that the rustic Germans of his part of north-west Spain attached a great deal too much importance to these matters. A few French words betray a pagan ritual ancestry, as for example, *joli*, from Frankish *jeohl*, the feast of Yule. As in Anglo-Saxon England, this was an important occasion of sacrifice, when a communal meal of ritual significance was eaten; and from this the *gild*, a meal and sacrifice commemorating the dead, is thought to derive. As elsewhere, major pagan festivals were to some degree subsumed by the Church. Thus their winter commemorative feast in November was to become All Saints' Day. Other words derived from pagan practice are Old French

---

[50] Cf. W. von Wartburg, 'Les noms des jours de la semaine dans les langues romanes', *Von Sprache und Mensch* (Bern, 1956), pp. 45–60.   [51] *Hist.* iii, 15.

truiller (from *trulljan*) to bewitch; and *guiler* (from *wigila*, a spell), to deceive. But this can be pressed too far. Only in the field of archaeological evidence do we find widespread remains of a kind that point to the same general beliefs. In the end, the Frankish peasant will not have had much interest in the war gods of his superiors, but gods he plainly did have who protected his family, his house and his livelihood, linked him at the graveside with his dead kindred and ensured him and his a future in their company. When he feasted and danced before his gods he was having a good time and a holiday. But he was having something more: an ecstatic experience shared with his kindred and neighbours, bringing them all into communion with the dead. This sense of community between the living and the dead persisted. Witnesses to it are the monastic necrologies and *libri memoriales* of Christian Francia. Traditional Christian prayers like the *Commendatio Animae*[52] would have appealed to converts, since they invoked in a historicizing way protection for the dying from a god whose Bible gave repeated proof of his willingness to save. All this, for the Franks as for the Germans, indicated the general lines along which conversion might prove safe and profitable. But they had not entered Gaul a united people. They became so as a result of their conquest of Gaul under a dynasty that had a short way with rivals. Victory will have done something for the repute of the gods the Merovingians acknowledged, but the Franks at large will have worshipped whatever gods took the fancy of this or that kindred or following. Similarly, each small group will have made its own terms with whatever Celtic gods it encountered in the countryside, and much the same may hold true for its reactions to Christianity, as and when it reached them. In the end, Christianity was to have an advantage not often enjoyed by any pagan cult: at one and the same time it offered victory to the warrior and protective magic to the peasant. It was socially cohesive.

It is not to be supposed that barbarian kings, let alone their peoples, would have accepted conversion unless they felt some sense of religious continuity. A spiritual revolution was never in question. On the other hand, neither were the serious implications first of paganism and then of Christianity to the barbarians ever in question. The business of national conversion was long and complex. Yet there is, even at so early a stage, some realignment of spiritual values of which some barbarians will have been dimly aware. Their Gallo-Roman mentors included men of intellectual and spiritual calibre, involved in theological issues of real moment, as, for example, the threat of Arianism, which preoccupied Caesarius of Arles at the beginning of the sixth century and was still preoccupying Gregory of Tours and his colleagues at its

---

[52] Text in Salin, vol. 4, p. 341.

end. We do not have to wait very long before there are bishops of Frankish blood; and several members of the Merovingian family showed either an interest in theology or a practical concern for the spiritual life of the cloister. Nevertheless, the first stage of the transition to Christianity was, as we have seen, a matter related not to theology but to the substitution of one kind of folk-magic for another. It could not have been otherwise.

III

THE CONTRIBUTION OF HISTORY

OF the major historians of the early middle ages, only Bishop Gregory of Tours, who died in 593 or 594, paints a lurid picture of society. Unlike Bede, a century later, the people of whom he writes were heirs to an illustrious past, of which they seemed to him to have proved unworthy. The Gallo-Roman Church had been a great Church. To it the bishop himself was firmly anchored, descended as he was, through both father and mother, from senatorial families of high standing. His family had provided bishops for the sees of Langres, Lyon, Clermont and Tours (indeed, many of the bishops of Tours). This proud background will often explain his reaction to events in particular dioceses. By birth and upbringing he was thus involved in great matters in a way that Bede was never to be. That he should be a writer as well as a doer is not surprising. Some of his writings – on the martyrs, fathers and confessors of his Church – will concern us later. For the present it matters that he also wrote history and stood alone in his generation in doing so: not specifically a history of the Gallo-Roman or Gallo-Frankish Church nor a history of the Franks, but what he entitled *Libri Historiarum Decem*, ten books of history, no more and no less.[1]

One purpose, if not the main purpose, of Gregory's History was to give the Church, the Gallo-Frankish Church, and within it the Church of Tours, a record of its past. Time and again his thoughts about the present lead back into the fourth and fifth centuries, the age of the great aristocrat-bishops, when asceticism assumed the function of martyrdom as the road to sanctity and whole communities were moved by miracles. It was the age of the saints, in which his own forebears had played their part; in retrospect a golden age. The thoughts of a bishop would perhaps inevitably lead back there, though the mere discovery of the past would not provide a motive for writing about it. The past that Gregory discovers is not so much that out of which the present had grown; it is not development that interests him. The Gallic past is more a standard by which the present can be assessed. It bulks large in his mind because it was accessible to him. Yet the same standard, the immutable standard of Christian behaviour, can be found elsewhere

---

[1] The best edition is that of Krusch and Levison, MGH SRM 1, i (1951). The English translation by O. M. Dalton, *The History of the Franks by Gregory of Tours* (Oxford, 1927) is reliable though his introductory volume should be used with caution. There is a more recent French translation by R. Latouche (Paris, 1963).

and at other times. It can be seen in the Primitive Church. In a word, there was an undifferentiated Christian past, dear to the early medieval mind. By turning to it and by isolating those features of it that seemed significant to him, Gregory makes all of it the past of his own present. His sixth-century Church was thus rooted in the tradition of whatever was best. But the reason why he turned to it is to be sought in the present.

In the historical sense, it can be said that the present for Gregory was a matter of some three generations, beginning with the conquests of Clovis and proceeding through the lifetimes of his sons to those of his grandsons, Gregory's own contemporaries. One has only to look at the proportions of his History to see that Clovis, however heroic in stature, belongs to Gregory's own time in a way in which the pre-Merovingian Frankish past and the Gallo-Roman past did not. The secular record of these remoter times is principally included, as Gregory insists, to provide a chronological framework. Book I of the History spans the ages between the Creation and the death of St Martin in 397, and Book II covers the Frankish advance to the death of Clovis in 511. There remain eight more books, devoted to the eighty years 511 to 591. It may well be that the significance of this chronology for Gregory lay in the calculation of when the year 6000 from the beginning of the world would fall; for that would be the year of Antichrist. In the late sixth century that year seemed not so comfortably distant but that premonitions and presages might be expected. Indeed, the fear seemed to grow on him as he moved in fits and starts through the writing of his History. The reasons for his writing history therefore lie within the happenings of a few Gallo-Frankish generations. It cannot be denied that for Gregory those eighty years had seen an accelerating decline from hope to something near despair. It was not political decline: Gregory makes no judgement as to the efficacy of Frankish rule over Gaul and has no objection to what we call barbarian kingship. He is not troubled by competing influence in high places of Franks and Gallo-Romans. Nor is he concerned with problems of social integration. His fears lie rather in what had been happening to Gallo-Frankish society as a unit of the Church; they are moral, not political. And this is precisely what he says, and repeats: there has been much good and much evil, with the latter preponderant; and what he therefore has to record is a tale of warfare – of kings with enemies, of martyrs with heathen, of churches with heretics, and, he might have added, of individuals in all walks of life with the moral problems that are raised by opportunities for cupidity, power, lust and so forth. The society that he sees is not a pleasant one, but it is in the nature of a history constructed from the multiplicity of doings and misdoings of individuals that it should look unpleasant. If Bede had wished to write an English history on the same principles he must have painted a picture equally dark. We must not think, therefore, that Frankish society was exceptional in contemporary terms of violence and vice. Gregory believed that the world was approaching its promised end, though he assumed that he would yet have successors in the see of Tours to profit from what he had written. But this was at most a general ground for modified dismay. His sense of despair was based on something more immediate. He judged that the men he knew had lost their way; which meant that the Church, too, had lost its way. It was for this reason that he wrote history. He does not say, as Bede does, that his record of good and evil deeds should actively assist his readers as encouragement or deterrent. All he claims is this: 'I have been moved, in my crude way, to preserve for those who came after a record of what has happened, including the conflicts of the wicked and the lives of those who have lived well.'[2] His purpose is not to teach but to record. And it is this, the record of the thing as it happens, that lends his History a vividness that any historian might envy. Bearing in mind this purpose, it is easier to assess what he has to say of the Gallo-Frankish Church he had been brought up in and served all his life.

First, and perhaps most significant, is the atmosphere of Gregory's century. The society he knows is in some ways a nightmare-society, living in fear. It is suffused with the miraculous – with the performing of miracles by the living and the dead and by the reaction of society to miracles. There is nothing in this that is specifically Frankish; it is no part of any barbarisation that can be attributed to the Franks alone. Indeed, Gregory takes pains to link his miracle-stories with the Gallo-Roman past, so that we cannot claim them as evidence of any break between the fifth and sixth centuries. The most notable link is St Martin, whose miracles, both in his lifetime and after death, are a vital part of the historical background. Martin broods over the Merovingians, who have taken him as their patron; the father of the Tours tradition of anti-Arianism, a bishop and a miracle-worker. It seems likely that it was Bishop Remigius who first introduced Clovis to St Martin's cult, since Martin was honoured at Reims. Under Martin, Gregory tells us, and with the added assistance of St Hilary, Clovis defeated the Visigoths; through Martin's intervention, secured by the prayer of Queen Chrotechildis, the horrible Chlotar I was saved by a thunderstorm from the armies of his brothers; for fear of his vengeance Chlotar remitted the taxation of the citizens of Tours; and to him the same king confessed his sins shortly before his death. Chilperic I even wrote a letter to the saint, to which he expected a reply. To these could

[2] *Hist.*, praefatio prima.

be added many instances of the dire consequences to lesser men of violating the sanctity of the saint's tomb or *territorium* or property wherever situated. Perhaps the best proof of Martinian patronage of the Merovingians is the elaborate poem on Martin written by Venantius Fortunatus (Gregory's contemporary) which is based – but only based – on the work of Sulpicius Severus.[3]

But St Martin did not have the field to himself. One is struck by the number of saints the Merovingians thought it prudent to enlist the help of; and this could easily be illustrated from the church-dedications of the Parisian region alone.[4] Gregory gives a careful account of how the city of Saragossa was saved from the besieging Franks through prayer to St Vincent. This prayer was a corporate act by the whole body of citizens, who abstained from food and drink, wore hair shirts and processed round the walls with their martyr's tunic. Their women-folk accompanied them in the garb of mourning widows. The watching Franks thought that some kind of magic was being practised, which indeed it was; and when they learned whose tunic was being carried round, they lifted the siege in fear and withdrew. The Frankish army believed in the protection of relics just as much as did the Saragossans. Not long afterwards the Merovingian pretender Gundovald made great efforts to obtain a relic of St Sergius from a Syrian named Eufronius, seeking, as Gregory says, 'every possible way of furthering his cause'.[5] It did him no good. But Gregory gives equal attention to miracles worked by living men. The tradition of the holy man clearly flourished in the atmosphere of sixth-century Gaul. We have the priest Julian of Clermont, hair-shirted and worn out with standing, who made nothing of healing the blind. Gregory himself once watched him cure a crazy man with a single word. Bishop Germanus of Paris worked miracles in his lifetime, at the time of his burial, and from the tomb. Patroclus of Bourges, a recluse, specialized in curing fever and pustules. The abbot Aredius was a water-diviner and a diverter of rain, as well as being good at curing toothache. Bishop Domnolus of Le Mans, a simple man credited with many miracles, refused the southern see of Avignon because he feared the teasing of 'sophisticated sena-torials or philosophizing counts'.[6] All these, as Gregory describes them, were considerable persons, and none more so than King Guntramn, whose robes had thaumaturgical powers and the invoca-tion of whose name could compel evil spirits to declare themselves. But miracles were associated with lowlier people, too. The chains of unnamed prisoners at Clermont fell off them during the night, not

---

[3] In four books, ed. F. Leo, MGH AA IV, i (1881).
[4] See M. Roblin, *Le Terroir de Paris* (Paris, 1971), pp. 157 ff.
[5] *Hist.* vii, 31.   [6] Ibid. vi, 9.

once but twice; and an essential point about the dramatic tale of the escape of Attalus from his master is that the yard-gates of his master's house were miraculously opened for him. One could multiply examples of this kind as Gregory recounts them. What they will have signified to Gregory's first readers is evidence that they expected: for them, miracles must happen as proofs of God's providence. Does it also follow that they could have little effect on the normal routine of life of a society seen by Gregory as set on a collision course?

Naturally it was a short step from miracles associated directly with Christian belief to something more deeply engrained. There are plenty of religious maniacs in Gregory's pages who imposed on the rustics. Some did a good trade in false relics such a moles' teeth, bears' claws and the bones of mice. Queen Fredegundis was convinced that her son's death was the result of witchcraft by certain Parisiennes; and by witchcraft a man's mistresses were said to have affected his reason. There were signs, good and bad, for all who were on the alert. Guntramn was notably awake to them, as for example to a good sign at his nephew's birth. Gregory's bad signs, which are numerous, are often phenomena of weather, such as a rain of blood, roses in January, a frost that kills the swallows and certain well-observed cloud-formations. All such could presage disaster on a local or national scale, Gregory is a careful observer of natural phenomena. There might, he thought, be rational explanations for some such, though not for others. All, however, signified God's intervention in the affairs of the world. They should be looked for and interpreted. The question that he asks himself is not 'how' they occur but 'why'. Yet there is often a remedy to ward off evident signs of God's displeasure. The saints and their relics, prayer and repentance, are for that very purpose. His History, then, can rightly, from this viewpoint, be called a theophany or manifestation of God's continuing activity in the affairs of man.

The Gallo-Frankish God thus presided over a society ever on the look-out for evidence of his pleasure or displeasure. It can hardly be surprising that he was greatly feared. Chilperic was especially concerned about the connection between his misdoings and divine displeasure. One Easter he entered Paris preceded by many relics to avert, if he could, the divine curse that must be incurred by entering the city without his brothers' consent. Urged by Fredegundis, his queen, he burned the tax-lists in a vain attempt to save his young sons from the plague, and after their deaths, now convinced that God had thus taken vengeance on him for his sins, made great gifts to cathedrals and churches and to the poor. In the end, he believed that these same sins had deprived him of any direct male heir. His brother Guntramn was no less worried, for all his reputation for miracle working and generosity to the Church. He once banished two atrociously ill-living bishops to monasteries, only to release them when it was suggested to him that if by chance they had been unjustly banished and his own sin thereby increased, his heir might die as a result. 'Free them at once', he ordered, 'and beg them to pray for my young sons.'[7] The safety of the dynasty seemed at all times to rest on the prayers of the Church and no king felt that he could afford to forgo them.

Such, then, is the atmosphere of Gregory's History; an atmosphere of guilt in the sight of a God who would take instant vengeance on those who misinterpreted his will or misused his saints or appropriated their relics and their properties. A counterpart to this is the recurrent theme of human vengeance and violence. Gregory has many tales of this type and never spares his readers the details of torture and death. He is not shocked by them and sometimes even approves of them. They are there because he means to describe the thing happening; greed, violence and retribution; *saevitas* turned in upon itself. And he does so with unexampled skill in what is a highly-wrought picture. His contemporaries might have been mystified by some of the motives he assigned as causes of human action but would not have questioned his general position on the relationship of the spiritual to the material world.

Gregory's Church in its physical and material contexts was a Church that had always had patrons and despoilers; and there they still were. Franks, like Gallo-Romans, often appear on the ecclesiastical scene in one or other of these roles. But the Gallo-Frankish bishops and monasteries now had masters as well as patrons and despoilers, where before there were none. The early Merovingians were good masters, less because the Church provided them with men competent to understand the remnants of Roman provincial administration than because they stood in fear of the Church's god and in constant need of the Church's support of their exclusive claim to rule Franks and Gallo-Romans. Gregory makes a revealing observation about this claim; the victories of Clovis, he writes, were the proof that his family was the original long-haired race of Frankish kings. On the whole, the bishops of the sixth century were an impressive body; yet many of them – some, laymen – were appointed directly by kings and all with royal approval. A few were terrible, as for example Cautinus of Clermont, Salonius of Embrun and Sagittarius of Gap. One can easily see that Gregory's own ideal of the good bishop was old-fashioned. He liked Sulpicius, preferred to see the Bourges by King Guntramn. The king dismissed rival candidates who expected to bribe their way into his favour with the words 'It has not been my custom to put

[7] Ibid. v, 20.

bishoprics up for sale'. Gregory describes Sulpicius thus: 'he is a man of most noble blood, son of a senatorial family and among the first in Gaul; he is a learned rhetorician and second to none as a poet'.[8] He might almost be describing Sidonius. At least he is not of the opinion that the late sixth century requires bishops essentially different from those of the late fifth century. Blood still counted, and polite learning if it could be had. But it was not always for these virtues that kings respected bishops and took care over their appointments; the office itself impressed them, with all that it implied as to spiritual patronage and guardianship. This was why Guntramn allowed Salonius and Sagittarius to appeal to Rome; and why King Sigebert supported the bishop and archdeacon of Marseille against his own local governor. Kings knew well enough what spiritual dangers they ran in ignoring the advice of bishops or the judgements of church councils. Gregory goes so far as to assert that it was heresy to disobey a bishop, and no one would have disputed his opinion that God himself avenged wrongs done to bishops. Kings accustomed from their youth to look back to their forebears for examples of courage and success would not have failed to mark that bishops equally stood in a proud line of succession, each conscious of his predecessor's example. Nowhere does this stand out more clearly than in the final chapters of Gregory's History, where he lists the bishops of Tours, not a few of whom he counted as relations. There they stand, an accumulation of virtues, renowned for their buildings, their parish-foundations and their loyal guardianship of St Martin's relics, all in a sense encapsulated in the person of the reigning bishop. Certainly it was possible for a king to turn nasty. Guntramn was understandably furious with the southern bishops who supported the pretender Gundovald, though even then he kept stricter control over his passions than kings often showed. Egidius of Reims did more than enough to justify the charge that he was an enemy to King Childebert and a traitor to his country. Perhaps we can best see the complex nature of the relationship of kings with bishops in two celebrated rows: that over Bishop Praetextatus, and the trouble with the nuns of Poitiers.

As Gregory describes the matter,[9] it is quite clear that King Chilperic, by nature a suspicious man, had some reason to suspect Praetextatus of Rouen of hostility and even of disloyalty to himself. Because of this, as much as for their fear of the king, most of the bishops assembled at Paris to try their brother were disposed to find him guilty of aiding and abetting the king's son in rebellion, and perhaps also of theft. Certainly the king had lost confidence in him and recognized him as a personal enemy of his queen. Whether or not the

[8] Ibid. vi, 39.   [9] Ibid. v, 18.

charges were trumped up, as Gregory asserts they were, the fact remained as Bishop Bertramn of Bordeaux stated it to Praetextatus: 'you are out of favour with the king and therefore you cannot have our friendship either, until the king pardons you'. Formally at least, Chilperic pursued his vendetta with Praetextatus through the approved channels; he did not simply spirit him away and have him assassinated, as he might have done with an offending layman. He was far too impressed by the corporate power of his bishops to do any such thing. The very office of bishop commanded his respect. But over and above the spiritual requirements of the office, the king expected personal loyalty. In the Merovingian kingdoms, political stability depended on the trust that public men could place in each other. Chilperic distrusted Praetextatus.

The case of the nuns of Poitiers raises different problems.[10] Here we have a rebellion of aristocratic nuns, if nuns they were, in no less a convent than that founded by St Radegundis, herself a queen. Two of the nuns, both daughters of kings, rebelled against their abbess and caused at least forty others to join them. Leaving the convent, they decided to put their case to their kinsman, the king, against the advice of Gregory of Tours and presumably of their own somewhat hostile bishop, Maroveus of Poitiers. King Guntramn proved sympathetic up to a point but ordered an episcopal enquiry. Meanwhile the rebellious nuns barricaded themselves in a church with a gang of ruffians to protect them. The bishops made their enquiry on the spot, at some personal risk, excommunicated the nuns and reported back to Guntramn that they still refused to return to their convent. Gregory gives us the letter from the bishops then at Guntramn's court acknowledging the report. A full episcopal council was to be summoned to consider the next step. Meanwhile Guntramn's nephew, King Childebert, 'ceaselessly vexed', says Gregory, 'by both parties', sent a court-priest to arbitrate, but without effect. The rebels next broke into the convent, pillaged it and carried the abbess to their stronghold. The abbess was duly rescued but the rioting in the city of Poitiers increased to the extent that the local count was at last told to restore order by force. This he did, though met by Chrotechildis, the ringleader, with the words: 'Do me no violence: I am a queen, a king's daughter and cousin of another king. Restrain yourself, or one day I shall have my revenge on you.' When the council met she hurled abuse at the abbess. But the charges amounted to nothing; the abbess was cleared, the rebellious nuns ordered to do penance and the implementation of all this respectfully handed over to Kings Guntramn and Childebert. In the event, Childebert begged that his two kinswomen might be

[10] Ibid. ix, 39.

pardoned and received back into communion, the less guilty to re-enter the convent and her cousin Chrotechildis to retire to an estate granted to her by the king. And this apparently is what happened. The scandal was at an end, after having caused two kings and many bishops some very anxious moments. It had been a matter of national importance and reveals several significant points: the necessity of obedience of nuns to their Rule, their abbess and bishop; the power of royal ladies to ignore this obedience and to appeal on grounds of kinship to kings; the anxiety of kings to uphold the Rule of a great convent established and enriched by their predecessors; and the capacity of bishops to speak as one, if after some hesitation, in a real emergency. Chrotechildis did not succeed in getting rid of her abbess; but on the other hand she was not treated as a rebellious nun of lowlier birth would have been, and had undoubtedly felt that her grievance at not being deferred to as a royal lady within a convent's walls would justify her extraordinary conduct in the eyes of her kinsmen. The balance between conflicting claims of obedience and blood, and perhaps also of property, was a fine one and easily upset. On the whole, one is impressed by the sense of responsibility shown by those most concerned in re-establishing peace, as well as by their constant appeal to the past: that is, to the intentions of founders and benefactors as set out in documents that could be produced and considered. Gregory judges the incident to merit careful and vivid recording for posterity.

Church property, whether in land or treasure, was by this time an inevitable cause of friction; and of this Gregory gives many instances. It was inevitable because the gifts that placated saints and ensured spiritual benefits for the donors' families were by their nature withdrawn in perpetuity from the market, constituting an ever-accumulating stock of wealth that attracted privileges of exemption from normal burdens. Privilege indeed was the hallmark of ecclesiastical ownership, whether of land, treasure or relics. The privileges enjoyed by the lands of St Martin are often referred to by Gregory, usually in the context of their protection against attack or invasion. Once only is there a clear indication of a king grasping the significance of unceasing donations to churches, when Gregory imputes to Chilperic the characteristically shrewd outburst: 'See how my treasure has been drained away and my wealth transferred to churches! Only bishops rule nowadays! My royal honour has deserted me for the bishops in their cities!'[11] In fact the Merovingians still had large resources, but Chilperic had no illusions about episcopal wealth and the power it implied. He was not in practice as hostile to bishops in general as Gregory pretends he was, and knew full well how to manage them. It

[11] Ibid. vi, 46.

was their wealth and not their spiritual patronage that roused his scepticism. But though Chilperic saw the problem, and Gregory rather naïvely betrayed that he saw it, he could do nothing to solve it. Churches and monasteries all over Frankish Gaul continued to attract gifts from the laity, from kings downwards; nor can we understand sixth-century society unless we appreciate that the ferocious Franks of Gregory's History were precisely those who endowed religious foundations and trusted in the saving power of saints. The uses to which the Church put its wealth were not called in question by the laity; there is evidence enough that traditional duties of charity on a very large scale were not neglected, and the upkeep of comparatively magnificent establishments honoured the saints under whose invocation they stood. Attacks on church property, at least as Gregory reports them, were motivated by the simple impulse to rob where it was worth robbing, not by any deliberate intention to rob the saint who owned the property. For example, thieves broke into the Church of St Martin at Tours, stole what they could and decamped to Bordeaux, where they quarrelled. One was killed and the others were taken to King Chilperic, who would have had them executed but for the bishop's plea for clemency. This is a straightforward case that could have come from any medieval century. Or again, Sigivald seized a church estate in the Auvergne and promptly went mad. But he also seized much else that had nothing to do with the Church. Laying waste of church property could be incidental to a more general intention to do the maximum possible damage to an enemy, as when Chilperic sent his son Theudebert to ravage Sigebert's western cities, in an area, that is, particularly rich in church property. In Gregory's words, 'he burned churches, stole sacred vessels, slew clergy, destroyed monasteries, used nunneries with contempt and laid all waste. There was greater lamentation in the churches then than in the time of Diocletian's persecution.'[12] But this he did because they lay in Sigebert's kingdom. Similarly the lands of St Martin suffered when the freebooter Chuppa carried out an extensive plundering raid round Tours, only to excite a successful resistance by the inhabitants. He was after what booty he could get, lay or ecclesiastical. There were, in fact, two distinct dangers: first the private raider or robber, who would almost certainly find the civil power against him in the long run; and secondly the ravaging army that was inseparable from the family wars of the Merovingians. These wars were the *belle civilia*, often inter-city wars, so much dreaded by Gregory and which indeed form one of the recurrent themes of his History. He dreaded them as a manifestation of greed but also because of their terrible destructiveness. But why

12 Ibid. iv, 47.

should armies refrain from destroying churches when they destroyed everything else, and how were they to distinguish between a vineyard belonging to a saint and another belonging to a layman? Gregory puts the matter like this, in an address delivered by King Guntramn to his commanders:

> How are we to win victories when we no longer respect what our fathers respected? They built churches, put all their trust in God, honoured the martyrs, venerated the clergy, and so won their victories . . . Whereas we show no fear of God but devastate his holy places, kill his ministers, disperse and destroy the relics of the saints and mock at them. There cannot be victory while we do such deeds. This is why our hands are powerless, our swords are blunted and our shields no longer the defence they once were. If I am to blame for all this, let God's punishment fall on my head. But if it is you who have been disobeying my royal commands, the time is ripe for burying the axe in your heads.[13]

One could not have a clearer statement that in the eyes of a pious Merovingian victory depended on not ravaging churches.

But restraint in such matters was not enough. Something positive was expected: a steady stream of largess, both in property and in treasure in its various forms. Gregory assumes this and gives some evidence that it was forthcoming. He does more: by frequent reference back to earlier donations and to documents confirming them he shows that continuity in donations was also expected. Families that had once proved generous were to make a practice of it and were to be reminded of their duty for the sake of their forebears' souls as well as their own. There was, for instance, enough documentation in the case of the nuns of Poitiers to prove that records of donations had been carefully preserved since the foundation of the house.[14] Recipients would in general be careful to keep written evidence of transactions important to them when they could do so. The trial of Bishop Egidius of Reims, accused of disloyalty to Childebert, illustrates the point. The bishop claimed that certain estates had been granted him by royal charters, which he produced in evidence. Their authenticity was questioned, and so the referendary who was alleged to have written them was summoned, and declared the handwriting a forgery. Next, damaging letters were produced, which the bishop in his turn denied having written. But again he was caught out because a clerk could be produced who had kept shorthand copies of them in the bishop's archives. Further evidence against him was found among documents 'in one of the cases of papers in the muniment room of King Chilperic', which

---

[13] Ibid. viii, 30.
[14] On the documents cited by Gregory see K. H. Debus, 'Studien zu merowingischen Urkunden und Briefen', *Archiv für Diplomatik*, 14 (1968), pp. 53ff.

papers 'had passed into King Childebert's possession after Chilperic's death'.[15] Here is some indication that the making and keeping of documents in the sixth century was less haphazard than we might infer from the few survivors. Donors knew what they and their ancestors had donated. Gregory has no need to tell his readers that this or that donation was recorded in writing. There is no mention of writing in the interesting case of Duke Chrodin – interesting because we do not have many accounts of donations by landowners below royal rank. There is no reason to think this case exceptional. Gregory writes as follows:[16]

In this year died Chrodin, a man outstanding in goodness and piety, a great almsgiver and supporter of the poor, generous to churches and in providing for the clergy. He often established new domains, planting vineyards, building houses and putting land into cultivation. Then he would invite bishops of poorly-endowed sees to his table, and afterwards distribute among them these buildings, together with labourers and tilled lands, as well as money, wall-hangings, utensils, servants and slaves; and he would address them thus: 'Let all these things belong to the Church so that the poor who obtain relief may win me God's forgiveness.'

Here we have repeated and carefully thought-out generosity by a substantial layman. He endows churches in order that the profit from the estates may be used for the poor; and he does this for his soul's relief. It is a classic instance of outright giving for a clearly-defined purpose. One could cite royal gifts of a like nature. But some were otherwise motivated. It is not clear, for example, what moved Guntramn to generosity on the death of his brother Chilperic. Gregory says that he restored what had been wrongfully taken from others but went further and made large gifts to churches unspecified, and to the poor. He also revalidated wills containing bequests to the Church that Chilperic had suppressed. One assumes that he was bent on winning support in Chilperic's former kingdom, and that may be the only explanation of his generosity. Church-building was equally and specially a part of royal munificence. When Bishop Médard of Soissons died, King Chlotar personally saw to his burial in his city and began to build the church over his tomb which his successor Sigebert completed. The motive here was respect for the high reputation of the bishop, a holy man whose relics might well afford protection to a prince; and Gregory bears testimony to the power of the saint. The same king from the same motive came to the rescue of the city of Tours after a fire had destroyed many churches. He re-roofed St Martin's church with tin and completely restored it.

<hr />

[15] *Hist.* x, 19.   [16] Ibid. vi, 20.

These must suffice as evidence of Merovingian involvement, as Gregory saw it, in the material affairs of the Church, both its properties and its officers. It was a growing involvement. Bishops could not manage without kings nor kings without bishops. The ruling caste of the Franks had now accepted the Church's teaching on what would bring them good luck, on where help lay, and on what perils awaited non-conformers. Merovingian stability, in so far as it existed, depended on this acceptance. For Gregory, pagan *fortuna* has long since been subsumed in Christian *sanctitas*. The bishops for their part have become involved in the daily routine of royal business. They will be a good deal at court if they are wise, ready with their advice, singly or in groups, providing what might be called a running commentary from the Church's viewpoint on what kings do, or mean to do, or have done. They are, too, a point of historical reference, a collective memory always present. But they have another function at court. They represent the interests of their cities as Christian communities; and cities that were by no means predominantly the haunt of the Franks. The separate identities of these communities, apparent in the fifth century, is no less sharp in the sixth. It runs through Gregory's History. At the political level the Merovingians thought largely in terms of cities and their *territoria* when the kingdom was divided and re-divided among them; and this is what makes it so difficult to draw accurate maps showing royal boundaries at any one time. In so doing they merely acknowledged the situation they inherited. The Church thought in the same way, and so did the inhabitants of the cities themselves. Citizens expressed this feeling of separate communal identity in hatred for those of other, and particularly neighbouring, cities. They were competitors for much. Thus the cities of Tours and Poitiers were ancient rivals. They could dispute fiercely over the body of St Martin. There was no less hatred between Tours and Orléans. When a palace official named Eberulf took refuge in St Martin's church, the guard that was mounted to keep watch over him was drawn from the citizens of Orléans and Blois, who finally went home with as much plunder as they could collect from Tours. Again, the men of Orléans and Blois took advantage of the death of a king to make a surprise attack on Châteaudun, carrying off everything they could lay hands on; whereupon the men of Châteaudun, with assistance from others in the territory of Chartres, attacked Orléans in reprisal. Only when the Orléanists threatened a further attack did the counts interpose and stop the fighting. The citizens themselves had taken the initiative and gone to war. There are hints elsewhere in Gregory that citizens were far from being the docile tools of kings or counts – or bishops. One of the charges against Bishop Praetextatus was that he had bribed the men of Rouen to rebel against their king. Another and much less reputable rebel, condemned to death for treason, was lynched by the people before sentence could be carried out; and the commanders whom Guntramn rebuked for their destructiveness pleaded that discipline had broken down generally among the people. In effect, they were out of control. These occasions, when authority could no longer manage quite large groups of townsmen, reinforce the point that it was at the level of the city that a meaningful sense of identity was experienced. Bishops might still as in the past go a long way towards controlling or canalizing this sense. The more closely they could identify themselves with the cultus of the presiding saint the likelier it was that the citizens would listen to them. The shrine of St Martin unites the bishops and citizens of Tours against all outsiders. Gregory has no more important lesson to teach his successors in the see, for whom in large part he writes his History. The hostile world begins at the boundaries of the city's *territorium*, for bishop and people alike. But sometimes, for a bishop, it is inside the boundaries. Like Caesarius of Arles, who once thanked a congregation for coming to church, bishops needed to woo their volatile communities. It has been well observed that public opinion mattered as much as family, wealth and royal favour in securing their status. Not only townsmen but clergy were directly involved in some of the riots described by Gregory. The sensible bishop would turn to the saints and their relics for help, especially in emergencies and on feast-days, when all could be identified in a single act of propitiation. It is then that *reverentia* can best manifest itself; and there is nothing pagan or neo-pagan about that. The alternative was boorish *rusticitas*.

Scholars often repeat that learning was dead in sixth-century Gaul. Some qualifications can be made, but in general it is true, as Gregory himself lamented, that traditional learning counted for little and was scarcely to be had. None the less, we find learning of another kind revealed in a steady shift of interest towards what was more congenial to the age. The shift was towards the Bible, of which the historical books were nicely attuned to the taste of the Franks steeped in the deeds of their own heroes. Gregory himself was at home in the Bible as in no other literature, hagiography excepted. It colours his style and outlook as a historian to a greater extent than Bede's were coloured. Bede was a better-educated man, perhaps in classical literature, certainly in the writings of the Fathers. For Gregory it is the Bible that counts most. We can see this not only in his numerous direct quotations (over 300 of them) but in the way in which his narrative is affected by biblical reminiscenses, phrases and words. Max Bonnet, a close student of Gregory's style, was of the opinion that the New

Testament, together with the Psalms, most influenced him.[17] Stylistic-
ally this may well be true, but there is no part of the Bible that does not
influence him and from which he does not quote. Liturgical usage
would have imprinted the Gospels and Epistles on his memory, and
the saints' Lives with which he was intimate would have been another
source for biblical quotations. But his direct knowledge of the biblical
text is beyond question. He uses the Vulgate and also earlier versions –
versions, in Bonnet's phrase, 'faites pour le peuple par les gens du
peuple', direct, rough, replete with barbarisms. (One thinks of such a
text as the Heptateuch of Lyon, written in Gregory's lifetime.)[18] It is
rather in the Old Testament than in the New that he would have found
historical circumstances most nearly suggestive of those of his own
day: the heroic age of a Chosen People's struggle; days of warfare,
kings and prophets; days of the revelation of God's providence in
miracle and retribution. He does not see the Franks he knows as the
Chosen People; he disliked Jews too much for that; but he thinks of
them in a context in which, to his successors, they will seem a Chosen
People. He is linking the Franks with a historical process that goes
back to the People of Israel; a process of national salvation, if only men
would listen.

Gregory starts his History with a profession of faith. He stands in
the orthodox Nicene tradition and wishes it to be known. He is no
Arian. He would not have claimed to be a theologian, and in so far as
he is one, his theology is more scriptural than patristic. From this
profession he moves on to the Creation, here following Eusebius,
Jerome and Orosius, quoting extensively from the Old Testament,
and thus to the biblical narrative. Ancient secular history is irrelevant
to his purpose. From the Bible he proceeds to the age of persecution,
and thence to the Franks. Providence is what matters, and the revelation of Providence in action is for him a proper concern of historical
investigation, in the field both of human deeds and of natural phenomena. Above all, it is by miracles that God reveals his providential
purpose. Miracles are in themselves proof of that purpose and proof,
too, of the orthodoxy that God favours in man. This is clearly shown
in Gregory's accounts of orthodox disputes with Arians, as for example
when he describes how the Arian Theodoric's widow was killed by
poison placed in the communion chalice, and goes on to comment:
'how shall these wretched heretics answer the charge that the Devil is
present in their holy place? Those of us who confess the Trinity equal
and omnipotent would be completely unharmed even if we drank
deadly poison in the name of the Father, Son and Holy Ghost.'[19] This

[17] *Le Latin de Grégoire de Tours* (Paris, 1890), p. 54.
[18] See CLA vi, 771.   [19] *Hist.* iii, 31.

God who reveals his providence through the miracles of his saints is as much a figure of the Old Testament as a recognizably Christian God; a god attuned to the moral conscience of the sixth century, whose principal attribute is heroic action. This is what makes it possible for Gregory to turn to the Bible for justification of royal deeds of violence. Thus, King Chlotar can go with an army to destroy his rebellious son Chramn 'like a new David to fight against his son as another Absalom', invoking God to justify him with the words 'Look down from heaven, O Lord, and judge my cause, for I suffer wrongful injury at my son's hands. Look down and judge justly and pass that judgment that of old you delivered between Absolom and his father.'[20] The parallel possibly did occur to the outraged father, well schooled as he was by his bishops. The Merovingian concept of law was clearly Mosaic in respect of the role of vengeance; for God was the avenger of his injured servants, and his judgement in such matters was closely connected with miracles. In one further way we can see how the religion of Gregory was adapted to the Frankish mentality. The Bible could be used for prophecies. The clergy of Dijon, anxious to know what fate awaited Chramn, placed on the altar the Books of the Prophets, the Epistles and Gospels and prayed for a revelation at mass. The reading from each Book in turn contained a passage presaging his downfall. So they knew which side to be on. The scriptures were in this way associated with a magic. We may see in it the paganizing of Christianity; but it might be more accurate to think of it as a facet of its germanizing.

A last instance of how the Bible and present events came together in Gregory's mind is his account of the discussion between Chilperic and a Jew named Priscus, at which Gregory was present.[21] It is told with the vividness that he reserves for such occasions, far removed from the dry style he prefers for narrating political events. Descriptions of comparable biblical confrontations in part explain this remarkable change, but also in part it may be due to hagiographical precedent.[22] The story, as Gregory gives it, is that he came to say goodbye to the king, who was preparing to leave his villa of Nogent for Paris. They were joined by Priscus, who was intimate with the king on account of business dealings. The king took Priscus gently by the hair – beard, perhaps? – and said to Gregory, 'Come, bishop, lay your hands upon him.' Priscus resisted, whereupon a debate took place between king and Jew, the bishop intervening where necessary, on the nature of God the Son. In the course of the debate, in which the Christians seek mainly to convince the Jew out of the Books of his own Testament,

---

[20] Ibid. iv, 20.
[21] Ibid. vi, 5.
[22] The point is made by L. Bieler, Spoleto x, 308.

the following books are cited, some several times: Deuteronomy, Isaiah, Psalms, Jeremiah, Genesis and Baruch, in addition to some appeal to the New Testament. The debate is conventional enough as to matter. One may wonder whether all three participants would have had the necessary quotations at their fingertips at what was a chance meeting as Gregory describes it, though it is worth remembering that Chilperic piqued himself on his theological knowledge. It ends with the Jew unconvinced. The king, defeated, orders water so that he and the bishop may wash their hands. They then take bread and wine together and bid one another farewell. Had the Jew been converted there would have been more reason than there is to doubt whether the episode ever took place; but as it stands it seems to witness to an authentic confrontation. The arresting point is not that Christians should have sought the conversion of a Jew; this was common enough; but that the minds of all three – Jew, king and bishop – should move so naturally over the books of the Old Testament. The Bible is the past of all three as well as their term of reference. Moreover, the Jew was not forcibly converted. He belonged to what was a society within a society, a pearl forever irritating the oyster. Gregory gives several instances of how irritating his contemporaries found it. Life could be made very uncomfortable for Jews, as for any who threatened a conformity desirable alike to kings and Church; but there they remained, a constant reminder to Christians that it was the New Testament that held them apart. The ethos of the Old Testament was more easily assimilable by men of the sixth century; but it was not for that that the martyrs had died.

In sum, what does Gregory as historian tell us of the Christian society he knew? A Gallo-Roman of senatorial rank, as were many of his episcopal colleagues, he describes a society that in the higher echelons of its Church, and indeed numerically, was still predominantly Gallo-Roman or Gallo-Celtic. Orthodox though he was in the basic doctrines of Christianity, and conscious as he was of the great aristocratic-ascetic witness of earlier days, he does not see the role of the Church as a bishop of the fifth century would have seen it. The Franks have made a permanent difference. Germans with deep-seated ethical and religious ideas of their own, they have not been converted overnight. Indeed, their own social ends have not been much affected by conversion. But in the process of conversion they have done something to the Church's idea of religion. Gregory is deeply impressed by the seriousness of the problems facing the Church. The Franks have somehow changed things. By their acceptance of Christianity they have shifted its social emphasis towards warfare, and in their daily life require a religion in which the elements of miracle and magic, though present before, move more decisively to the forefront. It is a church for Germans; but it has been made for them by Gallo-Romans. Furthermore, the Church is attempting to change the Franks. It wishes to canalize what is distinctively Frankish about them to its own ends, towards a resumption of mission. With the Merovingians of the early seventh century, it did just this. Gregory's History, then, reveals a society whose values are no longer those of Late Antiquity. His Church faces new problems which he makes intelligible in the broad context of God, the saints and sinful man.

IV

THE MEROVINGIAN CLOISTER

LIKE the fifth century, the early sixth has much to offer in the way of monastic foundations in Gaul or at least in parts of it. Caesarius of Arles, the last great pupil of Lérins, is the monk who links the centuries, but his influence was confined to the south. It was to his Rule for nuns that Queen Radegundis turned when she and her royal kindred decided to found a nunnery at Poitiers in 547, and from Arles she got it.[1] Perhaps she preferred its firm articulation to the Martinian observance common in Poitou at the time. The Poitiers foundation was something exceptional in importance and in other respects, but there are hints that the earliest Merovingians did take some further interest in monks; and if it were no greater, the reason might be that monasteries, like bishoprics, struck them initially as a Gallo-Roman preserve. Their conquest of Aquitaine would have familiarized them with Martinian houses, and as they penetrated into Burgundy and the Saône and Rhône valleys they would have come into contact with houses founded under the influence of Lérins; houses of the Old Gallic tradition, flourishing in urban centres and expanding in and around Lyon and Vienne. The Arianism of the Burgundian rulers, soon to give way to Catholicism, seemed not to affect their prosperity. At Grigny, for instance, facing Vienne across the Rhône, was to be found the headquarters of what amounted to a confederation of monasteries. Clovis himself, though several later claimed him as founder, cannot be proved to have founded any monastery, and this despite his veneration for St Martin. We know too little about the circumstances in which late Gallo-Roman landowners founded monasteries to suppose that Clovis would have seen it as part of his religious duty to follow suit. But if he did not found them, he made large gifts to the houses of St Martin and St Hilary: such is the report of the historian Fredegar,[2] writing in the seventh century. His queen, Chrotechildis, is likewise the victim of false ascriptions of later times. She cannot be shown to have played any part in the monastic foundation of St Germanus at Auxerre, the church of which she certainly rebuilt. Neither king nor queen seems to have thought of establishing monks at their new church of the Apostles (later Ste Geneviève) in Paris, the dedication of

---

[1] Ed. G. Morin, *S. Caesarii opera omnia*, ii (Maredsous, 1942), pp. 101–29; trans. M. C. McCarthy, *The Rule for Nuns of Caesarius of Arles* (Washington, 1960).

[2] *Chron.* iii, 24 (MGH SRM ii, p. 102).

which must surely signify a wish to please Constantinople and Rome. Nevertheless, the Merovingians of the next two generations – and bishops and laymen, too – showed active interest in monastic foundations and endowments. St Columbanus, at the end of the century, was not alone responsible for the revival of Gallic monasticism. Gregory of Tours must himself have been partly responsible as the promoter of the cult of St Martin to a national level. Not much less important was the influence of Radegundis at Poitiers. When the nun Baudonivia came to complete Fortunatus' Life of Radegundis early in the seventh century, she saw Radegundis in a conventional way, as one of an orthodox company of saints in the current idiom;[3] but she did not hide the important fact that Radegundis, together with Genovefa and Chrotechildis before her, had made a profound change in the life of Gaul. Great ladies turned to religion, and they sanctified public life in a way quite unlike that of the martyrs and confessors. The desert-mentality was not for them. In their active involvement they belonged more to the tradition of St Martin than to that of Lérins. Genovefa, a virgin dedicated to religion after a meeting with Germanus of Auxerre, had settled in Paris, built a tomb for St Denis and was the inspiration of the Parisians during Attila's invasion of Gaul in 451.[4] A female protectress endowed with *providentia*, her reputation was as dear to Franks as to Gallo-Romans; and it even reached Simeon Stylites in the East, who sent her his greetings and begged for her prayers. Thus she became a western prototype of the *puella Dei* with a significant role to play in the Christian *patria*. Baudonivia too portrays Radegundis in terms of the new Frankish *patria* (a word she likes), at once national and Catholic. The queen is an evangelist of charity and peace; her nuns must pray for all and must not be solely concerned with their personal salvation. She is a female Christian hero set in a context transcending national boundaries, as witness the dedication of her house to the Holy Cross and her acquisition of a suitable relic from the East. A significant Gallo-Frankish development in religion occurred at Poitiers. As proof of the wide influence of Radegundis we have the great number of parish churches subsequently dedicated to her in Aquitaine. They fall within the provinces of Bourges and Bordeaux – that is, within that zone of Aquitaine colonized, though sparingly, by the Franks from the sixth century. South of Bordeaux, where Franks did not settle, there are scarcely any dedications to Radegundis or to any other saint dear to the Franks. Yet Radegundis was not a Frank; she was a Thuringian, as Chrotechildis was a Burgundian and Genovefa, though a citizen of Nanterre, apparently not a Frank. The three enter at different times the

---

[3] Ed. Krusch, MGH SRM ii, pp. 358–95.
[4] Ed. Krusch, MGH SRM iii, pp. 204–38.

stream of Frankish affairs, never relaxing their concern for their royal kindred in peace or war, affording an example that proved attractive to high–born Frankish women. They withdrew from secular life only to bring their standards to bear upon it from the cloister. The serious ascetic purpose of Radegundis in particular cannot be questioned; yet it could be achieved in a setting of princely values. The royal princesses who later rebelled against the second abbess appear to have observed their Rule (that of Caesarius for nuns) while Radegundis and her first abbess, Agnes, were alive. Nor is it clear that the Rule was differently interpreted by the second abbess. The difference seemed to lie in the abbess herself. The charges brought against her were largely nonsense; but behind them lay contempt for an abbess who was no princess. A royal nunnery was a royal nunnery, whatever the bishops and the canons of councils might say. The Merovingians could not afford and did not tolerate the hiving-off and total loss of their best female exponents of Christianity.

What, then, with these examples before them, did the early Merovingians do to further monasticism? The trouble with the sons of Clovis, as with Clovis himself, is that many monasteries later chose to claim one or other of them as founders, or at least as benefactors, when everything suggests that the claims were baseless. We are in a world of forged charters and spurious Lives of saints that sometimes do, and sometimes do not, contain elements of truth. However, the sons of Clovis clearly did support monasteries, here and there. Childebert I may well have placed monks at his Parisian foundation of St Vincent (later St Germain-des-Prés) where he was buried, and was co-founder of St Peter's monastery at Arles in 548 for which, later, we have a letter from Pope Gregory I to the bishop,[5] warning him that the house should enjoy the basic conditions of independence (i.e. control over its own property and freedom to elect its abbots) granted by Pope Vigilius at the request of Childebert. He may also have founded a monastic *xenodochium* or hospice at Lyon in 549. St Calais (or Anisola) in Maine, St Samson in Brittany and St Marculf at Valognes may equally have benefited from his generosity. There can be no serious doubt that Selles-sur-Cher did, after his victorious campaign against the Visigoths in 531. For all the uncertainty of the sources one is left with the firm impression that Childebert was a friend to monks, and that over the full extent of his kingdom. Chlotar I, his brother and the husband of Radegundis, was associated with Radegundis in the foundation of St Croix. Indeed, the house was established 'per ordinationem praecelsi regis Chlotarii'[6] and he gave it lands. This was

---

[5] *Registrum*, ix, 216 (MGH Epist. ii, p. 203).
[6] *Vita Radegundis*, ch. 5 (MGH SRM ii, 381).

the first recorded major foundation of the Merovingians. The claim that he founded a monastery at his church of St Médard at Soissons is difficult to sustain.

So much for the sons of Clovis. A grandson of Clovis, Guntramn, is said to have founded the house of St Marcel at Chalon in 584, organizing it on the model of Agaune (the Burgundian house in the Swiss Valais where, around 515, King Sigismund had established the first monastic community in the West dedicated to the performance of *laus perennis*, unceasing chant performed by groups of monks in strict rotation). So at least Fredegar informs us.[7] Though as usual we have no genuine written instrument of foundation for St Marcel, it seems likely to be true on a number of grounds. He may also have assisted in the endowment of St Bénigne at Dijon; at least a genuine *placitum* of Chlotar III, of 663, says as much.[8] Equally there can be no doubt that Guntramn's brother, Sigebert I, and still more Sigebert's wife, Brunechildis, were interested in monks. The queen was a great benefactor of monks in her favourite city of Autun, whose bishop, Syagrius, was her closest supporter. Concerning one of her three establishments there, we have a letter from Gregory the Great in which he confirms the royal right to choose an abbot in collaboration with the monks and without episcopal intervention.[9] Nothing is said of the Rule that the monks were to observe though it is likely enough that the monasteries of the Rhône valley, Burgundy and Austrasia favoured versions of the practice of Lérins. This is the best of the evidence that can be adduced in support of early Merovingian encouragement of monasteries by foundation or endowment, though there is more that it may be wrong to dismiss too summarily. At least we can be sure that something had happened. The Merovingians and their friends, particularly among the bishops, were prepared to alienate treasure and lands to create privileged and professional societies of prayer enjoying immunities of one kind or another; that is, freedom from public burdens or from interference by secular or clerical officials. As such they were an active part of the Frankish world, not a separate world. They ensured perpetual intercession with the spiritual world for the security of rulers; and they were distinct in the minds of rulers from churches – which rulers also founded and endowed. One might say that a church was exclusively a bishop's business, concerned with the welfare of all who lived within its boundaries. A monastery had a more private purpose: it was the founder and his or her kin and other

[7] *Chron.* iv, 1.
[8] Pertz, *Diplomata* i, no. 41, p. 38; Pardessus, *Diplomata* ii, no. 349, p. 132.
[9] *Registrum*, xiii, 11–13 (MGH Epist, ii, pp. 376–81).

benefactors who reaped the reward of intercession, and by extension whatever causes interested them.

So far we have had to do with monasteries following Rules about which little can be said beyond the fact that they were local adaptations to suit the convenience of founders. The Rule of St Benedict, if known in Gaul, was certainly not widely known.[10] In the early seventh century it appears at Haute Rive (Altaripa) in the diocese of Albi and in a Rule for nuns at Jussa-Moutier composed by a former monk of Luxeuil, Bishop Donatus of Besançon. We cannot tell how it reached these distant spots. Its proliferation is from Luxeuil and is associated with the circle of St Columbanus. But the pre-Columbanic Rules are not to be dismissed as of little spiritual significance. An example is the Rule of Feriolus, bishop of Uzès, a local affair compiled from whatever material was at hand, notably from Lérins and Arles.[11] Possibly it was typical of Gallic Rules of the time, at least in southern Gaul. One arresting point about it is the dependence of the writer on conciliar decrees affecting monks, especially those promulgated by Gallic councils. Monks had been a concern of councils ever since Chalcedon in 451, and bishops had supervised the behaviour of monks and the foundation of monasteries within their own dioceses; in a word, they exercised *providentia* over monks and nuns as distinct from the *potestas* they enjoyed over clerics. No part of the Church was more liable to go astray without supervision than were monasteries. It was a matter not simply of supervising the behaviour and the property of monks but of watching over their spiritual practices and beliefs. Unsupervised orthodoxy faced obvious dangers in remote communities. It almost invited deviation into heresy. All this Feriolus had in mind. His Rule is not well constructed and is rather repetitive. However, what matters about it, as about any Rule, is whether the author had an ascertainable view of the spiritual life that is the *raison d'être* of monasticism. Feriolus certainly had. His monks are offered a clear objective – the perfect life, *ambitio perfectionis*. Their aim is not the avoidance of sin but the pursuit of virtue, and the chief virtue, as in the New Testament is love. The writer's ideal is the Early Church of Jerusalem, a community that felt itself one body. This was the monastic tradition passed on by St Basil, greatest of Eastern monastic legislators. Sin, here, is the disturbance of unity, and in consequence the monastic virtues are social rather than

---

[10] I follow David Knowles in rejecting the view that Benedict's Rule had its beginnings in Francia ('The Regula Magistri and the Rule of St Benedict', *Great Historical Enterprises*, London, 1963, pp. 135–95). No better case can be made for the Gallo-Frankish origin of the Regula Magistri, which Benedict used (cf. A. de Vogüé, *La Règle du Maître*, SC 105, p. 232).

[11] PL 103, cols. 339–664 and the commentary of G. Holzherr, *Regula Ferioli* (Einsiedeln, 1961).

individual. Such was the *corpus congregationis* of Feriolus: a community
that guided its steps towards perfection by the Bible (which indeed the
Rule cites 93 times). It was a view of the ascetic approach that seemed
to call for no minute regulation. The daily guidance of the abbot and
the overseeing eye of the diocesan were enough, the guide-lines
clear. Feriolus was no great legislator but at least he knew what he was
after. We cannot tell whether his house prospered or whether his Rule
attracted other founders. But it gives us some idea of what bishops
considered to be a monastic programme worth endowing and protecting. Such Rules were enough to justify the expectations of those
with lands to spare for monasteries.

What were the expectations of founders and benefactors? One of
them was the hope of winning salvation through the traditional means
of the relief of poverty; for the poverty of many religious houses was
certainly in excess of what was required by even the austerest religious
practice. Not all monasteries were initially well endowed, which is
one reason why some survived only for a few years. The ones we
know about are the successful foundations that attracted the generosity
of important people. This increasingly popular practice of winning
salvation through the relief of monastic poverty is what Émile Lesne
meant when he compared the giving of the sixth century to that of the
Early Church, a piety that seemed to him 'semblable à la fraicheur d'un
matin',[12] a view that may not be so naïve as it sounds. However, it can
be but one of the expectations that moved men to endow monasteries
and churches. More significant was the wish to ensure perpetual
intercession for donors and their families. It was a commonplace
provision of founders that their monks or nuns should remember
them in prayer, and that they should pray for the peace of the Church
and the safety of king and *patria*. For example, there is this in the
Formulary of Marculf (probably compiled about the year 700 at St
Denis): 'let them pray earnestly to God for the Church and for the
safety of king and *patria*'.[13] The same formula, or one very like it, can
be found in episcopal instruments addressed to monasteries, particularly in the seventh century. Bishop Bertramn of Le Mans leaves
presents to St Germain-des-Prés at Paris and to the Church of Metz,
both outside his diocese, so that his name might be recorded in their
libri vitae[14] (martyrologies to which were added the names of brethren
and benefactors). The intention was plain: monasteries were professional communities of prayer, and for whom should they intercede if

[12] *La Propriété écclésiastique en France*, i, p. 80.

[13] MGH Form., bk. i, i, p. 40; also ed. A. Uddholm, *Marculfi Formularum* Uppsala, 1962),
p. 24.

[14] Pardessus, *Dipl.* i, no. 230, p. 202; G. Busson and A. Ledru, 'Actus pontificum Cennomannis
in urbe degentium', *Archives historiques du Maine*, ii (Le Mans, 1901), pp. 102–41.

not for their benefactors? This was not alien to the deeply-engrained Germanic desire to be remembered as a generous kindred that had done its duty. But if the prayers of monks were specially valuable, the reason would be not only that monks had the opportunity to lead pious lives but also that they were the guardians of relics of holy men whose protection was worth praying for. There was a growing tendency through the sixth and seventh centuries for monks to take over the guardianship of churches that housed the relics of martyrs and holy bishops, and this more particularly in towns or their *suburbia*. It was to such communities that donors seemed specially attracted, and thus we sometimes find several monastic establishments in one small city, each guarding the relics of its saints and each favoured by its own benefactors. So Tours prospered, and also Poitiers, Lyon, Trier, Autun and other cities. Queen Brunechildis, benefactor of the church of St Peter and St Paul at Autun, caused it to be rededicated to St Martin, to whose cult she showed a strong attachment. So too Bishop Magneric of Trier, a friend of the queen, who transformed the church of Ste Croix of Trier into a Martinian house. Not long afterwards the most celebrated of Martinian relics, his *cappa* or cloak, makes its first rather equivocal appearance. It may have been from Dagobert I that it descended in the Merovingian house. Curiously enough, the emergence of this famous relic coincided with the partial eclipse of Martin's cult by that of St Denis.

These, then, were among the reasons that led men of property to endow monasteries. But there were others. The grip of a founder's kin on a particular locality was certainly strengthened by a family monastery there. The founding of monasteries in the countryside, notably in northern Francia and Burgundy, was caused by benefactors in the sense that their generosity alone made it practicable. The time had come in Frankish history when others than kings interested themselves in the real property market. Purchases could of course be left by the purchaser to his family, though there was no guarantee that the family might not sell what they inherited or see it lost in the civil disturbances of the time. Property left to a monastery was less likely to change hands and, whatever the Church might say, a kindred could retain a certain ascendancy over a monastery founded by a forebear and further endowed by his heirs. It was an ascendancy that could have practical consequences. It would surely be an exceptional family that would relinquish all claims on a monastery established upon its land, assisted by its gifts and administered by its members; and in fact cases are known in which founders looked upon their foundations as their own, to do as they liked with, and this as a matter of course, not of argument. For example, the Frank Gammo established a nunnery on his property of Limours, placing two daughters in it, one as abbess. Yet later in a charter dated 697[15] he and his wife made over the house to St Germain-des-Prés, apparently because he thought that so small an establishment of nuns would in future need the supervision of a powerful monastery. The reason was a good one but it rested on the assumption that he could still do what he wished with his own nunnery. The process of acquisition and disposal can be seen in the will of Bishop Bertramn of Le Mans, made in 616.[16] It is, like other wills of the period, a complex document, but the picture it gives of a lifetime's acquisitions is clear enough. Bertramn probably enjoyed a position of exceptional power in Maine. During his reign we can see something of the development of a place, always difficult for the Merovingians to control, from a *civitas* with antique institutions into a complex of ecclesiastical nuclei under the control of the bishop. The monasteries fit into this pattern. The crown apart, the Church was certainly the biggest landowner in the diocese by the early seventh century. Bertramn had made many purchases of property, urban and rural, in his diocese, and these he apportioned with sharp attention to detail between his episcopal church, the monasteries and his relations. The monasteries were subject to episcopal control with the one exception of St Calais, which enjoyed some immunity, probably for a generation before Bertramn's time. Why it should have been thus favoured is not clear. The foundation of the house on a gift of land made by Childebert I was said to have been a result of the favourable impression made on the king by a holy man he came upon in his hunting-forest; but this affords no substantial evidence of any grant of immunity. We know from Gregory of Tours that in 576 King Chilperic used St Calais as a prison for his rebellious son Merovech; but it was more likely Guntramn than Chilperic who granted the immunity. By Bertramn's day St Calais uniquely enjoyed immunity of a sort from the bishop. No other monastery in his diocese is known to have done so.

So much for founders and benefactors. As for the monks and nuns themselves, we can suppose that a variety of reasons brought them to make their vows, as was natural in a cross-section of the population that embraced everyone from royal kindred to emancipated slaves. There was salvation to be won certainly, and there was the living of a life held to yield the advantages of a form of public penance; but also there was the chance of a securer life than could be found anywhere outside a monastery's walls. The Lives of the saints give credit to the good motives of those taking vows, but the *acta* of successive Church councils suggest something different. They witness to continuing episcopal anxiety about laxity of morals, the leaving of monasteries without sufficient reason, the abandoning of the religious life and so on. In a word, the attraction of the religious life was sometimes not religious, and when it was, discipline was not firm enough to hold all monks and nuns to their vows. Even so, the situation was not anarchic. The growth of coenobitism during the sixth century was essentially healthy and accounts in part for the welcome given to sterner forms of coenobitism at its close. But with a social phenomenon of this order of magnitude, and from the chance evidence that survives, there can be no simple conclusion about motives or practice.

At the close of the century comes a figure of major importance – St Columbanus, a Leinsterman and pupil of St Comgall of Bangor. In 590 he left Ireland for the continent. Scholars have paid special attention to two aspects of his career: the penitential severity of his behaviour, and his learning. Both were real enough but neither takes us to the heart of his influence over Frankish society; and it was an influence that needs explanation since it affected a world already alive in many ways to the claims of monasticism, to which it had not failed to respond. Circumstances placed Columbanus in the company of Frankish kings and bishops not ignorant of these claims. He knew his kings. He accepted from Guntramn and solicited from Theudebert fiscal lands for his foundations, he appealed to Theuderic for help and he asked Childebert for a privilege of protection for his principal monastery of Luxeuil. His reliance on kings, then, was considerable, if not on bishops. A priest with a passion for evangelization, he had no official mission to the Frankish Church or even permission to operate within its territories. Ecclesiastically speaking he was on his own. His initial success was the conquest of a king by a sermon.[17] This says something about the king but more about Columbanus; and when we look at his surviving sermons, some of which were preached in Italy, and make allowance for the fact that they were probably worked over for publication, we can sense the power of the man. It is in his sermons and letters rather than in the better-known penitential and Rules (*Regula Monachorum* and *Regula Coenobialis*[18]) that he can best be seen. What immediately strikes the reader is the gulf between the piety of the Frankish Church, centred upon relics and the patronage of local holy men, and the piety of Columbanus, focused upon God and the relationship of God with man. It was indeed a gust of fresh air. Columbanus' influence was personal, not institutional. His sermons or *instructiones* are about God, not about saints. The first in the dossier of thirteen is on faith. 'Understand the creation', he writes, 'if you

[17] Jonas, *Vita Columbani* i, ch. 6 (ed. Krusch, MGH SRG in usum schol, pp. 162–3).
[18] Ed. G. S. M. Walker, *Sancti Columbani Opera* (Dublin, 1957).

wish to know the Creator; if you will not know the former either, be silent concerning the Creator; but believe in the Creator.'[19] He insists on the avoidance of learned talk and ceaseless discussion, which is not the way to God. We must, he says, quite simply cling to him – 'semper tenendus est profundus Deus, immensus, secretus, excelsus, omnipotens Deus'. He does not deny that the intercession of the saints will help; for like all great spiritual teachers he is haunted by the problem of access to God. Again, he preaches on how a monk should aim to please God,[20] and continues with a sermon on the nature of training – which he perfectly well understands is painful, as all training is. There is never any question of his not understanding man's weakness or not sympathizing with it, even when he makes few concessions to it. In the sixth sermon comes a wonderful passage on the nature of living from day to day, beginning with the words 'for what, I ask, is the difference between what I saw yesterday and dreamt this night?'[21] The fact of constant daily change obsesses him. The seventh sermon is on poverty: not on the need to give as the Frankish Church taught it, but on the need to have nothing to give. 'Let us eat with the poor, drink with the poor, share with the poor.'[22] He is a poet by nature (particularly when not writing poetry) who understands the heart and sees God as creator of the natural world. The eleventh sermon, on remorse, ends with a magnificent meditation on love.[23] There is a sharp contrast here with contemporary Frankish thinking, in so far as we know it. One glimpses what it was about Columbanus that seemed new and arresting.

The same man emerges, if less vividly, from his two Rules for monks. They are not Rules as St Benedict understood a Rule, not legislation carefully thought out to guide the whole life of a community. Perhaps there was no need for it while Columbanus was himself present to direct the monastic world of Luxeuil and its dependent houses. What he does provide in writing are the principles of monastic living as he understood them. He insists on obedience – *mortificatio*. This is not the first step of humility, as Benedict taught, but something that stands by itself as the Irish understood it: obedience not to a Rule but to a superior, the master who is abbot. With obedience he demands poverty and charity, silence and abstinence. Yet these are not the summits of endeavour. His real concern is with moral perfection. Like Benedict, his thoughts are fixed on the necessity for prayer, though in detail his conception of the *Opus Dei* is rather different. The Night Office is less significant to him than Lauds and his requirements for the recitations of the Psalms are tougher than

---

[19] Ibid., pp. 60–7. [20] Ibid., pp. 72–9. [21] Ibid., p. 89.
[22] Ibid., p. 93. [23] Ibid., p. 115.

Benedict's, making fewer concessions. Altogether, Columbanus' practice of asceticism is much in the Eastern tradition as transmitted to the Irish Church through Cassian. Perhaps it was the sort of coenobitism that Benedict had in mind for experts. There is a shape and purpose about Columbanus' coenobitic thinking that goes far beyond mere austerity. It is anchored in a view of penance that calls for a word of explanation. It seems unlikely that Columbanus introduced private penance to the continent. What is certain is that it formed a vital part of his moral teaching directed not only to his monks but to all who came under his influence. He acknowledged that there was always a time and place for canonical penance – that is, public penance and re-conciliation by a bishop; for instance, in cases of heresy. But the penance he is interested in is a state of mind. It is not merely regret for sin committed but the avoidance of further sin. In other words, it is medicinal as well as punitive, and hence the giver of penance must be an expert in the direction of conscience, a physician of souls whose expertise must embrace the whole possible range of individual sin. The absolution he gives is in the nature of a sacrament. He is both physician and judge. Moreover, confession and absolution are not confined to a single occasion, as with canonical penance. They could occur frequently, even for the least of sins. This has rightly been called a step towards a moral theology. It implies a constant relationship between the sinner and his confessor. Within Columbanus' own monastery, private confession was required before eating and going to bed.[24]

An unknown foreigner, Columbanus established an intimate priestly relationship, based on confession and penance, with the laity in the neighbourhood of his monasteries. As much as any Frank or Burgundian, he propagated the idea of monasteries as local centres of aristocratic cultus, such as he had known in Ireland. Yet the Frankish bishops accepted his practice without much ado, perhaps feeling that he was regularizing something towards which they themselves had been groping. A society burdened with a sense of guilt required the remedy of readily accessible reassurance; and not only accessible but repeatable. Confession and penance became a part of daily life, because the sense of guilt was. The Council of Chalon of about 650 officially recognized private penance: 'we judge it to be of use to all'.[25] The later spread of private penance owed much to bishops who had been the pupils of Columbanus. But bishops had differed from him on other issues, which can be summarized as his stubborn refusal to yield on

---

[24] Ibid., p. 142.
[25] MGH Conc. i, cl. 8, p. 210. It is unclear whether the *sacerdotes* who are here enjoined to give penance include priests.

any matter where Irish practice clashed with Frankish. A well-known
instance is the clash about the date of Easter, but this was not uniquely
important.[26] It was more significant that Columbanus broke every
Gallic conciliar decree on the right relationship of monks with diocesans; and these decrees had unimpeachable canonical tradition behind
them.[27] He meant to claim, and did claim, a degree of exemption from
diocesan supervision that was hitherto unknown in Francia and even
brought with him an Irish bishop to carry out episcopal functions for
his own monks. He defended his position in a discourse addressed to
the council held at Chalon in 603 when he appeared to be facing the
risk of expulsion.[28] The Easter controversy does not bulk large in it.
He repeats – what he had presumably often said before – that he does
not think much of the moral laxity of the Frankish Church and hopes
that the bishops will consider not only the Easter question but also
wider matters of canonical observance too long neglected. He sees
himself, a monk, in opposition to the secular Church, the Church of
bishops, taking no account of the many Frankish monks who were in
no way subject to himself. But when it comes to the point he begs for
charity, knowing that the big guns are all on the other side: 'for we are
all joint members of one body, whether Franks or British or Irish or
whatever our race may be'. Gaul can contain everyone. Hence his
simple plea, 'that I may be allowed with your peace and charity to
enjoy the silence of these woods and to live beside the bones of our
seventeen dead brethren' as in the preceding twelve years. Somehow
or other, he had caused a great deal more fuss than he meant to. His
quarrel was not with particular bishops; some helped him in exile and
his own diocesan is not known to have quarrelled with him; it was
rather with Frankish practice as expounded by the body of bishops,
and with the laxity of Frankish religious life as compared with the
Irish. But he could recognize some good in Frankish religious tradition; for example he could venerate St Martin: *domnus Martinus* he calls
him in his letter to the bishops, ranking him with *domnus Hieronymus*.
It has sometimes been thought that St Martin was eclipsed in seventh-
century Francia and that the Irish were responsible for it. The truth
seems to be more complex. The rise of the cults of the Virgin and of
the Apostles, as evidenced in church-dedications, did not mean that St
Martin was overlooked. Martinian cells continued to be founded, and
in general the saint took a more appropriate place in the hierarchy

---

[26] It did however give occasion for a famous letter to Gregory the Great (Walker, pp. 2–13).

[27] For the texts of the Gallic councils see C. de Clercq, *Concilia Galliae*, 511–695 (CC 148A,
Turnhout, 1963); s.v. monarchus, monasterium (p. 348) for index of relevant decrees.

[28] Walker, pp. 12–23.

among the great confessors but below the Apostles and the martyrs. Such at least seems to have been the intention of the monks.

All in all, Columbanus remained what he meant to be, a foreigner in a strange land, ready to rebuke sin wherever he saw it but essentially concerned with the salvation of his immediate disciples. His differences with the Frankish bishops went deep, though they were never as dramatic as his differences with his chosen protectors, the kings, on matters of morals. The fact is that though he ended his days at Bobbio in Italy, and not in Francia, the Frankish Church had absorbed a surprising amount of him and from him. It says much for the Church that it did so. What exactly it absorbed is seen only after his death. What could survive from a mission so immensely personal?

To answer this question we must go back in time to the beginnings of his mission. There was one class of Frank that listened to him at least as willingly as did kings: the local Frankish gentry settled on their estates. Some of them were among the earliest disciples of the Irish. They were at Luxeuil and elsewhere in the first decade of Columbanus' mission and must quickly have outnumbered the small band of Irishmen. But the most striking evidence of how they became attracted to him belongs to a slightly later time. In 610 he was making his return journey through Francia after the failure of an attempt to ship him home from the port of Nantes. Passing through the diocese of Meaux, he was taken by his companion, the monk Chagnoald of Luxeuil, to stay with Chagnoald's father, Chagneric, at his *villa* of Pipimisium.[29] The family, apparently of Burgundian origin, was a substantial one. During his stay, Columbanus was asked to bless Chagneric's young daughter, Burgundofara (the future Ste Fare).[30] Both the girl and the saint took this blessing to be in the nature of a dedication to God, though the father had initial regrets about losing her in this way to a nunnery. In due course she became head of her own nunnery – a double house, indeed – established on a family-property at Evoriacas. Presumably because of her youth the house started life under the supervision of her brother Chagnoald (later bishop of Laon) and of Walbert, another well-born monk from Luxeuil. It was no mere collection of cells but an establishment suitable for gentry. Several of Burgundofara's relatives were among the first inmates. Faremoutiers (as it came to be called) was from the start a family-monastery on a fairly big scale. Meanwhile, Burgundofara's other brother (or perhaps kinsman) Burgundofaro, became referendary to Dagobert I and finally bishop of Meaux; and possibly yet another brother, Chagnulf,

[29] *Vita Eustasii* (AA SS 29 March, vii, p. 783).
[30] Jonas, *Vita Columbani*, i, 26 (ed. Krusch, p. 209).

was count of the same city. The ramifications of the family's grip on the neighbourhood stands out clearly in Burgundofara's will,[31] which she draws up with her family's consent. Merovingian wills were not necessarily wills in our sense. This will may have been no more than a formal attestation of what the donor had already given or intended to give to others. She had many *villae* to dispose of, as well as lesser properties, notably within the walls of Meaux. The beneficiary is the nunnery. This large switching of property to monastic uses arose from one visit and the impact of Columbanus on the members of one family.

But Columbanus paid a second visit on his journey, to some connections of Chagneric living not far away at Ussy, the *villa* of a Frank named Authar. And here, at least two sons were presented for a blessing: Ado and his brother Dado, better known as Audoen or St Ouen, a courtier who later became bishop of Rouen.[32] Again we find a substantial family of landowners ready to welcome and make common cause with Columbanus. Ado founded a nunnery on family-land at Jouarre where the family-mausoleum built by Bishop Agilbert can still be seen in the crypt, which alone survives. It contains the sarcophagi both of Theudechildis, the first abbess, and (important for its figure-sculpture) of Agilbert, her brother. The relationship of the pair to the founder's kin is unclear but there is likely to have been one. Audoen built a monastery at Rebais[33] on royal land, and was moreover indirectly responsible for the foundation of the two great northern houses of St Wandrille and Jumièges. He was an influential man, related not merely to the family of Chagneric but also to the Agilulfing dukes of Bavaria; influential in a political as well as a religious sense, since he was one of the leaders of opposition to the extension of Carolingian power in western Francia. But he should not baldly be classified as a 'political bishop'. He was an evangelist whose authority embraced every aspect of public life. We may notice two further monastic founders of the same generation. A father and son named Friulf and Otmar (or Omer) left their estate near Coutances about the year 615 to enter Luxeuil as monks.[34] They could have found monasteries nearer at hand but instead chose to cross Francia to Luxeuil. In due course Omer was given the bishopric of Thérouanne in the northern territory of the still largely pagan Morini on the Flemish frontier. It has been suggested that his special qualification for the job

---

[31] Pardessus, *Dipl.* ii, 15–17.

[32] A third brother, Rado, later Dagobert's treasurer and founder of the monastery of Rueil-en-Brie, is recorded in the *Vita Agili* (AA SS Aug. vi, c. iv, 20, p. 582) though not by Jonas.

[33] Pardessus, *Dipl.* ii, no. 275, pp. 39 ff.

[34] *Vita Audomari*, ch. 2 (MGH SRM v, p. 755; also SRM viii, pp. 848 ff.).

was that he was a Saxon and could thus make himself understood by the Morini. One of his companions from Luxeuil, a westerner like himself, was Bertin, whom he established in a monastery at Sithiu (the future St Bertin) on land given to him by one of his converts. Lastly there is St Eligius, a man of humbler birth, a native of the Limousin who owed his advancement in life to his abilities alone, particularly as a goldsmith.[35] This skill brought him to the royal court. The foundation charter of his monastery at Solignac, in his native territory, survives and belongs to the year 632. It places the house firmly under royal protection and exempts it from episcopal control. The land, an old Roman *villa*, was a royal gift. Eligius recruited some of his first monks from Luxeuil but others were slaves on the estate whom he freed for the purpose of becoming monks. Not all monks, then, were aristocrats. Indeed, it is precisely the wide cross-section of Frankish society living at close quarters in small religious communities that may best explain some of the difficulties and upheavals of monastic life. Eligius also founded a nunnery in Paris and another, after he became bishop of Noyon, in his episcopal city.

It would be easy to add the names of other founders and other houses of monks or nuns, such as Marchiennes and Nivelles in the north and St Gallen, far away in modern Switzerland on the route to Italy. But we can take the families of Chagneric and Authar, together with Omer and Eligius, as probably typical. Under the influence of Columbanus they became monastic founders. Most of them were already men and women of local position and wealth, whose family fortunes may have been recently won or may have stretched back to the sixth century. What is clear is that those fortunes, as revealed in the form of new monastic endowments, were closely tied up with royal service and royal favour. Two kings in particular showed a liking for helping the Church by rewarding service: Chlotar II and his son, Dagobert I. It was to them that the Frankish Church owed the concentration of able young men at the court who were later to become bishops and monastic founders; and it was to them that the Church owed the impetus of the missionary drive into northern and eastern Francia and the neighbouring territories. Already in the *Regula monachorum* of Columbanus we find reminiscences of St Benedict's Rule; and it was through the followers of the great Irishman and particularly through Walbert, his second successor at Luxeuil, that St Benedict came to influence Frankish monasticism. The immediate result was the diffusion of what is called the Mixed Rule: a mixture, that is, of St Benedict, Columbanus and sometimes others, such as

[35] *Vita Eligii*, ch. 5 (MGH SRM iv, p. 672).

Caesarius; but a mixture that varies, from house to house. The construction of a monastic Rule was what it had always been, a piece of private legislation reflecting the tastes of the legislator and the local needs of his community. The legislation of Columbanus was moral and penal in flavour, admirable as a guide to ascetics, whereas that of Benedict was a way of life, beautifully orchestrated to the needs of a community. They blended well, though in the end it would be the contribution of Columbanus that would atrophy. Bishop Donatus devised a clever mixture of St Benedict, Columbanus and Caesarius. One would have supposed that the latter's *Regula virginum* would have sufficed for his mother's nuns, but such was not the case. He made that kind of use of St Benedict that can only point to a background of mature consideration of the Rule in the diocese of Besançon as early as the 630s. This, then, was the manner in which St Benedict penetrated Frankish monasticism.

The flourishing of Frankish monastic life over a brief period owed most to Columbanus, but would have been impossible without the active patronage of the Merovingian family; of Chlotar II, Dagobert I, Dagobert's son Clovis II, and Clovis' wife Balthildis, to mention the most notable. The historian Fredegar, writing a generation later, devoted much space to Dagobert as a great and fearsome king who began well but later turned to Church property when he felt a need to enrich himself.[36] Fredegar says nothing of his relations with monasteries with the exception of the Parisian house of St Denis. Here he was remarkably generous, not only in redecorating the abbey church but in his gifts of land in widely scattered places. It is curious that Dagobert did not or could not introduce a mixed Rule or any Columbanic practice at St Denis, since both he and his father, Chlotar II, were certainly influenced by the new movement. Important adherents of it had been present at Chlotar's court in Paris. It was principally through others that Dagobert exercised an influence over monasticism. He can in practice be counted as co-founder, with Eligius, of Solignac, having given the land for it; and he meant to keep his eye on it. Nobody, including the diocesan, was to interfere with its life 'with the sole exception of the most glorious king'.[37] Its life was the life of the mixed Rule – 'the Rule . . . of fathers Benedict and Columbanus', supervised by Luxeuil. The ghostly patrons of Solignac were all saints of the north: Denis, Médard, Remigius and Germanus. Dagobert's intention to control his northern frontiers will account for his support of the foundation of the monastery of St Amand (or Elnone) on the present-day frontier of France and Belgium. Again he provided the land; the

---

[36] *Chron.* iv, ch. 60.   [37] MGH SRM iv, p. 747.

will of the founder, St Amand, refers to the king's munificence. A third monastery indebted to him was Audoen's foundation of Rebais, which again was protected from episcopal intervention by royal authority and again was to live by the mixed Rule. The great monastic patterns he had in mind were St Maurice of Agaune, Lérins, Luxeuil and St Marcel of Chalon. The privileges these enjoyed were to be enjoyed by St Amand.

Dagobert's work was continued by his son Clovis II, who established the Irish refugee, Fursy, in a monastery at Lagny, near Paris, granted an immunity to the monastery of St Bertin and gave lands for the endowment of Montier-la-Celle, near Troyes. And there were other, comparable benefactions. Again one notes the concentration on the north, the continuing influence of Columbanus and collaboration with other benefactors, such as Erchinoald, mayor of the palace. But more important was the generosity of Clovis's queen, Balthildis, once an enslaved Anglo-Saxon. Whether or not she was the driving force behind her husband, it is certain that her interest in the monastic movement was as evident before his death as after it. Of her two great foundations the first was Corbie, once again north of Paris, on the Somme, between the years 657 and 661. It was formally a joint foundation with her son Chlotar III. They gave the house no less than ten domains or *villae*, together with some forest. The monks were to live 'under the holy Rule', by which was meant the mixed Rule, as is made clear in the privilege granted by the diocesan, the bishop of Amiens.[38] The close connection of Corbie with Luxeuil was there from the beginning; so too that with the Merovingians, as some hold is demonstrated by the resemblance of the late sixth-century Corbie cursive hand with that of the royal diplomas. Balthildis's second great foundation was the nunnery of Chelles, once more on royal property. It may in fact have been a re-foundation of an earlier Merovingian house.[39] The queen took nuns from the neighbouring house of Jouarre to enlarge her community, and these included her first abbess, Berthila. Probably the connection of Chelles with the Anglo-Saxons goes back to the queen herself. It is likely but not certain that a mixed Rule was again imposed, perhaps under the influence of Audoen, to judge from the queen's donations to Jumièges and St Wandrille.

Other Merovingians of the seventh century encouraged monasticism in practical ways. Their particular form of encouragement came precisely at the time when the work of Columbanus stood poised between expansion and contraction. It was on a large scale. All the houses so far

---

[38] Pardessus, *Dipl.* ii, pp. 126 ff. Another edn. by Krusch in NA 31 (1906), pp. 367 ff., who casts doubt on the authenticity of the bishop's privilege, in my view wrongly.

[39] *Vita Balthildis*, ch. 7 (MGH SRM ii, p. 489).

considered were major foundations from the start. They were meant to make a significant change in north-west Francia and to launch a formidable missionary drive, with political overtones, on the northern frontiers. This was characterized by encouragement of missionaries from the south, and from Aquitaine in particular. There had been a traditional link between the south and the Rhineland: the earliest missionaries had reached the Rhine from Lyon, and Trier had drawn on the resources of Poitiers, Bordeaux and Clermont. But in the seventh century, Burgundy and southern Austrasia had become a special area of Columbanic work and the southerners were ready to look further north. They were to be found in northern Austrasia and Neustria. Unlike their predecessors, these southerners kept no formal link with their mother-churches; there was no bond of property, as in the past, linking south with north. Like the Irishmen, they were on their own and also like the Irishmen they were dependent on the goodwill of local landowners, and above all on that of the Merovingians themselves. Their combined efforts, especially under Dagobert, are an essential background to the work of St Willibrord in the Low Countries, though much that they did was destroyed by Frisian expansion southward and westward in the late seventh century. We know, for example, that Dagobert attempted to make Utrecht the base for a Frisian mission with the assistance of the bishop of Cologne; but this too was destroyed. The missionaries of the mid-century were certainly a group. Its members were connected in varying degrees with each other and all with Luxeuil. It comprised at least nine members, bishops and abbots, of whom the senior, and the vital link with the Merovingians, seems to have been Acharius of Noyon, a man of Luxeuil. Their influence spread from Picardy in the south to Antwerp in the north. The greatest of them was St Amand, who came from Nantes or near by. The curious fact about his missionary career is that it took him so very far afield. Beginning as a recluse at Bourges, his wanderings took him to the Basques and to the Slavs as well as to the Frisians. This is made clear in his Life, which is of exceptional value because it was written soon after his death.[40] St Amand was also a visitor to Rome and to the Merovingian court, where he had a celebrated quarrel with Dagobert over the king's morals and over his own right to extend his missionary work in any direction he chose. Interpreting literally the message of St Matthew (28: 19), 'docete omnes gentes', he held that his mission was to all peoples in the ethnological sense, not to individuals. The king, on the other hand, felt that missions should only be sent to heathen whose political

---

[40] *Vita Amandi* (MGH SRM v, pp. 431–49).

submission concerned him. In the end it was agreed that Amand was safe and useful among the unconverted northern Franks and southern Frisians. But where did Amand acquire the idea of a mission to all people? It has been argued that he got it not from Luxeuil but from his visit to Rome. Yet the fact is that Columbanus himself, whatever priority he gave to *peregrinatio* as personal salvation, also had a sense of mission. It had taken some persuasion to make Columbanus and his followers settle in the Vosges, and his successors at Luxeuil interpreted his intentions thus: 'that neighbouring peoples should be fed on the faith'. It is thus not possible to divorce Amand's interpretation of his mission from his Columbanic background, however much it may have been reinforced at Rome by his veneration for St Peter. The same view was held to some extent by his colleagues in the north and equally by his Anglo-Saxon successors. Certainly the monkish conception of mission combined with the ascetic life takes on new force with him; and here in the north, among monk-bishops dependent on the Merovingian court, was born the idea of missionary work allied with political assimilation that the early Carolingians were to carry much further, both in the north and on their eastern frontiers. Not that political back-up made life much safer for such as Amand. The illustration of the saint destroying a pagan temple in an early eleventh-century copy of his Life nicely captures the tense atmosphere of early missionary work.

Merovingian penetration and settlement of the Rhine area, and east of it, long antedated Amand, and partly it involved regions that had been Christian for centuries. The picture is rather of Frankish enclaves penetrating east from the Rhine up the rivers that led into the heart of Germany – that is to say, among Germanic peoples who were not Franks. Some of them were pagan (for example, Frisians and Saxons) while others (like the Bavarians) were Christian or part-Christian. Moreover, they were ruled by dynasties that were often hostile to the Merovingians. Frankish missionaries of the seventh century were faced here with a much more complex situation than they met in the north. It may well be that the example of Amand in reaching the Slavs of the Middle Danube was an inspiration to others; there was something attractive to missionaries about *gentes* who were, so to say, uncorruptedly pagan, and those missionaries who reached Bavaria may have had the Slavs on the eastern Bavarian front as their objective. Emmeram, Corbinian and Rupert were Frankish missionaries in this area, all abbot-bishops or wandering bishops typical of Franco-Irish monasticism. Emmeram[41] came from Poitiers to Bavaria, and there he

---

[41] Ed. B. Bischoff, Arbeo, *Vita et Passio Sancti Haimhrammi Martyris* (Munich, 1953); also by Krusch, MGH SRG in usum schol., 1920.

stayed, apparently at the duke's request, though his intention had been to reach the 'gentes Hunorum', that is, the Slavs. Corbinian,[42] a native of Melun, reached Bavaria rather later, to live by the mixed Rule at Freising with his Frankish companions. The third, Rupert of Salzburg, belonged to a noble Frankish family of the Rhineland: his biographer calls him 'episcopus et abbas'.[43] What these three had in common was Frankish blood, Franco-Irish monastic practices, and the patronage, more or less willing, of the Bavarian dukes. One can understand why that patronage should be less willing because Frankish enclaves in Bavarian territory could have political consequences. This seems to have been tolerable for the ducal family, itself of Frankish origin and perhaps related to the Burgundofaros, so long as the Merovingians ruled, but less so when the Carolingians succeeded them. Carolingian family interests in the Rhineland were rather too near for Bavarian tastes. In the northern and middle Rhineland, indeed, it was the Carolingian family, at first with Merovingian approval, that made the running as monastic patrons in the seventh century. Between the two, the dukedom of Alsace under the family of the Etichonen formed a barrier to Merovingian expansion east of Burgundy. It was not the only barrier, but it serves to emphasize that missionary work from central Francia towards and over the Rhine was bound to have for client or independent peoples the appearance of Merovingian penetration. Like the work of Columbanus' Frankish followers in Francia it was a Merovingian success, on a more modest scale. Wherever monastic colonizers settled under royal or aristocratic patronage can be seen the beginnings of a new social stability. Properly managed and protected, houses of monks and nuns stood a good chance of growing with time into centres of cultus and education for their localities, nuclei of exploitation and magnets attracting endowment and personal ability.

[42] Ed. Krusch, as in preceding note.
[43] *Vita Hrodberti* (MGH SRM vi, p. 157–62.

V

THE MEROVINGIAN SAINTS

IN the Codex Amiatinus, written in Northumbria when Bede was a youth, is a picture of the Jewish priest and scribe, Ezra. He sits in his library, writing. On his left is his open book-press, in which we can see nine separate volumes of the Bible. But he is not only Ezra; he is also to be seen as Cassiodorus, who, like Ezra, saved the sacred books by copying them in troubled times; and the book he is writing is quite possibly the *codex grandior*, the great volume of the Old Translation that the monks of Wearmouth-Jarrow obtained from Italy. The writer is a symbol, both of biblical study and of the Bible itself as the book that dominated the whole field of Frankish, as of European, literary activity. Some idea of the predominance of the Bible may be had by looking at the sixth or French part of E. A. Lowe's *Codices Latini Antiquiores* (manuscripts, that is, written prior to the year 800),[1] the contents of which break down as follows: three pagan literary texts, five grammatical or glossarial, seven legal, seven liturgical, thirty-two biblical and eighty-three patristic texts. However much we multiply these figures to arrive at what we may think the age actually possessed in the way of books, the proportions would remain as they now are, except that the liturgical manuscripts will surely have bulked larger. The Bible and the Fathers lead the field by many lengths. Small wonder that Lowe, an excellent classical scholar as well as a great palaeographer, could see it as a melancholy tale of decline, a prolonged exhibition of contempt for Antique learning. 'Reading and writing', he concludes, 'were taught only because they were needed by the Church and by those who explained Scripture.'[2] If the Merovingians earn any good marks from him it is because they accidentally preserved a few classical texts as palimpsests (for example, Jerome on Sallust and Cassian on Pliny and Gaius) and gave birth to two famous centres of calligraphy – first Luxeuil and then Corbie. The age may have known what it wanted but it plainly wanted the wrong thing. We can modify Lowe's picture, based as it is exclusively on extant manuscripts, at least to the extent of allowing that the rhetorical tradition, notably in letter-writing, survived longer than he believed, particularly in southern Gaul. But nothing can change its essential shape. We

---

[1] It should however be appreciated that this part contains MSS now housed in French libraries, not all of which were written in France. Other parts also contain French MSS.
[2] CLA vi, p. xiii.

either accept Frankish readers and writers as men of the Bible or we pass them by.

The Frankish Church looked upon the Bible less as a source of doctrine than as inspired literature to sustain religious emotion. Its message was hagiological, so standing at the beginning of the record of a long religious tradition of holy men who had done wonders through God, and did them still. It had a lyrical appeal. This causes the author of the Life of St Liafwin to say that the saint discovered his paradise in the melodies of David's Psalms and the mellifluous readings of the Gospels.[3] He could have added other books of the Bible, all held to require prayer as much as instruction for their understanding. The Psalms in particular, once memorized, became part of mental furniture and could cease to be thought of as a written text. This reminds us that the Bible was studied as a series of separate books, separately bound in general; and even their contents were most familiar in a liturgical guise. Biblical texts were thus mediated through the liturgy of the Church and the commentaries of the Fathers. It sometimes looks as if love of well-known liturgical texts was stronger than the wish for better biblical texts and that the Old Latin versions were deliberately preserved when better Vulgate versions were available. To judge from lectionaries alone, one can see that scattered Merovingian centres continued to cherish ancient liturgical usages drawn from the whole range of biblical books. What counted most was neither accuracy nor authenticity but the transmission of the well-loved versions that together constituted the heart of the Bible. Their home was not the library but the church; their companions were music and chant, meditation and prayer. They thus involved laity as well as clergy, as Caesarius often insisted in his sermons. An approach so very un-dogmatic explains a passing appetite for verse-versions of the Bible. Avitus of Vienne, who died in 518, made a paraphrase in verse of the first books of the Old Testament which he said was for children.[4] Though a stout Christian effort, it had pagan overtones, for in it the beginner could find God hurling his thunderbolt like Jupiter, an angel like the messenger Iris giving orders to Noah, and Adam and Eve enjoying their nuptials.[5] Avitus admitted later on that it was all too difficult; it smelt too much of the rhetorical past of pagan letters and had no future for those brought up to sing barbaric *cantilenae*. Other versifiers were no more successful, though the attempts of Juvencus and his kind did penetrate Frankish Gaul. Together, these efforts betrayed a good classical instinct that the Bible must be presented as

---

[3] *Vita Liuini*, PL 87, col. 332.
[4] Epist, 43, p. 73, 7–8.
[5] *Carmina* i, 144 ff.; iv, 133 (MGH AA vi, 2, pp. 207 and 239).

inspired literature to Germans only recently converted. In what other context could they accept the great biblical progression of God's miraculous intervention in human affairs that stretched from Moses, Elijah and David to Christ, Peter and Paul?

From this corpus of literature – comprising the Bible itself, some apocryphal books, commentaries and the texts of the liturgy – stems what is best in the writings of the Frankish Church. It falls naturally into place in the literature common to the whole Western Church, but it has its peculiarities. One may instance a remarkable product of the monastery of Ligugé, near Poitiers. There, in the late seventh century, a monk named Defensor composed a moralizing collection from the Bible and the Fathers, called the *Liber Scintillarum*.[6] It was to be much read in the middle ages and is indeed a forerunner of the medieval *sententiae, quaestiones* and *summae*. It is no mere *florilegium* but a real attempt at synthesis. Defensor means to interpret his biblical texts, and so he groups them according to subject-matter, and, uncommonly, even cites many of his patristic sources.[7] His groupings are a valuable guide to the meanings of words fundamental to seventh-century asceticism – for example, *securitas* and *curiositas* – and as he addresses, or purports to address, various social categories (as, physicians, judges, monks, parents, pupils and servants) he displays to them through the Bible their characteristic vices and tells them how the corresponding virtues are to be preserved. Defensor knows the world outside the walls of Ligugé and he knows his own brethren. It is his moralizing tendency that needs emphasis. Like Caesarius before him, he is considering the vices of the society before his eyes and he is bringing the Bible to bear on the problems they raise. His is an insecure and introspective world – still the world of active demons; and where one has demons one must also have protectors. Against this background there grew up the most characteristic form of Merovingian literature, the Lives of the Saints.

The Lives of the Merovingian saints are a formidable collection when one looks at them in the huge volumes of the *Monumenta Germaniae Historica*.[8] They are even more formidable when one considers the enormous number of manuscripts that contain collections of them. Most of these collections are of the twelfth to fourteenth centuries, though some are earlier. A few belong to the eighth, and one at least (and it would be easy to miss something in so vast a field) to

---

[6] Ed. H. M. Rochais, CC 117, i (1957). See also Rochais in *Études mérovingiennes* (Paris, 1953), pp. 257–63.

[7] Some unidentified citations come from the Latin version of St. John Chrysostom according to M. C. Díaz y Díaz, *Hispania Sacra*, 11 (1958), p. 483.

[8] Mostly edited by Bruno Krusch with additions and revisions by Wilhelm Levison. For a partial defence of Krusch, in general too sceptical, see Wattenbach-Levison, i, p. 121.

the seventh or even sixth century – namely the *Passio* of the martyrs of Agaune, perhaps written at Lyon and now in Paris.[9] This scarcity of early manuscripts tells us nothing of the popularity of saints' Lives for a period from which so few manuscripts of any kind survive. It merely tells us that at a later date these same Lives were useful enough to be re-copied, embellished and put together in new collections to suit local tastes. They would constitute, one might suppose, a wonderful reservoir of political and social material for the historian; and so they might if they were biographies in our sense of the word. But they are not. Considering their bulk, little of this kind can be culled from them. They stem from the *Acta Martyrum* and the earlier saints' Lives, Gallic and other, and are doubtless also influenced by the tradition of *laudationes* recited at the graves of Gallo-Roman aristocrats. Even in the seventh century, Bishop Bertramn of Le Mans could require in his Will that his obsequies be so conducted that his *laus* should be delivered to the people. We meet a serious corpus of Lives in the late sixth century in the writings of Gregory of Tours and Venantius Fortunatus. In the century following they develop in the direction best suited to the purposes of the Church, which Gregory might not have anticipated. But if we cannot claim that their purposes remained constant throughout the Merovingian period, we certainly can claim that they always formed part of a great and unchanging whole: namely, the local cult of the holy man, centred on his presence in a shrine. The writings that fostered such cults embraced calendars, martyrologies, breviaries, sacramentaries, litanies, hymns and inscriptions as well as the *vitae et passiones*. In other words, we are faced with a very elaborate literary exercise designed to harness and propagate cults that look more 'popular' than they were. They were only 'popular' in the sense that they were aimed at the common people, not in the sense that they derived from them. Had it been otherwise, the writings we must consider would have contained a much larger element of folklore than in fact they do. They are the work of the Church, a literary attempt to do three things: to attract and hold popular devotion (for the Lives were read aloud on saints' feast days), to define the nature of sanctity, and to keep the cult of holy men within the structure of the Church.

These lives were generally successful as Lives just in so far as they were unsuccessful as biographies. An example of a successful biography is Eddius' Life of St Wilfrid. It brims over with biographical facts and is a vivid picture of the career of a controversial bishop. But it achieved no sort of popularity that we know of. It was a bad saint's Life. The

---

[9] CLA v, no. 589.

good ones – that is, the successful ones – are by comparison dull and unrewarding. Yet they were copied and disseminated and plainly achieved what they were meant to achieve. Their object was to depict the local holy man as a living example of an ancient pattern fixed once and for all in the Bible, without regard to what kind of saint he was. He could be a martyr, a confessor, an ascetic, a bishop or monk, a king or even a queen, or a wild man of the woods. His sanctity was still determined by his conformity to the pattern. The types might vary and so might the virtues expected of them. Indeed, it is often surprising to find that the great biblical virtues are subordinated to or supplemented by the preferred Merovingian virtues, such as austerity, affability, purity, patience and hard work. But the pattern did not change. And it was a heroic pattern. All holy men, from biblical times onwards, had been instruments of God's purpose. For each in turn God had miraculously intervened against the course of nature to demonstrate his favour. It was the same God intervening in the same way through his chosen medium, the saint. Sameness, in a word, is proof of authenticity. The saint must perform acceptable miracles to enter into the glorious tradition. Gregory the Great was specially anxious to demonstrate in his *Dialogues* that modern miracles had biblical forebears: what God had done for the People of Israel he continued to do for the people of Italy in the sixth century. It was a continuous manifestation, always revealed by the same signs. This is why Gregory of Tours starts his *Liber in Gloria Martyrum* with three chapters on Christ's nativity, miracles and death. This too is the point that he made when he wrote, 'some will ask whether we ought to speak of the *Life* or the *Lives* of the saints . . . obviously it is better to say *Life* . . . because, though their merits and virtues differ, they are all sustained in this world by one bodily life.'[10] The saint reveals the same sanctity whenever God intervenes through him. This is why the successful Life will contain few personal details: it is God's personality, not the saint's, that counts. One might be led to infer from this that the public for whom the Lives were intended would live in constant fear of the immediate power of God. But this was not the case. The public saw the holy man, not God: and if they no longer saw the holy man in person they saw miraculous evidence that he remained a living force. So they worshipped a local manifestation of God, the holy man still active from his shrine, as powerful in death as in life. He is not disembodied – indeed, his body is incorruptible – and he can easily reveal himself physically. Gregory of Tours has some vivid descriptions of the tension among the crowd of faithful as they await

---

[10] *Vita Patrum*, praef. (MGH SRM ii, p. 662).

miraculous proof of their saint's presence among them.[11] The saint might be angry or pleased, and he demanded constant propitiation, including votive offerings of which records were kept.[12] If propitiated, he could intervene through miracles to the advantage of the daily affairs of those he patronized.

When we turn to Gregory of Tours as hagiographer we find at once that his saints fall into two distinct types. They derive from different social traditions. First, there are the aristocratic bishops, including some relations of his own. This kind of saint's Life had a respectable ancestry. Some were written in the fourth century and one, Pontius' Life of St Cyprian, in the third. But Gregory had models nearer home and nearer in time, as for instance the Lives of Germanus of Auxerre and Caesarius of Arles. Secondly, there are the hermits and monks, simple folk for the most part and attached rather tenuously to the structure of the Church. Gregory, a bishop, brings them within the fold by writing about them; but they are not a class with much future. Gregory's corpus of Lives – aristocrats, hermits and monks – is a massive contribution to hagiography, comparable to the *Dialogues* of Gregory the Great composed soon afterwards. Indeed, the pope may have seen the bishop's collection. The difference lies in the presence of a central figure, St Benedict, in the pope's collection. There is no central figure in the Lives of Gregory of Tours, or at least none comparable to St Benedict.

Though Gregory's motives were not dissimilar from those of other hagiographers he differs from most of them in his historian's care to get his facts right and his chronology straight. Two great themes preoccupy him. First, the miracle-history of the sees he knows best, Clermont and Tours; and secondly the collective summarization of the miracles of the holy men of Gaul; and these he sees as an entity and a cumulative witness. He does not mean to record all that he knows, but to leave an indelible impression of the Gallic heritage of heroic sanctity. The foundation of this weighty picture of national achievement is necessarily Sulpicius Severus' Life of St Martin with the appended Dialogues. The birth of Martin, his arrival in Gaul, his consecration as bishop and his death are chronological linchpins for Gregory, though exceptionally he does not get them quite right. St Martin is the beginning for him, a huge figure, at once monk and bishop, bestriding both worlds. He cannot add to Sulpicius' facts but he can enumerate the miracles performed by St Martin since his death. Gregory can give literary shape to the miraculous evidence of the continuing power of the most famous of Gallic saints. Not that he

[11] *De virt. S. Mart.*, bk. 2, ch. 25 (MGH SRM ii, p. 618).
[12] *De virt. S. Juliani*, ch. 16 (ibid., p. 571).

used, or could use, a tithe of the local embellishments to which the cult continually gave birth. But he took the best. And he can do much the same for St Julian of Brioude, the presiding saint of the Auvergne and a national figure not much inferior to Martin. Gregory's Julian is an arresting personality. He is not the historical figure that Martin was but he is the tutelary saint of a mountain region where Mars and Mercury were once worshipped, and he seems to have taken over some of their attributes. For example, he can control weather and the elements; he is swift to avenge any slight such as robbery; and he has temple-cattle. Perhaps there is a hint of some Woden-like pagan god here. It is clear enough that his cult reveals a popular regional deity, capable of benevolence and anger, protection and destruction, and of miraculous intervention. In a sense, the roots of such a cult must be popular, and to that extent will lie outside the Church. Gregory brings Julian inside by composing an account of his miracles that can be used liturgically.

But when all is said it is Gregory's smaller men who rivet attention. They are more numerous than his bishops and he plainly loves them. He enjoys the simple-living hermit, the rough man of the people who practises terrible privation (not necessarily to be copied by the faithful) and is rich in miracles. But it was a difficult field for the hagiographer to work in. How was he to draw the line between the cults of acceptable ascetics and mere wild men of the woods of whom nothing was known apart from their popular, and perhaps temporary, veneration? The time was near, if it had not actually arrived, when the hermit was to be told plainly that the place for him was the monastery where his oddities would be subject to a Rule and checked where necessary by a bishop. There was nothing much, for example, that Gregory could say about the entirely local cult, at Bouillac, near Bordeaux, of two priests whose names even had been forgotten. He just records that they had lived, once, holy lives and were buried in the same church, where they were remembered.[13] His Life of St Friardus shows us the kind of recluse he felt he could accept.[14] Friardus lives the life of what Bernoulli calls a 'Waldbruder', attuned to nature and asking nothing for himself. When he happens on a wasps' nest or falls from a tree he simply says 'Our help is in the Lord's name who made heaven and earth', and no harm comes to him. He is a specialist in reviving sterile trees. Another is Gregory's hermit Caluppa, whom he had actually visited.[15] Caluppa's asceticism was such that he lost the strength to work and took refuge on a cliff in the Auvergne. One of his miracles is of special interest. He faces two dragons and puts them to flight by

---

[13] *In Glor. Conf.*, ch. 46 (ibid., p. 776).
[14] Ibid., pp. 705–9.   [15] Ibid., pp. 709–11.

prayer and the sign of the cross. One dragon Gregory can identify: it must be the Devil himself, 'in my opinion the very Prince of Temptation'. But the other dragon he cannot identify; and indeed there seems no special reason for a second dragon. The right inference is surely that Gregory is here taking a story from folklore, in which the second dragon once had his role. In Gregory's account his second dragon lingers on; it seemed a pity to drop him, and perhaps the people still liked him. A third 'Waldbruder' is Emilianus, a gardener, at home with beasts and birds.[16] A wild boar took refuge in his garden from the dogs of the hunter Brachio (which means bear-cub, adds Gregory). Overwhelmed by the saint's fearless simplicity, Brachio was in effect converted. He was unable to read or write, though he could sing; so Emilianus instructed him in the Psalter. These wild men have no theological quirks. They ask no questions and their asceticism is rewarded by God with the ability to perform miracles. All are near to nature; they are at home with animals and birds, much in the manner of the Eastern saints; and they live what amount to idyllic lives. They do not of course face the temptations of greater ascetics, men of the standing of Quintianus, Gallus, Nicetius of Clermont, Nicetius of Lyon and Gregory of Langres, who merit warmer commendation. But still they are brought inside the Church as subjects of official cultus and so are rescued from the semi-pagan countryside. Gregory treats them as a class. Thereafter they appear spasmodically in Merovingian hagiography. Looking as a whole at the saints' Lives he had composed, Gregory sees their composition as in itself a sort of miracle. He expresses it thus in the preface to his *De Virtutibus beati Martini*; 'after all, I think God is able to express these matters through my words, as he once brought forth water from the hard stones of the wilderness to quench his people's thirst. Surely he can once more speak through the mouth of an ass by opening my lips.' He meant what he said.

The pastoral strain, put to higher uses, also emerges in the writings of Gregory's contemporary, Venantius Fortunatus, bishop of Poitiers.[17] Venantius' writings had widespread influence, reaching beyond the continent to Anglo-Saxon England. One can too quickly dismiss him as a time-serving Italian who made a good thing out of occasional eulogies of Merovingian princes who had done nothing to deserve them. But he was bigger than that. Trained in the schools of Ravenna and so in touch with contemporary Byzantine thought, he had made his way to Francia with the intention of giving thanks to St Martin for curing him of a youthful eye complaint. But his route was circuitous

---

[16] Ibid., pp. 711–15.

[17] *Opera poetica*, ed. F. Leo (MGH AA iv, i); *Opera pedestria*, ed. B. Krusch (ibid. iv, ii). For textual emendations see S. Blomgren, *Studia Fortunatiana* (Uppsala, 1933).

and he spent some two years at the court of the Austrasian king Sigebert before reaching St Martin at Tours and finally Poitiers, where he was to spend the greater part of his career, probably as a lay agent to the nunnery of Radegundis. Only in the last years of his life did he become a bishop. There was plenty of antique learning in Venantius; Virgil, and to some extent Ovid, were at his fingertips. This can be gauged not merely from direct citations but from verbal reminiscences. Their poetry is alive and active in his mind. But it was coupled with familiar knowledge of the Bible and the Christian writers, especially Sedulius and Arator. It is Christian learning that predominates in his writings. We have from his pen both poetry and prose. There are panegyrics, epitaphs, elegies, hymns, letters, narrative verse, theology and saints' Lives. He was a professional writer in a society with an insatiable appetite for his work; and the Franks were the cause of it. It is impossible to imagine him in any other setting.

Venantius' writings during his stay in Austrasia were mostly court pieces, no doubt depicting their subjects as they ought to have been, rather than as they actually were. There was a fashion in such things. But this by itself is insufficient explanation. The number and variety of his addressees, lay and clerical, to say nothing of what remains of their own letters, show that the Austrasian aristocracy had a longing for eulogy of a special kind. Its keynote was friendship and tenderness. A word that recurs is *dulcedo*. The idea it expresses was familiar to Antiquity but it permeates the wide circle of Venantius' acquaintance. Nor is it lost in the still wider circle that gathered round him when he moved on to Western Francia. These same magnates were already accustomed to eulogy of a different kind in the form of vernacular *cantilenae*. It looks as if the mode of Christian–Roman eulogy encapsulated what was essential to the barbarian mind in the old; namely, the search for a basis of moral repute in the deeds of real or imaginary heroic forebears, Germanic or Roman. Thus, Venantius compares the fall of Thuringia with that of Troy,[18] and this at a time when legends of the Trojan origins of the Franks were beginning to circulate. Fredegar, a Burgundian writer as it seems, gives some attention to them.[19] Polite eulogy is not the only form of literature in which this emotional transfer is apparent; but it does serve to explain something of the appetite of educated barbarians for a new form of Latin literature designed to attract them.

Poitiers is the heart of Venantius' poetic inspiration; and, in Poitiers, Radegundis and Agnes. He found the service of ascetic women attractive and in it he wrote what are probably his best poems. The first was

[18] *De excidio Thoringiae* (MGH AA iv, i, append. 1, p. 271).
[19] *Chron.* bk. ii, ch. 5 (MGH SRM ii, p. 46).

occasioned by the appointment of Agnes as abbess of Ste Croix.[20] He calls it *De Virginitate*. In it one catches echoes of distinguished predecessors in the same genre: notably Sedulius, Arator, Avitus, Juvencus and Paulinus of Nola. Venantius' poem is not about Agnes but about the nun's vocation; not about morality or even asceticism but about the visionary world that virginity conjures up in his mind. The bride of Christ sees the heavens opened and dreams of her union with her Lord. For her it is all a dream-world and for the poet an ecstasy of song and light, a paradise of flashing gems and brilliant flowers, where Christ takes up his bride into the senate of saints. The flavour is decidedly erotic, and the vision of heaven points straight to medieval mysticism. The participation of nature in the great moments of salvation, though older than Venantius, is new to the society he addresses. Allied to this cult of virginity were the beginnings of the western cult of the Virgin Mary, to which Venantius and his friend Gregory of Tours, with their Byzantine connections, made a vital contribution.[21] Venantius' *In Laudem Mariae* (if it is his, as seems likely) is a major poem in which the Virgin appears as queen of heaven, receiving homage. It has rightly been called a romanticized view of female virginity which seems to owe little to Byzantine thinking; indeed it suggests a first shy approach to the theme of courtly love, somewhat as exhibited in Venantius' poems to the great ladies he knew. The beginnings of the western cult of the Virgin thus owe much to Poitiers and Tours; and connected with it comes the cult of holy images. Another great poem is rather different. *De excidio Thoringiae*[22] is written as if by Radegundis and is addressed by her to her cousin Amalafrid in Byzantium. It is an elegy on their youth spent at the Thuringian court before their country was overwhelmed by the Franks and she herself taken away as their captive. It recalls a whole childhood of shared joy and sorrow, and especially the ruin of their home and the deaths of their kindred. Basically the story must be Radegundis' own; but the dream-world is the poet's. One other poem about a woman (and there are several) deserves notice: that on the death of Galswintha,[23] Chilperic's queen and Brunechildis' sister, who was assassinated by or on behalf of Chilperic. But the poem is not about assassination nor does it apportion any blame. It is about the cruelty of fate, out of which good can come, and about the grief of three women. First, that of the princess's mother, Queen Goiswintha,

---

[20] MGH SRM iv, i, pp. 181–91.

[21] Gregory was in fact the first western writer to report the Assumption of the Virgin, in *De Glor. Mart.* 4 (MGH SRM, 1, i, ch. 4).

[22] MGH AA iv, i, append., pp. 271–5.

[23] Ibid., pp. 136–46.

who laments long and prophetically at her daughter's departure from Spain to marry a Frankish king. Forebodings of grief accompany Galswintha as she leaves the weeping court, and Nature, as so often with Venantius, reacts sympathetically. Her death, which soon follows, is not politically significant for the poet; it is only the occasion for the grief of her nurse and then (very different) of her sister Brunechildis; and again, Nature grieves with them. Finally, the old queen back in Spain learns of the inevitable tragedy and weeps for her lost daughter. The poem is an elegy on shared suffering – of mother, sister, daughter and nurse.

Despite these poems, and admitting that the large body of his work can only be called court pieces, it may come as a surprise that Venantius was esteemed more particularly as a writer of saints' Lives by the centuries that followed. It was the first point made by Alcuin in an epitaph composed probably for the Church of St Hilary at Poitiers.[24] His saints' Lives are all *pièces d'occasion* in prose or verse, composed for such as wanted them, according to where he found himself at any one time. The prose Lives fall into two main groups; an Aquitanian (St Hilary, St Radegundis and St Severinus of Bordeaux); and a Neustrian (St Albinus of Angers, St Marcellus and St Germanus of Paris, and St Paternus of Avranches). In verse are his lives of St Martin (in four books) and St Médard of Soissons, and numerous shorter notices on sanctuaries he had visited and their builders. Their flavour is episcopal. It is the bishops who feel the need for commemoration, for themselves and for their saintly predecessors. Two poems on St Vincent of Agen were addressed to Bishop Leontius II of Bordeaux. The Life of St Albinus was written at the request of the reigning bishop of Angers and constructed from material available at Angers, of a distinctively Celtic type, and written, says Venantius, 'to edify the people'. The Life of St Marcellus was written for St Germanus from material so scanty that Venantius has to fill it out with an enormous preface. He can record one or two miracles that sound popular, as when Marcellus lifts red-hot metal with his bare hands from a smith's furnace and tells the smith how much it weighs;[25] and when he faces a troublesome dragon and kills it with his staff.[26] But most of Marcellus' miracles are connected with the church itself and are clerical in origin. The little Life of St Paternus (or, in French, St Pair) is of interest on several counts.[27] It is a Life of a hermit and monk who became a bishop, continuing throughout to live ascetically in great simplicity and to work miracles. Venantius manages to weave the miracles and the hard living very skillfuly into a factual account of a

---

[24] MGH SRM Poet, i, no. xvii, p. 326.
[25] MGH AA iv, 2, p. 51.
[26] Ibid., p. 53.
[27] Ibid., pp. 33–7.

busy career. Though well-born, Paternus starts life as a hermit in the
cave of a pagan divinity on an island. But it is with the support of King
Childebert, none the less, that he is able, later on, to found many
monasteries; and one suspects that royal favour was behind his promotion to the see of Avranches although Venantius only says that
what moved Paternus to accept was a vision of three departed bishops,
who consecrated him. He died, worn out, at Avranches about the year
563 but was buried, as he wished, in his monastery of Sciscy (now St
Pair sur Mer) and it was for the monastery, not the bishopric, that
Venantius in his old age composed the Life. Paternus was not a bishop
of much political importance, but he clearly combined efficiency as an
administrator with a hard-won name for asceticism, and so attracted
royal attention. One may note one of his miracles. He strikes the
ground to produce water – just, adds Venantius, as Moses had produced water from the rock. His miracles are biblical miracles. The Life
of St Germanus,[28] who was personally known to Venantius, tells us
almost nothing of biographical interest, not because nothing was
known but because it would have been irrelevant to an orthodox
saint's Life as understood by its readers and hearers. But we are given a
glimpse of the man, 'sitting there, grave and anxious, severe in expression and austere in speech'. The Life is a tribute to an old acquaintance
as well as to his successor, Bishop Ragnemod. Venantius is moved by
the circumstances of Germanus' miracles and is particularly good at
imagining Germanus coping with demons – no very demanding task
for a man who could perform a miracle at the antenatal stage:
Germanus had prevented his own mother from aborting him. Unfactual the Life may be, but at the same time it is warm and even
affectionate. Almost equally unfactual is the Life of St Radegundis,[29]
who was even better known to Venantius. He confines himself to the
ascetic and miracle-worker and reveals nothing of the person who
inspired him to write the *De Excidio Thoringiae* and many affectionate
occasional pieces. But in this case he seems to have leaned too far
towards orthodoxy since not much later the nun Baudonivia was
commissioned to make another attempt in a warmer vein. But we
must not forget that Venantius' strings of miracles were the right
miracles, falling into expected patterns; and he does not miss their
symbolic significance.

But it is on his Life of St Martin[30] that contemporaries chiefly judged
him. This huge effort seems to have been made for Gregory of Tours
as a thank-offering, if it was not actually commissioned by him. As to

[28] Ibid., pp. 11–27.
[29] MGH AA iv, 2, pp. 38–49.
[30] Ibid., iv, i, pp. 293–370.

facts, he cannot of course improve on the great work of Sulpicius, which he excerpts and reshapes without too much regard for precision. But he still thinks this a very important literary occasion for him. He feels he is contributing to a noble tradition and therefore starts by listing his predecessors as Christian poets. These include Paulinus of Périgueux, who wrote a verse Life of Martin and was in fact more faithful than Venantius to the text of Sulpicius. In the field of miracles subsequent to Sulpicius' Life he has free rein and indulges his fancy. We are given Martin's vision of heaven, his conversation with angels and visits paid to him by the saints, including the bejewelled Virgin. He sees heaven less as a court than as a great army of legions, squadrons and cohorts, gloriously equipped and commanded by Christ, its king. Such visions are not traditional. They are the visions of Venantius himself. The Life of St Martin may leave on the reader the impression of a rather formless epic; but it pleased the poet greatly. He had done what he meant to do for St Martin. He had turned him into an epic figure, a visionary admitted to the splendours of heaven. All this had little or nothing to do with the historical figure of the saint but it does tell us how the sixth century liked to conceive of the most powerful of its miracle-working patrons. St Martin, in the eyes of the poet, shared with St Hilary and (of all people) King Chilperic, the ultimate in fame: to be known in India. Venantius' vast poem (completed in two months) was his contribution to a literary genre especially dear to early medieval writers of saints' Lives: in conjunction with Sulpicius, he had achieved an *opus geminatum*, a prose and verse version of the same Life. Some liked their saints' Lives in verse and others in prose, as Bishop Aunarius of Auxerre pointed out to a contemporary of Venantius whom he was anxious to bully into composition.

Venantius and Gregory are almost the only Frankish hagiographers of their generation that we know of. Neither was a Frank by birth though what they wrote was Frankish hagiography for Franks; and neither is conceivable outside the Frankish field. The great opportunity that both seized was to standardize the image of the holy bishop. Without exactly making the bishop a saint because he was a bishop, they showed how the exercise of episcopal power and authority could assist the right man with God, so that his miracles in life and after death sustained his claim to perpetual patronage of his people. To his sainted predecessors, the reigning bishop owed much of his influence. But it must be the right man; a man of action rather than of intellect. Asceticism still counted, learning hardly at all. St Martin is the link between bishop and hermit. Gregory makes the last serious attempt to incorporate the hermit into the Merovingian Church. The simple world of Nature in which the hermit moves is to some extent an imaginary world to him, and more to Venantius, who goes so far as to claim that Nature as well as man is saved by Christ. And this world of the sanctified countryside fits well enough into the mental background of the superficially Christian Frank, still hankering for his tutelary divinities of stream and spring, hill and wood. The hagiographer may not take much from folklore or popular hearsay to construct his picture of the holy man, but the picture he does provide is precisely suited to a time of transitional beliefs. It could not long survive as a dominant form.

The seventh century already betrays some marked changes in the sort of saint's Life that the Church wanted. Clearly the Irishmen made a difference. Columbanus himself was too formidable and too near in time to be entirely submerged in miracles in Jonas of Bobbio's famous Life of him.[31] Jonas does not write a biography but personal details are plentiful enough; details, however, that mainly demonstrate the saint's ways of dealing with moral turpitude. The rebuking of kings was nothing new; the tradition of resistance to authority had been acknowledged in Gaul since the time of St Martin; but it was a dangerous precedent, proper only to the exceptional man. Columbanus was exceptional and that alone makes Jonas' Life unique. There was no one else like Columbanus. When Jonas consents to write a Life of a more commonplace man the result is correspondingly ordinary as, for example, his Life of the sixth-century John of Réomé, founder of the monastery of Moutier-St-Jean, written at the request of the monks and dedicated to the abbot Hunna.[32] It is an ahistorical seventh-century view of an unimportant holy man of the Lérins circle, viewed against a background of forest-clearing, farming and prayer. His miracles arise from simple occasions, proper to a hermit, and his house is an asylum for the poor and fugitives. All the same, John was much respected by royalty. Jonas' other Lives are in effect appendices to his Life of Columbanus. Even when he deals with the career of a northern missionary as idiosyncratic as St Vedast of Arras[33] he does not fully avail himself of the plentiful information he could have had locally (as from St Amand, whom he visited) but is content with a hurried sketch of the work of conversion. It was more important that Vedast should emerge as an orthodox miracle-worker: and so he does. Upon the whole, the Lives of what may be called the Luxeuil school are unimpressive. An exception is the Life of St Germanus of Moutiers-Grandval, in the Jura. A friend of Arnulf of Metz, Germanus qualified for martyrdom through death at the hands of brigands.[34] But it is an

[31] MGH SRM in usum schol. ed. Krusch (1905).
[32] MGH SRM iii, pp. 505–17.
[33] Ibid., pp. 399–427.   [34] MGH SRM v, pp. 33–40.

exception only in the sense that it affords welcome insights into the life of an East-Frankish magnate of the seventh century.

The Irish apart, the significant change of the seventh century is towards the Lives of political bishops. These are classified by modern German historians as *Adelsheilige*, though the term is surely too narrow. Undoubtedly the bishops who were the subjects of written Lives were men concerned in public affairs, sometimes as supporters of kings and occasionally as their opponents. Some, but not all, were of high birth. It was not claimed that their careers made them saints but rather their deaths, or the miracles attributed to them after death. An earlier example of this class, though in some ways unique, is the Life of Desiderius of Vienne by the Visigoth king Sisebut.[35] It was the first attempt to make a martyr out of a political bishop who committed treason and was executed for his pains. He had involved himself too closely in the career of Queen Brunechildis, which was why her countryman Sisebut was interested in the matter. But none of this prevented the performance of the expected miracles at his grave. Politics could provide a fresh route to martyrdom, still the best claim to sanctity. But Desiderius was exceptionally lucky. The Lives of the churchmen who came later contain few martyrs, though many of them took great risks. The Gallic Church had never been rich in indigenous martyrs (though Gregory did his best with them), and this may be one reason for the extraordinary proliferation of Lives that showed other roads to sanctity. To become a martyr through missionary work was not to be quite as prestigious as the traditional hero who had met his end through passive resistance. Even less prestigious were the political martyrs. All could be counted as martyrs but their claims had to be weighed against those of a sterner time, like St Maurice of Agaune or St Denis of Paris, whose cults were firmly anchored to important places. But the *Adelsheilige* were big men. The most important are: Sulpicius of Bourges, Audoen of Rouen, Eligius of Noyon, Wandrille of Fontenelle, Philibert of Jumièges, Arnulf of Metz, Leodegarius of Autun and Desiderius of Cahors. There is a separate but related group, stretching farther back, of those of royal blood: Sigismund, Chrotechildis, Chlodomer, Radegundis, Dagobert II and III, Geretrudis and Balthildis. St Arnulf overlaps both groups.

The core of the episcopal group was formed by the able young men who rose to power at the court of Chlotar II and his son Dagobert I. One not belonging to the group was Leodegarius (or Léger) of Autun, a bishop who fell foul of the powerful Ebroin and so met his end.[36] No man was more involved in palace revolutions than Leodegarius or

---

[35] MGH SRM iii, pp. 620–7.
[36] MGH SRM v, pp. 249–362; see also vii, p. 845.

played the game he had to play more ruthlessly. But in Burgundy in particular, where his influence lay, he was thought to have behaved as a responsible bishop should behave. The *Passio* we have of him (a good deal worked over) gives his side of the story, which ends in execution seen as martyrdom.[37] Or rather it begins there; for thereafter come the miracles at his resting-place that prove sanctity. It is difficult to believe that St Leodegarius meant to the pilgrim or the pious peasant what the local saints described by Gregory of Tours meant to an earlier generation of rustics, but there is some evidence that he did. No less than three bishops thought it worth while to compete for the honour of housing his remains, which excited local veneration from the moment of his death. Only a miracle could decide the matter. Accordingly the bishops met, and placed on the altar under a cloth three slips of parchment containing the names of their dioceses. The slip that was drawn turned out to be that of Poitiers, which therefore got the saint's remains. Such at least was the story as known to Ursinus, who composed his version of the Life in the eighth century.[38] It sounds circumstantial. But the circle of King Dagobert is altogether more attractive. Eligius and his pupil Audoen,[39] who wrote his Life, are political saints of a better complexion. Both were missionaries and neither had enemies. In the case of the southerner Eligius, the great goldsmith, his biographer gives the impression that his life changed radically on his appointment to the see of Noyon, for he then gave himself entirely to missionary work. Audoen's account of him is indeed biographical in a sense that most earlier Lives were not. However much stress is laid on his sanctity, his doings are described and we are left with a picture of a real man who enjoys power and does good. The writers of these mid-century Lives wish to justify their subjects' careers as well as to insist on their claims as miracle-workers. St Amand,[40] on the other hand, does have enemies and does face the ill-will of a king. He courts martyrdom without obtaining it among the various heathen peoples he works to convert. His earliest Life does afford an authentic picture of the career of a remarkable man, as difficult in his way as Columbanus or Boniface; but if one looks merely at the titles of the twenty-six chapters one sees at once that the writer has not abandoned the traditional view of what constitutes sanctity and indeed makes a Life worth writing. His guide-lines are firm in the Life of St Martin and Pope Gregory's *Dialogues*. We find

---

[37] Another view is provided in the Life of St. Praejectus of Clermont, equally involved in politics and equally unfortunate (ibid., pp. 212–48).

[38] Ibid., ch. 24 of Passio ii, pp. 346–8.

[39] Ibid., pp. 536–67; see also vii, p. 847.

[40] Ibid., pp. 395–485; see also vii, pp. 846 ff.

Amand, as a lad, putting to flight a serpent of great size by prayer; we find him at St Martin's shrine; we learn of his abstinence; in an ecstasy he speaks with St Peter on two occasions; he quietens a storm at sea; he can restore a hanged man to life; a blind man receives sight from the water in which the saint has washed his hands; a disobedient monk stricken with paralysis is healed by his prayer. The writer sums it up thus: 'what miracles did the Lord not perform through him who gave life to the dead, sight to the blind, movement to the paralytic, cleanness to the lepers, hearing to the deaf, health to those oppressed by demons?'[41] When we move among these later Merovingian Lives that are richer in personal and political detail, it is right to remember that the proofs of sanctity as traditionally understood were still the basic reason for their composition.

We have reached the frontiers of the Carolingian age, when saints' Lives, popular as ever, were to develop new features. They were to show an inventive exuberance quite foreign to the Merovingians as a whole, whose *œuvre*, naïve by comparison, was plundered and embellished without compunction. Yet still within the Merovingian age we have one last group of Lives that forms the most significant link with the future: the Lives of some of the founders of the Carolingian dynasty itself. In this respect the earliest Carolingians were unlike their predecessors. Three Merovingian queens – Chrotechildis, Radegundis and Balthildis – achieved sanctity, but the kings did less well. None was acknowledged as a saint by reason of his kingly qualities. Indeed, those very qualities seemed to debar them from sanctity. To protect Church property, to fight the Church's battles and to support its bishops made a good king but not a good saint. Nor was any claim to sacral status through blood a road to sanctity. Like many of their predecessors, the Carolingian founders did interest themselves in the Church and especially in the establishment of monasteries. It was not difficult to make saints out of pious ladies like Geretrudis of Nivelles,[42] the daughter of Pippin I and Itta, who, alive or dead, loomed large in the religion of north-eastern Francia and in the Rhineland. Round her cult, locally, surviving pagan practices also seemed to coalesce, and it may not have seemed irrelevant that the site of her nunnery was once a place of pagan sacrifice and that she herself bore the name of a Valkyrie, Keretrud. But the going was harder when it came to a major political figure such as Arnulf of Metz, 'a man high and noble by birth and wealthy in the things of this world'. The repute of the see of Metz and probably also of the family required his sanctification, and the fact that he had been a bishop made it possible.

[41] Ibid., p. 449.
[42] MGH SRM ii, pp. 453–74.

The first Life[43] was composed by a monk who had known him
personally, and the occasion was, as often in the past, the translation of
his remains, from the monastery of Remiremont, where he spent his
last years, to Metz. He showed, necessarily, abstinence and humility,
but the illustration of these virtues comes almost verbatim from the
Life of Radegundis. His birth was hailed by a pilgrim as that of one
who should be 'great in the sight of the Lord' (Luke 1: 15). He had all
the right virtues. He accepted his bishopric unwillingly and with tears
and in the end resigned it to become a hermit. He performed miracles
before and after death. Indeed, had the author recorded them all they
must, he says, have filled an 'enorme volumen'. In a sense, one could
not have a more traditional bishop's Life. It fits well into the accepted
pattern. Arnulf, if anyone, is an *Adelsheiliger*. This first Life, unlike the
second which was to follow it, is kept well within traditional bounds,
and the political ambitions of the family are not in evidence, even if
they may be suspected. In a word, it is a Merovingian Life. The family
that gains most from the sanctification of the Frankish nobility is the
Carolingian family.

The cult of the saints was not primarily ethical: that was holy which
was attached to a holy man, and loyalty to him rather than how one
behaved to others was what won his patronage. Yet the saints' Lives
did provide a platform for the teaching of social morality and to some
extent also of theology. They did insist that murder, theft, perjury and
so on did not pay, any more than did manual work performed on
Sundays. We have seen that most of these Lives demonstrated the
sanctity of well-born men and women, and increasingly so as time
passed. But the moral lessons that could be taught through them were
directed at humbler people and had therefore to take account of what
they were able to appreciate. Not surprisingly, then, the humble are
commonly seen as objects of sympathy. A saint will not stand against
the unfree in the interests of masters. On the other hand, to be poor is
meritorious only if one has become poor deliberately for the service
of God. Otherwise, the social role of poverty is what it always had
been: to afford the rich a chance of salvation through almsgiving. The
saint will often make himself poor and work at menial tasks with his
own hands – but in the service of God. The ascetic ideal is still active.
This is not to say that the hagiographers set themselves against wealth
and authority. Far from it. The *potens* as such is not a bad man, above
all not when he is an ecclesiastical *potens*. The wicked judge familiar in
the *Acta Martyrum* is almost unknown in the Merovingian Lives,
however harsh he may be. The saint will not readily oppose the

---

[43] Ibid., pp. 432–46.

severity of a judgement though he may try to mitigate its consequences. Thus he may rescue a thief from the gallows by miraculous intervention but will not condone the crime for which the thief was hanged. He is simply exercising the charity proper to himself in a situation which provides him with an opportunity. Not infrequently a saint will free captives and prisoners. A case in point is Gaugericus of Cambrai, interesting also because he was the product of a local priest's school in which he learnt to commit the Psalms to memory. The miracles in Gaugeric's Life are all to do with the freeing of prisoners through prayer despite the opposition of officialdom.[44] The common man listening to the reading of his own saint's Life will learn the virtues proper to a saint and some, but not all, of them may be meant to apply to him. But there is certainly nothing in the corpus of Lives corresponding to the careful lessons in social morality conveyed by sermons such as those of Caesarius. One cannot claim that the saints of the Lives were object-lessons in living that the layman would do well to follow in detail. This was never their purpose. The saints were there to personify supernatural power and to give protection against the demon-world. They were the common man's patrons against forces that could and would destroy him and his. They were at the same time mediators between man and a very remote God. It cannot be by chance that so few Merovingian churches were dedicated to Christ himself. Although the miracles in saints' Lives were derived as types directly from the Bible, Christ as God remains somewhat outside the daily experience of the peasant in search of ghostly protection. He may be envisaged by such as Venantius as a splendid warrior-figure fit to be sought by the ascetic and won by the virgin, but the common man will prefer the more accessible shrine of his own tutelary god, the local saint. To serve this single purpose the shrine with its elaborate cult proliferated throughout Merovingian Francia; and part of that cultus was the saint's Life. It tells us more about the religion of the Franks than does any other source of information.

---

[44] MGH SRM iii, pp. 652–8.

VI

THE CHURCH IN COUNCIL

THE first council of the Church is described in Acts 15: a meeting at
Jerusalem, a debate and the dispatch of letters summarizing its conclusions. The pattern persisted. Thereafter we know of seven councils
of the Church that were agreed to have been general: Nicaea I (325),
Constantinople I (381), Ephesus (431), Chalcedon (451), Constantinople
II (553), Constantinople III (680–1), and Nicaea II (787). The canons
or decisions of these seven general councils were regarded as binding
on the whole Church for all time. How these canons were preserved
and disseminated is difficult to determine. Their contents at least
showed clearly that the great issues that justified the summoning of
general councils were doctrine, discipline and cultus. But equally from
an early date there were councils or synods at a lower level – national,
regional, metropolitical and diocesan – that implemented the general
canons and issued canons of their own; and it is such that must be
considered at the level of Frankish Gaul.

Primarily but not exclusively (and obviously not at diocesan level)
the councils we have to consider[1] were the preserve of bishops; of men
who were lords of their people and keenly aware that they stood in an
apostolic succession. A bishop is sometimes called *princeps populi* and,
more affectionately, *papa*. Thus there survives an early inscription
from Vienne which describes its bishop as *Dominus papa*, and another
from Le Puy which ends with the words *Papa vive Deo* ('may our
father live in God'). So far, then, as titles reveal anything, the Gallic
bishops were a brotherhood of apostolic successors, each charged with
the care of one Christian community. There was a clear awareness of
common roots and shared traditions, and never more so than when
assembled in council. What we do not find is Merovingian abbots as a
group associated with bishops in council, though individual abbots
might sometimes attend. Only under the Carolingians do abbots
achieve the necessary prestige.

For the Merovingian period there survive the canons of over twenty
councils in which more than one ecclesiastical province was repre-

[1] The Merovingian councils are published by F. Maassen in MGH Conc. i and the Carolingian
in Conc. ii. Good though these editions are, I cite Merovingian councils for convenience from
that of C. Munier, *Concilia Galliae*, CC 148A and 148, covering the years 314–506 and 511–695
respectively. Reference should always be made to C. J. Hefele and H. Leclercq, *Histoire des
conciles*, 8 vols (Paris, 1907–21).

sented, two provincial councils and one diocesan synod. Of these, the first was the council of Orléans held in July 511, after the defeat of the Visigoths of Aquitaine by Clovis.[2] It was attended by thirty-two bishops including four metropolitans. The bishops of northern Gaul were absent; overwhelmingly it was an Aquitanian occasion, marking the glad submission of the Roman churches of the South to the new Catholic overlord and their sense of relief at the overthrow of his predecessor, the Arian Alaric, whose concessions to them had been too late and too few. The canons make it clear that the bishops had assembled at Orléans on the orders of Clovis, that he himself had specified certain matters for discussion and that the canons required his approval. It was a new departure: the Merovingians meant to control the Church wherever they conquered fresh territory. However, the issues faced by the bishops were neither unconventional nor surprising. They defined with some care the conditions on which candidates for clerical orders were admissible and generally such candidates had to obtain the prior authorization of the king or the local count. The cohabitation of clergy with women was regulated in accordance with the ancient canons; and this indeed is a reminder that the first duty of any church council was to reaffirm its obedience to former canons, especially of the great general councils. The bishops went on to affirm their authority over monasteries within their dioceses, the relations of an abbot with his bishop and of monks with their abbot; and there should be no more setting-up of independent cells by vain, ambitious monks without the permission of bishop or abbot. Two important groups of canons concerned ecclesiastical property. Royal gifts of land were to be immune from public charges but were to be used to keep churches in repair, to support bishops and to succour the poor and prisoners. Presumably the king was distributing the property of the Arian clergy of the Visigoths and plainly meant to keep his eye on it. He had much to distribute in the way of *beneficia* and patronage. A second group of canons were concerned with the apportionment of diocesan income; and finally, conditions were laid down for the admission of Arian clergy to the Catholic hierarchy and for the reconsecration of Arian churches. Other matters, concerning for example the liturgy and sacraments, were not overlooked; but the main concern of the council was the disposal and control of property falling to the Aquitanian churches through Frankish conquest and reallocated (in part at least) by the conqueror himself. The Aquitanians had been freed from Arian supervision but had acquired new masters who might acknowledge the Roman Law by which the South lived

---

[2] *Conc. Gall.*, pp. 4–19.

and might not even be much in evidence except in scattered garrisons, but who intended to retain control.

Once again, in 533 under the sons of Clovis, the bishops assembled at Orléans in council:[3] twenty-six of them, representing the three kingdoms of the sons but predominantly from northern Aquitaine. The presence of the metropolitan of Vienne will have been due to the tightening grip of the Franks on the Burgundian kingdom to their east. In the intervening twenty-two years there had been other, regional, councils and some had been important. But what now, after a generation's experience of the Franks, had the bishops to say? They say it, briefly, in twenty-one short canons. They are bothered about themselves; about the support of the metropolitan by his suffragans; about the annual summoning of provincial councils; about the duties of bishops when a colleague dies; about the election of bishops, clerical ordinations, negligent clergy, married clergy and – a shaft of light that was to penetrate far into the future – about the inadmissibility of candidates for ordination who could not read or were ignorant of the rite of baptism. Abbots who disobeyed their diocesans were to be excommunicated until they submitted. There is concern about the annulment of marriages and about the cultus of pagan idols. The bishops thus look fearlessly at problems old and new, many of which they will never be able to solve. Their remedy is always to look back to earlier conciliar legislation where this is possible. This time, then, their minds are less taken up by problems of property and more by those of discipline. They speak with one voice. The point about pagan practices is taken up in an edict, now incomplete, promulgated by one of the brother-kings, apparently Childebert I.[4] He is extremely concerned that pagan shrines and idols continue to attract devotees despite the efforts of bishops. His people is a *populus christianus* and he himself is dedicated to serve God. Pagan practices must cease throughout his kingdom. Thus he adds his voice to the voices of the bishops in council.

Another council, national in one sense but regional in another, assembles at Clermont in the Auvergne in 535;[5] in Aquitaine, therefore. The occasion of it appears to have been the extension of Frankish conquest in Burgundy and in the South. Bishops from these parts are present, as well as some northern bishops who had not previously attended councils. Additional churches are thus drawn within the conciliar fold, making a total of fifteen. For all their subservience to the king (Theudebert) who has summoned them, they sound a note of

[3] Ibid., pp. 98–103.
[4] MGH Capit. i, no. 2, pp. 2–3.
[5] *Conc. Gall.*, pp. 105–12.

uneasiness; the election of bishops shall be by the clergy and people concerned, with the assent of the metropolitan; they are no matter for the exercise of patronage by the powerful. Thus the bishops close ranks against local interference by lay magnates. Perhaps also it was a warning to kings themselves; and if so, in vain. The bishops go on to require the presence of priests in charge of private oratories at the great feasts of the cathedral church. They mean to keep an eye on all the clergy of the dioceses, oratory priests as well as city clergy and parish priests. A further warning note is sounded: clergy shall not enlist the help of great men to resist their own bishops, nor shall a man escape excommunication who unjustly seizes church property by turning to the king. Finally, they decide to write to the king to ensure that church property shall remain unmolested when, through changes in boundaries of kingdoms, such property shall be transferred to a different kingdom. Clermont is significant. The bishops gain courage in council and identify potential threats to their order and to their properties; threats from lay magnates, perhaps from kings and certainly from clergy. It would be a great mistake to imagine that bishops and their clergy were always like-minded or a happy brotherhood. It was only too easy for clergy to identify their interests with those of the townsmen, rustics or patrons they served and to see their bishops as mitred *potentes* to be kept at arm's length. The same episcopal mistrust of clergy and determination to control them is apparent in the third council of Orléans held in 538[6] and attended by an increased number of bishops from Burgundy and Francia north of the Loire. For all their wealth and experience, the Aquitanian bishops gain strength from the adherence of their more distant colleagues; and all can look to their king as to the natural protector of a national Church.

The mid-sixth century sees a marked expansion in conciliar legislation, beginning with yet another council at Orléans in 541.[7] It coincides with the disappearance from the scene of the aged Caesarius, the great metropolitan of Arles, whose contribution to the smooth transition of the southern churches from Visigothic to Frankish overlordship can hardly be overestimated. It is worth pausing to consider his career, round which there lingers a flavour of the Antique and the heroic. Born around 470 in the territory of Chalon-sur-Saône, then Burgundian, and tonsured as a monk at eighteen years of age, we find him shortly afterwards at Lérins. There he spent several years. From Lérins he was sent to Arles to recover from an excess of mortification; or so at least his biographer reports. The metropolitan, to whom he was related, retained him, ordained him, and allowed him to seek

---

[6] Ibid., pp. 114–30.
[7] Ibid., pp. 132–46.

instruction from the great African *rhetor* Pomerius. Thus early he emerges as an adept at enforcing monastic discipline and not less as a young man well received in the best families. In 503 he was elected metropolitan of Arles on the nomination of his predecessor: a nice case of episcopal nepotism, and entirely justified in the event. The new metropolitan at once secured from the Visigoth Alaric II – what he might not have obtained a few years earlier when the Visigoths felt less threatened – a perpetual exemption of his Church from tax. In 506 he presided over a council at Agde, the canons of which were of value to succeeding councils. He survived, probably without difficulty, the conquest of the region by the Franks but with considerably more difficulty the temporary re-conquest by the Ostrogoths, who cited him to appear before Theoderic at Ravenna. He returned home by way of Rome, winning papal approval and the confirmation of the privilege of Arles as papal vicar in Gaul and Spain. One result was the extension of Caesarius' jurisdiction over the southern Burgundian churches. Between 524 and 533 he presided over no less than five councils of the South and in the same period produced his definitive version of his Rule for the nuns of Arles, soon to be adopted by Radegundis at Poitiers. In 536 Arles fell to the Franks, and in 542 Caesarius died. Such is the outline of the reign of a great monk-bishop of the Gallo-Roman type, who could survive Burgundians, Visigoths, Ostrogoths and Franks; courageous certainly, but also secure in the unwavering support of the southern senatorial families. The great influence on his life was certainly Lérins, the practices of which he transmitted to Arles. With Lérins, too, it seems best to associate his first acquaintance with Augustinian theology, thereafter so clear in his teaching on grace and free will. We can watch Caesarius at work in the daily duties of a metropolitan; as master of his clergy, defender of orthodoxy, monastic legislator, reliever of distress (no small matter in a disrupted world), expert in the canons of the Church and the writings of the Fathers; but especially we can watch him as a preacher in the great series of his surviving sermons.[8] How to reach the people of a large and populous province was the problem he posed to himself and his clergy. The answer was teaching and preaching and, by extension, how and what to teach and preach. After his death his sermons continued to be read and circulated. There are traces of them everywhere in the middle ages, often under other names – and naturally, since he himself had been an excerptor and simplifier of the best sermons of others. However, his hand is plain to see upon them all. His message is to the parish. The zeal and rather touching lack of

---

[8] Ed. Morin, CC and in part Delage, SC.

discretion of this great man were applied to a new scene. They survived to inform the best of the Merovingian episcopate.

It was thus the south of Gaul, not the North, that produced the great episcopal exemplar at the critical moment. Such a man and no other could draw colleagues to him in successive councils and show them how bishops in unity could define the purposes of their Church. They could apply the wisdom of the canons and the Fathers to a new situation. At least in this respect the way ahead was clear. The two great councils summoned at Orléans in 541 and 549[9] are evidence of a shift in emphasis away from the South. They were truly national in composition, in the sense that all three Frankish kingdoms were represented, though no bishop attended from the far North or the East. The concern of the bishops, reflected in thirty-eight canons, points to a clear realization that no major ecclesiastical issue should be passed by without comment. Thus they give their minds to the need for an agreed date for Easter, liturgical matters, the obligations of bishops, the position of the clergy, Church property, penance and marriage. Archdeacons, the principal administrative officers of the bishops, make their first shy appearance in Frankish legislation; but monastic communities seem not to have invited special attention. Throughout there is a strong sense of churches drawing together to define dangers and propose remedies, always with an eye to the legislation of the past. The *potentes* press upon them locally, secure in the feeling that if they endow private oratories they also control the priests of those oratories and can expect priests to come begging to them for patronage. The bishops will have none of this. They even suspect one another: as a body, they must watch over the conduct of colleagues. The *potentes*, protectors and benefactors, present a problem because they are *potentes*, and this in the Roman provinces of Bordeaux and Arles as much as in the Frankish province of Rouen. Improper influence, then – one might call it *gratia* – and property come to the fore; so too does the moral conduct of the ordinary man: homicide, adultery, marriage, slaves and Christians subject to Jewish masters. It sounds as if most of this were appropriate to purely Frankish communities; but the legislation holds good for a province as distant as Eauze in the Pyrenean approaches, where Franks hardly ever set foot. The *Romani* of the Midi had their own troubles. Nor were the vestiges of paganism confined to the North: Christians everywhere were not to consume sacrificial offerings to idols nor to take oaths on the heads of wild beasts or cattle. One is still a long way from a well-ordered parochial society, content to obey its village-priests and venerate its allocation of saints.

[9] *Conc. Gall.*, pp. 148–61.

The 549 council of Orléans is national in two senses: all three kingdoms are represented and so also are all parts of the Frankish world, East as well as North. It meets at the order of the *clementissimus princeps* Childebert I, to recapitulate the ancient canons and to consider what else needs attention. The bishops look outside Francia to the controversy over the Three Chapters. Like the pope, they condemn the heretical sects of Eutyches and Nestorius. Thus they express at the doctrinal level their sense of unity with Rome: not Rome of the secular Empire, once so dear to the senatorial class, but Rome of the popes. They make it their first canon. Thereafter they give the best of their attention to problems of hierarchy and to the gifts received by the Church. Ecclesiastical hierarchy is not just a comfortable human matter of manœuvring for place and prestige. The emerging institution is very complex. Thus the relationship of metropolitan to bishops and of both to councils cannot be too precisely set forth. Moreover, who shall be a bishop? Can a layman be consecrated bishop? Kings held that they could: who better to rule a diocese than a man trained and proved under the royal eye? Perhaps the bishops are scenting future danger when they enact that the election of a bishop shall be made 'with the king's permission after election by the clergy and people [sc. of the diocese] as laid down in the ancient canons'. Monasteries, or at least nunneries, now receive consideration. The terms on which girls may receive the nun's habit are laid down. What is more, excommunication awaits the girl or widow who has been professed and then goes home and marries. As with monks, the line between the cloister and the hearth is notably fluid: one can be both in and out; and men are always seeking brides where they should not. The two societies blend, whatever the bishops may say.

King Childebert and his queen, Ultrogotha, had recently founded a *xenodochium* (a guest-house for pilgrims, travellers and the poor) at Lyon, and this provided an occasion for once more threatening those who seized property donated to the Church. The point is also made that the property of the Church is in trust for the relief of the poor and distressed; and thus to seize it is to slay the poor. The matter will have appeared in another light to those who watched family property increasingly alienated to the disadvantage of prospective heirs.

Bishops had agreed to discipline erring colleagues; they were each other's comforters, but also judges. This is precisely what happens at Paris in 552. Childebert 'invites' them to a council[10] to consider the case of Saffaracus, bishop of the city. Suspected of a grave but unspecified crime, the bishops of Meaux and Chartres had examined the

---

[10] Ibid., pp. 167–9.

evidence and reported unfavourably to his metropolitan (Sens), who seems to have deposed him. The assembled bishops – some from distant dioceses – confirm the sentence and instruct the metropolitan to proceed to a new election to the bishopric of Paris. One may guess that the crime of Saffaracus, whatever it was, had affronted King Childebert: no bishop could hope to survive long who had lost the goodwill of his king. On the other hand, it was in the royal interest to protect the bishops where they felt most sensitive: the property of the Church. Hence a remarkable capitulary (or decree)[11] promulgated by Childebert's brother and successor, Chlotar I, who in 558 became sole king of the Franks. It is a directive to the royal agents to observe all concessions made to the Church by the king and his predecessors; and some of these were new. In particular, privileges of immunity granted by kings to churches or monasteries are to be honoured; that is, royal agents are not to enter immune properties for fiscal or judicial purposes. Ecclesiastical property was not automatically immune, nor were immunists exempt from all public duties (for example, military service); but it is clear enough that the Merovingian Church as a whole benefited enormously from such concessions and probably true that the crown's resources were diminished. Such are the early stages of a process that had its roots in Late Roman privileges and was to enjoy its heyday under the Carolingians. A clear Roman thread runs through Chlotar's directive, as through so much of Merovingian legislation; and the bishops at Paris were preponderantly from the Roman South. Curiously, most of the surviving Merovingian grants or confirmations of immunity benefited bishoprics and monasteries of the North. This may warn us not to draw too sharp a line between the barbarian North and the Roman South. Not a few of the most prominent northern bishops of the sixth century were southerners to whom the royal courts of the North had acted as magnets.

The Frankish kings now enter their *selva selvaggia*: the time of Gregory of Tours and a little later, when royal kinsmen fought each other in what looks like a free-for-all but was in fact a calculated groping for security. These kings – brothers, sons and nephews – were not barbarians, if by that we mean the kind of warrior who followed Clovis into Gaul a century earlier. The Church inevitably suffered. But its bishops continued to meet together to take counsel at national, regional or provincial level, often but not always at the command of kings. Some of them were now of Frankish or mixed descent, though their corporate flavour could still be described as Roman. Over approximately fifty years, councils are recorded at Tours, Paris, Lyon,

[11] MGH Capit. i, no. 8, pp. 18–19.

Mâcon and Valence, the last[12] reflecting the energy (and equally the problems) of the eastern or Burgundian part of Francia under the rule of that cultivated but unreliable uncle-figure, King Guntramn. The canons of some of these councils survive. They reiterate the claims of the Church to look after itself, to be free in its elections, to preserve its properties intact and to safeguard the moral sanctions of society; and they do so with increasing fervour. Now and again they betray uneasiness at the behaviour of kings. Bishops can say as a body what they cannot say individually and this was the great strength of councils. Moreover, they could say it repeatedly, and even publicly, as we learn from the Tours council of 567:[13] a canon 'has been publicly read in that same holy Church and thus approved by all [? those present at the council] and by the people'. At Tours also the bishops bewail attacks on ecclesiastical property for which there is increasing opportunity 'while our masters rage against each other'. In the canons of the Paris council,[14] perhaps soon afterwards, comes a sharper cry: no man shall be consecrated bishop except by the free choice of clergy and people. He shall be accepted neither by royal command nor on any condition that is opposed to the wishes of the metropolitan and the bishops of the province. But he was. Nevertheless, the bishops go on to insist that any such improper elections drawn to their attention shall be investigated. When it comes to alienation of Church property they can look even further back in a good Gallo-Roman spirit: property should be restored that was lost to the Church 'in the time of King Clovis of blessed memory'. The bishops themselves should set a good example by restoring property that does not legally belong to them, even if they held it through the liberality of a king. Anathema awaits anyone who seizes property or who makes off with a widow or daughter against the wishes of her kindred – even if this is done with royal support. This is in fact a brave but useless defiance of a recognized Germanic method of obtaining a bride by violence. It was still being practised centuries later, when the French had forgotten that they were once Franks. The bishops at Paris were thus prepared to be uncommonly outspoken at a time of disturbance and distress. This was felt so keenly by the bishops of the province of Tours that they sent round a pastoral letter which is no less than a directive for a time of war.[15] How shall God's forgiveness be won? Those contemplating marriage are asked to accept delay, and all should give the Church a tenth part of their goods and slaves. One purpose of this was clearly to provide the means to ransom the greater number of captives expected in the wars. Thus we meet tithe in a Merovingian context. It had long

[12] *Conc. Gall.*, pp. 235–6.   [13] Ibid., pp. 176–99.
[14] Ibid., pp. 205–10.   [15] MGH Conc. i, pp. 136–8.

since appeared in southern Gaul and elsewhere and always specifically as a gift to the Church for distribution in alms to the poor. By extension this would apply to captives. In his extravagant way, Caesarius had warned that whenever a poor man died of hunger the man who had not paid his tithes was guilty of murder in God's eyes. The first council of Mâcon[16] met in 581 or soon after 'on the order of King Guntramn, to consider both public matters and the needs of the poor'. The complaints of the poor were equally to be considered at his council of Valence.[17] The second council of Mâcon[18] in 585 clarifies the giving of tithe as a matter of ancient custom: priests will distribute tithes for the relief of the poor and to ransom captives. Thus tithes were launched on their long and often troubled career in medieval France. Captives, pilgrims and the poor – in brief, the lost, without natural protectors – remained a dominant concern of the Frankish bishops, and sometimes of kings. They acknowledged their duty to assist the vast floating population of *les misérables* and a large part of their resources was dedicated to this. Tithes played their part in the relief of distress, not in the enrichment of bishops.

Episcopal courage did not always yield returns, or even perhaps often. A nice instance of failure resulted from the division of the territory of Chartres between three royal brothers. One brother, Sigebert, decided to found a see in his part of Chartres and chose Châteaudun, to which he nominated Promotus as bishop. The new see lay in the province of Sens, whose metropolitan was subject to a different brother, Guntramn. So Sigebert turned to the more malleable metropolitan of Reims to consecrate the new bishop. This was highly uncanonical. Guntramn then convoked a council at Paris, at which the bishop of Chartres expressed his indignation at the division of his diocese. The assembled bishops directed a fierce letter of protest to the metropolitan of Reims:[19] Promotus had no business to exercise episcopal functions and would be excommunicated if he persisted in laying hands on the property of Chartres. Six metropolitans, as well as others, signed this letter, including of course the metropolitan of Sens. They also wrote to King Sigebert:[20] 'we understand, assembled in council at Paris, that a new and unheard-of appointment to Châteaudun, which belongs to the diocese of Chartres, has lately been made, not without the connivance of your glorious self. We really cannot credit that this was done with your majesty's consent', and so on. All very brave; but what was the outcome? Promotus remained bishop of Châteaudun till his death. The king took no notice. One could adduce

[16] *Conc. Gall.*, pp. 223–30.
[17] Ibid., pp. 235–6.   [18] Ibid., pp. 238–50.
[19] Ibid., pp. 212–15.   [20] Ibid., pp. 215–17.

other instances of the disturbance to provincial and diocesan boundaries caused by the periodical re-division of Frankish territory between
competing kings. Obviously it disrupted the Church and protests
were seldom effective. On the other hand, bishops were drawn
together in council to define and clarify their rights in the light of
written law, and this with some frequency. Nothing was forgotten
and little overlooked. What was never overlooked was the authority
of kings, who reigned by God's grace and were in some sense his
viceregents, and this long before anyone had thought of a royal
inauguration as an ecclesiastical ceremony. For example, the bishops
assembled at Lyon[21] insist that all bishops should celebrate Christmas
and Easter in their cathedrals, unless prevented by sickness 'or by the
king's command'. And how happy they were, as at Valence[22] in 584,
to receive a royal envoy with a letter from the king, asking them to
confirm his family's donations to the Church; yes indeed, it was
pleasing not only to bishops but to God as well.

The records of a council at Mâcon[23] in 585 allow an unusual glimpse
of procedure. Priscus of Lyon, here called *patriarcha*, presided. He
started by thanking God for their reunion. The metropolitans present
echoed his sentiments and added their prayers for their king (Guntramn).
The other bishops then requested their superiors to set forth the
matters on which decisions must be taken. The metropolitans assented
to this and added that the canons must be observed everywhere. They
then got down to business with a consideration of no work on
Sundays. As it turned out, other matters than those propounded by
the metropolitans were raised: as when two bishops asked that the fate
of slaves should be debated. The twenty canons that we have – it must
have been a long council – close with the decision that the bishops shall
reconvene in three years' time. The metropolitan of Lyon shall himself
arrange this at a place reasonably accessible to the bishops and after
consultation with the king. The procedural outlines were clear.

From the early years of the seventh century, and indeed for over
fifty years, the Merovingian barque sailed in smoother waters. In 613
Chlotar II became king of all the Frankish lands and in the following
year summoned a grand council to take stock: in effect, two councils,
one ecclesiastical[24] and one secular, followed by a royal edict[25] and a
further ecclesiastical council in 626. This impressive body of legislation, looking back as it does over a very rough century, shows the
Merovingian Church at its best. Chlotar could gather together no less
than eighty representatives of churches, including twelve metropolitans

[21] Ibid., p. 232.   [22] Ibid., p. 235.
[23] Ibid., pp. 238–50.   [24] Ibid., pp. 274–85.
[25] MGH Capit. i, no. 9, pp. 20–3.

out of fourteen. He was not to be content with a repetition of old canons; new measures should be taken for the salvation of his people and the well-being of the Church. And so they were. Once again the bishops insisted on episcopal elections by clergy and people; but the king, in his edict, went a little further: the chosen candidate could only be consecrated if the king judged him to be worthy. If the candidate were already at court, a member of the royal entourage, he would be certain of approval 'by reason of his personal merits and his learning'. This sounds terrible. In fact, both Chlotar and his son Dagobert not infrequently chose bishops from the court-circle. Eligius of Noyon is one example out of at least six distinguished bishops, often from the South, who owed their sees to royal favour won at court. They were a new race of bishops with a strong sense of mission and a happy confidence in royal support. What was the alternative? A bishop would designate his own successor and take steps to ensure his election; and this could be more disastrous than any royal choice. The king in his edict ratified the oft-repeated canons of his Church on the relations of judges and bishops in civil and criminal jurisdiction, on clergy seeking the support of *potentes*, on Jews, on Church property, on nuns and on much else. Then came a revealing warning: the bishops were great proprietors and must not abuse their position. The agents they employed should belong to the places where they exercised their duties and must abstain from violence. In this respect, then, the king saw the dangers inherent in the administration of Church property much as he would those inherent in the administration of secular estates, including his own.

At Clichy, near Paris, a rather smaller body of bishops assembled in 626: they wished to ratify what had been decided in 614 and complete their work. This they did in twenty-eight canons.[25] It is clearly to be inferred, as so often, that the earlier canons were not being observed. In other words, once bishops had left a council and reached home, they either would not or could not enforce the canons they had agreed to. All knew what to do: few could do it. This time, they lighted on a new provision which would seem to run counter to the king's edict. An episcopal candidate must belong to the vacant diocese (if 'diocese' is not too broad a translation of *locus*). Put another way, he must be a member of his predecessor's entourage. This had no future. But the bishops wished to limit royal authority in another way. The edict of 614 had permitted civil judges to summon clergy in minor orders to their courts without the sanction of their bishops. This was now declared illegal. Episcopal sanction was always to be necessary, under

[26] *Conc. Gall.*, pp. 291–7.

pain of excommunication. Thus the bishops returned to normal canonical practice, and a loophole permitted in the euphoria of 614 was plugged. It is not known whether the king objected. In brief, one can say that the bishops present at the councils of 614 and 626 felt their strength. They had one king only to deal with, and a king in general sympathetic to the Church. But it was the strength of numbers; and a strength also in the assured possession of a large corpus of earlier canonical legislation. They were strong enough to define more closely the relation of their jurisdiction to that of the civil power. But still they had a master.

We have no conciliar legislation for the reign of Dagobert (629–39) though much evidence of his concern for the business of the Church. The pressing-forward of missionary activity to the edges of the Frankish world explains the establishment of a bishopric at Thérouanne in the north and probably also at Constance in Alemannia, in the extreme south-west of modern Germany. Then followed the customary Frankish fragmentation of kingdoms with its inevitable effects on the Church. Councils of the Church thereafter follow the pattern of the kingdoms; as for example, a largely Neustrian council at Chalon about the year 650.[27] The assembled bishops were understandably worried and some of their canons betray new causes of anxiety. There must not, they insisted, be two diocesans in one diocese. We know that there were two bishops of Digne, either rivals or a bishop and his designated successor. One cannot tell which. Neither must there be two abbots in a monastery, though an abbot may choose his successor, who must not, however, share his authority. The property of a see or a monastery must never be divided, nor shall bribes be offered for promotion to any ecclesiastical rank. No layman shall take charge of a parish nor shall the patronage of the great be sought or the king approached without episcopal permission. Put another way, ecclesiastical property was being divided, laymen were administering parishes, bribery for office was widely practised and lay patronage was an accepted means of circumventing difficult bishops. We have met with much of this already. What we have here is a concentration of abuses that would naturally result from the weakening of central authority and the lack of means to check the retreat into local patronage. This impression is strengthened when we look at the canons of an Aquitanian council held somewhat later at Bordeaux.[28] Though it was summoned on the orders of Childeric II, it looks as if the duke of Aquitaine, Lupus, had some responsibility for the council and that great laymen were present as well as bishops and their representatives.

[27] Ibid., pp. 303–10.
[28] Ibid., pp. 312–13.

The bishops here complain of lack of discipline among the clergy, who are behaving and dressing like laymen, seeking lay patronage, bearing arms and living with women. Moreover, they were insolent to their bishops. So even in Aquitaine, most civilized of the regions of Gaul, discipline had collapsed. Bishops could not control their clergy. All they could do was to beg their duke to back up their decisions. The same sense of despair echoes through the decisions of a Burgundian council summoned by King Childeric at St-Jean-de-Losne.[29] Grimly determined, they repeated the burden of former councils, and not as a matter of form. The business of the Church is to go on insisting. However, there were new emphases. Deposed bishops and abbots, and such as have abandoned their duties, should not resume those duties. Clergy and monks must not travel without written permission of bishop or abbot. There is movement, then, and dereliction of duty. We are very near the end of any semblance of control. Writing in 742, the aged Boniface reported to the pope that Carloman, Carolingian ruler of eastern Francia, wished to revive ecclesiastical discipline (*ecclesiastica religio*) for it had been trampled under foot for sixty or seventy years: 'old men say that the Franks have held no synod for over eighty years, nor had an archbishop, nor established or renewed any canons of the Church'.[30] This takes us back to the 660s. Boniface and his informants were not quite accurate. There had certainly been some spasmodic activity since then, and probably more of which no record survives. But in general the statement may be accepted as correct.

Such is the general impression of continuing activity of bishops in council over a period of rather more than a century and a half. Their feet firmly planted in Gallo-Roman tradition, successive generations of bishops met at one territorial level or another to reaffirm the discipline of the Church by the promulgation of basic canons. They faced a changing political situation, and a bewildering number of Merovingian masters, with singular courage; a courage that owed much to the fact that they did often enough meet together to comfort one another. Many were aristocrats, some ascetics and others the proven servants of kings. Yet they could speak with one voice. It seems as if their exhortations fell increasingly on deaf ears. On the other hand there is some slight evidence that bishops attempted to enforce at diocesan level what they had agreed to at the provincial or regional level. Even in the Carolingian age, when bishops frequently issued diocesan statutes, it is uncertain how, or how often, statutes

[29] Ibid., pp. 315–17.
[30] Tangl, *Die Briefe des heiligen Bonifatius und Lullus*, no. 50, p. 82.

were enforced at the parochial level. What matters is less the degree of enforcement than the clear perception of what was wrong.

Less has been said of the underlying social problems referred to in canonical legislation. Social relations, the behaviour of men to one another, were certainly rendered no easier by the political fluctuations of the time, but more significant was the mingling of moral standards of Gallo-Romans, Celts, Germanic settlers and minorities such as Basques and Alans. They were tenacious standards. How was the Gallo-Roman bishop of a northern diocese to deal with remnants of paganism, the persistence of the blood feud, Frankish views on the inheritance of property or customs of concubinage and marriage? Councils told him how. The status of women, therefore, was a paramount considera-tion. We speak of Franks or Gallo-Romans; yet within a generation or two of the arrival of the Franks there were mixed marriages. Personal names may reveal little. A girl with a Frankish name may have had a Frankish father but a Gallo-Roman mother, whereas a boy with a Roman name may have had a Frankish mother. What law would such persons observe in the matter of inheritance or marriage? Canon law stuck firmly to Roman usage and this is what the bishops insisted on in council after council. But those to whom it was meant to apply might belong to solidly Frankish milieux. The bishops were not faced with mere barbarism but with the delicate sub-structure of Germanic social practices. Nowhere was this more obvious than in the no man's land between clerical and secular life; for example, in the lives of nuns, whether confined to nunneries or living at home; and in the lives of parish clergy or clerics attached to private oratories or courts. To any such, continence could seem un-Frankish, not to say offensive. In the sphere of moral behaviour the bishops faced problems beyond the reach of legislation; but we should know little about them if councils had not attempted to define them. Nor were the bishops themselves exempt from them. Their canons persistently urge bishops to live as they would have others live; not, in other words, to be content with the moral standards of the *potentes* they actually were. They were to watch each other, to correct one another and to deal with episcopal abuses at councils called by the metropolitans. They were secure in spiritual affinity and not infrequently in blood-relationship. There were families of bishops, if none so prestigious as the family of Gregory of Tours. The biographer of the Frisian Liudger, first bishop of Münster in Westphalia and a pupil of Alcuin, praised his mother for having given birth to two future bishops and, through her daughter, to still more bishops. In short, the Liudgers were an episcopal dynasty; and there were others, earlier and later. This hardly entitles us to look on church councils as family affairs but an element of it was always present. It made for mutual trust. Together and only together, they could seize the opportunity to impose a shape of belief, a liturgical cycle and sacraments and some conception of new social values upon a whole community still only nominally Christian. In council the episcopate showed up best.

VII

THE MEROVINGIANS AND
THE PAPACY

THE special warmth felt by the Anglo-Saxon Church for Rome, and
by Rome for the Anglo-Saxons, can too easily conceal another relationship: that of Rome with the Franks. Papal strains echo through the
barbaric music of the Gallo-Frankish Church like an oboe – sometimes
in majestic solo passages but more often so blended with the orchestra-
tion as only to be discernible to the keen ear. But they are there.

The background, Gallo-Roman, was a long tradition of generally
happy relations with Rome. The pope was seen by Gallo-Romans as a
fatherly figure, *Papa Urbis*, from whom advice on many matters could
be sought. It was a warm relationship, especially with the churches of
Provence, and correspondence survives to illustrate it. Cases of
ecclesiastical discipline were referred to him, the initiative lying with
those who sought guidance. This could result in the statement or
re-statement of what we call papal prerogatives, as, for example, in the
celebrated row between Pope Leo and Hilary of Arles; but what brings
this about is not a papal desire to advance new claims over western
churches but the need to explain the papacy's traditional authority to
warring parties that have invoked papal intervention. The pope
remained, as he had long been, the ultimate judge in *causae majores*,
major issues, often concerning the behaviour of difficult bishops. The
pope, then, was a judge and acknowledged as such. He was also the
guardian of orthodox doctrine. The churches of southern Gaul, and
especially of Provence, saw in him their natural shield against heresy.
The early sixth century was for all of them a time of disturbance, both
political and social. How could their world remain comfortably
Roman, caught as it was between Goths and Franks? How, on top of
this, were they to face the divisive rumblings, now a century old, of
the debate between St Augustine and Cassian on free will and grace? In
its heyday, it had been a debate specially associated with the name of a
Briton, Pelagius. It had involved more even than a deep theological
issue: the very nature of the Church had been called in question. Was
humanity so tainted by sin as to be unable to escape the consequences
without God's unsolicited grace? Or did baptism do that for the elect,
the minority of true Christians, which would enable them, by great
efforts, to earn the further help of God's grace? Cassian's own position

had been something of a compromise. His Gallic sympathizers have thus been called semi-Pelagians, though semi-Augustinians might more accurately have described them. Feelings were still running high in the early sixth century. In the summer of 529 fourteen bishops assembled at Orange for the dedication of a church newly erected by 'our son the Patrician Liberius'. They were worried men: there was little comfort to be had from the lovely Roman arch of Orange, reminding them of imperial patronage long past. So they constituted themselves a council under the leadership of Caesarius of Arles and issued a set of canons to define their orthodoxy in the matter of free will and grace.[1] Faith was the free gift of God, as Augustine had taught, and without it the human will was powerless. It is an impressive document, shot through with anxiety for the world of laymen committed to their pastoral care: 'and because we earnestly wish that our decisions, here recorded, shall be medicine not only for the clergy but also for the laity, it has seemed right that the illustrious laity who have been present at the dedication with us should also subscribe the document'. And so they did, to the number of eight. But what matters most in the present context comes in the introductory canon. Caesarius has had a word with the pope: 'it has seemed just and reasonable to us, in accordance with the advice and authority of the Apostolic See, that we should subscribe the few *capitula* sent to us by the Apostolic See, which contain the judgements of the Antique Fathers garnered from the holy scriptures'. Thus we know that the canons of this council, wholly concerned with doctrine, were effectively what had reached Caesarius from Rome. This is a prominent example of the Gallic clergy's reliance on Rome for doctrinal guidance; guidance in no arid debate but in their fearful responsibility for the salvation of their flocks' souls. Salvation of which souls? Salvation by what means? The pope would know.

It was his principal duty, as Pope Leo informed the bishops of Gaul and Spain, to protect ecclesiastical cultus from the sin of diversity, to defend it against novelty, to act in such matters as an intermediary between the churches of the East and the West. The date of the celebration of Easter was such a matter. Pope Boniface I in 422 reminded the bishop of Narbonne that all were governed by the *statuta* of the Fathers. 'Our business', he adds, 'is to be the diligent guardian of what our Fathers established.' Thus the popes were not only judges but also guardians of orthodoxy and tradition; and these duties they fulfilled both by correspondence and by frequent interviews with Gallic bishops visiting Rome. But they were more than judges and

[1] MGH Conc. i, pp. 44 ff.; CC 148 A, pp. 53 ff.

guardians. So far from wishing to impose a blanket of uniformity, they proclaimed the ancient rights of local churches. The great Pope Innocent I regretted that Gallic churches that owed their beginnings to Rome should diverge from Roman practice in the liturgy, and particularly in the celebration of the Eucharist. He regretted, but that was all. In the manner in which Gallic bishops were chosen, the popes drew attention to the established rights of local churches and metropolitans, refusing to fish in troubled waters. Bishops were touchy about their rights and showed no reluctance to let the popes know it.

In one other respect, perhaps the most important, the popes enjoyed a unique authority. In them successively was vested the *principatus* of St Peter. This unquestionably betrayed overtones of imperial authority inasmuch as the same word was employed by the emperors to evoke their authority over the *Respublica*. It was not resented by churchmen, to whom the western home of the emperors, whether Rome or Arles, enjoyed a special prestige that added lustre to the resident bishop. Apart from this, the bishops of Rome were apostolic in a special sense, as successors to St Peter, each in his turn the direct heir of the great founder. Thus, in 450, the bishops of Provence drew a parallel that they felt sure would be pleasing to Pope Leo: just as Rome enjoyed a universal *principatus* through St Peter, so too should the bishops of Arles enjoy a Gallic primacy through St Trophimus. Nobody defined the extent or nature of this Petrine *principatus*; it was merely felt to be there, a reality to be invoked as the need arose. So far from being resented, it was welcomed as a solace. There was always St Peter to look to, and Peter's Rome, and Peter's man, the pope.

So far as the evidence goes, it could not be claimed that Rome and the Gallo-Roman Church were regularly in touch with one another. The evidence is spasmodic and possibly their relations were little better than that. But there was communion and affection and mutual respect. The judgement of the popes might be challenged from time to time, but not their authority. Such is the background.

The first Frankish settlers saw themselves as heirs to the last Gallo-Roman rulers and so to the relationship of those rulers with the Church, itself a Roman institution. There were bishops at hand to remind them of this. We cannot tell whether Clovis himself was ever in touch with the papacy, but the dedication of his Parisian church to the Apostles betrays awareness of St Peter as a patron worth having. His incursions, and those of his sons, south of the Loire would have brought them in touch with clergy still more obviously loyal to the Roman connection, if only because the link was geographically easier to maintain. In Arles sat Caesarius, not only metropolitan but papal vicar over all Gaul. Pope Symmachus sent him a pallium, a vestment hitherto worn only by popes, to signify his personal dignity and authority. Moreover, it was sent at the request of a Frankish king, Childebert I, and without proper reference to the emperor. The pallium was a vestment directly associated with the cult of St Peter, from whose tomb it was held to derive the saint's *virtus*. Caesarius was to regard himself as having jurisdiction, pastoral authority, and the duty to defend dogma. He wrote to the pope for confirmation of the canons of the council of Orange: it was the pope's authority that was to determine doctrine for the whole Church. Doctrine, however, was unlikely to bother the Frankish kings overmuch, apart always from Gothic Arianism; for to accept, as they did, orthodox Catholicism was to align them with Rome as its exponent and defender. They were the men of the emperor and the men of the pope, at least in so far as it suited them. Clovis or his sons on his behalf sent a votive crown to St Peter; clearly a sign of respect, and perhaps of submission. Gregory of Tours described Clovis as the *Novus Constantinus*, a powerful image linking rulership with the papacy. But with the sons of Clovis we reach some firmer evidence that the bond between Rome and the rulers of Gaul was not to be broken. The first known letter (it is no longer extant) from a pope to a Frankish king was sent by Pope Vigilius to Theudebert I in 538, and he sent it through his vicar, Caesarius of Arles, the natural intermediary. Theudebert ruled over the Austrasian, or eastern, part of the Frankish dominions; and it is rather with this part than with the Neustrian, or western, part that Arles and the papacy were to have contact. But it was not only clergy from Arles who already in the sixth century were making the pilgrimage to the shrine of St Peter. The attraction of a visit to Rome was felt by Frankish clergy as well as the southerners; and this was happening long before Gregory the Great established his relationship with the Anglo-Saxons through Augustine of Canterbury. In other words, it was not from the Anglo-Saxons that the Franks learnt about the cult of St Peter and the primacy of Rome.

If the connection between the earliest Frankish kings and Rome was tenuous, it would be a fair guess that it was through no ill-will on the part of the kings. Communications were hazardous. The popes themselves were uneasily placed between the Ostrogothic rulers of Italy and emperors far away in Constantinople and often indifferent or even hostile to the North. Yet Arles and the region of Provence continued to provide one means of communication. Indeed, the popes had a special reason for keeping in contact with Provence, since in it lay a significant nucleus of papal estates, an integral part of that scattered patrimony of St Peter which lay predominantly in Campania, south of Rome and in Sicily. This Provençal patrimony is wrapped in mystery. It emerges in the mid-sixth century in two letters from Pope Pelagius I to Bishop Sapaudus of Arles. These request that what is due to Rome shall be sent in cash or in warm clothes (very acceptable to Romans suffering from Gothic assaults).[2] It is clear from the letters that, as elsewhere in the patrimony, the pope employed a *rector* or manager over his distant estates; and it is with the *rector* that Sapaudus was expected to intervene. We cannot tell when these estates were acquired: they simply surface in 556, and in 613 we hear the last of them. It is in fact only under Gregory the Great (590–604) that much is to be learnt of them, though even then they defy identification. Most of them probably lay in the dioceses of Marseille and Arles. At least they were important enough to papal finances to make Gregory anxious about regular annual payments and proper auditing of the revenue. He wrote frequently and in detail to his Gallic agents on such matters. In 595, a letter accompanied his agent Candidus to Gaul, together with words of commendation to the Frankish king, Childebert II. The pope no longer wanted his dues in cash – Gallic coin being unacceptable in Rome – but in clothing or in the form of Anglo-Saxon slaves for training as monks. Already, then, Gregory is likely to have been planning his Anglo-Saxon mission. We do not know what happened to the Provençal patrimony after his time: the last reference to it is in a letter of Pope Boniface IV to Arles on 23 August 613. It may have been absorbed by the Frankish kings or by local bishops and magnates. Rome could easily have been denied access to Provence by the Lombard kings of northern Italy.

In that brief period of fifty years, the patrimony was to play a significant part in Rome's relations with Franks and Anglo-Saxons. Light comes, as it habitually does, with Gregory the Great. From his voluminous correspondence with the West, preserved for the most part in his Register of Letters, we can see much of his anxious provision for the Anglo-Saxon mission and of his equally anxious care for the Franks. First, as to the Anglo-Saxons. Several of his letters are addressed to those Gallo-Frankish clergy and rulers through whose territory his missionaries from Rome had to pass. If it be asked why the Franks themselves had not already sent missionaries to England, the answer must be that they were in no position to mount so difficult an operation, even if they had wished to do so. Nor was it their business: Rome was, and remained, responsible for launching missions to pagan peoples. However, the Franks had long been in close touch with the people of Kent. Franks were certainly settled there; there were important trading contacts; and the royal Kentish dynasty was allied to the Merovingians through the marriage of the Merovingian princess

[2] *Pelagii papae epistulae quae supersunt*, ed. P. M. Gassó and C. M. Batlle (Montserrat, 1956), pp. 12, 29.

Bertha with the Kentish king Aethelberht. In Canterbury Bertha had her own church, dedicated to St Martin and served by a Frankish bishop, Liudhard; but this was her personal affair and in no sense the spring-board for a mission. We cannot tell how far the political influence of the Franks was exercised over Aethelberht but at least it is clear that they alone were in a position to facilitate the Roman mission. All this was known to the pope. Hazy about the Anglo-Saxons, he was quite clear that the Franks were the key to the exercise. He therefore wrote letters to the clergy along the route through Gaul, begging their good offices. Arles, Vienne and Lyon were obvious recipients. These powerful bishops were not only to see the hesitant missionaries on their way north but also, in the event of their success, were to continue to support them. Not that the new province (indeed, two provinces) of the Anglo-Saxon Church was to be subordinate to them; it was to remain directly under the care of Rome. But much would turn on Frankish goodwill. Once the mission had made a good start in Kent, Augustine was to return to the continent to be consecrated bishop; whether in the south or in the north is unclear. It might have been at Arles, as Bede was to infer. However, a letter written by Gregory to the Patriarch of Alexandria in 598 implies that Augustine was consecrated on his way to Kent: and consecrated, moreover, by 'the bishops of Germania'. This may mean Frankish bishops, presumably in Neustria and not far away from the crossing to Kent. If this is right, one understands why the pope was specially anxious to enlist the support of the Merovingians. He had authority over their Church, however independent in practice they might be, and may well have read a letter from his predecessor, Pelagius II, to the bishop of Auxerre, sharply reminding him of the Roman origins of the Gallic Church. So he wrote to the Merovingians, and did so some twenty times in the short period of seven years.

These Merovingian letters of Gregory deserve more than passing reference. They say little or nothing that would have surprised his predecessors, but they say it with an intensity and persistence that reflects what they lacked: the faith of a monk. The Augustinian mission was uppermost in his thoughts as he wrote, interwoven with passages of exhortation, rebuke, advice and consolation. The churches of the Franks were in sad need of attention and he understood how much would turn on the co-operation of kings. So, writing to Childebert II in August 595[3] to accede to the king's request for a pallium for the bishop of Arles, he raised the question of simony – that is, the buying or selling of ecclesiastical preferment. 'It has come to our

---

[3] *Registrum* v, 60.

ears', he wrote (and how often he writes it), 'that some have been
promoted to bishoprics direct from the laity'. The king would surely
never tolerate promotion in the army of untrained men? Moreover,
and horrible to relate, such promotions were said to involve the
pestiferous sin of simony. Let the king look to it as he hopes for
salvation. A little later he sent the king a present: keys of St Peter in
which were enclosed portions of the saint's chains. By the same post
went a letter to Queen Brunechildis, Childebert's mother, praising her
for her government and the education of her son and urging her for
love of St Peter, 'as we know you love him with all your heart', to
welcome the priest Candidus as the new controller of the pope's 'little
patrimony'.[4] There was flattery here, certainly, as always in Gregory's
subtle wooing of queens, but we need not infer from what is known of
Brunechildis' stormy political life and miserable death that she was not
in fact a pious woman. She, too, was worthy to receive relics of SS
Peter and Paul, though not without severe warnings as to their treatment. Once more, in September 597, she was warned about simony
and the promotion of laymen to bishoprics as acts of patronage; and
she was also to watch out for recurring outbreaks of pagan practice.
He sends her a book for which she asked and regrets that he cannot
send a pallium to her supporter, Bishop Syagrius of Autun. The
correspondence clearly went both ways. He later gave way about the
pallium because Syagrius had been so helpful to Augustine's mission.
But he wanted her to summon a synod, where his own representative
would be present, to deal with the evil of simony. A year or so later he
asked permission to send another representative empowered to deal
severely with her clergy. Plainly there was much to be put right in the
Frankish hierarchy. Gregory's standards, moral and spiritual, were
unattainably high. But he managed to insert a *douceur*: the more the
queen submits to God, the more she binds her subjects to herself. In
other words, to submit to God was to strengthen her control over her
subjects. The piety of rulers brought a material reward, as he reminded
other barbarian kings. It was all part of his huge initiative in winning
Germanic souls. The message went out to Francia, England, Spain and
Italy. But Brunechildis had a further reward. The pope wrote in
November 602 to say that he granted the privileges she sought for the
Church of St Martin and her nunnery of Autun: 'the Franks are happy
above all other people in deserving to have such a queen'.[5] He knew
that the old lady was already in terrible trouble and he would do all he
could to patch up peace between her and her adversaries. It was his last
letter to her. The constant coming and going of representatives, to say

---

[4] Ibid. vi, 5.
[5] Ibid. xiii, 7.

nothing of letters, between them witnesses to the pope's increasing knowledge of the state of affairs not merely in Roman Aquitaine and Provence but also in the Frankish north. Through all his minute consideration of practical issues there shines his sense of *providentia*. The great moral teacher will save the souls of Franks through the right ordering of their Church. Such is the purpose of a Christian society. The Franks were not Anglo-Saxons, lost in idolatry, but straying members of an ancient Church; a Church indeed that had provided Gregory with serious reading-matter on the cult of national saints. They were the heirs of St Martin. He assured them that they were equally heirs of St Peter.

Others besides Brunechildis were made aware that the eye of the pope was on them. Bishops anywhere, north or south of the Loire, could expect to hear from him. Simony is a constant theme of such letters and could be deftly inserted among other matters. We may take one or two examples. The bishop of Saintes received relics of SS Peter and Paul and other Roman saints for his church: let them be housed and guarded with all due reverence, the pope insists.[6] (Doubtless they were. In relic-collecting there was always a whiff of competition, for relics attracted the faithful but also the merely curious, and were thus a source of revenue.) The papal agent, Candidus, was informed that the four brothers of the bearer of a letter had been enslaved by the Jews of Narbonne. It was a serious, indeed shocking, thing that Christians should be in servitude to Jews. Let Candidus see to it that the men be ransomed forthwith. The large Jewish population of the cities of the Midi and the problems it raised for the Church are better left for consideration at a later stage; but it can at least be said that Gregory was well aware of these problems, and not only in southern Gaul. He accepted that Jews had a right to practice their religion under Roman Law and should never be persecuted or forcibly converted. On the other hand, Christians should be protected from Jewish proselytism, and particularly Christians serving Jewish masters. The pope could write to Aregius, bishop of Gap, to console him on the loss of 'your men' (unspecified): it was a cause of grief to him: 'love makes us one, and thus our heart is specially moved at your sorrow'.[7] But the bishop was not to prolong his grief. The pope goes on to build more generally from this theme a picture of the pastor's moral stance. And more: he allows the bishop and his archdeacon the privilege of using the vestment known as the dalmatic. Finally he advises Aregius that Bishop Syagrius had been ordered to summon a synod, in which he is to interest himself. To this same Syagrius of Autun, a frequent cor-

---

[6] Ibid. vi, 48.
[7] Ibid. ix, 219.

respondent, he wrote sharply to order the return of two Italian bishops who had decamped in disgraceful circumstances.[8] Syagrius and his colleague of Arles were even more sharply rebuked in another letter for having failed to prevent the seizure and forced marriage of a nun; nor were they to take this fraternal rebuke in the wrong spirit.[9] To these fourteen memorable years of papal vigilance the Frankish bishops, like their rulers, seemed to react with docility. They did not feel that new and terrible powers were being claimed and exercised by their pope. And they were right. Gregory did no more than implement the authority over the Western churches always implicit in the papal claim to be the voice of St Peter. What was new was the persistence and moral fervour of the voice. No letter failed to clarify the moral grounds on which the pope intervened, whether the issue itself were great or small. Dark days lay ahead both for the papacy and for the Western churches; but the voice was not forgotten.

In another but related field the links between Rome and the North held firm through the Merovingian age. The liturgical usages of the North never ceased to be nourished by Rome. How this happened is not clear. We can only observe the results. Private initiatives seem often to offer the key. Frankish pilgrims to Rome, from the time of Clovis onwards, brought home with them not only relics but books; and among these were liturgical books. They were probably not often Roman books but copies of them made by or for interested parties. Their effect was to add to the fruitful confusion so characteristic of Frankish liturgy. The same text might be copied more than once from different Roman versions. The use made of them would depend entirely upon local tastes without there being any overall directive. This did not disturb the popes: the Roman rite was proper to Rome herself and the Italian dioceses subordinated to her. However desirable it may have seemed that other churches should conform to the rite, no pressure was put on them to do so. Not until the eighth century do we find a pope who instructs a non-Italian church that it should follow Roman usage in the celebration of the Eucharist, the administration of the sacraments and the hours of the Office. So the churches of the Franks went their own way, spasmodically admitting that there ought to be uniformity but never getting to the point of envisaging a national liturgy. We ought not to be surprised. The furthest they went was at the council of Vaison in 529,[10] under the leadership of the Rome-orientated Caesarius of Arles. It proposed that the Kyrie eleison

---

[8] Ibid. ix, 223.   [9] Ibid. ix, 224.
[10] MGH Conc. i, pp. 55 ff.; CC 148A, pp. 77 ff.

should be chanted as it was *in sede apostolica*, together with a Roman addition to the *Gloria Patri* and a mention of the reigning pope in prayers. And that was all. As for the popes themselves, they remained indifferent. They probably held that by this time all churches of ancient foundation had evolved usages that suited them best.

There was, therefore, no one Gallic liturgy inherited by the Frankish Church. There were several, perhaps many. Even so, they always showed signs of Roman influence. So early do these signs appear that it could reasonably be supposed that there never had been a time when this or that Gallic church had not looked to Rome for guidance. Augustine of Canterbury was surprised to find that the Gallican rite of the mass as celebrated at Arles differed from what he had been brought up to in Rome. He therefore wrote to tell Gregory the Great, who replied that Augustine should stick to the Roman rite but accept whatever rites of other churches struck him as better: 'I am perfectly content that you should welcome whatever you find in the rites of the Roman or Gallic or any other church that might seem more pleasing to Almighty God.'[11] This was in effect an invitation to Augustine to put together a new liturgy for his Anglo-Saxon mission, based no doubt on the Roman, but profiting from the experience of neighbouring churches, themselves indebted to Rome. In several surviving versions of so-called Gallican liturgies of the seventh and early eighth centuries the influence of Roman formularies and prayers is apparent. In a word, these early liturgies are already hybrids. Their successors of the eighth and ninth centuries betray increasing Roman influence.

The liturgical book of central importance was the sacramentary. It originated in small collections of prayers for the liturgical year, recorded for the convenience of celebrants of the mass on separate sheets or in booklets. Basically a mass-book, it could also contain other matter, such as rites for baptism, ordination, monastic profession, sickness and death. The sacramentary proper emerges in the later eighth century but the collecting of suitable prayers, especially for saints of local interest, was happening in seventh-century Francia and probably earlier. Gregory of Tours reports that Sidonius Apollinaris, bishop of Clermont in the fifth century, composed masses and moreover, when his mass-book was mislaid, carried on with his celebration without it – like an angel, his hearers thought.[12] Even the frightful King Chilperic, Gregory's contemporary, tried his hand at composing hymns and masses. Would that we had them. All this is evidence of liturgical life. The Frankish clergy were familiar with various types of sacramentary that stemmed ultimately from Rome. It was natural,

[11] Bede, *Hist*, ii, 22.
[12] *Hist*. ii, 22.

then, for copyists to attribute them to the *ecclesia romana*. Later generations attributed them to particular popes, notably Gelasius and Gregory
the Great, though without much justification.

A Roman type of sacramentary attributed to Gelasius was used in
Francia in the seventh century but already adapted to local requirements. Doubtless it had been brought back by a pilgrim and quite
possibly by a monk. The Gregorian (distinct from the later Gregorian
sent by Pope Hadrian to Charlemagne), may also have owed its
transmission to some pilgrim who had been impressed by what he had
heard in Rome. Once more, we are left with a piece of private
enterprise; there was nothing official about it. Yet another pilgrim will
have brought home his copy of a type of sacramentary known as the
'Leonine', and this perhaps in the seventh century. Thus the Frankish
churches knew and used several related types of Roman sacramentary.
How many intermediaries there were, or how soon local additions
were made, we may never know. What is certain is that the liturgies of
Francia in the Merovingian age were progressively, and in part un-
consciously, romanized. At least to the earliest users, who knew
where the sacramentaries had come from, the link with Rome as the
mother of western liturgy will have seemed natural and comforting.
When in Rome one copied what one could and brought it home as so
much treasure, to be cherished as Roman relics were cherished; but
unlike relics, sacramentaries could be interpolated, and of course
misread, by curious neighbours. Busy centres of cultus like St Denis,
Corbie and Chelles were not slow to learn of the latest garnering from
Rome. It is this, and what looks to us like hopeless confusion, that
compels us to see Francia and not Rome as the natural home of
liturgical experimentation in the early middle ages. But Rome provided the material, directly or indirectly.

Equally significant for the Frankish churches was the arrival of
practical guides to liturgical performance, known as the *Ordines
Romani*. Sacramentaries contained rites but they did not say how such
rites were in practice to be conducted. The *Ordines* provided this
information. Indeed without them the sacramentaries would have
been virtually useless. Also unlike the sacramentaries they were
known to have behind them the direct authority of Roman practice.
Collections of such *Ordines* were circulating in Francia in the early
eighth century and perhaps earlier, and the separate *Ordines* comprising any collection must have been there earlier still. Of course
they, like the sacramentaries, had already invited Frankish additions.
The Franks seemed unable to leave well alone; usefulness, not clarity
or uniformity, was their aim. So with *Ordines* and sacramentaries alike
they had their way. One thing they clearly gained from this influx of

Roman texts was familiarity with the biblical texts incorporated in the Roman rite. There is the curious instance of St Magnobodus, a sixth-century priest at Angers. Finding himself in Rome, he took part in the celebration of Lauds and read so well that the Roman priests, affronted no doubt at this exhibition of barbaric competence, blew out his candle. But on he went, reciting from memory. So well did he know his Roman liturgy and its patristic and biblical texts. Such at least is the story in the saint's Life, the date of which is uncertain.[13] One can readily imagine an abbot on a visit to his diocesan or metropolitan. He is present in the cathedral at the celebration of mass and there witnesses or hears variations on the rite that are new and attractive to him. On his return home he dispatches a monk from the scriptorium to make a copy of the cathedral mass-book or better still the whole sacramentary. The copy will undergo some alteration as like as not; but it will carry a fresh version of a romanized text to a new house. It is thus that the forms of religion travel.

Rome was the home of SS Peter and Paul but also of very many other martyrs. A collection of the *acta* or *passiones* of these Roman martyrs will be a martyrology. We find one such in Francia before the end of the sixth century. Naturally it attracts local additions since Frankish Gaul has her own martyrs. Auxerre, Lyon and Autun were notable contributors. Auxerre indeed added the names of all her departed bishops, as saints who if they did not actually achieve martyrdom would certainly have done so, given the chance.

Textual anarchy has nothing to do with spiritual decadence. In our present context it rather argues a pathetic anxiety to get the best, to do the right thing, to feel the assurance that Rome is somehow or other behind the forms of one's liturgy. Had it not been so, there was nothing to prevent a happy perpetuation of the Gallican usages handed down from a venerable past. Furthermore, textual experimentation presupposes the availability of many liturgical books; perhaps ten or more if one wished to do the thing properly. This entailed much copying, much time and not a little expense. More important, it entailed much determination, sometimes in the face of Roman indifference or even inability to help. Thus Pope Martin I could tell St Amand that though he could provide relics he could do nothing about books since his library was exhausted; he had nothing to give in that way, and the bearer of his letter could not wait to make copies.[14] Against such a background, and with the absence of any controlling authority, one can only wonder at the resultant kaleidoscope of the vibrant life of Frankish religion.

[13] AA SS 16 Oct. vii, 941.
[14] PL 87, col. 138B.

With the disappearance of the Merovingians and the arrival of the Carolingians the Frankish Church enters a new phase; a phase of reform, of uniformity and of yet closer ties with Rome. This should not blind us to what had gone before. The authority of St Peter had never been questioned nor had he ceased to be loved by the northerners. Frankish churches celebrated the feast of the *cathedra Petri* – but characteristically on a variety of dates. To live within the peace of St Peter was the aim and hope of every Frankish bishop and abbot. How to do so was another matter.

VIII

THE BURDEN OF PROPERTY

The churches and monasteries of Roman Gaul emerged from the barbarian invasions and settlements as landed proprietors on a large scale. Roman Law defined and protected their properties and movable wealth: their buildings, cemeteries, oblations, treasures and lands. Moreover, it specified the uses to which this wealth should be applied. A church was the administrator of what it controlled. It was for its bishop to ensure that it was applied in the right proportions to the expenses of the clergy, the upkeep of buildings, the needs of the poor, the ransoming of captives and much else. Not only in his city but throughout his diocese, where the earliest parish churches and private oratories were now to be found, he exercised his legal rights and duties. Monasteries too fell within his jurisdiction for certain purposes. He was the father of all his people and the administrator of all his church's property. If that property had been confined to his diocese his task, and that of his archdeacon, deacons and bailiffs, would have been comparatively easy; but often, and increasingly, it was scattered over a much wider area.

Normally, as we have seen, the Gallo-Roman bishops and sometimes abbots were men of rank and personal wealth. A proportion of their wealth, often much of it, reached their cathedrals or monasteries as gifts or by will: and this at the expense of their families. Others also contributed. Rich laymen were increasingly ready to add to the properties of saintly patrons; and this is witnessed to in many a foundation-charter or confirmation of such. Churches were clearly great proprietors before the coming of the Franks. Above all in terms of property, the early Frankish Church meant much more than the aggregate of churches in areas populated by Franks. The Merovingians made themselves masters of regions where Franks settled sparsely, if at all. Thus Aquitaine and Provence in the South, and Burgundy in the East, came by slow degrees under Merovingian control. Gallo-Roman bishops might continue to reign over their rich southern sees but their masters lived north of that great dividing line, the Loire, and there were Frankish garrisons scattered over the huge region to see that those masters were obeyed. The wealth of the south of Gaul and of parts of the east was certainly much in excess of that of the north, and was accordingly coveted and battened upon. But the north was only comparatively poor. Neustria and Austrasia, the western and eastern divisions of Francia proper, had rich farming lands and many cities; their wealth should not be underestimated.

An early surviving will from a northern church can serve to illustrate what means were at the disposal of an episcopal contemporary of Clovis. Remigius, bishop of Reims, who died at a great age in 533, left estates and those who worked on them, both free and unfree, to a number of beneficiaries. Chief of these was his own Church of Reims, though his relations and other churches were not overlooked. There was also a balance in money and personal effects. His lands, comprising fifteen lots, all lay within the territory of Reims, the most considerable being at Château-Porcien. He names his *coloni* and says how he acquired the property. His will[1] is detailed and complicated; so detailed, indeed, that he does not forget his swineherd, Mellovicus, now freed and with a slave of his own. The names of many he disposes of are Germanic, not Roman. It is clear that neither Remigius nor his church was exceptionally rich, but still, a Gallo-Roman important enough to have baptized Clovis in his cathedral can leave property in the north of Gaul, and can make his church the chief beneficiary.

Vast accessions of property reached the northern churches and monasteries from the sixth century. It was not for nothing that King Chilperic complained, in 584, that his treasury was impoverished: 'see how our wealth has gone to the churches! Only bishops rule nowadays!'[2] The poor fellow exaggerated, but charters and wills confirm that increasing amounts of land, in parcels great and small, were passing to churches and monasteries in outright ownership or with varying rights of usufruct; and having so passed, had continually to be defended by often-distant beneficiaries against depredations and thefts, to say nothing of outright purloining by kings and local magnates who could not easily be challenged. To this difficulty in holding on to what was theirs we owe the often excellent documentation that is our main source of information. The upsurge in donations to churches and monasteries witnessed by such documentation was very considerable from the sixth century but was to increase enormously under the Carolingians. Nor was it only in lands, labourers and money. Relics also were a valued legacy. To take an eighth-century example, the great Abbot Fulrad of St Denis could leave to his foundation of Leberau in Alsace 'a third cell which I built in the hills of the Vosges, where Saint Cocovatus now rests'. We do not know how the abbot came by the remains of this obscure saint from Barcelona but he was

---

[1] MGH SRM iii, pp. 336–47.

[2] Gregory, *Hist.* vi, 46. To much the same effect, the gibe of Leo of Poitiers about the wealth of SS Martin and Martial (ibid. iv, 16).

proud to place them in a new cell, 'now called Fulrad's', and leave
them in his will to Leberau.[3]

The Carolingian age was to be characterized by a series of splendid
estate-surveys (known as *polyptycha*), most of which are ecclesiastical.
Until recently it was believed – there being nothing to disprove it –
that the Merovingian age knew no such sophisticated documentation.
However, we now have the tattered remains of just such a survey from
the late seventh century and it comes from St Martin's of Tours,
hitherto wretchedly documented for the period.[4] The survey lists the
names of tenants grouped in localities on its properties near the confines of Touraine, Poitou and Anjou. The yields of these localities
(called *colonica* mostly) are then jotted down as owing to St Martin's, a
quantity being earmarked for the upkeep of the monks. The returns
are not in money but in kind: wheat, rye, barley, oats, honey, wax and
so on. Over 900 personal names of *coloni* are still readable; and all we
are considering are scraps of what must have been a much bigger return.
So St Martin's is found to be registering its local returns in the seventh
century and the presumption must be that it also happened elsewhere.
We owe the scraps to the chance that they were later used in the
bindings of books.

It must next be seen how the churches and monasteries of the north
profited from the Merovingian conquest of Aquitaine, the largest and
richest region of Gaul. Great estates continued to dominate the
Aquitanian landscape, as also to a lesser extent in Neustria; and many
of these, whether in whole or in part, came into the hands of churches
and monasteries as royal or local gifts. Salt, oil and above all wine were
acquisitions that any northern house might covet. Merovingian
charters for Aquitanian properties are uncommon but all those that
survive mention vineyards. Nevertheless, it is clear that Merovingian
donations of such properties to northern churches were very extensive;
and the Aquitanian bishops, and missionaries to the north, followed
Merovingian example by willing estates to the same churches. Not
surprisingly, the Aquitanian secular lords reacted against such wholesale surrender of huge properties to northerners. Gifts of over a
thousand hectares were not uncommon; and one well-known donation
made by a certain Nizezius of 679–80 endowed the Aquitanian
monastery of Moissac with an immense estate of nearly 10,000
hectares.[5] He was obviously disposing of a Roman *fundus*. So, too,
were Balthildis and Chlotar III in their gifts north of the Loire to the

[3] Tangl, 'Das Testament Fulrads von Saint-Denis', NA 1907, pp. 171–217; B. de Gaiffier,
Recherches d'hagiographie latine, p. 8 on the Leberau property.
[4] P., Gasnault, *Documents comptables de Saint-Martin de Tours à l'époque mérovingienne* (Paris,
1975).   [5] Devic and Vaissete, *Hist. gén. de Languedoc*, ii, preuves, cols. 42–3.

monastery of Corbie in 659 or thereabout. No part of Aquitaine was more coveted than the Auvergne, where the church of Reims and the monastery of St-Pierre-le-Vif of Sens received very large gifts of land. Those of the latter, which also extended to the Limousin, are recorded in detail in a surviving fragment of its eighth-century estate-survey.[6] What was in question were not only estates in cultivation but tracts of land for clearing. Among known donors were Yrieix of Limoges, whose will in 572 greatly benefited St Martin's of Tours;[7] Bishop Bertramn of Le Mans, who left Aquitanian property to his see in 616;[8] and Desiderius of Auxerre, whose southern properties went to several Burgundian churches.[9] But it is hard to find a northern church or monastery of any standing that gained nothing in this manner. St Denis and St Germain-des-Prés in Paris, St Wandrille, Metz, Trier, Verdun and especially the church of Reims were outstandingly successful. However, properties so acquired could be a long way from the headquarters of their new owners. It was not easy to prevent pillage or plain seizure by local magnates. The excellent records of Reims illustrate how persistently the church had to fight, over centuries, to retain and enjoy the gifts of the faithful. Even so, it would be true to conclude that the Frankish Church gained more from this steady penetration into the South than ever the Frankish warriors did from the garrison-settlements there allotted to them by the early Merovingians. But if it strengthened the hold of the North on the South it sharpened the southern sense of hostility to the North and its periodical demonstrations of independence.

A good way of illustrating the ever-accumulating wealth of a Frankish church is to trace the fortunes of the greatest of all Frankish monasteries, St Denis of Paris. The material is plentiful and in the general line of its fortunes there is no reason to think it untypical of the greater monasteries and churches, so far as we know at present. In the words of Georges Tessier 'Le monastère de Saint-Denis est le type de nos grands éstablissements religieux du moyen âge'. But in another sense St Denis was, or was becoming, unique. It enjoyed a special relationship with the Frankish kings, and would merit close attention on that ground alone. It is reasonable, then, to watch developments through dionysian eyes.

The abbey stood on the site of the Gallo-Roman property of Catulliacus, at a bend of the Seine some six miles north of the Île de la Cité but within the Parisian territory. By it ran the road to Rouen and

[6] Pertz, *Diplomata* i, spuria no. 2, pp. 116–18. See also Rouche, *L'Aquitaine*, pp. 467–70.
[7] Pardessus, *Diplomata* i, no. 180, pp. 136–41.
[8] Ibid. i, no. 230, pp. 197–215.
[9] Ibid. ii, no. 323, pp. 100–1.

round it (as all round Paris) stretched forest-land that the Gallo-Romans and the first Merovingians left largely uncleared and unoccupied, apart from hunting-lodges. The nearest royal villa was Clichy, less than three miles to the south. Catulliacus was the resting-place of the bones of St Denis, first bishop of Paris, martyred in the mid-third century; and also from an early date the place of his cultus. Towards the end of the fifth century St Genovefa erected an oratory over the tomb. Soon afterwards the first *Passio* of the martyr was written; in other words, a local cultus was launched. Not that the first Merovingians took much notice, if we can rely on the few references in Gregory of Tours. The earliest clear evidence of interest is archae-ological. Beteen 565 and 570 Arnegundis (or Aunegundis), wife of Chlotar I and mother of Chilperic I, was buried there. From the contents of her coffin, recently excavated, it is possible to form a fair idea of the splendour of a Merovingian burial in a Christian basilica.[10] Near her lay, as it seems, her young grandson, Dagobert, son of Chilperic and Fredegundis, who died in 580. It would be going too far to speak of St Denis as the royal burying-place; but at least some Merovingians, and certainly others of rank, were buried near the martyr's tomb. A religious community of some sort guarded the shrine, and it seems likely to have been a monastic community. The earliest extant St Denis charter (or indeed Frankish charter) is a frag-ment recording a gift from one Desiderius, and the date is 619 or 620.[11] Certainly St Denis is a monastic community by then; before, that is, the succession as king of its greatest patron, Dagobert I. In fact, not only Dagobert but his father, Chlotar II, regarded the saint as his *peculiaris patronus*, though Chlotar preferred in the end to entrust his bones to St Vincent. What was important for St Denis at this stage was the proximity of the royal villa of Clichy, much favoured by both kings. In a religious sense it was bound to bring business. For example, the council of Clichy in 626 was stated to have met in the *atrium* of St Denis. Chlotar is not known to have been personally generous to the monastery but on two occasions at least he confirmed the gifts of others. Certainly by this time St Denis looks to have ranked with the greatest of the *loca sanctorum* of Francia: that is, with St Médard of Soissons, St Aniane of Orléans, St Martin of Tours, St Pierre-le-Vif of Sens and St Germanus of Auxerre. Not that St Denis had a clear field, even in the territory of Paris. South of the Seine it had to compete for patronage with St Vincent (later St Germain-des-Prés) and with Ste

---

[10] A reconstruction in colour is attempted in P. Lasko's contribution to *The Dark Ages*, ed. D. Talbot Rice (London, 1965), following p. 198.

[11] K. H. Debus, 'Studien zu merowingischen Urkunden und Briefen', *Archiv für Diplomatik*, 13 (1967), pp. 11 ff.; text at 86 ff.

Geneviève. By the ninth century the three together are believed to
have owned more than half of the extensive territory of the *civitas*.

A dramatic change in the fortunes of the house came with the reign
of Dagobert, who allegedly felt gratitude to the saint for having once
protected him from his father's wrath. Some such personal reason will
best explain his devotion to St Denis and his steady belief, reinforced
by many gifts, that the saint's patronage could alone sustain his good
luck. Chlotar II was scarcely in his grave before Dagobert made the
abbey a present of the royal estate of Etrépagny in the Vexin. This was
followed by a stream of further gifts, culminating in the many
properties that reached the house by his will. Which these properties
were cannot now be established because the will itself and many of the
records of earlier gifts only exist in later, interpolated forms. Some
were in and around Paris, by which means the king bound closer to
him the principal monastery in the most critical area of his kingdom.
By the same means he ensured the beginning of that process of
assarting round Paris which thereafter was to be a monastic not a royal
work. But some properties were further afield, as for example in
Aquitaine (the Limousin and Poitou). A large Poitevin patrimony
came to the abbey from the confiscated lands of the Aquitanian *dux*
Sadregisel. Even further afield, in Provence, St Denis was given an
annual rent of 100 *solidi* from the fisc at Marseille. The purpose of this
was probably to provide oil for lighting in the abbey church, as it also
was when a comparable gift was made to Corbie. With it went toll-free
transport for six carts. Then came a further annual gift of 100 cattle
(*vaccas inferendales*) from the fisc of Le Mans, which may have been
taken in cash. On top of this, Dagobert granted the abbey an immunity,
shortly after doing the same for Rebais. This was an immunity for one
property only, a general immunity for all abbey properties coming
later. Its effect was to make the immunist responsible to the king for
whatever the royal officers had hitherto been responsible for within
the area specified; and it was an important step in the business of
building up an ecclesiastical lordship. This generosity was sometimes
at the expense of others. Furthermore, Dagobert could press hard on
monasteries and churches with taxation when he wished. Like his
successors, the king was generous where he was sure of loyalty and
support, and not otherwise. But we have not yet reached the heart of
his generosity to St Denis, or the reason for it. The abbey gained
something more than the transformation of its territorial wealth. The
chronicler Fredegar describes how Dagobert rebuilt and embellished
the abbey church in a way that astonished everyone.[12] With this went

---

[12] *Chron.* iv, 79.

the establishing of perpetual chant at the abbey, on the model of St Maurice of Agaune, with the sole object of ensuring prayer for the king and his house. This must have involved an increase in the number of monks as well as their reorganization, and it may well have been for the sustaining of this enlarged community that so much property came to the house. The perpetual chant lasted for at least a generation and perhaps longer. There is some evidence that the community was not entirely happy about the change.

It may also have been with an eye to provisioning the enlarged establishment that Dagobert instituted an October fair for the abbey. No contemporary source says that he did so, let alone why he did so, but there seems to be no reason to question the tradition. Only a king could have authorized a fair; and this is the earliest-known instance of a king forgoing such a source of profit out of affection for his spiritual patron. No Merovingian source tells us (what we know to have been true by Carolingian times) that the goods traded were honey, wine and madder, nor that the fair lasted for four weeks at a stretch to allow merchants time to arrive from distant parts. All this suggests later development. What is certain is that the abbey benefited quickly and largely from the fair and that its proceeds attracted the rapacity of royal agents and magnates just as much as did its far-flung estates.

Dagobert's last gift to St Denis was his own body.[13] He meant the abbey to become a royal burying-place. Not only he but his queen, their son Sigebert and the queen's brother were buried there. It is not surprising that to future historians of St Denis Dagobert seemed to be not merely their greatest benefactor but their founder.

However, the next generation proved equally generous in its way. Dagobert's son, Clovis II, together with his formidable queen, Balthildis, did two very important things for the abbey. In the first place, Balthildis imposed on it a monastic rule, perhaps the mixture of the Rules of St Benedict and St Columbanus so common in mid-seventh-century monasteries. The community did not welcome the disturbance, and the echoes of their disapproval lasted till the ninth century. But St Denis was made to toe the line. Other ecclesiastical lordships were treated far more roughly. The queen's celebrated clash with a body of dissident bishops led by Aunemund of Lyon (she allegedly executed nine of them and the young Anglo-Saxon Wilfrid only just escaped)[14] is an early example of territorial politics involving the Merovingian Church in a major clash. Burgundy was always

---

[13] P. Lehmann, *Erforschung des Mittelalters*, iv (Stuttgart, 1961), p. 201 publishes the St Denis epitaph for Dagobert from the Rapularius of Hinricus Token (mid-15th cent.). See also Levison on Dagobert's will, NA 27 (1902), pp. 333–56.

[14] B. Colgrave (ed.), *The Life of Bishop Wilfrid by Eddius Stephanus* (Cambridge, 1927), ch. 7.

separatist and difficult, and the fate of Aunemund did nothing to check the independent spirit of the Church of Lyon, which was in effect a territorial principality on its own. No abbot of St Denis got himself into trouble of this magnitude, though one early Carolingian abbot – Hilduin – was temporarily deprived of his rule for taking the wrong side and had to make a suitable apology. In fact, the abbey owed the most critical of its privileges to Balthildis and Clovis. This was the royal confirmation in 654 of the privilege of emancipation of the abbey granted by Landri, bishop of Paris.[15] Clovis obviously regarded this as a very important step. He stated in his confirmation that the bishop had freed the house from episcopal control and had done so at the king's request. The monks can now more easily pray for the stability of the kingdom. Henceforth no bishop – and not just the bishop of Paris – may touch the possessions of St Denis wherever they may be. The effect of this was to place all the lands of the abbey under immediate royal protection. It would be to the king direct that future abbots would go – and did go – whenever the house was threatened in its properties by what Lesne had called 'une armée de rongeurs'.

Over the next generation St Denis stood up as well as it could to the consequences of general political disintegration. But weak kings were better than no kings, and the abbey knew how to use its special relationship with them. The record is one of gains and losses. The gains still predominated but they required fighting for. The losses were not yet serious, though the abbey, like other monasteries, may already have been feeling the first exploratory bites of secularization. The local official who was most likely to resent the special position of the abbey was the count of Paris. In the 670s Count Gairinus proved a difficult customer. Though he had been a witness to the diploma of Clovis II confirming Bishop Landri's emancipation, he yet managed to lay hands on the abbey's toll from the fair, dividing it between the abbey and himself *per forcia*. The occasion was the temporary removal of the fair from the abbey precincts into Paris during a time of disturbance. The dispute was referred to Childeric II, who confirmed the abbey's right to all tolls from foreign merchants wherever the fair might be held. Though this judgement was confirmed by later kings, it was by no means the end of the matter so far as the counts were concerned. Paris, and therefore St Denis, now lay at the centre of chronic political upheaval and so of strained loyalties. Gairinus was the brother of a more important figure, Leodegar, who deprived St Denis of at least two northern properties which he bestowed on the monastery of St Wandrille. Loyalties had to be bought, and normally at the

[15] P. Lauer and C. Samaran, *Les Diplômes originaux des mérovingiens* (Paris, 1908) have a facsimile, plate 6.

expense of someone else. Leodegar's rival, Ebroin, apparently re-warded the assassin of Dagobert II with the large St Denis property of Taverny, to be held precarially: that is, the abbey was forced to rent the land. But, as against this, he presented the abbey with valuable rights over the mill at Chailly. A further sign of the abbey's political standing was its use as a prison. In 677 Bishop Chramnelin of Embrun was deposed by Theuderic III and retired to St Denis, where he was authorized to enjoy his episcopal revenues. The king himself was imprisoned there for a while by his own brother. Clearly, then, the abbey was a safe place for the dynasty, if not for every member of it. The abbot continued to turn for protection to the king nominally in power, as when he appealed successfully over some disputed properties in the Beauvaisis and again in a dispute with the bishop of Rouen. If Merovingian kings continued to be buried in the abbey their graves, with one possible exception, have not survived.

In 688 the Austrasian magnate Pippin II won control of Neustria, and thus of Paris, at the battle of Tertry, near St Quentin. It by no means marked the end of the Merovingian dynasty but it did raise critical problems for Frankish churches and monasteries everywhere. Some churches that disliked the new order of things suffered in their properties: Reims, Rouen and St Wandrille are examples. One cannot so early speak of a Carolingian policy of secularization but it was plain that loyalty had to be secured and paid for. Donations to churches continued, some by the Carolingian family and some by Merovingians under Carolingian control. In fact, Pippin's own endowments seemed to follow a definite pattern of rehabilitating smaller monasteries and placing them under the control of safe men. St Denis itself did not do badly. The early Carolingians were obviously anxious to win its support. The abbey was prepared to co-operate as long as its Merovingian loyalty was not strained too far. It looks as if Pippin deprived St Denis of its property of Gamaches, and probably more. On the other hand, under Childeric III the abbey gained some valuable concessions and confirmations from Pippil. Lagny-le-Sec, which came its way in 689, was a useful Parisian accession and a special mark of favour, since it had been for some time the property of the mayors of the palace. In 694–5 it gained Nançay (Bourges) and in 706 Solesme. In 695 it exchanged its rent from Marseille and other rents worth in all 300 solidi a year for the domain of Nassigny, and almost certainly gained by the exchange. But it may have done even better; for in 716, two years after Pippin's death, the Marseille rent was confirmed. Either the exchange had been cancelled (and of this there is no evidence) or it was a piece of fraudulent dealing by the abbey. In 691 Clovis III gave a judgement for St Denis on the appeal of Abbot

Chaino concerning the property of Noisy-sur-Oise, and six years later his successor had to intervene again to protect the property against no less a man that Drogo, Pippin's son, Pippin himself being present on the occasion of the appeal. Nor was Drogo the only Carolingian of his generation to try his strength against St Denis. His brother Grimoald, count of Paris, invoked the precedent of Gairinus and laid hands on half the toll from the St Denis fair. Both parties appeared before the king (Childebert III), who inspected the abbey's charters and gave judgement for it. Grimoald accepted the judgement and indeed made some attempt at restitution with a view to winning over the abbey. So it looks as if he had misunderstood the position in the first place. He was reputed a just man. The incident demonstrated how constantly a religious house had to be on its guard to defend its privileges, even against those who might be genuinely unaware of them. The incident caused the king to issue a diploma (the original is extant[16]) rehearsing the circumstances of the establishment of the fair and the privileges granted by his predecessors.

The short period between the death of Pippin II in December 714 and the victory of his illegitimate son Charles Martel at Vinchy in 717 was an anxious one for St Denis, as for many other religious houses; for during it Neustrian opposition to the Carolingians expressed itself in the rule of the last vigorous anti-Carolingian mayor, Ragenfred. St Denis approved of Ragenfred and presumably of his attempt to clean out the Neustrian monasteries that had become centres of Carolingian support. But they must have quaked when, at the moment of crisis, the Carolingians bought Bishop Turnoald of Paris with the gift of the abbacy. They were unable to rid themselves of this dreaded link for some years, but eventually secured not merely an independent abbot but also a monastic bishop of their own, apparently on the Celtic model. The office seems to have lasted into the ninth century. Meanwhile their loyalty to Ragenfred and his king had brought them some rich rewards. Chilperic II's five gifts to them included part of the estates of the Merovingian villa of Clichy, and this linked St Denis territorially with the heart of Paris.

The victorious Charles Martel meant from the start to win over St Denis, which could do more than anything else to secure him in the territory of Paris. Consequently he treated the abbey with a degree of consideration that he showed to no other church or monastery within his power. Yet even here he not only gave but took away; and this illustrates the deep complexity of the problems facing him. He undoubtedly secularized some of the abbey's estates; that is, he handed

---

[16] Ibid., plate 31.

them over to his supporters to be held precarially of the abbey, or else failed to prevent them from seizing such estates. This was not necessarily to the abbey's disadvantage provided it could draw its rents and be assured of legal ownership. Land might in this way be improved at no cost to the owner. But things did not always work out so well, and the abbey fought back. The high value now attached to written contracts is illustrated by the case of St Denis reclaiming an oratory in Hainault from a certain Hormungus, *rector* of Marseille, who produced in justification the first known authentic forged diploma. St Denis also won back a property from the abbess of Septmeules, who seems equally to have tried her hand at forgery. It was not easy, even for Charles Martel, to prevent others from nibbling at the scattered properties of so rich a house. He cannot have been unaware of yet another attempt on the St Denis fair – which indeed came nearer to ruining it than anything that had happened hitherto. His wife, together with her son, Grifo, and the count of Paris helped themselves to the tolls to the extent of a capitation of four *denarii* on every merchant visiting the fair. Twelve years later another count was to attempt the same, with embellishments. What Charles really felt about St Denis is better shown by his gift to it of the remainder of the great villa of Clichy, which included the forest of Rouvray (of which the Bois de Boulogne is the surviving remnant). Rouvray-Clichy covered 2,000 hectares. His munificent present made St Denis easily the biggest landowner north of the Seine in the Paris area, and perhaps anywhere in it. In 742 Theuderic IV (though in effect the mayor of the palace, Charles Martel) issued a very important confirmation of the abbey's privileges, new and old, adding that the house should freely elect its own abbot. It is doubtful if in practice it ever did. Charles can be said to have bought his right to do what no Carolingian had done before: he had his son, Pippin III, educated there under the abbacy of his own kinsman, the pluralist Hugh, and was himself buried there when he died in 741, after making suitable deathbed gifts.

If we look at the Chronicle known as the *Liber Historiae Francorum*, probably composed at St Denis in 727,[17] we can see that Charles was rather slow to win the abbey's confidence. It speaks politely but somewhat remotely of him, acknowledging his prowess as a warrior but not troubling to conceal a defeat. It is more interested in the Merovingians under whom it had grown up, and less indignant about Carolingian usurpations than about the impious Clovis II, who had once dared to lay hands on a precious relic – the arm of St Denis. The abbey cannot be called whole-heartedly Carolingian before the death of Charles Martel.

[17] MGH SRM ii, ch. 53, pp. 326 ff.

Nothing in the St Denis *Liber* suggests that contemporaries saw Charles as the great originator of mass-secularization of church property. Indeed, the only record we have that such a view was held is a famous addition in Archbishop Egbert's copy of the letter of St Boniface and others to King Æthelbald of Mercia.[18] According to the addition, Charles had recently died after a long and painful illness because of his seizures of church property. It is the first step in the potent anti-Charles legend (that of St Eucher) which Archbishop Hincmar took some pains to propagate in the ninth century: Charles had to burn in hell, in effect for the sins of a whole generation. Looking back from the vantage-point of St Denis in the year 1706, Dom Félibien, the abbey's historian, was uncertain of the justice of this: 'c'est un point qu'il valoit beaucoup mieux abandonner aux secrets jugemens de Dieu'. He was right. It is in fact very difficult to decide what Charles did with church property, and why he did it. But it matters to know, since the Frankish Church was critically affected.

The taking of church lands, whether outright or on a temporary basis, whether with some legal colour or without it, goes back in time far behind Charles Martel. The richer churches became, the likelier it was to happen. There were several possible reasons for it. Plain robbery was one, and the pages of Gregory of Tours provide many early instances. The rewarding of faithful followers was another, particularly at times when rewards could not be provided outside Frankish territory, as for instance they once were east of the Rhine. A third reason was the replacing of politically untrustworthy bishops and abbots with more amenable candidates, who might even on occasion be laymen. The early Carolingians unquestionably secularized land for the last two reasons – namely, to reward and to remove nuclei of disaffection. But the first, plain robbery, was prevalent enough in their time and they cannot always be held responsible for it nor blamed for failing to check it. St Boniface is an unconscious witness in their defence. Though he seemed to believe that it was only recently that churches had been given to laymen he was quite clear that secularizations had started long before – indeed, from the time, some eighty years earlier when, as he asserted, church councils had ceased to be held in Francia. His own work had lain largely in what from the Frankish point of view were the ecclesiastical marcher-lands of the Rhine, where dynasties of bishops, as at Trier and Mainz, managed as best they could. Such men were not so much hostile to as ignorant of the reforming practice of Anglo-Saxon missionaries. Here, and in the half-exploited territories east of the Rhine, many forms of aberrant

---

[18] Tangl, *Die Briefe des heiligen Bonifatius und Lullus* (MGH SRG, 1955), no, 73, p. 153.

Christianity could and did flourish; and they could conveniently be laid at the door of negligent rulers. However, it was not only here that trouble occurred. Some of the worst abuses of ecclesiastical rank and property took place in areas where neither Merovingians nor Carolingians ever exercised more than spasmodic control. Burgundy was a case in point. Here as much as anywhere the Church suffered from the steady breakdown of secular authority. Long before the time of Charles Martel the whole area between the Rhône and the upper Loire had been transformed into what amounted to principalities ruled by bishops, and sometimes by dynasties of bishops. The Late Antique structure of these nuclei of power was undisturbed; the bishop still ruled from his *civitas* over the *municipia* and *castella* of his diocese. The counts and the *duces* had lost control. It was better for them, if they wished to retain power, to become bishops. This sounds bad; nepotism always does; but it may well have been the best way of securing some sort of order in a world where central authority had broken down. At least there was continuity. Families long used to exercising local authority continued to do so under other titles. More than anyone else they had an interest in preserving the old shapes of life at a time when political chaos threatened. Not that they were unwilling to fish in troubled waters. In Pippin's last years the bishop of Auxerre was Savaric, a worldly bishop if ever there was one. By force of arms he took control of Orléans, Nevers, Tonnerre, Avallon and Troyes, and finally turned upon Lyon, where he met his end.[19] In Auxerre he was succeeded by Ainmar and in Orléans by Eucher, his nephew, a monk from Jumièges. It looks as if Ainmar was a layman who employed a consecrated bishop to perform his spiritual duties. This was an arrangement not uncommon at the time. Charles Martel, fresh to power, could interfere very little in Burgundian affairs and therefore contented himself with approving these arrangements. Only after the defeat of the Arabs – when they had devastated Burgundy – could he call the Burgundian magnates to order. Meanwhile Bishop Ainmar had it all his own way. He so extended his power, comments the author of the *Gesta* of the bishops of Auxerre, 'that he pretty well ruled the entire *ducatus* of Burgundy'. He even seems to have accompanied Charles on an expedition into Aquitaine, an area that touched the interests of both. But once Charles had settled with Aquitaine and felt secure in the south, he turned without hesitation upon Ainmar and got rid of him. The property of the see now shrank to a hundred *manses*, we are told, and the bishop was deprived of control over his monasteries. Charles was doing two things: he was availing himself of

---

[19] *Gesta epis. Autisiodorensium*, 26 (MGH SS xiii, p. 394).

ecclesiastical property to reward his loyal followers and he was removing a bishop too closely identified with the interests of the local aristocracy. The Church of Auxerre may well have suffered in consequence; but it was no well-ordered or politically innocent see when he laid hands on it, nor had he created the disorder in the first place. Other sees fared even worse. There are many gaps in the episcopal lists for Burgundy, as also for the area between the Seine and the Loire; and these were precisely the areas most involved in the early eighth-century struggles between the Carolingians and their rivals. On the whole it was better for a see to be given a layman than to be left vacant and pillaged by all, as happened at one time or another to Verdun, Lyon, Vienne, Metz, Le Mans and Utrecht – and doubtless others. In some ways the fate of the Burgundian Church was exceptional, both in the extent to which it had fallen into the hands of local magnates before Charles Martel arrived on the scene and in his subsequent treatment of it. But not in all ways. The characteristics of his dealing with the Church are the same everywhere; a mixture of spoliation, eviction and liberality, varying in proportion according to the situation. His enemies were not Merovingian loyalists, for he was himself one. They were the supporters of Merovingians backed by his rivals, and above all they were supporters of local autonomy. With them lay political control and therefore they had to be dispossessed. The trouble was that dispossession opened the door to further local struggles for power that Charles was unable to control. The solution he often favoured – and he was not the first to do so – was to group collections of sees and monasteries in the hands of men he knew he could trust. Thus his nephew, Hugh, accumulated ecclesiastical possessions in Neustria. Starting with the see of Rouen about 719, he added Bayeux and Paris together with the abbacies of St Wandrille and Jumièges in Normandy. He seems to have been in episcopal orders and certainly left a good name behind him at St Wandrille, which he richly endowed. The *Gesta* of the abbey make it clear that the monks recognized all this as uncanonical but at the same time it was not done simply out of cupidity. He was, they concluded, a *gloriosus praesul*.[20] There followed some less glorious *praesules*. The abbot Teutsind, who also ruled St Martin's at Tours, had no compunction about secularization. He may have taken as much as a third of the lands of St Wandrille for his followers, granting them as *precariae*. We do not know if this was done on orders from Charles Martel or with his knowledge; but it happened, just the same.

In Austrasia, where Charles had hereditary enemies to face, the need

[20] *Gesta sanctorum patrum Fontanellensis coenobii*, ed. F. Lohier and J. Laporte (Rouen–Paris, 1936), ch. 8, pp. 26–8.

to be sure of the loyalty of bishops was even greater. Thus, Felix of Metz took over the administration of the see of Châlons at his request, and Felix's successor at Metz also ruled Laon. At Trier we find Bishop Milo succeeding his father, Liutwin. Both held other sees, namely Laon and Reims, and both were firm supporters of Charles. Clearly they stood aloof from the reforming activities of the Anglo-Saxon missionaries, Boniface and Willibrord, who had their aristocratic adherents in the vicinity; but they did not at once clash with them. It seems unlikely that Milo ever received episcopal orders since we find others performing the spiritual duties of the diocesan in Reims and Trier. The *Gesta Treverorum* record the churches robbed by Milo and other *tyranni*, and the list is impressive;[21] but it omits any mention of the greater churches of Trier, which Milo presumably protected. He did not prevent Charles from endowing his cathedral and St Maximin. His own monastery of Mettlach remembered him gratefully, though nobody else says that they did. Nothing much could be said against him, apart from the undoubted fact that he hunted and took no care of ecclesiastical discipline. But he did see to it that the spiritual duties of his office were performed by others. If he took away much he gave something in return, and presumably kept good order for his master in a critical area. The reforming councils did not depose him.

Less fortunate was another friend of Charles Martel, Bishop Gewilib of Mainz, whom St Boniface classified not among 'the drinkers and slackers and hunters', like Milo, but among the *clerici adulterati*, a more reprehensible category.[22] Worse, if possible, Gewilib took part in a bloodfeud to avenge his father, Gerold.[23] For this and for his opposition to Boniface's plans for the neglected churches over the Rhine, Gewilib was deprived of his see of Mainz in 745. This *praesul* was not *gloriosus*; he was *rudis*. None the less, his succession to his father as diocesan had been regular and he was probably a consecrated bishop. Probably also he was no worse than some other bishops of the Rhineland and certainly he satisfied Charles Martel's requirements. Apart from moral behaviour more appropriate to a layman, his crimes were negligence and, much more, opposition to the activities of Anglo-Saxon monks in Hesse and Thuringia; and in this respect he had more to put up with than his colleagues in Burgundy, Aquitaine and Neustria.

Whatever we make of Charles Martel's motives, the Frankish Church at the time of his death in 741 had lost much. But it was still very rich. For example, in the next generation the abbey of St

---

[21] *Gesta Treverorum*, 24 (MGH SS vii, pp. 161–2).
[22] Tangl, *Briefe*, no. 50, pp. 82–3.
[23] Ibid., no. 60, p. 122.

Germain-des-Prés still had some fifty domains covering an area of
66,000 hectares; St Wandrille had over 4,000 *manses* (of unknown
extent) and St Riquier 2,500. There were still monasteries that owned,
even if they did not directly exploit, up to 8,000 *manses*, which might
be of the order of 100,000 hectares, and no doubt St Denis was one of
them. These great immunities were exempt from temporal service,
their dependants were untaxed by the crown, they were often exempt
from customs and tolls and they enjoyed profitable rights of justice.
Altogether they cannot be said to have been bankrupt. But this in no
way lessened the impulse, felt by them as by all medieval landowners,
to implement old claims when they could and to remember acts of
robbery, great and small. A monastery like St Denis or a see that
attracted powerful bishops, like Reims, could use influence to redress
wrongs and did so remorselessly. But smaller houses and poorer sees
were in no position to do likewise; and it was these, of which we have
little knowledge, that suffered correspondingly most and recovered
least. The great establishments did best. But we need to be clear what
we mean by this. The landed wealth of the Merovingian Church may
have been more impressive in theory than it was in practice. If we
reckon its possessions in terms of *dominium*, legal ownership, it may
easily have owned a third of the cultivated land of Frankish Gaul. But
dominium is not the same as the power of profitable exploitation; and
much of its property was let to lay tenants in return for a census or
quit-rent, the cultivator enjoying a wide liberty to dispose of his
profits, and sometimes land, as he wished. We need not underestimate
the value of a steady return in rents to a large proprietor nor the
ultimate benefit to him of having his land improved at no cost to
himself, always supposing that he could lay hands on it one day. But
he may, even so, have done better under the early Carolingians, when
a greater proportion of what he owned he also cultivated to his own
advantage. A new kind of property is born, exploited by or for the
owner. This is what David Herlihy meant by saying that 'the shadow
of the saint falls ever more widely across the fields of Europe' in
Carolingian times. If he was right in his interpretation of a wide range
of evidence from Church inventories, Church property throughout
Europe greatly increased between 751 and 825. Whether this means
primarily an absolute increase or an increase in terms of the building-
up of greater nuclei of directly-exploited land, is uncertain. Clearly the
movement towards greater nuclei was in a general direction of which
the Carolingians, with their extensive manors, would appreciate. It
made for efficiency and larger profits. On the other hand, it opened the
way to precisely that kind of cornering of the land market of which
they disapproved.

Such was the material condition of the Frankish Church inherited from Charles by his sons, Carloman of Austrasia and Pippin III of Neustria. What the Church required now was what it had required a century earlier: general restitution of properties taken by laymen. It was not what it was to obtain. Both Carloman and Pippin were sympathetic, but Francia was still on a war-footing and neither could do much outside the lands he directly controlled, and there not always. Carloman, the readier of the two to promise if not to perform, was clear that the Austrasian Church needed radical reform; but he was very nearly powerless when it came to church lands. His council at Les Estinnes in 744 makes an important modification of the promise of general restitution given at an earlier council. Canon II enacts that wholesale restitution cannot in fact be made, 'because of war and attacks by other peoples'.[24] He must hold on for a time unspecified to ecclesiastical lands held *sub precario et censu*, it being understood that twelve *denarii* be paid annually by the holders for every church property so retained. This was quite a substantial rent. There was no guarantee that such a property, if it fell in, would not be regranted on the same terms to someone else, 'if we are driven by necessity'. On the other hand, any church or monastery that could show poverty should have the necessary amount of land restored to it. This seems to adumbrate a new approach: that a religious establishment was morally entitled to the land it required to perform its proper functions, and no more. The ruler would exercise his *defensio* to that extent. Pippin, for his part, enacted at Soissons that his Neustrian monasteries should be 'consoled' with a proportion of their lost property, those holding on to the remainder paying a *census*.[25] There was no hint of any final and total restitution. Pope Zacharius seemed satisfied with the arrangement, at least on a temporary basis; St Boniface less so, suspecting that it would in fact prove permanent. What was being worked out was a policy of regular re-division of church lands by the crown, partly in the interests of reform. As a principle it was not legally expressed till 768, but in practice it operated twenty years earlier. It may well be, as has been argued,[26] that when Carloman and Pippin used the words *reddere* and *restituere* of church lands they never did mean outright restitution but only symbolic investiture that recognized a right but no more. On this reading, no one need have been deceived. Strictly speaking, Pippin did not renew the practice of secularization but applied a new principle which extended even to the control of new

[24] MGH Conc. ii, i, p. 7; de Clercq, *Législation*, pp. 120 ff.
[25] MGH Conc. ii, i, p. 24.
[26] By W. Goffart, *The Le Mans Forgeries* (Harvard, 1966), p. 10, though originally by Brunner.

endowments. In other words, he did not want an affluent Church that could abuse opportunities of political power but a Church whose possessions he could justify and protect and guarantee. The principle of *divisio* was not to go unchallenged. It was certainly operative throughout Pippin's reign, may have been tacitly abandoned by Charlemagne and was finally renounced by Louis the Pious in 819.[27] Yet it had important repercussions on Carolingian policy over church lands through most of the ninth century.

Once again, the history of St Denis shows clearly the conflicting claims that beset any Frankish ruler. Pippin did not forget that he had been brought up in the abbey, nor that it was the scene of his second royal unction in 754. Moreover, he intended to rely heavily on Fulrad, ultimately his arch-chaplain and the first great abbot of St Denis. Like the Carolingians themselves, Fulrad came of a landed family from the Maas-Moselle area, where he retained his possessions. He was probably brought up at court and by 749 was sufficiently trusted to be sent as a delegate to Rome on the mission that ultimately led to the downfall of the Merovingian dynasty. His reward, in 750 or thereabouts, was the abbacy of St Denis. At about the time when Pippin became king, in 751, Fulrad became in addition arch-chaplain, an office of high significance under the first Carolingians.[28] Pope Hadrian I clearly considered him the leading ecclesiastic in Francia, and Boniface's letter to him begging his protection for Lul suggests that this was indeed the case.[29] He accompanied the king everywhere. Fulrad's four immediate successors as abbot were also either arch-chaplains or chaplains, and thus the link between royal administration and the abbey was firmly cemented. We do not know how the remaining Merovingian legitimists among the monks of St Denis regarded their new abbot's political background; perhaps there were not many left; but it is only with the arrival of Fulrad that St Denis can be considered irrevocably in the Carolingian camp. Not merely this: it moved to the forefront at the expense, seemingly, of houses under Anglo-Saxon influence, to which it had never succumbed. But the monks had nothing to complain of with Fulrad. Through him they won a degree of consideration from Pippin, already well-disposed as he was, that no other religious house and no bishopric could boast of. No sooner was he crowned than Pippin restored to St Denis forty-six properties.[30] We do not know

[27] MGH Capit, i, no. 138, pp. 275 ff.
[28] See J. Fleckenstein, *Die Hofkapelle der deutschen Könige*, i (Stuttgart, 1959), pp. 45 ff.; and by the same, 'Über die Herkunft der Welfen: Fulrad von Saint-Denis und der fränkische Ausgriff in den süddseutschen Raum', *Forschungen zur oberrhein. Landesgeschichte*, 4 (1957).
[29] Tangl, *Briefe*, no. 93, p. 212.
[30] Pertz, *Diplomata*, i, no. 23, pp. 108–9.

over what period these losses had been sustained nor what proportion they bore to the total of losses actually claimed; but the restitution was a large gesture. At a later date Pippin restored to the abbey the valuable property of Essonnes, hitherto held by a certain Raucho. But he plainly did not restore everything, nor cancel every precarial holding that the abbey had had to surrender. A general confirmation of restorations by Charlemagne in 755 makes it plain that neither Pippin nor Carloman had been able, or perhaps willing, to evict from the abbey's lands men who had probably seized them on their own initiative. No one could say that St Denis was short of property. At least Pippin had been generous enough to ensure the prayers of the community for his family and his following; an intangible benefit can be underestimated. When he died, Pippin was buried in the abbey.

One last attempt was made on the fair of St Denis. In 753 Gerard, count of Paris, imposed a capitation tax on the merchants, adding for good measure a tax on serfs. Fulrad appealed to Pippin, claiming that this ruined the fair. Pippin's judgement in his favour was very explicit. But Gerard tried again in 759, in vain. The abbey took care to have the judgement of 753 ratified by subsequent kings. After this there was no more trouble. Gerard's attempts are a final illustration of the tenacity of royal agents who tried to reverse exceptional privileges for the Church that impoverished themselves and the fisc.

The subsequent relations of St Denis with the Carolingians cannot concern us here. They are characterized by the growing political importance of the abbey. For a time, Charles the Bald was himself lay abbot and defender of the house against the Vikings. It seems also that the abbey was already set on its career as a historiographical centre, if, as seems likely, the so-called *Annales Mettenses Priores* were compiled there about the year 806.[31] A little later, the abbot Hilduin and the monk Hincmar (soon to be archbishop of Reims) were certainly involved in historical writing that aimed to glorify the past of the abbey and to link its fortunes as closely as possible with those of the crown. No other religious house had better materials from which to construct such claims or perhaps the skill to elaborate them. But, making allowance for its special good fortune, the abbey's history under the Merovingians and early Carolingians is not unlike that of other great monasteries. In a material sense, the gains had been enormous, the losses considerable, and the balance to its credit very handsome.

What, in the end, can be said for the Frankish Church as it awaited

---

[31] See H. Hoffmann, *Untersuchungen zur karolingischen Annalistik* (Bonn, 1958), pp. 24, 29; and I. Haselbach, *Aufstieg und Herrschaft der Karlinger in der Darstellung der sogennanten Annales Mettenses Priores* (Lübeck–Hamburg, 1970), p. 24.

the Carolingian efficiency-experts? It was disorganized, corrupt and without spirituality – or so one would guess. In brief, it was suffering the fate of any Church trying to survive in a half-century or more of political disruption. But the Franks were still there, with their churches and monasteries and convents and tutelary saints – indeed, with more of them than ever. Plainly they had learnt the uses of institutionalized religion. More than that: in the early eighth century they were already teaching their letters to children who were to become the rank and file of the first stage of the Carolingian Renaissance.

IX

THE MAKING OF THE GERMAN CHURCH

THE conversion of the Germanic peoples bordering the Frankish world is something that could never have happened in Antiquity. The concept of a barbaric hinterland, so essential to the thinking of the Later Empire, was gone; and in its place was born the conviction that those outside should be inside. The Christian world should be one, its frontiers bounded only by the reach of its missionaries. It looks now like an immense demonstration of self-confidence by a society which, whatever else it was, was not Roman. It would be nearer the mark to call it, quite simply, Christian. The Merovingians were the Christian princes whose military power made all this possible. No missionary penetration into Germany could ever have been successful that lacked strongholds on the Rhine and outposts beyond it. The inference can be drawn that missionary activity was thus no more than the cultural aspect of a successful military take-over of the areas whence the Frankish Rhine was threatened. But not all missionaries did what authority expected of them or enjoyed the same measure of support. Nor were kings moved solely by considerations of military security. To understand the making of the German Church is to understand the birth of the idea of crusade, at least in the sense of armed penetration into a strange world in the name of Christ. It was an idea that as a prerequisite demanded pagans. These were not in short supply nor always difficult of access. The trouble, and the essence of the whole story, was this: the initial missionary field turned out to be a demi-world of lapsed Christians, lost communities practising what had survived of Christian cultus in isolation. Only now and then did one hit the genuine article – a real, uncontaminated pagan.

The beginnings of this activity lay in the earlier part of the seventh century, when missionaries under Merovingian protection set to work in the northern and eastern regions of Francia itself. The pioneers had not been Franks but Aquitanians and Irishmen. One of the greatest, St Amand, had been clear that his mission was not to any one people but to all whom he could reach; and these turned out to be Gascons and Slavs as well as Germans. His was a universal mission to all pagans, without regard to race. His outlook was shared by some at least of his contemporaries and their successors. It could prove awkward for kings who did not want the Gospel preached indiscriminately.

The next stage is dominated by missionaries from Anglo-Saxon England. We may ask why. Why should many of the finest products of a newly-converted land turn their attention overseas? One reason – and it was never absent – was the urge to *peregrinatio*, to sacrificial exile from home; and a very strong sense of home is requisite before this is possible. The Irish had it; and from their Irish masters the Anglo-Saxons learnt that this was the essential route to ascetic fulfilment. Another reason was the influence of Rome, powerfully directed towards universal conversion. Stronger than either was the teaching of the Bible, because of which *peregrinatio* dissolved into *missio*. And what goal more natural for an Anglo-Saxon so inclined than the lands of his Germanic kindred over the sea? Bede, writing a generation later, observed this activity of his countrymen with pride and a certain awe; and he drew together their scattered efforts into a coherent pattern of success and failure. He made a historical process of it which, had he written a decade later, must have reached its true culmination in the career of St Boniface.

Bede tells his story in three successive chapters of the *Ecclesiastical History*,[1] leaving out only St Wilfrid's adventure (the earliest chronologically) for later treatment in the section devoted to Wilfrid's career.[2] All are concerned with missionary work in Frisia and the neighbouring Saxon territories. Whether by accident, as Bede says, or intentionally, as Wilfrid's biographer Eddius insists,[3] Wilfrid found himself in Frisia in the year 678, on his way to Rome. There, by permission of the Frisian king, Aldgisl, he began the *opus evangelicum* that Willibrord was to carry further. It was a winter's occupation only and destined for many a set-back, but Bede was probably right to see it as a beginning that neither Frisians nor Anglo-Saxons could forget. A more serious effort was made about ten years later. Egbert, an Anglo-Saxon exile in Ireland, intended, according to Bede,[4] to undertake a mission to 'many peoples', starting with the *Garmani* from whom the Anglo-Saxons sprang. Bede lists them. But Egbert was prevented from setting out and in his place sent his pupil Wihtberht, who spent two years preaching to such Frisians as he could reach through their king Radbod. The mission, the goal of which was probably the Saxons, was a failure; Wihtberht returned to Ireland. He in his turn was followed by another of Egbert's men, Willibrord (a Northumbrian, like his fellows), and by two other exiles in Ireland, the White and

---

[1] *Hist. Eccles.* v, chs. 9–11.   [2] Ibid., ch. 19.
[3] Life of Bishop Wilfrid, ch. 26.   [4] *Hist. Eccles.* v, ch. 9.

the Black Hewald. The Hewalds went to the Saxons over the Rhine. It was too far from base and they were unprotected. Their mission ended almost at once in martyrdom. Bede offers an interesting explanation: the Saxon chieftains feared that 'gradually the whole land would be compelled to change its old religion for a new one'.[5] They saw the mission as a national threat. If their gods went, what else might not follow? They could see clearly and at once that two poor missionaries were a challenge to the old life. Bede saw it, too.

But Willibrord was no Hewald. He belonged to no lunatic fringe but could learn from what had already happened that enduring success must depend on more than the chance benevolence of a pagan ruler. A Benedictine monk and a former pupil of St Wilfrid, he knew something of the resources of the papacy. He arrived in Frisia in 690 and turned at once to Rome for permission to preach. The pope was the man to license missionary work, as every Anglo-Saxon cleric knew. Moreover, Willibrord wanted Roman relics for the churches he hoped would replace pagan shrines. Where would one be without them? During his absence a certain Swithberht was consecrated bishop of the Frisians by Wilfrid, but soon left to go to the Bructeri in southern Westphalia. This again was too far from base. He ended his days in a monastery at Kaiserswerth on an island in the Rhine which Pippin II gave him. In 696 Pippin sent Willibrord again to Rome to be consecrated archbishop of the Frisians, and then established him in the *castellum* of Utrecht. The consecration is noted in Willibrord's calendar, probably in his own hand. Till his death in 739 he was to devote most of his time to the work of conversion among those Frisians over whom the Franks exercised spasmodic control. We know that he built churches and consecrated some bishops whose names are lost. Bede ends his account by saying that Willibrord is still alive as he writes, honoured for his great age and longing for his heavenly reward. He had made what he could of Frankish support, though from Rome he had received little that we know of except encouragement.

Willibrord's links with home remained unbroken. There was correspondence, which does not survive; and his belated biography, written half a century after his death by his kinsman Alcuin (and possibly based on an earlier life)[6] tells us little of interest apart from an account of his visit to the island of Fositeland (Heligoland) where his treatment of the shrine of the god Forseti enraged the Frisian Radbod. But we do have charter material concerning his properties that is superior to what survives for St Boniface. They stretched from

[5] Ibid., ch. 10.
[6] Ed. Levison, SRM vii, chs. 9–11; and by A. Poncelet, AA SS Nov. iii, pp. 414 ff.

Brabant in the north to Thuringia in the south. That was the way to establish a mission. We know how and from whom he acquired his property at Echternach in Luxembourg, the site of his favourite monastery. The donors of this and neighbouring properties included the abbess Irmina, Pippin II, Pippin's wife Plectrudis and his son by a mistress, Charles Martel. In other words, the Carolingian family had decided to endow him liberally in the heart of their private property, which can only mean that they regarded his mission as a permanent institution. Echternach is often seen as Willibrord's place of retreat. It seems likelier, however, that when Frisia was closed to him, as during the troubled days between Pippin's death and Charles's accession to power, his retreat was Antwerp, once the residence of St Amand, whence he could continue the work of earlier missionaries in Brabant. Echternach may have been meant for penetration into Saxony. The Carolingians seem to have made no difficulty about his probing into German territory that was certainly not Frisian. The last Thuringian duke, Hedeno (or Hetan), an ally of the Carolingians, gave him two possessions that indicate a willingness to see his mission extended into Thuringia. Penetration up the course of the Main seems to have been expected. Many Frankish families had gone that way and begun the settlement of what was to become Franconia; and some of the Rhineland bishops had actively supported them. The route was marked out that Boniface was to take. There can be no question, then, that Willibrord and his disciples were active, as circumstances allowed, among the Frisians, the Thuringians and even the Danes. (He made one trip to the *ferocissimos Danorum populos* and brought back thirty boys for baptism and training.) They made an impression that may not have been fleeting, and could indeed have claimed that their mission was to all peoples within their reach.

However, it is as the apostle of the Frisians that Willibrord is chiefly remembered. His intention was presumably to found a Frisian Church on the model of the Anglo-Saxon Church: that is to say, a national church dependent on the support of rulers but in close communion with Rome. It is another matter to be precise about what he would have understood by a national church. Certainly he would have seen no contradiction, emotional or jurisdictional, in a Roman-Frisian Church dependent on Pippin II. He would not have supposed that it would have been wholly subordinate to Rome, any more than the Anglo-Saxon Church was. In practice Willibrord was unable to establish an ecclesiastical province such as Rome would have favoured. Frankish power was restricted to south-west Frisia until he was too old to undertake distant missions. It may also be the case that Frankish magnates offered passive resistance in Frisia as in Francia itself to a new form of ecclesiastical organization. Though an archbishop and the recipient of a pallium, Willibrord found his resources quite insufficient for what was expected of him. His lasting achievements were the see of Utrecht as a centre from which the Frisians would ultimately be converted; the initiation of the Anglo-Saxon missionary drive into Thuringia; and the demonstration that the way to set about such work was under papal guidance with adequate Frankish backing.

This first investigation of the Lower Rhine area by the Anglo-Saxons was part of a larger phenomenon. There were other missionaries at work who were not Anglo-Saxons and not interested in the Lower Rhine. They were the children of the union of the Columbanic houses with the Frankish Church, and for this reason we may say that the missions to and beyond the Middle and Upper Rhine in the late seventh and early eighth centuries were Franco-Irish. It is important to know who these missionaries were, and how successful they were, because St Boniface was shortly to tread in their steps and occasionally on their toes. The first was Kilian from Worms, who made his way with two companions into Thuringia, where he was active in Würzburg. Nothing certain is known of his career there apart from his martyrdom about the year 689. His mission was not to introduce Christianity to the Thuringians but to sharpen its impact, much as Columbanus had once sharpened it in Francia. The cult of Kilian in Würzburg was started not by any Irishman or Frank but by Boniface's own nominee, the Anglo-Saxon Bishop Burghard (or Burchard) in 752. Perhaps most significant is the evidence Kilian's career affords us of Frankish penetration up the Main and the ready co-operation of the Thuringian ducal dynasty. A second missionary of rather later date was Rupert, an aristocratic Frank, also from Worms, who had reached Bavaria by the year 696 to settle at Salzburg under the protection of the Agilulfing dynasty. He was a bishop indeed, but a wandering bishop of the Irish tradition, an *episcopus et abbas*, not a diocesan in the Anglo-Saxon sense. Once again, here was no missionary settling in the wilds among savages. Something of Roman Salzburg had survived, and there were Romans as well as Bavarians living there. In re-establishing St Peter's monastery in the *oppidum*, Rupert called on the services of Roman monks he found on the spot. It is rather in his establishment for nuns, the Nonnenburg, that we come across aristocratic Germanic names. Though the Bavarian duke provided for him, Rupert was none the less kept well away from Regensburg, the capital, presumably because he was looked upon with some mistrust as a Frankish missionary. The Agilulfings were themselves of Burgundian origin and saw well the potential danger of too much

Frankish interference in Bavaria, even while they were prepared to make use of Frankish missionaries. Two other missionaries who had made their way into Bavaria from Francia were Emmeram and Corbinian.[7] Emmeram, a native of Poitiers, was in Regensburg by 670 (he died *c*.690) and was clearly looked upon by the duke as a reformer, not as a converter. He too belonged to the Irish-Frankish tradition and also suffered from the disadvantage of rousing the political susceptibilities of the Agilulfings. Corbinian came from the neighbourhood of Paris (probably Melun) and had enjoyed the confidence of important Franks, notably the Carolingian mayors of the palace. He twice visited Rome. He was probably a monk following the mixed Rule, like others of his generation. When he settled on the hilltop at Freising in western Bavaria, already a religious centre, the spiritual patron he chose was St Martin; and this, in conjunction with the clear Frankish nature of Freising's earliest charters, is proof enough of Corbinian's ties with Francia. Some of his Frankish companions survived him (he died in 730) and lived on for years at Freising, observing, it seems, the rites of their mother-church. Finally we have St Pirmin, who died in 753, only one year before St Boniface. Whether Pirmin was a Frank, an Irishman or a Goth is undecided, though he reached the Upper Rhine from Gothic Septimania. He is the least opaque of the missionaries independent of Boniface. A protégé of Charles Martel, his stamping-ground stretched from southern Alemannia as far north as the territory of Metz, where he was to die in his monastery of Hornbach. The characteristics of his career were, first, his capacity to manage potentates, whether Frankish or Alemannic, and secondly and consequently, his success in attracting endowments for monasteries observing the Rule of St Benedict and intended for a missionary role. His major foundations were Reichenau on an island in Lake Constance (724), soon to become a centre of Carolingian learning, and Murbach in Alsace (728). With Murbach he had the support of the Etichonen family, who were none the less suspicious of Charles Martel's interest in it. With local diocesans, especially Strassburg, Pirmin got on very well. An exception was the bishop of Constance, who disliked extra-diocesan monk-bishops quite as much as Boniface was to do. Not far from Reichenau was St Gallen, a great Irish-Rhaetian foundation with a distinguished future, once the Carolingians had won control of it by ousting the Alemannic dukes. (Their subjection was completed by Carloman at Cannstatt in 746.) In Rhaetia and Alemannia, then, missionaries worked in an area very critical to the Franks, who were prepared to push their fortunes there against local opposition if neces-

---

[7] Arbeo's Life of Emmeram gives a pro-Frankish view of the difficulties of his Bavarian career. Arbeo also wrote a Life of Corbinian (both ed. Krusch, MGH SRG in usum schol., 1920).

sary. Pirmin survived quite happily among those conflicting pulls, founding and reforming religious houses as and where he could win support. How he meant his monks to go to work is shown by his *Scarapsus de singulis libris canonicis* or *Dicta*,[8] a little handbook composed for their use. He does not envisage work among pagans; the inhabitants of the area were Christians. His target was the scattered Christian communities among whom pagan practices still persisted. To this extent his problem was not unlike that of Caesarius in Gaul, two centuries earlier. He starts off with a résumé of biblical history up to Christ's Resurrection, together with some comment on the Decalogue. It is the moral life of the whole community that he seeks to regulate. His summary of persisting pagan practices (ch. 22) is of particular interest. There are also recommendations about offerings suitable to be brought to church, tithes, and about penance. Perhaps most important is his insistence that the congregation shall teach itself, thus perpetuating what could so easily be forgotten or overlaid with other matter; 'Hold fast to the Creed and the Lord's Prayer, and teach them to your sons and daughters so that they too shall hold fast to them' (ch. 32). Altogether it is straightforward, elementary teaching: but it lays bare the nature of Pirmin's problem and suggests why the bishops and magnates of so large an area tolerated his presence. This, finally, may be said of him: his capacity for getting on with people extended to St Willibrord and even to St Boniface. His pupil, Bishop Heddo of Strassburg, carried on his work in friendly collaboration with Boniface's men.

Such evidence as remains of the labours of this group of missionaries – and only the most important have been mentioned – leads to certain conclusions. Frankish penetration over the Rhine, the motives behind which were more complicated than mere aggression, coincided, in the later seventh and early eighth centuries with isolated missionary activity which the Franks did not initiate but did encourage. There was nothing planned or co-ordinated about this activity. From Frisia in the north to Rhaetia in the south it assumed different forms and met with different fortunes. But its impetus was *peregrinatio*. Irish in origin, this affected Anglo-Saxons, Franks and possibly Goths. From Northumbria to Septimania, monks would now risk their lives in missionary journeys into the same hinterland of Germanic tribesmen, some pagan but mostly Christian, there to establish themselves under the protection of local chieftains and ultimately under that of the Frankish rulers. Of papal support there is little evidence apart from Frisia and Bavaria.

---

[8] Ed. G. Jecker, *Beiträge zur Geschichte des alten Mönchtums,* 13 (Münster, 1927); also by U. Engelmann, *Der heilige Pirmin und sein Missionsbüchlein* (Konstanz, 1959). For a critique see Lehmann, *Erforschung des Mittelalters,* iv, pp. 142–7.

(Dedications there of churches to St Peter may not necessarily betray acceptance of Roman influence, canonical or liturgical.) Rhineland bishops whose sees, except for Basel, all stretched east of the river were ready to collaborate and even to help with the setting-up of new monasteries. They did not feel that wandering monks or even monk-bishops threatened their prerogatives, nor that it mattered much whether the new or reformed monasteries followed the Benedictine Rule, an Irish Rule or a mixture. As between themselves, diocesan claims within the Rhine–Main–Neckar area were clearly understood. But plainly the lack of co-ordination and the variety of practices so introduced afforded every chance for the sort of developments that would strike a man like St Boniface as so much eccentric doctrine. And this was no mere tidy-mindedness on his part. His objection to diversity was fundamental and reasonable.

St Boniface was not only a bigger man than those we have been considering; more is known about him, if less than we could wish. Unlike Willibrord, he was the subject of a biography soon after his death[9] and, also unlike Willibrord, his correspondence survives in great part – a collection of 150 letters, more remarkable for their revelation of purpose and character than for their number.[10] (We have, after all, 300 of Alcuin's letters and 850 of Gregory the Great's.) Formidable in life, he became a Christian martyr and hero from the moment of his death. He was the son of substantial parents, who named him Winfrith: Boniface was the name given him by Rome. He was born in Wessex (perhaps at Crediton) in the 670s, and after some education at Exeter entered the monastery of Nursling, near Southampton. He became and remained a learned man, brought up in the reformed Benedictine tradition of Theodore's Church though not uninfluenced by the Irish. He knew the great Aldhelm of Malmesbury. Grammar and the teaching of grammar left their mark on him and clearly he was no enemy to secular literature. By 712 he was a coming man, a man of weight in the West Saxon Church with an assured future. His diocesan, Daniel of Winchester, held him in high esteem. All this he cast aside to turn to the mission-field, inspired by reports of Willibrord. Accordingly he set out for Frisia in 716. It was a bad time. Willibrord's mission was threatened with collapse, and Boniface was back in England the following year. At least he had learnt to respect Willibrord.

In 718 Boniface set out again, but not for Frisia. This time he went straight to Rome. Why he did so is not clear. What we do have is the outcome: a mandate from Pope Gregory II, dated 15 May 719,[11] which

---

[9] Ed. Levison, MGH SRG in usum schol., 1905.
[10] Ed. Tangl, MGH Epist. Select. i, 2nd edn., 1955.   [11] Ibid., no. 12.

entrusted him with a mission to the heathen in an unspecified area, though it looks as if Thuringia were understood. He was to be the pope's *conminister*, charged with the duty of inspecting the situation of Christianity in Germanic territory and subsequently of reporting on it. The time was ripe for some such investigation, for Charles Martel was now counter-attacking against the Saxons and pushing into central Germany. But what is remarkable is the chance nature of the conjunction. An unknown Anglo-Saxon priest arrives in Rome with no more than a letter of introduction from his bishop and, after some doctrinal testing, is dispatched on a fact-finding mission that could mean anything – or nothing. It says something for Gregory II's appreciation of Boniface's potential and something also for his anxiety for the state of German Christianity, a prey to syncretism, heresy and laxity. He wanted to know what had been the result of a generation of Franco-Irish mission-work in the Rhineland and beyond; what were the intentions of the Carolingian mayors in the same area; what was the condition of the Frankish Church itself. Rome had the answer to none of these questions but could take an opportunity to find out. Indeed, the seizing of unforeseen opportunities is characteristic of the entire process of conversion across the Rhine. The papacy even more than Boniface stood at a moment of decision. But while we delimit in this way the papacy's special interest in Frankish moves that might affect what may be called its Alpine preoccupations (namely, the Lombard–Bavarian–Rhaetian complex) we should not lose sight of its sense of the urgency of universal mission. Time was running short: 'advesperascit dies'.[12] It was therefore as the pope's man, now and ever after, that Boniface made his way north to Thuringia and thence to Frisia, where Willibrord was again in a position to push forward his mission. From 719 to 722 Willibrord and Boniface collaborated in the re-establishment of the Frisian Church under Frankish protection. The older man saw the younger as his natural successor; but Boniface may have had no particular interest in Frisia and certainly felt that he lacked papal authority to remain there. So he returned south into Hesse, where Christianity was hardly distinguishable from paganism. At Amöneburg, a Frankish fortress and later the site of one of his monasteries, he encountered two chieftains – the twins Dettic and Deorulf – who, according to his biographer, worshipped idols 'under some kind of nominal Christianity'.[13] We may suppose them typical of many. The Franks and the Irish had been there before, under the aegis of the bishops of Mainz, and things had gone badly since their departure. The bishop of Mainz was not pleased at the interference of

[12] Ibid., no. 21, a crucial missionary statement by Gregòry III in the Pauline tradition.
[13] Willibald's Life, MGH SRG in usum schol., ch. 6.

Boniface, whose success among the Hessians was sufficient to justify a progress-report to the pope which resulted in a summons to Rome and further cross-examination. From this encounter he emerged a consecrated bishop, without a see indeed but charged with a mission to all the Germans east of the Rhine. We have the text of the oath he took to the pope on this occasion. It was written in his own hand and placed on St Peter's relics.[14] Some have seen in these events a deliberate advance in papal policy, a claiming of a new kind of authority. Whether or not this was so, it is less the claim than the vision of *all* Germania that is striking. Yet the pope was placing his representative in an awkward position, for he had given him episcopal authority over territory that was at least theoretically under the charge of the Rhineland bishops. There was bound to be a clash, and a clash from which Boniface would emerge the loser if he remained unrecognized by the effective Frankish ruler, Charles Martel. At this point, therefore, Charles was requested by the pope to take Boniface under his protection, which he did in a formal letter.[15] Charles is often accused of passivity towards Boniface and of helping him less than he might have done. But we know too little to be sure. Charles may have encouraged Boniface to found German sees. But neither was the papacy anxious to see any hurry in this matter. Charles might, had his motives been solely political, have used Boniface in ways that he did not use him. But the fact remains, as Boniface ruefully admitted, that without Charles's protection his episcopal mission east of the Rhine would have been impossible. We should not see Boniface as a pawn in a political game.

There followed a decade of work in Hesse and Thuringia. It was inaugurated by a spectacular demonstration at Geismar, where on the advice of local Christians, the bishop felled a great oak sacred to Woden. The effect on the work of conversion was as dramatic as it was intended to be, and was followed up by an action even more characteristic of Boniface: from the timber of the felled oak he built the first oratory at Fritzlar. The construction of mission churches served by Benedictine monks, and later of nunneries, is the hallmark of his labour. Some of these houses perished during Saxon attacks; no less than thirty were destroyed in the one year, 752.[16] But others survived to play a vital role in German ecclesiastical life. Boniface's activity as founder of monasteries, often on lands donated by local magnates, demonstrated the possibilities of the Rule of St Benedict as a missionary tool. Already, however, the Rhineland bishops, and notably Mainz, showed displeasure at this large display of appropriation in the name of Rome. Boniface was caught up in a situation of great com-

---

[14] Tangl, no. 16.   [15] Ibid., no. 22.
[16] Ibid., no. 108 (one of Boniface's two letters to his fourth and last pope, Stephen II).

plexity where local families of long standing were jostling for position with *novi homines*. It was not easy for bishops used to the game, let alone foreigners. However, Bishop Daniel encouraged his disciple with a long letter of advice on how to convert pagans.[17] Some of it was good advice that did not underestimate pagan intelligence: pagans should be argued with in a moderate way. We do not know to what extent Boniface made use of the advice, nor what he did about interpreters, but his work was sufficiently impressive to cause a new pope, Gregory III, to send him a pallium, probably in 732. He thus became archbishop of the German churches east of the Rhine; but still he had no see. Though he moved thus ever more clearly away from his initial *peregrinatio* among the heathen towards the work of organization and reform, both he and the pope saw this extension in spiritual terms. They were organizing the work of salvation in the quickest way they knew, not laying the foundations of the medieval German Church. Their objective was a strong provincial-diocesan framework controlled by Rome and operating in the field through missionary-monastic units. Always they sought to enforce *canonica rectitudo*, the time-honoured observances of the Roman Church. It was a challenge to Domesday rather than a piece of empire-building. The letters of successive popes are concerned less with boundaries than with orthodoxy and problems of Christian practice. Those of Boniface, whether to Rome or to his Anglo-Saxon friends, reveal consistent distaste for the new work. He was more interested in their prayers and the recruits and books they could send him than in making contacts with Frankish notables, whom he detested. He found it hard to be an archbishop and at the same time to observe the exact terms of his original oath to St Peter. This apparent literal-mindedness was not, however, a Bonifacian quirk but a characteristic of most thoughtful men of his time.

In 738 Boniface paid his third and last visit to Rome. His hope may have been to push forward from his advanced bases in Thuringia into Saxon territory – always the goal to Anglo-Saxon missionaries sensitive to ties of blood. But the pope was cautious. He sent his distinguished missionary back to Thuringia, with an additional duty to perform in Bavaria. Boniface had not hitherto done much about southern Germany. Alemannia seemed to be reserved by Charles Martel for Pirmin, and Bavarian ecclesiastical ties, so far as the dukes were concerned, were rather with Italy and Rome than with the hated Franks. Avoiding their Frankish-orientated western region,[18] the

---

[17] Ibid., no. 23.
[18] One may instance the Huosi at Freising as an example of a West-Bavarian family ready to collaborate with the Carolingians.

dukes chose to concentrate on the founding of monasteries comparatively free from episcopal control in eastern Bavaria and to support
missions even further east into Slav territory. Here at least they were
safe from the Franks. Their discussions with Rome about the reorganization of the Bavarian Church as a whole had been going on since at
least the year 716, and there can be no doubt that the popes, preoccupied as they were with Bavaria's southern neighbours, the
Lombards, had a direct interest in the fate of the Bavarian Church.
Boniface, then, arrived in 739 at Duke Odilo's court as a papal representative, not as a Frankish one, and as such was welcomed.[19] Like
Theodore in England, he now undertook the delimitation of dioceses
on the basis of existing political subdivisions. Therefore his work
lasted. He made not an ecclesiastical province but a ducal Church. The
resulting dioceses had their bishops at Passau, Regensburg, Salzburg
and Freising. In Passau, Bishop Vivilo remained undisturbed, for he
had been consecrated by Gregory III and was certainly not what
Boniface most mistrusted, a wandering bishop of the Irish tradition.
The first step towards diocesan stability had thus antedated Boniface's
mission. But Boniface found plenty of 'heretical' bishops and priests to
remove, as the pope had anticipated. Some survived his reforming
zeal. The only one of the four sees that remained firmly under his
influence was Freising, in the west. On Bishop Virgil of Salzburg, an
Irishman, he could make no sort of impression, and his nominee at
Regensburg, Gaubald, disappeared with Duke Odilo. Apart from
demarcating dioceses, Boniface's most lasting work in Bavaria was, as
elsewhere, the introduction of Benedictine monasteries and their
integration with indigenous monastic traditions. But once his work
was done his personal influence in Bavaria ceased. In Alemannia it
never existed. It was to Virgil, not to Boniface, that Pippin III turned
when southern Germany was in his power.

In 741 Boniface returned to Hesse and Thuringia. In the same year
died Charles Martel and Gregory III. Boniface thus acquired two new
masters – or rather three, since Charles's power was initially divided
between his sons Carloman (in Austrasia) and Pippin III (in Neustria),
with both of whom Boniface was to get on rather better, or at least
more fruitfully, than he had with their father. The new pope,
Zacharias, was to take a more detached view of his mission than had
Gregory II or III. However, the opportunity now arose[20] to do for the
central German churches what had already been done for Bavaria.
Bishoprics could be founded in areas made secure by Frankish arms. If

[19] See Gregory III's two letters about Bavaria, Tangl, nos. 44, 45.
[20] The events of 741–3 are chronologically susceptible of other arrangements. I give here what
may be called the classical sequence.

Boniface had had his way there might have been bishoprics still further advanced into the no-man's-land where Saxon raiding made life unsafe. That Boniface still had his eye on the Saxons is shown by a letter addressed in about 738 to the Anglo-Saxons, asking their prayers for the conversion of the continental Saxons. But nothing came of it; Frankish control of the Saxons remained spasmodic. Boniface greeted the new pope in a long letter [21] which is sometimes thought to have been injudicious; but this takes no account of the tradition of rebuking popes and gravely overestimates the moral condition of Rome itself. Boniface submitted, but asked why heathenish festivities that offended foreign visitors were permitted in Rome. Zacharias replied tartly that they were not, or at any rate not any more. [22] More important, Boniface informed the pope that he had consecrated three new bishops. These were: Burghard, [23] to Würzburg; Witta, to Büraburg; and Willibald, to Erfurt. All three were Anglo-Saxons. The boundaries of these dioceses were determined to the south and west by existing dioceses, to the north and east by the frontier of paganism, and internally by tribal frontiers. Würzburg, a *castellum* and once the ducal residence, was the see for southern Thuringia (i.e. northern Franconia); Büraburg, an *oppidum* near Fritzlar and well-sited for defence, was the see for Hesse; and Erfurt, a mere *locus*, was the see for exposed northern Thuringia. The group was completed in 745 by the addition of Eichstätt in southern Franconia, to link Würzburg with Regensburg once Bavarian resistance to the Franks had collapsed. Boniface was ill at ease about his creations – though, after ten years as archbishop he had a perfect right to make them – and felt the need of papal confirmation. After considerable delay Pope Zacharias sent it – but unwillingly, since he disapproved of the sites selected and doubted whether the numbers of the faithful justified the creations: 'you will recall, dear brother, the canonical injunction that bishops should not be appointed to villages or little towns, since this cheapens the name of bishop'; but he allowed them. [24] There is in fact no evidence that Bishop Willibald ever left his abbey of Eichstätt for Erfurt. Boniface seems to have remained personally responsible for that part of Thuringia, terribly exposed as it was to Saxon attack, and eventually to have left it in the care of his successor at Mainz, Bishop Lul. Büraburg also proved to be too exposed. As a see it lasted only a few years, and then Hesse, too, reverted to the jurisdiction of Mainz.

[21] Tangl, no. 50.

[22] Ibid., no. 51.

[23] A library catalogue of *c*.800, written on the last folio of a MS once at Würzburg, is sometimes said to be Burghard's (now Bodleian MS Laud. Misc. 126; see CLA ii, 252 and B. Bischoff, and J. Hofmann, *Libri Sancti Kiliani*, Würzburg, 1952, pp. 142 ff. and plate 14).

[24] Tangl, no. 51.

Boniface had in practice been too rash, though in principle he had simply done what Rome had intended.

But there was more in Zacharias' letter. He approved the proposal made in Boniface's letter that Carloman's wish for an Austrasian church council should be granted and went on to insist on the need to enforce canonical decrees and cleanse the hierarchy of all whose conduct violated the canons. The fact of the matter is that the council may already have been held.[25] It was closely followed by a second council at Les Estinnes in Hainaut and a third at Soissons, for Pippin's territory. All were meetings of some bishops with their clergy, together with lay *optimates* and the mayors of the palace under whose authority the consequential decrees were promulgated;[26] and over all Boniface's was the presiding spirit. The capitularies are statements of intent, not of achievement. Indeed, not much that Boniface hoped for from them was achieved in his lifetime. Again he hoped for too much, though Rome knew well that the mayors had in practice a very limited field for action when it came to displacing clergy on whose loyalty they depended, and to restoring to the Church properties that had been alienated over a long period of civil strife. However, the councils are very significant. After many years the Frankish clergy had once again come together to discuss the state of the Church. They did so much in the spirit that had inspired the Anglo-Saxon reform councils of the previous century. Their aim was a return to the old order; the restoration of the rule of canon law and of moral order among clergy and laity. The early Church and the teachings of the Fathers were before their eyes. Above all, there was to be continuity. Provincial councils were to be held annually. But it was easier said than done. Natural development though it was, work of this kind was not what Boniface had come to the continent to do. It was equally not what earned him prestige in the eyes of contemporaries.

In 744 Boniface founded a little monastery at Fulda in Hesse. It was to be for him what Echternach had been for Willibrord. If it was a place of retreat it was also a potential base for future advance into the Saxon hinterland. Its first abbot was a Bavarian disciple, Sturmi. He went to Rome and Monte Cassino to study the Rule of St Benedict at source. Some years later the pope granted a privilege, the first for any German house, that placed Fulda under direct papal jurisdiction, thus exempting it from diocesan control.[27] It was Boniface's *Eigenkloster* or personal monastery, standing on land given him by Carloman. Also exempted was Fritzlar, and possibly his other foundations. Fulda was

---

[25] MGH Conc. Aevi Karo 1., i, no. i. (This is a better edn. than Capit. i.)

[26] MGH Capit. i, nos. 10, 11, 12.

[27] Tangl, no. 89; also E. E. Stengel, *Urkundenbuch des Klosters Fulda* (Marburg, 1958), no. 15.

a very modest affair, and not beyond the reach of Frankish protection. But though modest it rose from no virgin site in primeval forest. Fulda had been occupied periodically since Roman times – in short, was a decayed Merovingian stronghold. In it Boniface's community erected a building and lived some kind of life. The beginnings of most Bonifacian houses were no doubt like this.

Though an archbishop, Boniface still lacked a see of his own. Territorial archbishops were an essential part of the structure of the reformed Anglo-Saxon Church as Boniface remembered it; not simply respected seniors, like metropolitans, but masters of their provincial suffragans, bound by the gift of the pallium to dependence on Rome. The Franks did not take kindly to the idea. They vetoed his plan, approved by Rome, for archbishops at Reims and Sens, only permitting one for Neustria - at Rouen. The hierarchy of western Francia was firmly committed to its old metropolitical grouping. As for Austrasia, the mayors at first seemed ready to give Boniface the see of Cologne, and Zacharias confirmed the appointment. Cologne was a strong point in Frankish planning for advances beyond the Rhine and one at least of its bishops, Kunibert, had penetrated the pagan hinterland as far away as Utrecht and Soest. But something went wrong; either the opposition of local magnates used to bishops of a different complexion or Carolingian recognition that there had been a shift of political emphasis to the south. Instead, then, Boniface got Mainz as sole archbishop in Austrasia. Agilolf, a member of an old Frankish family, got Cologne. One would have imagined Mainz a see better sited than Cologne for control of the central German churches lying along the rivers that emptied into the Middle Rhine, and thus more significant in Carolingian eyes. But Boniface was not pleased. It may be that he had hoped to push forward the work of Willibrord from the more northerly vantage-point. From Mainz he ruled in effect over the entire Franco-German Church. But the next bishop of Mainz succeeded to no more than the diocese; Lul, Boniface's pupil, was not granted a pallium till 781. The drive to reform was already passing from the Anglo-Saxons to a new generation of Franks, and most conspicuously to Abbot Fulrad of St Denis and Bishop Chrodegang of Metz.

Boniface's last known public act was the unction of Pippin III as Frankish king in 751, or so the Frankish annals state.[28] It is possible. However, the envoys who negotiated for Pippin at the papal court were Fulrad and Burghard, not Boniface. Always it is unsafe to suppose Boniface the only link between Francia and Rome. He would have been surer of himself had it been so.

[28] *Annales Regni Francorum*, MGH SRG in usum schol. (1895), s.a. 750–1.

Our view of why Boniface hoped for Cologne gains some support from the final phase of his career. In 753 he obtained Pippin's permission to visit the northern Frisians, possibly with a view to organizing the Church there, and set out with a few companions. An old man, he may have had martyrdom at the back of his mind but there is no evidence that he did. At Dokkum in the sea-marshes beyond the Zuider Zee he and his companions were set upon and killed by a band of pirates, who behaved more like men after booty than outraged pagans. The day was 5 June 754.[29] He was not so far from the reach of Frankish power that his body could not be brought back by difficult stages to Utrecht, and thence up the Rhine to Mainz, and finally (after a wrangle over where his body should rest) to Fulda. His biographer finishes his task with an account of a seasonable miracle at Dokkum; he, Willibald, had had it from Lul, Lul from King Pippin, the king from an eyewitness. What better authentication could be looked for? Miracles go with martyrs, and Boniface was at once a martyr, more powerful in death than in life. Even the Franks were impressed. It was his martyrdom that was remembered and admired; that, and his learning. Almost at once Bishop Milret of Worcester wrote to Lul acclaiming the martyr, 'the glory and crown of all whom the *patria* has sent out'.[30] The bishop went on to identify the glory of martyrdom as the proper end of such a *peregrinatio*, pursued as it had been, 'in the sweat of his brow'. There was no word about the reorganization of the Germanic churches. Milret was not to know that without the work of Boniface in Germany, drawing north and south towards a common middle ground within a single ecclesiastical pattern, the work of Charlemagne and even the eventual unification of Germany must have followed a very different path.

With Boniface at the moment of his death were certain books among which may well be those that one can still handle at Fulda. They remind us that he was a man of books; and if we are to get anywhere near his mind we must take his books into account. The three famous books, the *Codices Bonifatiani* 1, 2 and 3, now in the Landesbibliothek at Fulda, owe their preservation to the original decision to house them as martyr's relics in the treasury rather than in the library. The first is a Gospel harmony written by order of Bishop Victor of Capua, read by him in 546-7, later taken north and glossed in an Insular hand, possibly that of Boniface himself.[31] The second book is an early eighth-century copy, probably Burgundian, of a collection of patristic texts, some anti-Arian. It is known as the Ragyntrudis-

---

[29] Such is the tradition of Fulda derived from Sturmi. The Mainz tradition is 755, and this was followed by Willibald.

[30] Tangl, no. 112.   [31] This was Lowe's guess (CLA viii, 1196).

codex, from the name of the lady for whom it seems to have been written.[32] But its chief claims to distinction are two or more violent cuts through the margins: Boniface tried to defend himself with a book against his attackers, and this may be the book. To look at it is to be a little shaken. The third book is an early eighth-century Gospel-book written in part by an Irish scribe named Cadmug.[33] There is no reason to question the tradition that these three books were the property of Boniface, whether or not they were among the books he certainly had with him when he was killed. The Gospels and the Fathers: what more authentic relic of the learned *peregrinus*? Scattered through his correspondence with his friends in England we come upon a wider range of his literary interests. For example: the abbess Eadburg of Minster in Thanet reported that she had not yet obtained for him a copy of the *passiones martyrum* but would welcome some selections of Scripture from him; later, he thanked her for her gifts of *sanctorum librorum* to console 'the German exile whose task it is to lighten the dark corners of the Germanic peoples';[34] he asked Archbishop Nothelm of Canterbury for a copy of the correspondence between Gregory I and Augustine, which he had failed to obtain from Rome; he asked a former pupil, the abbot Duddo, for some commentaries on St Paul to fill gaps in his own collection; from Eadburg, again, he begged a text of the Epistles of his master, St Peter, written in gold to impress the carnally-minded in his congregations, and sent her gold for the purpose; from Bishop Daniel he sought a particular copy (Abbot Winbert's) of the Prophets – six Prophets in one volume written in large, clear letters, for his sight was failing and he could not get such a text where he now was; Archbishop Egbert of York was thanked for a present of books and was asked for copies of the commentaries of 'the lector Bede'; the request for Bede's commentaries (but not his History) was repeated to Abbot Hwaetberht of Wearmouth; Egbert was again approached about Bede, but this time especially his homilies. It may well be asked why some of these books were not available to Boniface in Francia. They probably were. But he had freer access to old friends in England than to learned circles in Francia. The constant interchange of books and other presents between Boniface and the Anglo-Saxons is as impressive as the absence of it between Boniface and the Franks. Of the books he asked for, it can be said that they were the tools of teaching and preaching, the texts necessary to any missionary. Yet he was a learned man whose writings are full of quotations from and recollections of books out of the common run, and was himself the author of a Grammar.[35] He

---

[32] CLA viii, 1197.   [33] Ibid. 1198.   [34] Tangl, no. 30.
[35] See Levison, *England and the Continent in the Eighth Century* (Oxford, 1946), p. 70.

could not be mistaken for a product of the Northumbrian school of learning; he was not like Bede; but his affinities with the school of St Aldhelm are obvious. To his contemporaries his learning seemed entirely appropriate to a monk-missionary. It might well have surprised St Benedict.

What is to be made of this extraordinary career? It looks so successful. It even looks successful in a worldly sense. To Boniface it was a failure. He had gone to the continent in the wake of other Anglo-Saxons to be a *peregrinus* and a missionary to pagans. He had no doubt hoped, like Willibrord, to bring light to his Saxon blood-brothers, and was disappointed. His advances towards and retreats from this goal were precisely conditioned by the military fortunes of his Frankish protectors, who were still a long way from even that measure of success that Charlemagne was to have in Saxon territory. Moreover, the Franks were not the blood-brothers of the Saxons but their bitter enemies. The objectives of the Franks and of Boniface were to that extent irreconcilable from the start. But we must not dismiss his relations with the Franks as uniformly bad. In the days before he became a bishop he could win Frankish recruits. One such was Gregory of Utrecht, whom he met at the home of Gregory's grandmother, Adela of Pfalzel, at Trier. This was a noble Frankish family and young Gregory had only recently left school at Aachen. Yet Adela let him abandon a promising career to follow the missionary.[36] It was the bishopric, not the mission, that made the real difference and led to clashes with the Rhineland episcopal clans. Gewilib of Mainz and Milo of Trier were two bishops of whom Boniface strongly disapproved on canonical grounds, close though they were to the Carolingians; and the absence of the bishops of Worms and Speyer from the great synod of 742 (the *Concilium Germanicum*) could well have been due to their dislike of his episcopal activities in and beyond the Rhineland that traditionally fell under their jurisdiction. There were others; Boniface wrote scathingly of 'Milo and others like him'.[37] But again, not all Frankish bishops were his enemies. And as for the Frankish rulers, it may be thought remarkable that they were so tolerant of a difficult foreigner with a curious directive from Rome. They had their own links with the papacy, were benefactors as well as despoilers of the Church, warmly supported Willibrord and Pirmin, and had problems of their own, unrelated to Germany, that Boniface did not have to understand – as, for example, the threat of Islam. Yet Charles Martel protected him, and Carloman and Pippin went a good deal further.

If, then, Boniface's sense of failure was not the result of Frankish obstruction – and he does not say that it was – we must seek the reason

---

[36] Liudger's Life of Gregory, MGH SS xv, 67.
[37] Tangl, no. 87.

elsewhere. It lay in his own mind. First, he was a monk of strict Benedictine observance, trained to obedience; and this obedience he transferred to the service of four successive popes: Gregory II, Gregory III, Zacharias, and Stephen II. He was St Benedicts's man and he was St Peter's man. The startling uses to which he and his friends put the Rule, above all as a missionary and educational weapon, were not those of an earlier generation nor those of the ninth century; yet they were those of recent Anglo-Saxon practice and were approved by Rome. It cannot be questioned that they made the observance of the Rule difficult in new ways. One has only to read Boniface's emergency directions for the arrangement of affairs at his monastery of Fritzlar to appreciate how precarious life could be for a tiny com-munity set up to serve an exposed place.[38] Here was an initial strain on Boniface's moral resources. Secondly, his intellectual and spiritual background was ill attuned to the organizational tasks imposed on him by Rome. His repeated requests for help in prayer – help against inner more than external dangers – are the cry of a man upon whom Satan presses close. He looks often to the Bible for analogies to his own unhappy situation. There is much of Ezekiel in him and more of St Paul. In the Pauline Epistles he found the ever-present motive of heavenly reward for sufferings rather different from those he anti-cipated; and here also he found the tension that he too had to endure between what he could offer to the world and what he wanted for himself. It grew with the years. His patron was St Peter but his mentor was St Paul. His deepest troubles cannot therefore be laid at the door of the Franks. To them, indeed, in the person of Abbot Fulrad and perhaps also King Pippin himself, he turned, towards the end, in a spirit not ungrateful but clearly hopeless.[39] He knew that his time was short because of his infirmities, not because he contemplated martyr-dom, and he knew that his followers, mostly Anglo-Saxons, now faced a precarious future: 'they are nearly all of them *peregrini*', he added. Would they be scattered at his death or be cared for? His priests working in outlying places were the most urgent consideration: 'they can get enough bread to eat but are short of clothing unless they have advice and help from other quarters'. It was a pathetic swan-song for a hero.

There are no short cuts to an understanding of St Boniface. There could hardly be so in so strange a conjunction of coincidences as that of his arrival on the continent with the forward push of the Carolingians into Germany and the awakening of the popes to the missionary possibilities of the same area. Somehow, Boniface keeps his privacy to the end. For all his letters, we know little about him; just enough to afford us a glimpse into the tortured heart of the eighth century.

[38] Ibid., no. 40.   [39] Ibid., no. 93.

X

PIPPIN III AND THE PULL
OF ROME

A WELL-bottomed Merovingian king was master of his own Church. If he had the will and the means he could attract clergy to his court, use them and reward them. He could endow, renovate, despoil or protect, more or less as he chose. He could summon councils of clergy, with or without lay participation, and to some extent control deliberations. He might of course invite rebuke, as from Columbanus, or find dissident bishops siding with dissaffected magnates. But by and large he got away with it. Always there were the unseen brakes upon his actions of fear for his soul's future and reliance upon clergy and their ghostly partners, the saints, to protect him from the powers of evil. With the later Merovingians the means, and to some extent the will, had atrophied. They mattered much as figure-heads of traditional regality but decisions affecting the Church were taken by the rep-resentatives of whatever powerful clique of magnates happened to be in the ascendant. Rarely a pretender was made king; but when this happened, it seemed prudent to invest him with a Merovingian name and with a claim of some sort to Merovingian blood. An earlier chapter has sketched some of the effects of this development on the landed property of the Church and on the personnel of the episcopate. Moreover, the growing divisions between the eastern and western parts of Francia, namely Austrasia and Neustria, could only weaken kingship, and with it the Church.

This weakening process covered about a century; one could say from the middle of the seventh century to the middle of the eighth. The future was to see it as the gestation period of the Arnulfing or Carolingian clan, the period of its rise from comparatively modest beginnings to dominance within Austrasia, control of Neustria and finally to kingship. Contemporaries were less sure. They could not see what we see. Panegyrists of the full-blown Carolingian age could represent it all as the inevitable rise of a dynasty ordained by God to save Francia. In fact, there were set-backs and challenges. The decline of the Merovingians was not progressive. However, the rise certainly took place. The Carolingians were warriors. They could put down resistance at home and extend Frankish power further afield; over the Rhine into German lands, into northern Italy, and into Aquitaine as conquerors both of independent Aquitanian rulers and of Arab invaders of the Rhône valley. This last was the special achievement of Pippin III, who stands out as a military commander of the first rank. Here, if anywhere, contemporaries could identify a kingly role; a house that could extend its power so profitably was royal in fact if not in name. Who but God could ensure this triumph? In brief, each successive victory in arms was one more proof of a kind of Christian miracle. This at least contemporaries could see. Franks had been bountifully supplied with *gesta Dei* since the time of Clovis, and their chroniclers and liturgists and poets were at hand to reassure them of the same. Here was one more instance of God's special concern with their destiny. So it could be represented.

All this sounds uncommonly cynical. But cynicism was not a weapon of the age. Plainly these first Carolingians were ruthless and brutal. They were also pious. Charles Martel was no enemy of the Church, however he may have disposed of its properties and offices in his time of need. Foreign missionaries, and in particular St Boniface, owed everything to his support. Still less hostile were his sons and successors, Carloman and Pippin III. Carloman indeed retired to Monte Cassino, thus following the example of a succession of Anglo-Saxon kings dear to Bede. He did not, as it happened, cease to be a factor in Frankish politics, but he had ruled and fought as if he were a king and had resigned his power under whatever pressures to end his days as a monk – again, as if he had been a king.

Pippin III is another and a larger matter. He had been educated at St Denis, was to celebrate his second inauguration as king there, and finally was to die within its walls and to be buried, as he desired, in front of the doors of the basilica. He had no closer adviser than its abbot, the Frank Fulrad. In brief, he was the man of St Denis. No other Frankish ruler, except Dagobert, had been so intimately associated with one monastic community. The winning of the support of St Denis was decisive in swaying the loyalties of the Frankish Church from the Merovingians to the Carolingians; without this, no amount of secular support could have ensured Pippin his throne. One can easily see how successive victories in the field and subsequent donations of land (often from the Church) won over secular magnates already impressed by the Carolingian way with doubters and rebels. But ecclesiastical support cannot so easily be accounted for. Among the bishops and abbots were good conservative Merovingian loyalists whose houses were replete with Merovingian grants and confirmations of property and privilege.

Pippin, like his brother Carloman, had inherited his father's commitment to missionary expansion over the Rhine while still mayor of the palace. He had also been involved from an early date in the reform of the Frankish Church – what is best seen as the domestic aspect of missionary work further afield. A series of councils show what this entailed. Carloman's two councils in Austrasia were followed by Pippin's, held in 744 at Soissons in Neustria. Its decisions were promulgated in a capitulary;[1] and the contents as well as the date make it clear that the reforming councils of the two brothers were closely related and convened to solve the same problems in the same way. Pippin styles himself *dux et princeps Francorum* but dates his capitulary as falling in the second year of the reign of King Childeric. No hint, then, that the days of the Merovingians were numbered. Twenty-three Neustrian bishops with their clergy were present, but also lay magnates. Boniface was attending the council of Carloman in Austrasia but in any case might not have expected to be present at a Neustrian council. What did reform entail for Pippin? His capitulary contains little or nothing that would have surprised an earlier generation: the true faith is proclaimed, a heretic is condemned, and the ancient observances of the Church are paraded. Each see shall have its legitimate bishop and there shall be two archbishops, at Reims and Sens (both already metropolitans), to whom their suffragans and others of the faithful could turn for judgement. More particular provisions are then made as to the duties and behaviour of bishops and priests. Monks and nuns shall live strictly by their Rule. Their properties shall be restored to them, at least in so far as to assure their subsistence, and rent shall be paid for properties not restored. It is to this last provision that historians have given most attention. Indeed it is important, but it is only one aspect of the general problem of disorder. The laity is not overlooked. Laymen are reminded to abide by the rules of Christian morality and in particular to shun fornication, perjury and false witness. Behind 'fornication' lie wide problems of social relations, including the nature of marriage, that are better reserved for later treatment; and 'perjury' covers the whole range of difficulties faced by men who could never be certain who the ruler of tomorrow might be. Reims and Sens failed, for the present, to achieve the status of archbishoprics; but Rouen, not mentioned in the capitulary, succeeded.

Three years later, in 747, the brothers planned a united council for both their principalities, though Carloman, hitherto the more active, seems to have departed for Monte Cassino before it met. What moved them to renewed activity was a collection of canons sent by Pope Zacharias from Rome. Pippin had asked for guidance on certain matters; and he had not asked Boniface.[2] In reply, the pope sends

---

[1] MGH Capit. i, no. 12, pp. 29–30.   [2] See Zacharias' letter, Tangl, no. 77.

excerpts from former canonical legislation (mostly from the collections made by Denis the Little) on the required topics: organization, the ministry of souls, illicit marriage. However, the pope has some personal decisions to convey. If bishops or priests wish to live, or to continue to live, under monastic discipline, he is in general in favour of their doing so; and further, he insists on the well-known impediments, natural and spiritual, to marriage.[3] He is giving a directive for the future and is not requiring a general inquisition into those already married.

No capitulary survives for Pippin's council of 747 but the correspondence of Boniface casts some light on what then and earlier had been decided. Boniface writes to Archbishop Cuthbert of Canterbury to tell him of these happenings.[4] The council had sent a profession of faith and unity to the pope; it had insisted that it was up to the metropolitans themselves to write to the pope for the *pallium*; and a synod was to be summoned every other year. Continuing supervision, then, was envisaged. Finally, the respective duties of bishops and clergy were once again specified. Boniface was quite clear what ought to be done. It will have been equally clear to Frankish clergy now rising to positions of responsibility, some of whom were present at the council. The pope wrote to thank Boniface and the bishops for their profession of faith and unity. Perhaps at the same time he wrote to thirteen of the secular magnates, possibly East Franks, giving them canonical instruction about the churches and monasteries built by them on their properties.[5] It cannot be doubted that in 747 Rome was much better informed on the problems of the Frankish Church than it had been a generation earlier. A steady relationship was being established – something very different from the spasmodic exchanges of the previous century.

As we approach the crisis that was to make kings of the Carolingians we should remember that the Merovingians were not guttering out like so many candles. They remained what they had always been: the ancient dynasty under which the Frankish Church had grown up. A little poem may remind us of the true state of affairs.[6] Though its date is uncertain, it seems to suit best the political situation shortly before 751. It concerns the celebration of Easter at the Merovingian court. Three final strophes describe the occasion as the poet himself witnessed it, and the second of these reads as follows: 'the priests sing hymns in the court of the king, and of the illustrious man who has suppressed all profane talk, remembering the splendour of the divine feast; for an

---

[3] Preserved as letter no. 3 in Codex Carolinus (MGH Epist. i, pp. 479–87).
[4] Tangl, no. 78.   [5] Ibid., no. 83.
[6] Ed. D. Norberg, *La Poésie latine rythmique du haut moyen âge* (Stockholm, 1954), p. 58.

unbridled tongue must burn in flames'. It is the illustrious man, the *potens persona* – who but the mayor of the palace? – who had done the suppressing; and there, in happy conjunction with his king, he sits to celebrate Easter. The poet sees no hostility, no jockeying for control, no *coup d'etat* in the making. Easter unites all.

Whether the *potens persona* was Pippin or one of his Carolingian predecessors there are no means of telling. But it was Pippin who in 750 sent two emissaries to Rome; one an Anglo–Saxon (Burghard) and the other a Frank (Fulrad). They were to ask the pope this question: should a ruler enjoying no power rightly continue to bear the title of king? How could one be a king without *potestas*? The question may not have startled a papal court familiar with the view of St Augustine and of Isidore that a king's title implies that he rules. The teaching of the Bible pointed in the same direction. In a word, the pope had been invited by two churchmen of very different backgrounds to pronounce the Merovingians an anachronism. And so, in effect, he did. How could he have done otherwise when he reflected how much the fate of the Frankish Church, and indeed of Rome itself threatened by Lombards, depended on the Carolingians? Certainly it was a matter of *potestas*. But what is most arresting is that the pope's opinion should have been sought. Plainly he would be most helped by a Frankish king conceived somewhat on the lines of the good king of the Old Testament. Others thought likewise.

It was no great step, therefore, for men to begin to see a new and powerful king as a New David, even a New Moses. Imagery of this sort makes its appearance soon after the change of dynasty had been effected. And what would a New David lead if not the columns of a New Israel? Frankish liturgies were not slow to make the connection, which is also to be found in the earliest Frankish *Laudes Regiae*, the liturgical acclamations of a priest-king that invoke the martial qualities of king and Christ alike; to be found also in the proud sentences of the prologue to the Merovingian Salic Law composed in Pippin's reign.[7] Pope Gregory VII, looking back on the part played by his distant predecessor Zacharias, commented that the last Merovingian was not deposed for moral defects but because he was not useful. A king must be suitably gifted; he must have *utilitas*. The Frankish clergy who supported the first Merovingians would have agreed wholeheartedly.

Our sources betray less interest in the unmaking of the ancient dynasty in 751 than in the making of the new one. They are of course sources favourable to the change that occurred. If any hostile sources survived, they would probably express more interest in alternative Carolingian candidates (such as Carloman, safely tonsured in Italy)

---

[7] Best text in *Legum*, iv, 2 (ed. K. A. Eckhardt, 1969), pp. 2 ff.

than in the Merovingians. One writer, bringing up to date the chronicle of Fredegar in the Carolingian interest, reports that after consultation with the pope Pippin was made king and his wife queen. This was done by choice of all the Franks in accordance with ancient practice.[8] To this extent Merovingian precedent was being followed. But there was something more: Pippin was then, at Soissons, consecrated by the bishops (probably including Boniface), and his magnates did him homage. A new king and a new dynasty were thus inaugurated in a traditional ceremony that included a new element. The Carolingian Royal Annals are terse but explicit about the eclipse of the Merovingians: 'Childeric, wrongly called king, was tonsured and put in a monastery.' Poor King Childeric and his son thus endured the ultimate humiliation for long-haired kings at the hands of the Church. They presumably ended their days in peace at St Bertin, comfortably remote from the areas of strongest Merovingian loyalism. The Church had no further use for the *rex falsus*. It needed a useful king.

Very little is known of the inauguration ceremony of 751. Consecration by bishops certainly implied the use of chrism for anointing. King-making of this kind was not unknown in Visigothic Spain and in Ireland, as the Frankish bishops may have been aware. But there were Old Testament precedents that could have influenced them just as much. Anointed kings like Saul and David stood in a special relationship to their consecrators, more particularly, as now, when the anointing was all that compensated for a specially dramatic case of oath-breaking to a reigning king. So the Merovingians were dismissed, quietly and suddenly, and plainly after careful preparation. They had not petered out.

Despite what the bishops had done for him, Pippin III (III because the third of his family to bear the name) felt insecure. There may have been local troubles. But a greater problem was Rome. The Merovingians had often fished in the troubled waters of Italy. An expedition to northern Italy, on whatever pretext, could bring back booty to Francia and at the same time divert the attention of warriors from domestic ambitions. The Carolingians understood this. Indeed, their involvement in eastward expansion and in missionary work had brought them still closer to the problems of Italy. By 750 the papacy could legitimately feel that Rome was threatened by the Lombards, as were equally the remaining outposts of imperial power in Italy. Only the Franks could save Rome. Such was the conclusion of Pope Stephen II, who succeeded Zacharias in 752. A secret mission was dispatched to Pippin to emphasize the menace that faced Rome and to beg for an interview with him. No doubt the pope would have preferred the

---

[8] Chron. cont., ch. 33.

intervention of the emperor, Rome's traditional protector; but for that
he asked in vain. Pippin, however, proved ready to see him on
Frankish soil. Two envoys, Pippin's brother-in-law, the duke Autcar,
and Chrodegang, bishop of Metz, were sent to Rome to conduct him
through Lombard territory to Francia. This they did, handing him
and a considerable entourage over to the Abbot Fulrad at St Maurice of
Agaune in the narrow Alpine pass south of Geneva. Pippin awaited
him at his villa of Ponthion near Châlons and sent his twelve-year-old
son, the future Charlemagne, to bring him to his presence. Thus
Charlemagne made his début in company with a pope. The procession
entered Ponthion on 6 January 754, Pippin holding the pope's bridle.
Negotiations followed. Pippin, as a result, undertook to oust the
Lombards from the exarchate of Ravenna and to restore the territories
and rights of the 'Roman republic' to the pope, though in fact they
belonged to the emperor. All these were now represented as the rights
of St Peter. It may well be that at this stage the pope exhibited for
inspection a Roman forgery, in which there may well be elements of
truth, known as the Donation of Constantine.[9] According to this,
along with much else, Constantine had endowed Pope Silvester I and
his successors with Rome, Italy and the West. The forgery bears all the
marks of a literary composition by some member of the Lateran staff
who knew how to make intelligent use of a much older composition,
the so-called Acts of Silvester. Plainly it is an early step, perhaps the
first, towards the birth of the Papal State as the future was to know it.
There is no certainty that the Donation was composed or produced at
Ponthion in 754; the first clear evidence of its existence comes some
twenty years later. However, the claims it makes were certainly such
as would impress the Franks in 754, and something to this effect was
certainly conveyed to them. The Lombards were alarmed, at least to
the extent of rescuing Carloman from Monte Cassino and sending
him north in a futile attempt to stir up the pro-Lombard element
among the Franks.

What Pippin promised on oath, for his sons and for himself, was to
accept the *defensio* of Rome as interpreted by the pope. First, Pippin
tried negotiating with the Lombards, while the pope retreated to St
Denis for the rest of the winter. The Lombards were not interested.
Rather reluctantly the Frankish magnates agreed with Pippin that an
expedition against the Lombards must be mounted. But before it set
out, the pope solemnly repeated the inauguration of Pippin and his
sons as kings of the Franks at St Denis. Pippin was anointed. What lay
behind this first royal unction in Francia is unknown and probably
unknowable. There were the precedents already referred to. From

---

[9] Best text by H. Fuhrmann, *Fontes Iuris Germanici Antiqui*, in usum schol. x (1968).

such sources, among which should be included the *Collectio Canonum Hibernensis*,[10] Pippin's advisers may have seized upon the value of royal unction for one who was no Merovingian. A St Denis monk, now or a little later, asserts that in addition to anointing the kings the pope 'forbad all, under pain of interdict and excommunication, ever to dare to choose a king of any other blood than that of the princes whom the divine piety has seen fit to exalt and at the intercession of the holy apostles to confirm and consecrate by the hand of their vicar, the blessed pope'.[11] Pippin's queen, Bertrada, was at the same time blessed by the pope. It seems likely that the blood that Pippin feared might supplant his was not so much that of the Merovingians as that of some rival Carolingian. The pope thus did rather more than repeat the consecration of 751, which from the Frankish point of view was sufficient; he did all that he could to ensure the succession of Pippin's heirs, not merely to the Frankish throne but to the protection of the papacy. They were the men of St Peter in a sense that no Merovingian had ever been. To make the point quite clear the pope also bestowed on the three kings the title of *patricius Romanorum*; that is, protectors of the Romans. Hitherto, only the emperors had made patricians and that without adding any particular denomination. This suggests that the emperor played no part in honouring Pippin and his sons, though he may have been aware of it. Thus fortified, Pippin ventured with his army into the Lombard plain. The Lombard king, Aistulf, capitulated and surrendered some of his conquests, but was soon back again, investing Rome. This brought Pippin to Italy a second time. Once more the Lombards capitulated, though on much severer terms. But it was not until 759 that Rome felt tolerably safe, by which time Pippin was in any case too preoccupied with expeditions into Septimania and Aquitaine to mount any more campaigns in Italy. Effectively he had done what had been required of him, and that without causing any final breach between himself and Constantinople. But Rome did not loosen its grip on the Franks. A Frankish presence at the Concilium Romanum of 769 is evidence of the process of drawing-together that began in 754. Years later, Charlemagne put together a great collection of papal correspondence with his grandfather, his father and himself. All that now survives is the first part, containing the papal letters only. It is known as the *Codex Carolinus*. The first forty-three letters are earlier than Charlemagne's accession and effectively cover the whole of Pippin's public life. The Carolingians thus saw their correspond-

---

[10] Ed. H. Wasserschleben, *Die irischen Kanonensammlung* (1885: repr. Aalen, 1966).

[11] *Clausula de unctione Pippini*, MGH SRM 1, i, pp. 465–6. For the extensive literature on the Clausula see Wattenbach-Levison, ii, p. 163, and Oppenheimer, *Legend of the Ste Ampoule*, append. 2.

ence with Rome as a record continuing from one generation to the next; and it begins with Charles Martel.

These years saw the upsurge in Byzantium of iconoclasm; that is, a reaction against the veneration of images of Christ, the Virgin and the saints, and more particularly by monastic communities. Whether or not such veneration had come to exceed its traditional bounds, emperors puritanically disposed felt the veneration of images to be sufficiently near to idolatry to impede any attempt at the conversion of Jews or followers of Islam. Furthermore their soldiers agreed with them. What ensued was widespread destruction of images and persecution of the monks who were their chief defenders. Other Eastern Churches and Rome were drawn into the controversy. The passionate rivalry between iconoclast and iconodule was to last well into the ninth century. Nor is this surprising. The implications of the quarrel reached the bedrock of Christian dogma, affecting even what was to be understood by the manhood of Christ. One should never underestimate the insecurity of orthodox Christianity in the early Middle Ages. From all this the Frankish Church, now intimately linked with Rome, was not immune. At Gentilly, in 767, it seems probable that iconoclasm was debated at a council the decisions of which have been lost. Charlemagne himself, a few years later, was to become deeply involved and largely misled.

As king, Pippin continued to govern, or at least to supervise, his Church through gatherings of higher clergy and magnates in council. One such meeting must have taken place soon after his accession, and seven of its articles survive to reveal what seemed most urgent to the mind of the *domnus rex*.[12] Widespread cases of incest preoccupied him and his advisers: a man should not marry his niece or his cousin or two sisters in succession or a nun. This was already well known from Merovingian legislation. Pippin repeated it and laid down civil penalties of varying severity for different classes of delinquent. Clearly such liaisons of deep-rooted Germanic practice were not going to be lightly abandoned, whatever the Church said. We do not know what the remaining articles of the council contained; doubtless questions of Church property were not overlooked. But what chance has preserved betrays the consistent preoccupation of the Frankish Church with issues of social morality, if anything more intensely under the Carolingians than under their predecessors. At his royal villa of Ver (or Verneuil) in 755 Pippin held another council, and of this we do know the decisions.[13] Most of the bishops and probably the secular magnates were present. All that ought to be known, says the preamble, is to be found in the ancient canons; but what has been forgotten

[12] MGH Capit. i, no. 13, pp. 31–2.   [13] Ibid., no. 14, pp. 32–7.

has to be restated. The first group of decisions concerns the duties of the hierarchy: metropolitans, bishops, priests, monks and other clergy. There are two *ordines*, that of monks and that of secular clergy. Monks must live according to their *ordo* in monasteries and clergy according to the canonical *ordo* under their bishops. The king will keep a special eye on nuns. It sounds like the voice of Boniface, now silent for a year, but is probably that of his successor as archbishop, Chrodegang of Metz. It is also the voice of the king himself: 'but the lord king says . . .'. Then comes a group of decisions that resume earlier canons, notably those of Orleans in 538. They too are concerned with ecclesiastical discipline. The council is equally concerned that churches and monasteries shall retain enough property to meet the needs of subsistence. Beyond that, ecclesiastical lands granted as benefices to others shall remain strictly accountable to the king or to the bishop concerned. Finally, there shall be no clandestine marriages; even peasants must marry at a public ceremony. What this last entailed is anyone's guess. Pippin plainly meant to rule his Church through his bishops. Secular clergy directly and monks when necessary were to be subjected to regular episcopal supervision. The Carolingian Church was above all to be an episcopal Church. At the level of the diocese the Christian community could be controlled. What is new is the firm intention to make it work.

Once again, at Compiègne in 757,[14] the king and his bishops (but not those of the Midi) give their minds to that continuing solvent of social stability, the bond of marriage. What was to be done about marriages already contracted between parties who should not have married? When were such marriages to be dissolved? The bishops considered a wide variety of cases, some but not all turning on the question of consanguinity. Others were less straightforward but clearly arose from situations that actually occurred; as, for example, what should happen when a father violated his son's betrothed or when a husband found that his wife had been seduced by his brother. One senses the immediacy of the provision that if a vassal felt compelled to accept a certain wife as a condition of receiving a *beneficium*, and later regretted it, he might legitimately put away his wife and marry someone of his own choice. Or again, unwitting marriage with a person of servile rank was a ground for separation. But the consequences of separation were not the same as those of nullification or divorce. There were difficulties that defeated the bishops, however. A married woman might take the veil without her husband's consent. What happens? She could stick to her decision, says one clause; but another clause qualifies this: she might do so if her husband did not

---

[14] Ibid., no. 15, pp. 37–9.

summon her home. In a word, nothing has been decided. Attached to these decisions at Compiègne are found a further set of decisions on these matters, attributed to a meeting at Verberie.[15] They differ slightly and may have been an alternative draft. Papal delegates were present at Compiègne and there is a possibility that Italian usage in rules of marriage may have crept in through their intervention. We cannot be sure. What is certain is the deep concern of the Frankish Church, shared no doubt by the secular magnates who were also present. Behind it all must lie a simple social fact: a small landowner would not normally expect to move far from his locality. His choice of wife would therefore be limited to an extent that is difficult for us to appreciate. The chances of his wishing to contract a union, knowingly or not, with someone within the prohibited degrees (say, a second cousin) were correspondingly higher. One wonders that any sense was made of it at all.

One further council merits special attention. It met at Attigny in 762 or slightly earlier, and was largely attended by bishops and abbots, making a total of forty-four. Its decisions do not survive. What does survive is the text establishing a confraternity of prayer binding all those present.[16] There were precedents for something of the kind. The liturgical recitation of the names of the living and the dead reached far back into the past. In the more recent past both Bede and Boniface had borne witness to the practice. Plainly it had received some impetus from Anglo-Saxon *peregrinatio* to the continent; a man cut off from his former colleagues and friends would passionately wish to be remembered by them. However, the practice was not exclusively Anglo-Saxon. It was one thing for a religious community to remember its own founders, benefactors and brethren, and especially the royal kindreds whose protection was so vital, but another to embark on the programme of the clergy at Attigny. They formed themselves under Chrodegang's leadership into what the Germans call a *Totenbund*, a society of men bound to recite so many masses and psalms for the death of any one of them, their communities being equally bound to participate. They were carefully organized to carry out this rather complex operation and behind them lay the support of the king. Lists of names must clearly have been drawn up and distributed; and the intention would have been to keep these up to date. We may call the result a synodal *Totenbund*. The bishops of southern Gaul were not present, nor were those of Bavaria. However, a few years later, probably in 770, the Bavarian bishops made a similar arrangement at a synod held at Dingolfing under the aegis of Tassilo,

---

[15] See de Clercq, *Légis. Relig.*, p. 142.
[16] MGH Conc. ii, i, no. 13, and see K. Schmid and O. G. Oexle, *Francia*, 2, pp. 71–122.

the Bavarian duke, and probably under the leadership of Bishop Virgil of Salzburg.[17] These two associations, Attigny and Dingolfing, were to have deep impact on the future. Their example and their lists of names were to lie behind comparable arrangements of associations for liturgical commemoration of the living and the dead for many sees and monasteries. An early and very important follower was to be the abbey of Reichenau, whose great book of association survives in all its complexity.[18] The example not only of Anglo-Saxons but of the Early Church itself was the bedrock on which Chrodegang built. Nor can it have seemed alien to the Germanic mind, prone as it was to think in terms of confraternities – as, for example, of guilds and sworn friendships. Thus communities led by their bishops and abbots drew closer together; they were to know about each other and pray for one another. Least of all can this initiative have seemed alien to the mind of Pippin himself, who in 750 or thereabouts had made a gift of a fishpond to the monks of Flavigny, recorded, if we can believe the charter, on ivory tablets. The substance of the charter seems unexceptionable. Pippin adds that the monks should pray earnestly for him and for his family, present and future; 'and I beg that you should chant a psalm daily'.

Pippin turned to his Church, as any Merovingian would have done, for help in special emergency; as in 765, after a famine, when he ordered his bishops to arrange for prayers of gratitude for a good harvest. God had ordained the preceding famine and God had brought them fertility. Fertility was still a king's concern. On second thoughts, but quite logically, the king adds that all should be paying their tithes, whether they wished to or not. The copy of the king's letter that survives is addressed to Bishop Lul but other bishops certainly received it.[19]

Only towards the end of his reign was Pippin's subjugation of Aquitaine and the Rhône valley sufficiently advanced to enable him to give thought to the Church beyond Neustria and Austrasia (the Frankish Church proper). Indeed, it is in the last year of his life (768) that a capitulary deals with the South,[20] though its implementation was to rest with his son. The southern churches were in disarray, many of them having had to face Arab attacks from Spain. Bishops, abbots and abbesses were now bidden to resume a regular way of life, and in this and the general work of restoration they would be assisted by the king's representatives, his *missi*. Much ecclesiastical property

---

[17] Ibid., no. 14B.
[18] *Das Verbrüderungsbuch der Abtei Reichenau*, ed. J. Autenrieth, D. Geuenich and K. Schmid (MGH Libri Memoriales, nova series i, 1979) with an important introduction.
[19] MGH Capit. i, no. 17, p. 42.   [20] Ibid., no. 18, pp. 42–3.

was in the hands of laymen and buildings had been abandoned. Northern regulations about restoration of property would apply to the South. That is, laymen were to hold such property on the precarial basis, for a rent, so long as churches and monasteries retained direct control of sufficient property for their needs. There was to be no wholesale and outright restoration.

The name that most frequently recurs in Pippin's ecclesiastical decisions is that of Chrodegang of Metz; so much so, that it seems right to consider him in some detail. He belonged, like Fulrad and Gregory of Utrecht, to that class of educated Frank upon which the early Carolingians reconstructed their Church: efficient, energetic, ruthless and pious; and, as so often, a little probing reveals his connections with others – founders, abbots, abbesses, bishops – who, as a kindred with its associates, exhibited that spirit of confraternity that was a hallmark of the Carolingian Church. They worked together, consulted each other and prayed for each other. We know most about Chrodegang from Paul the Deacon's summary in his book on the bishops of Metz, written about 783,[21] and there is no reason to doubt his witness. Chrodegang was born around 712 in the Hesbaye, of aristocratic stock. His connection with the district, and especially with Liège, had important repercussions later on; for St Trond in the Hesbaye was a dependent monastery of Metz. A relative was Cancor, founder of the great monastery of Lorsch, and a brother was the first abbot of Lorsch. He was brought up at the court of Charles Martel, where he rose to be a referendary; thus a trained administrator. Shortly after Charles's death we find him bishop of Metz, at the age of thirty therefore, and at the very time when the reforms of Boniface were beginning to take effect in Austrasia. Whether, so early, they affected Chrodegang we cannot tell; for he does not again surface before 748 when with the support of Pippin III he founded the monastery of Gorze. Thereafter he accompanied Pope Stephen to Francia, as we have seen. His reward was the pallium and effective succession to Boniface as controller under Pippin of the Frankish Church. He was present at all the subsequent councils of Pippin's reign and died in 766.

Metz stood high in Carolingian esteem. A royal city, it boasted some forty churches in addition to the cathedral and several monasteries and nunneries. It was at least as important as Trier, the city of its metropolitan. The Carolingians' ancestor, St Arnulf, had once been its bishop, though his cult had not yet taken root; or, if it had, was a local affair. Paul the Deacon casts light on two significant documents emanating from Chrodegang. The first is what may be called his foundation-charter for Gorze in the neighbourhood of Metz.

---

[21] MGH SS 11, pp. 267–8.

His monks are not envisaged as missionaries with pastoral duties in the surrounding countryside but as strict followers of the Rule of St Benedict within their own cloister. Their role is spiritual. To ensure this, they are under the control of the bishop but would naturally enjoy the traditional autonomies of a Benedictine house so long as they behaved themselves. In the bishop they had a supervisor but also a protector. They were monks, and as such to be clearly distinguished in function from secular clergy such as Chrodegang presided over in his own cathedral city. For these last he composed a famous Rule.[22] Many of its provisions were borrowed direct (though without acknowledgement) from St Benedict's Rule, and this is something that will be found in no other regulation for Frankish clergy of the period. Yet much of it is not from St Benedict but from Chrodegang himself. It has a Roman complexion that hints at papal influence during Pope Stephen's visit in 754. It was nothing new that cathedral clergy should live in the *domus ecclesiae* under their bishop and archdeacon; Merovingian councils had sometimes insisted on it. The usage had clearly fallen into desuetude. Chrodegang revives the practice for Metz. His clergy must live as the ancient canons prescribed; indeed, they are *clerici canonici* bound to the service of their cathedral. They were to become an important feature of the Carolingian Church – more important than modern concentration on Carolingian monks would suggest. Years later, one can watch Bishop Aldric of Le Mans reorganizing his cathedral canons much after the model of Chrodegang. Chrodegang provides in detail for their common life and their duties, and means to supervise them personally when at home in Metz. But he casts his net a little wider to include, for certain purposes, the clergy of the city and suburbs who do not live in the building attached to the cathedral. All are drawn in, though not all in the strict manner enjoined for those who serve the cathedral. Here and there in his Rule Chrodegang refers to Roman usage, to what was practised in Rome – the *mos Romanae ecclesiae* or some such words.

The Roman slant of Chrodegang's thought is most clearly marked in his liturgical provisions. It was for the correct and regular celebration of the Divine Office that a community of trained clergy was required. It was for this that the relics of Roman martyrs were brought to Metz. Paul the Deacon records that it was Chrodegang who introduced Roman chant, *Romana cantilena*, to Metz, where it should be practised as it was in Rome. Here then is deliberate borrowing of the Roman liturgy by a Frankish bishop. It looks as if the initial fervour did not outlast Chrodegang, at least if Paul the Deacon was right about Metz in his own day; but Metz certainly became the most significant

[22] Mansi, *Sacrorum conciliorum nova et ampliss. coll.* xiv, pp. 313 ff. Also PL 89, cols. 1059–1120.

centre for the propagation of liturgical music in Carolingian Francia. One sees that Chrodegang's episcopal preoccupations were very different from those of St Boniface. Though a monastic founder, his sense of mission was most clearly revealed within the walls of his cathedral; for him, a Carolingian bishop must start there.

It remains to be asked how he got on with his two great contemporaries, Boniface and Pirmin; for these three men, so different in race and background, dominated the mid-century. As a monastic founder, Pirmin's reach was impressive. His personality was clearly more attractive to diocesans than was Boniface's. Starting with Reichenau in 724 in the diocese of Constance, he moved south to Chur on the eastern route to Italy and north into Basel, Strassburg, and finally Metz. Alsace, and particularly parts of northern Burgundy were his stamping ground. Chrodegang's predecessor showed no hostility to him; neither did Chrodegang himself. One may instance a monastic privilege granted in 749 by Bishop Heddo of Strassburg, a former pupil of Pirmin; it is witnessed by bishops of Pirmin's circle and also by some associated with Boniface; Chrodegang figures in the list. Heddo and Chrodegang are here the link between two circles. If Chrodegang appears to have been less active in helping Boniface it may only have been that Boniface's main field of work lay beyond Chrodegang's range of interest. Within Neustria, however, were bishops close to Pippin who were certainly in touch with Chrodegang. One such was the bishop of Meaux. When Pippin founded his monastery of Prüm in 762 it was from Meaux that he drew his first contingent of monks. Eugen Ewig, the closest student of these events, is of the opinion that Pippin's entire reorganization of the Frankish Church was made possible by the collaboration of Chrodegang, who in effect carried out much of what Boniface had foreseen but had been unable to achieve: the appointment of suitable bishops to sees long vacant, the restoration of diocesan organization, the re-establishment of ecclesiastical provinces and the first serious attempt at dealing with the shifting problems of marriage. What this amounts to is that under the leadership of king and archbishop the Frankish episcopate was beginning to think and act as a unit. Whether originally inspired by Boniface or Pirmin, bishops were conscious of their existence as a confraternity: *confraternitas* is to be a keyword to Carolingian churchmen, both secular and regular. Clergy of different racial origins were learning to pull in one direction. It was a precedent, sometimes overlooked, for the remarkable mixture of men who were to assist Charlemagne.

So much activity inspired or supported by the king and his friends should argue an interesting court-circle. No doubt it was; but we have little information to go on, and certainly none to justify us in imagining a court school. Pippin had been sent to Lombard Pavia as a youth, to be taken under the patronage of the formidable King Liutprand. There at least he would have seen with his own eyes what a sophisticated court-circle was like. His experience of the good things of Italy was thus not limited to what reached him from Rome. If he patronized no court school on a permanent basis he saw to it that religious instruction was available at court. Virgil of Salzburg spent two years there, and Pippin enjoyed his preaching. Round the king were educated clergy, some of them administrators of a high order. Their efforts were reflected in the quality of royal charters, which show improvement upon Merovingian charters and equally upon such contemporary charters as survive. Moreover, what looks like a juridical revival can also be associated with the court. This was the age of the refurbishing, or commiting to writing, often for the first time, of the national customs of some of the Germanic peoples. Their language was Latin, the drafting was the work of clerics, and the authority behind them was royal or ducal. Thus we have from the eighth century versions of Ripuarian, Alemannic and Bavarian custom, to say nothing of the much more elaborate legal codes of the Lombard kings. Behind Pippin we ought to see Liutprand, at least so far as a reissue of Salic Law goes. Law is closely associated with history. Charles Martel's nine-year-old son, Jerome, is reported to have written or copied a Life of his ancestor, St Arnulf; and the same interest in illustrious origins is exemplified in the Carolingian continuation of Fredegar's chronicle and in a different way in the curious *Liber Historiae Francorum* in which Francus, companion of Aeneas, leads his people from Asia to the Rhine. At a later date, Paul the Deacon was to confirm this link by seeing Anchises in the Frank Ansegisel. Such was the historicizing atmosphere that seemed congenial to the first Carolingian king.

But it was still the Roman link that mattered most, both to Pippin and to other Franks. Not only St Denis but St Riquier, St Vaast in the North, St Martin's of Tours in the West and Murbach in the East were among the monasteries which certainly sent representatives to Rome at one time or another. Grimoald of Corbie (a house already poised for its great career as a writing-centre) returned from Rome in 741 with books. Pippin's brother Remigius, bishop of Rouen, visited Rome in 760 to ask for a teacher of clergy in the Roman chant and also sent clergy to learn the chant in the Roman *schola cantorum*. Contrariwise, Italians found comfort in Francia, as had Venantius Fortunatus long ago. Willichar of Nomentana became bishop of Sens, and George of Ostia bishop of Amiens. This coming and going certainly involved books, perhaps especially liturgical books; and this, in part at least, betrays a general if unorganized turning to Rome. One well-known book may be instanced; that forest of symbols, the sacramentary of Gellone,[23] so called because it reached Gellone in the early ninth century. Its original home has never been determined, though some northern Frankish monastery – possibly Meaux or nearby but surely not St Denis – seems likely enough. It is a version of the Gelasian sacramentary apparently put together for use by a bishop; therefore a version of what was ultimately Roman. Yet it was not consciously its Romanity but its utility that caused its diffusion over the Frankish dioceses. It was helpful on the chant, the *ordo psallendi*, the rite of baptism and the mass. To his Gellone sacramentary the first scribe, whose name was David, added illustrations; vivid abstractions, sketches of animals and birds, a mermaid or so, portraits of saints and clerics and a repulsively realistic nobleman – a true *homo utilis*. Altogether the book looks like what it is: a barbaric adaptation, at who knows how many removes, of a liturgical contribution that had drifted over the Alps from Rome to the Franks. Let it stand for the provincial aspect of that romanizing drift of which Chrodegang and Fulrad were the sponsors.

The hairy nobleman in the sacramentary is a salutary reminder that the substance of the Frankish Church (as of any Church) was the laity. Warriors surrounded the king, himself a warrior. Their religion there-fore was martial in flavour. Bishops, too, were warriors. The Church had long insisted that clergy were not to fight or to bear arms. In the eighth century, however, there comes a change. Ordinary clergy were still not to fight but the higher brethren, bishops and abbots, were implicitly exempted from the canonical prohibitions. The distinction was made clear by the synod of Soissons in 744. Pippin expected his bishops and abbots to raise contingents for war; and still more so did Charlemagne. Boniface, outraged at the exploits of the warrior-bishop Milo, would not have approved; but Pippin could not do without the military service of the great ecclesiastical landlords; nor do we know that they were unwilling to fight beside their secular kins-men. The turning to Rome does not, then, imply a retreat from arms.

We know that Charlemagne was to follow Pippin and can see, as did Charlemagne himself, that the father laid the foundations on which the son was to build. Pippin may not have envisaged things so clearly. In many ways he seemed to look back to the palmy days of the Merovingian Church. There was an air of insecurity, even a con-sciousness of impermanence, about his efforts. Only in building can

---

[23] For a fresh treatment of Gellone see B. Moreton, *The Eighth-Century Gelasian Sacramentary* (Oxford, 1976), *passim*. For its illustrations, B. Teyssèdre, *Le Sacramentaire de Gellone* (Toulouse, 1959).

one infer that the first Carolingians expected their work to last. There were beginnings here that were not to be reversed, and at least one aspect of them can be associated with Chrodegang. The introduction of Roman chant and of regular life for canons serving a cathedral church affected ecclesiastical architecture at Metz and elsewhere in Francia. Monasteries too were affected, perhaps even a little before Chrodegang's time if the regularly-planned claustral buildings at Manglieu, near Clermont, can safely be dated to about 700. More important was the layout of the church and monastic buildings round a quadrangle that appeared at Lorsch in 763; for this certainly was influenced by Chrodegang. It was to be the classic shape of the medieval monastery. The extension and re-designing of crypts to give the faithful easier access to relics is also apparent by the mid-eighth century, as at St Viâtre and equally at St Denis; and in this, Roman influence is very clear. The visit of Pope Stephen in 754 may well have left an architectural as well as a liturgical legacy to the Frankish Church. At Jouarre[24] can still be seen the most remarkable proof of the spirit of change. Here lay the body of the first Merovingian abbess, Theudechildis. By the middle of the eighth century she was venerated as a saint. Her tomb was then moved to the centre of the crypt and the church above was re-designed to allow access to the faithful. The tomb was surmounted by a cenotaph with a long inscription and the west wall of the crypt magnificently decorated with tiles, somewhat after the manner of the later *Torhalle* at Lorsch. The architect had taken a decisive step away from the plan of the traditional Roman *confessio* towards the developed Carolingian crypt, such as may still be seen at Soissons, Auxerre and Flavigny. But to return to the cathedrals: the clearing of ground and the erection of permanent buildings for canons in the heart of cathedral cities may best explain the large areas within such cities that were later to be available for the construction of the great medieval cathedrals. It is almost always unsafe to think of architectural change in terms of reigns, but at least it is clear that the major changes associated with Charlemagne's reign had their beginnings under his father. Already the influence of Rome and, distinct from Rome, of Lombardy can be discerned here and there in the planning and even in buildings that we can still see. When we consider the magnificent book-illustrations of Charlemagne's Church we should not lose sight of a harbinger: in 754 – perhaps a coincidence – the scribe Gundohinus completed at *Vosevium* (unidentified) a Gospel book made to the order of a lady, Faustina, and a monk, Fuculphus.[25] Its illustrations are something new in Frankish art and plainly derive

[24] See La Marquise de Maillé, *Les Cryptes de Jouarre* (Paris, 1971).
[25] See Hubert, Porcher and Volbach, *Caro. Art,* pp. 71–4.

from Lombard models. It has rightly been seen as standing at the birth
of Carolingian book-painting. But, as with painting so with architecture: the beginnings lie in the generation before Charlemagne.
They are scattered and equivocal but leave a strong impression that a
warrior-king beset by political difficulties could still feel his way
towards a new interpretation of the Church while doubtless believing
that he was resurrecting the past.

XI

CHARLEMAGNE

i. The Metropolitan Line

Of Charlemagne we know more that is true, and more that is untrue, than of any other early medieval ruler. Not long after his death, Einhard wrote a terse and masterly account of his life and reign (both long by medieval standards) that set the old man in the context of approved imperial comportment as seen by the Roman historian Suetonius in his *Lives of the twelve Caesars*. This was something new.[1] With certain prudent omissions, Charlemagne could be seen quite comfortably as a successful warrior replete with the expected virtues. The picture is substantially true. But there was a difference: Charlemagne was an ardent Christian. It would have been easy for Einhard to cast him in the mould of a saint, such as we can read of in many a conventional Carolingian saint's Life. But this he did not do. His emperor is a secular figure going about his proper business as warrior, judge and counsellor; but a secular figure that rules a Church and lives a Christian life. In many respects Einhard's Charlemagne is like his father, whom he greatly admired. The fact that it was Charlemagne and not Pippin who merited such a biography points less to changed circumstances than to a real difference in standing between the two men.

Charlemagne's unprecedented series of conquering campaigns, stretching over thirty years and more, cast a lurid light on secular Christianity as understood by Franks.[2] Every campaign was embarked on for what we should call political reasons; yet most of them wear a decisively religious aspect. Those least obviously religious in intent involved the defence of outlying territories from marauders and the establishment of marches under military command. Such were his operations on the Breton frontier, northern Spain and Bavaria, though the annexation of Bavaria, a Christian duchy in close contact with Rome, led inevitably to Carolingian assumption of Bavarian missionary work among the Carinthian Slavs to the east. The subjugation of the Frisians wore a distinctly religious complexion; no Carolingian settlement of a conquered people led to more fiercely anti-pagan

[1] Of the many editions the best remains O. Holder-Egger's revision of Pertz and Waitz, MGH SRG in usum schol. (1911).

[2] The Carolingian annals, and particularly the Royal Annals (*Annales Regni Francorum*), are the main source of information.

measures.[3] These, however, seem to have been imposed at a late stage in the settlement. Since at least the time of Willibrord, missionary churches had struggled hard for life in Frisia. Contact with Frankish forces had never been sufficiently reliable to discourage sudden changes from acquiescence to hostility among the Frisian chieftains, often supported by their Saxon and Danish neighbours. Several Lives of missionary saints of the ninth century bear witness to the difficulty of establishing firm outposts north of Utrecht, or even Antwerp. The dangers that faced Willibrord continued to face his successors in Charlemagne's day. One such was Liudger, a Frisian by birth and a pupil both of Bishop Gregory at Utrecht and of Alcuin at York. His biographer, Altfrid, writing in the 840s,[4] describes a career that must have been characteristic of many who undertook the northern mission towards the close of the eighth century. Parallels with the experiences of Willibrord show that Altfrid had access to Alcuin's biography of Willibrord without affecting the likelihood that what Liudger did must almost inevitably have followed the main lines of Willibrord's career. Thus we find Liudger embarking on a mission of idol-destruction and settling down hopefully with his companions among the northern Frisians; but only to see his work ruined by the rising of the Saxon Widukind, who invaded Frisia, 'deflected the Frisians from God's ways, burnt their churches, drove out God's servants and compelled the Frisians to relinquish Christ and sacrifice to idols, as far as the river Vlie'. The expelled Liudger then visited Rome and reached Monte Cassino where he learnt St Benedict's Rule, which he later instituted in his own monastery at Werden on the Ruhr. His fame now reached the ears of Charlemagne, who gave him a teaching mission within five Frisian districts. This as usual involved the destruction of idols. Again at Charlemagne's behest he paid a visit to Heligoland on the confines of Frisia and Denmark. Willibrord had been there before and had infuriated the Frisian Radbod by defiling the sanctuary of the god Forseti. Liudger did more: he actually destroyed the sanctuary, built a church and baptized the inhabitants. This of course led to a reaction, though the priest whom Liudger left behind him is said to have taught among the Frisians for many years. As for Liudger himself, Charlemagne chose him as first bishop of the newly-subdued Westphalian Saxons, with his see at Münster. There he seems to have remained for the rest of his days, destroying idols, building churches, ordaining priests and baptizing. All in all, Altfrid leaves a bald account

[3] Ed. K. A. Eckhardt, *Germanenrechte* 2, iii (1934). See the comments of R. Buchner in Wattenbach–Levison, Beiheft (1953), pp. 42 ff.

[4] Ed. W. Diekamp, *Die Vitae Sancti Liudgeri* (Die Geschichtsquellen des Bistums Münster 4, 1881).

of a heroic life of mission among outraged pagans. Liudger not only survived: his work survived too. Such men made possible the Carolingian mastering of outlying peoples.

The long series of campaigns designed to quell Saxon resistance brought Charlemagne face to face with pagans who had been raiding Frankish outposts in central Germany, and even as far west as the Rhineland, for generations. There were not many years between his accession in 768 and his death in 814 when he was not preoccupied with the Saxon menace. Each Saxon campaign opened up wider problems of defence in depth and of conversion as a weapon of subjugation. Charlemagne's first campaign of 772 was a reprisal raid of a familiar type, deeply though he penetrated Saxon territory. But he did destroy the Irminsul, the tree trunk that supported the Saxon heaven, much as St Boniface had once destroyed the sacred Donar Oak at Geismar; and he further embarked on a course of mass-baptism that led to endless Saxon reprisals against Frankish mission posts. Thus military occupation and forced conversion went hand in hand. To the Franks, then, no pacification of hostile peoples seemed possible until those peoples spoke the same religious language and accepted the moralities of dealings as between Christians. King Alfred was to face his Danish enemies in the same spirit. The destruction of a Frankish army in 782 led to more serious counter-measures. After a victory at Verden near the Aller Charlemagne massacred 4,500 prisoners, perhaps in reprisal for the killing of some of his trusted friends, or perhaps as a sign that fire and sword were necessary concomitants of Frankish Christianity. Their leader, Widukind, got away; he had escaped to the Danes or *Nordmanni* as the Royal Annals call them. Three years later he surrendered and was baptized at Attigny. His people were subjected to draconian measures of control, summed up in a *capitulatio de partibus Saxoniae*.[5] It leaves nothing unsaid. The first clause sets the tone: 'let the churches of Christ now built in Saxony and dedicated to God's service receive not less but more, and more surpassing, honour than had the sites of idol-worship'. Death will be the penalty for any kind of attack on a church; for ignoring regulations for observing Lent; for killing a cleric; for burning the dead; for refusing or avoiding baptism; for plotting against Christians; for breaking faith with the king. Moreover, tithes shall be paid to the churches and clergy. There is much more to the same effect. To us it seems obvious that Christianity thus imposed could only lead to further rebellion – which indeed is what happened. To Charlemagne and his advisers things looked otherwise. A few voices only were raised in warning,

[5] MGH Capit. i, no. 26, pp. 68 ff.

Alcuin's among them. After a further decade of revolts and suppressions a milder capitulary was promulgated in 797.[6] The agreement of the Saxon chieftains was sought to its terms and the normal Frankish penalties of compositions and fines replaced the blanket-coverage of the death penalty. But not even this pacified the Saxons of remoter areas, particularly those of the north in touch with the Danes. Another six years of trouble led to the most savage of all solutions: mass deportation of Saxon communities for settlement in territories where constant supervision was possible. Now at last the Saxons could be said to be subjugated, though not without leaving much trouble for the future. The role of the Church had been critical. Paganism had been identified as lying at the heart of Saxon aggression though in fact it had lain more obviously at the heart of resistance. It was a large, simple target. Charlemagne personally inspired the terrible use of Frankish religion as an instrument of suppression; but others – bishops, clergy and monks – were his willing lieutenants in the field. They suffered for their faith. This is what the Frankish churchmen were like, once they saw a good, clear pagan target. What is astonishing is that the Saxons settled down to make the best of a bad job. Clearly there were material advantages to be had from living under Carolingian control. Their *Poeta Saxo*, writing at the end of the ninth century,[7] could represent the Saxon nobles as deeply loyal to the Carolingians and grateful for their conversion; and it is certainly true that Saxon nobles were stout supporters of the East Frankish Carolingian kings throughout most of the ninth century. They belonged, now, to the *populus Christianus*; heirs, like the Franks themselves, to a culture that was not rooted in German forests. Not for the *Poeta* the boring details of the painfully slow process of the conversion of Saxon yokeldom as it must actually have happened.

Even more critical for the development of Charlemagne's Christian empire were his relations with the Lombards and Rome. Like other northern rulers before and after him he found himself drawn into the affairs of the Lombard plain and thus to Rome and to the south. His control of Bavaria might alone have necessitated this: but in fact it was the papacy that involved him ever more deeply in Italian politics. Here he was heir to his father's commitments. As anointed king and Roman patrician he inherited obligations to Rome that he was not to be allowed to forget. Two years after his accession he had married the daughter of the Lombard king Desiderius. The match had apparently been engineered by his mother. The new pope, Hadrian I, hard-pressed by Lombard incursions into papal territory and well aware of Lombard intentions to control the papacy itself, was dismayed.

---

[6] Ibid., no. 27, pp. 71 ff.   [7] MGH Poet. iv, pp. 7 ff.

Charlemagne decided to break with the Lombards and as a first step, in 772, repudiated his Lombard wife; a risky decision since Desiderius held prisoner the young sons of Charlemagne's late brother and co-ruler, Carloman. A revolt in Francia was not unlikely. There was no question here of obvious political gain to Charlemagne; rather the reverse. What he so clearly appreciated was the dependence of his rule · in the eyes of Frankish churchmen on loyal implementation of solemn undertakings made to Rome by his father. For his part, Hadrian barricaded the gates of St Peter's and sent urgent messages north for immediate help: how, he asked, could the king delay any longer to follow the example of his father? It was not Hadrian personally who feared danger: he feared for St Peter. Charlemagne now intervened with two army groups and by June 774 had reduced Desiderius to the point of submission. Unlike Pippin, he remained to see that the submission was permanent. He assumed the Lombard crown, styling himself *rex Francorum et Langobardorum*. Not only the Lombard provinces but their cities also, and especially Pavia and Verona, were to remain in his hands; and this was to have some significance for the development of his religious and cultural plans within Francia.

Charlemagne now paid his respects to the pope, who received him in Rome as became a patrician. Twice he was received within the city with great pomp. The occasion was a religious one: the king had come in person to the tombs of the apostles, and not without some fear for his safety. The two men proceeded to ratify in a formal manner the engagements entered into by their predecessors in 754. According to the papal account, which is all we have,[8] the precise limits of the territories to be restored to the papacy were agreed on; namely, whatever the Lombards had formerly seized, including the imperial territory of the exarchate of Ravenna. The archbishop of Ravenna, however, had no notion of submitting to papal control within the former exarchate; nor did Charlemagne remain in Italy to see that the terms of his agreement with the pope were carried out. He had more urgent business to attend to on the Saxon frontier. Hence a series of angry letters from Hadrian: why was not the king still in Italy to ensure the full restoration of papal property? Why was the Church of Rome, his spiritual mother, thus humiliated and why were their common enemies mocking the papacy? In so far as the Frankish masters of Lombardy concerned themselves with local affairs it seemed to be to the detriment of Rome. How very unlike the behaviour of Constantine of sacred memory!

In 780 Charlemagne found time to be back again in Pavia for

---

[8] *Liber Pontificalis*, i, p. 498 (ed. L. Duchesne, Paris, 1886–92).

Christmas, and in the following spring paid a visit to Rome to celebrate Easter. The occasion was taken by the pope to bestow royal
unction on the king's two younger sons, Pippin and Louis, the former
receiving the title of *rex in Italiam* and the latter *rex in Aquitaniam*.
Whatever Charlemagne may have intended Pippin to do in Italy, it
plainly did not include the restitution of all papal properties annexed
by the Lombards and now in Carolingian hands; and this the pope
soon noted, with mounting bitterness. Charlemagne wished to have
no further trouble with Italy. Yet in 786 he was back again in order to
subdue the southern Lombard duchy of Benevento. This time the
pope obtained some territorial concessions, though not nearly what he
demanded. It was now clear to him that one Lombard king was much
like another, whatever his nationality. One could hardly claim that the
special spiritual relationship between Rome and the Carolingians was
making any difference to the way in which a Carolingian conqueror of
Italy behaved. The pope could go on protesting at the difficulties and
injustices to which his properties and agents were subjected, but the
fact remained that he was simply Charlemagne's man. This was what
Frankish protection entailed.

At the moment of Pope Hadrian's death on Christmas Day 795
Charlemagne was clearly master of the western world; Italy was his,
all the Saxons except those of the extreme north were subjugated, the
western areas of the Slav world had been penetrated, and even the
Avars had been defeated. The new pope, Leo III, was no Hadrian; he
saw the world as it was and submitted to his master, who sent him a
famous letter of congratulation, presumably composed by Alcuin
who preserved it,[9] but certainly expressing the king's views. He
grieves for his dearest father Hadrian but welcomes Leo; herewith
some presents actually intended for Hadrian; let Leo rest assured that
the *pactum* between Hadrian and himself will be renewed. Then comes
an interesting little lesson, which is consequential upon the *pactum*:

My task, assisted by the divine piety, is everywhere to defend the Church of
Christ – abroad, by arms, against pagan incursions and the devastations of
such as break faith; at home, by protecting the Church in the spreading of the
Catholic faith. Your task, holy father, is to raise your hands to God like
Moses to ensure the victory of our arms. Helped thus by your prayers to
God, ruler and giver of all, the *populus christianus* may always and everywhere
have the victory over the enemies of his holy name, and the name of Our
Lord Jesus Christ resound throughout the world. May your prudence adhere
in every respect to what is laid down in the canons and ever follow the rules of
the holy fathers. Let the sanctity of your life and words be a shining example
to all men.

[9] MGH Epist. ii, no. 93, pp. 136 ff.

In brief, the king will fight for the faith and the pope will pray and give a good personal example. The beneficiary will be the *populus christianus*; and it is this rather than the not unexpected division of function between king and pope that is too easily overlooked. Charlemagne now ruled over many peoples. What held them together was that they were potentially or in fact a *populus christianus*. Angilbert, bearer of the letter, was further instructed how to emphasize its message. The pope's was no passive role. On the contrary, he was to be very active in rooting out simony everywhere in the Church and was expected to govern it and to observe the highest standards in his own behaviour. Thus he would be the king's *pius pater* and his particular intercessor with God. There was nothing cynical about this.

The king was right to feel some anxiety about Leo's capacity to behave as a strong pope should, for in April 799 he was attacked and manhandled by a gang of disaffected Romans. They accused him of a wide variety of crimes. Leo managed to make his escape to Charlemagne at Paderborn, the Franks' advanced base for operations in Saxony. Only the king could save the pope, and perhaps the papacy. Contemporaries saw this clearly. Alcuin summarized the situation neatly in a letter: the pope was a refugee, the Emperor Constantine V had been deposed by his own people, and the only hope for the *populus christianus* lay in the royal dignity of Charlemagne himself. At about the same time we find Alcuin using the phrase *imperium christianum* in the context of the western world. It described accurately enough the true situation; Charlemagne's nucleus of kingdoms and territories was in fact an *imperium*, a magnified version of the high kingship of an Anglo-Saxon Bretwalda. So Alcuin could have interpreted it, at least in a political sense. But it would be another matter to suppose that he was urging his king to assume an imperial title. The claim of the Empress Irene, who in 797 had herself deposed her son, Constantine VI, to rule as an emperor was certainly repugnant to the West, as was equally her support of those who, in western eyes, appeared to favour the worship of images in churches. It did not follow that Charlemagne was her natural replacement. More significant in western eyes was the total inability of any Byzantine ruler to intervene in Italy and do for the papacy what Charlemagne alone could do. Alcuin's point was clear as it stood: only one man had the power and authority to rescue the papacy, and that man already exercised *imperium* over most of western Europe. Moreover, that *imperium* was not merely political but spiritual in the sense that the king was God's chosen instrument for the establishment of a Christian society. Another, unidentified, writer who saw things very much as did Alcuin expressed his views in a long poem now known as the

Paderborn Epic,[10] and may well have done so in the critical year 799. It is a panegyric: Charlemagne has all the virtues, a hero, an Augustus, the light of Europe and so on. These are borrowed plumes. More significant, his new capital of Aachen is a new or second Rome, he is St Peter's instrument and the ironclad avenger of the insulted pope. But imperial crowns are not won by rhetoric. If any man stood to gain by Charlemagne's promotion to the imperial title it was the pope himself, whose position in Rome against his enemies would be immensely strengthened; for an emperor enjoyed legal powers that a patrician did not. King and pope probably discussed this at Paderborn before the latter was sent back home with a suitably prestigious escort.

The protector of the pope had clearly no option but to take yet another return ticket to Rome, to ensure that Leo was safely re-established and that his persecutors were punished. But what authority had Charlemagne to sit in judgement in Rome? And would that judgement cover the pope himself? Here were large areas of doubt. Arriving at St Peter's with much ceremony in late December 800, the king lost little time in holding a formal inquiry into the charges levelled against Leo. Our sources differ as to the details. It seems likeliest that the embarrassment of a judgement was spared the king by the pope's asseveration of his innocence – indeed, ignorance of whatever he was accused of. This seemed to be enough; and there were clergy present who would have been most reluctant to involve themselves in any judgement of the pope, which in their view would have been to judge St Peter. On the same day, his mind relieved, the king received an embassy from Jerusalem conferring on him authority over the Holy Places and city. What more was lacking to assure him that only from Byzantium could he expect opposition to his assumption of the imperial title? And what could Byzantium do beyond vainly proclaiming that there was no vacancy in the empire?

On Christmas Day, while at mass, the pope placed a crown on the king's head as he rose from his knees, whereupon the congregation, or part of it, acclaimed him as emperors were wont to be acclaimed: 'Charles, most pious Augustus, crowned by God, great and peace-loving emperor, life and victory!' Then, say the Royal Annals, the pope adored him: he was no longer patrician but emperor and Augustus. The papal source adds that he was also anointed, which seems probable enough. Thus there would have been three constituent parts to the ceremony: he was acclaimed by the people of Rome, crowned in a way that Franks could have understood, and anointed

[10] Karolus Magnus et Leo Papa, ed., with important commentary by H. Beumann, F. Brunhölzl and W. Winkelmann (Paderborn, 1966); and see the arguments of D. Schaller, FMSt 10 (1976), pp. 134–68 that Einhard may have been the author.

according to the usages of the Church. Einhard alone reports that the king was surprised, whether by the bestowal of the title or by the manner in which it was bestowed is unclear. Scholars love to debate the point. It seems that he must already have discounted hostile Byzantine reactions; nor does natural modesty sound much like Charlemagne, even in St Peter's. It is a fair guess that, if indeed he was annoyed, it was because the pope had presumed to take an active part in emperor-making. At all events, emperor he was – and must have known that he would be. He could now sit in judgement on the pope's enemies and condemn them for the crime of *laesae majestatis*; and his name could soon appear on papal coins and, together with the pope's, on papal documents.

But what difference did this make to Charlemagne? In political terms, little or nothing outside Rome. His remaining thirteen years were to be full of troubles, though not only of troubles. His administrative measures, his resolute pushing against the Slav territories to the East, the activity of his churchmen in Dalmatia, his handling of the Danes and his measures of defence against the first Viking raids – all these exhibited no slackening of grip, if also no very obvious connection with his new title. With the Byzantines he continued to negotiate, first with Irene and then with her successor, so that by the time of his death he could claim that his title had been recognized by the Eastern Emperor. Yet that title was seen as personal to him: it was not meant to hold his possessions together after his death. In 806 he informed his magnates that his possessions were to be partitioned between his three legitimate sons, and no mention was made of the empire. The deaths of two of them, however, left his son Louis, king of Aquitaine, as heir to all. He now decided to leave his title of emperor to Louis, and a council of his great men heartily agreed that such was God's will. On 11 September 813 he placed a gold crown on the altar of his palace chapel at Aachen and told Louis to take it and place it on his head. This he did. Contrary therefore to Charlemagne's original intention, the *nomen imperatoris* was passed on. And the pope had played no part in the matter. This surely casts light on Charlemagne's reported objection to the nature of his own inauguration in 800. In little more than three months the old man was dead. The inscription over his tomb at Aachen is revealing. What it proudly records is the length of his reign as king – forty-seven years – and the increase under him of the Frankish realm. An orthodox emperor certainly; but it was not of the implications of this that the author of the inscription was thinking.

One is bound to ask whether the *nomen imperatoris* made any difference to its first Frankish holder. The answer is that it did, if in a rather intangible manner. The tone of Charlemagne's capitularies and other pronouncements becomes noticeably more religious after 800. There is an intensity about him, an emotional pressure, that was less obvious before. He feels his obligation as God's chosen representative to care for the *populus christianus* committed to him, to watch over them, to protect the poor, to supervise his clergy. It was of these last that he thought when in 811 he made his will. Nearly three-quarters of his vast accumulation of treasure was to go to the twenty-one metropolitan churches of his empire, not to his heirs. Einhard gives the text in his biography of the emperor and alleges that Louis scrupulously carried out his father's behests in 814. It was salvation that the emperor was concerned about, his own and his people's. This is equally apparent in other respects; for example, in the decrees promulgated for the province of Lyon at a synod at Chalon in 813, when Charlemagne was present.[11] They range over the shortcomings and sins of Christian society – of bishops, priests, monks, nuns, and especially the laity. Confession is insisted on, of the sins of the mind as much as those of the body, together with fasts, almsgiving and the regular administration of the sacraments. The synod most gladly decreed that all should ceaselessly offer prayer for the life and safety, the soul and body of the lord emperor and his family, for the safety of the kingdom and the remission of sins. The emperor was searching ever more closely into the moral life of society and its spiritual consequences. It can be argued that an old man nearing his end would naturally dwell more on these things. But it is clearly the assumption of enhanced responsibility for the *populus christianus* since 800 that brings social shortcomings into sharp focus for him and causes him to see portents and omens of disaster if God were not swiftly appeased. Here, if anywhere, with his Church ranged behind him, Charlemagne most clearly betrays the meaning of *nomen imperatoris*.

ii The Inner Circle

Several Merovingian kings had had cultivated men in their entourages and so, too, the first Carolingians. This was implicit in the requirements of a writing-office and a staff to serve their private chapel. Such men could for a limited time form groups about the court and could feel a certain unity; and some clearly spanned more than one reign, thus ensuring continuity of a kind. Nor was this peculiar to the Frankish kings. The Lombard kings in particular did better. Their circle of learned men, secure in a capital city like Pavia, cannot have failed to impress visitors from the North. Pippin III, as we have seen,

[11] MGH Conc. ii, i, no. 37, pp. 273 ff.

relied heavily on the services of the abbey of St Denis and was able to attract clerics of standing to his court, not all of them Franks. To take an example: one visitor was the Italian theologian, Ambrosius Autpertus, of the monastery of St Vincent on the Volturno. A manuscript of one of his writings was at St Denis by about 770; and he may well, with his wide interests in teaching, preaching, and education of the clergy have been a forerunner of Charlemagne's reforms. Pippin was by no means always at or near Paris, though wherever he was some sort of instruction could be had at his court. Charlemagne thus inherited a court circle, both secular and clerical, capable of providing efficient service and schooled in the tastes of a king with a strong religious bent and a desire to push forward the frontiers of Christianity.

Charlemagne accepted a court and a tradition. No very marked changes took place at first. His early years were mainly devoted to campaigning, when he could count himself lucky to reside at any one *villa* or *palatium* for a few weeks at a stretch. There were, as before, favourite halting-places – notably Herstal – where he might hope to find himself at certain seasons and where, accordingly, he might assemble round him a larger court than usual. Its composition would be to some extent secular, since military planning had to be discussed at leisure. The secular element of the Carolingian court always counts. However, during these first years there were developments. The annexation of Lombardy in 774 had brought him in contact with a court more sophisticated than his own. Shortly afterwards he was in touch with the Italian scholar Paulinus, later patriarch of Aquileia, as well as with Beornred, known as Samuel, an Anglo-Saxon abbot who was to become archbishop of Sens. A later writer asserts that the first teachers at Charlemagne's court were two Irish scholars, which is not impossible since a steady Irish influence is discernible. Their presence cannot be ascribed to the cultivation of the court. Rather it was due to the evident signs of Charlemagne's growing political power. He could provide a safe refuge from the distractions brought upon Ireland by Viking attacks. On the other hand, the king was plainly open to outside influences. In the 780s he could attract scholars of real standing from Italy, such as Peter of Pisa and Paul the Deacon, both in a sense refugees from the turbulence of newly-acquired Lombardy. Better still, in Parma he first met the Anglo-Saxon Alcuin. Still he had no fixed residence in Francia where continuity of teaching could be assured, always supposing that such was his aim. The example of Lombard Pavia was clearly an inspiration to any would-be patron of learning. Moreover, Charlemagne had the means to support many learned men, for by the 780s he was a very powerful and wealthy king.

A patron of learning? There was much to be said for it. Scholars wished to be patronized. An Alsatian abbot had already dedicated to him a copy of a manual of grammar, and the great Bavarian Arn had left home for Francia. The men attracted to his patronage represented several learned interests: notably grammar, liturgy and theology. Masters in a wide variety of disciplines were available. Systematic instruction at court, such as had not been known earlier, was possible. Within the king's family-circle lay the prospect of respectable pupils from the aristocracy, and security of a kind hardly to be found in England, Ireland, Spain and Italy. What was new about the early court-circle was the influx of learned refugees.

This time of movement coincides with the appearance of the first important books that can be associated with the court. A certain Godescalc – not the later heretic – was attached to the royal entourage when Charlemagne visited Rome in 781. Not long afterwards, at the king's command, he copied a splendid book on purple vellum,[1] partly in a new script called minuscule though chiefly in the old-fashioned uncial. It was a Gospel lectionary of the Roman usage. The link with the papacy is clear. From Rome and from northern Italy the king may very well have brought books home to Francia. As Bernard Bischoff has pointed out, this is the likeliest route by which the court obtained the Graeco-Italian models for the court style of painting. In the same way it may have acquired the famous Gothic text known as the *Codex Argenteus* and the great Virgil manuscripts that were later distributed to St Denis, Werden and Lorsch. From Italy, then, Charlemagne already had men and books; as also from England, Ireland, Bavaria – and, quite soon, Spain. One begins to wonder if some plan were not formulating in his mind.

There is a possibility (again suggested by Bischoff) that around 780 Charlemagne sent out a general letter asking for books. If he did, the letter does not survive. But it would explain the gifts that soon began to reach him, some of them very uncommon books such as a copy of the grammar of Diomedes from the abbot of Masmünster. A court library was being assembled; books were obtained, copied and some-times distributed. The distribution in turn hints at what books the king considered should be in libraries used by teaching clergy else-where in his kingdoms. St Amand, Salzburg, Lorsch, Trier, Lyon, and especially St Riquier were recipients of books from the 780s. One should never dissociate the court enterprise from its roots in provincial libraries: there was always, and increasingly, contact and exchange. A list of books survives that may reveal what the court holdings were around the year 790. They are impressively wide in subject and

[1] See Hubert, Porcher and Volbach, *Caro. Art*, pp. 75 ff., with plates; CLA v, no. 681.

notable for the number of classical authors – and above all, poets. They include texts of Lucan, Statius, Terence, Juvenal, Martial, Horace, Cicero and Sallust; though not, oddly, Virgil, Livy or Pliny. The list appears to have been the work of an Italian scribe. We cannot tell how many of the books then at court he records; certainly there were many others at different times, and others again of which we have little or no knowledge. Of books actually written in the court scriptorium a vivid impression can be had from the catalogue of the wonderful exhibition of Carolingian manuscripts and other remains arranged at Aachen in 1965 and subsequently published.[2] It was the only occasion in well over a thousand years when all these books were reassembled in their original home. But again it must be remembered that Charlemagne's books were simply what he could lay his hands on. Unlike his heirs, he seems to have had no policy of acquiring associated texts.

At this point it may be well to say something of the secular classical holdings. It is to Carolingian manuscripts that we owe much of our knowledge of classical Latin authors. Because of this, we may easily conclude that Carolingian scribes and readers saw the classics as we see them. Certainly they were used as convenient sources for grammatical study, but equally there can be no question that there was a deeper sense of classical revival among men who reflected. Otherwise, classical texts would not have been dug out of provincial libraries and sent to court, often to be copied there for monastic and cathedral libraries. The famous *Puteanus* manuscript of Livy, for example, must have been housed in the court library around the year 800, and both Corbie and Tours obtained copies. It was the houses specially patronized by Charlemagne that seemed to do best in forming early collections of classical texts. Lorsch, near the Rhine, is a case in point. It looks as if by the end of the ninth century the long period of more or less haphazard acquisition was over and favourite authors established; and of these the list is long. It would be absurd to pretend that readers failed to enjoy texts that they took the trouble to acquire, to master and then to expound to others. It opened a new world to them. One cannot read Virgil or Horace and fail to be affected. Doubtless some kind of picture of Antiquity emerged in their minds. Charlemagne himself, brought up on a diet of vernacular heroic lays, would have listened to readings from some classical authors, and those that told of warlike and heroic deeds would have been entirely congenial to him. Perhaps he saw himself as the patron of a new Augustan circle. One cannot tell how he would have placed Antiquity in a chronological sense, nor how he would have related it to the world of Christian beginnings, let alone that of the Old Testament. Classical texts came to his court from

---

[2] *Die Ausstellung Karl der Grosse – Werk und Wirkung* (Aachen, 1965).

churches and monasteries, reaching him in company with other, more numerous, texts that were not pagan classics. Why, then, compartmentalize the two? Both belonged to the Christian heritage and had always done so. In the rulers of Antiquity the court would have recognized patrons of learning, fathers of their people, extenders of frontiers. They had been men with moral problems. Moreover, pagan and Christian pasts blended in emperors like Constantine, Theodosius and Justinian; and these could have made as great an impact as Augustus. Probably Charlemagne saw himself as heir to an undifferentiated series of rulers that started with David and progressed to emperors who were either prototypes or realizations of the Christian ruler. Pagan rulers, like pagan authors, could be re-interpreted in a Christian sense. If Pliny, Seneca and Cato could be seen as harbingers of Christianity, so too could Augustus and Trajan. We need not, then, be surprised that pagan writers were happily subsumed by the court and its dependants. If a text were judged suspect or unsuitable for general study, it was not because that text derived from Antiquity.

In 794 or a little earlier Charlemagne decided to make his home at Aachen. He was not to be there all the time but it became in effect his permanent headquarters. Aachen had obvious strategic advantages: it was near the Rhine and the German frontiers but at the same time accessible from central and southern Francia and a good route from Italy. It had been a Roman settlement and had also been used in Merovingian times. Apart from these advantages it boasted warm springs for bathing and good hunting. Whether it still had any buildings worth consideration is doubtful; but at all events Charlemagne decided on something new and certainly grander than what he found there. He proceeded to build himself a *palatium* (the foundations of which lie under the present town hall) on a scale presumably suggested by what he had seen in Italy; and adjoining the *palatium* a series of other buildings proper to a permanent court. The only one that survives is the chapel (now the cathedral), a solid building impressive in conception and splendid in execution of detail. Its bronze-work alone merited a chapter to itself in the Charlemagne *Festschrift* published in 1965. The inspiration of this building may have been Italian – perhaps in part San Vitale at Ravenna – though some features recall Carolingian work at St Denis and St Riquier. A case has been made for the revival in the Carolingian age of fourth- and fifth-century Roman architectural models, and specifically Christian models, in which context St Denis, Fulda and in part Aachen can be seen. But like all Carolingian buildings, Aachen is not a direct copy of anything but Charlemagne's idea of a royal chapel. Interesting features are the king's throne and the decoration of the vault (now replaced by a copy) showing Christ in

Majesty, conceived much as in court manuscripts. And thus, as Professor Bullough points out, the Divine Ruler looked down upon his earthly representative, the Frankish king; and the king, one might add, looked down from his throne in the gallery upon his subjects – or would do if he craned sufficiently forward. If he took, as is possible, any of his inspiration from the Roman Lateran, he confined the use of the word to one part of the complex, the building where treasure was housed. Such a windfall as the great Avar treasure that reached Aachen in 795 or soon afterwards would clearly have needed special accommodation. The king will have looked on his fine headquarters as in some sense a *Roma Nova*. Such at least is implied by the author of the Paderborn Epic. Here he could be at home, to bathe and hunt with his magnates and discuss business both with them and with the clergy. Here too was a home for a library and a school.

The first company of the king's learned friends were dispersing, though without necessarily losing touch with the court. Paulinus went off to Aquileia in 787; Peter of Pisa seems to have gone home before 790; Paul the Deacon had reached Monte Cassino by 787; Theodulf was bishop of Orléans before 797; and Alcuin retreated to Tours in 796. All these, then, were no longer permanently resident with the king when Aachen was enjoying its great period of productivity, though their mark upon it was heavy enough in the person of their pupils and successors who, unlike their masters, were often Franks. These included Angilbert, Einhard, Modoin and Aldric – and, among non-Franks, at least two Anglo-Saxons (Fridugis and Osulf) and an Irishman (Joseph). Frequent visitors to court were bishops trained by Alcuin: Riculf of Mainz, Ricbod of Trier, Arn of Salzburg and Franco of Le Mans. Most of the bishops and abbots who witnessed Charlemagne's will in 811 had been trained at court in a manner fitting them for important ecclesiastical posts elsewhere. This presupposes facilities for serious study and education. The fruits of these can equally be seen in the administrative documents issued in Charlemagne's reign – above all, in capitularies – which show a marked improvement in composition. The court chapel expanded to meet new demands on its administrative services under the supervision of an impressive succession of arch-chaplains.

What did the court understand by study and education? Primarily, the furtherance of religion at home and abroad. This involved teaching, as it always had. But the mere scale of Charlemagne's possessions argued agreement about what was to be taught, how taught, and from what texts of what books. Could one identify the pure sources of devotion? Such problems and their solutions will have emerged quite naturally in the minds of the men gathered round the king. The earliest of them were already accomplished scholars before they joined him, though they may not till then have seen what needed to be done. Charlemagne's own contribution may have been no more than an insistence on some very concrete principles, such as: clarity, order, reason and justice – all derived from God and none in isolation at all new.

The book of books to them all was the Bible, the book of Christian society and of life itself. All the books of the Bible, together with their commentaries, reached the clergy as the fruit of Graeco-Roman Anti-quity, in this respect indistinguishable from the pagan authors. For them all, God's purpose was revealed in these holy books, so that the *Renovatio* or *Restauratio* or *Reformatio* which they had begun to glimpse was also a *Revelatio*. Their Renaissance (and it is a perfectly permissible term) was a revelation of the pure sources of Christian life, in all their variety, granted to those who mastered the Bible. But the Bible was a Latin book. Latin therefore was a living language, not an intellectual exercise; the language of God, of Christ, of prayer, of liturgy, of psalmody and of the Fathers; in a word, the *Vatersprache*, the tongue of inspired communication, whereas the vernacular, the *Muttersprache*, was the tongue of common, everyday life. One senses particularly the veneration and love of the Carolingian scholar for the Book of Psalms. It comes out in a woman, Duoda, wife of Bernard of Septimania, in her manual of devotion composed for her young son William in the 840s.[3] William must above all else read and meditate upon the psalms; for in them, she tells him, all wisdom is contained and all things foreseen. Much the same emotional response was roused by the Book of Job, the account of a secular man's struggle with sin. Writings of this kind are highly introspective, requiring a man to look deep into himself and to face some basic problems of life. They set the tone for the Carolingian revival. It was one of immense seriousness.

To face the Latin Bible and the literature and liturgy of the Church one needed first to learn some Latin. The mastering of the elements of Latin by clergy was therefore the first priority in Carolingian educa-tion. How teaching was organized at court is not known: probably on an *ad hoc* basis. Alcuin indicates that certain groups existed at court – *sacerdotes*, *ministri*, *versifici*, *turba scriptorum*; but these were not in practice clearly differentiated. Whatever the arrangement, there were *magistri* as well as youngsters at court. This may not in any formal sense have differed much from what was done at York or Tours or Lyon. Scholarship as we understand it was certainly not the aim of instruction. Alcuin's object was fairly clear: to prepare young men in the liberal arts so that they could read and understand the Bible. The

[3] *Manuel pour mon fils* (SC, 1975).

end, in other words, was spiritual, and the means were the liberal arts. Grammatical grounding was thus vital; a grounding chiefly in some well-known texts, or parts of them. Not that the texts in themselves had no virtue. On the contrary, Alcuin saw them as a road to wisdom, to *philosophia*; and herein he differed not at all from the Fathers of the Church. Education in his eyes must have some practical shape and a philosophical justification, as it had once had for Cassiodorus. True wisdom, even when not specifically Christian, must reveal God's purposes. Alcuin refers to pagan philosophers in his correspondence, and significantly several of these references are in letters addressed to Charlemagne, who would have shared his enthusiasm for a New Athens in Francia.

It is possible that all seven of the liberal arts were taught at court, for which special manuals were prepared. It is possible; but it is chiefly in grammar that one has a clear idea of Alcuin's plan of instruction. How this affected Latin can be seen in the next generation of writers; for only after a good grounding in grammar could they have moved on to acquire that familiarity with books that they so obviously had. The art of reading widely was to have a direct bearing on improved literacy in the ninth century. So in the end one can see what Alcuin believed to be the objects of education, though not so well how in practice he set about it; and without question he was the chief *magister* of the court.

Alcuin includes *versifici* among his groups at court. Versifying in Latin was an accomplishment practised by men of widely differing specialities and tastes. It was a predominant occupation that one has to come to terms with. Carolingian poetry, whether at court or outside it, was abundant. Much of it survives and should therefore be taken seriously. Judged by the standards of the classical poets familiar to the ninth century, by no means all of it is of high quality; but some of it, composed by men of learning and intelligence, certainly is, and merits careful study. Poetry at court was composed in an atmosphere of comradeship: *amicitia* is a word that recurs. Not only Charlemagne but his whole family including the women was bathed in its warmth. Pseudonyms emerge from Alcuin's circle of pupils that indicate the familiarity of friendship. Not everyone had a pseudonym, classical or biblical, but many did. We know twenty-three of them and they were not confined to scholars and teachers, or indeed to court residents. Alcuin wrote a letter to Gundrada in which for the first time he addressed her as Eulalia.[4] He explained that this change of name was a mark of familiarity and goes on to point out that the Lord had changed Simon's name to Peter and the names of Zebedee's children to 'sons of thunder'. Charlemagne himself was referred to on occasion as

---

[4] MGH Epist. ii (*Alcuini Epistolae*), no. 241, p. 386.

Solomon or Moses or Constantine, but particularly as David. *Novus David* is significant of the role he saw for himself in his new Christian society. However, the importance of pseudonyms lies in the group they constituted: a closed society of people who passionately shared a common outlook. This outlook explains the nature of their efforts at versification.

Court poetry was of two kinds. First, there was panegyric, and a lot of it, directed at Charlemagne; and behind it lay a respectable tradition of prose panegyric for emperors.[5] An element of toadying was to be expected; and sure enough, there it is. The great patron was praised for virtues he was unlikely to have had. In fact he became to his panegyrists an idealized figure, a collection of royal attributes. Verse of this kind was circulated among admirers and formed a corpus in its own right, constructed according to acknowledged rules and welcomed as a vital element in court literature. An unknown scholar or someone doubtful of his prospects would naturally try his hand at it but so, too, did men of real standing, such as Alcuin or Theodulf. The circle of those at court, who drank and bathed and hunted and chatted with their patron and his family genuinely saw themselves as an élite, the fine flower of Christian society. And so with the versifying it becomes very difficult to distinguish mere toadying from a delight that sprang from being carried out of themselves by a living ideal.

It was in poetry, both direct panegyric and the occasional pieces that form an equally important part of it, that scholars could readily show their awareness of Antiquity and their skill in following classical models. A man who could persuade others that he had mastered the hexameter and the distich was entitled to be taken seriously, whether his models were strictly classical or fourth- and fifth-century Christian poets like Juvencus or Prudentius. Some Virgil and Ovid he might be expected to know. Alcuin himself referred to *vester Vergilius* in a letter to Charlemagne, who must at least have heard of the poet. In brief, poetry seemed a natural vehicle for expressions of praise, friendship or dedication. Philosophical and theological problems could suitably be aired in the form of verse-letters.

But sometimes poetry was used as a vehicle for satire. Thus in two great verse-letters Theodulf could paint a sharp, but not unrelievedly sharp, picture of the personalities of the court-circle.[6] Where Irishmen were concerned he could turn to straight invective. 'Hic Scottus sottus cottus trinomen habebit' is how, in an untranslatable phrase, he sums up the wretched Cadac, an Irish teacher whose sophistry and methods of biblical commentary infuriated him. Not but what Charlemagne

---

[5] Ed. R. A. B. Mynors, *XII Panegyrici Latini* (Oxford, 1964).
[6] MGH Poet. i, pp. 437 ff.

stuck to his Irishman, perhaps even giving him a bishopric. The same Cadac may have been the addressee of an elegant *planctus* or lament written on the death of Charlemagne. Theodulf's verse-letters, doubtless meant to pass from hand to hand, reveal rifts within the circle of *amicitia*. Of this there is further witness in a poem addressed by Theodulf to Hraban Maur, the *corvulus* or young raven when a boy at court. (In fact, the poem is meant for general consumption.) It is an elaborate composition, allusive and puzzling and full of bird-imagery for which there were classical models. The birds of the poem are the young scholars at court – the time is shortly before 800 – and what Theodulf is saying is that they are all a bit above themselves, too ready to irritate and gird at older scholars. They are owls, geese and so forth; and among them is a *cuculus* or cuckoo. One thinks naturally of Alcuin's pupil, the subject of his cuckoo-poem[7] and referred to in correspondence. Theodulf is satirizing a whole group of *corvuli*, birds specially associated in the Christian literary tradition with sin. One can imagine that Alcuin's pupils, brought up in the Anglo-Saxon tradition, might have spoken their minds about Frankish or Visigothic or Italian masters. There were limits to *amicitia*.

Yet another literary group associated with the court was the historians. The roots of court-associated historiography go back a long way, certainly as far as the first Carolingians. In the year 727 the chronicle known as the *Liber Historiae Francorum* was put together, possibly at the abbey of St Denis.[8] An Austrasian version, completed in 736, was appropriated and tacked on to the earlier chronicle attributed to Fredegar. To this was added another continuation made under more obvious supervision. The writer states, under the year 751, that up to that point the work had been composed by order of Count Childebrand and thereafter by order of his son Nibelung.[9] Childebrand was the uncle of Pippin III. The chronicle leaves no doubt that Childebrand's family actively assisted the early Carolingians in their rise to power. Here we have, then, a record of Carolingian doings as seen from their point of view. Though secular, it reveals something of the new view of kingship and a feeling for the qualities of Old Testament kings. A king should be a *Novus David*. The chronicle ends with the accession of Charlemagne and his brother Carloman in 768. Other chronicles, rather different from the short annals of an earlier generation, were now being compiled by religious houses. Charlemagne himself was not immune to this widespread concern to keep records of events. A set of Royal Annals (the *Annales regni*

[7] Ibid.   [8] MGH SRM ii.
[9] Ed. Krusch, MGH SRM ii; Wallace-Hadrill, *The Fourth Book of the Chronicle of Fredegar with its Continuations* (London, 1960).

Francorum)[10] was composed at court. It records expertly whatever redounds to the credit of the Carolingians and seems to have been the work of a court cleric with access to records and court memories; one supposes a chaplain or chancery clerk. The first section of these annals appears to have been written about the year 788. By 796, when the court was established at Aachen, a change of writer can be discerned, though not a change of objective; and another writer completes the series, as we have them, for the period 808 to 829. With each change the interests of the royal chapel and especially of the arch-chaplain emerge more decisively. We can be fairly sure that Einhard was not one of the writers, as has sometimes been claimed. On the contrary, he made use of the Royal Annals in his Life of Charlemagne. Neither was he responsible for the special edition known as the so-called annals of Einhard, put together some time after 801 and probably in response to a royal demand for a new edition that made use of extra material. Whoever composed them, the Royal Annals leave an indelible impression of how a Christian warrior wished his deeds to be seen.

But in one man at least Charlemagne had a historian of real stature. Paul the Deacon deserves to stand by Gregory of Tours and Bede as a major historical writer.[11] A Lombard from Friuli, he was brought up in the court of Pavia in the tradition of Late Antique grammar and also of theology. He accompanied the Lombard king's daughter to the southern court of Benevento, where he was composing verses and an abbreviated world history in the 760s, and a *Historia Romana* shortly afterwards. The Roman history was an improved text of Eutropius continued as far as Justinian's reign. In 774 he entered Monte Cassino and there composed a major commentary on the Rule of St Benedict. He felt himself to be an exile, one of the Lombard intellectuals with court contacts who had suffered from Charlemagne's annexation of the Lombard kingdom. His brother was taken prisoner to Francia and his whole family reduced to want. This induced Paul to send an elegy to Charlemagne begging forgiveness for his brother; and this he followed up by a trip to Francia which he imagined would be brief. In fact he stayed for several years, caught up in the first enthusiasm of northern court learning. To this time belongs his history of the bishops of Metz, written at the request of its bishop, Angilram, who was also Charlemagne's arch-chaplain. The history is also a justification of the rise of the Carolingian family, the success of which he attributes to the sanctity of their ancestor, Bishop Arnulf of Metz. Charlemagne must have been delighted, not least since it also justified

[10] MGH SRG in usum schol. (1895); R. Rau, *Quellen zur karolingischen Reichsgeschichte*, i (Berlin, n.d.).
[11] The best summary of his writings is Wattenbach–Levison, ii, pp. 203–24.

his freeing of Rome from Lombard oppression – something that Paul could only have attempted to describe as a convinced Catholic opponent of Arianism. By 787 Paul had returned to Monte Cassino but without losing contact with the Frankish court. His intense piety outweighed his sense of race; and to this piety we owe not only his commentary on the Rule but also a homiliary composed for Charlemagne and perhaps a sacramentary. Though a member of a humiliated people, he was able to see Charlemagne as the great initiator of restored Christianity in the West. It is a good proof of Charlemagne's magnetic power that he could conquer Paul the Deacon and persuade him that the overthrow of the Lombard kings was a kind of dreadful necessity imposed by Providence. This is not to say that Paul did not feel as a Lombard. He always intended to continue his Roman history to cover Italy up to modern times, which in effect meant writing a history of the Lombards in the context of their assumption of power in a Roman and Catholic province. His six books of Lombard history[12] end with the death of King Liutprand – that is, at the high-water mark of Lombard achievement and before the final triumph of the Carolingians. This may have been chance. There are thought to be signs that his powers were failing and that he died an old man, perhaps in 799, before he could complete his work. On the other hand, he might have found any further continuation an embarrassing job, exposing his divided loyalties. So his great history can be read like a work of resignation: he knows what the end of the Lombard kings will be. He composes an epic which is also an epitaph. If it is the product of any school, it is the product of the Italian, not of the Frankish; in other words, of the tradition on which the Carolingians themselves drew when Pavia and Verona were theirs. In this sense it belongs to the Carolingian renaissance. And also in another sense: Paul freely used oral Germanic material, and this involvement in the Germanic past was equally part of Charlemagne's thinking. It was all relevant to an immediate situation; how, namely, a new Chosen People, chosen by God, had arrived at a point where they dominated the Christian, Latin West.

But the type of the successful court scholar was not so much Paul as Einhard, and this because Einhard was a many-sided and above all practical man. A Frank from the Maingau born around 770, he had been employed for some time in the scriptorium of Fulda when Baugulf, his abbot, sent him to court early in the 790s. We know what he looked like. Men who knew him there described him as a little man, a *homuncio*, busying himself about the place like an ant. They add that

---

[12] MGH SRG in usum schol. (1878); trans. by W. D. Foulke, *History of the Langobards by Paul the Deacon* (New York, 1906).

there was a great soul in the little body; he was what the pupil is to the
eye. And we know his court nickname or pseudonym - Bezaleel; and
this is interesting. In Exodus, chap. 31, God informs Moses that he
had called Bezaleel the son of Uri: 'and I have filled him with the spirit
of God, in wisdom and in understanding and in knowledge and in all
manner of workmanship, to devise cunning works, to work in gold
and in silver and in brass, and in cutting of stones, to set them, and in
carving of timber, to work in all manner of workmanship', and so on.
This not only reveals what seemed significant about the young
Einhard to Charlemagne, namely his skill as a craftsman; it also
identifies more than one object associated with him and a general
group of objects that were symbolically important in court thinking.
Einhard was a craftsman first and foremost, not a scholar; though he
was also a scholar and teacher, especially after Alcuin left court for
Tours in 796. Indeed, Alcuin saw him as an expert in Virgil and
charged him to overlook Charlemagne's personal studies in literature
and mathematics. He was equally a student of Vitruvius, a theorist in
the arts of building and embellishment who could turn his hand to the
making of things, and conversant with Carolingian book-illustration
and its classical models. But first a craftsman. Charlemagne made him
overseer of his buildings and in particular 'overseer of the king's works
in the royal palace at Aachen'. That is, he was not the architect of the
palace but general superintendent with special responsibility for the
opera regalia, presumably the decorative features. Already he was
Bezaleel as well as a learned man and a trusted diplomat. In 806 he was
sent on an embassy to the pope, and in 813 was chosen by the magnates
to convey to Charlemagne their wish that his son Louis should become joint-emperor.

We know of two of Einhard's pieces of craftsmanship. Both were
liturgical, both were associated with the church of St Servatius at
Maastricht, and neither survives. What survive are partial descriptions, copies, and a later drawing of one of them. Einhard himself
describes the translation of the relics of SS Marcellinus and Peter,
which came to rest as fragments distributed by him not only to
Maastricht but to Mülinheim, (or Seligenstadt), Ghent, Valenciennes
and other places. The *Translatio*[13] was an important composition of the
author's maturity in retirement at Seligenstadt. It describes how
Einhard was provided with his relics by a Roman deacon, Deusdona,
who appears to have made a business of finding Roman relics for the
North. Among his other clients were Soissons (which stole part of
Einhard's acquisition) and Fulda. More significant is the *Translatio*'s
revelation of its author's extreme piety and total reliance on the

[13] *Historia translationis beatorum Christi martyrum Marcellini et Petri*, MGH SS xv, i. pp. 238–64.

miraculous intervention of saints for the benefit of those who housed and visited their relics. Einhard also made what is now known as his triumphal arch, an *arcus argenteus triumphalis* crowned with a jewelled cross, of which there is a later copy.[14] The whole complex, in effect an adaptation of the Roman triumphal arch, had this inscription: 'To sustain the trophy of eternal victory, Einhard, a sinner, raised this arch and dedicated it to God.' Its symbolism was heavy, for it embraced both the triumph of the Cross and Charlemagne's identification with Constantine. It must have been a very important product of the court workshop. The work was probably completed some time after the emperor's death and is thus evidence of the continuing activity of court craftsmen under Louis the Pious. Curiously, none of this is referred to specifically by Hraban Maur in his epitaph for Einhard. The nearest he comes is this: 'Look, in this grave lies a noble man. The name his father gave him was Einhard. He had a clever mind and a ready tongue, and was honest in his dealings and serviceable to many in his art. Charlemagne brought him up at his court and through Charlemagne he brought much work to completion.'[15]

Though contemporaries may have seen Einhard's greatest contribution as lying in the field of craftsmanship rather than of authorship, his *Vita Karoli Magni* written around 830[16] in his retreat at Seligenstadt is for us a momentous achievement of the renaissance. What is remarkable is that Einhard should deliberately have departed from the popular genre of biography, as represented for him in Sulpicius Severus' wonderful Life of St Martin, and turn to a classical model: Suetonius' Lives of the twelve Caesars. Some have seen in this a reaction against the monk-dominated court of Louis the Pious but there is no evidence of this. It seems more likely that his decision to depict the emperor somewhat after the manner of Suetonius on Augustus, Vespasian, Titus and Tiberius, rested solely on his experience that in the last resort an emperor was a secular figure: a warrior, a judge, a father of his people. An emperor's ideals should be Christian – and Einhard shows clearly that Charlemagne was committed to a political ideal that was theocratic – but his business had to be secular. He might, as did Charlemagne, live a pious life among his friends and family, attending divine service daily, but his Christian ideals – *magnanimitas, animositas, constantia* – were equally those of Antiquity. Therefore while giving an affectionate sketch of the man he had known at close quarters, Einhard was able to arrange the affairs of

---

[14] Illustrated and discussed in *Das Einhardkreuz*, ed. K. Hauck (Göttingen, 1974).

[15] MGH Poet. ii, pp. 237–8.

[16] Ed. O. Holder-Egger, MGH SRG in usum schol. (1911) and L. Halphen, *Éginhard, vie de Charlemagne* (Paris, 1947).

Charlemagne's life under the moral headings by which they should be assessed. One could call the resulting picture secular-moral. And it was a resounding success. Lupus of Ferrières was delighted when he first read the book, and soon after 840 Walahfrid Strabo produced what in effect was a critical edition, divided into chapters and adorned with a prologue. Even today there remain more than eighty manuscripts of the work, quite apart from the innumerable borrowings from it made by chroniclers and historians (for instance, Asser). One has only to compare it with the *Gesta Karoli Magni* written by Notker of St Gallen some fifty years later to grasp that Einhard's picture was grounded in fact. It is a distinguished piece of historical biography in the Antique tradition – with modifications. To Charlemagne's heirs it would not have seemed a trumpet-call for a secular state; far from it. Quite simply it was a splendid piece of literature and an honour to a self-conscious generation. It was not a court production since it was not written at court; but it is unthinkable except from a pen trained in the court school and steeped in its ideals.

Charlemagne's scriptorium and library were not dispersed at his death. His books were not all distributed as he had intended. There is evidence of continued activity, if on a reduced scale, under his successor. The school, and, round it, the gathering of learned men were too vital a part of the inheritance to be sacrificed. Objectives and tastes might change but the creation of Charlemagne remained.

XII

RECEIVED WISDOM

i. Alcuin

ALCUIN is a knowable man. To tell us about him there survives a large body of his writings, much of his extensive correspondence and a *Life*[1] which is not negligible simply because, some twenty years after his death, contemporaries wished to see him take his place in the venerable series of saintly men. We can see him too, in the warm glow of the comments of friends. We may even see his hand in the margins of a St Martin's copy of the canons of the council of Ephesus (now in Paris, BN Lat.1572),[2] The man who emerges is a scholar and a teacher.

The date of his birth is unknown, though doubtless it fell between 735 and 745. Certainly he was a Northumbrian of good birth, connected by blood with men who had made their mark in the mission-field; but he seems not to have been interested in his social background. Indeed, he later asserted that York was his father and mother, and meant it. At the cathedral school of York he was educated under Eanbald and Albert, masters in the teaching tradition of Bede. He succeeded Albert as master in 767, becoming directly responsible for the school and library in 778. It was Albert who sent him on a mission to Charlemagne, whom he met a second time at Parma in 781 on a return journey from Rome. The next year he was invited to Charlemagne's court, but was back in England in 786 and again in 790-3. At the synod of Frankfurt in 794 he took a leading part. He was now an important man. By 796 he had accumulated several monasteries: Ferrières, St Lupus of Troyes, Flavigny, perhaps Berg, and finally St Martin of Tours, to which he retreated permanently as abbot in 801. He seems to have been a monk and a deacon but no more. He died in 804. What immediately stands out is his long period of incubation at York. He was not a young man when he took up permanent residence in Francia. It follows that his intellectual outlook would be, and would remain, that of a Northumbrian, and more particularly of a York scholar.

Little is known of Alcuin's York and its library, though some at least of the books used by him he enumerated in a poem on the saints of the Church of York,[3] written or at least revised in Francia. The remainder

[1] Ed. W. Arndt, MGH SS xv, i.
[2] Plate 1 in B. Bischoff, *Mittelalterliche Studien*, ii.
[3] Ed. E. Dümmler, MGH Poet. i, pp. 169–206.

of his poetry is lyrical, panegyric and dedicatory and nearly all belongs to his Frankish period. The York poem is important for several reasons. It is a historical epic that puts one in mind of the Bible, sometimes of the *Aeneid*, and sometimes of poets nearer in time, like Venantius Fortunatus. Even so, its 1,650 lines in hexameters are the first of their kind in medieval Latin; an epic in praise of the author's *patria*, Northumbria, and more particularly of the city of York. In this sense it belongs loosely to a special class of panegyric in praise of cities. A *laudatio urbis* had to be seen against a Roman background, as did eighth-century York. But Alcuin's concern is with Christian York, the home of his heroes. He turns to Bede's *Ecclesiastical History* for most of his historical material and creates a verse counterpart, for which he had much precedent. His own *Life* of his kinsman Willibrord[4] was written as one version in prose and another in verse but conceived as a unit. But he was no slavish copier of Bede. He selected what he required, shortened, omitted and expanded, and always the Roman link was in his mind. Paulinus and Wilfrid are seen as the agents of Rome, initiators of asceticism and learning under the aegis of benevolent kings. It has been suggested that Alcuin saw Edwin as somewhat of a forerunner of Charlemagne. But in the poem's final section he moves chronologically beyond Bede into his own day – happy days originally, when King Eadberht and his brother Archbishop Egbert had ruled kingdom and church in amity. Egbert indeed was an episcopal hero, an ecclesiastical *potens* in a comparatively new mould; indeed, precisely the sort of bishop that emerged in Francia under Charlemagne. Then there had come political disruption, which may perhaps explain Alcuin's own decision to make his home abroad. The Church of York, however, remained as a witness to learning; and he was never to lose touch with it. The clergy of York would have seen the poem as an exposition of the moral purposes of a *patria*, full of exemplary lives of men who had championed the faith of Rome and St Peter. The clergy of Francia would have seen it likewise; and it was in fact on the continent that it was to exercise most of its influence.

Alcuin in Francia speaks to us as a voluminous writer on many topics. He would sooner have been remembered as a teacher, the director of Charlemagne's court school and then of the monks of St Martin's. A teacher's success is to be judged by his pupils. Alcuin's pupils were many and distinguished in their day, and the differing nature of their specialities is a witness to his own wide range. In one direction goes Hraban Maur and in others go Candidus and Fridugis – all in one respect or another advancing beyond their master. And there

---

[4] Ed. W. Levison, MGH SRM vii, pp. 81–141.

were many others. In a word, Alcuin was the schoolmaster of the central period of the Renaissance, and was lovingly remembered as such, at least by his pupils. His teaching embraced the liberal arts as the basis of all education; the liturgy and prayer; exegetical instruction; theology; and perhaps nearest his heart, the nature of Christian devotion. At the end of his life he was thinking of devotional exercises and above all of the Psalms, the great source of devotional experience and meditation. It is the warmth of the man that stands out, not the scholarship; and the same could no doubt have been said, if enough were known, of his great predecessors: Albert, Eanbald, Egbert and ultimately Bede with whom all good things begin.

With his learning and some books – conceivably the Moore manuscript of Bede now in Cambridge? – Alcuin took with him to Charlemagne's court the deep conviction that *amicitia*, friendship, was the bedrock of any fruitful association of master with pupil. For him, it was the enduring personal link, whether of men face to face or of men separated but joined in an association of prayer. The linkage in prayer – itself nothing new – was felt by him with special intensity and led naturally into the realm of private devotion, the heart of medieval spirituality. And with prayer went confession and penance. Alcuin's long *Confessio*, with its combination of private vices with public failings, was composed for Charlemagne.[5] Perhaps the stress on penance owed most to Irish influence at York; and indeed his approach to the liturgy in general shows no disposition to scrap Irish usage. Much stronger, however, was his determination to preserve whatever he thought was genuine Roman usage; and of this, too, York had been a guardian. Alcuin's influence on liturgical and biblical reform in Francia was Rome-orientated.

Alcuin's teaching manuals for the liberal arts show clear traces of Northumbrian concern for moral and ethical values; and so also their form. One may instance the use of the Anglo-Saxon poetic device now called kennings as a way of making instruction more memorable: 'what is death?' – 'The tears of the living'; 'what is a ship?' – 'a wandering home'; and so on. Also Anglo-Saxon is the introduction of dialogue. One can see these usages in the so-called *Disputatio regalis et nobilissimi iuvenis Pippini cum Albino scholastico*,[6] a kind of mirror of princes. The aim is to achieve vividness, and it succeeds. Such an essay on kingly virtues inevitably raises the question whether Alcuin's views on kingship influenced the king and in particular the imperial coronation of 800. Clearly he had views. He had not read the highly moraliz-

---

[5] *Teste* D. A. Bullough.
[6] Edd. W. Suchier and L. W. Daly, in *Altercatio Hadriani Augusti et Epicteti philosophi* (Illinois Studies in Language and Literature, 24, no. 1–2, Urbana, 1939).

ing Irish tract *De duodecim abusivis saeculi* for nothing. Bitter experience had taught him what weak kingship meant for Northumbria and he was very much alive to the claims of royal blood. It may be that Bede's picture of the Anglo-Saxon Bretwaldas or high kings sorted well enough in his mind with the facts of Charlemagne's expansive rule. But too narrow or technical a use can be read into his use of the word *imperium*. It cannot be shown that Charlemagne's assumption of the imperial title owed much to Alcuin. What Charlemagne owed to him was something different: the adaptation to Frankish purposes of the great Northumbrian tradition of teaching with its powerful moral basis, its spirituality, its orthodoxy and its deep sense of responsibility.

We must look briefly at two of Alcuin's treatises of instruction for laymen. The first in date of composition is *De virtutibus et vitiis*,[7] addressed to Count Wido. It has been called a handbook to guide a secular man in the moral conflicts that might occur in the everyday affairs of a military man and royal judge. Certainly its aim was practical, like everything Alcuin wrote. In this sense it is a secular counterpart to Pope Gregory's *Pastoral Care* and ranks with the Lady Dhuoda's manual of advice for her young son, written after Alcuin's time. Alcuin sees the secular life as a moral battleground between the vices and their corresponding virtues; the struggle for a man's soul. And as always he takes his stand in a solid patristic tradition. What he has done is to make a neat treatise out of his patristic material, doubtless with the help of somebody's collection of apposite passages, suitable for a busy count. In effect he tells the count that he is no more exempt than a cleric or the king himself from following the severe moral guide-lines of orthodox teaching. And this blending of instruction for clergy and laity is characteristic both of Alcuin and of the circle of Charlemagne generally. In the eyes of later and still sterner reformers this was to seem a dispersal of effort and even a spiritual hazard. A slightly later treatise was Alcuin's *Disputatio de rhetorica et de virtutibus*,[8] composed between 801 and 804. It has the form of a dialogue between the author and his master but, as the title suggests, is not confined to a single theme. Certainly it is an essay in rhetorical exhortation, a discussion of rhetoric on a narrow front and a contribution to literary theory. Whether it is really a tract on kingship or good government falling within the genre of the *via regia* tracts may be doubted. It employs rhetorical conceits familiar to others and builds upon well-known sources (predominantly Cicero's *De inventione*) but is conceived in the Alcuinian manner. The writer thus fulfils the duty

---

[7] PL 101, cols. 613–38. The most convenient edition of Alcuin's writings is PL 100, 101. Later editions of separate works are to be preferred where available.

[8] Ed. C. Halm, *Rhetores latini minores* (Leipzig, 1863), pp. 525–50.

of the man of God in dangerous times to issue a warning. Let the just ruler appreciate his moral responsibilities to his subjects who in their turn should learn to obey him by observing his laws. This was the route to stability. The *De Rhetorica* is thus in part a description of the ideal of political morality as presented to Charlemagne; but in part also an essay on the use of rhetorical forms and devices, adapted as a dialogue; not however an essay on rhetoric in its full classical range but on the selection of topics or arguments – *inventio* as understood by Cicero, Cassiodorus and Boethius. Behind Alcuin lay the example of the Fathers, many of whom had begun their careers as teachers of rhetoric. These were the masters who must come to the help of a ninth-century ruler.

Beyond teaching lay deeper and less welcome preoccupations. Alcuin's biographer puts these words into the mouth of his teacher, Albert, on sending him off to Rome and Francia: 'be a fighter against that fearful heresy that tries to make Christ adoptive, and be the strong defender and powerful preacher of faith in the Holy Trinity'. This is perhaps hindsight but accurately describes Alcuin's dominant role as defender of trinitarian orthodoxy in the great dispute over the heresy of Adoptionism. Doctrinal stability was at once imperilled by any claim that Christ in his human form had been only God's adoptive son, son in his nature but not in his flesh; a metaphorical son, distinct from the eternal Logos. Have we, then, two Christs or one? The trouble had started as a local confrontation between the primate of the Spanish Church, Archbishop Elipand of Toledo, and a curious sect in southern Spain led by an ascetic radical who appears to have taught that God had revealed himself successively in David (as Father), in Jesus (as Son) and in St Paul (as Holy Ghost). There was a smack of ancient heresy about it. Elipand had no difficulty in dealing with this nonsense but his own sense of being the defender of strict orthodoxy was sharpened at the very moment when he needed to tell a more formidable opponent precisely what he did consider orthodox. In the nature of things, the Spanish Church under Arab surveillance enjoyed little contact with churches of the outside world. Septimania, how-ever, was now under Carolingian control: a Spanish Church with a Frankish master nervous about the spread of disturbing teaching. Elipand's opponent was the priest Beatus of Liébana, who informed him that he preached an adoptive Sonship, duly supported by the Spanish Mozarabic liturgy. Beatus and his supporters appealed to Pope Hadrian against Elipand's furious rejoinder; and they also appealed to the Franks. Elipand thereupon looked round for sup-porters of Mozarabic orthodoxy and found one in Felix, bishop of Urgel, which lay in Frankish-controlled territory. It happened that

Felix's entry on the scene coincided with Charlemagne's involvement with Byzantium over orthodoxy; about 788, namely. He could not have been more sensitive to heresy in dioceses under his control. Felix was condemned as a heretic and sent to Rome, thence retreating to the protection of Toledo. Elipand now turned to Charlemagne direct. At the great council of Frankfurt in 794 Adoptionism was a main item on a heavy agenda. Representatives of most of the western churches, including England, joined in condemning it. Alcuin, who was present, wrote two letters to Elipand and the Spanish bishops, explaining things in moderate language. Others also wrote, Pope Hadrian among them. But Elipand was beyond the reach of Hadrian and Charlemagne, and Adoptionism began to spread in northern Spain and Septimania. This alarmed the clergy of southern Francia, and notably the archbishops of Narbonne and Lyon and the powerful abbot Benedict of Aniane. Alcuin was now thoroughly involved, as we can tell from a letter to Felix (who, interestingly, replied direct to Charlemagne). Alcuin was collecting patristic ammunition for a final assault. He also advised the intervention of orthodox theologians and named several, including the new pope, Leo III. One of these, Theodulf of Orleans, must have felt personally involved in what was happening so near to his own diocese; but another, Paulinus of Aquileia, is the only one who is known to have written against Felix, apart from Alcuin himself. Pope Leo confined his intervention to an anathema, delivered in 798. Matters came to a head at Aachen in 800, when Alcuin and Felix confronted each other in public debate; and Felix was defeated. But Alcuin continued to write: first, a considerable statement in seven books against the arguments of Felix, and then one against Elipand, together with a handbook of anti-Adoptionist texts for the *missi* of the South. It was the end of the heresy in Frankish territory and Elipand must have died soon afterwards. But Felix was still being attacked by the archbishop of Lyon in 816, and Adoptionism lingered on in Spain till the second half of the ninth century.

The quarrel reveals how firmly Elipand stood for the historical right of Toledo to interpret dogma for the Spanish Church; dogma inherited as local tradition and enshrined in a venerable liturgy. What Spain had not absorbed was the Petrine cult so active in Rome, England and Francia from the eighth century. First Beatus and then Alcuin were right to insist that the Bible, the six great councils and the creeds of Nicaea and Ephesus knew nothing of Adoption, but they were wrong in arguing that Adoptionists denied the unity of God and made four persons out of the Trinity. Alcuin was unimpressed by the Spanish liturgy, preferring the witness of the Bible, the councils and the Fathers. Repeatedly we find this emphasis on the triple bedrock of orthodoxy in Alcuin and his contemporaries. There in the past lay the basis of orthodox stability. Hence their concern to secure accurate texts. For Alcuin there was no room for doubt: Christ as Son of God became man through incarnation without losing his eternal character of Son of God. Birth, not baptism, made Christ what he was. One notes, too, Charlemagne's own anxiety for exact information about any teaching that threatened the unity of orthodoxy. It had to be understood and refuted. Alcuin captured this spirit. He could face Elipand and Felix not simply because he was told to do so – he was reluctant to take action – but because he saw a challenge to what he thought fundamental. He looked for no fresh interpretation of dogma and cared very little for sophisticated Spanish arguments. All that needed to be established was what the Church had already decided. How could Christ not be God-begotten in his humanity if men had the potential to be godlike? His refusal, perhaps inability, to consider seriously the theological arguments of the Adoptionists says much about his mind. He looked back.

Controversy unwillingly engaged in revealed Alcuin's powers as a clear and persistent exponent of accepted dogma. He had shown no taste for theological speculation. Much the same can be said of his treatise *De fide sanctae Trinitatis*,[9] dedicated to Charlemagne towards the close of his life. He would use dialectic as Augustine had recommended in defence of the doctrine of the Trinity. And indeed Augustine was the bedrock of his argument. He examined the evidence for the trinitarian God in Old and New Testaments; the nature of God in relation to eternity, time and creation; the implications of the incarnation; man as body and spirit; and finally the coming reign of Antichrist and the certainty of resurrection and judgement. The most perceptive English student of Alcuin long ago followed the lead of Hauck in suggesting that the formal theology of Alcuin and his successors suffered from its divorce from vitalizing faith; it was simply a thing apart, a repetition of what the Fathers had said. But it is not every theologian who can go beyond Augustine. Moreover, Alcuin's theology glows with passionate faith in God's goodness and the consequent demand on man for trust, contrition and penitence. To this end baptism was offered, the mass celebrated and the saints invoked. Repeatedly he seems to approach the domain of the mystic but draws back. If he repeats an old lesson he does so with deep conviction that the answer to man's problems is already provided.

So much in Alcuin is related to this central theme of what was

---

[9] PL 101, cols. 9–58.

established. It can be seen very plainly in his liturgical interests. His attention was fixed on the creed, clearly of the type preserved in the Irish Stowe Missal. But liturgy embraced not only the creed but the entire range of formulae that governed the ritual aspect of religion: sacramentaries, lectionaries, homiliaries and *ordines*. A book of sacramentaries to take one example, was a collection of variable prayers for the mass as arranged through the year, taking into account special prayers for saints' days and sometimes containing other matters. It was for the use of the celebrant and was the forerunner of the medieval missal and pontifical. Such collections, showing local needs and tastes, were made spontaneously in Francia, Italy, Spain and elsewhere. By the eighth century two forms of sacramentary had come to predominate: the so-called Gelasian and Gregorian. Neither had official status and neither can be attributed, at least in their complete forms, to the popes in question. The result for Francia was variety. No one sacramentary was imposed on the Frankish Church by Pippin III or Charlemagne. The famous sacramentary of Gellone, compiled not at Gellone but probably in the diocese of Meaux, is an example of an efficient local collection. Prominent in it are saints' feasts of northern and central Francia, and the inclusion of many episcopal benedictions points to its intended use by a bishop. In the year 831 the northern monastery of St Riquier possessed nineteeen Gelasian sacramentaries, three Gregorian and one 'Gregorian and Gelasian missal recently put together by Alcuin'.

How did Alcuin come in? It is always rash to assert anything about Carolingian liturgy, or equally to deny it. However, it is clear that in 786 or thereabouts Charlemagne was worried that he had no sacramentary that he could call authentic and so asked Pope Hadrian, through Paul the Deacon, for a copy of the sacramentary 'put in order by Pope Gregory'. Hadrian seems to have been caught out. What he eventually sent may have been a de luxe manuscript, of which the sacramentary of Bishop Hildoard of Cambrai was probably a copy, made in 812. There are other traces of it. This, known as the *Hadrianum*, was placed in the court library as an *authenticum* available for copying. What Charlemagne got was in fact no more than a copy of some papal sacramentary compiled a century earlier. Its contents were local to Rome and rather peculiar and indeed was not even up to date by Roman standards. Though rich in prayers, it had several big gaps and its real use can only have been for a pope on special occasions some time ago. In many respects it did not answer the needs of the Frankish Church. But in due course (probably between 801 and 804) it was taken in hand by an expert. The result was a composite document: first the text of the *Hadrianum* and then a supplement introduced by the word *Hucusque*.[10] No source says that Alcuin was that expert though he did not lack the necessary skill; no source apart from the monastery of St Riquier, a decade later, whose great lay abbot, Angilbert, was a friend of Alcuin. The best authority deems that it does not fit easily into what else is known of Alcuin's work. A likelier author is Benedict of Aniane. The supplement incorporates masses for Sundays not supplied by the *Hadrianum*, taken from older sacramentaries, and adds additional offices for saints, special masses and a rich series of prefaces for masses and other matter. The compiler had pillaged familiar Frankish sacramentaries and supplied much of what was needed. The proof of success lies in the popularity of the new compilation though not to the exclusion of older sacramentaries. The mass-structure of the Frankish Church, fed from Rome through many springs, remained Frankish.

Equally linked with his concern for the liturgy was Alcuin's Bible and its exegesis. Here as always the background was Charlemagne's personal interest in authentic texts. As with Pope Hadrian's sacramentary, Paul the Deacon's homiliary and the Rule of St Benedict supplied by Monte Cassino, so with the Bible. And the Bible, central to everything, was a jungle. A jungle, in the first place, of versions: whether Old Latin texts of several kinds, Jerome's Vulgate in more than one form, conflations of the two, or new versions; and in the second place, of sizes. One could have separate biblical books, collections of books, (for example, the Gospels) or pandects (that is, all the books in one volume). In addition there were those biblical texts proper to the liturgy, the form of scripture most familiar to clergy and laity; and in particular the Gospels and Psalms. Charlemagne made certain statements about the Bible which presumably reflected his own views. These appear in his *Admonitio Generalis* of 789, his circular *De litteris colendis* and elsewhere. The Bible fell into a context for him. There were schools for studying grammar, computus, chant and so on, all of which suffered from corrupt texts. The books were faulty, thus standing between his pupils and God. So too with the Gospels, the psalter and mass-books. They were now to be transcribed with care – and by adults. The need was for correct biblical texts that could be understood and expounded. This was not to envisage a new critical edition of the Bible so much as a revised text, purged of grammatical and orthographical blunders. It is uncertain what active steps Charlemagne took to ensure the kind of text he wanted; and if any scholar or scholars were charged with the responsibility, no agreed text was officially distributed. Instead we find a variety of more or less

---

[10] Ed. H. A. Wilson, *The Gregorian Sacramentary under Charles the Great* (Henry Bradshaw Soc. xlix, 1915).

improved texts all produced within a generation. One of these texts constitutes the so–called 'Ada' group, produced between 781 and 814, apparently at Aachen. It stands quite near the famous text produced independently by Alcuin and is specially memorable for its illustrations. One supposes that Charlemagne had personal knowledge of this group, if of no other. He certainly sent Bibles to deserving recipients, of which survivors are the Dagulf Psalter made for Pope Hadrian and Godescalc's Gospels made for Pippin's baptism in Rome in 781. But out of all this we get no official text.

It may be that the first-fruit of Charlemagne's concern for biblical reform was the Bible of Maurdramn, abbot of Corbie from 772 to 781, of which only five volumes out of at least twelve survive. Again, the text is fairly close to Alcuin's; and it is written in fully-developed Caroline minuscule. There is also a Metz Bible, probably due to Bishop Angilram, who died in 791: not a good text but the earliest-known Carolingian pandect. Most scholarly of all was the Bible of Bishop Theodulf.

So to Alcuin's Bible. It was commissioned by Charlemagne, though not in the sense that he required Alcuin single-handed to produce an official text for general use. Alcuin explains, in a letter, that his other work is being held up because of Charlemagne's order that he should emend the texts of the Old and New Testaments. Perhaps this means no more than that he was tidying up a particular Bible at Tours for the king's personal use. He actually prepared several Bibles. One was for Gerfrid of Laon, another was for someone named Ava, the third was Charlemagne's (probably finished early in 800), and a fourth, distinct from the third as it seems, was a Christmas present for Charlemagne in 801, destined for the Church of Aachen. There was even a fifth, for Tours. None of these survives. At least one more Bible (now at St Gallen) was written under Alcuin at Tours and sent away. This makes a total of not less than six Alcuinian pandects, and it may be that they all differed in one way or another. The well-known Tours Bibles, of which we do have examples, belong to the next and following generations. Over the fifty years following Alcuin's death there is evidence of the dissemination from Tours of twenty-three Bibles, fifteen gospels and other biblical material. The texts differ slightly but must substantially represent the text of Alcuin. He clearly used Vulgate texts as his basis. Curiously enough, his corrections and even orthography seem less good than those of Maurdramn and Angilram. It is not clear that he used Northumbrian texts brought from York; he rather favoured local Gallican texts. He never specifies biblical books among those books he sought from home. His pandect text of St John seems to have differed from the text he was using at the same time for purposes of comment. What this comes to is that Alcuin was no outstanding textual scholar of the Bible. He had the resources at Tours to tidy up and produce a clean Bible when asked to do so; and he did so on several occasions. However, he has a significant place in the Carolingian biblical movement that started under Pippin III and stretched on to Charles the Bald a century later. It was a time of enormous biblical production. Bibles were being copied everywhere and in considerable variety. They were central to the Carolingian revival.

Then came the problem of understanding the biblical text: in a word, exegesis or commentary, of which there was a greatly increased output in the eighth and ninth centuries. In general this amounted to the transmission of patristic commentaries or their reduction into shorter handbooks, such as collections of *Quaestiones* to help the clergy, and so the laity, with difficult scriptural passages. There survive many such collections, often anonymous; but men of distinction were ready to make them for their communities, and their work showed clear signs of personal preference in choice of sources. Alcuin played an important part: his exegetical writings bulk large in his literary production. It was what he called 'culling the beautiful flowers from patristic gardens' and expanding them, in Gaskoin's words, 'into a continuous exposition of the threefold sense of Scripture, literal, allegorical and moral'. Especially in allegory he put things in a personal, not to say fanciful, way that looks to be characteristically Anglo-Saxon. He composed commentaries on Genesis, some of the Psalms, Ecclesiastes, Proverbs, St John and some of the epistles. Genesis was specially near to his heart. He often cites Genesis 1: 26 ('And God said, let us make man in our image, after our likeness') and it becomes a key-passage in the dispute about images. Man as God's image is in the forefront of his thinking. His commentary on St John allows him latitude for allegorization and spiritual interpretation, as also for something peculiar to him: the symbolism of number, which he again indulges in his commentary on the Psalms. Few others, apart from Cassiodorus and Honorius of Autun, shared this intense interest in numerology. Alcuin had a central text from the Book of Wisdom 11: 21: 'God disposed all by measure, by number and by weight'. Number was the silent voice in the Psalms, what Bede in *De Templo* called its wordless characterization; and the key to this silent meaning was the interpretation of number. It casts light on Alcuin's mind. However humbly he might follow Augustine, Jerome and the other giants he saw mystical problems in Scripture in his own way; and these formed a link between his Bible and his view of prayer, both public and private. The Bible flows into the liturgy to become, properly ordered, the source and expression of contemplation. The biblical texts of the liturgy were, in Dom Leclerq's words, 'collected and arranged in such a way as to make of them a poem of inexhaustible meaning and profundity'; they developed man's inclination to read the Bible itself in search of spiritual treasure. Particularly is this true of the Psalms. Through the liturgy they entered everyday life to become 'the normal and spontaneous expression of the soul's contact with God'. Often one finds their texts preceded or followed by some title, summary, prayer or collect asking that their meaning should be understood. Often, too, they were abridged for special or private use, as breviaries. Prudentius of Troyes, who died in 861, composed such a breviary for a lady to recite on journeys. This was how Alcuin saw the Bible as he read it and commented on it: the word of God, all that man required if it were properly understood. The key to such understanding was the Fathers – Augustine and Jerome certainly, but also Gregory, Bede, Isidore and away in the distance the Greek Fathers transmuted as Latins. These had formulated the answers to two great problems of scriptural exegesis: how do you discover the New Testament in the Old, and how do you cope with the different senses of Scripture? The bulk and variety of biblical manuscripts, together with the exegetical and liturgical texts related to them, demonstrate that here lay the abiding concern of the best minds of the eighth and ninth centuries. Alcuin's was one of them. A traditionalist Alcuin may have been, and this sometimes makes him seem more mediocre than in fact he was. But he could also show striking originality. Nowhere is this clearer than in his application of logic to theology, in which he and his pupils take a big step towards the better-known experiments of men of the next generation. This is a side of him that has only recently begun to be explored.

One scratches the surface of Alcuin. His writings defy brief evaluation by their very variety; and to them one ought to add writings that may have been his, or in which he may have played a part, or which have been attributed to him, rightly or wrongly, at one time or another. An example of the difficulty is the authorship of the *Libri Carolini*, attributed by some scholars to Alcuin but by others more plausibly to Theodulf. Yet Professor Bullough showed that chapters 14 to 27 of Book 4 strongly recall Alcuin's work on dialectic and may have been transmitted by Alcuin to Theodulf on request. Like many of his contemporaries and his pupils his writings leak into those of others; and this because their thoughts had already done the same. They fuse into a common instrument, intellectual, moral and spiritual.

ii. Theodulf

Theodulf was one of the few Visigoths who gained access to Charlemagne's court and made his mark there. Born about 750, he reached Francia in the 780s and was certainly active in Charlemagne's circle by 790 at latest. In 798 he was performing the duties of a *missus*, by which year he was also bishop of Orléans and abbot of St Aignan at Orléans as well as of Fleury and Micy. In 800 he took part in the trial of Pope Leo III; in 806 he dedicated his personal oratory at Germigny-des-Prés; in 818 he was accused, rightly or wrongly, of complicity in Bernard of Italy's plot against Louis the Pious, deposed from his see, and exiled to the monastery of St Aubin at Angers, where he probably died in 826. It seems likely that one beneficiary from his fall was Count Matfrid of Orléans, an enemy skilled in the art of *damnatio memoriae*. That is almost all the firm chronology we have of his career, apart from the dating of some of his writings. Whether he came from Gothic Septimania or from Spain cannot easily be determined. The balance is in favour of Spain, partly because his writings suggest Spanish education, and also because, in a poem to Charlemagne, he speaks of his presence in Francia as being the direct result of *immensis casibus*, an overwhelming disaster. Another refugee. There were no such disasters in Septimania in the critical years, or none that we know of; but northern Spain suffered severely, and at the right time, at the hands of the Arab ruler, Abd-al-Rahman I, who was determined to put down Carolingian sympathizers there. Saragossa in particular bore the brunt of Arab attentions in 782; a city of repute as an intellectual centre interested in those fields of study in which Theodulf was an expert. Add to this the fact that Theodulf's favourite poet, Prudentius, was a Saragossan and it becomes plausible that it was from this city or its neighbourhood that Theodulf set out to find Charlemagne, by way of Septimania.

One of Theodulf's skills that may quickly have engaged the interest of the court circle was in poetry; and much of this, composed over the course of his career, is preserved.[1] A skilled poet, his verse fits comfortably into the Christian-Latin tradition; and he can even be seen as a court-Pindar on a modest scale. His long and famous eulogy on Charlemagne, *Ad Carolum Regem*,[2] was composed to celebrate the victory over the Avars in 796. To find an enconium like this one has to look back to the circle of Theodoric at Ravenna or to Venantius at Poitiers. Charlemagne's *prudentia*, he claims, knows no frontiers: it is

[1] Ed. E. Dümmler, MGH Poet. i, pp. 437–581.
[2] Ibid., p. 483.

broader than the Nile, mightier than the Danube, bigger than the Euphrates, no less than the Ganges. Obvious river-rhetoric derived from Antiquity, it is a conventional way of saying what is seriously meant: the king is a mighty man, and everyone knows it. Theodulf goes on to describe the person of the king, feature by feature; an idealized portrait of a *homo caelestis* with whose reign the spring has come again; the spring of Charlemagne, his family, his friends and his peoples. There is no satire here. The court-circle is then described in some detail – the royal family and then the courtiers, one by one, under their classical pseudonyms. Some of this is indeed satirical, especially when Irishmen are in question. The poem, then, is a mixture of hyperbole, satire and seriousness. If Charlemagne's face can be hailed as brighter than thrice-refined gold it is a salutation in a good tradition; and what it means is 'this is the face of a man who is pretty nearly godlike' – and everyone would have understood and agreed. Pretty nearly but not quite. There remained the Trinity; and on this Theodulf also composed verses, *De Spiritu Sancto*, in the preface to which the poem itself is required to address the king, claiming that it will help those who go astray.[3] 'Can you really do this?' asks Charlemagne; 'yes indeed' answers the poem, 'I really can, so long as God helps me!' Theodulf has culled his dogmatic flowers from the Fathers and, like Alcuin, he must be right.

But there is another poet in Theodulf, who can address his king in a very different way, as an official. It is thus that he writes in a poem on the restoration of Pope Leo III and again in a long poem *ad Judices*[4] – formally addressed to the judges of the South among whom he had recently been at work as a *missus* but in practice to the king. The poem is meant to urge the king to a heightened sense of law and justice; all he has to do is to command and the Frankish world will become a better place. The Old Testament had portrayed the long Jewish struggle for justice that culminated in Josiah, the great restorer of justice. That is how Charlemagne should be. Apart from this, a *missus* and other judges ought not to be offered bribes, let alone accept them; but in the loving care with which he describes some of the bribes he himself had turned down, Theodulf betrays that he was a connoisseur of *objets d'art*. The arresting fact is not that Theodulf should have reported his feelings to the king but that he should have done so in an elaborate poem, and a poem that was preserved. Almost any public occasion, one could infer, or any serious issue might lend itself to such treatment. They could be set in the measured terms of archaizing verse and set, too, in the context of respectable exemplars from the Bible. So far as the king was concerned, poems such as Theodulf could write hit the

[3] PL 105, cols. 239–76.   [4] MGH Poet. i, p. 493.

mark. He was a trusty who could be commissioned to compose a
funerary inscription for Queen Fastrada and an epitaph for the king's
old friend, Pope Hadrian. Theodulf is full of Ovid and Virgil. But
what his poetry most clearly reveals is that the Carolingian Renaissance had by now brought about a revival of patristic synthesis, not of
the old classical spirit. He cited Ovid and Virgil because his masters
cited Ovid and Virgil; and these masters were the Christian poets of
Late Antiquity: Claudius, Paulinus, Venantius and particularly
Prudentius – *parens noster*. A Spanish poet steeped in this tradition
could serve Charlemagne very well; but not Louis the Pious. There
survives an exchange[5] in verses between the exile at Angers and his
friend Bishop Modoin of Autun in which he pictures himself somewhat as Ovid in the *Tristia*: the happy times have gone, when literary
skill counted at court. To this Modoin replies by citing examples of
Roman and other intellectuals who had endured exile with patience.
All the same, he concludes, what Theodulf had better do is to say that
he is sorry and he will be forgiven. He had been the court poet *par
excellence* and the royal circle had been genuinely impressed by the
Theodulfia Musa. But he had other claims on the court besides his
poetry.

In 787 the second council of Nicaea legislated for the restoration of
images. A copy of the document reached Rome, where it was badly
translated from Greek into Latin and then sent on by Pope Hadrian to
Charlemagne for his inspection. The West did not understand the
issues involved in the iconoclastic controversy and especially not in the
translation of Nicaea II provided by Rome. However, Charlemagne
saw significance in the document, both political and theological, and
was convinced that he was being asked to approve the worship of
images. The issue was not entirely foreign to the western world. Since
the sixth century miracle stories had tended to be associated with
images of saints. The earliest evidence of this comes from Marseille,
where Bishop Serenus had reacted violently against what he saw as the
cult of images in local churches; and Gregory of Tours was not much
less disturbed by the popular tendency to place an *imaginem pictam* of
Christ in churches and private houses. A council at Tours, slightly
earlier, also seems to have objected to images on altars when the
eucharist was being consecrated. These rumbles may still have been
heard two centuries later. At all events, Charlemagne assembled a
team of theologians on whose advice he sent back to Rome a list of
capitula or headings of points that he wished to refute. The pope took a
rather more informed view and replied with a letter showing that the
Greek position was not so summarily to be dismissed. Unimpressed,

[5] Ibid., pp. 563–9, 569–73.

Charlemagne proceeded to embark on a detailed refutation on his own account. The work took about three years (from 790 to 792) and involved many sessions of his committee, over which he seems occasionally to have presided. The decisions taken certainly represented his own views. The refutation finally sent to Rome (where it seems to have been pigeon-holed) was rightly sent in his name. It is known as the *Libri Carolini*.[6]

Which of the theologians available was the author of the *Libri*? An obvious candidate would be Alcuin; obvious in the sense that he was a leading theologian in close touch with Charlemagne. However, he was absent in England during the critical time of composition, and there is only one section of the *Libri* that specifically suggests his interest or his style. This indeed he may have supplied. As for the rest, whatever suggests him equally suggests any other Carolingian theologian. If we look for peculiarities of style we are led inevitably, as Ann Freeman showed, to Theodulf. We are greatly assisted by the survival of a unique if incomplete manuscript of the work, now in the Vatican, which was plainly the working copy, though not originally intended as such. Neatly written with attractive initials, it must have been meant for Rome, after correction. Such corrections exist, but they get more numerous and fundamental till the point was reached where it could no longer be regarded as a fair copy. The scribe adds marginal words of comment – like *bene, recte, verissime* – which might possibly betray the intervention of the king in person. This working copy, as it became, reached Rome, presumably at a later date than the fair copy actually sent at the time.

How do we know that Theodulf and none other compiled the work so ruthlessly revised? We know it, first, from the language: it is the work of a Visigoth. Visigothic spellings have in places been corrected to normal Frankish usage by the revisers. The style is Theodulf's and so, too, the employment of some favourite words. But what really betrays Theodulf is not the language but the matter. The Old Testament and certain patristic writings were his specialities; and wherever the *Libri* touch these, corrections are few. The Frankish correctors felt more at home when it came to the Psalms, presented to them in non-Frankish versions. Curiously, the biblical quotations appear from no known biblical text. What the author seems to have done was to quote biblical passages from memory, and not from the Bible direct but from biblical texts in the liturgy of the Visigothic Church as preserved for us in the Mozarabic rite. One is not looking at the odd

---

[6] Ed. H. Bastgen, MGH Conc. ii, suppl. (with emendations in Freeman, *Speculum*, 40, 2 (1965), pp. 287 ff.). See Bastgen's articles in NA 36 (1911) and 37 (1912), and W. von den Steinen, ibid. 49 (1930–1).

Spanish usage creeping into otherwise impeccable northern texts but at biblical quotations recollected from Spanish sources. The Mozarabic liturgy was ornate and elaborate and old, and particularly rich in antiphonal texts – that is, biblical texts set to music and adjusted to the music. This rearrangement was peculiar to the Spanish Church. So, what Theodulf did was to quote scripture from memory in the form in which he knew it best; namely, in the phrases of his native liturgy. This is apparent throughout the *Libri*. He may even have forgotten that he was not quoting from the Bible direct. The same happens in the only other prose work that is certainly Theodulf's – his *De ordine baptismi*,[7] addressed to Magnus of Sens. The texts he might have liked to check his quotations from were doubtless unavailable to him. He simply had to do a rush job for Charlemagne.

On images the *Libri* have some revealing things to say; revealing not only for the Carolingian outlook but also for authorship. They betray what can only be called an advanced artistic sense. Already in his poetry Theodulf shows his connoisseurship, and much more in his oratory of Germigny, to which we shall come. What were statues and portraits of saints for? Obviously not for worship as Charlemagne imagined the Greeks thought. For what, then? They are, says Theodulf, *opificia*, artefacts, the work of man's hand and not of God's. They have no mystic function. Artists' work, they are images of what is in the artist's mind. He is merely a craftsman, dependent on his employers and his models for inspiration. If he is pious, this may to some extent rub off in his work, without of course making that work an object of piety in itself. Painting ought not to be called pious because it depicts good deeds nor impious if it depicts violence. The Holy Spirit has nothing to do with it. Only one work of art was ever inspired by God; and that, as we learn from the Old Testament, was the building of the Ark of the Covenant. So, an image derives no value and no mystical significance from the saint it represents. What is valuable about it is the material of which it is made, the artist's success, and sometimes the antiquity of the thing. Nobody else in the eighth century seems to have said or thought anything like this about art. Theodulf's *coup de grâce* for what he assumes to be the Eastern argument is this: if an image is removed from its proper place and has no inscription or identifying symbol, how do you know that the Virgin you think you see was not actually meant for Venus? No inherent venerability is present to help you to decide. Or again, how do you know that an image of a pretty girl with a baby is the Virgin and Child and not Venus and Aeneas? 'They have the same shapes, their colouring and the materials used are the same. The only difference is the

[7] PL 105, cols. 544–8.

superscription.' Plainly you are not looking at a piece of divine inspiration that merits worship. The *Libri* contain references to many kinds of works of art which together betray Theodulf's deep knowledge and love of them. He can draw on practical experience and knows how craftsmen work. He can describe a representation of the four seasons as if he were recalling an actual panorama of the months; and when he comes to the personification of the Earth he is thinking of what he describes in a poem.[8] He possessed a depiction of Earth with her attendant rivers, winds and so on, made to his own design. To sum up, his approach to images was highly sophisticated and, so far as is known, unique. The *Libri Carolini* contain abundant proof of it. Unique, but influential in an unexpected direction. He himself was only concerned to argue that in the exposition of dogma the word had absolute primacy over the image and that one could not defend the veneration of images of Christ, the Virgin and the saints on the ground that the Greeks had shown the way by venerating imperial portraits. Nor could one defend the representation of New Testament heroes on the ground that the Old Testament Cherubim could be so represented. In fact, Theodulf never condemned images, as distinct from their worship, in so many words. But he came near enough to it, and was respected enough, to delay for a few years in the 790s any development of ruler-representation in Carolingian court art. Representations of emperors in Constantinople and in Rome were to be seen from the early eighth century but did not affect Carolingian artists. Only at the very end of the 790s did northern artists feel strong enough to react, and then in a modest way. The court chapel at Aachen is thought to have been unlikely to have had a mosaic Christ in Majesty so early. The first large-scale portrayal of a Frankish king is that of Charlemagne in the famous papal mosaic at Rome, which dates from about the year 800; but there was no follow-up in Francia itself. In the mid-ninth century we encounter what are held to be royal portraits in Frankish manuscripts; but it was left to the Ottonians to develop the art. These hesitant beginnings owe nothing to any incapacity to represent kings or Christ pictorially. They are due to an interpretation of dogma directly associated with Theodulf's reaction to what he saw as Greek image-worship.

When Alcuin produced his Vulgate text of 800, Theodulf was also busy with the Bible under the same impetus of Carolingian encouragement. Theodulf's work was not like Alcuin's. It was differently

---

[8] MGH Poet. i, p. 547.

conceived and, although copied and disseminated, never won the same wide acclaim. It was in fact a working text built up from a variety of sources and designed as a scholarly reference book. If it can be said to have had a predominant forebear, it could only be the kind of Bible produced in the scriptorium of Saragossa by Bishop John: a Bible with its books arranged in the old Spanish order, with prefatory verses. Copies of this and other Spanish biblical texts presumably reached Orléans some time after the completion of the *Libri Carolini*. In brief, what Theodulf produced was not a new biblical text but a critical appraisal of the materials from which correct copies might be made. He set to work in his own way. Instead of marching through the Bible book by book he worked at whatever book was available to him in manuscripts. This is one reason why none of the copies of his Bible exactly resembles any other. The work was a continuous process of addition and adjustment that strictly speaking never came to an end. What he envisaged was a handbook in one volume (a pandect, namely), small in format, the writing in triple or double columns, such as the Visigoths favoured. The books should be divided just as Isidore had said they should. He would stick to the currently-accepted canon of Scripture and leave out the Apocrypha. Basically his text was Jerome's Vulgate, with improvements from Hebrew texts; Jerome, however, derived from several distinct traditions, each of which affects the biblical books in different ways. Two of his pandects survive, one now at Paris and the other (probably a copy of it) at Le Puy. They are beautiful books written in tiny Caroline minuscule but with Visigothic features; and they were written at Orléans, not at Fleury as was once believed. The Paris manuscript is full of added variants and corrections, the work of a contemporary Orléans hand though not necessarily that of Theodulf himself. The variants are not confused with corrections of errors and are carefully noted in the margins, with sources given. Theodulf uses his own system of signs for his sources, some of which also appear in the *Libri*. And he had the benefit of an Alcuinian text for purposes of collation. All this argues good scholarship, but never scholarship as an end in itself. Critical work on the Bible by Carolingian scholars was part of a larger theological programme, the outcome of which was to be teaching. Theodulf was an active diocesan, laden with cares that Alcuin never knew. There survives a manuscript that is a kind of *vade mecum* of biblical commentaries belonging to Theodulf's own programme. It belongs to the class of patristic *florilegia*, cullings from the Fathers. It seems to have been put together before the *Libri Carolini*, which make use of it, and then kept handy and finally tacked on to the end of his Bible as a help in interpretation. It is thus further proof that Theodulf never envisaged a free-standing biblical text like Alcuin's but a working model within a greater scheme of instruction.

We are left with one final witness to Theodulf's mental processes: his oratory at Germigny-des-Prés, dedicated in 806 and falling to the crown at the time of his disgrace. So far as it now exists, it is not, as some have thought, very like the royal chapel at Aachen. It is rather more what a Byzantine who knew Ravenna might have constructed; but its stucco-work, now fragments only, suggests neither Aachen nor Ravenna but something Islamic, perhaps Spanish, and is closely related to the canonical tables in Theodulf's Bibles. The inspiration must be Theodulf's. He seems to have conceived of his oratory as a new Temple of Solomon set in the midst of Paradise; and this fits in well enough with his own Old Testament preoccupations and to some extent those of the court as well. Charlemagne was seen as a new Solomon as often as a new David, particularly by Theodulf; and in due course Charles the Bald was also Solomon, the fount of wisdom to his people. This cult – for it was a cult – together with its iconographical trappings was more than a piece of loose typography conceived to flatter: it had a direct bearing on Charlemagne's own view of his royal office. Germigny was not built to flatter any Carolingian but simply expressed the personal preference of one bishop and his own opinion of what needed saying iconographically in his own oratory.

What chiefly remains at Germigny is its apse-mosaic, and the interpretation of this depends on the philosophy of the *Libri* and the decoration of the Bibles.[9] The mosaic has an inscription which explains what it is: it represents the Ark of the Covenant and the Cherubim (spelt, as Theodulf preferred, 'cerubin'). What one sees is the Ark with two small and two large angelic figures bending over it. No other western church gives the Ark this kind of prominence or shows it in this manner. There is no accustomed Virgin here, or Christ in Majesty, but a dogmatic statement of a different kind that affords no opening for superstition or veneration. However, the description of the making of the Ark in Exodus reads: 'make one cherub on the one end, and the other cherub on the other end; even of the mercy-seat shall ye make the cherubim on the two ends thereof'. So too in I Kings and II Chronicles. There are two cherubim and no more. What, then, are the other two cherubim doing in the mosaic? The *Libri* clear the matter up. There were indeed four cherubim: two who guarded the Ark of Moses and two for Solomon's Temple. Moreover, the two for Solomon's Temple symbolized the extension of salvation from the Jews to the Gentiles. This is clear evidence that the Germigny mosaic was a portrayal of the doctrine of the *Libri* and came from the same

---

[9] Illustrated in Freeman, *Speculum*, 32, 4 (1957), plate iv.

mind. It would be quite another matter to argue from the mosaic that it had direct political significance, foreshadowing the *regnum Christianum* over which the modern Solomon presided. It was enough that God had made his covenant with his Chosen People of biblical and later times. Theodulf looked to his Bible to discover, among much else, what could and what could not be represented in art as a dogmatic statement. So Germigny comes together with Theodulf's writings; they cannot be divorced or understood apart from each other.

Less is known about Theodulf the man than about Alcuin or Einhard but much is known about what went on in his mind. He was atypical of Carolingian court-scholars but not on that account an inhabitant of some outer circle, at least in the earlier part of his Frankish career. He could address a variety of occasional verse to the king, could compose hymns, could recite at court, could be asked to undertake delicate commissions such as a royal epitaph, and could be required to prepare the most momentous theological statement issued in the name of any Carolingian king. His episcopal statutes (best reserved for later consideration) were the work of a bishop who fully accepted the challenge of Charlemagne's reforms. His reward was great: the see of Orléans and a collection of first-rate abbeys. On the other hand, he came from Visigothic Spain – always a source of suspicion and irritation to Franks, and not least when Frankish conquests had cleared the route by which heresy moved north. This seemed not to matter. He was a Visigoth who could accept the political theology prevailing at Aachen and the king's role in Christian society. When it came to the *Libri Carolini* his Visigothic oddities could be pruned by Franks who knew better. He seems to have taken no offence. As a collator of texts in chaotic condition, as patristic interpreter and as champion of the Old Testament he made a vital contribution to the Carolingian concept of a Christian society.

XIII

THE NEW ISRAEL AND
ITS RULERS

i. Louis The Pious

THE reign of Louis the Pious was the testing-time of the Carolingian experiment in Christian *renovatio*. In part at least it was so because of the reverberations of three distinct events: first, that Louis, as nobody could have anticipated, was the sole survivor of Charlemagne's legitimate sons in 814 and thus his sole heir; secondly, that Louis in his turn made a solemn and carefully considered provision for the present and future rule of his empire in 817, which his three legitimate sons – Lothar I, Louis the German and Pippin I of Aquitaine – accepted as binding; and thirdly, as a result of the birth of a fourth son, Charles, later called the Bald (son of a second wife, the Bavarian Judith), Louis reallocated his dominions and so brought about civil war, his own deposition and finally his restoration. The turmoil, especially near and round Louis himself, powerfully affected men who were well able to think and write.

Louis was a better-educated man than his father, though not on that account an abler. If he did not share his father's tastes (apart from hunting) this was largely due to his having been brought up in Aquitaine, where Charlemagne sent him while still a small boy to be king. To this, and to his Aquitanian friends, he owed his monk-like propensities. Once emperor, he found himself the centre of a learned court at Aachen that had not been dispersed. Charlemagne's friends were still there, together with an entourage of capable administrators. Evidence of continuity can be seen in the capitularies of Louis's reign, which in quality even surpass those of Charlemagne. They are a major monument to the culture and efficiency of court administration. Apart from this, it looks as if Charlemagne's great library was not dispersed, or not to any serious extent. In parts of this heritage Louis certainly had an interest. Before he became emperor he had accepted a copy of Augustine's *De doctrina christiana* from his father's friend, Angilbert of St Riquier. In 827 the Byzantine emperor Michael sent him a famous manuscript of the theological works of Pseudo-Dionysius that Hilduin of St Denis, and later Eriugena, in part translated from Greek into Latin. Greeks were not unknown at court. Theodulf sent him an inscribed copy of his *De spiritu sancto*. Books were dedicated to him:

for example, Dungal's *Responsa* to Claudius of Turin and Dicuil's *Astronomia*; and not only to him but also to the empress Judith (poems and biblical exegesis). In one of them, a Fulda manuscript of Hraban Maur's *De laudibus sancti crucis*, there remains the only representation – one can hardly call it a portrait – of Louis dressed as a *miles christianus*, authoritative rather than pious, holding a great cross and garbed as a warrior.[1] This is by no means all. We know the name of his first palace librarian: it was the monk Gerward of Lorsch. We also know that he made a present of a magnificent set of Gospels, written at court around 800, to the monastery of St Médard at Soissons. Bernard Bischoff made a study of the manuscripts, and especially of their handwriting, produced or probably produced at court in Louis's reign and the list is impressive. It includes classical as well as biblical and patristic texts. When he came to die, the emperor handed over to his most intimate friend, his half-brother Bishop Drogo of Metz, not only his insignia and vestments but also books: liturgical texts, it is presumed. In sum, the court at Aachen under Louis continued to prepare, disseminate, receive and copy a wide variety of books, some of them of great magnificence. There was no break in 814, at least in this respect.

One man who played a part in this activity in the early days was Archbishop Ebbo of Reims, later to be deprived of his see for disloyalty and to end his career as a German bishop. He had been Louis's foster-brother and they had been brought up together; and he had been humbly born, as was often the case with one child in fosterage. His birth was very much to his discredit in the eyes of future colleagues: one could never trust the man of mean origins in a position of responsibility. The close connection between Louis and Ebbo came out in their joint patronage of art. Louis had contacts with Italy. Apart from having estates near Brescia, he had made a long stay in Ravenna in 793 and had accompanied his brother Pippin on an expedition against Benevento. One outcome of this was the presence of Italian artists with Greek tastes (if they were not themselves Greeks) at Aachen after 814. One can detect the direct influence of the imported illustration-types used at Aachen on the book-illustrations of Reims under Ebbo, as also on the dependent Reims house of Hautvillers, which produced the great Utrecht Psalter. In the field of art Ebbo may have been to Louis what Einhard was to Charlemagne. Charles the Bald knew Ebbo well at court and admired him; 'the vigour of his mind', Charles recalled, 'combined with his tremendous energy would naturally have enabled him to enter the ranks of the bishops and rise high in them'; or, in other words, to enter an aristocratic circle from which his birth would normally have excluded him. Charles also

[1] Illus. plate v, p. 304, in *Karl der Grosse* catalogue (Aachen, 1965).

told a story about him to the pope.[2] When Ebbo was in disgrace and hiding in Paris in 833, he sent to the empress Judith a ring she had given him while awaiting the birth of her son Charles. Judith wept at this reminder of the old friendship between the foster-brothers but could do nothing to help him. Up to the time when Ebbo unwisely sided with Lothar against Louis, he was certainly a formidable figure both at court and at Reims; but backing the wrong horse cost him his job, as well as the hatred of most of his colleagues. He acted very differently from Bishop Drogo, who was consistently loyal to Louis and benefited, as did Ebbo, from the artistic activity at Aachen. One can see clearly from work of the circle of Ebbo and Drogo how court influence in art spread out to the provinces. Some of Charlemagne's artists had left Aachen for the provinces in 814, and some of Ebbo's left Reims after his disgrace. In the illustration of books, then, as well as in their writing and collection and dissemination, there was no lack of activity at Louis's court and at centres connected with the court. To what extent he inspired new building it is hard to tell. At least of his palace at Ingelheim we know that it was decorated with frescos, derived from the History of Orosius, which depicted scenes from Antiquity up to the reign of Constantine, and thereafter the deeds of Theodosius, Charles Martel and Charlemagne. Apart indeed from the Aachen complex there is nothing much but occasional foundations on which to base any idea of Carolingian palaces such as existed at Ingelheim, Paderborn, Frankfurt, Forscheim, Basel and elsewhere. But whatever his contribution as builder, Louis unquestionably ranks high as endower and protector of churches and monasteries, not least St Denis, Corbie, Inda and the southern houses when he ruled in Aquitaine.

The emperor was not a patron of poetry to the extent that his father has been. There seems to have been no poet at court before the arrival of Walahfrid Strabo in 829. Louis was reported to have despised the shows and the *poetica carmina gentilia* he had known in youth; which is what might be expected of one whose real interest, to judge from dedications alone, was theology and whose court-scholars were theologians. These included Clemens, Aldric of Le Mans and the *magister* Thomas. However, his tastes may reflect a more general shift in interest among men of a new generation, perhaps more serious-minded and clearly facing graver problems. Deeply religious, Louis shared the interest of even his most learned contemporaries in the study of the stars and of portents, generally as a means of predicting the future and of averting disaster. Calamity was never far from his thoughts, and *fortuna*, that old ally of the Merovingians, seemed to

[2] PL 124, cols. 872–3.

him to be deserting his dynasty. God would need much appeasement. So one finds him praying and fasting and distributing alms in a lavish way with appeasement in mind; to the extent indeed that his bishops thought well to warn him that propitiating God was their business, not his. He may have believed that propitiation of an angry God fell within his professional role as emperor; it belonged to his *ministerium*; the unity of his Christian empire was encapsulated in his person. Thus he could proclaim in a capitulary that the Catholic Church was Christ's body 'in which we by good works desire to become a member'. Louis was himself Christ's vicar and representative: the unity of the Church was inseparable from the unity of society. It may seem odd, then, that he should have been a notable protector of Jews – sufficiently to incense some of his southern clergy. His own deacon, Bodo, was converted to Judaism and fled to Spain, where he had a notorious debate with Albar, a convert from Judaism to Christianity. Jewish influence was plainly at work at or near the court. But it was in an economic sense only that Louis protected Jews, and this chiefly in the south where he was once at home. It did not affect his intensely religious outlook.

Charlemagne had not owed much to southerners. Like his predecessors, he had not found them co-operative with Franks. Things were quite different with Louis. His early years as emperor at Aachen were much influenced by southerners, and most of all by Helisachar, his chancellor, and by Benedict of Aniane. With their approval he at once set about cleaning up the court. His sisters were 'invited' to retire to nunneries and all loose or superfluous women were expelled. The court was to be as far as possible monastic, and to a large extent the happy old arrangement of co-operation of secular with clerical was to be discarded in favour of the clerical. Benedict, whose original name was Witiza, was born some time before 750 and is first met with at the monastery of St Seine, near Dijon, in 774. He was the son of a count of Maguelonne, in which diocese he founded his own monastery at Aniane around 780. Already however he was well known at court, a trusted servant both of Pippin III and Charlemagne. After experimenting with a variety of eastern Rules he picked on St Benedict's as the most suitable for his house. He went further, visiting monasteries over a wide area of the South, and in some at least he gave instruction in the Rule: evidence, surely, not only that the Rule had been misunderstood but also that communities wished to understand it. But overmuch influence can be attributed to Benedict. Certainly he restored lapsed communities and founded some, but there were influential men in the South, including diocesans of standing, who were independent reformers on their own account, both of monasteries and of chapters of canons. Leidrad of Lyon, to take one example, seems to have reformed local communities without reference to Benedict. So it looks as if a new Benedictine spirit was stirring. Louis's ideas about reform were much those of Benedict and were possibly derived from him. In Aquitaine they collaborated; and the council of Chalon in 813 recorded that nearly all the Burgundian houses now followed the Rule.[3] Once at Aachen, Louis summoned Benedict from Aquitaine, established him in a monastery at Inda (now Cornelimünster) near Aachen, and started reforming the Frankish houses. The important synod of Aachen in 816[4] re-established what is called an *ordo regularis* with *una consuetudo*. Its first provisions cover the clergy, canons and canonesses, together with twenty-seven provisional *capitula* for monks. Certainly it excited opposition. Notwithstanding, next year the emperor summoned a synod of abbots and monks to Aachen, to meet under Benedict's direction.[5] Benedict's biographer, Ardo, explains how Benedict expounded his views on the Rule. The resulting capitulary, which not everyone liked, was effectively a revised Benedictine Rule which did in fact deal with issues not foreseen in the original Rule and also removed superannuated matter.[6] The chapters of the new Rule were to be learnt by heart. Inspectors were appointed to report on monasteries to their diocesans; and this they did. Furthermore, monasteries were to send representatives to Inda for training under Benedict. The report of the Reichenau representatives to their abbot survives. So Inda became, if not for long, a *schola monachorum*. A further synod at Aachen in 818/19 met to determine the rights and privileges of monks, notably in the election of abbots – an issue that was to trouble religious houses for a long time. Over all this the emperor exercised direct control and showed the importance he attached to monastic well-being by exonerating monasteries from excessive burdens; contributions should be strictly related to means.

Benedict composed several supplementary works of guidance, including a *Codex Regularum* of somewhat antiquarian flavour and a *Concordia Regularum* that was vital. To this should be added his revision of Pope Hadrian's *Dionysiana* and its famous supplement. He died in February 821. What he had achieved with imperial support was monastic uniformity of practice and discipline over a wide area and had shown how to keep it that way. His monks were to be completely cut off from the world for the purpose of prayer and work, always a

    [3] MGH Conc. ii, i, no. 37, pp. 278.
    [4] Ibid., no. 39, pp. 307–464. See also *Corpus Consuetudinum Monasticarum*, i (Siegburg, 1963), ed. K. Hallinger, pp. 433–563 for Aachen legislation and Benedict.
    [5] MGH Conc. ii, i, no. 40, p. 464 and Conc. ii, ii, p. 465.
    [6] MGH Capit. i, no. 170, pp. 343 ff.; *Corpus Consuet*. i, pp. 515 ff.

monastic ideal and never realized for long. Fasting was to be stricter and the Office, increasingly heavy in its demands, exclusively important. This reflected with some accuracy the demand of the century for professionalism of prayer and particularly, as the emperor saw it, for the prosperity of his empire. The attempt at centralization of control could never have survived the social upheavals of the next years though it did serve as a model for Cluny in the remoter future. It is probably true that by the mid-century the Frankish monasteries were in a worse way, their properties more widely secularized and their practices just as diffuse as they had been before Benedict. Major problems of property could not easily be solved on the reformers' terms. Beyond this, however, one glimpses the real object of monastic reform, the spirituality of the Renaissance. Advancing beyond Charlemagne, Louis saw the clergy, and still more the monks and canons, as a class set apart from the laity; professionals of higher standing. This may have seemed implicit in Charlemagne's work but was not quite what he had intended.

Louis's *ordinatio imperii* of 817[7] was as solemn a document as the Carolingians ever produced. It recorded a religious occasion, when the bishops and magnates met together at Aachen and agreed to the emperor's disposition of his empire for the present and the future. It was preceded by fasting, prayer and almsgiving, so that God's will should be made known. Its provisions were witnessed by Louis with his own hand: *propriis manibus*; and this was done for the good of the empire, for the keeping of the peace and for the protection of the whole Church. It rested upon the most significant concept of the Renaissance, not yet elaborated but generally felt: namely, that the empire was a Christian unity, and more than that, was itself the Corpus Christi, indivisible and sacred. To disturb this unity by dissension, let alone by rebellion and warfare, would be to dismember the Body of Christ. Such was the sense in which peace, resting on a delicate equilibrium, was understood. The empire was an earthly reflection of a greater reality, providing the opportunity for all men to achieve salvation. The *Ordinatio* was thus a religious and legal statement of the utmost gravity. Louis's second marriage, the birth of Charles the Bald and the provision of land for the new son at the expense of what had been so solemnly decided are readily explicable in human terms; and it is tempting to say that there was nothing else Louis could have done but go back on the *Ordinatio*. There were those who agreed with him. But many did not, and these included not only his disillusioned elder sons with their followings and others who saw a

[7] MGH Capit. i, no. 136, pp. 270–3.

chance to fish in troubled waters but also clergy who were horrified at the casting aside of the *Ordinatio*. The motives of some may have been mixed; it is not easy to see where political pressures were exerted: but the tone of the opposition to Louis, as it comes to us in writing, is one of moral outrage. It is this aspect of the consequent rebellion that betrays the thinking of men brought up in the reformed tradition.

One opponent was Agobard, archbishop of Lyon. Of Frankish blood but born in Spain, he had reached Aquitaine around 782, had been a pupil of Leidrad at Lyon and in 816 became his successor as archbishop; a suspicious man: suspicious of relics in an age that set great store by them, and suspicious also of ordeals as proofs of God's judgement. He could think for himself. Further proof of this were his views on law. Perhaps he was influenced by Benedict of Aniane; it seems likely; but certainly he was present at Aachen when the *Ordinatio* was promulgated. No bishop was more convinced that it had been divinely inspired, and none more certain that the evils of discord that followed its abandonment were precisely what were to have been expected. Theological and social unity had been sacrificed, and of this the increasing alienation of church property was one manifestation. He urged their complete restitution upon his puzzled emperor, though sensibly blaming Louis's predecessors more than Louis himself for the beginnings of a process that nobody could have checked. This did not please the emperor, mindful as he must have been that Agobard had been one of his earliest appointments to a see. No ruler would have cared to be reminded, as was Louis, of the precedents of Ahab and Manasseh. Even the court reformers thought Agobard too radical – and rude with it. Then again, Agobard blamed the court for its protection of Jews: Jewish beliefs propagated in his own province seemed to him to threaten Christian unity. It was enough that his clergy had to combat superstition without having to combat Jewish proselytism. His position over the first revolt against the emperor, in 829, is clarified if we accept that his famous letter to Louis, known as the *flebilis epistola*,[8] belongs to that date and not to 833, as has generally been thought. In it he urges the retention of the *Ordinatio*, which could only be undone by God, its maker. He did not himself envisage rebellion. What distinguished the second and greater revolt of 833, which temporarily unseated Louis, was the intervention of Pope Gregory IV, who arrived on the scene as an open supporter of Lothar. Agobard wrote to assure the emperor that the pope came only to make peace, and this in fact may have been true. Agobard's own position was logical, as he made plain in his manifesto, or *Liber*

---

[8] PL 104, cols. 287–92.

Apologeticus.[9] At all costs peace must be preserved and bloodshed avoided. His bugbear was the empress Judith, and to him as much as to anyone else was due the widespread belief that she was the Scarlet Woman who had brought dissension among Christians. Oaths had been broken, the moral fabric of the empire had collapsed and the heathen were attacking it from outside. Such was the judgement of God on sin. Everywhere there were Augustinian signs of Antichrist. On Agobard's correspondence the rebellious bishops based their case, or *Relatio*, against Louis: he had been negligent, unjust, cowardly and depraved; his court was a sink and his advisers evil. In brief, he was a self-declared tyrant and no king. Lothar, already co-emperor, must be considered to rule alone. All Louis could hope for was time for penance in a cloister. The moral drama of Louis's annihilation was thus very much Agobard's responsibility; and one can see that it had some bearing on the actions of Louis's sons, who can too easily be dismissed as merely self-seeking. But what caused the rehabilitation of Louis was also something moral: namely, Lothar's harsh treatment of his father and the consequent anger of the other sons. One simply could not treat a penitent emperor, once chosen by God, as if he were a common malefactor. Agobard was not one of the bishops who fled with the defeated Lothar. He remained at Lyon till Louis reached the city to examine him; and then he lost his see, for contumacy. When Louis and Lothar were finally reconciled, Agobard was restored; and by that time the death of Pippin of Aquitaine had given young Charles the Bald an endowment that was not at the expense of Lothar. Ironically, Agobard died, shortly before Louis, at Saintes in Aquitaine while assisting Charles (and thus Judith) to put down a rebellion in favour of Pippin's son. He had been notably consistent, clear-headed and courageous. Speculation, as personified in Felix of Urgel, was anathema to him: it disturbed the unity of Christ. What mattered had been decided by the Bible, the Fathers and the canons of the councils. Similarly with the *Ordinatio*: everything had been decided with God's help and there was no going back and no room for argument. He saw things from a conservative southern viewpoint but could support his belief in unity to its logical extremity. Louis had to go. But Louis returned; and that was God's judgement, too. Persistent though he was, he could not see far into the politico-theological puzzle raised by the birth of Charles the Bald. That puzzle was the nature of rule in a Christian society.

A larger-minded participant was Wala, who, together with his brother Adalhard, was the bright light of the great monastery of

---

[9] Ed. G. Waitz, MGH SS xv, pp. 274–9.

Corbie, a confidant of Charlemagne towards the end of his reign and equally of Louis to begin with; and Wala, fortunately, found a biographer in another Corbie monk, Paschasius Radbert.[10] What Radbert wrote was no biography in the ordinary sense, nor yet a panegyric. Rather it was a lament for a lost ideal as it had been embodied in Wala. It was written in two parts, or at least has been held by many to have been so: the first part completed in 838 and the second some fifteen years later, during the reign of Charles the Bald. Looked at in one way, it could be argued that after so long a gap there was still need to defend the reputation of the reformers who had revolted against Louis; they were still not safe. Looked at another way, one could say that Paschasius had at last elaborated a full defence of what had been sacrificed. It was an essay in political theology. He called it his epitaph for Arsenius (that is, Wala). Why he chose to use transparent pseudonyms for his characters is not clear. He was not the first to call Wala Arsenius and it may have been no more than literary convention. The age loved pseudonyms and nicknames; but it may have been mere prudence to call Louis Justinian.

Paschasius had already written a biography of his brother Adalhard.[11] It was a conventional saint's life for Corbie, to which he appended what he called his Eclogue of the Two Nuns,[12] by which he meant Corbie and her daughter-house at Corvey (or Korvei), in Saxony. It was a kind of panegyric in dialogue form; and this same form he later used in his epitaph for Wala. But the epitaph is in other respects quite different. He was not concerned to map Wala's career nor to paint him as a conventional saintly figure but only to exhibit him as defender of the reforming ideal, and as a man betrayed. Loyalty to an ideal is the keynote; and it was because Wala and his friends failed that the epitaph took the form of a lament for what collapsed with him, never to be recovered. In fact, Wala emerges as the Jeremiah of the reformers. Paschasius had himself been involved in the troubles of the 830s and in due course was removed from Corbie by Charles the Bald. He looked to Wala as the champion of reform as envisaged in the early years of Louis the Pious. More clearly than anyone else he grasped the true nature of the crisis they had all passed through. The ideals of 817 had been lost, and many still grieved for them. It seems unlikely that the epitaph had any political objective, nor was it ever widely read. It was simply a personal lament and a written record that should remove any possibility of argument that the opponents of

---

[10] *Epitaphium Arsenii*, ed Dümmler, Abhand. d. königl. preuss. Akad. (Berlin, 1899–1900), on which ed. see Weinrich, *Wala*, pp. 93 ff.

[11] PL 120, cols. 1507–56.

[12] Ed. L. Traube, MGH Poet. iii, pp. 38–53.

Louis were all, or even principally, self-seekers. Perhaps also it was a counterblast to the justifications of Louis's actions which were certainly in circulation.

Louis's supporters also had their ideals but expressed them in a more prosaic way. First and foremost, we have the continuation of the Royal Annals, known as the St Bertin Annals because of the survival of the earliest manuscript in that monastery.[13] The Annals were in fact kept up at Aachen, as under Charlemagne, and were official at least in the sense that the annalist had access to official documents and recorded events from the viewpoint of his employer; obviously, then, one-sided but not necessarily untrue. They were already a venerable record, having been composed at Aachen since 788. The annalist for the section from 819 to 829 was the great arch-chaplain Hilduin, abbot of St Denis, St Germain and St Médard. It says something about the seriousness of the revolt of 830 that Hilduin himself was involved in it. But the Annals continued to be kept, presumably under the direction of his successors as arch-chaplain. The long section from 835 to 861 was the work of Prudentius, bishop of Troyes from 843 or thereabouts, and it continued to be written at Aachen till the death of Louis the Pious in 840. Prudentius then fled for safety to the empress Judith in Aquitaine, whence he returned to resume his annal-keeping under Charles the Bald, who himself had a copy of the Annals. Official documents continue to be recorded, and particularly for the important years 843 and 845. The treaty of Meersen in 851 is given in full. Prudentius died in 861, at which point the official Annals stop, only to be continued at a more personal level by Hincmar of Reims. Thus we have a continuous record, partly official and generally well-informed, from 788 to Hincmar's death in 882. Within it, the picture of Louis the Pious does not suggest a hopeless weakling but rather a king battling with disloyalty where he least expected to find it: namely, among his sons, his magnates and the most influential churchmen in the land.

Unofficial and more partisan – even exculpatory – were two biographers of Louis. One, known as the Astronomer[14] because of his expertise in the subject, was a younger contemporary of Louis and a court official. Louis gave him an observatory; but apart from astronomy he was strong on medicine and might have been a court physician. His picture of his employer is not idealized. He seems not quite at ease in accounting for Louis's personal puritanism, notably in his dealings with the more old-fashioned bishops. On the other hand he accepts the emperor's undoubted attachment to the ideal of a Christian empire as a single body under the direction of a God-given ruler. And it

---

[13] Ed. F. Grat, J. Vielliard and S. Clémencet (Paris, 1964).
[14] Ed. R. Rau, *Quellen zur karo. Gesch.* i, pp. 257–381.

may surely have been Louis's conviction that he and nobody else encapsulated this unity that enabled him to go back on his own *Ordinatio* without feeling that any principle had been abandoned. The Astronomer could write from personal knowledge of Louis's last ten years (830–40); and what emerges is a picture of an emperor who was as traditionally Carolingian as a puritan could be. He was certainly weak; not because he listened too much to the wrong people (Judith and her kinsmen, and then her alleged lover, the great Bernard of Septimania) but because he forgave too easily. In the ninth century there was no future in forgiving rebels and expecting them to be grateful. He could be brusque, as with the pope, and savage, as in his treatment of his rebellious nephew, Bernard of Italy. Indeed, his penitential reaction to Bernard's death may explain his subsequent mildness in dealing with rebels. Yet he had some of the instincts of the warrior and was a stickler for honour, fidelity and the ceremonies of the court. His spirit was firm and was founded in the practice of obedience to his father – which virtue he also expected from his sons. Hence, as the Astronomer saw it, his refusal to accept his fate at the hands of his son, Lothar: it was one thing to do penance to appease God but quite another to admit that he had been deprived of his imperial rank. If he had admitted as much, he might not so easily have been reinstated after the collapse of the rebellion. Nor did his piety prevent him (or any of his contemporaries) from being wholeheartedly credulous. The Astronomer's account is replete with portents, eclipses and plagues that presage disaster and, in the end, Louis's own death. The death-bed scene is vivid. He spent his last moments in the company of his half-brother, Bishop Drogo, to whom he confessed. Even so, he was bothered by an evil spirit, to whom he cried out 'Hutz! Hutz!' – presumably meaning 'Avaunt!' And then he was buried at Metz by Drogo, there to lie near his mother. Such is the Astronomer's picture.

The second biographer, Thegan,[15] is rather different. An aristocrat and a chorbishop (a suffragan bishop as it might now be) at Trier, he stood less close to Louis. But his passions were more engaged; he was readier to indulge both in adulation and in railing. He sees political issues more clearly than does the Astronomer and is less concerned at the breaking down of ideals. His biography was written in the comparatively peaceful closing years of the reign, probably in 837 or 838. He has his own picture of the young Louis, brought up by Charlemagne, as he says, 'in the liberal arts and in law'. He does not disapprove of Louis's early pieties nor of his attempts as emperor to deal with local repression and robbery, to restore patrimonies (except

---

[15] Ibid., pp. 216–53.

his own, which he continued to alienate like all his dynasty), to ratify deeds and to free those unjustly enslaved. Perhaps following Einhard, he describes Louis's physical prowess and his skill in interpreting scripture. On the bad side, he relied too much on advisers in order to give himself more time for prayer and psalmody (one point that Agobard noted with approval) and, much worse, continued the disgraceful custom of promoting *vilissimi servi* to bishoprics and high office. Scripture showed how unwise this was – one had only to look at Jeroboam – and all experience went to prove that such promotions always turned out wrong. Thegan has a long passage on just how wrong. And this was the gravamen of his charge against an emperor who was basically good and suitable. But the best proof of the folly of trusting the lowly-born was that after Lothar's humiliation of his father, Louis's worst enemies in Lothar's camp were bishops raised from humble circumstances – and foreigners; and above all the rest, Archbishop Ebbo. It was the emperor's fault: 'He made you [Ebbo] a free man, though not of course noble, which would have been impossible. Your fathers', he goes on, 'were goatherds, not royal counsellors.' It would take a Homer, a Virgil or an Ovid to sing the man's misdeeds. It was Ebbo who had brought his king and benefactor low. After Louis's resumption of rule, the bishops persuaded Ebbo ('vile clodhopper') to resign his see, no doubt fearing that if they formally judged and condemned him he might divulge things about their own behaviour that were better kept dark. One would not guess from Thegan that others thought well of Ebbo as a reforming bishop, and a scholar and promoter of missionary work on and over the northern frontiers of the empire. It is Agobard who reveals that Ebbo always had the Scriptures with him, even on horseback. Clearly, Ebbo played no very meritorious part in the revolt and its aftermath; he lacked political courage, if nothing else. But Thegan's attack was personal: Ebbo had been no friend to chorbishops. It was easy to reach the conclusion that if only Louis had trusted well-born advisers and left the bishoprics to them, all would have been well. What was worse, he went on trusting the wrong people after his restoration. So Thegan acquits Louis of being naturally unsuitable to rule or of not measuring up to his predecessors in capacity. He simply had this weakness for the low-born. In other words, the golden age of Charlemagne had been when aristocrats, a king's natural advisers, were bishops and counts. *Novi homines* might be efficient, and ruthlessly so, but they were also insatiably ambitious and thus prone to give self-interested advice, and in the last resort to disloyalty. It is a significant reflection on a social shift, in so far as it is true. Thegan of course had failed to get a diocese.

Two other men felt impelled to say something about the emperor

and to place him in the context of his times. That so many were moved
to leave some record in writing of how he appeared to them is itself
vital evidence of the questioning spirit of the New Israel. One of these
was Ermold, known as Nigellus, the Black. Probably an Aquitanian
cleric, he had held some appointment at the court of Pippin of
Aquitaine but was exiled to Strassburg around 824-8, perhaps because
suspected of disloyalty to the emperor. Whatever the suspicion, he
tried to clear himself in two letters to Pippin and a panegyric to Louis
written in 826-8.[16] Unlike Thegan and the Astronomer, he wrote
before the crisis-years and could afford to be optimistic. He believed
that he saw Charlemagne's programme of militant Christianity coming to fruition; the conversion of the Danes seemed a possibility. Louis
was the head of Christendom, the equal of the Apostles, a ruler whose
glory derived from his faith. He should be merciful, as Christ was: no
hint of weakness here. Judith, moreover, was the perfect consort; her
beauty and her motherhood deserved nothing but praise. Ermold's
panegyric is, then, essentially a summary chronicle in verse of Louis's
best actions, with something of the flavour of an epic dependent on
classical models. Certainly there is nothing else like it for the time. He
can describe vividly: as, for example, the interior of the church of
Strassburg, the paintings in the palace and church of Ingelheim, or
Bigo comforting Louis on the news of Charlemagne's death. Allowing for a good measure of flattery, his picture of the God-fearing,
militant emperor cannot have been so wildly out as to excite derision
at court, even among those who already hated Judith and her clientele.
Thegan was not an important man with big interests at stake but
merely a disgraced cleric who hoped to win forgiveness by saying as
elegantly as he could what many will have admitted: that the emperor
was worthily implementing the Carolingian programme.

Unlike Ermold, Nithard moved in altogether more exalted circles;
for he was the grandson of Charlemagne and thus the nephew of Louis
and the cousin of Charles the Bald and his brothers. Charles was no
sooner king than he asked his cousin to write the history of his reign,
presumably on a yearly basis;[17] but he died, in company with two
other Carolingian kinsmen, in June 844 in a skirmish with the Vikings,
and his writing thus covers less than three years. He was, according to
his epitaph, wise and learned in Scripture, and a good soldier; and
plainly he was a court-educated layman of firmly secular outlook. He
admits in his prologue that he had meant to say nothing about
Charlemagne and Louis but found that their reigns were an essential

---

[16] *Ermold le noir, poème sur Louis le Pieux et épitres au roi Pépin*, ed. E. Faral (Paris, 1932).

[17] Ed. R. Rau, *Quellen*, i, pp. 385–461; also P. Lauer, *Nithard, histoire des fils de Louis le Pieux* (Paris, 1926).

prelude to what he had to record; and he was right. His admiration of Charlemagne was boundless; his was the golden age. As to Louis, Nithard is not unsympathetic to the man personally but is critical of his handling of the events that led to rebellion. Since the work was meant for the eyes of Charles, much had to be omitted; as for example the reasons why his brothers felt outraged by Louis's arrangements for Charles. Nor is there any concern with the religious aspect of the troubles. Unlike Paschasius and Wala, the champions of the divinely-unified empire, Nithard is content with less; a number of *regna* living in amity under kinsmen struck him as an acceptable political solution; indeed as a reversion to a venerable Frankish tradition. These together constituted the Christian *res publica*, so easily shaken by sin and discord. Nithard agrees with Paschasius that there was ground for pessimism in the gulf that separated ideal from reality. Both could discern the inevitable results of personal ambition, brutality and incapacity to govern – the results, as others would have put it, of sin. The significance of Nithard's history is that a Carolingian layman, writing on commission for his cousin, should be able to stand back and view the preceding half-century with a certain degree of detachment. He could not see to the bottom of the problem; could not see, that is, that Charlemagne's ideal was unworkable, was stillborn in his own lifetime and inevitably started to collapse under his son. Moreover, the collapse gathered momentum. Louis's resumption of power solved nothing, any more than did the accession of Charles the Bald.

When one has finished with these contributors to the record, there still remains a select company of theorists, experts in the tradition of Mirrors of Princes, little books of advice and exhortation for rulers. The earliest example is the *Via Regia* of the abbot Smaragdus.[18] This was long thought to have been addressed to Louis the Pious while king of Aquitaine but now seems likelier to have been a thank-offering to Charlemagne for the gift of the abbey of St Mihiel. Certainly he was a southerner, the protégé of Theodulf rather than of Benedict. Smaragdus maps out the course of kingly duties by taking examples from the Bible, and especially from the career of King David. The king is an anointed vicar of Christ, almost a crowned abbot. (Indeed in a second book, the *Diadema Monachorum*,[19] he could borrow large portions from the *Via Regia* because the offices of king and abbot were not dissimilar.) He gave the king a prose and verse version of the *Via Regia* and also worked up a Merovingian Mirror of Princes for one of Louis's sons. The moral was clear: kingship was theocratic; the ruler must accordingly take counsel from the Church, love his subjects, behave in a manly way, care for the poor, be wise, just and pious, and put down

---

[18] PL 102, cols. 933–70.   [19] Ibid., cols. 593–690.

the proud. Such had been the practice of the successful kings of the Old Testament. In short, the Carolingian king had a definable job, a *ministerium* within the *imperium Christianum* which he could perform well or ill. Above all, he must listen to the Church; essentially no new message, since within Francia alone several Merovingians had been told as much. But now there was an intensity lacking before. Whether or not Louis read the *Via Regia* everything suggests that advice of this sort reached him and was taken seriously. He was God's king, employed to exercise the power of *correctio* and *defensio* over Christ's people. This may sound delimiting now but certainly did not do so in the ninth century.

There can thus be no question that the difficulties in which Louis found himself caused many to reflect on the nature of rule in a Christian society and to express their views in biographies, histories and treatises, in prose and in verse. The tone of some is exculpatory and of others admonitory. Archbishop Agobard could write a long letter that is in fact a treatise in order to compare ecclesiastical with what he calls political rule. Bishop Jonas of Orléans writes a lengthy treatise *De institutione regia*.[20] A respected scholar and poet, he had been chosen by Louis to succeed Theodulf at Orléans and had been the redactor of measures taken at the council of Paris in 829 after a critical debate on the nature of civil power. These *acta* were used by Jonas when he came to compose *De institutione regia* and a companion treatise, *De institutione laicali* (written as a moral guide for Count Matfrid). The *De institutione regia*, written in 831, was intended to recall Pippin of Aquitaine to his duties as a Christian ruler and to help him to avoid misfortune, the cause of which, for society as well as individuals, was sin. The business of Jonas, as of any bishop, was the salvation of souls; pastoral solutions presented by the Bible and the Fathers could be applied to Carolingian society. Bishops had to answer to God for kings as well as for others. The authority of a king derived from God alone, not from the people for whom he was answerable to God. Derivation of authority from God was thus vital to Jonas. He was not concerned with the initiation ceremonies by which a man became king but with the proof, in a king's life, of sanctity, that he evidently was God's choice. Why was a king needed? Because people did not live Christian lives, as they would do if they listened to the clergy. A king, then, is the enforcement principle in Christian society. He is there to see that justice is done and the Church protected, and that his household is above reproach. Indeed, injustice or weakness could affect the succession. Jonas does not fail to point out that Louis

[20] Ed. J. Reviron (Paris, 1930) but see Dom Wilmart's critique in *Rev. Bén.* 45 (1933), pp. 214–33.

had not enforced justice within his own household. The bishop is a political moralist, not much concerned with the nature of a unitary empire and blissfully unaware of the real weaknesses in the position of any ninth-century ruler, whatever his ideals. Exhortations of this kind may have been largely ineffective but they were grounded in actual experience of society threatened by disloyalty, upheaval and incompetence. Nobody wrote a treatise on warfare. The answer of the moralists was clear: look back to the biblical rulers and see how they managed under God's guidance. It was an outcome of fifty years' experience that churchmen like Jonas could look at events in this light and express themselves in writing. Nothing suggests that kings resented it or thought their position weakened thereby. What the crisis of Louis's reign did was to concentrate thought on the moral problems of rule; to enquire what a ruler was for, to whom he owed his authority, and how he should exercise it. This was no narrowing of royal authority but its exaltation as a divine office; and it supposed that that office was a realizable ideal. The solution should naturally be sought, not in a fresh look at the material problems actually besetting rulers, but in the guidebook for good living that all agreed was basic: the Bible.

ii. Charles the Bald

The four sons of Louis the Pious – the Emperor Lothar, Pippin I of Aquitaine, Louis the German and (their half-brother) Charles the Bald – were all educated men surrounded by intelligent servants and committed to the protection of the Carolingian Church. Nothing is clearer than the deep sense of reliance upon that protection felt by all churchmen; so deeply felt, indeed, that whatever looked like its withdrawal evoked passionate reaction. The matter was practical, not theoretical. This said, the brothers' approach to the churches under their care was not uniform; in so far, that is, as the evidence goes. More is known about some brothers than others. Louis the German can clearly be seen as a ruler over the bishops and abbots of East Francia. The documents of his chancery and his attitude to the intellectual and pastoral concerns of his Church confirm this impression. More must be said of him at a later stage; and something, too, of Lothar, since Lotharingia, his Rhineland kingdom, was a nodal point for the Carolingian renaissance. But it is of Charles the Bald that most is known. Furthermore, the renaissance of the Frankish Church initiated by the early Carolingians, organized by Charlemagne and deflected into unexpected channels by Louis the Pious, resumed course and reached its fruition under him.

Charles of all the brothers has most claim to stand in the tradition of his grandfather, Charlemagne. A true renaissance prince, he emerges as a sophisticated, pious and masterful ruler, and always a dangerous man to cross. His beginnings lay in the court of his grandfather and father at Aachen; and they were dismal beginnings. He was neither to forget nor to forgive the humiliation of his father and of his mother Judith at the hands of his elder half-brothers. He remembered, too, that he alone of his generation bore the name of his grandfather, which he in turn bestowed on his eldest son. Always he showed awareness of *nomen* and of the past of his dynasty. This sense of the past will have gained something from the teaching of his tutor, Walahfrid Strabo, editor of Einhard's *Vita Karoli Magni*. Much as he honoured his father, Charles took Charlemagne's court for his exemplar as a centre of learning and a magnet to the wise. It was for him to combine secularity with piety and to exercise his God-given authority as Charlemagne had done; but perhaps with less stress on the secularity. This was the road to *fortuna*, the good luck of the house. Like others, Walahfrid recognized his pupil's intellectual precocity; he was a youth with a future. Paul the Deacon was impressed by his Latin culture. He was well educated in the liberal arts and probably also in law and theology. Hincmar later reported that he had learnt the latter from childhood, meaning at court; and Ermold described in verse how the boy had dispatched a deer under the eye of his anxious mother, thus displaying the *virtus* of his father and the *nomen* of his grandfather. Freculf of Lisieux sent the second part of his universal chronicle to Judith for her son's education: he was to consider the glories of his family in the wider context of Rome.

Charles's effective reign over western Francia started not in June 840, when his father died, but on the battlefield of Fontenoy, twelve months later. It was a frightful slaughter though curiously little is known about who was killed there. It was the first of a series of fratricidal engagements stemming from Louis's arrangements for the succession; and it was indecisive. What the young king gained was a breathing-space of some years in which to impose his authority on Aquitaine, where it was reasonably disputed by the supporters of Pippin I's heir, Pippin II. Also, and less successfully, he attempted to master the independent Bretons on his western frontier. Already the menace of Viking assaults along the coast of western Francia complicated matters. Thus early he was called on to face rebellion exacerbated by invasion and was seldom to be free from either. Lupus, abbot of Ferrières, reassured him in a series of letters written between 843 and 845.[1] He was not to submit to overmighty subjects – '*potentes*, whom you have made and can put down'. He must rule with an iron

---

[1] Ed. Levillain, i, nos. 31, 37; ii, 124.

fist and follow the example of the blessed King David by keeping clear of evil men: personal virtue brings immediate gains. Lupus then sent him a résumé of imperial deeds 'so that you can easily see what to imitate and what to avoid. Above all I advise you to consider Trajan and Theodosius.' (Sedulius Scottus also recommended the example of Theodosius I). Not content with this, Lupus sent a copy of Augustine's sermon on oaths as Lenten reading: perjurors could expect to forfeit eternal life. All this was practical advice. Charles must learn to be an iron king, like his grandfather, and not the victim of other men's counsel, like his father. Churchmen with ideas about defining royal power were to find that Charles knew his own business.

The Royal Annals (the St Bertin Annals) continued to be kept by palace clerks, the link between the reigns of Louis the Pious and Charles being the Spaniard Prudentius, later bishop of Troyes. He was responsible for the record from 835 to 861, when he died. His information is scrappy, no doubt because he was never long at court and thus missed important information; but it is accurate when it can be checked. He can be critical of Charles on occasion and does not always write as if he were a court official. Hincmar, continuing where Prudentius left off, reports that the king had a copy of the annals to the year 861; but it is not clear that he had them in Prudentius' lifetime. Perhaps for this reason Charles commissioned a second and more personal record. His cousin Nithard was to provide a partisan account that accepted the infamy of his brothers in challenging his claims: an account for the future to read. Already he saw, as the continuators of the chronicle of Fredegar had seen, the value to his house of a written record. But others, too, used their pens in the new king's interest. An anonymous poet dedicated a *Carmen de exordio gentis Francorum*[2] to him, reminding him of his ancestry by parading before him the virtues of St Arnulf of Metz, Charlemagne and Louis the Pious. Here were his exemplars.

Another side to Charles that emerged in these early years and equally tied him to his predecessors was his concern for theology. This was more than a matter for learned clergy; it touched the king himself and the objectives of his rule. One can see this clearly in his intervention over the dispute concerning predestination started by the monk Gottschalk. This calls for longer consideration elsewhere; but so far as the king was concerned it involved the salvation or damnation of his own subjects. He was consulting Lupus about it in 849 and obtained opinions from other experts. His frequent bullying of Archbishop Hincmar to get the matter settled and his subsequent treatment of the wretched Gottschalk betray dismay at the prospect of predestined damnation for unknown numbers of his subjects but plainly also his

[2] MGH Poet. ii, pp. 141–5.

indignation that his clergy should be thrown in confusion. He demanded clarity of doctrine and certainty of belief, like any other Carolingian, and meant to understand theological issues. Evil times – and they plainly were – demanded the reinforcement, indeed the imposition, of orthodoxy. Hence his resolve to inform himself about the nature of the Eucharist, the heart of Christian practice. Ratramn of Corbie provided him with a suitable résumé in 843, while the abbot of Corbie, Paschasius Radbert, sent him a copy of his own treatise written some time years earlier on the same subject, with a special dedication and poem invoking the Virgin's help for a king strong in virtue who bore the name of his great ancestor. These learned men addressed him as their intellectual equal. What interested them, as pressing issues, interested their king. It was his business, too. In this sense the great abbey worked for its king. But the second part of Paschasius' *Epitaphium Arsenii* by no means suggests that everyone at Corbie had accepted Charles's rule as permanent, even after thirteen years. The son of the detestable Judith might yet be overthrown. Such at least is one possible reading of this extraordinary outburst from a house as well-established in the business of political intrigue as of scholarship.

Other monasteries were less equivocally loyal to the king. St Denis certainly was, and also (among the greater) St Riquier and St Amand in the north, and St Martin's of Tours on the Loire. Tours was placed under a lay-abbot the king could trust: Vivian, also count of Tours and formerly his chamberlain. This was in 844, the year in which Charles' mother, Judith, died at Tours. She had been a remarkably influential woman, ill-used by opponents of the Emperor Louis's second marriage and its consequence, Charles: a second Jezebel to some, and allegedly the mistress of Bernard of Septimania, but to others a cultivated queen with a strong interest in religious foundations and a natural resolve to defend the interests of her son and her German kinsfolk. From Tours the king received a superb copy of Boethius' *De Arithmetica*, dedicated to the Caesar who bears the unconquered name of his grandfather. Charles was not often the recipient of secular books and the Boethius may not have interested him much except as a splendid exemplar of one of the arts of the *quadrivium*. But he was unlikely not to have shared the Carolingian fascination for computistical texts, allied to which were works on astronomy. Indeed, one scholar claims that 'the Carolingians had opened up for themselves and their inheritors the whole complex tradition of ancient astrological imagery'. Latin versions, often illustrated, of Aratus' Greek poem on the heavens fully support the claim. Nor can Charles have been unaware of the stirring of interest in medicine, not simply in the preservation of medical texts but in medicine as an intellectually respectable study. It was to be incorporated in Christian wisdom and to be taught, at least in parts of northern Francia, within a school curriculum. The men most interested in this happened also to move in the circle of the king.

Charles received a yet more significant gift from Tours. This was a Bible, now known as his First Bible. It was a thank-offering from Count Vivian. Like the *De Arithmetica*, it is a book one can still look at. It is rich in historical illustrations, notably that showing the donor presenting his book to the king, who sits enthroned among his monks under the protecting hand of God.[3] There are no bishops present. The picture is a reminder to offer prayers for the king, his family and his subjects; and a reminder to the king himself. The book is a Bible; largely, the sacred account of God's first Chosen People, the people of David, Solomon and Josiah, whose mission was now entrusted to a second Chosen People, the Franks. Continuity of mission was always present to Carolingian minds. Later on, Charles was to give the great book to the Church of Metz.

In June 848 Charles caused himself to be chosen, crowned and anointed King of the Aquitanians at Orléans. His consecrator (soon to desert him) was Wenilo, archbishop of Sens. Almost all the Aquitanian magnates, together with bishops and abbots, were reported to have been present. Whether they were or not, the king was never to find it easy to control so huge a region as Aquitaine, however alert he may have been to the need to appoint loyal Franks to significant offices, both secular and clerical; and above all to the critical see of Bourges. Pippin II continued for years to be a magnet to the disaffected. Though seldom to return to Aquitaine, Charles was its anointed king. It seems unlikely that he felt the need to strengthen his claim to rule his Neustrian Franks by submitting to a comparable ceremony: it was enough that his father had crowned him in September 838. But a solemn inauguration with unction as well as crowning was no bad substitute for unchallenged hereditary succession. Orléans was the first occasion when the clergy gave Charles this substitute for what he lacked: the gravely religious provision for his elder brothers made by the Emperor Louis in the famous *Ordinatio* of 817, and later revoked, in part, in the interests of Charles. Magnates, including clergy, wavered in their loyalties. Their difficulties, in which self-seeking was only one element, were vividly illustrated when Louis the German invaded Aquitaine in 858. The bishops were not at first united in their opposition to the coming of a senior Carolingian. Louis the German was a formidable elder brother and the only one of them to have good

---

[3] Illus. in Hubert, Porcher and Volbach, p. 139. For dedicatory verses, MGH Poet, iii, pp. 243–8, 249, 250–2.

sons. His hopes of supplanting Charles in western Francia were no idle day-dream. He probably never abandoned them. What turned the scales was the intervention of Archbishop Hincmar of Reims, henceforth to be the most powerful influence in West Frankish affairs. His letter to Louis,[4] written on behalf of the clergy of the provinces of Reims and Rouen, not only excuses their attendance on him but questions his motives in invading his brother's lands. Louis went home.

Charles was present when Hincmar's new cathedral at Reims was dedicated and the relics of St Remigius translated. Thus he acquired the patronage of a national saint to add to that of St Martin; and shortly afterwards he acquired another: St Dionysius or Denis of Paris, ancient protector of Frankish kings. It was Charles himself who turned to the great Irish scholar, Eriugena, for a new translation into Latin of the Greek writings of Denis the Areopagite, sent by the Byzantine Emperor Michael to Louis the Pious. Charles shared the common belief that this Denis and St Denis bishop of Paris were one and the same man. The translation – addressed *meo Karolo*[5] – was so pleasing that the king invited Eriugena to translate a second Greek work, the *First Ambigua* of Maximus the Confessor. Thereafter Eriugena proceeded on his own to a great career as a translator, theologian and philosopher. But what mattered was the personal link between the king and the foreign scholar. Eriugena's occasional verse addressed to him reveals how close they were to each other.[6] The patron could be hailed in all seriousness as 'heir of David' and 'king and theologian'. Thus Charles could be enticed to see himself as philosopher-king of a new Athens (the image was Alcuin's); and something of Greek patristic thought must now have been reaching him in Latin guise.

Charles had other routes to the Greek world. Almost at the end of his life he wrote a letter to the clergy of Ravenna in which he refers to a celebration of the Constantinopolitan mass of St Basil in his presence. The liturgy of St Basil was the chief eucharistic formulary of the Byzantine rite. He seems also to have been familiar with the liturgy of St James of Jerusalem, and perhaps other liturgies. This may reveal a royal penchant for liturgical experimentation. It would not be surprising, considering the number of Greek clerics in the West and his connection with the Church of Metz and its *schola graeca*.

To the abbey of St Denis the Carolingians had turned for some of their best administrators. Charles did likewise and rewarded the monks accordingly. He assumed the lay-abbacy in person when the house was directly threatened by the Vikings; and here his bones were ultimately to find rest, along with those of Charles Martel, Pippin III

---

[4] PL 196, cols. 9–25.   [5] PL 122, cols. 1029–1194.
[6] Ibid., cols. 1221 ff., 1227, 1229, 1234.

and his own infant son Charles, child of his second queen, Richildis. From St Denis we have the best evidence of his revival of the earlier practice of *Natales Caesarum*, that is, the official commemoration of his anniversaries and those of his consort by chant and prayer, in return for which a feast was granted. Several monasteries and churches became involved in this new form of commemoration, which required rather more of them than the traditional prayers for the royal family. But St Denis was the king's *pretiosissimus protector*, in whose church his tomb was prepared before one of the principal altars. The good fortune of his family was tied up with the cult of national holy men; and their patronage mattered as much to him as what the Church at large could provide for him in a material way: as, for example, for his court's upkeep, for lands to reward faithful service, and for men-at-arms and trained administrators.

The central part of Charles's reign brought him east, to Metz and St Arnulf, father of the dynasty; that is, into the central region of Francia ruled first by the Emperor Lothar and then by his son, Lothar II. Perhaps with an eye to a possible path to Italy, Charles started by challenging the younger Lothar's claim to Provence, but withdrew. Aggression was built into the Carolingian idea of Christian kingship. God was himself a war-lord. This emerges clearly from contemporary essays in the genre of the *Via Regia*. Charles now saw himself as the likeliest successor to Lothar II if only he could push his claim before Louis the German made a move. The new emperor, Louis II, was tied up in Italy and not a serious contendant. Meanwhile, Charles did what he could to weaken Lothar by supporting the cause of the wife he was trying to divorce. At least this earned him the good opinion of the great Pope Nicholas I. From now on, Charles seemed to be playing a papal game that some of his bishops, including Hincmar, deeply mistrusted. It is likely enough that his ambition was the imperial crown, which by no means suggests that he was the instrument of his clergy; not, at least, in a political sense. On them he relied for the sophisticated administration revealed in the splendid series of *acta* from his reign and in the heavy record of meetings, arrangements and recriminations recorded in his capitularies. But politically he followed his own counsel. He could be sharp with clerics at court and merciless with bishops whose loyalty he doubted. 'We kings of the Franks', he once declared (using the pen of Hincmar), 'are not the surrogates of bishops but *terrae domini*.'[7] When he was bored by the chatter of bishops, he said so. Bishops had to know their place.

Did Charles have a court school resembling the school of his grandfather? No one can deny the intellectual activity of his court or the

[7] PL 124, col. 878 and again col. 886.

attraction of his patronage to scholars and artists. But whether the court itself was a place of book-production and a workshop for skilled craftsmen is more doubtful. Certainly instruction could be had at court. We know of men who made their way to court precisely for this purpose. Lupus, advising Bishop Aeneas of Paris how to approach the king, writes in terms that reveal the king's personal interest in teaching.[8] Heiric of Auxerre, an advanced scholar, observed that Charles's palace deserved to be called a school since there were daily lessons as well as military instruction and noted that foreign scholars, and particularly Irish philosophers, came to court *ad publicam eruditionem*.[9] Plainly, then, teaching took place, and much talking. Hincmar was of the opinion that moral instruction was a hallmark of any *schola*; and perhaps this also was catered for. However, the essential requisite of a school was a permanent base. Though often at Compiègne from the 860s, Charles had no fixed headquarters corresponding to Charlemagne's Aachen, which he longed to possess. If, then, there were limits to what his court-circle could achieve, there remains a marvellous outpouring of what can only be described as court-inspired productions, the work of masters closely associated with the court, as of (or at) St Denis, Tours, Metz, Reims and St Amand. The spread rather than the concentration is remarkable.

Charles was unlucky in his children. In the course of 865 and 866 four of his sons died. This left Carloman, soon to break into open rebellion, and Louis the Stammerer, his ultimate successor whom he detested. He therefore caused his consort Ermentrud to be crowned queen in the hope that she might yet bring him better sons. Her death in 869 was rapidly followed by the acquisition of a new queen, Richildis, from whom also better sons were devoutly but vainly expected. This second marriage was an occasion for a new Bible, now known as his Third, or San Callisto, Bible. Its splendid illustrations were pasted into a still incompletely decorated text, presumably for the special purpose of celebrating the marriage. As a series, these illustrations are a remarkable reflection of Carolingian thought about the nature and origins of kingship. Among them can be seen Joshua as an exalted figure, Saul inaugurated as king in the Carolingian fashion, David as king and author of the Psalms, most beloved of the Old Testament books to ninth-century readers. A Byzantine model was certainly used by the artists, but not slavishly. The frontispiece to the Book of Numbers shows peace and order disturbed by paganism, heresy and magic – artistically a new idea that mirrors a common Carolingian concern. (Charles himself, in 873, betrayed great anxiety

---

[8] Ed. Levillain, ii, no. 122.
[9] Pref. to *Vita Germani*, MGH Poet. iii, p. 429.

to extirpate 'those who work evil and magic', thus bringing death to his people). Above all, the Bible contains a dedicatory illustration of Charles enthroned, with his consort veiled before him.[10] Below this picture is a long verse-inscription on purple, now rather worn. It draws attention to the 'noble consort on the left, by whom distinguished issue may rightfully be given to the realm'. It is an invocation. Two years later, Charles issued a charter in which the Church of Paris and the monks of St Eligius were required to hold the customary annual celebrations of his family's anniversaries, and these should include any future offspring 'if it should come to pass that such be granted by the prolific Virgin; and a refection shall be held . . . on the day of the birth of new offspring if, as we said, such shall have been granted by the Mother of God.'[11] The Virgin, Queen of Heaven, had been represented in Charlemagne's Aachen, in an unique ivory, as a warrior-figure of the Byzantine tradition, her son omitted. There she was *Virgo Militans*. But here in the charter she is conceived differently, as *Maria Genetrix*, who can be importuned, as if she were the old Roman goddess *Fecunditas*, to do what unction and coronation had so far failed to do. But in vain. Charles sits there, hopefully, with his new queen in the San Callisto Bible; but he is only one in a company of kings, his predecessors; and of these, the most significant is Solomon, bearded and crowned in the centre of one illustration but appearing also in two smaller scenes at the top of the page. One of them shows his anointing as king. He stands, a beardless young man, between Zadok and Nathan. In an unfinished Metz sacramentary, a kind of coronation manual and so perhaps dating from 869, we can see a strikingly similar scene of a young Frankish prince, presumably Charles himself, being crowned by the Hand of God.[12] He stands between two haloed bishops, probably Popes Gelasius and Gregory, fathers of the Frankish liturgy. So like were Charles and Solomon to minds that made pictures; the centuries separating them were obliterated. Charles seems to have presented the Bible to Rome on the occasion of his imperial coronation.

But first, there was a coronation at Metz, in Lotharingia. Lothar II had died unexpectedly and Charles was on to his kingdom in a flash, no doubt arguing that his father had presented it to him in 839. Others considered it pure aggression. But Hincmar rallied the Lotharingian bishops to his cause; and Hincmar composed the *ordo* for coronation and unction that took place in Metz cathedral on 9 September 869. It

---

[10] Illus. in Hubert, Porcher and Volbach, p. 140.
[11] G. Tessier, ed., *Recueil des actes de Charles II le Chauve*, 3 vols. (Paris, 1943–55), ii, pp. 314–15.
[12] Illus. in Hubert, Porcher and Volbach, p. 152.

was an inauguration to a new kingdom that momentarily gave Charles his heart's desire – Aachen. In his allocution,[13] Hincmar dwelt on history, appropriately enough in the place where the initiative had been taken in devising a genealogical link between Merovingians and Carolingians. Long ago, he informed the congregation, St Remigius had received holy oil from heaven to anoint Clovis, ancestor of the Carolingians. This same oil, preserved in Reims, he had with him. He now used it to anoint Charles. But what, the historian asks, did this do for the king? Did it make him a churchman's king? In a certain sense it did. Before unction, the clergy insisted on a promise or *professio*, which marked out a specifically Christian path for the exercise of royal power. The advice of the clerical experts would clearly be required. Nothing, however, suggests that Charles resented this or thought that it made him anyone's servant but God's. He would have regarded it as an enhancement of power. He knew from experience that oaths were reciprocal; one may instance his oath at Quierzy in 858, when he had sworn to honour his faithful subjects as a *fidelis rex* should.[14] Further, he had acknowledged in 859 that his consecrators at Orléans had the power to authorize his deposition if he failed as a Christian king. No doubt such would have been his fate if Louis the German had defeated him. Even as early as 844, at the council of Ver, there had been an implied threat of excommunication, or possibly more, in the final words of the bishops to their king. However, he was safe in his person and office so long as he did not manifestly act 'against God and against you'. Indeed, he required obedience from his bishops, who knew that they were helpless without him. If we wish to see a king crawling before his bishops we must wait for the *Responsio* of Boso on the occasion of his election as king of Burgundy in 879. Charles's bishops stood in awe of him. To usurp royal functions or to emulate royal power was, as Hincmar pointed out, to behave like Lucifer; 'we cannot all be kings'.[15] Moreover, all those not designated by God to be kings were subjects, clergy and laity alike. Step by step, such views crystallized as crisis followed crisis over the ninth century.

Whatever his claims to rule in Lotharingia, there were those who saw in it the king's ambition for yet higher things. The Fulda annalist detected a menace to Louis the German: Charles, he alleged, ordered that he should be called *imperator et augustus*, as lord of two kingdoms.[16] This lacks confirmation but in any case would have no more constitutional meaning than had the words of Eriugena some years earlier when he hailed Charles as *eusebestate igitur regum*,[17] most

[13] MGH Capit. ii, p. 340.
[14] Ibid., p. 296.
[15] Ibid., p. 305.
[16] *Ann. Fuld.* s.a. 869.
[17] PL 122, cols. 1196.

pious king; a Byzantine borrowing proper to a Grecian but presumably arcane to Charles.

Some art historians ascribe to the Metz coronation the making of the little bronze statuette of a Carolingian ruler on horseback.[18] Certainly it is contemporary work of the Metz metal school. It could be Charles or, as was once thought, Charlemagne. It does not matter which. There was a Carolingian image in plastic art as in painting. Differentiation from his ancestors was not what Charles sought. To the same occasion may be ascribed a famous unfinished Metz sacramentary; unfinished presumably because Charles's occupation of Metz was brief. At least it can be inferred that an occasion religious as much as political produced the book to mark it.

For a little while, as ruler of Lotharingia, Charles had Aachen, and from it brought back treasures that reached other destinations. But the Metz venture did not work as intended. There was a successful counter-attack. He may now have begun to think of founding his own Aachen at Compiègne, safe within his western territory. Works of art (metal-work and carved ivories) and fine books associated with him may well belong to the early 870s and clearly imply his patronage of craftsmen and writers from several centres, notably Metz and St Denis. The splendours of the liturgical books of Metz were an obvious inspiration. Among the books directly associated with the king are a sumptuous personal prayer-book, in which the king in full regalia kneels before a triumphant Christ on the Cross. Charles's humility, like that of Christ himself, is a royal attribute. The book's ivory covers are decorated with Old Testament relief motifs associated with humility, and especially with David's. The covers of Charles's personal psalter convey much the same message. The psalter contains what is claimed as a portrait of the king. From Charlemagne's day there had been representations of Frankish kings, but not until the mid-century do we find any that could be claimed as portraits. A very early one is the portrait of the Emperor Lothar in his gospel-book: one seems to see a real man.[19] Nor is there any reason why one should not. Paschasius Radbert could say of painters who knew their job that they could often achieve a speaking likeness of a face without the assistance of letters or voice. Then we have Charles in more than one book but he fails to look other than symbolic till we reach his psalter, for which there is no certain date. The portrait is idiosyncratic:[20] drooping Carolingian moustache, greying hair, puffy cheeks, a strained look (shared by the Emperor Lothar), crown at a rakish angle. The king is not apparently bald. But if it was painted from the life, the portrait is

[18] Illus. in Hubert, Porcher and Volbach, p. 225.
[19] Ibid., p. 145.　　[20] Ibid., p. 147.

still heavily symbolic. Charles is ranked by the painter among the divine kings of old, and sits there under the protecting hand of God. He vividly recalls the Carolingian idea of King David – author of the Psalms (as was believed) but also prophet and warrior – though it must also owe something to contemporary Byzantine practice. Above the portrait runs an inscription in gold on purple, in which he is compared with Josiah and Theodosius. This is not vainglorious but a reminder to the king of two great exemplars. He is to reflect upon Josiah who reformed Israel and Theodosius, whether the codifier of Roman Law or he who submitted to penance imposed by St Ambrose. Both Theodosii were heroes to the ninth century, and indeed were celebrated in a single sentence by the poet Sedulius.

In the great *Codex Aureus* of St Emmeram in Regensburg we see Charles once more;[21] this time under a magnificent baldacchino, blessed by the hand of God, attended by angels and receiving the homage of his provinces. And again there is a long inscription. Other illustrations in this Bible, for example that showing Gregory the Great, help us to grasp something of the intellectual setting of Carolingian kingship in its historicizing and biblical context. Yet another Bible, called his second, is associated directly with the king, but it belongs to a group of Franco-insular manuscripts and so is a book of patterns, not portraits. It comes from St Amand, of which he was patron. In the verse dedication the writer alludes to the king's loss of his son Charles in 866 and to the rebellion of his son Carloman in 870. The scriptorium thus had a direct interest in the fortunes of the royal family. It speaks to the king of recent, painful events and does so in a splendid Bible.

St Amand also contributed to a special interest of this aggressively pious king: saints' Lives. Milo sent him a new edition of his Life of St Amand with verses praising the royal power and peaceableness. A poem on sobriety, also intended for him, was presented after Milo's death by his nephew Hucbald, who also perpetrated an appalling poem on baldness – which he had the good sense not to present to the king, though it finishes with a eulogy of him. A greater man, Heiric of Auxerre, dedicated to him a verse Life of St Germanus, praising him for perpetuating the wise rule of his father and grandfather; Greece, he adds, plainly referring to Eriugena and his friends, grieves to see her privileges pass to Charles's kingdom. And it was at Charles's instance that Usuard, monk of the favoured house of St Germain-des-Prés near Paris, compiled a famous martyrology. The king thus saw himself as the prosperous bedesman of as many saints as he could muster. It was nothing unusual; but it reveals a vital aspect of his practical mind.

[21] Ibid., p. 149.

Many were anxious to tell Charles how to be the kind of king the Church desired; and foremost among them, Archbishop Hincmar. First around 869 and certainly on request, he provided a treatise on virtue and vice. It followed good models, showing the king the ageless virtues and vices in a traditional way and probably reassuring him that he was already on the right path. But it seems to emphasize the special vices of the time: gluttony, cupidity, sensual indulgence and particularly violence – that is, unjustified violence, not wars against enemies or repression of rebels. A year or two later Hincmar was ready with a weightier contribution on the person and office of a king.[22] Charles had asked for comment on certain texts bearing on his royal office. The reply takes the form of a Mirror of Princes; an essay, that is, in a well-tried literary genre with which recent Carolingians had been familiar. Hincmar pays attention to the person of the king within the *res publica*, the nature of royal mercy and the punishment of wrong-doers. It is a stern master he depicts and no passive servant of the Church. Like Charlemagne, Charles's business is *correctio* and active warfare against his pagan enemies, the Vikings. The profession of arms was not to be despised, as by some it clearly was. What is curious is that armed might seemed to require any justification. All we know of Charles from earlier years suggests that harsh measures came naturally to him. His vengeance could be terrible: executions and blindings punctuated his reign. Hincmar's intention will have been less to correct royal backslidings than to show the king that he was well set on the *via regia*, the Christian's way through the world to heaven. No less for his own sake than for that of his hard-pressed, bewildered magnates Charles would welcome theological backing in the business of resisting Vikings. It enforced his claim on them to give him the support in the field he so often lacked in years of grim pressure. Encouragement and advice, then, he received from the Church; and it came to this: of royal blood and born to rule, he was to see himself in a clear context as an office-holder on whose personal comportment hung the well-being of Christian society, and as heir to a complex tradition of classical, patristic and Jewish roots. He must never forget the timeless unity of God's people that reached back to the Israelites and to their kings. Among the virtues, he must fasten on to *sapientia*, as the poets also tell him. Solomon would be his model here. The *sapientia* of a Christian ruler demanded a positive outlet in good government, sensible counsellors, sometimes severity to inspire terror, a will not only to defend his people with arms but to extend the bounds of Christian society. God was a god of war, and so too should be his servant, the king. So Charles was invited to take his place in a great succession:

[22] PL 125, cols. 833–56.

David, Solomon, Josiah, Trajan, Theodosius, Constantine, Charle-magne. More than his grandfather, he was surrounded by worried men, who looked to the past for lessons and examples. Only in a special sense did they presume to tell him his business: they related it to Christian morals. But since a bad king must in practice be tolerated, much more must a good king be left to his own devices. One can see the application of all this ethical guidance in an immensely long edict promulgated at Pîtres in June 864,[23] which rehearses the perils and horrors brought upon Francia by the Vikings; and it does so in the light of moral shortcomings at home. Only through repentance could Charles and his people hope to win divine aid in their resistance. Repentance, not capitulation, was the Church's remedy.

Since at least 872 the papacy had seen Charles as the most suitable successor to his nephew, the Emperor Louis II. In papal eyes this meant an emperor in Italy, fit to carry on Louis II's endless campaigns against dissidents and Arabs in the hostile south. But it meant more. The popes held an exalted view of the emperor's office. He was *salvator mundi*, established by God in imitation of Christ, the true king; and what Christ had had by nature, the emperor attained by grace. The Christ-imitating ruler, the *christus Domini*, was no stranger to Charles; and no stranger, either, to his elder surviving brother, Louis the German. Both kings would have seen the imperial crown as a means of re-uniting Charlemagne's world. Even Louis II, who could play no part north of the Alps, had informed the Byzantines that he reigned as emperor over all the Franks 'since it can be said that we rule all the territories of those who are of our own flesh and blood'.[24] It was a formal statement of Frankish political theory. There was one *regnum*, not three or four. Louis II died in August 875, and Charles at once made for Rome where he was crowned emperor by the pope on Christmas Day, as Charlemagne had once been. He found himself in a byzantinizing atmosphere that hung about him for the remaining two years of his life. There were discussions with the learned papal librarian, Anastasius, who had already interested himself in the works of Pseudo-Denis, so revered by Charles. Anastasius was very fulsome on the subject of the sublime ruler of the Franks. Charles also listened while in Rome to a recitation of a parody in verse of the *Cena Cypriani*, in which the guests were biblical characters; and to this John the Deacon appended an epilogue on the imperial coronation. Neatly if not quite plausibly, he summarized Charles's triumph over the dissi-dence that started long ago on the field of Fontenoy. He grasped that the new emperor required praise above all else; reassurance that his reign had now reached its natural culmination. For his part, Charles

[23] MGH Capit. ii, pp. 310–28.   [24] MGH Epist. vii, p. 388–9.

gave presents to the pope (seen as bribes by the Fulda annalist). These included the San Callisto Bible and a remarkable ivory throne, the work of Metz craftsmen either in Metz or in Charles's court-workshop, assuming that one existed. The throne's ivory panels – possibly inspired by Solomon's throne in I Kings 10: 18 – show Charles at the moment of being offered two crowns by angels. It is a most impressive piece of work and bears no resemblance to Charlemagne's stone throne in the chapel at Aachen or to the metal travelling-throne known as Dagobert's which Charles allegedly took from Aachen and gave to St Denis. If he had given the pope nothing else, the ivory throne would have left a vivid impression of the new emperor as patron of religious art and as a ruler who saw himself in the line of succession from David, the evident choice of God.

The papacy did its best to support Charles in the difficulties that faced him, first in northern Italy and then at home, where he returned to find that Louis the German had invaded his territory in his absence. Many in western Francia would support the outraged Louis, feeling that Charles had deserted them by an irrelevant trip to Italy. However, Louis retreated. Charles then (June 876) held a great council at Ponthion,[25] the purpose of which was to persuade the bishops and magnates of west Francia and Lotharingia to recognize his titles of emperor and king of Italy. There were many sessions, largely taken up with Roman rehearsals of his claims, and with the business of imposing his new confidant, Archbishop Ansegis of Sens, as papal vicar over the north. To this last the bishops of Hincmar's persuasion objected; they feared the threat to the autonomy of the Frankish provinces of the Church. The last session of the council was a liturgicized occasion. The emperor arrived, according to Hincmar, robed and crowned in the Greek fashion, followed by the Empress Richildis, whereupon the two papal legates intoned the imperial litany. The Fulda annalist is equally sour about Charles's tendency to go Greek on formal occasions as, for example, by wearing a diadem with silk veil in church. The Ponthion council closed with official *laudes* or acclamations of the pope, the emperor, the empress 'and the rest according to custom'. The Frankish Church as there represented thus formally accepted the new emperor crowned by Rome. But it did not remove him from the hurly-burly of Frankish affairs into the more rarefied atmosphere of pope's man in Italy. The value, to him, of the imperial title lay north of the Alps. It lent colour to his immediate entry into Aachen on the news of the death of Louis the German and to his further advance east, only to be checked by a decisive engagement at Andernach. This last bid for pan-Frankish dominance disturbed the eastern Franks more than the

[25] MGH Capit. ii, pp. 348 ff.

westerners, who simply wanted the king to defend them from increasing Viking pressures. The impressive measures he then took show that he did indeed mean to defend them.

Work on the *palatium* at Compiègne, already begun, and the foundation of a royal chapel there, dedicated to the Virgin – 'for we wish to imitate the practice of Charlemagne'[26] – suggests that he meant to stay where he was; and it may be that he himself named his new headquarters Carlopolis; clearly it was known as such by the tenth century, according to the lost annals of St Quentin-en-Vermandois, and the giving of such names was much in the spirit of the ninth. Hadrian II himself suggested renaming Tours Karolidonum. Eriugena wrote a poem for the dedication of the chapel, which he describes.[27] And even now, in 877, Eriugena can wish him a long and prosperous reign. Charles, for his part, provided the hundred *clerici* of his new collegiate establishment with a lavish foundation-charter (or what was seen as one), in which he states plainly that his model had been the chapel at Aachen, dedicated to the Virgin by his grandfather of sacred memory. This he had done because Aachen had not yet come to him. So he founds Carlopolis but goes on hoping for Aachen. He was not to be buried there; but his successor, Louis the Stammerer, was, and so also, by a strange irony, Louis V, last of the Carolingians.

Urgent cries for help from Rome, pressed by enemies, sent Charles south once more. First, he made detailed provision for the government of his kingdom in his absence, knowing that trouble was brewing. But it was the business of an emperor to defend Rome against infidels and rebels; go he must. To many Franks it looked like desertion in the face of the Vikings. Revolt broke out. It was on his hasty return from Italy to deal with this that Charles died unexpectedly in an Alpine hut, on 6 October 877, from dysentery or poison or both. It had proved too much for one man.

Before his last journey south, the emperor had named his executors and provided for the disposal of some at least of his books.[28] He was a sick man and knew that he might not return alive. The books were to be divided between St Denis, Nôtre Dame of Compiègne, and his son and successor, Louis the Stammerer. This will probably explain some of the treasures of the two great houses. The executors appear to have deflected certain books to the cathedral of Laon as gifts from themselves. So Charles, at the end, was thinking of his collection 'in our treasury'.

It was a long way from the field of Fontenoy to the Alpine hut, and the journey had taken a long time: thirty-six years of rebellion,

---

[26] Tessier, *Recueil* ii, p. 451; see also p. 360.
[27] PL 122, cols. 1235 ff.   [28] MGH Capit. ii, pp. 358–9.

dissatisfaction and invasion. One wonders whether the clerical advice he constantly got and the pictured images of kingship that came his way had any effect on his actions. He had been required to 'be a Solomon in wisdom, a warrior like David, a champion of religion like Constantine, an observer of law like Theodosius, a father of his people like Charlemagne. A tall order. Clearly he tried, believing that his models enhanced his authority. The recurrent themes of his capitularies are the rule of law, civil and canon, as established by his predecessors; and the pursuit of justice, reason, moderation and peace as bulwarks of a stable Christian society. His had been the responsibility for *correctio*, for the eradication of infidelity and sin – the harbingers of social disruption. He filled no passive role. The opinion of his clergy was that he succeeded to a large degree. We do not know what his secular magnates thought: certainly they did not object to the kind of king he was, though many objected to his measures affecting them personally at different times. The moral basis of Charlemagne's rule had been severely shaken by the débâcle of Louis the Pious and the divorce proceedings of Lother II, but Charles continued to accept that his rule was hedged about by the texts of Christian morality. His job remained traditionally Carolingian. He was no mere warrior; but still less was he a kind of monk or bishop. His models, unlike his father's, lay more in the Old Testament than in the New. It was not, then, absurd for the often critical Hincmar to warn a pope that Charles was a Christian, learned and law-abiding, and so above reproach. His acts of violence could be misdirected, his attitude to his kindred and their lands excusable only on the ground that to strike first was the way to survive. But he knew what being a king of a new kind entailed. He had a view of Christian society and his place in it. In excess of any other member of his dynasty he was made to understand that kingship was a special form of Christian life. It started at birth, was shaped by baptism and by education to his *ministerium*, was confirmed by the acclamation of his people and by the rites of inauguration, was proved by his capacity to rule and rewarded at last by access to the heavenly kingdom. The clergy of the ninth century knew what they wanted: not simply or formally a Christian king (the Frankish kings had long been such) but a king conceived on a biblical pattern interpreted in the light of the Carolingian renaissance.

XIV

REFORM AND ITS APPLICATION

i. *Legislation and Exhortation*

ONE speaks of legislation; but if it is difficult to give a precise meaning to the word in the Merovingian context, it is more so in the Carolingian, when material for study is more abundant. There survive many documents; capitularies wholly or partly devoted to the business of the Church, and directives and synodal acts at a lower level that seem to give effect to what had been decided at a higher level. Alas, there is no assurance about the legal standing of most of this material. It survives in private, often later, copies; and when there is more than one copy textual divergences often emerge. Bishops or others might acquire copies of directives that immediately affected them, but none had legally authentic versions of what had once been promulgated, even in their own presence, let alone of the entire corpus of legislation. The imperial or royal chanceries are sometimes taken to task for incompetence: the clerks should have kept authenticated copies of whatever was decided; and this they did not do. But there is no evidence that it was their duty to do so. It was the word of the ruler and not any writing that gave legislative force to whatever decisions were arrived at by or for the Church in his presence. Thus it came about that when Louis the Pious wished to consult his earlier capitularies he had to turn to a large private collection made inaccurately enough by a certain Ansegisus, abbot of St Wandrille and other houses.[1] Some years later, a collector known by the pseudonym Benedictus Levita made his own selection of capitularies and other matter.[2] Without these two, our knowledge would be sadly diminished. However, when every allowance has been made for gaps, confusion and contradiction, what remains can only be called copious evidence of Carolingian legislative intention. How far down in society these initiatives penetrated is a separate issue.

Reference has already been made to the new start given to ecclesiastical legislation in Francia by St Boniface, Carloman and Pippin III. Derived from Anglo-Saxon practice, the models and inspiration were Roman; and it was upon the canon law of the Church that royal legislation rested. Relevant conciliar decrees and references to them are reiterated throughout the Frankish material. The Frankish Church

[1] MGH Capit. i, pp. 382 ff.   [2] PL 97, cols. 697–912.

was plainly being required to put its house in order. Charlemagne would have said that his work for the Church was no more than a development of his father's. This was essentially true, but did not prevent his successors from seeing in him the planner and initiator of the reform of the Church.

It was at the siege of Pavia in 774, after he had been king for eight years, that Charlemagne received from Pope Hadrian I the great collection of canons known as the *Dionysio-Hadriana*;[3] that is, the canonical collection made by Dionysius Exiguus (Denis the Little) in the early sixth century, with additions. It was some while before the effect of this was apparent in Frankish canonical practice. Meanwhile, it was in his fresh conquests – Lombard Italy, Saxony and Bavaria – that the first evidence of his ideas on religious legislation was made apparent. Italian capitularies in particular were to form a substantial contribution to ninth-century legislation. A capitulary promulgated at Herstal in 779[4] reveals in its ecclesiastical articles that the king was already tightening his grip on the higher clergy; and typically, it survives both in a Frankish version and, with some variations, in a Lombardic version. He followed this up with a sharp letter to his secular officials complaining that 'our bishops' were seeing clergy other than those designated by themselves jobbed into benefices, to say nothing of secular interference in the Church's precarial holdings and tithes. The local secular hold over Church property, sometimes for understandable reasons, was a problem never satisfactorily solved by the Carolingians.

It was in March 789 at Aachen that Charlemagne issued the first, and in some ways the greatest, of his capitularies affecting the Church.[5] It comprises eighty-two articles and a prologue in which he informs the bishops that he is sending special representatives (his *missi*) to assist them in remedying abuses. From now on, the *missi* were to be the most effective channel between the royal will and the bishops. Yet the tone of the prologue is apologetic: the king justifies his intervention, which he trusts will be well received, by invoking the precedent of Josiah, reformer and lawgiver of Israel ('not that I rate myself his equal in sanctity'), who recalled his people to true religion through visitation, correction and advice. These three words, *circumeundo, corrigendo* and *ammonendo* – were to weave their way through all his legislation. The capitulary is known as the *Admonitio Generalis*. Its first sixty articles are a résumé of material from the *Dionysio-Hadriana* concerning mainly the functions of bishops and the behaviour of clergy. In a

---

[3] Ed. J. Hartzheim, *Collectio Dionysio-Hadriana, Concilia Germaniae*, i (Cologne, 1759), pp. 131–235.

[4] MGH Capit. i, no. 20, pp. 47–51.   [5] Ibid., no. 22, pp. 53–62.

word, the way things should be had long since been laid down in the
canons, and the hierarchy should not plead ignorance as an excuse for
non-observance. This was no mere window-dressing. The remaining
articles, which are new, pin-point immediate needs in the light of
those canons. No doubt they reflect the concerns of the king himself
but are put together, after much consultation, by royal clerks. They
would not otherwise be larded with scriptural quotations (the *Lex
Domini*). Preaching is stressed as a prime obligation of the clergy; and
to this the bishops must look, as well as to how clergy administer
baptism, celebrate mass, chant the Psalms and explain the Lord's
Prayer. Bishops are also responsible for the upkeep of churches, the
supervision of monasteries and houses of canons. Monasteries and
cathedrals shall provide instruction in reading for children of all classes
(*scolae legentium puerorum*), and shall further provide for instruction in
the Psalms, chant, computus and grammar; and the 'catholic books'
(biblical texts?) shall be corrected with great care since erroneous ideas
come from faulty texts. The copying of these books is the business of
experienced scribes. So much does the Carolingian programme hinge
on correct texts widely distributed and uniformly expounded. The
clergy are in fact being made responsible to the king for the religious
life of the laity; and more than that: also for its moral life – for
understanding the nature of peaceful coexistence, of perjury, superstition, envy, vengeance, theft, illicit unions, false witness, penitence.
Most of this had been said before. Charlemagne's clergy bring it
together as an act of royal policy. Then comes the real problem: did
every bishop and abbot receive a copy of the *Admonitio*? It seems
unlikely. Perhaps it was left to the *missi* to ensure that the gist of it was
passed on – who knows with what success? Probably some of the
higher clergy present at Aachen at the critical time made what copies
they could. All that is clear is the intention.

Revolts, unsuccessful campaigns and famine were the background
to an impressive gathering of clergy summoned by Charlemagne to
Frankfurt in June 794. The resultant capitulary[6] and some consequential documentation survive. The initiative was the king's: he
summoned clergy from far and wide (there were English representatives), specified the agenda and presided personally. It was his synod,
and therefore intensely practical. Much that was discussed and decided
upon affected secular life but always under his overshadowing sense
of Christian morality. Weights and measures, coinage and the keeping
of archives fell within this category. But there were deeper issues.
None moved him more than the burning questions of the heresy of
Adoptionism and the cult of images: these came first. The assembly

---

[6] Ibid., no. 28, pp. 73–8.

went on to consider political matters but soon came to what was strictly ecclesiastical: the jurisdiction of bishops; the undesirable movement of clergy from one diocese to another; the territory of rival metropolitans, the rehabilitation of one bishop and the condemnation of another; the monastic life; the organization of the Church (this largely from the *Dionysio-Hadriana* by way of the *Admonitio*); authorization for Bishop Hildebold of Cologne to reside at Aachen to advise the king on the business of the Church; the admission of Alcuin to the confraternity of prayer that embraced those attending the council. The jurisdiction of the Church was further extended: clergy were justiciable in any cause, civil or ecclesiastical, only at the bishop's court; counts were to be present at such courts to enforce episcopal sentences, but a joint court of count and bishop would hear cases between clergy and laity when the latter brought the charge; churches standing on land held in benefice by the laity were to be maintained by them, and tithe paid. The clergy came in for stricter control: palace clergy were to be protected against influences of indiscipline from the outer world; clergy might not form sworn associations leading to conspiracy; bishops were to instruct their clergy with a view to promotion; bishops were to avoid material preoccupation – though how this was to be done is not stated; bishops were to supervise private churches. But if the authority of bishops over their clergy was thus strengthened, so too was that of metropolitans over their bishops. A firm hierarchy of control would be the basis of order and stability, and from this the innumerable straggling communities of monks and nuns were not to be exempt. Some articles of the capitulary cover strictly spiritual matters, such as religious teaching, the cult of saints, the right of the pure in heart to pray in any language. As one reads the huge capitulary one is reminded of the councils of Toledo. A great assembly of important men gathered from all over Francia and beyond can raise matters, particular and general, as opportunity serves; and these, disparate enough, are reflected in the decisions recorded. What holds it all together is the overriding sense of urgency and the will of Charlemagne himself.

We come to the year 802, when Charlemagne could speak as emperor. A long capitulary, known as the *Capitulare Missorum Generale*,[7] reiterates the principles of the *Admonitio* in rather more urgent language. It starts off by emphasizing the supervisory duties of the *missi*. The Lorsch Annals reveal that *missi* of real distinction were not being chosen; only through men who were above bribery could the emperor counteract local influence and protect churches and those without protection. The capitulary enjoins a new oath of fidelity on free men, lay and clerical,

[7] Ibid., no. 33, pp. 91–9.

above twelve years of age; an oath that effectively made every man directly responsible to the emperor for preserving social stability. Clergy, monks and nuns are tied even more rigorously to their prescribed duties. Special attention is paid to deviations common to the laity: homicide, feud, incest, perjury. A Christian society that overwhelmingly comprises laymen will require heavy supervision and stiff penalties for going astray. The emperor is saying that all this is his responsibility. It may well be thought that clerical indoctrination was placing him in an intolerable position, where directives issued in his name could not possibly be enforced and for the failure of which he and his successors might be made answerable. Yet the palace felt that enforcement ought to be possible: the capitulary was followed up by further special directives to *missi*. Evidence of such for Orléans, Paris and Rouen survives. Hardly a year passes for which there is not some trace of consultation over or clarification of decisions taken earlier on; much repetition, therefore, and not a little exasperation, punctuated by national fasts to expiate a generation's sins and to propitiate an angry God.

As the end of the reign draws near, Charlemagne's sense of frustrated mission boils over in a series of programmatic statements. The first, of the year 811, is an angry letter to bishops, abbots and counts,[8] rebuking them for failing to collaborate and for treading on each other's toes; 'are we really Christians?' he enquires, perhaps not ironically. Plainly he is preparing them for a major assembly and more soul-searching. Then comes what does not look like a capitulary but is so classified, of 811 though from an unknown place, *De Justitiis Faciendis*.[9] The emperor is coming down heavily on all conflicts and disputes, some dating back to his father's time, that still disturb his empire. He will judge personally all outstanding quarrels involving bishops, abbots, counts and *potentiores*, and the *missi* are reminded of their duties.

The year 813 witnessed a final round of deliberations and proposals for reform. In Italy an assembly was summoned at Mantua, formally at the instance of the young king Bernard but in fact at Charlemagne's, 'so that the evils that at present submerge God's Church shall be rooted out and cast forth'.[10] Its decisions are reported in two parts, the first ecclesiastical, and the second general but inevitably touching social problems affecting the Church. The Lombard Church, like the Frankish, had been unable to protect its properties from secular invasion or its clergy from failure to observe the ancient canons. In Francia itself the emperor decided to summon the regional assemblies of bishops under chairmen of his own choosing. There were five such. The southern bishops met at

[8] Ibid., no. 71, pp. 161–2.
[9] Ibid., no. 80, pp. 176–7.   [10] Ibid., no. 92, pp. 194–5.

Arles and drew up a list of canons to present to the emperor. Their colleagues elsewhere met at Reims, Mainz, Chalon and Tours; and they too drew up canons for their master. The results were co-ordinated at a great assembly held at Aachen in September 813.[11] Important political issues were decided: Louis the Pious was crowned co-emperor in his father's presence and Bernard was confirmed in his kingdom of Italy. Then came the affairs of the Church; and these were summarized under the emperor's direction. But what survives is not the imperial capitulary but the agreement of the bishops present, after all five reports had been considered. Various versions of the agreement, different as they are, reveal that the regional assemblies had failed to face all the problems submitted to them and were convinced that nothing further could be done without the support of the emperor and his local representatives. At least they had all given attention to the control of monasteries, nunneries and houses of secular clergy, as also to the problem of wandering or unattached clergy, the proper observance of Sunday and, perhaps most important, baptism. Some great capitulary would doubtless have followed; but the emperor died in January 814, a bare three months after the assembly.

Charlemagne's bishops met in provincial assemblies from time to time, presumably to accept and hand on what had been decided in general assemblies or had reached them as capitularies. Reports of some such come down to us from Friuli and from several Bavarian councils; and there must have been others. All of this may in a loose sense be termed legislation for the Church. In intent, it is very impressive. There can be no question that Charlemagne himself was deeply concerned to activate the reform not only of the Church narrowly conceived but also of the Christian society entrusted to him. In this he was heir to his father and to the teaching of some very sophisticated clergy. Their dependence on him is always apparent; but on the other hand, they have moved to the front as initiators of reform in detail. Their cathedral libraries were already well stocked with canonical material; and so too were monastic libraries, as for example Corbie, St Denis and Tours. Abbots, though some were powerful, enjoyed nothing corresponding to the collective authority of bishops.

With Louis the Pious we move into a different atmosphere, rather monastic than episcopal and heavily flavoured with the reforming ideals of Louis's Aquitanian mentor, Benedict of Aniane. For a while it was to be men of the South, notably Benedict and Helisachar, who called the tune at Aachen. Their intention was traditional: to reform Christian

---

[11] Ibid., no. 77, pp. 170–2.

society according to principles long since determined. But their approach was rather different. At once we encounter an astonishing series of reforming councils, stretching over four years (816 to 819). More than under Charlemagne one can feel the reforming thrust of the emperor; a thrust soon deflected and weakened by the arrangements he felt it necessary to make for the future government of his empire (the *Divisio Imperii* of 817) and his second thoughts on the matter following the birth of Charles the Bald in 823. These political events, together with Louis's treatment of the rebellious Bernard in Italy, had grave religious overtones, outraging many clergy as well as laity. However it would be true to say that nobody in 814 doubted the religious zeal of the new emperor. Indeed, it has been thought that his role in the earliest councils of the reign was sufficiently preponderant to offend certain bishops who had been accustomed to a bigger say in the business of the Church. One of these was Theodulf of Orleans.

The first Aachen council, of 816, at once turned its attention to clergy and more particularly to canons and canonesses. Its decisions were bolstered with a vast deal of reference to patristic and canonical literature.[12] The Rule once devised by Chrodegang of Metz was not only to be enforced but expanded. The secular canons in their comfortable city quarters could not anticipate an easy time, nor much relish the intervention of monks at Aachen. However, the monks themselves, already forewarned by some provincial *capitula*, were in their turn considered in 817, at a synod of abbots and monks under the direction of Benedict. The Rule was expounded, difficulties and errors cleared up and some useful additions made; such is the account of Benedict's biographer. The decisions arrived at were then submitted to the emperor for his approval, so that they could be enforced throughout Francia. The resulting capitulary[13] runs to over seventy chapters: all monks were to learn it by heart. It is hardly surprising that it raised controversy and, in parts, opposition. The emperor thought it necessary to appoint inspectors charged with the duty of visitation. The new chapters of the revised Rule required explanation; so much so, indeed, that one of those present at Aachen, the influential Abbot Smaragdus of St Mihiel, composed a very elaborate *Expositio* of the Rule. It was a measure of the passionate attention to detail that is more apparent in Louis's religious legislation than in Charlemagne's. No previous Frankish ruler had shown anything approaching this degree of concern for uniform monastic observance throughout his realm. It seemed for a time to work. The inspectors were very busy and the bishops, as was proper, were involved in their appointment and in seeing that their recom-

---

[12] MGH Conc. ii, i, no. 39, pp. 312–464.
[13] MGH Capit. i, no. 170, pp. 344–9; see also *Corpus Consuet. Mon.* i, pp. 423 ff.

mendations were carried out. In case of doubt there was always appeal to Benedict's own monastery of Inda, near Aachen, the true *schola monachorum*. The report survives of two delegates from Reichenau to their abbot after a training course at Inda.

Still Louis had not finished. A new synod was summoned for the end of 818 and the beginning of 819. This considered many matters, confirmed much of what had previously been determined and probed into affairs hitherto left untouched. The rights and privileges of monasteries, the size of the burdens, financial and other, imposed on them, their protection from over-zealous or irregular abbots, and the filling of abbatial vacancies were now investigated. This last was vital if monasteries were to play a greater part in religious life. Genuine free election by monks, as laid down in the Rule, was never really contemplated. Only specified royal monasteries were to have this privilege, but even they were enjoined at every vacancy to seek royal permission to proceed to an election. As for the rest, the ruler was free to approve or impose any abbot he thought most suitable. Needless to say, the administration proved incapable of supervising all abbatial elections throughout Francia; but the right to intervene remained and was often exercised over houses of special importance because of their wealth, their political standing or their geographical position. Not content with what he had achieved through a willing emperor, Benedict went on to compose his own explanatory works on the Rule, the most significant of which was a concordance of Rules that to some extent placed the work of the great Benedict in a historical setting. He died in 821, having done more for the Rule than anyone since its author. Ironically, his insistence on the isolation of monastic communities cut off from the world and following a strictly ascetic path of prayer and work ran counter to the new imperial policy of involving them more in the life of Frankish society. On the other hand, his anxiety to promote the monastic Office to a position of importance not envisaged in the original Rule did indeed bear fruit. The liturgy moves to the front. Monasteries were above all to be communities of prayer and of intercession. As with monks so with canons and canonesses: imperial approval was given to measures already taken to ensure uniformity and discipline.

But this was by no means all. It is impossible to summarize the legislation of 818–19, or often to determine what parts of it stemmed from episcopal consultations, what parts from the lay magnates or from the emperor himself. This is significant, for it means that the legislating Church was for the first time moved by one common and powerful impulse. It looks to the very roots of society. One may instance measures to ensure a supply of properly-equipped parish clergy and clergy serving private churches; the repair of ruined churches; the protection of widows; provision for the upkeep of parish clergy; conditions on which boys and girls might be admitted to the religious life; how gifts to the churches were to be apportioned between the poor and the clergy, tithe, regulations for marriage and definitions of incestuous unions.[14] All this placed, and was meant to place, large additional burdens on diocesans. The emperor himself wrote to his metropolitans to ensure that their diocesans understood the decisions taken. They applied, moreover, to the Church in Lombardy. One may conclude that the enormous effort of 818–19 and what had preceded it since 816, has been unduly overshadowed by the pioneering work of Louis's father and grandfather. This is the culmination of Carolingian reform. There was to be nothing comparable till the twelfth century. Further legislation was to follow but increasingly it was weakened by palace disputes and traditional Frankish preoccupation with successions, to the point where it looks more like mending fences than erecting a new structure. Only while Louis was confident in his personal righteousness could he control reform.

There was more legislation in 825, in 829, and a final burst after Louis's death. A great synod at Paris in November 825 issued a *Libellus* loaded with patristic and canonical justification;[15] and the emperor backed it up with an *admonitio* 'to all'.[16] The impression left is that the bishops were beginning to press for the things they thought mattered most. They could, for instance, petition the emperor to "assume the burden' of personally hearing cases (presumably vital ones) affecting the Church and the poor. It is the emperor, however, who reminds them of their duty to establish schools in suitable places for the instruction of the sons and ministers of the Church. Schools open to all, laity and clergy alike, were not at all what he had in mind, though his hopes may have been less narrow than those of the Emperor Lothar, who at the same time was establishing named centres where more advanced instruction would be available for picked students from the Lombard dioceses. Nine clauses of the *admonitio* insist on a close and friendly collaboration between all those in authority of any kind, whether lay or clerical. It could hardly be said more clearly that the peace and stability for which every Carolingian longed were still a dream. Louis finishes by urging that copies of his capitularies shall be obtained from his chancery by all bishops and counts. It is clear enough that they were not. Further imperial missives betray his irritation that the duties imposed on *missi* remained unfulfilled.

The bishops appear to be behind the deliberations and decrees of an

---

[14] e.g. MGH Capit. i, no. 138, pp. 275–80.
[15] MGH Conc. ii, ii, no. 44, pp. 480 ff.
[16] MGH Capit. i, no. 150, pp. 303–7.

important synod held at Paris in 829.[17] As so often, it is hard to tell in what sense the surviving records are to be seen as legally constitutive, or in what sense worked-over memoranda for bishops' use. The episcopate was by now a highly effective body of learned and dedicated reformers; memoranda for such, enlarged with supporting texts not used by the assembly in session, are not out of the question. But again it was through imperial initiative that they met. The co-emperors, Louis and Lothar, state that their longing to hold a general assembly to correct what is wrong cannot be fulfilled because of hostile disruption; and instead they require archbishops to hold such investigations locally and report to them. We know that such meetings took place at Paris, Mainz, Lyon and Toulouse, though only the decisions of Paris survive – perhaps because the presence of Louis himself ensured proper recording. The work of writing-up these decisions was in part at least the responsibility of Jonas, bishop of Orléans, and the second section is either a résumé of his *De Institutione Regia* or a draft of it. The first section covers much already familiar material though with more stress on personal conduct and on lay–clerical relations. Four chapters are devoted to social morality, starting with an appeal to all to observe Sundays strictly, a duty now largely neglected in the interests of trading and the labours of the countryside. Then follow cheating over weights and measures, oppression of the poor through the avarice of the powerful, and usury (this at great length with heavy biblical support). The second section starts with a statement that it will be concerned with the role of kings, princes and generally all *fideles*, and how avarice, envy and hate threaten the Church. It asks some familiar questions: what is a king and what should he avoid? What is the proper nature of his office (his *ministerium*) under God? How should he delegate authority for the suppression of vice and the protection of the poor? How does justice lend stability to the kingdom and injustice overturn it? What follows the recognition that a kingdom is bestowed not by men but by God? Why should all men subject themselves humbly and faithfully to the king's power? There is more to the same effect. None of it threatens the emperor: he is simply implored to recognize that his office is God-given and that its proper exercise conditions the health of Christian society. The report of the proceedings closes with an addendum in which the emperor is begged to ensure that the authority and dignity of the clergy are better observed and that the laity be instructed to assist the clergy in their work of *correctio* and not stir up idle suspicion and scandal against them. In brief, then, the bishops at Paris (and no doubt their colleagues elsewhere) can look from the hopeful plans of Pippin and Charlemagne

[17] MGH Conc. ii, ii, pp. 606–80.

and the urgent legislation of Louis to the firm reality of life as it is actually lived in the empire. Much had been attempted, little had been realized: could the emperor do anything more? The answer was that he could not. The political crisis of his reign was upon him; and had it not been, the answer would still have been much the same. But the remarkable fact remains that even in 829 the bishops believed in the radical transformation of society. An assembly held at Worms in the same year saw the promulgation of the last of Louis's capitularies that aimed at reform;[18] but it also heard of his intention to endow his son Charles with part of the lands allotted to his brothers by the *Divisio* of 817, and heard of it with dismay. A deeply religious provision was to be swept aside. So far as reform went, confidence was undermined and the end was in sight. In 836, after his penance and restoration, a council was held at Aachen to repair some of the damage and to reassure the bishops that the reform measures agreed to in 829 were still to be enforced; but emphasis on fidelity to the emperor does not suggest that confidence was to be depended on.

The bishops and lay magnates, shocked and much divided by the upheavals of a decade, were determined to save what they could under the rule of Louis's quarrelling sons. This is swiftly apparent in the decisions promulgated by Charles the Bald for his western kingdom at Coulaines in 843.[19] He has accepted what he calls a *foedus concordiae* and he and those present have put their hands to it. It is a painful document that lays bare the horrors of discord and the vital need for concord as a condition of Christian stability. All will turn on a common recognition that the Church and its property and clergy are to be honoured, and so too the king. He for his part shall honour his faithful subjects and treat them reasonably and equitably; and if he fails in this obligation he shall be admonished in such a manner as is fitting to his royal sublimity. A threat? Perhaps. But he was a young man at the beginning of his reign, and this was a treaty. The bishops had no intention of circumscribing his power but rather of bolstering it. The direction in which they pointed him was authentically Carolingian. Their distinction and their bitter experience alike justified them in setting him on the right path. The treaty, then, was a formal act, setting out in very general terms the conditions on which king and bishops could collaborate in the prosecution of reform. The same sentiments were to be repeated on many occasions during both Charles's reign and those of his brothers. Next year, at Toulouse, Charles met his Septimanian

---

18 MGH Capit. ii, i, nos. 191–3, pp. 12–20.
19 MGH Capit. ii, ii, no. 254, pp. 253–5.

bishops. We have the resulting capitulary.[20] It is largely concerned with parish clergy; that the bishops shall not press too heavily on them but that they shall be properly watched over by the bishops' officials, visited annually by the bishops, encouraged in the work of evangelization, protected in their properties and equipped to know the canons. It had been said before.

But also in 844 the three royal brothers met at Yütz, in Lothar's middle kingdom, to consider the affairs of the church under the presidency of their uncle Drogo of Metz, now papal vicar north of the Alps. Uncle Drogo was an important link with Carolingian policy as it had developed over many years. No bishop had more loyally supported Louis the Pious in his troubles. One therefore expects to find a firmly traditional stance and no nonsense about clipping royal wings; and this is what one does find.[21] Drogo and the assembled bishops make use of the Coulaines decisions; build on them indeed. Not but what the kings are seriously warned to observe fraternal amity as recently agreed on at Verdun: 'we venture to tell you without offence that our Holy Church, redeemed by Christ's blood and restored at great cost by your predecessors, has been torn apart, turned upside-down and overwhelmed by your quarrels.' Strong words. The bishops are fulfilling their duty but are not assuming fresh responsibilities. Having begged for peace in this manner they can proceed to ask their masters to fill vacant sees, restore bishops unjustly expelled, watch over abbatial elections, return church property and lend active support to whatever measures the clergy think necessary for the salvation of the faithful. Let there be a general penance for the evils of the past. What distinguishes these hopeful propositions from anything in Charlemagne's legislation is that the unity he could count on had dissolved for ever. To impose religious unity upon a scene of political disunity was impossible. This the bishops knew. Their powers of analysis were admirable; they knew what ought to be done; but they could not do it. The message they never hesitated to convey was that kings, and only kings, could enforce the restoration of ecclesiastical property.

Again in 844 the same troubles occupy the clerical mind at a council held at Ver, near Senlis.[22] It would, say those present, take too long to enumerate the evils of the present time and the burden that rests on Charles to make peace and to rescue the Church from the weight of its sins. Let the king pursue mercy and judgement and justice. He is

---

[20] Ibid., no. 255, pp. 256–8.
[21] MGH Capit. ii, i, no. 227, pp. 113–16 (the bishops' propositions only; the capitulary does not survive).
[22] MGH Capit. ii, ii, no. 291, pp. 383–7.

reminded of Solomon, David and Hezekiah, who overcame the enemies of God's people in arms and by prayer; and especially he is reminded of Charlemagne. All this they suggest because it is their duty to watch over and care for his soul. Once more he is told that churches and monasteries are in disarray; monks and clergy are wandering about; nuns are forming illicit unions; military demands are too heavy; the Church of Reims has for too long been leaderless; and above all, ecclesiastical property is widely retained for secular use, so that clergy and poor face destitution. Finally, the king is advised to part with evil counsellors – presumably those who prevent the restitution of Church property; and if he does not, the bishops will look to it. An empty threat, certainly, and one that tells us less about how the bishops thought they could control the king than about their consternation at the material state of the Church. It was very much worse than it had been for fifty years. The decisions of Ver border on panic; and in such an atmosphere very bold things could be said.

One could go on to council after council in which the bishops passionately urge measures against disruption that were no consequence of Charlemagne's reform programme; and seldom do they omit reference to appropriate canons from early Church councils and to the Bible. At Beauvais, for example, in 845[23] the clergy assemble for the purpose of preferring Hincmar to the see of Reims but take the occasion to tell Charles still more about the restitution of their property. This is shortly afterwards reiterated at Meaux-Paris.[24] All the time one is moving from legislation to exhortation; and when it can be called legislation, it is repetitive legislation. Meaux-Paris resulted in a formidable statement of eighty-three articles. These are important both as a summary of recent decisions and as a hardening of some of them in a manner that brought about a direct clash with the lay magnates. The bishops start by setting the scene: evils and corruption face Church and society on every side; the Northmen, ruthless persecutors of Christianity, have been at the gates of Paris; the king must act. Laymen are acting as abbots over monasteries without episcopal authority and contrary to all canons and rules; cathedral clergy are ceasing to live communal lives; common crimes, especially sexual crimes, are everywhere rife; the king must ensure that vigorous *missi* are dispatched throughout his realm. Particular stress is laid on property, its misappropriation and maladministration; and this includes precarial holdings. Obviously this is aimed at the laity, both magnates and smaller landowners in distant places who were more difficult to control. The king himself made some attempt to restore Church lands, notably to Reims; but much remained unrestored.

[23] MGH Capit. ii, ii, no. 292, pp. 387–8.   [24] Ibid., no. 293, pp. 395–421.

What the bishops failed to note was that ecclesiastical property had also been purloined by some of themselves, as well as by clergy and monks. The bishops conclude thus: 'and we furthermore admonish you fully to observe and implement those *capitula* which by God's help you promulgated and confirmed with your own hand and have now promised to observe'. Leaving aside the more familiar issues of social morality and clerical discipline, there is dramatic evidence that the king was stung into preparation for practical measures involving large-scale restitution of land; for at a general assembly at Épernay, convoked shortly afterwards, the lay magnates reacted furiously. Details of the meeting have not survived. All that is clear is that only nineteen of the *capitula* of Meaux-Paris were confirmed; and none of these, unless possibly that affecting precarial holdings, offered any threat to lay landholders as such. Charles had had to choose between his lay and ecclesiastical magnates. His choice reflects no hostility to what the bishops had wanted but rather his immediate reliance on the loyalty of his lay magnates at a time of political instability and threatened invasion. In fact, he had no choice. Nor should we assume that all ecclesiastical property in the hands of laymen had been acquired by violence. Many may have believed that their family lands had been wrongly alienated to the Church in the first place; others that properties granted as *beneficia* by kings could or should not be revoked; and others again that as lay abbots and rectors they did more for their communities than properly-elected abbots would have done. The situation was extremely complex. Bishop Prudentius of Troyes summarized the outcome of Épernay like this: 'less respect was paid to the urgent advice of the bishops on ecclesiastical matters than perhaps at any other time of which there is evidence in the whole Christian epoch'.[25] Reform, if it may be called that, had had a severe set-back. It reminds us how closely lay magnates were involved in the business of the Church. The clergy had no wish to ignore them; indeed, depended on their protection and continuing generosity. A head-on collision, as at Épernay, was a rare and grave event.

The seven years from 852 to 859 were years of upheaval in all three kingdoms, but for Charles they were years of acute crisis. His nephew Pippin II was in revolt in Aquitaine, the Vikings were pressing severely on northern and western Francia, Louis the German invaded his brother's kingdom and magnates everywhere were uncertain where their loyalties lay. They were years of frequent colloquy between the king and his bishops, and records of some of these discussions and decisions leave an impression of an episcopate that meant to be heard. Often, but not always, it was Hincmar with whom the initiative lay.

[25] *Ann. Bert.* s.a. 846.

His vigorous legal mind, increasingly well-stocked with canonical precedents, could distinguish and enumerate the evils that beset the church. He was not afraid of demanding instant redress. However, it would be quite wrong to infer that he or any other bishop aimed at taking over the government of the kingdom. What can be inferred is that the frequent meetings of bishops at several levels had accustomed them to speak with one voice. There was an episcopal point of view. When Hincmar and his colleagues sent their famous letter to Louis the German in 858 denying him their support in West Francia, they did not omit to state their views on the restoration of the Church. This was still uppermost in their minds. A notable feature of the meetings of these years is the seizing of the opportunity to deal with special problems. Thus at Soissons in 853,[26] Hincmar raised the question of the validity of the ordination of thirteen clergy by his predecessor Ebbo during the short period of his restoration, and did so because it affected the validity of his own reign at Reims. But the council also dealt with more general issues. The *missi*[27] were to join with diocesans in visiting and inspecting all houses of canons and monks; owners of private churches were to admit the authority of diocesans; church property granted away as benefices was to be restored; church lands enjoying immunity must not be taken as freehold by laymen; church treasures and books must be inventoried; payment of ninths and tithes must be enforced. Clearly much of this was an attempt to regain the ground lost at Épernay; and it was a vain attempt. The king was probably anxious to comply. At Attigny in 854[28] he was prepared to enumerate no less than thirteen separate assignments for his *missi* that should have enforced the decisions of Soissons and of so much else. One has the impression of many bishops and counts almost perpetually engaged in the task of inspection, correction and report. It is a false impression. Hence at Bonneuil in 856 the bishops could protest that nothing had been done. Indeed, the situation was much worse, since revolt had forced the king to hand over new monasteries as benefices to loyal supporters. He had no option. Next year at Quierzy[29] the bishops and lay magnates assembled separately to consider Viking depredations exacerbated by 'the mobility of some of our *fideles*'. This was to be looked into on the spot by the bishops, *missi* and counts; and it is not easy to see how the responsibilities of any one group of examiners could have been separated from any other. In short, all royal resources were to be mobilized to face a crisis equally alarming to clergy and laity; and soon afterwards the king and his magnates, lay and clerical, exchanged oaths of mutual support. Kings were not used

---

[26] MGH Capit. ii, ii, no. 258, pp. 263–6.　　　　[27] Ibid., no. 259, pp. 267–70.
[28] Ibid., no. 261, pp. 277–8.　　　　　　　　　　　[29] Ibid., no. 266, pp. 286–91.

to treatment of this kind. One can see why it was now necessary; nor would the clergy have claimed that they were asking their king to do more than guarantee their traditional rights.

There followed a welter of assemblies and meetings at various levels in which the bishops took the initiative, and, for some of these, documentation survives if not always in reliable form. Their characteristic business is consideration of particular, urgent matters together with reiteration of previous canonical legislation. An example is a meeting at Savonnières, near Toul, in 859,[30] of clergy from West Francia, Lotharingia and Provence in the presence of their kings. Earlier canons were read and approved; peace was to be made with Louis the German, the schism ended which had disrupted the Church, by now 'almost collapsed', and peace and justice restored to Christian people. Charles made his case against Wenilo, his recalcitrant archbishop of Sens, and against the still more recalcitrant Breton bishops. Finally, a confraternity of prayer was agreed on by the bishops present, to which the abbots would be admitted if they so desired. It is a good example of a mixed agenda: there is royal business and episcopal business, all of which can be recorded in thirteen canons or articles.

The councils of the 860s are haunted by an issue at once political and religious; the proposed divorce, namely, of Lothar II from his queen, Theutberga. It was a complicated matter involving the self-confessed relationship of the queen with her own brother before her marriage as well as that of Lothar with Waldrada, his mistress. The bishops showed an understandable tendency to divide according to their political allegiance. More important, Pope Nicholas I became involved. He was not a man to pull his punches. It reminded the Franks that they had a spiritual master. The hostilities stirred up by the divorce were evident enough when the bishops met at Tusey, in Lotharingia, in 860.[31] The five resulting canons that could be called genuine betray the disciplinary drive of Archbishop Hincmar. They are concerned with wandering clergy and monks, with nuns and widows, perjurors, thieves, sexual offenders and the seizure of ecclesiastical property. Moreover, the bishops were to exchange lists of wanted malefactors. But it is clear that much of what Hincmar proposed met with successful opposition from his Lotharingian colleagues. The chances of radical reform remained, as they had long been, hopeless. The sense of mounting crisis informs the proceedings at Pîtres in 862.[32] All those present – the king, bishops, abbots and

[30] Ibid., no. 299, pp. 447–50.
[31] PL 126, cols. 122–32; Labbé, *Sacr. Conc.* viii, 702–34.
[32] MGH Capit. ii, ii, no. 272, pp. 303–10.

counts – were agreed in recognizing the Viking attacks as the natural reward of sin. The articles of the meeting are in effect a lengthy homily on shortcomings general and particular. 'We cannot all be kings.' 'Let us all make reparation through penance, confession and almsgiving, each according to his means.' All must strive to do justice and live justly, as under Charlemagne and Louis the Pious. Things had reached a pretty pass if the reign of Louis could be considered a good example of peaceful living. Penalties, secular and ecclesiastical, are to be strongly enforced. One is reading a text drafted by bishops; but there can be no reason to question that its mood accurately reflects the despair of all those present at Pîtres.

By now it will be clear that no year passes without at least one assembly of bishops, with or without lay participation, urging the king to do his duty; and something of the same could be said of the other Frankish kingdoms. Whatever his personal inclination, Charles could not enforce wholesale restitution of ecclesiastical property; he could not protect the indigent and helpless; he could not implement canonical legislation. But he could from time to time have his own way over ecclesiastical appointments, and this in a ruthless manner. At Verberie, in 863,[33] he could be very firm in support of the claim of the monastery of St Calais that it was a benefice held of the king since the time of Louis the Pious and not subject to any proprietary claim by the bishops of Le Mans, whose documents were forgeries. Pope Nicholas, as we learn from correspondence, had expected the dispute to be settled in favour of Le Mans; but it was not. It was an example of the increasing readiness of monasteries to appeal to the king and the pope against diocesan pretensions. However, the assembly at Verberie did not confine its attentions to St Calais; it also considered the case of the bishop of Soissons, Rothad, deposed without consultation with Rome, and allowed him to visit Pope Nicholas in Rome. He was restored to his see. Furthermore, at the instance of the pope, the marriage of Charles's daughter Judith with Count Baldwin of Flanders (with whom she had eloped) was permitted.

Still the bishops' pressure on the king was not relaxed: Hincmar had no intention that it should be. Thus we find Charles again at Pîtres next year,[34] agreeing that ecclesiastical privileges and immunities must be respected; that counts who fail to help the bishops are answerable to him; that refugees from the Vikings are to be protected and not subjected to any form of taxation; and finally, that copies of capitularies are to be sent by his chancery to all archbishops and counts, who in their turn will make copies for their bishops, abbots and lay officials.

[33] J. Havet, *Œuvres*, i (Paris, 1896), pp. 187–90.
[34] MGH Capit. ii, ii, no. 273, pp. 311–28.

No doubt some of them did. Probably the king was more successful in his insistence that bishops, abbots and abbesses should send contingents to campaign against the enemies of the kingdom, notably for the protection of shipping. He showed his teeth again at Soissons, in 866,[35] where the bothersome case of his favourite Wulfad was decided. Wulfad, once employed in his service, had been one of the clergy ordained by Ebbo, Hincmar's predecessor. The king wanted him to be archbishop of Bourges so that, as he informed the pope, he could watch over his young son Charles, now king of Aquitaine. Hincmar naturally would have none of this. None the less, Pope Nicholas was prepared to accept Wulfad as a special case though he felt that the bishops had not thoroughly examined the evidence. It so happened that Wulfad was an efficient and learned man; we know something of the contents of his library; but he certainly owed his promotion to the royal will. In 867 the great pope died. He had intervened consistently in the ecclesiastical disputes of Francia, without fear but on appeal. The record of his interventions is clear in a large body of correspondence to and from Rome, on matters great and small. One may instance his reply to Humfredus, bishop of Thérouanne bidding him not to desert his flock when threatened by Vikings; his letters in defence of Robert, bishop of Le Mans, in his dispute with Charles the Bald over the monastery of St Calais; and his masterly résumé, in a letter to Egilo, archbishop of Sens, of the reasons why he disapproved of his promotion to Sens from a monastery (Flavigny) in another province – after which, *licet difficulter*, he sent him his pallium.

For a few years from 868, councils were remarkable for, and sometimes dominated by, a rancorous quarrel between Hincmar of Reims and his nephew and suffragan, Hincmar of Laon, whom he had brought up. One is alternately repelled and attracted by these two learned, virulent prelates. Their quarrel was concerned with the canonical relationship of a metropolitan with his diocesans and of the right of the latter to appeal to Rome over the head of the metropolitan. But it was initiated by the king himself, who had given diocesan land to a faithful count – only to see him forcibly ejected by the bishop; and it was made no easier by the intervention of the pope. Both bishops were steeped in canon law; indeed, the legal learning of Hincmar of Reims calls for proper consideration at a later point. A new feature of the quarrel was the employment of a collection of canons known today as Pseudo-Isidore, the most famous legal forgery of the middle ages. The collection seems to have been put together around the year 850 in the province of Reims, apparently by clergy who sympathized

---

[35] Labbé, *Sacr. Conc.* viii, 816–30, 833–6. See also F. Lot, 'Une année du règne de Charles le Chauve: année 866', *Recueil*, ii, pp. 415–60.

with their deposed metropolitan, Ebbo. They must have had a good library at their disposal. In no sense was their work official. It was put together in a hurry, over two or three years, for a particular purpose. Certainly it was not the long-sought answer to all their problems. Some of Ebbo's clergy had fled for shelter to the neighbouring province of Trier, apparently taking a version of Pseudo-Isidore with them; for in 852 Archbishop Theutgaud was able to cite a passage from it that occurs nowhere else. Soon the Hincmars were using it, though in different ways. Thereafter it reached further afield, and finally to Rome. It was, in brief, one more collection of canons and decretals that could prove useful. There was no reason to question its general authenticity, though parts of it could indeed be questioned by anyone bright enough to spot its inconsistencies.

Pseudo-Isidore comprised a familiar canonical collection known as the *Hispana-Gallica*, the capitularies collected by Angilram and Benedictus Levita, the decretals of Pseudo-Isidore (the Isidore referred to was in fact an early pope who had had nothing to do with it) and finally the Donation of Constantine[36] to Pope Silvester which owes its dissemination largely to its incorporation in Pseudo-Isidore. Much of this mass of material was genuine, if sometimes doctored, canons and decretals; the rest of it was the invention of the Pseudo-Isidore workshop, and this particularly applies to the decretals. In short, it was a confection of genuine and invented material, of hard law and mysticism, put together in the belief that what ought to be, but did not lie to hand, should be provided. It was a matter of revealing the intentions of Providence. The forgers presumably believed that their forgeries truthfully represented certain fundamental usages of canon law that were being challenged by Church and State. This might be called a pious forgery. It plainly does reflect the anxieties of provincial clergy and equally plainly reflects a vision of what the Church should be. In particular it champions the role of bishops as masters in their own dioceses against the encroaching power of metropolitans such as Hincmar. The natural protector of bishops was the pope. Therefore direct appeal to Rome was the last and proper recourse of every diocesan. The object of the forgers was not to erect the medieval papacy as we know it under Hildebrand and Innocent III, nor did any canonist seriously develop the papal position implicit in Pseudo-Isidore before Gratian. There is more than the short-circuiting of metropolitans in the collection; but it is the substance of what was used by the two Hincmars and to some extent by the papacy in the great quarrel.[37]

---

[36] *Constitutum Constantini*, ed. H. Fuhrmann, *Fontes Iuris Germanici Antiqui*, in usum schol. (Hanover, 1968).

[37] Ed. P. Hinschius, *Decretales Pseudo-Isidorianae* (Leipzig, 1863; repr. Aalen, 1963).

The course of the quarrel was, briefly, as follows: the bishop kicked out the interloper from his property, appealed to Rome and addressed his clergy on the subject of episcopal rights, basing his case on Pseudo-Isidore. He further accused his uncle of concurring in his arrest by the king and placed his diocese under an interdict until such time as he was liberated. The metropolitan thereupon released the clergy from the interdict but persuaded the king to release the bishop, who next set about a full statement of his authority *vis-à-vis* the metropolitan and issued this as a broadside to his clergy, from whom he demanded full obedience. The metropolitan reacted with a counterblast, also making use of Pseudo-Isidore and obviously fearing that his other suffragans might be drawn in. This counterblast, issued at the synod of Attigny in 870, is a massive work entitled 'the *opusculum* of 55 chapters'.[38] The bishop, it argues, was now at risk because of what he had put his name to. It examines the bishop's sources and refutes any canon (i.e. such as define episcopal authority) that conflicts with the fundamental canons of Nicaea. What clashed with the old law was no more than a figment. The bishop's appeal to Rome continued to be blocked by metropolitan and king. In addition, he was now accused of treason and submitted to a council at Douzy in 871,[39] which deposed him. He was imprisoned, and later blinded, apparently on the king's orders. When Pope John VIII visited Francia in 878 he allowed the deposed bishop maintenance from his former diocese and permission to celebrate mass. The poor man died some two years later. The quarrel had been fought from a basis of canon law, genuine and forged, with a sophistication that would have been impossible in the Francia of Charlemagne. Whatever might be said of the fate of reform, the weapons of canon law were now clearly appreciated; and there were bishops able enough to wield them.

But still synods and councils reiterated the business of reform, and particularly discipline; still the Church clamoured for order. Thus at Pîtres in 869[40] ecclesiastical honours and immunities are once again to be protected; bishops and counts are to collaborate; archbishops and bishops shall obey the king and make reparation to laymen they have wronged; bishops shall strictly observe the privileges granted to their churches by pope and king and watch over the collection and distribution of tithe; they shall enforce the obedience and respect of parish priests to their secular lords and shall accept for ordination all qualified persons presented by laymen and religious houses; and they shall take special care to settle quarrels, pacify those involved in feud and enforce penance. The royal *adnuntiatio* that follows allows the king wide

---

[38] PL 126, cols. 290–494; Labbé, *Sacr. Conc.* viii, 1837–44.
[39] Labbé, *Sacr. Conc.* viii, 1547–1658.
[40] MGH Capit. ii, ii, no. 275, pp. 333–7.

powers of intervention and enforcement. Behind this seems to lie mounting secular frustration, less with the king than with the bishops. The king for his part is required to do more and more: to defend the Church, restore its properties, preside over the social morals of an entire generation, protect his realm from the Vikings and satisfy his lay magnates that he remains their good lord.

One last great occasion remained. Charles, now emperor, returned in a hurry from Italy in 876 and summoned an assembly at Ponthion.[41] There were present two papal legates and no less than fifty bishops. Indeed, only those of the provinces of Tours, Bordeaux and Eauze were prevented from attending by their duties in the Viking-infested West. The main business of the assembly was to accept the king as emperor and to recognize his new archbishop of Sens, Ansegis, as papal vicar in Frankish territory. It was not a happy occasion but liturgically it was splendid; and it must have seemed in retrospect, once Charles was dead, a fitting conclusion to so many years of fruitless ecclesiastical gatherings, that is, in terms of the achievement of what had been aimed at for a century. In many other respects, however, it had been the reverse of fruitless. Never had so many clergy met so often to define the work of the Church, to examine its canonical heritage and to analyse the dangers that faced it. Their legislation remains an overwhelming proof that the clergy of the early middle ages were never concerned with the hereafter to the exclusion of the world they lived in.

ii. *The Bishops and Reform*

Councils and synods stretching over a century told the Carolingian clergy what they should be doing. Had they done it, there would have been no need for such remorseless iteration. But it would be wildly untrue to conclude that they did nothing. As a body, the bishops were notably able, learned and zealous; as individuals, they differed sharply. Some were familiar with the court, others not; some occupied sees within metropolitan Francia, others were far away and isolated; and all faced special local problems of their own. Tours, for example, or Soissons had little knowledge of the problems of the border-world of Salzburg or Utrecht. The problems of Corbie were not those of Reichenau. Thus, different religious centres interpreted the *Admonitio Generalis* and its offspring in different lights – and increasingly so, as Charlemagne's grip loosened and they were left to their own devices. The wonder is the amount of agreement there was about what to do and how to set about it.

[41] Ibid., no. 279, pp. 348–53.

We must assume that the bishops and abbots received the directives that affected them; some can be shown to have done so. The library catalogue of Reichenau, made in 821 or 822, lists its holdings of *capitula* and laws, among much else;[1] and there were collections at Bourges, Lyon, Le Mans, Orléans and Liège. A great collection was made at Reims under Archbishops Hincmar and Fulk. We have chance evidence of collections of canons in cathedral and monastic libraries. Hildebold of Cologne had a good one, and that of Baturic, bishop of Regensburg and abbot of St Emmeram's, was plainly intended for regular consultation. So, too, was the collection of Bishop Ghaerbald of Liège, in whose diocese lay Aachen itself. He assembled texts of capitularies, diocesan statutes, correspondence and laws, all of which had immediate application to his own diocese. It is what one would expect of an efficient diocesan at work in close proximity with the emperor.

Certain well-defined types of record reveal a general episcopal resolve to take action. One of these is diocesan *statuta* or statutes; handbooks, in effect, for the guidance of priests. There are some thirty-four of these, mostly in manuscripts of later date and often combined with collections of canons. Their contents are various: conduct, rites, faith, property, discipline and duties. The mixture is thus spiritual, liturgical, administrative and social. St Boniface made one such. Ghaerbald's statutes[2] suggest a diocese that was still fairly insecurely Christian and his successor, Weltcaud, added some more that highlight the local preoccupation with remnants of paganism.[3] These northern efforts look primitive in comparison with the statutes of the sophisticated South. Theodulf of Orléans composed two sets[4] which really do seek to implement the *Admonitio*, especially on the teaching side, and are boldly aimed at the salvation of souls without regard to social or political implications. To Theodulf, the priest is a shepherd, living the good life he teaches, intent on prayer and reading. The life of the layman should in effect be a life of penance conditioned by confession. It was an ideal almost monastic, presented to congregations living under close clerical discipline and accustomed to regular attendance at church. The same ideal could hardly have been urged on the laity of Liège.

Two successive bishops of Bourges, Rodulf and Wulfad, who reigned from 845 to 876, followed Theodulf's example. They, too, had high pastoral aims that, if realized, would have shaped their parishes as Christian societies ruled by priests. At least three further

[1] G. Becker, *Catalogi bibliothecarum antiqui* (Bonn, 1885), p. 8, sect. 142.
[2] Ed. C. de Clercq, *Légis. Relig.* i, pp. 352–62.
[3] Ibid., pp. 363–6.
[4] PL 105, cols. 191–224; a better edn. of the second statute in de Clercq, *Légis Relig.* i, pp. 323–51.

bishops shared their outlook. Others, however, seemed more con-
cerned with discipline and the eradication of the sort of abuses that
might characterize well-established parishes. Their champion was
Reims under Ebbo and Hincmar. It was a matter largely of tone.
Government and instruction were the keynotes of these statutes.
Hincmar's voice was sharp and masterly, but also fatherly.[5] If he saw
the laity as sheep they were at least to be very active sheep. Tours, and
Orléans under Theodulf's successor, adopted much the same tone.
Further east Heito of Basel preferred Theodulf's notion of the parish
priest as teacher and guide when he came to expound their duties to his
Alemannic clergy. Working through the bishops' statutes of whatever
flavour one senses the influence of monastic ideals, of penitential
practice and of the sermon-collections of the past. Their flocks were to
feel the core of their religion in a great mystery, centred on the mass. It
is majestically portrayed on the ivory panels on the back of Bishop
Drogo's sacramentary, made around the year 830.[6] The mass set the
priest apart, as to some extent it always had. We can accept this
without supposing that a wedge was deliberately being driven
between clergy and laity, to the benefit of the clergy. Statutes, then,
were one kind of evidence of how the bishops meant to carry out the
policy of *reformatio*.

Another kind was provision for instruction of the laity by preaching. Ninth-century sermon collections do show, if not that the laity
were instructed or converted, as the case might be, then at least one
way in which they were meant to be instructed or converted. Preaching had the sanction of law. The *Admonitio* (ch. 82) states that priests
were to preach to their people in every parish and specified that
sermons were to cover the essentials of the faith and the works of the
devil. There was to be instruction on all Sundays and feast-days, and a
sermon at mass after the Gospel and before the final blessing. Thus the
sermon was firmly incorporated in the liturgy. Sometimes particular
sermons were recommended, such as Gregory's homilies on the
Gospels. It was further emphasized that sermons should be preached
in language that was understood – a recognition that Latin was not
understood everywhere. This apart, the exercise of translating Latin
sermon-material into a vernacular afforded the chance to simplify and
to stress essentials. It was not that such a vernacular as Old High
German was in itself a vehicle inadequate to express the full Latin
message; indeed, the wider uses of vernacular for Christian instruction
are sufficiently important to be reserved for later consideration. The
difficulty lay rather in the limited grasp of Germanic priest and

---

[5] PL 125, cols. 773–804.
[6] Illus. in Hubert, Porcher and Volbach, *Caro. Art*, pl. 215, p. 235.

peasant. The basic collections of Latin sermons on which the clergy could draw were mostly those of the fifth- and sixth-century Gallic Church. Eloquence, then, was seen as a principal weapon for bishops and priests by the Carolingian reformers. It was necessary to learn how best to put things to their vastly differing flocks. The sermon collections, or homiliaries, covered the requirements of the liturgical year in an explanatory way; and since so much of their material rested ultimately on scriptural commentary, the homiliary was closely related to the lectionary (or *Comes*) – a collection of gospel and epistle readings for each day in the liturgical cycle. A priest would therefore see his lectionary as a sort of running scriptural narrative background to his pastoral work. Further, and obviously, it would constitute that part of the Bible that he knew best – indeed, by heart. This was a significant limitation on how much of the Bible was actually read and understood. Apart from homiliaries designed for use within the liturgy there were others intended for private devotion. Hraban Maur composed two collections, one for the Emperor Lothar, which was judged suitable for public use.[7] What finally disappears in the ninth century is the distinction between a homily (or exposition of a text) and a sermon properly so called (dogmatic or moral instruction).

Charlemagne commissioned Paul the Deacon to compose an authoritative homiliary purged of error.[8] He wanted, as always, a clean text. Paul started with a dedicatory poem, begging his patron to use his *sagax sapientia* in putting right whatever was at fault in the homiliary. His models were mostly Italian, as was to be expected. The collection was fairly widely copied in Francia, as it was meant to be, and leaked through into private collections. Frankish homiliaries betray a good deal of variation and this was the result not only of the sources used but also of the intended users. Hraban Maur's great collections were in a class apart. He put together seventy homilies at Fulda for the people (as distinct from those addressed to Lothar), firmly anchored to the traditional exposition of virtues and vices. His method was, first, to expound the relevant Gospel reading and then to launch into an exposition suggested by the text. Plainly he saw his hearers as ignorant, credulous, rural and numerous, and so he himself was direct and simple and often colourful. The saints were held up as the great exemplar. But Hraban provided sermons on topics, as distinct from occasions; for example, an affectionate scolding of those who attempted to aid 'the distressed moon' (presumably an eclipse) by blowing on horns.[9] Another sermon rebuked extravagant mourning

[7] PL 110, cols. 13–136 (first collection); cols. 135–468 (for Lothar).

[8] Ed. F. Wiegand, *Das Homiliarium Karls des Grossen auf seine ursprüngliche Gestalt hin untersucht* (Leipzig, 1897; repr. Aalen, 1972); PL. 95, cols. 1159–66.   [9] No. 43.

at death, which was no more, he explained, than the gate to life.[10]
There is no reason why these sermons should not have been preached
to the people in the form in which we have them, unlike Paul's which
would certainly have required paraphrasing. At St Père of Chartres a
collection was made of models designed to help priests instruct their
flocks on doctrine, morals, feasts, and saints and martyrs as examples
of endurance and charity. Moreover, congregations were to be
warned to listen in silence and to obey their priests. Abbot Lautpert of
Monsee made a collection of 140 homilies on the Gospel readings for
the year and sent it to Bishop Hildebold at Cologne for use by his
clergy and people. This was a Bavarian collection. A complete sermon
survives, possibly by Paulinus of Aquilaea, that is clearly a bishop's
address to a congregation on his visitation of a parish. He urges that
illiteracy is no excuse for ignorance – a familiar Carolingian precept
that applied to parish priests almost as much as to their flocks. Whatever else one makes of all this homiletic material, various as it is, it
cannot be called a vehicle for propaganda or polemic. Sermons of this
kind were straightforward exhortations to virtue, together with rudi-
mentary instruction. Their use in the liturgy becomes more general-
ized and higher standards are demanded, if not obtained. We can only
conclude that bishops and abbots had taken the *Admonitio* seriously.
The parish church was to be the pivot of the reformation.

Beyond statutes and homiliaries lay a still more vital channel of
instruction. The whole liturgy could be seen as such, and within it
pre-eminently the mass itself: the symbol of Christ's sacrifice and the
renewal of the community of participants in him. This was firmly
stated by Carolingian liturgists, notably by Ratramn and Paschasius
Radbert of Corbie. What the liturgists emphasized was not so much
the celebrant as the transmitter of God's grace as the united congregation, the *plebs sancta*, all equal in God's eyes. People therefore needed to
understand the mass, and not least the pagan converts and semi-
pagans of newly-acquired territory. They needed to understand and
then to participate. Pippin III permitted them to sing parts of the mass
while Charlemagne grasped the role of the homily in the mass as a
means of instruction. Hence his concern to acquire an authentic mass-
book or sacramentary; and thus the sacramentary was more fundamental to Carolingian liturgical practice than any of the associated
texts. An established order for the mass, together with its prayers and
blessings, was what he thought he had in the *Hadrianum* with its
supplement. The mass, so conceived, was a performance and a drama,
and its rituals sometimes highly emotional. Its vital elements, the
priest's part, remained in Latin, the sacred language, but some of the

[10] No. 68.

prayers and the sermon were in the vernacular, though even then not necessarily more comprehensible without instruction. The people had an active role: they brought their oblations to the mass, their presence was essential since no priest could then celebrate mass alone, and they received communion both of bread and of wine. If one thing marked off the priest more than another, it was the moving of the altar from a central position in the church, where the priest had faced the congregation, to a distant position at the east end, where he stood with his back to them. The far-off altar was the place for the sacrament, the Gospel book and the relics of saints; and thus it was a raised shrine, approachable only by the priest. Carolingian church-architecture took account of this change, and churches tended to become more spacious, more impressive with their wall-paintings and mosaics (such as may still be seen at Oberzell and Germigny), more adapted for processions and choirs. It was an important contribution to popular piety. As to instruction on the mass, it seems that insistence on mystery was uppermost, that the spiritual value of the mass was not seen to lie in literal understanding of every word; in brief, that the mass was above human discourse. Instruction must have been as simple as it was derivative, though some expositions were more sophisticated.

But equally within the liturgy should be included the huge, floating corpus of saints' Lives and miracles read to congregations on occasions of commemoration. These included not only original compositions of the Carolingian age but also a quantity of reworked Merovingian material. The sophisticated Aquitanian cathedrals and monasteries seem to have been specialists in the business. Lessons of all kinds could be drawn by the faithful from regular attendance at such readings; and they were lessons, particularly in social morals, that had remained unvaried since the fifth century. A ninth-century peasant might have had a clearer notion of *sanctitas* than is possible today. In brief, saints' Lives and miracles were means of instruction.

The people could be reached through yet another literary medium: *florilegia* or collections of moral teaching, to help them to discern right from wrong. The roots of such teaching lay deep in Antique literature and the Bible. In so far as there was a generally recognized ethic of right and wrong it was to be found in St Augustine's *De Doctrina Christiana*. Further help was obtainable in penitential books. The canons of the early councils had been quite clear about the sacrament of penance, which was a public act and therefore humiliating. Already this must have been very difficult to enforce, even before varieties of Irish penitentials became available in Francia in the Merovingian age. These, though less rigorous in some respects, still envisaged public penance. Confession to the priest, however, which was the first step towards a penitential sentence and ultimate absolution, was increasingly permitted in private. In fact, private penance steadily increased while public penance, though never abolished, tended to atrophy. The penitential books of the eighth century were sufficiently various (and in some instances extraordinary) to rouse episcopal opposition. Bishops felt that exuberant tariffs of sins and penances, acquired no one knew where, were unsafe manuals for use by parish clergy. The inevitable Carolingian reaction ensued. Bishops started to compile their own manuals of penance for their clergy. One interesting group of such texts comes from the north and east of Francia. Bishop Halitgar of Cambrai produced a manual around the year 830[11] that contained both Roman and insular elements. Material from the *Hadriana* was well to the fore. Though he stated that his texts had been collected by his forebears he was right to add that he was no mere compiler. He showed some ability to choose for himself from among the rather bewildering selection of vices available, favouring on the whole the selection once made by Gregory the Great. He sent his penitential to Archbishop Ebbo of Reims, who in his turn appears to have taken a copy with him to exile at Fulda. There it became known to Hraban Maur, abbot of Fulda and later archbishop of Mainz, himself a prominent compiler of penitentials. Hraban acted as consultant on such matters to his own archbishop, Otgar, and to Bishop Heribald of Auxerre. Materials were thus handed round. But Hraban, too, was no mere compiler. He often turned to the Bible as a final court of appeal, which is what one would expect of a great biblical commentator. He could make up his own mind on penance for clergy who committed major sins, no doubt with Ebbo in mind. One can imagine that he was much exercised about the validity of restoring clergy who had been reconciled after penance. Other lively issues were penances for killing in battle and for slaying of kindred; conciliar legislation gave him no guidance about the latter. He decided that penance in such a case should not involve perpetual wandering as an outcast: there were already too many such wandering killers for the good of a stable society. Hraban's penitentials and those associated with them were strictly personal compilations for local use – one more indication that we should not envisage the reforms of the Carolingian clergy as uniform in distribution or application. But this does not make it the less remarkable that at least some bishops earnestly bent their minds to the universal problem of sin, its identification and expiation.

There is a close connection between manuals of penance and *florilegia* of moral teaching. The so-called Ecclesiastical Capitulary,[12] issued late in Charlemagne's reign, laid down that the nature of right and wrong,

[11] PL 105, col. 651–710.   [12] MGH Capit. i, no. 80, pp. 178–9, esp. cl. 15.

of virtue and vice, was to be taught to and by priests in a special kind of handbook or set of canons: 'every priest shall have lists (*capitula*) of the greater and lesser vices, so that he can recognize them and preach them to his flock (*subditi*); and thus they can be warned of the snares of the devil'. Sometimes it was the corresponding virtues that were specified, as by the synod of Paris in 829[13] and in the statutes of Bishop Walter of Orléans. Admonitions of both kinds were often called 'excerpts from the Fathers', which indeed is what they largely were; but *florilegia*, 'cullings', was also used. Some were derived mainly from classical writers, as for example those compiled by Heiric of Auxerre, Hadoard of Corbie and Sedulius. More were firmly based on the Bible and the Fathers, and notable among them the book of exhortation written by Paulinus of Aquilaea. The faithful were to be warned of eight principal vices which, as a set, go back to the Desert Fathers. Cassian had had them, and Gregory the Great refined them as spiritual and carnal sins. This set, with the corresponding virtues, affected both the penitentials and the *florilegia* of the ninth century. Individual laymen of standing might seek special guidance. For example, Paulinus composed a *florilegium* in 795 for a layman who clearly needed a lesson in humility, and Alcuin's *De Vitiis et Virtutibus* was also addressed to a layman and quickly disseminated. Bishop Halitgar's book of penance was appended to a *florilegium*, most of which was taken from the scriptures, Augustine and Gregory the Great. The inference is that all men – bishops, laity and even kings – needed clerical guidance on virtues and vices; they needed teaching. A *florilegium* composed by Haimo for a Pater Guilelmus is in effect a book of consolation for a retired official, whereas one written for a certain Alagus, possibly a canon of Auxerre, is decidedly monkish in slant and goes to some trouble to show how the Christian virtues were to be attained. There were plenty more designed for some particular need, as for example Adalgar's composition for a German *mater carissime*, strongly ascetic in flavour and emphatic in its insistence on obedience and on the *caritas* that gives meaning to *virtus*. But when all is said, we still do not know how far or how widely these *florilegia* were used. Those designed for private use and often specially commissioned, presumably were used, but those for general consumption by priests and monks may have fared less prosperously. What they certainly embodied was an ethical standard for clergy and laity alike. No age was made more conscious of sin, damnation and reward.

The most arresting of all texts that can broadly be classified as *florilegia* is an exhortation[14] addressed by the lady Dhuoda, wife of the

[13] MGH Conc. ii, ii, no. 50, p. 610.
[14] *Manuel pour son fils*, ed. P. Riché, SC 225 (Paris, 1975).

mighty Bernard of Septimania, to her young son William on the occasion of his *commendatio* to Charles the Bald, with whom he was in effect a hostage for the loyalty of his father. She wrote in the family stronghold of Uzès, in the south, some time between 841 and 843. What she wrote was a manual of moral and spiritual instruction that followed a common pattern, though it was more elaborate than most. Her tone is warm, affectionate and worried; for she did not know what would happen to the boy or to his father. Loyalty is one keynote of her message. But the real interest of her manual lies in its witness to Carolingian spirituality as seen by a highly literate lady. She believes in a firmly trinitarian God, probably sharpened in her mind by the Adoptionist controversies in Aquitaine, and she sees the lot of frail man as a lifelong struggle between virtues and vices as exemplified in the literature she knew. In a world of exemplars, the best model for her son was the suffering but triumphant layman, Job. William was to read his Bible and manuals of devotion regularly, to attend the canonical hours, to associate with good men and to reverence the clergy. Private reading and prayer called for more emphasis than the sacraments. Especially he was to attend to the lessons of the Psalms, which contained and foresaw everything. In short, he was presented by his mother with a programme of spirituality that might have strained a monk. Dhuoda's learning came, perhaps largely, from manuals and collections, but her biblical and patristic and liturgical knowledge was direct and extensive. Her poets were Christian poets and her Latin neither barbarous nor quite that of the Carolingian humanists. What matters is not whether her manual was attended to but that an Aquitanian lady, tucked away on a hillock in the Midi, should have composed an elaborate guide to the spiritual and moral life. She holds up to her son a mirror in which he can see both Job and himself. One could not ask for a clearer aperçu of Carolingian intro-spection at its best. But alas, both Bernard and William were to go the way of many Carolingian rebels. They were executed.

The tangled skein of the relations of reforming bishops with the parish clergy and monasteries of their dioceses can be unravelled a little further. The bishops were heirs to a constantly shifting situation that had started far away in the days when all parishes in a diocese were established by them and all parish priests directly answerable to them. From the settled communities or *vici* of the diocese the parish priests exercised a missionary role over the countryside. But in addition to *vici* there were *villae*, the estates of landowners who were willing to establish their own oratories or private churches, each served by a priest. Regino of Prüm, writing in the tenth century, was clear that the basic distinction between churches of the *vici* and the *villae* still held good, though of course the proportion varied from diocese to diocese. The churches of the more important *vici* were often collegial in organization, presided over; by an archpriest with a staff of clergy to visit outlying areas, wherever a Christian nucleus existed, and closely controlled by the bishop. There were some thirty-five such arch-presbyteries in the diocese of Auxerre in the seventh century, but not all were centred on *vici*. The private churches of the *villae* tended to multiply, especially in the north, and over these the bishops found it more difficult to keep control. The rights of a founder-proprietor could never be overlooked. Therefore it is not surprising that church councils of the early Merovingian period (there were few in the later) were mostly held in the areas where traditional parish organization was little impeded by private establishments: namely, in the south. From the later seventh century, episcopal control, like so much else, seemed to slacken. One cannot call it anarchy; there were always strong bishops somewhere; but monastic foundations grew in number, long vacancies in sees became commoner, wandering clergy of the Celtic type appeared, and so too country-bishops, *chorepiscopi*, of ill-defined status. Variations of this type did not help diocesans. Missionary activity passed from episcopal clergy to monasteries, themselves heavily endowed by landowners. The rise of a great monastery such as Corbie rested firmly on immunity from comital control within its properties and to some extent from episcopal control, legally embodied in a charter of emancipation granted by the diocesan; and it is to charters that grant emancipation, immunity, gifts and confirmations that we are largely indebted for knowledge of episcopal and other activity at the level of the parish, the private church and the monastery. Largely but not exclusively. Early Carolingian capitularies reveal that new duties were being imposed on parish priests that in their turn called for closer supervision by diocesans. Parish schools had now to be provided for, though with what success no one can tell; and the collection of tithe fell on the parish priest, who was required to keep a register of tithe-payers. It was the priest, too, who led his flock to take their oath of fealty to the king in the presence of the count. Small wonder that bishops were required to examine the qualifications of candidates for the priesthood. Over such, as over canons, nuns, monks and the laity itself, each diocesan was to keep constant watch, naturally with the assistance of a larger body of administrators, such as archdeacons.

An effective parish priesthood depended, as the Carolingians and their bishops saw it, on freedom from dominance by local proprietors and benefactors. One reform to this end – and it is insisted on in an ecclesiastical capitulary of 818–19[15] – was that all parish clergy should be free men. No serf was to receive orders; he must have been freed. Moreover, parish clergy were to be assured sufficient property to maintain themselves in independence. Canons similarly were to enjoy what a later age would call a *contenementum*. But autonomy of this sort implied corresponding duties, religious and social; and thus burdens increased with autonomy. Over-large parishes (and there were many) could be subdivided to increase efficiency of administration. In 808 the archbishop of Sens sanctioned the division of just such a parish. He clearly defined the boundaries of the new parish, dedicated a new church and specified that its inhabitants were to attend the new church to hear mass, to be baptized, to pay tithe and to hear sermons. However, subdivision of parishes could be taken too fast and too far. Such was the opinion of Hincmar of Reims as expressed to Charles the Bald; but he was as much worried at the multiplication of new dependent churches – *capellae*, he called them – as of new parish churches proper. There was a case for *capellae* in remote districts so long as they were firmly subordinated to their mother-churches. He then specified what the priest in charge of a *capella* might and might not do. Needless to say, he promulgated minute regulations for his archdeacons, archpriests, rural deans and others, to ensure that his supervision was effective; all, in the words of Lemarignier, 'dans un esprit très carolingien', which few if any of his colleagues exhibited to the same degree. He demanded annual reports: where precisely is the church? How is it equipped? Does the priest visit the sick, care for the poor, keep a school, distribute alms? What of the cemetery and the presbytery? And in respect of the last, what land sustains the priest? Finally, what other properties are in the parish, whether free or servile, and how many inhabitants have they? Upon these facts depended the collection of tithe, in itself a matter of such significance as to require brief consideration.

Tithe was the tenth part payable on the produce of whatever kind upon which a man lived, whether he were king or serf, and it appears with wearisome frequency and no little confusion in a wealth of ninth-century documents, including charters. The Carolingians aimed to enforce legally a universal tax of ancient, indeed biblical, lineage. Bishops were not immune, at least in principle, and on bishops fell the burden of enforcement. And there can be no doubt that there was enforcement, even among the newly-converted on the eastern frontiers. The lone voice of Alcuin was raised against this, as an inadvisable introduction to Christianity. Tithe was payable to the

---

[15] MGH Capit. i, no. 138, cl. 6, p. 276.

baptismal church of the payer, which in practice meant the parish priest who administered the sacraments to him. More than one bishop stated as much in his diocesan statutes. The difficulty arose when more recent foundations claimed tithe that had hitherto gone to the parish churches. Both Charlemagne and Louis the Pious reacted strongly against the tendency, as weakening the structure and stability of parishes, but not to much effect. Others than parish priests continued to lay hands on tithe; as, for example, cathedrals, monasteries and landholders who were strong enough to get away with it. Councils of the later ninth century were forced to admit that such things happened and would continue to happen; which meant in effect that any church that performed pastoral functions, whether parochial or not, could claim tithes or a proportion of them. Once collected, however, there remained the still more troublesome question of distribution. Ancient practice was clear: tithe was for relief of the poor, of pilgrims and of captives. The Carolingian bishops did not deny this but took the view that so handsome a piece of revenue was a superflux that should be shaken in more than one direction. In brief, it should be divided between bishop, clergy, fabric and poor in varying proportions. It was the bishop who decided, and he did so with the support of kings, councils and canon law (including Pseudo-Isidore). He further required an account of distribution from those responsible. Some bishops declined to take a share of tithe for themselves, while others claimed it on grounds of necessity. What all of them did was to take seriously their responsibility for collection and distribution. It is probably the most clearly-marked instance of the bishop's increasing authority over the parishes of his diocese. It can never have been an easy matter for him to do battle over tithe with landowners to whom his diocese already owed much in the way of endowment and protection, nor with prestigious monasteries who claimed to collect tithe from their own demesnes and distribute it as abbots thought best. Corbie, for example, took no notice of royal or episcopal threats but went on collecting tithe from its tenants. It was not unknown for a bishop formally to allocate a proportion of tithe to a monastery; perhaps, then, to accept a *fait accompli*. The monastic claim to tithe was naturally strengthened if a monastery exercised parochial responsibilities, as many did. It was even possible for a monastery to obtain a direct grant of tithe from a king. One is left with a situation of mounting complexity. Plainly tithe was collected. What happened next depended largely on the strength of mind of the diocesan.

Surveillance of monasteries presented worried bishops with a fresh problem in the ninth century, or with an old problem in a fresh guise. The election of an abbot had always been, in theory at least, the

business of the community. Approval of the choice and institution of
the abbot was the diocesan's business. Interference by the local landowner on whose generosity the house counted, or by the crown, was
to be expected. One cannot generalize about what happened under the
Merovingians; everything happened. A possible conclusion is that
monasteries seemed insufficiently important to invite any attempt at
the imposition of uniform control of elections. There were great
abbots, certainly, and monasteries with wide estates; but numerically
and in bulk they were less weighty than the episcopate. To the
Merovingians they were never a coherent force to be reckoned with.
This changed with the Carolingians. By the end of the eighth century
the aggregate landed wealth of monasteries had so increased as to
make them a political force of which both kings and bishops had to
take account. The election of abbots became a matter of moment. For
the first time there is evidence of lay abbots. There had always been
abbots who hunted, kept dogs and falcons, possessed weapons, employed *joculatores* and entertained as became men of rank; but they had
not been laymen, and no Merovingian bishop claimed that they were,
even while he castigated them for their shortcomings. There might of
course be a lay protector or administrator hiding behind any one of a
variety of titles, such as *rector*; but he was no abbot. A lay abbot, in
brief, was a laymen exercising full abbatial authority. If he were a cleric
(a bishop, for example) exercising such authority on a brief tenure, he
was no lay abbot. In practice it seems that free monastic choice of a
new abbot was a privilege seldom conceded, and not a right. The
Carolingians kept a close watch over elections. Curiously, the bishops
in council appeared not to be much concerned with how abbots were
elected but only with the shortcomings of abbots who failed to live
canonically. If some of them were laymen nobody minded, or said
that they did. However elected, they increasingly invited the attention
of diocesans anxious about their behaviour, their wealth and their
political muscle: they were not to attend royal assemblies without
episcopal permission. Abbesses were even more strictly supervised.
The Carolingians faced a dilemma: anxious as they were for monastic
reform, they could not ignore the wealth and usefulness of abbots.
Charlemagne in particular felt the need to put loyal supporters in
control of monasteries, sometimes to the weakening of episcopal
control. He would grant confirmation of privileges and immunities to
specially-favoured houses, like St Denis, Fulda or Lorsch, when he
saw advantage to himself in doing so, but it by no means followed that
they automatically enjoyed freedom to elect their own abbots. This
does not mean that the abbots he imposed, or of whose election he
approved, were necessarily bad abbots; it cannot even be asserted of

lay abbots, who could be perfectly competent to administer a great monastic complex and leave strictly liturgical duties to monks in priest's orders. Louis the Pious was certainly more generous in bestowing privileges, perhaps more obviously in the interests of reform. But it was a matter of degree rather than of change of policy. He, too, was grudging about free elections. St Martin's, for example, enjoyed the privilege (unlike St Denis). Yet it was Louis's own seneschal, Adalhard, a layman, who was elected abbot in 840. He only relaxed his vigilance in less sensitive areas where many of Benedict of Aniane's reformed houses lay. This illustrates how difficult it was for pious kings to reform monasteries with the zeal with which they reformed the secular Church. Bishops would occasionally express dismay. Their mood of exasperation at the condition of monasteries generally, and of the failure of Charles the Bald in particular to check his magnates' appropriation of monastic property, was clearly expressed in 845-6. There were signs of an episcopal challenge to lay abbots inspired both by self-interest and by a genuine desire for reform. It was no easy matter for them when Charlemagne and Louis the Pious possibly, and Charles the Bald certainly, had been or were themselves lay abbots for short periods. What else had Einhard been, or Alcuin? However, the issue was not again seriously raised by the bishops till the council of Trosly in 909. In the meantime, some of them were feeling their way towards an inevitable compromise between reformers and laity, all of whom had ineradicable interests in the control of monasteries.

Bishops were capable of facing the solvent of private churches and expanding monasteries and of ensuring at least their spiritual jurisdiction within their dioceses. Hincmar directly controlled several monasteries in the diocese of Reims and was not alone among bishops in so doing. Charlemagne's Bavarian bishops seem to have deprived their monasteries of any sort of parochial control; but such ferocious conservatism may not have been general. Monasteries for their part were entirely capable of looking after their own. One proof of this is their ability to survey in a detailed professional manner the estates they owned. The resultant documents, known as polyptychs, were very detailed registers of lands, revenues and personnel. A famous one was drawn up at St Germain-des-Prés for Abbot Irmino[16] in the closing years of Charlemagne's reign, plainly influenced by the format of surveys of royal estates. Incomplete as it is, we can see from Irmino's survey how a great monastic immunity comprising some 80,000 acres scattered over Francia was managed. From it his agents could see at

[16] *Polyptyque de l'abbaye de Saint-Germain des Prés*, ed. A. Longnon, i (Paris, 1886); also ed. B. Guérard (Paris, 1844).

once what returns to expect and how to meet unforeseeable demands from the crown. A slightly later example is Abbot Adalhard's poly-ptych for St Bertin;[17] a smaller matter but very efficient. It may indeed owe something to Hincmar's searching questionnaires.

When one has surveyed the field of diocesan legislation, *statuta*, sermons, liturgy, *florilegia*, charters and polyptychs, a clear impression remains that the principles of reform set out in Carolingian legislation were earnestly attended to. The bishops did what they could in widely different circumstances. Much turned on whether their diocese were in the eastern or western part of the empire; whether their main problem were lack of trained clergy, over-mighty lay patrons or monasteries, shortage of authentic texts for teaching, deviant dogma or just plain paganism. It can never have been easy to teach brotherly love and self-sacrifice to societies still drawn to the ethic of the blood feud. Surviving texts show how bishops meant to set about their task – though not, inevitably, how far they succeeded. One is left with a strong impression of sense of purpose and mission, and above all of energy.

iii. *An Exemplary Bishop: Hincmar*

A galaxy of distinguished men formed the nucleus of the Carolingian episcopate; theologians, canon lawyers, liturgists and scholars, them-selves the fine fruit of the renaissance. A body that included Theodulf and Jonas of Orléans, Ebbo and Hincmar of Reims, Agobard of Lyon, Drogo of Metz, Hraban Maur of Mainz, Wulfad of Bourges, Pardulus and Hincmar of Laon, to name no others, could stand comparison with any other body of bishops, medieval or modern. At the begin-ing stood Chrodegang of Metz, the first considerable Frankish bishop in the series of reformers; and at the end, Hincmar of Reims. Chrode-gang died in 766 after a reign of twenty-two years, Hincmar in 882, in his thirty-seventh year as bishop. But it is Hincmar and not any of the others about whom enough is known to justify a sketch in the round of a great Carolingian bishop. He was not as learned as some nor as pious as others, and whatever else he was, he was emphatically neither loved nor lovable. But there he stands, formidable to the end. To grasp the significance of Hincmar is to take a sizeable step towards understand-ing the Carolingian reform movement.

Hincmar was born, around the year 806, in northern Francia. His family was substantial. About the year 814 he entered the royal abbey of St Denis as an oblate and in due course became a canon there, the

---

[17] *Le Polyptyque de l'abbaye de Saint-Bertin (844–859)*, ed. F. L. Ganshof, F. Godding-Ganshof and A. de Smet, Mém. de l'Acad. des Inscriptions et Belles-Lettres, xlv (Paris, 1975).

abbey not yet being subject to St Benedict's Rule. The abbot was Hilduin, who must be seen as Hincmar's first teacher. In 822 or soon after Hilduin (also arch-chaplain to the Emperor Louis) took Hincmar with him to court at Aachen, where he remained for some years. By 830 at latest he was back at St Denis; late enough, however, not to be involved in Hilduin's disgrace and banishment to Saxony. He still decided to accompany Hilduin into exile and then pleaded successfully for his restoration. It was now that the abbey was reformed by two visiting archbishops – Ebbo of Reims and Aldric of Sens – and Hincmar became a monk and a priest. In 834 he witnessed the deposition and later the restoration of the Emperor Louis, who took him into his service in some undetermined way. From this point he was in the royal circle and an associate of the young Charles. It was Charles who gave him his first two preferments: the abbeys of Compiègne and St Germain-de-Flay at Beauvais. These he proceeded to reform. In 845 he was elected archbishop of Reims, a province with nine suffragan sees lying partly in Lotharingian territory outside the jurisdiction of the West Frankish crown. It was an exposed and disordered province, much battened upon by all and sundry during the vacancy caused by the deposition of Ebbo. Two of Hincmar's abiding problems were to be the validity of clerical orders bestowed by Ebbo (and so by implication the validity of his own election) and the resumption of church lands seized by the laity and the crown. In 847 he received the pallium; not at the request of Charles, his more immediate sovereign, but at that of the Emperor Lothar.

From the moment of his election Hincmar found himself involved in public business of every kind. In 858 he was leading the opposition to Louis the German's invasion of West Francia. In the 860s he was fiercely engaged in Lothar II's divorce proceedings, which divorce he opposed on strictly legal grounds that seemed not to apply years later, when the man concerned was his own master, Louis the Stammerer. Out of this came his treatise *De divortio Lotharii et Theutbergae*.[1] Also in the 860s came the deposition of one of his suffragans, Rothad of Soissons, who appealed to Rome and was reinstated by the pope. In 868 he had his first brush with another of his suffragans, Hincmar of Laon; and next year he anointed Charles king of Lotharingia at Metz – which was, in fact, the conclusion of an act of naked aggression. On the other hand, he opposed Charles's further plan of accepting the imperial title from the pope, partly because this necessitated two journeys to Rome that left Francia leaderless and partly because it would tend to subordinate Frankish metropolitans to direct papal supervision. It was Hincmar who anointed Charles's son and suc-

[1] PL 125, cols. 623–772.

cessor, Louis the Stammerer, in 878, after whose early death he did the same for Carloman; and for Carloman he composed *De ordine palatii*[2] on the basis of an earlier treatise, from which the new king might learn how administrative matters had been arranged under Charlemagne. In the same year (882) he died at Épernay after a retreat from Reims in the face of a Viking attack.

Whether faced with a national crisis or a brush with a parish priest, Hincmar approached the matter as a lawyer. This is so unlike what one would have expected a century earlier that it merits special consideration. It lies at the heart of ninth-century thinking. It is, first, to be remembered that Hincmar and his colleagues knew no official law of Church or State in the sense of a universally-accepted written code; nor was there such till long after their time. For their canon law they had indeed a fundamental collection, the *Dionysio-Hadriana* which, apart from its contents, had marked the official Carolingian recognition of the priority of Rome over national or local collections. It could be supplemented by the *Hispana*, an important collection of canons made by the fourth council of Toledo in 633. This included not only Greek and African canons but also those of ten Gallic councils, fourteen Spanish councils and a long series of papal decretal letters. In Francia it achieved a special form known as the *Hispana-Gallica*. At the beginning of the ninth century *Hadriana* and *Hispana* were being combined as one collection, which in its principal shape is known as the *Dacheriana*. The Carolingian bishops thus had plentiful canonical material at their disposal. It was inherently difficult to use, even self-contradictory, to which must be added the confusion arising from variant versions of the same material in different libraries. Its inadequacies are shown by the need people still felt to make local collections that seemed to solve the problems they were specially interested to solve; hence the Pseudo-Isidore, individual collections such as that of Florus of Lyon, and the continuing affection felt for older collections like the *Vetus Gallica*.[3] What none of this collecting solved was the pressing problem of the defence of church property against secularization. The ninth-century Church failed to achieve freedom from lay control and usurpation. But there was also secular law. Churchmen as well as laymen were subject to the inherited provisions of Roman Civil Law, which included important provisions for the government of the Church, most notably Book 16 of the Theodosian Code, promulgated in 438. Further provisions had been

---

[2] Ed. T. Gross and R. Schieffer, *Fontes iuris Germanici Antiqui*, in usum schol. (Hanover, 1980), to be preferred to the older edns. by M. Prou (1885) and V. Krauze (1894).

[3] Ed. H. Mordek, *Kirchenrecht und Reform im Frankenreich* (Berlin–New York, 1975) with important introduction.

made by Justinian, whose *Corpus Juris* was brought to Francia by Pope John VIII in 878. Civil law, therefore, was a vital element in the law governing the Church. Ignorance of it at no time exempted clergy from the obligation of obedience to it.

Where Hincmar learnt his law is uncertain. St Denis is a possibility; there is clear evidence of interest in legal texts in its library in the ninth century. Charles himself, who had considerable legal knowledge, may have acquired it in the same place. Another possibility is the court circle, where legal texts were also studied under the Emperor Louis with the help of good teachers and an excellent library. In short, the study of law was not confined to one place. If Hincmar could bend his mind to it at St Denis or Aachen, others could do so at Orléans and Lyon. Legal studies flourished in the earlier ninth century and in an attenuated form towards its close. Hincmar's voluminous writings are peppered with quotations from Roman law as also from Carolingian law, which he considered its natural corollary; and these quotations derived not only from well-known recent collections but directly. Where he found a useful reference in patristic writings he could go to the source and quote it more fully or exactly. And he knew some uncommon sources, as for example the fourth-century *Collatio Mosaicorum et Romanorum Legum*, to which King Alfred also seems to have had access not many years later. Hincmar knew enough civil law, and was widely enough respected for his knowledge, to be sent a dossier of correspondence with Byzantium for refutation. The sender was Pope Nicholas I, himself a skilled lawyer. We further know that Hincmar had legal collections made for his own use, and built up an efficient legal library at Reims. What is more, he taught there: one of his pupils was his nephew, Hincmar of Laon. A particularly weighty use of civil law is apparent in writings addressed to Charles in 868, when he parades seven Roman texts to convince the king of the injustice of confiscating the property of the see of Laon. He was not interested in verbiage; he preferred, he said, the written evidence and proof of 'many texts long conserved, that stem from all those who have reigned wisely and judged justly'. These texts the Church should guard and observe as the Fathers did.

But canon law was the main arsenal from which Hincmar drew most of his ammunition for his ceaseless battles with suffragans, popes and kings. The Church was heir to a great body of written law, though not all of it of equal authority. What was basic were the canons of the first six general councils, which were binding on all Christians equally and for all time, and above all the canons of the first council of Nicaea, summoned by Constantine in 325; ' and this', says Hincmar, 'was the holy and mystical synod'. He often speaks of 'Nicaea' as a short way of referring to the *Dionysio-Hadriana*. The last of the seven general councils was the second of Nicaea, convened by the Empress Irene in 787 to end the Iconoclastic controversy. Not much less authoritative in Hincmar's eyes were the canons of other councils and synods, for even regional ones were, by and large, a repetition of general canons with particular reference to local needs: all were inspired by the same Spirit that informed Scripture. Here was the ultimate court of appeal. But a second branch of canon law was the decretal letters of the popes. These he saw as interpretative; they were a guide to enforcement, a clarification of canons. It followed that any decretal that did not clarify was in effect a nullification of conciliar legislation; and this view could have the effect of limiting papal authority. Hincmar was cautious here but could cite in support a distinction made by Pope Gelasius. But in practice he was not lacking in respect towards the papacy, sharply as he quarrelled with it. He was clear that popes had overriding authority so far as metropolitans were concerned: 'we metropolitans follow the holy canons and the decretals of the Roman see under the supervision and judgement of the apostolic rock . . . and are dependent upon it, from which flows the stream of religion and of ecclesiastical rule and of canonical justice'. The pope was thus an interpreter, a controller, a pastor and a judge of appeal; but not a legislator. A more significant limitation of papal authority in Hincmar's eyes was that the pope had no power to change the customary law and privileges of a national church (such as the Frankish) and therefore none to challenge its temporalities or indeed its political stance. But again, he did not press this unduly. These attitudes of Hincmar, and his realization of what could be done with law, developed steadily over the length of his reign. They are most apparent in his long quarrel with his nephew; a quarrel that turned on the interpretation of law.[4] At the end of the quarrel when the bishops met in council at Douzy in 871 they unanimously deposed their colleague of Laon but did so on a variety of grounds. Some gave most weight to his defiance of the king, others to his defiance of his metropolitan, and others to what he had done with canon law; for he had, they said, contaminated the Scriptures and the Catholic words – that is, had produced versions of canons inauthentic in themselves and contradicted by better authority. No doubt they had his use of Pseudo-Isidore in mind.

What does this tell us of the archibishop's conception of law? There can be no question of his deep knowledge of the sources, and no question either that he was prepared to bend the law to suit his own purpose. To that extent he was a forger in his own right, and of this Pope Nicholas was well aware. He accused Hincmar of cooking the

---

[4] The writings and letters generated by the quarrel are in PL 126, cols. 279–648.

account of the synod held at Soissons in 853: 'by cutting out words, by adding words, you deliberately altered the acts of the council in the copy you forwarded to us . . . and you did this to drive these clergy to despair, by keeping them from appeal to Rome'.[5] Ratramn of Corbie, too, pointed out Hincmar's errors in quoting the Fathers in his admonition to his clergy on predestination, though this was possibly because he had not had time to check his sources. It can be argued that he was no true champion of law and justice in the abstract but simply a skilled manipulator of law in his own interest. This may be true but is still compatible with his having and expressing a view of law that overshadowed his use of it. The quarrels in which he was involved were not the cause of his interest in law; they merely sharpened it and canalized it. For Hincmar and his colleagues the supreme law was Christ. Scripture defined the norms of faith. That was all a good Christian needed, but the fact was that no Christian was a good Christian. Nobody lived entirely in accordance with the law of faith as set out in Scripture and culminating in Christ. Human law, then, was a necessary complement of divine law. It existed for those of insufficient faith and was by its nature repressive. Formulated for the weak, its conformity with Scripture gave it majesty. Seen in this way, human law intermingled with divine. They could be cited side by side. Thus Hincmar often linked Civil Law with Scripture, and especially with the Pauline epistles. The maker of human law was the Christian ruler; and what he made was sacred in so far as it conformed to Christian morality. A Christian's duty was to conform to all law, whether he were a subject or the ruler himself who, if he transgressed the law, would deny his royal function. To transgress was, for a king, to deny his own *subscriptio*, which for Hincmar was a heinous sin. Moreover, human law was permanently binding on the successors of those who promulgated it. So one arrives at the conception of the full flood of written law, unceasing and majestic, flowing from Moses and the pagan emperors through to the Franks themselves. What had been decided and written mattered most, and was unalterable. Any case, however humble, should rest on written testimony. Thus Hincmar could rebuke his king for going back on promises made at Quierzy in 858: the promises were written and the matters determined. He could equally rebuke his nephew for failing to obey royal law, from which the clergy could by no means escape. Pope Hadrian II had levelled accusations against the king without advancing written proof, and therefore they fell to the ground.

What Hincmar thought about law and the nature of authority is neatly summed up in chapters 7–9 of his *De ordine palatii*. The whole of

---

[5] MGH Epist. iv, no. 80.

the earlier part of this important study is Hincmar's own. The later part, which treats of royal administration and the organization of the court, is based on a now lost *libellus* from the pen of Adalhard of Corbie; but through it all sounds the authentic voice of the archbishop with a lifetime's experience and reflection behind it. Law was the only route he recognized to social order in an age when order was hard to come by. His views were entirely comprehensible to his contemporaries. He could describe Charles the Bald to Pope Hadrian as 'brought up from youth in canon and civil law'; and if Charles, then to some extent his advisers, whether lay or clerical. King Alfred would have understood very well what Hincmar's concept of the unbroken heritage of law signified to a ruler. The artists of the San Callisto Bible grasped it equally well, after their fashion. The miniatures of their Bible are eloquent: that preceding Exodus shows Moses the lawgiver at the high moments of his career, that preceding Leviticus depicts the raising of the Tabernacle with the Ark of the Covenant on an altar – the embodiment of the Old Law, the peace and order of which prefigure the New. The frontispiece to the Book of Numbers shows peace and order in disarray, confused by violence; law has been undermined. Deuteronomy has Moses delivering his final words before death, thus concluding the Old Law and, by his benediction, ushering in the promise of the New. The reception and transmission of the Law is thus fundamental to the Carolingian artistic concept of what the Bible is about: it is a book of revealed law for Christians, the heirs of the first Chosen People. The San Callisto Bible probably had nothing to do with Hincmar; indeed, there is more reason to associate it with the school of his predecessor, Ebbo. But it is still a remarkable iconographic reflection of how the generation of Hincmar saw the background to the law it lived by. Within that generation, Hincmar remains the greatest exponent of the uses of law as the intellectual shield of a struggling Church. He accepted the aims common to every Carolingian bishop: to protect and instruct his clergy, to supervise their lives and to provide the tools that might in the end lead to the education of the laity. The aim was a Christian society; the means were legal.

Ever practical, Hincmar never supposed that he ruled a Church of the Saints. His *populus christianus* embraced all men, saved and sinners. Salvation for the individual was impossible if society were not ordered and hierarchized. Order and hierarchy were what ensured social stability for the working-out of God's purposes; a stability always threatened by war, violence and theft. The work of the Devil was disruption; his triumph always was to rock the boat. Social classes seemed to Hincmar to have divine approbation. Freedom lay in fulfilling God's purposes by assuming the responsibilities proper to one's own class. Of the unfree Hincmar had very little to say, his thoughts being concentrated on the *potentes*, the men of property, and the *pauperes*, free men reduced to want. *Potentes* were to use their wealth wisely and by no means to seek to increase it at the expense of lesser men. One can see a vast social problem here, not indeed peculiar to the ninth century but characteristic of it. It lent special urgency to the Church's duty of poor-relief. Hincmar's Church was numerically a Church of the destitute or near-destitute. Mobility of any kind, social or economic, at once threatened disorder, something uncontrollable that Hincmar often summed up as *avaritia*. As the overriding evil, it was what the Fathers called *superbia*, pride or self-interest. The *potens* who pursued his private ends to the detriment of others shook the foundations of Carolingian morality. In a word, personal sin affected society. Against such, the Church should react by denunciation, teaching, law and the sacraments. Hincmar was no believer in a Golden Age to come: the Devil was permitted by God and the struggle for man's soul would go on. Only by surveillance and the enforcement of social discipline could those be saved who should be saved. Had it worked out, Carolingian society would have been a police-state.

One social sphere in which the clash of fact and hope can be most vividly seen is that of sex and marriage, and on these matters Hincmar had much to say. They are better left for separate consideration.[6] He can be said to have penetrated as deep into social *mores* as any ninth-century reformer could get. It was a long road from the *Admonitio Generalis* to the slaughter-houses he asserted that husbands led unwanted wives to.[7] He knew his councils and he applied the canons. He cited the canons, the Fathers, and above all the Bible, thousands of times in his writings. One might ask what else he knew. Classical pagan literature struck him as mostly irrelevant, though he was not hostile to it, and was a good grammarian at heart. Christian literature was another matter. He could cite quite long passages from Arator, Boethius, Marius Victorinus, Orosius, Rufinus, Prudentius and Sedulius. But books were always to him instruments of work. This is abundantly clear from the library he built up at Reims; the conservation of the heritage of the past meant little or nothing to him. Rich in patristic texts, it was notable for collections of useful material, books of reference, glossaries and dictionaries of a specialized kind. One does not get the impression that the literary tools of the past existed for him as a means of re-creation: his culture was Christian-Frankish, not Roman, a way to action and salvation. It has been claimed for him that he was more cultivated than most of his episcopal contemporaries.

[6] See below, ch. xvi (ii).   [7] PL 125, col. 657.

This seems very doubtful. He was no intellectual but a remorseless pursuer of whatever written records might assist him in his pastoral work.

With very few exceptions (notably Paul the Deacon), men of the ninth century showed little interest in the past for itself. Their sense of chronology was weak. There was no William of Malmesbury among them. But this did not prevent them from using the past. Hincmar was himself a great user. The Roman past had little to offer him, the past of Israel much more, at least in an exemplary sense. His contemporaries were equally alive to the exemplary history of the first Chosen People, their kings, judges and prophets; and in the end their failure to accept the New Covenant in Christ. But the Frankish past was special to Hincmar in a way not seen since the far-off days of Gregory of Tours. The beginnings of this interest lay in his years of apprenticeship to Hilduin in the abbey of St Denis. It was Hilduin, not Hincmar, who first saw fresh possibilities in the cult of St Denis and blended the first bishop of Paris, the Pseudo-Denis and Denis the Areopagite into a single heroic Gallic figure. It was important not only for the future of the abbey but also for the Carolingian kings. Louis the Pious was to rehearse the benefits derived by his predecessors (not simply his ancestors) from the saint, and the reciprocal benefits the abbey had enjoyed from Frankish rulers, starting with Dagobert, 'one of the old Frankish kings'. Crown and abbey were as closely linked under the Carolingians as they had ever been under the Merovingians. Hilduin's Life of the saint[8] is an elaborate exercise in historical criticism though based on several false premisses. Associated writings were a book of the miracles of the saint and a Life of Dagobert, the abbey's first considerable benefactor though not its founder. In these Hincmar may have played some part, perhaps as collector of materials. Certainly he had learnt how to use archival and liturgical sources and how these could be presented in the context of the deeds of a patron saint. He considered himself the heir of Hilduin (who died in 840) in what amounted to a hagiographical mission. The experience was emotional as much as intellectual. Had there been no literary side to his life at the abbey, the power of the saints would still have been impressed on him in his monastic office of keeper of the relics.

Thus prepared, Hincmar migrated to Reims as archbishop in 845; a migration from St Denis to St Remigius, from a Gallic to a Frankish patron. For a century at least the Franks had been learning to see themselves as a regenerate people. It was the lesson of the prologue to the Carolingian recension of *Lex Salica*, of the *Liber Historiae Francorum*, of the continuators of Fredegar's chronicle and of much liturgical

---

[8] PL 106, cols. 23–50.

acclamation of rulers. Hincmar was not short of information. He could see the whole Frankish past as a single developing experience. It had had its ups and downs. Some Frankish kings had striven to fulfil their people's divine destiny, others had not. Charles Martel had not. Hincmar castigates him, reporting the famous vision of Bishop Eucher of Orléans (under Pippin III) in which Charles was seen in torments in hell. As a consequence, St Boniface and the Abbot Fulrad had opened the king's tomb at St Denis. Out of its smouldering interior a dragon had flown; 'and I myself', adds Hincmar, 'have known those who lived into my time but were present on that occasion, and they assured me to my face of the truth of what they heard and saw'.[9] Clearly he was reporting an incident familiar to the monks of St Denis when he was one of them. In his personal continuation of the Royal Frankish Annals, known as the Annals of St Bertin, he felt unable to omit an account of the miracle of a blood-stained shirt at Thérouanne[10] and another of how Satan tempted Charles, son of Louis the German.[11] The miraculous runs through his thoughts at every stage of his life. It surfaces most notably on the occasion of Charles the Bald's unction and coronation at Metz in 869. In his allocution Hincmar speaks of the heaven-sent oil with which St Remigius had baptized Clovis at Reims. Some of it he will now use to anoint Charles. He thus links a Carolingian with the first great Merovingian and does it through the agency of a saint. He also believes (what was untrue) that they were connected by blood. He can subsume the whole past of Frankish kingship in liturgical form with the help of Remigius. Other saints came readily to his mind. He searched through many saints' Lives for examples of resistance to the injustice of the powerful. They were a vast reservoir of ammunition inherited from the past and worked up in the present. We should be wrong to think them less valuable to the ninth century than they had been to less sophisticated men of earlier generations.

Hincmar believed that his most important piece of writing was his Life of St Remigius.[12] It therefore merits some consideration. Already at St Denis he had discovered what could be done with a patron saint. At Reims he passed to the patronage of a historical figure, a bishop whose welcome for Clovis was vital both for a dynasty and for the bishopric of Reims. Already there was one Life of Remigius available at Reims; an earlier one, says Hincmar, had largely perished during the troubles of Charles Martel's time, 'when the few priests remaining at Reims made ends meet by trading in a small way, frequently wrapping up the money they took in pages torn from books. Thus the book of St

---

[9] MGH Capit. ii, ii, no. 297, p. 433.
[10] *Ann. Bert.* s.a. 862.
[11] Ibid., s.a. 873.
[12] MGH SRM iii, pp. 250–341.

Remigius, already rotted by damp and gnawed by mice, lost the greater part of its remaining pages. It has been hard work to find a few of the dispersed pages, here and there.' Equally informative was the material collected over the years by the clergy of Reims for the liturgical cult of their hero. What could be made of all this to further the cult of a still-local saint? Hincmar never rushed his fences. Not content with careful accumulation of what was accessible at Reims, he consulted others for any information they had. He delayed writing the Life, pausing on the way to translate the relics of his saint to a new crypt in the presence of the king, to whom no doubt the occasion was a reminder of the protective power of the patron of a Church much reduced by devastation and alienation of property. Four years before his death, Hincmar published the Life. It was a time when Charles seemed to be turning to other advisers than Hincmar. The Life would stake out the claims of St Remigius to defend his own against disorder, disruption, plain robbery and even from the challenges of vigorous suffragans to metropolitical authority. The result was a very elaborate composition. Broadly liturgical in framework, it is traditional in the sense that the saint's career moves from birth through virtues and miracles to public service, death, and subsequent miracles. The aim is instruction, primarily for the faithful of Reims and thereafter for the Frankish Church as a whole. Hincmar provides a reader's guide to explain his intentions: the Life is not to be read straight through by all. Some parts (and he marks them) are straightforward popular instruc-tion in the context of the liturgy, others are pastoral meditations for clergy, and others again are disquisitions on vital topics for the pondering of the learned. But the moral is clear: St Remigius continues to protect his flock as he always had in the past. *Exempla* of menace and retribution are not spared. For example, the villagers of Sault had refused to obey the saint's order; the men were forthwith stricken with gout and the women with goitre – and their children had inherited the curse to the present day. Pippin III had been chastised in his sleep for seizing a property from the suffragan see of Laon. Louis the German had been defeated in 858 because he had installed himself in a *villa* of Reims before giving battle. Such warnings might impress Carolingians; they would certainly impress local magnates with an eye to the main chance.

Hincmar reflects, as he comes to his saint's last days, on his great age and saintly character, possibly seeing himself in the dying bishop. The last words he ever wrote, the final entry in the St Bertin Annals for 882, record the delivery of Reims from the Vikings: 'but the city that neither walls nor human hands could defend was saved from assault by God's power and the merits of the saints'. So Remigius had ghostly companions in the protection of Reims, the Virgin among others. Hincmar bequeathes to Reims a saint's Life grounded in fact, round which legends of venerable age and stories of recent times had gathered. It is a complex piece of work, prepared with immense care; and it is very long. In the end, the saint matters most. Like other saintly patrons he broods over the scene of Frankish life, interceding with heaven for his people. When one has finished with Hincmar's stormy political career, his sturdy and often unscrupulous manipulation of law and his rigorous administration as an archbishop, one is left with a saint's Life. Other bishops were not unlike Hincmar. There was simply more of him.

XV

THE USES OF LEARNING

i. *A Classical Scholar: Lupus of Ferrières*

MUCH is known about the schools, teachers, pupils, curricula and books available in early western Europe; so much, that an impression can soon be had of a society devoted to education. One is left to imagine hosts of eager youths quietly pursuing their courses in the *trivium* (grammar, rhetoric and dialectic) and the *quadrivium* (music, arithmetic, geometry and astronomy). Some no doubt did, even if the *trivium* usually meant elementary grammar, and the *quadrivium*, if one attempted it as a cleric, boiled down to elementary mathematics. Beyond this lay the study of theology for the chosen few. Grammar necessarily involved some knowledge of the pagan classics. The library catalogues of cathedrals and monasteries show that texts of such were widespread. Sometimes the texts to which they refer show signs of use. They are, however, vastly outnumbered by Christian texts. Grammar was in fact taught from technical manuals and collections of material suitable to illustrate grammatical points. The presence of a Virgil, Cicero or Horace in a library catalogue cannot be taken as evidence that these were familiar to pupils. If they knew any literary texts as a whole, they would be likelier to be the Christian poets – Juvencus, Arator or Prudentius. In brief, the fact that the ninth century saved so much of pagan literature for the future does not imply that it was taught in the schools as it had been in the schools of Antiquity. Learning in general was elementary and spasmodic.

However, the chosen few certainly existed, and existed in numbers unknown to the Merovingian age. They were sensitive to the attraction of pagan literature for itself, and aware of one another. Among them were a sprinkling of laity, as for example Eberhard of Friuli, whose library catalogue survives; [1] but for the greater part they were clergy and monks. Most prominent among them was Servatus Lupus, abbot of Ferrières in the Gâtinais (Sens). He it is who best enables us to see what learning meant to a select company of ninth-century scholars. Born around 805, and so the exact contemporary of Hincmar, he had been educated at Ferrières. His family did not belong to those parts;

[1] Ed. De Coussemaker, *Cartulaire de l'abbaye de Cysoing et ses dépendances* (Lille, 1903), pp. 1–5; P. Riché and G. Tate, *Textes et documents d'histoire du moyen âge, v^e – xe siècles*, ii (Paris, 1974), pp. 414–16, with trans.

they seem to have migrated from the East, probably Bavaria. Ferrières was not a great monastery. St Eligius may have founded it in the seventh century. Its earliest surviving charter is a fragment from the reign of Clovis II. Alcuin and three of his pupils had held the abbacy in succession, and this will explain its literary interests. The last Alcuinian abbot, Aldric, sent off the young Lupus to study at Fulda under Hraban Maur, and there he remained for some six years. In 836 he was back at Ferrières, becoming abbot in 840 and dying in office about the year 862. Over his long reign he was a good deal involved in national affairs and often absent on the king's business or the abbey's. The best that survives from his pen is his correspondence, comprising about 120 letters.[2] We have a great many Carolingian letters, and Lupus' correspondence is not the biggest collection. No doubt several of his correspondents could have produced an equally large dossier. He ought not to be seen as an altogether exceptional letter-writer by Carolingian standards, anyway as to quantity. One reason why his collection was worth keeping as exemplars was that it covered a wide assortment of subjects, addressees and modes of approach. There were begging letters, letters of exculpation, advice and consolation, business letters, letters of recommendation, choking-off letters, and letters on points of theology and scholarship. Those about scholarship have attracted most attention, though in fact they constitute a minority in the dossier. But they are very illuminating.

Lupus was a scholar who could deal with textual problems as a learned man should. He was not by any means the first scholar to spot that texts got handed down corruptly or varied in their readings. Biblical and patristic texts were equally liable to corruption and variation, and those who studied them knew it. In terms of general textual expertise Theodulf was at least as sophisticated as Lupus, though not in the same field. Bede, too, without bothering his head about any theory of textual criticism or emendation, was keenly aware that texts of the same work could show serious diversity in his own special field of the Bible. As Paul Meyvaert has pointed out, nobody has yet studied the references to textual problems scattered about in the corpus of patristic writings. Lupus, then, was simply applying to the field of classical texts the criteria already familiar to scholars working in other fields. Serious study of classical texts was therefore a late comer on the scene. Those to whom Lupus wrote on such matters would have been familiar with what he meant when he wrote that texts varied and corruptions crept in all too easily. Was it not the very problem that Charlemagne had seen? His message had been that one

[2] Ed. L. Levillain, 2 vols. (Paris, 1927, 1935) hereafter 'Correspondance'. All Lupus' writings are in PL 119.

must arrive at an acceptable standard text, and the only way to keep it uncorrupted was good, clear handwriting. The same message had been taught by Cassiodorus, long before, in his *Institutes*. Thus, the fact of textual awareness was not new with Lupus. He merely applied old lessons in a neglected field.

What the letters of Lupus predominantly reveal is the daily working life of an abbot. They reveal the demands made on his time by public service; the need to attend the royal court, to lead the abbey's contingents on active service in the field, to act as a *missus*. They also reveal the struggles of a second-rate monastery to make ends meet. There are frequent letters, spread over many years, about the abbey's sufferings as a result of the loss of its distant Norman dependency of St Josse, from which it had drawn part of its sustenance. The crown had bestowed it on a magnate who needed rewarding and in consequence the abbey was hard put to find food and clothing for its inmates. St Josse was restored in the end, but only after Lupus had badgered everyone who had influence with Charles the Bald. Perhaps many abbots spent precious hours doing precisely this. A further major topic of the letters is the work of the Church itself: letters to metropolitans, bishops, abbots and priests on matters of discipline, promotion, organization, joint action and teaching. The abbot was clearly an influential man, a figure who counted in national affairs; but not so unswervingly loyal to his king as to end up in a bishopric. Whether or not we consider all this activity – the substance of his letters – as so much wasted time for a good scholar, this was in fact how he spent most of it. Occasionally he sighs for peace, as an abbot well might whose house was uncomfortably near the path of Viking raids.

Of the letters on scholarship which constitute his claim to fame, about twenty are really significant. The first in the dossier is one such.[3] It was written in 830, soon after Lupus' arrival in Fulda, and is addressed to Einhard at Seligenstadt. He writes to introduce himself to the man he considers the last survivor of the golden age of Carolingian learning, with whom he hopes to enjoy *amicitia*. It seemed appropriate to show off a little and so he quotes Horace and Cicero. Since he was a lad, he says, he had felt a passion for literature, despite the fact that most people considered profane letters superstitious and superfluous. There were few left who could teach it. It was in a bad way. He goes on: 'as I see the matter, wisdom should be prized for itself'. *Sapientia* is the word he uses, not *scientia*, learning. And so, he has been sent to Fulda to acquire not *scientia* but 'an introduction to scriptural study'. Modern writings he finds unattractive because they lack the *gravitas* of Cicero and other classical writers whom the Fathers had imitated.

[3] Correspondance, no. 1.

Einhard's *Vita Karoli* has now fallen into his hands; at last he catches an echo of the lost classical style. Having broken the ice in this manner he goes on to ask for the loan of books, especially Cicero's *De inventione rhetorica* to collate with his own faulty text. This wish to collate classical texts crops up more than once in Lupus' correspondence and places him in a category different from that of his friends – at least, as far as we know – who only borrowed texts of which they had no copy. In fact there survive at least a dozen manuscripts that reveal his handiwork as a textual scholar, of which the most important is a copy of Cicero's *De oratore*, written by Lupus himself. Texts annotated by him include a corpus of Cicero's philosophical writings, Valerius Maximus, Aulus Gellius, Macrobius, and Donatus on the *Aeneid*. He saw what to do with manuscripts. He could leave spaces where he suspected gaps, mark corruptions and record variants. He could equally collate biblical texts, though in this field he had a more distinguished predecessor in Theodulf.

Lupus stood in a scholarly tradition, thin but secure; and this he handed on to Heiric of Auxerre and others. But even in the first flush of scholarly excitement what strikes one most about the young Lupus is that learning and its techniques are not ends in themselves. There was much wisdom to be won from the classical authors, even if their immediate value lay in their capacity to say things well. For this reason the Fathers had cultivated them; and because Lupus had been sent to Fulda to learn the scriptures he also studied the Fathers and turned as they did to classical models. He felt no sense of incongruity. He was not in the modern sense a classical scholar in the making. Einhard was not deceived, as his reply shows; and when he got to know Lupus better, the book that he dedicated to him was his *De adoranda cruce*. This we learn from Lupus' enormously long letter of consolation on the death of Einhard's wife,[4] which abounds in quotations from the Bible and the Fathers. In a further letter to Einhard[5] he asks for help in interpreting a passage in Boethius' *De arithmetica* of which, without knowing it, he had a faulty text. He also wished to borrow something rather curious: a copy of the 'alphabet' composed by Bertcaudus, *scriptor regius*, written in capitals which some call *unciales*. Finally, he wanted advice on the quantity of certain syllables.

While at Fulda Lupus copied a good many texts, including a collection of Germanic laws for Eberhard of Friuli. But he explains to another friend that he was really there to read, and adds that he was not there to learn German, which would be a considerable undertaking. He presumably means, to write German. Back at Ferrières, he writes at great length to an enquirer on the quantity of syllables but refuses to

---

[4] Ibid., no. 4.   [5] Ibid., no. 5.

lend him a book because the messenger, however reliable, would have to travel on foot.[6] Further, there is this revealing query: what is their Irish friend Probus up to? Is he, as he used to say quite seriously, pursuing the liberal arts in the German forests, or is he admitting into the society of the elect Cicero and Virgil and all the others he thinks illustrious? Has the Saviour spilt his blood and endured hell in vain? Lupus writes again to the same correspondent, Altuin,[7] to lament the decay of learning, the ignorance of teachers, the rarity of books and the lack of leisure; and adds, in the course of further grammatical points, how important it is not to depart from your authorities without good reason. To another, obviously a pupil, he sends a message that he had better get on with the study of Virgil as best he can.[8] Next year comes a letter to abbot Adalgard[9] on irregular verbs, together with thanks for help in correcting a text of Macrobius (though he would sooner have had the whole book than a detached piece), and also for a copy of Boethius on Cicero's Topics: 'I don't know if I have got the whole of it, nor if it is your own copy, nor if you have collated it.' A year or so later he writes to the abbot Marcward of Prüm for a copy of Suetonius in two small volumes, since none is to be had anywhere near Ferrières.[10] He also wishes to send along his nephew and two other students to learn German at Prüm. German was clearly considered a useful acquisition for a West Frankish monk who might have to travel far and meet important people on his monastery's business.

A year later (845) Lupus was writing to Hincmar for help in the restoration of St Josse; and he ends thus:[11] 'in trying to win back our property I should even have contemplated imitating the ancients and turning to the artifice of erudition if experience had not taught me how pointless it is. If Virgil himself were to return now and expend all his skill to win hearts he would not find a single reader among our contemporaries.' This was nonsense, but certainly it meant that Lupus knew himself to belong to a small minority among the literate. The metropolitan of Tours is asked to lend the St Martin's copy of Boethius on Cicero's Topics; the copy written on papyrus 'or, as they say nowadays, on paper'. Lupus does not wish to be known as the borrower.[12] The following letter in the dossier, to an unknown correspondent, paints a gloomy picture of subsistance-living at Ferrières: 'our Demosthenes', he writes (apparently meaning himself), 'is often short of greenstuff, and bears with third-rate bread as best he can'.[13] Not only books are worth borrowing. He asks Abbot Marcward to send to Seligenstadt ('called Saligstat in German') the *tabulae* that

[6] Ibid., no. 8.	[7] Ibid., no. 9.	[8] Ibid., no. 12.
[9] Ibid., no. 21.	[10] Ibid., no. 35.	[11] Ibid., no. 48.
[12] Ibid., no. 53.	[13] Ibid., no. 54.	

Hilperic painted and dedicated to the two martyrs of Seligenstadt.[14] Then back again to books: Ansbald of Prüm is assured that Lupus will collate for him the Prüm copy of Cicero's letters with the copy at Ferrières, 'so that out of the two the truth shall emerge if that is possible'; and in return he would like Cicero on Aratus to supplement what he already has.[15] At the same time Prüm is thanked for teaching German to the Ferrières pupils – 'it is so necessary nowadays that only the idle neglect it'. Furthermore, Prüm is reassured that the courier with this letter is entirely reliable but does not like sleeping alone because it gives him the horrors.[16]

There were limits to what Lupus thought learning might do for a man. In a letter supporting the claims of a monk to the see of Amiens, he writes that the monk is possibly a little short on learning and then explains that he might not prove a very good teacher of *instituta divina*. Nevertheless, he would make a useful bishop.[17] He did get the see – and Hincmar formed a very low opinion of his basic knowledge. There was a little letter-exchanging with England, mostly urging the case for *amicitia*, which in practice meant sending books to Lupus. He tells Abbot Altsig of York in 852 that since they both burn with love of learning the abbot can start the exchange by sending him, via St Josse now restored, a list of books for copying;[18] apart from Quintilian's *Institutions* they are exegetical. Even a selection would be welcome. Learning is thus not confined to classical authors in Lupus' mind. The same mixture appears in a letter to Bishop Heribald of Auxerre (probably his half-brother):[19] Lupus sends him Jerome on the Prophets which he would like back as soon as possible, not having read it himself, and at the same time expresses his views on Caesar, who ought not to be classed among the historians of Rome, since all that survives is Caesar's commentary on the Gallic Wars. During the remainder of Caesar's life, when he was burdened with the business of the world, his secretary Hirtius kept a record in the form of another series of commentaries. Heribald shall have such of these commentaries as Lupus can find.

When he writes to Pope Benedict III[20] to introduce two Ferrières monks on pilgrimage, Lupus takes the chance of asking for the loan of Jerome on Jeremiah, in a copy of great age. He only wants Book VI onwards, the earlier Books being already available. Also he would like Cicero's *De oratore*, Quintilian in one small volume (only parts of these being accessible to him) and Donatus on Terence. To another correspondent due on a visit he advises great caution on the brigand-

[14] Ibid., no. 65.   [15] Ibid., no. 69.   [16] Ibid., no. 70.
[17] Ibid., no. 74.   [18] Ibid., no. 87.   [19] Ibid., no. 95.
[20] Ibid., no. 100.

infested roads:[21] he is to bring with him Sallust's *Catalina* and *Jugurtha*, 'the Verrines and such other books as you know we have only defective copies of or no copies at all'. His own metropolitan, Wenilo of Sens, is asked for a Livy of which he is in urgent need;[22] and at the same time he offers to discuss the doctrine of the redemption with him. From Odo, abbot of Corbie, he begs a manuscript of Faustus of Riez, but writes again to make it clear which Faustus he means: not the one Augustine refuted but the one condemned by Pope Gelasius.[23] He regrets being unable to lend Hincmar Bede's commentary on St Paul's epistles:[24] the book is so big that it cannot be hidden in clothing or a wallet and would certainly attract thieves by its beauty; it shall be sent later on, when a safe way can be found.

As the years pass, times get more difficult. Lupus by himself is sufficient evidence of the gravity of the Viking threat to the entire region south of Paris. Preparations had to be made to evacuate Ferrières; there was disruption everywhere. The king made repeated demands on Lupus' time and on the manpower of his monastery. However, he is able to write thus to Bishop Aeneas of Paris:[25]

Among other things, I have indicated to the king (who is very keen on teaching) my wish to resume, God permitting, my study of the liberal arts and equally the teaching of them – if he would indulge me so far. He agreed with a smile as well as some flattering remarks and promised to further my plans so far as it proved feasible. I tell you this at once, so that you shall know what arguments move him in such a matter.

In fact, Lupus seemed to get on very well with the preoccupied king. He even sent him some improving reading for Lent: Augustine on St James's epistle, with special reference to oaths and perjury.[26] But all the time he was bothered by correspondents seeking help on points of detail; as, for example, the meaning of the Roman title *pater patratus*.[27]

The last letter in the dossier[28] is addressed to his kinsman Ebrard, a monk, who has begged for a composition without specifying a subject. What he gets is a letter on the subject of wisdom. There is, Lupus thinks, something of a revival of study in his part of the world, though not everywhere with the same objectives. Many are content with literary ornamentation and only a few seek what is incomparably more important, the good way of life; 'and thus we alarm ourselves over linguistic slips and in trying to get them right we overlook the slips in our daily lives; and these increase all the time'. All wisdom, he goes on, comes from God.

[21] Ibid., no. 101.   [22] Ibid., no. 104.   [23] Ibid., nos. 106, 107.
[24] Ibid., no. 108.   [25] Ibid., no. 122.   [26] Ibid., no. 124.
[27] Ibid., no. 125.   [28] Ibid., no. 133.

How just it is that those who put learning above sanctity should ever be excluded from the feast of wisdom. This is why it is so much more important to devote our time to the acquisition of *honestas* and *iustitia* than to the polishing and repolishing of our style. But admittedly there are many ways to God, as also to philosophy, and the Church is open for each of us to pursue his own path of piety.

At the end of the letter comes this: 'Of course, while you occupy yourself in these (divine) studies, I would not want you entirely to neglect the noble arts proper to a man of birth; seek them from God, who gives all in abundance'. The tone of this letter is unlike that of the earliest letters to Einhard. Lupus seems to have got scholarship in perspective as a useful, dignified tool; but not as an end in itself.

Lupus knew, or sought to know, or sought to know better, a wide range of classical authors, most of them not unfamiliar in the ninth century. What is surprising is the number of correspondents to whom he could turn, or who turned to him for texts they could presumably appreciate. Within this context, discussion of classical, biblical and patristic writings seemed to blend without any sense of incongruity. One is left with the impression of a man who knew his classical authors in a way that Bede, for example, had not, and who cared deeply for them. But they were not all. The limits were set in the two compositions of Lupus that survive apart from his letters. Both are saints' Lives. That of St Maximin of Trier was written at the request of Abbot Waldo.[29] There is a letter to Waldo about it, dated 839. Clearly, Lupus writes, there should be such a Life, 'but one thing has rather troubled me: obviously much of what Maximin did in his lifetime has been swept into oblivion, and what remains are faint indications among which a proportion look like fairy-tales'. In other words, he had little to go on that satisfied his standards; but he cannot have been too dissatisfied because he believed his Life would secure him the patronage of the saint. It is a traditional saint's Life, a parading of the miraculous. However, Maximin had had the uncommon experience of giving shelter to no less a man than Athanasius, despite imperial hostility. St Jerome had seen him as the most courageous bishop of his time. Lupus goes further: 'O most holy man, fit to be ranked with the greatest in the Church, who could spurn the unjust charge of imperial power!' He then risks a comparison with the present time: 'but consider the degenerate standards of today! . . . Cash rates higher than justice.' Who now would accept an Athanasius under his roof? Who now, in other words, would stand up for a bishop who had fallen foul of his king? Lupus is careful to show that Maximin had also proved a

[29] PL 119, cols. 665–80.

valuable patron to the Carolingians. The saint was as powerful in death as in life.

Lupus' second Life, that of St Wigbert, was written at the request of the community of Hersfeld.[30] Again he complains of the scantiness of material, but he will do his best with it, 'so that a worthy memorial may be inscribed in fitting words and what is most splendid shall not be deformed by illiteracy'. In other words, the spirituality of the subject would be lost without good writing. The Life is beautifully composed. Lupus has taken heart, as he says, from those before him who had written about men they never knew personally: Sallust, Livy and – 'to come to our own' – Jerome and Ambrose. He has a further point to make: the reader must be charitable when he finds the Latin language roughened by Germanic words for people and places; he is not writing poetry, when one must stick to the 'sonority of Roman eloquence', but history. One can see why he was bothered about this aspect of his subject, for Wigbert, an Anglo-Saxon, had been one of St Boniface's right-hand men in the German mission-field and his first abbot of Fritzlar and Ohrdruf. Boniface, like Maximin, had known how to stand up to princes, 'being ignorant how to court royal favour by crawling adulation'; he had been all for 'ecclesiastical honour and rigour'. Thus Lupus played his part in the advance of the cult of St Boniface and his disciples in ninth-century Francia, West as well as East. Lupus' literacy skills found a further outlet as an official drafter. The canons of Carolingian councils are generally of a high standard; those of the synod of Ver, of 844, are exceptionally so and were drafted by Lupus.[31] He recorded the decisions of the assembled bishops directed to Charles the Bald and indeed written in the king's *palatium*. They start with a preface of notable pungency. It is built round a passage from the Book of Daniel: 'the Lord has power in the kingdom of men'. *Discordia* reigns. 'Return to peace with your brothers.' Strong words; but stronger still are those at the end of the preface: 'may the following not be applicable to you – you do not hear God's words because you are not of God' (St John: 8). The king's soul is in danger: 'restore to God what is his and so enjoy what is yours in peace'. 'You also, *clarissime rex*, flee the company and counsel of the perverse; for if you despise us, or rather God speaking through us, we shall be forced however unwillingly to carry out what our office demands.' This was presumably a threat of excommunication as a step to penance. Lupus was speaking anonymously; officially he was the mouthpiece of others and therefore did not risk the king's wrath. Yet in their emergency the bishops turn to the scholar to express what they feel about the spolia-tion of the Church. Lupus could do it best. He had style at his

[30] Ibid., cols. 679–94.   [31] MGH Capit. ii, ii, no. 291, pp. 383–7.

command, the right biblical quotations and obvious familiarity with the relevant canons of earlier councils and synods.

Finally, Lupus was no mean theologian. The controversy over predestination stirred up by Gottschalk in the 840s involved Lupus, as so many others. He put his own position in a letter to the king that was nothing less than a theological tractate.[32] He was by no means entirely hostile to Gottschalk. His interpretation of St Paul and Augustine on free will was not the one generally accepted. This presumably reached the ears of Hincmar, in whose custody Gottschalk lay, because Lupus had to write a further letter-treatise[33] which did nothing to help Hincmar. He also wrote direct to Gottschalk:[34]

Since it is not wrong to have opinions about a subject, so long as they are not contrary to faith, I will explain to you the thoughts that the holy and learned Augustine seems to me to express in the passage you ask me to comment on.

This he does, ending thus:

My advice to you, reverend brother, is not to go on bothering your head with these problems. They take up time that would be better given to work and teaching on more useful matters . . . what can we know with any precision about the ineffable vision of God? Meanwhile let us march into the vast field of the Scriptures, let us give ourselves wholly to meditation upon them and search there humbly, piously and always for the face of God.

And finally:

I do not know who stole those papers of mine you found. Anyway, the sense of the Greek words will be best explained by Greeks. Later on I will try to explain them but just at present they don't come to me, and I am so overwhelmed with work that I cannot look into the matter.

But Lupus did not leave it at that. He wrote a full-length treatise on predestination which he called his *Liber de tribus quaestionibus*, and a collection of supporting authorities to go with it.[35] Here particularly one can see the sense in which the classics were useful to him. Repeatedly he brings in a classical text to bolster the Bible or the Fathers, and does so without any straining after effect. Sallust, for example, puts the distinction between body and soul quite neatly and can be cited; and in the same way, without acknowledgement but quite naturally, Valerius Maximus slips in. He looks to see how the Roman writers dealt with the issue of self-reliance or reliance on others as opposed to reliance on God. Cicero and Virgil help him; and thus to the Fathers, 'our own writers so obviously more superior in wisdom': Cyprian, Jerome and above all Augustine. Later on comes an echo

---

[32] Correspondance, no. 78.   [33] Ibid., no. 79.
[34] Ibid., no. 80.   [35] PL 119, cols. 619–66.

from Tacitus, two more quotations from Cicero and a tribute to
Priscian. The balance is the same in Lupus' collection of authorities.
There is some showing-off with Horace but what matters is the
Fathers: 'nor is it wonderful that I should have found this in the two
greatest lights among our teachers, Augustine and Jerome, and after
them in Gregory and Bede, since their teaching stemmed from the
authority of the Gospels'. Any Carolingian teacher could have written
these words but they happen to be the words of the one among them
who had best claim to be called a classical scholar. His classical taste
obviously had a stylistic effect on whatever he wrote; all his writing is
exceptionally lucid and taut, even elegant. This apart, the wisdom of
the ancients is subsumed into the deeper wisdom of the Fathers, who
themselves had used it freely. There was no question of anything
more. Pagan literature was a moral *praeparatio*.

   The twenty years or so of Lupus' writing life were years of a crisis in
communication. This was partly physical. It was a time of invasion,
brigandage, civil war and wholesale seizure of church property. There
was equally a breakdown of confidence and trust. Authority was
challenged at every level and oaths were not kept. There was a breakdown of doctrine, of which the violent reaction to Gottschalk is a
measure of its seriousness. There was a breakdown of law. And there
was a breakdown of language. The vernacular, oral and written, was
becoming commoner as a means of communication between educated
men. The vernacular language of faith and teaching looks more direct
and purposeful; but it was not yet sure of itself and it varied from
region to region. The language of Christianity in the West was still
Latin, and the Latin required for exegesis of the Bible and defence of
doctrine was a sophisticated language. It was to this language that
Lupus sensed the challenge, and for this reason he gave time to the
copying and correcting of the classical texts that underlay the Latin of
the Fathers. It was a very different interest from that of Sidonius in the
fifth century. Lupus was not concerned to preserve an aristocratic
treasure or a way of life. He insisted only that men who wished to
understand the teaching of the Church had better start with Cicero and
Virgil.

ii. Scholarship, the Bible and the Liturgy:
Hraban Maur, Walahfrid Strabo, Amalar

As manuscripts of biblical exegesis and commentary greatly exceed
those concerned with classical authors, so do biblical scholars exceed
classical scholars. The former, not the latter, are characteristic of the
Carolingian Renaissance; and among them none was so respected and

productive as Hraban Maur. Let him stand for the many who saw the study of the Bible and the disciplines associated with it as the rock on which Christian society rested.

His name, Hrabanus, was the latinized form of Germanic *Hrafn*, raven; and Maurus, the name of St Benedict's favourite pupil, was added as a nickname by Alcuin. He was born at Mainz about the year 780 and was sent by his parents to the monastery of Fulda, some seventy miles north-east of Mainz. Fulda still retained the teaching traditions and library of its founder, St Boniface. Any monk trained there was permanently marked by the Anglo-Saxon Benedictine ethos. Nevertheless, some of its best pupils were sent to Alcuin at Tours or at court for a finishing-course; and one of these was Hraban. Alcuin's influence on his mind was deep: one can detect this specially in Hraban's theology and in his interest in the computus. Back at Fulda, he joined the teaching staff by 804 at latest and soon became head of the school. He seems to have taught everything, like Alcuin, but his specialities were theology and biblical exegesis. To judge simply from his pupils he was a great teacher. It is as an aspect of his teaching that his written work has to be assessed. Both teaching and writing had coincided with some anxious years for the monks of Fulda under Abbot Ratgar, an ambitious monastic builder who sacrificed the resources of the house, including the labour of his monks, to his building programme. For this, as well as for a devastating epidemic, Ratgar was blamed by the community, who appealed for justice first to Charlemagne and then to Louis the Pious. Hraban's books were confiscated during the troubles. But Ratgar was removed. The emperor replaced him with Eigil, a more intellectual man. The troubles were revealing in several ways: first, of how a building programme could get out of hand; second, of the community's determined efforts to appeal direct to the emperor; and third, of the emperor's personal concern to put things right.

In 822 Hraban succeeded Eigil as abbot, handing over most of his teaching to Rudolf, who subsequently wrote a sketch of his life that is hardly a biography.[1] It is clear that he was a pastoral and a missionary abbot; thirty new churches in neighbouring villages owed their foundation to him, and his liturgical innovations were designed to attract people to church. But a man in his position was likely to get involved in political upheavals. Hraban felt a strong moral obligation to support the reigning emperor: first Louis the Pious and, after his death, Lothar; and this caused trouble with Lothar's brother, Louis the German. For this reason he retired from his abbacy, in which he was succeeded by his pupil Hatto, and retreated to the nearby Petersberg.

[1] MGH SS xv, pp. 339–41.

By 847, however, Louis had sufficiently forgiven him to make him archbishop of Mainz, in which capacity he proved a strict reformer, especially in pastoral matters; the canons of his synods of 847 and 852 hark back directly to the great reforming synod of Mainz in 813. He died in February 856 in his seventy-seventh year and was buried at Mainz.

Such is the career into which Hraban's literary life has to be fitted. To judge from his pupils, his library and the output of his scriptorium, his influence on Fulda was second only to that of St Boniface. Whether this entitles him to be called the *praeceptor Germaniae*, as historians have been wont to call him for the last two centuries, is another matter. Though he wrote more than any other Carolingian scholar, his writings as a whole do not seem to have enjoyed an immediately wide circulation, even in Germany. Around a dozen copies of what seem to have been his most popular works are as much as survive. In other words his influence was local; and this is typical of the influence of ninth-century writers once one is clear of the generation of Charlemagne. They provided for the local situation that faced them.

Hraban's writings fill six volumes of Migne's *Patrologia Latina*.[2] The first in date of the more significant is a complex and uninviting piece, *De laudibus sancti crucis*;[3] a poem designed as letter-play and number-symbolism. It must have delighted Alcuin, under whom it looks to have been started, as later it certainly delighted the medieval mind. It gained Hraban the reputation of a poet which he did not deserve. The intricate, even repelling, format can conceal from our eyes the growing concentration of the ninth century on the cult of the Holy Cross. Thereafter came a theological handbook for priests (*De institutione clericorum*),[4] a chronological treatise (*De computo*);[5] a version of Priscian's *Grammatical Art*;[6] a famous variant of Isidore's *Etymologies* known as *De universo* (though its real title was *De rerum naturis*);[7] two homiliaries;[8] a martyrology[9] and penitential;[10] commentaries on most of the books of the Bible;[11] and a little treatise called *De inventione linguarum* (or *litterarum*)[12] which contained the remark that Boniface had taught two ancient systems of cryptogram to Hraban's predecessors at Fulda. There is a fair amount more of occasional writing, especially of correspondence and verse. The bulk is great.

[2] PL 107–12, except where better edns. available.
[3] MGH Poet. ii, pp. 159–66.
[4] Ed. A. Knöpfler, *Veröffentl. des kirchenhist. Seminars, Munich*, v (1900).
[5] CC xliv (1979), pp. 165–321, ed. W. M. Stevens.
[6] PL 111, cols. 613–78.
[7] Ibid., cols. 9–614.   [8] PL 110, cols. 9–468.
[9] CC xliv (1979), pp. 3–134, ed. J. M. McCulloh.
[10] PL 110, cols. 467–94.
[11] PL 107–10.   [12] PL 112, cols. 579–1584.

The first impression one gets from Hraban is of dullness; endless pages of excerpted material from the Bible and the Fathers, sensibly arranged but certainly not liable to inspire any pupil; which indeed holds true for a considerable part of Carolingian literary production. It is not creative, at least in the modern sense. But then one looks closer to find out what it was that he was trying to achieve. One begins to see that his enormous respect for the past did not prevent him from doing things with his material, so that the end-product was his own. Even in so obviously derivative a work as *De universo*, resting firmly on Isidore, there are subtle changes for what was in effect a guide to the interpretation of Scripture. He divides Isidore's twenty books into twenty-two, conceivably because that was the number of books in the Old Testament; and he introduces material that Isidore had not used; as for example from Arator, Bede, Sedulius, Josephus, Lactantius and Augustine, whether directly or indirectly. His emphasis is on the mystical significance of objects. One can study his method more easily in his chronological treatise, *De computo*, written in 820. This is a revised text of a computus originally composed for a monk, perhaps Irish, named Macharius. It had abounded in extraneous information that made it difficult for teachers to use. Bede had done much to rationalize it but again it got confused with more material. Various Carolingian attempts were made to straighten it out once more. For his part, Hraban went back to Bede. He arranged the whole in dialogue form and in sections: arithmetic, astronomy, Easter reckoning, world history and chronicle. This does not in fact tell us how the Carolingians taught any part of the *quadrivium* but it provides a shape. There was probably no standard system of *quadrivium* instruction; it depended on the individual master. The subject was vast. It invited him to proceed from elementary arithmetic at one end to the order of the cosmos at the other; dates therefore, and how to arrive at them, but also the *Opus Dei*. Hraban is often content to cite what Bede and Isidore had dug out, notably in his astronomical section; but his approach to cosmology is less scientific, more overtly religious, than Bede's. Half of his book is devoted to Easter reckoning, where he provides a modified Easter Table and makes omissions from Bede that are not always for brevity's sake. What stands out is this: he does not share either Bede's scientific concern or Bede's interest in and sense of the past. For Hraban, the past is an undifferentiated reservoir from which to draw up useful material, above all for the purpose of explaining biblical texts. One notices this in his section on the world chronicle, which he drastically shortens in order to concentrate on the biblical part. What Bede sought was to produce a critical argumentation that faced big issues in a scholarly way; whereas Hraban wanted a clear, logical text for students at Fulda; and he wanted it because a computus so devised was liturgically vital for half-pagan East Francia. He meant his student-priests to be in no doubt about the dates and times of the Christian feast days. How otherwise could they enforce them? His target was intellectually humbler than Bede's but a lot more useful in terms of the reform of Christian society; at any rate, the society of which Fulda was the heart.

The same mental processes are discernible in Hraban's version of Priscian's *De arte grammatica*, the principal subject of the *trivium*. Between Priscian and Hraban come many masters of the grammatical art, as for example Aldhelm and Bede. By no means all of Hraban's sources are to be found in Priscian, nor does he always follow Bede in preferring examples from Christian writers to pagan. His criterion is what is best for teaching. And he shows independence of Bede in other respects – as in his theory of letters and of consonants. His interpretation of syllables shows some originality and he can develop Bede's theory of accents. Altogether he has a clear notion of how to use, correct and combine material from different sources. Most interestingly he betrays some concern in the Old Testament as poetry, and not only accepts but develops the current idea that in verse-forms the Old Testament had priority over the Greek and Latin pagans. Poetry he sees as a form of spiritual knowledge, pagan and Christian poetry springing from a common root in the Old Testament. They belonged to one tradition; and if one omitted what was obviously unacceptable on religious or moral grounds from the ancient writers, pagan literature was not merely permissible but essential for Christian society. Grammar was not a dangerous necessity but a precious heritage, and the same could be said for much pagan literature that was not overtly grammatical. It taught wisdom. Thus far Hraban and Lupus were on common ground.

More significant still was Hraban's *De institutione clericorum*. Mainly based on Augustine's *De doctrina christiana* and Isidore's *De ecclesiasticis officiis*, it was intellectually nowhere near either of them; but it was not trying to do the same things. The result was a great pedagogical work, the first (or at any rate the first extant) teaching manual compiled for German clergy and monks. He no more attempts than did any other Carolingian scholar to define the Church in theological terms. He is content that its nature is universal, and this distinguishes its doctrine from any heresy. The Church's beliefs and practices, its liturgy and hierarchy, proceed from a single pattern. He must have delighted, if he knew it (as Cardinal Newman later did) in Augustine's limpid phrase in his attack on the Donatist Parmenian: 'securus iudicat orbis terrarum'. Hraban's business was to identify the hierarchy of clergy, monks and laity, and within that to consider the role of the order of clergy, the *ordo clericalis*, in its liturgical functions. When one reads Hraban on the celebrant of the mass, what stands out is his sense of the vital function of the priest as intermediary between God and man. Unlike Isidore, he does not regard bishops and priests as being effectively on the same footing. A good Carolingian, he has a sharper sense of hierarchy, whether between bishops and priests or between bishops and archbishops, bishops and chorbishops. The office of the priest is none the less high, as might be seen from Old Testament precedents. His vestments were symbolic; and his unction as well as his contact with the sacraments set him apart as one who must always be pure. By contrast, the laity's role is passive. The mass is for him, what it always was, the great sacrament, but not far behind it in Hraban's eyes is the sacrament of baptism. Germany was still in the ninth century a world of mass-conversion and mass-baptism; and thus the rite had to be simplified. Charlemagne had sent a circular on the matter to metropolitans. Hraban approaches it in that light. His concern is for the correct form of baptism and he is clearer on the reasons for this than on a theological explanation of its significance. It was a rite for the mission-field. He follows his master Alcuin to a large extent on the form of the rite, except that his ordering is different and he attaches more weight to renunciation of the Devil. Baptism marked the victory of the true God over false gods, not over some vague atheism. To make this quite clear Hraban puts things in lord–man terms of relationship suitable for his Germans; and when he became archbishop of Mainz his rite became fairly widely disseminated in the German mission-field. Confirmation he saw as a rite distinct from baptism. It was reserved for bishops, since only bishops could apply chrism. His famous hymn, *Veni creator spiritus*, can be seen in relation to this rite.

To return to the mass, Hraban's eucharistic teaching comes from Isidore, Bede and Alcuin, not direct from the Fathers; and yet it is patristic in flavour and less 'Frankish' than the teaching of some of his contemporaries. He plainly did not share Radbert's view of the Real Presence in the elements, seeing them as a path to God rather than God in reality; and here, as with the other sacraments, he argues that the saving function of the eucharist depends on the moral will of the recipient. This was also Augustine's opinion. Before Hraban there had existed short guides to the mass (called *expositiones missae*) but his is the first of the ninth-century commentaries. It is a straight exposition for priests. When he comes to the sacrament of penance he is no clearer than any of his contemporaries as to whether he is thinking of the traditional form of public confession or the newer private confessions.

Public confession might have political repercussions, and he seems to feel this. At least he is perfectly clear about the need for reconciliation as the fruit of confession and penance.

Hraban treats three other large themes in *De institutione*. The first of these is the feasts of the Church. He has nothing interpretatively to add to his source, Isidore, but his feasts are not quite the same. He adds a feast for the Virgin and, in the Frankish tradition, inserts Rogations and Good Friday. One meets a new stress on the significance of Whitsun; and this is in keeping with Hraban's view of a penitential Church in which salvation depends on the individual's own assessment of sin and what effort he is prepared to make in order to become accessible to the working of the Holy Spirit. Secondly, Hraban explains the nature of scriptural interpretation, abridging Augustine in such a way as to emphasize moral interpretation. He shows no interest in textual problems: the Vulgate is enough, and no one need waste time collating different texts of the Bible or in practice need bother much with Greek and Hebrew. Always one feels with Hraban that his Bible is something different from Bede's Bible or Gregory the Great's: it is more the source of the liturgy and the background to the sacraments. For the understanding of the Bible the liberal arts were necessary, as also for putting its precepts into practice. For down-to-earth teachers like Hraban, the liberal arts were entirely practical: music was a discipline for clergy who had to sing services, astronomy was geared to the computus, dialectic a weapon in the battle against heresy and rhetoric a tool for preachers. Geometry helped one to understand the biblical description of Solomon's temple. Only arithmetic retained something of its antique mystery. But it has to be added that Hraban's approach to classical literature was one of devotion; he saw it, as did Lupus, as an adjunct to Christian literature. One recalls Lupus' complaint to Einhard in 836 that he would have returned his copy of Aulus Gellius if the Abbot Hraban, complaining that he had none of his own, had not kept it back. Moreover, Hraban had said that he meant to write to Einhard to explain that he had seized the book from Lupus by force. The *Noctes Atticae* of Aulus Gellius do not look like essential reading; but they were a hodgepodge, and the Carolingian world loved potted information. Thirdly, Hraban looked hard at preaching (and teaching, of which it was an aspect). The preacher, he thinks, should operate within a clear scheme of virtues and vices – another Carolingian obsession; and in this respect the teaching of Augustine and Gregory could stand simplification: identify the vices and the triumph of the corresponding virtues should follow as a matter of course. It was equally the message of Hraban's first collection of homilies. It was the moral theme that the preacher should never miss.

As to teaching apart from preaching, his message is less to the individual (as with Cassiodorus and Augustine) than to the group, the priesthood or those destined for it; and this would appear to stem consciously from Carolingian legislation and its aims. It was all quite straightforward, even simple. The problems of the individual were neither here nor there. It is certain that he must have envisaged more specialized instruction for abler pupils and allowed for discussions with them; but of this we know nothing.

Looking at Hraban's writings in the round, one sees why he was an excerptor and encyclopaedist. The Carolingian clergy were trying, in a matter of a generation or so, to adapt to modern requirements the entire teaching traditions of Antiquity and the Early Church. What they needed was well-ordered, clear handbooks and compendia of relevant knowledge. What they did not need was problems and doubts. Hraban was quite specially the right man for the job. He had any amount of broad, ethical wisdom; he could rearrange anything to make it comprehensible; and he could see what to omit. There was really no room for complicated exegesis among the German clergy. Everything turned on understanding the liturgy and its precedents in the Old Testament, for the Jews, like the Franks, had been a people ruled by written law. And with the liturgy had to go an understanding of the role of the priesthood and of the sacraments it administered. Leaders of God's people, the priests dispensed the sacraments, and they expounded the meaning of the Bible as the revelation of God, the source of wisdom and the absolute law-book. In width of knowledge only Alcuin equals Hraban among the Carolingian scholars; and yet, for all his clear objectivity, Hraban is sometimes warmer and even more lyrical than his master. He never ceases to wonder at God's wisdom, which he identifies as the source of human knowledge. All knowledge, therefore, has the justification that it can be seen from the viewpoint of a Christian ethic. Knowledge is, in this sense, wisdom. It is learnable. One could class Hraban as an optimist. All he asks of his pupils is moral energy. They will not be misled by such pagan writings as come their way, any more than he himself was. His feeling for such writings rested on no markedly deep foundation of knowledge. He just knew that they belonged, that they were one more potential source of wisdom for Christians. Some of his contemporaries had deeper understanding of the texts they studied, whether pagan or patristic. Hraban had no sense of the historical niche to which any piece of writing belonged, no compunction about altering sources to suit his teaching, no time for doubts. He was thus as limited in one way as he was broad in another. His objectives were always before his eyes, and they were restricted objectives. He is by no means the most interesting of the Carolingian scholars but one sees, in the end, why everyone respected him. They saw him as a pastor whose teaching and writing recognized the objectives of reform: reform of people, not of institutions; of clergy and monks primarily, and through them of an ignorant, disorientated laity. His epitaph might well be some words in the preface to a collection of his homilies: 'herewith are sermons to preach to the people about all those things that they ought to believe'.

A second scholar of the same mould was Walahfrid Strabo (the squinter). He was an Aleman of humble parentage, born around 809 in the neighbourhood of the great monastery of Reichenau on an island in Lake Constance. He entered the monastery as a young boy. Reichenau was then at the height of its distinction as a centre of learning. Its abbot Waldo had been promoted by Charlemagne to the abbacy of St Denis and the next abbot, Heito, bishop of Basel, was also personally known to the emperor and a man of importance. It was under Heito's successor, Erlebald, who became abbot in 822, that Walahfrid made his profession as monk. Something is known of his teachers there: first, Reginbert the librarian, and then Grimald and Tatto, both of whom also taught at some time at the palace school. There was thus a continuing link between Reichenau and Aachen. Among much else, Walahfrid was taught to write metrical verse. He was not among the best of the Carolingian poets but could sometimes write with feeling, after the manner of Alcuin. In 826, at around the age of eighteen, he was sent to Hraban at Fulda. He has some claim to be considered Hraban's best pupil. Among his companions at Fulda was the Saxon Gottschalk. They studied Virgil together. A few years later he was summoned to Aachen to be tutor to the young Charles the Bald and held this position, on and off, for some nine years. It may be that his influence on the upbringing of Charles was his weightiest contribution to education; but nothing is known of how he set about his duties at court. What is clear is that he was devoted to his pupil's mother, the Empress Judith, who came from the same part of the world as himself. The political upheavals and fluctuating loyalties of the 830s horrified him. It was not simply that he and many others were put in a difficult position; the whole concept of unity on which Charlemagne's renaissance rested was threatened. When Charles no longer needed a tutor, the Emperor Louis gave Walahfrid the abbacy of Reichenau. That was in 838. Next year he was driven into exile by Louis the German and did not return until 842. He died in 849 on his way back from a visit to Charles. His career was not unlike that of Hraban, different as the two were in character. A St Gallen manuscript containing his own elegant handwriting is a vade-mecum or collection of materials made apparently in the year of his death. It reveals the width of his interests in grammar, poetry, computus, astronomy, classical literature, biblical exegesis, liturgy and history (at least as concerns prodigies and portents). It suggests a civilized and rather anxious mind, eager to note whatever might come in useful.

From Walahfrid's pre-Fulda days survives a fairly large collection of verse. There are early poems addressed to Archbishop Ebbo and to Thegan, a bishop in the diocese of Trier. There is also his first effort in hagiography. Like so many of his contemporaries he wished to contribute to the massive literary record of God's working through his saints and martyrs; at once a form of insurance for the future and a comforting witness to the works of the past. What Walahfrid wrote was a Life, in hexameters, of the third-century martyr Mammes, deeply reverenced by the Eastern Fathers.[13] Along with this he wrote a Life of a much more recent martyr, the Irishman Blaithmac,[14] who had fallen a victim to the Vikings in front of his own altar on Iona. Irish pilgrims to Reichenau told the story and the monks promptly commissioned a record in verse from Walahfrid. Martyrdom was a present reality and no longer a mere theme of the heroic past. Having proved his skill in this genre he next tried something rather more ambitious: his account in verse of the vision of the monk Wetti, one of his own teachers.[15] It is in fact a metrical version of an account in prose by the retired abbot of Reichenau, Bishop Heito, who was present when Wetti recounted his vision. Walahfrid seems also to have added an introduction to Heito's account and divided it into chapters: a form of editing at which he was to become very skilful. Wetti had clearly been overmuch devoted to learning, with the result that his other claustral activities were not rated above *mediocriter*. His vision took him on a well-trod progress through hell, purgatory and heaven; and in purgatory he encountered Charlemagne, of all people. Why, he asked his guide, is the defender of the faith here? Because he fell a victim to lust towards the end of his life. The moral reputation of the great emperor could thus be questioned a mere ten years after his death; nobody's reputation was safe. Wetti begged forgiveness for Charlemagne's sins, and this was granted at the intercession of the holy virgins – not of the martyrs or the priests. One notes the instant appeal of this vision of sin punished and forgiven to the consciences of a well-educated circle of monks; and again the Carolingian obsession with sin, associated with a clear judgement on the moral risks of learning. Wetti survived his vision by one day.

[13] MGH Poet. ii, pp. 275–96.
[14] Ibid., pp. 297–301.   [15] Ibid., pp. 301–33.

As an established hagiographer, then, Walahfrid went on to Fulda for a dose of sterner instruction under Hraban. Little is known of his doings there, but shortly afterwards he made an abridgement of Hraban's commentaries on the books of the Pentateuch, which argues that his instruction had been exegetical. About the same time he reverted to his favoured genre and composed or refurbished prose Lives of St Gallus[16] and of Otmar,[17] first abbot of St Gallus's monastery. The two St Gallus pieces, for which Walahfrid only claims a less barbarous presentation, were done at the request of the monks. More curious is his poem *De imagine Tetrici*[18] inspired by the sight of the statue of the heretic Theoderic brought from Ravenna by Charlemagne and set up at Aachen. This is a poem in dialogue form. It is long-winded, rather laboured and undoubtedly more suited to prose in some respects; on the other hand its emotional intensity seemed to require verse, which is what it got. There sat Theodoric, a splendid sight despite the pigeons nesting in his horse's mouth and nostrils. But he had been a heretic. Walahfrid's thoughts turned to the orthodox court he himself served, and above all to that glorious Caesar, the Emperor Louis, a second Moses replete with all the Catholic virtues, who talked with God. The poem is in fact a panegyric in a familiar court vein; but its hero is not Charlemagne but Louis and the con-quering power of Frankish orthodoxy. It purports to picture a state of peaceful stability that could scarcely have been further from the truth. In other occasional verses addressed by Walahfrid to the court the real state of affairs surfaces from time to time. They seem deeply felt and are notably amiable in tone; there is none of the satirical bite of some of Theodulf's court pieces. The best of them is one addressed to a layman named Ruadbern,[19] a *cubicularius*, whose claim to praise was his loyalty to Louis and Judith, as loyalty was equally the theme of Dhuoda's admonition to her son: loyalty is a virtue one notices when it is most threatened. Walahfrid's mind was full of the consequences of waver-ing loyalty; and a noticeable adjunct to this was a heightened sense of history.

While he was in exile Walahfrid wrote his most influential book, *De rebus ecclesiasticis* (or more properly *De ecclesiasticarum rerum exordiis et incrementis*).[20] It is not at all concerned with mystical interpretation. What he leads up to is a contrasting of spiritual and secular offices as he knew them at court, and he reaches this goal after lengthy considera-tion of the origins of certain ritual and liturgical usages. One can tell

---

[16] MGH SRM iv, pp. 280–337.   [17] MGH SS ii, pp. 40 ff.
[18] MGH Poet. ii, pp. 370–9.   [19] Ibid., pp. 388–90.
[20] MGH Capit. ii, pp. 474 ff.; also ed. A. Knöpfler, *Veröffentl. des kirchenhist. Seminars, Munich*, i, (1890).

this from the titles of the thirty-one chapters – accurate descriptions, whether or not they were Walahfrid's own. For example: on the origins of temples and altars; on sacred vessels; on the words applied to sacred things; how God's house is described in the German vernacular; on images and pictures; on dedications; on offerings; on how often one may take communion; on the order of the mass; on canonical hours, hymns, the increase of *cantilenae*, on baptism, tithes and litanies. Clearly the slant of the work is liturgical, in a historical perspective of sorts. He likes to go back to the scriptures, councils and Fathers though without much chronological awareness. He is trying to find out the reasons for usages, likes words and tries his hand at etymologizing. Also by contemporary standards he is something of a puritan. He is all for simplicity in worship and is worried that too much attention is being paid to the bedizening of churches at the expense of the poor; Pope Gregory had not laboured at building churches but at teaching and charity. Not that he opposes the building of churches for the right reasons. This casts an unexpected light on the direction of reform by the mid-century: neglect was scarcely more deplorable than over-enthusiasm about building and embellishment. In this respect his views were not unlike those of his contemporary Amalar, whom he certainly consulted.

Lastly, Walahfrid was the redactor of two famous pieces of narrative. One of these was no less a book than Einhard's *Vita Karoli Magni*; and thus, if he was prepared, in the reforming spirit of his generation, to see moral shortcomings in Charlemagne he was equally able to recognize a great man and a great biography when he met them. He adds a prologue that is in effect a eulogy of Einhard and a defence of his reliability. Einhard had been the bright star of a generation that understood the aims of learning, whereas today 'studies have suffered a setback and the light of wisdom is less prized than it was, and harder to find'. One meets with these ups and downs in the Carolingian assessment of its own achievements. He ends with the words: 'What I, Strabo, have done is to add titles and establish the chapters which seemed to me necessary to facilitate the use of the book by those who wished to consult it.' In fact he understood Einhard's intentions rather better than have some recent editors. His second work of redaction was Thegan's Life of Louis the Pious. But here he feels more critical of the author. Again, he provides the Life with chapters, titles and a prologue; but the prologue is no eulogy. He thought that Thegan was altogether too extravagant and even crude; too ready to attribute evils to the misfortune of the emperor. However, the work was basically truthful and useful, and therefore he adjusts it much as he adjusts more traditionally hagiographical writings.

What could be improved should be improved. It is not unlikely that he saw the Lives of saints and those of the two emperors as belonging to the same genre: all were records of great Christian warriors, some far distant in time and others of yesterday. There is even a sense in which the Lives of Charlemagne and Louis might be thought of as belonging to the liturgy. We do not know how contemporaries used them; but one possible use would have been at annual commemorations of their reigns.

Walahfrid cannot be dismissed as an amiable poet caught out by war. At court he learnt the need for political unity and personal loyalty as pre-conditions for the survival of the Church he knew; but his masters were the scholars of Reichenau and Fulda. His significant writings were on the historical reasons for the easily-abused rites and practices and liturgy of the Church. He seemed to feel a need for justification of these matters in excess of what his teachers felt. He saw threats and challenges everywhere. But like them he was a stern conformist.

Much less conformist was Amalar of Metz, most distinguished of the liturgists of the ninth century. Little is known about long periods of his life. He would have been born, either at Soissons or Metz, around 780, for he was old enough to have been noticed by Charlemagne and taught by Alcuin. He seems to have been a priest at Metz soon after 800 and possibly also commendatory abbot of Hornbach, near by. If he owed something of his special interests to Alcuin, he owed at least as much to his connection with the Church at Metz, centre of the cult of St Arnulf and recently the see of the great liturgical innovator, Chrodegang. For a while bishop of Trier, he was sent in 813 on a mission to Constantinople, which may account for some Byzantine colouring in his thought. On his return he seems to have lost his bishopric – the Emperor Louis may have disapproved of him – and to have retired to Hornbach, where he gave himself up to writing. He also visited Rome and Corbie. Then, in 835, he was put in charge of the see of Lyon, Bishop Agobard being in exile. It was a bad choice. Ecclesiastical traditions in Lyon were old and jealously guarded, and they differed from those that Amalar had learnt from Alcuin. Extremer than his master's, Amalar's practices led to a clash with the exiled bishop, the waspish Agobard, and with Agobard's clergy, of whom the most vociferous was the deacon Florus. Amalar used his position to disseminate views and writings that were bound to be challenged. A synod at Quierzy in 838[21] heard various charges brought against his

---

[21] MGH Conc. ii, ii, no. 57, pp. 768–82.

liturgical innovations and teaching. Some of them proved serious enough to cause his removal from Lyon. He then retires from our view, to die in 850.

Some of Amalar's writings have perished; others were of secondary importance, such as his rules for the canonical life of clergy and nuns; while others again had real importance, notably a work on the antiphonary[22] and his *Eclogae de ordine romano*,[23] later revised after visits to Rome. There remains his great work, the *Liber officialis*,[24] on the offices of the Church, of which he prepared perhaps four editions between 821 and 835 or thereabouts. It has a dedication in the form of a letter to the Emperor Louis; virtually a prayer with some litanizing colour that recalls imperial acclamations. He adds something entirely characteristic: it is a work of inspiration – *scripsi quod sensi*. In other words, he claims a certain freedom of treatment and interpretation because the spirit has moved him. Many a man condemned for heresy had said, or felt, the same. Behind his claim lies a growing pre-occupation with the working of the Holy Spirit, which will be experienced by the man who has prepared himself for its coming. His book, he says, will explain the offices of the Church and the functions of the sacramentary and the antiphonary. Book I rests on a firm patristic foundation and discusses the ceremonies of the ecclesiastical year. His method can be illustrated by what he writes of the vigil of Pentecost – a mixture, as has been pointed out, of fact and fancy, an allegory reminiscent of Bunyan. He writes:

Alleluia is sung in commemoration of the pristine innocence of Adam's life but because that innocence did not last the Alleluia is muted in the Tract. Let me illustrate this by an analogy. As a catechumen I was captured and carried off to Constantinople. My kindly Christian master sought and found me; he killed my captor and set me free so that I might return home. How joyful I was to be free again! But alas, because a long, laborious and perilous voyage lay between me and my home, exuberant joy gave way to weariness – just as Alleluia subsides into the Tract. Yet as I set out on the journey my deliverer sent companions with me to protect me from the wrath of the barbarians who beset my way. Such guardians are the baptismal rites . . .

Though fanciful, this is innocent. Book II treats of holy orders and vestments with their mystical significance and Book III is an elaboration of what he had written in his *Eclogae*. But these Books are not so innocent. Allegory and mystery of a highly subjective nature are given freer rein. It was one thing to find prefigurations of the mass in the Old Testament but another to infer (what had some historical foundation)

---

[22] Ed. J. M. Hanssens, *Amalarii episcopi opera liturgica omnia*, iii (Vatican, 1950), pp. 13–224.
[23] Ibid., pp. 229–65.
[24] Hanssens, ii (Vatican, 1950).

that the only essential orders were those of priest and deacon; the bishop, a vicar of Christ indeed, had emerged, he believes, from the office of presbyter. This ran directly counter to contemporary teaching on the bishop's office. More seriously still, in discussing the canon of the mass he argues that the first part constitutes a sacrifice for the elect only, and the second part a sacrifice for sinners generally; and this because Moses' tabernacle and Solomon's temple contained two altars, not one. And again, he allegorizes the fraction of the Host into three particles: the body of Christ is threefold – it rose from the dead, it lies in the grave and it walks upon earth. There was a background of dispute to this business of fraction, but Amalar was still being very fanciful and potentially heretical. He discusses the biblical signification of the various participants at mass and takes occasion to associate the idea of holy women with deacons and subdeacons in the liturgical symbolism of the Resurrection. This idea had a future; it was full of dramatic possibilities; but it must have struck conservatives as astonishing. In brief, Amalar was seeing the mass as a dramatic representation of Christ's life. When revising his three Books he added a fourth, on the Divine Office; and in this he traces back all offices to Old Testament types, adding some more dramatic interpretation of the mass. Again he claims divine inspiration: 'this has quite recently been revealed to me'. He claims no other authority.

The crisis came when Amalar was put in charge of the Church of Lyon, still smarting under the exile of Agobard, himself a respected liturgist in a traditional mould. Amalar's writings, which he himself circulated, and his teachings horrified the local clergy. The consequential charges of heresy brought against him at Quierzy were engineered by the deacon Florus but had been preceded by some fierce attacks in writing. Heresy could be exposed and dealt with; but behind the charges lay indignation, less easily satisfied, at Amalar's inventiveness, subjective interpretations and theatrical playing-about with the sacraments. All liturgies, his accusers urged, were the work of men and so, unlike the Bible, could have none of the mystical significance he attributed to them; and, if they had, it would not have been revealed to Amalar. Allegory, for example, should only be used, and then with great circumspection, in the interpretation of the Bible. Such had been Augustine's view. The specific charges brought against him at Quierzy were, first, his division of the prayers of the canon of the mass into two parts; then, his assertion of the threefold nature of Christ's body; his belief that the body and blood of Christ in the mass together constituted the whole Church; his speculations on the fate of the Host in the digestive tract; and finally, his use of allegory in the liturgy and his pagan allusions. Much of his speculation lacked any authoritative support in the Bible or in the Fathers. Amalar's defence was typical: 'whatever I have written I have read deep within my own spirit'. The council duly condemned his teachings as heretical; but he was allowed to retire from Lyon without further penalty. Agobard was restored.

Amalar was well aware that it was something new to apply allegory to the liturgy. He was equally conscious of his own brilliant imaginative powers. In a way, his approach had been inevitable. Strict biblical exegesis had its limitations. Scholars were now giving increasing attention to the liturgy. They were bound to do so if they continued to follow the guidelines of the great reforming councils of the early years of the century. And this is what binds Hraban, Walahfrid and Amalar together, different as they were. Training of the clergy and the work of conversion were not forgotten; far from it. Yet at the heart of it all lay awakening concern about the nature of the mysteries of the liturgy in the mass and baptism. It was much more than an exercise in hierarchy and vestments. Troubled times brought concentration on essentials. Perhaps, after all, everyone would not be saved? Perhaps the Empire would not endure as a harmonious body of Christian brethren? It seemed rather a matter of who could be saved, and what could be saved. These were the questions that exercised the best minds and finest scholarship of Fulda and Reichenau, Metz and Lyon.

iii. Collective Learning: the Eastern Courts and Centres

It is a matter largely of convenience to treat scholarship east and south of the Rhine separately from that of the west. What they had in common was fundamental; what separated them lay for the most part in simple facts of geography. Carolingians might rule them all and even feel a sense of kinship while they fought each other; but the regions they ruled were very different, each having its own traditions and problems. Even so, the cement holding them together, when it could be made to stick, was the programme of Charlemagne's *renovatio*; and this remained as political structures weakened. We should look in vain for any real sign of a German or a French separatist political outlook in the ninth century. Certainly the emergence of the vernaculars is no evidence of it. If anywhere one would expect to find it in narrative sources like the Annals of Fulda and the chronicle of Regino of Prüm.[1] The Fulda annals, composed by the monk Rudolf, teacher in the monastic school, certainly have more to tell of the Rhineland and Germany than of western Francia, and particularly of the small area bounded by Mainz, Worms, Trier and Cologne: this was home territory and attention to it was to be expected in the same

[1] Both texts ed. by R. Rau, *Quellen sur karolingischen Reichsgeschichte*, iii (Berlin, 1960).

way as Rudolf's devotion to his master, Hraban Maur. He had little use for the westerner Charles the Bald who was, he says, as timid as a hare. But what distinguishes his annals from western annals is not conscious political bias but lack of reliable information from any source. Unlike the St Bertin annalists he seems to have had no access to court circles. He is notably dull on the Slav campaigns on which one would have expected him to be better informed than western annalists. On the other hand he is more interested in recording natural phenomena: tempests, plagues, famine and the usual adjuncts of these – evil spirits and one good prophetess. Altogether his is an anxious, worried performance. This is not to say that the Fulda Annals do not record much that is historically important but only that they are politically less well informed and sophisticated than the St Bertin Annals. They afford no ground for concluding that East Francia felt herself distinct from the more latinized west.

Regino's monastery of Prüm lay north of Trier. He was its abbot in 892 and then moved on to St Martin's at Trier, where he finished his chronicle in 908. He knew more than did the Fulda annalist about events in western Francia, partly because Prüm had property in Brittany. He thought well of Louis the German but could castigate him for invading the kingdom of Charles the Bald. What he felt most strongly was the natural unity of the Frankish world, so sadly shaken by the disaster of Fontenoy; it had reduced men's desire as well as their capacity to stand together and resist attacks from outside. What he praised in Louis the German was his preference for the hardness of iron over the glint of gold; a judgement that echoes the opinion of the *Gesta Karoli Magni*, written at St Gallen not long before. This was the true measure of what a reforming but hard-pressed Church required of its kings. Regino wanted all Carolingians to be strong, like Charlemagne. Only then could they fulfil their role in world history, secure in *fortuna* and *virtus*. One can understand this in a monk who must have watched the Vikings burning his monastery in 882. There was little comfort anywhere save in the Frankish victory over the Vikings at Saucourt (celebrated in the *Ludwigslied*). Regino writes late enough in the day to be obsessed by the threat of total disintegration before the Vikings.

We shall not find a palace school in Charlemagne's sense outside Aachen. But we shall find evidence of royal interest in learning east of the Rhine; and learning in no essentials different from that of the West Franks. There is the identical moral impulse behind it even when deployed in a different manner. First one notices the *Hofkapelle* or court chapel of the East Frankish rulers. As in the west there are arch-chaplains in control and subordinate to them notarial sections under arch-chancellors. And as also in the West, high officials of the chapel could expect bishoprics and abbacies. For example, Louis the German's first arch-chaplain, Gozbald, probably of Fulda, became abbot of Niederaltaich and in 842 bishop of Würzburg. His pupil Ermanric calls him a most learned man. After his father's overthrow in 833 Louis the German strengthened his independent administration by making Baturic of Regensburg arch-chaplain and Grimald of Weissenburg arch-chancellor, in due course to succeed Baturic. Royal administration and ecclesiastical office were thus intimately linked. We know that Grimald was much at court; indeed, was Louis the German's closest adviser. His hand is apparent in appointments to major sees. That he was in a real sense the religious director of Louis's court is further suggested by his surviving vade-mecum, a manual for daily use that includes a litany with prayers for the royal family, benedictions, a necrology of court interest, a memorial poem for Louis's dead daughter Hildegard, a list of bishops and other matter. It looks as if he tried to escape from his court duties; certainly he had to return to court and take over on three different occasions, and was suitably recompensed with monasteries. He died in retirement at St Gallen in 872.

Grimald's most notable successor was Liutbert, archbishop of Mainz, to whom may be attributed the growth of Alemannic influence at court. He took his spiritual duties seriously; otherwise Otfrid would not have dedicated his gospels to him. But he was also a warrior against both Vikings and Bohemians: a reminder to us not to separate clergy from laity in the national business of defence. He remained arch-chaplain under Louis's successors. Under Charles the Fat in particular he and the personnel under him were the administrative link between the past and the future. The court chapel survived and at its core the ancient *capella* as the treasury of royal relics. Charles the Fat's last arch-chaplain was Liutward of Vercelli, an Aleman like Liutbert, educated at Reichenau. Such was his dominance that he was held responsible for Charles's failure before the Vikings in 887. The two men fell together. Louis the German had proved more adept than his successors in keeping lay and clerical aristocracy under strict control. His royal monasteries were supervised as they were not by the lay abbots of the West. When he took his bishops from these monasteries for court duties they did not sever their monastic links. Thus we find a large number of powerful abbot-bishops who owed everything to their king. This is reflected in the competence of royal administration and in the quality of charters. Moreover, trained personnel carried on from reign to reign, so ensuring continuity whether the court were at Frankfurt, Regensburg or elsewhere. There is a high degree of integration and a proficiency, themselves a fruit of the renaissance.

Less can be said of the intellectual and cultural interests of the Emperor Lothar I, largely because of lack of evidence. One would expect something of the pupil and friend of Einhard and Wala. No doubt his court at Aachen would have resembled that of Charlemagne and Louis the Pious if the arrangements of 817 had been implemented. As a young king in Bavaria, from 814 to 817, we do not know that he attracted a cultivated circle; but by 822 he certainly had a court of his own and in 825 promulgated a famous capitulary at Corte d'Olona, clause 6 of which concerned the reform or restoration of schools.[2] He there enumerates the teaching centres, of which the chief is at Pavia, under Dungal. The bishop of Ivrea is instructed to look after arrangements personally. But whatever its inspiration, the capitulary will not have been composed by Lothar. Naturally he was the subject of eulogies when he succeeded his father as emperor, as for instance from Walahfrid. For the twelve remaining years of his life he was mostly at Aachen, where there must still have been some sort of school. Bishop Franco of Liège was educated there. Lothar clearly had an interest in theology or scriptural exegesis, for he asked Hraban for a commentary on Jeremiah and also on the latter part of Ezekiel, not explained by Gregory the Great. Though ill, Hraban complied. Later on he asked Hraban for more commentaries. In 854 or the next year Hraban sent him on request a two-part collection of homilies on the biblical readings of the mass, asking that faults should be corrected by the emperor's learned readers. In 851 Lothar summoned to his palace a Luxeuil monk, Angelaumus, to teach the liberal arts; and the same monk composed for him an allegorical commentary on the Song of Songs, together with some words of consolation on the death of the Empress Ermengard. This entirely Carolingian concern with the Bible is reflected in the magnificent Gospel-book, containing his own portrait,[3] which Lothar commissioned at Tours around 850 and then presented to St Martin's. If he may be said to have had a court poet it was Sedulius Scottus (resident however at Liège) from the year 848. Sedulius of course was happy to write verses for any Carolingian; but he did welcome Lothar on a visit to Liège with a eulogy complete with all the accepted virtues; rather impersonal, in fact. He was a great deal warmer in his praise of Ermengard, who seems equally to have attracted Hraban. A war-song from Lothar's circle is a poem on the battle of Fontenoy; a lament, however, not a song of victory.[4] It depicts Lothar as taken to the battle by his magnates like Christ delivered to Judas. But this apart, the literary interests of his court

[2] MGH Capit. i, no. 163, pp. 326–7.
[3] Plate in Hubert, Porcher and Volbach, *Caro. Art*, p. 145.
[4] MGH Poet. ii, pp. 138–9.

seem to have been theological. Entering the monastery of Prüm one week before his death, he appears to have found that peace on which he congratulated Hraban when the latter retired to a life of contemplation.

Almost nothing can be said of the literary tastes of King Lothar II or of his uncle, the Emperor Louis II. We know that Archbishop Gunther of Cologne, Lothar's confidant, was generous to writers and that both Hraban and Sedulius dedicated works to him; which is only to say that Lothar II was a Carolingian king. Louis II, the Emperor Lothar's ablest son, clearly had a court at Pavia though we are largely ignorant of its literary activity. His chancery was capable of composing excellent letters. Louis's empress, the powerful Angilberga, attracted literary compliments much as did Ermengard.

Louis the German comes through altogether more attractively. His court circle was dominated by highly literate clergy and he was particularly close to Walahfrid, whom he restored to Reichenau, and to Hraban, his archbishop of Mainz. It is the personal closeness that is striking. In 844 we find Louis and Hraban discussing scripture in a monastic cell at Rassdorf, Louis further requiring an explanation of the chants intoned at mattins. Gerold, archdeacon at the palace, seems on occasion to have acted as intermediary between the two men. Among other writings supplied by Hraban to Louis were his twenty-two books *De rerum naturis*,[5] written to assist biblical exegesis and submitted for correction by the king's 'most wise readers', who, whether or not they really were expected to correct, must have been there. We know also that when Louis met his brother Charles at Tusey, he took the opportunity to consult Hincmar about Genesis and the Book of Psalms. Not surprisingly, both Notker of St Gallen and Regino record that he knew his Bible. He was as well versed in the ecclesiastical as in the secular disciplines. Several scholars sent him their work. There survives a short poem of thanks from Louis to Baldo of Salzburg for a gift of books, to which he adds a request for further elucidation. A really considerable scholar, Ermanric of Ellwangen, a pupil of Hraban, planned to write a work on the liberal arts for Louis and may have done so. He certainly held office in the chapel and chancery though most of his time was spent in one or other monastery. A good classsical scholar, he compares the king with Hercules for strength and Ulysses for cleverness. Sedulius, though living outside Louis's kingdom, composed a long dithyramb for him: 'the flower of the great Charles . . . the glory of his father' and so on. But Sedulius does commit himself to the view that the German peoples loved him, the pagans were terrified of him and under him the barbarous tongue, the

[5] PL 111, cols. 9–614 (there entitled *De Universo*).

vernacular, had been taught to sing Christian song. This fits in well enough with what is known of the upsurge of Germanic vernacular as a means of instruction and elucidation by translation. What matters here is that it was associated with the king. Otfrid of Weissenburg's translation of the Gospels was presented to him in the 860s. Louis's court, then, quite apart from royal interest in learning elsewhere in his kingdom, was a centre of study. This appears to cease after his death. Of his three sons, only the youngest, Charles the Fat, leaves serious indications of studious interest. He met Notker at St Gallen, where he questioned him on scientific matters and heard the anecdotes later incorporated in the *Gesta Karoli Magni*. St Gallen supplied him with books. One would expect Notker to speak of Charles with lively respect, and so he does; for nobody could doubt the king's piety. Thus it is clear that at least the major figures in the two generations following Louis the Pious were not ignorant warriors but educated men who had books and scholars about them. But they enjoyed few of the advantages of those who had served Charlemagne at his court and palace school. The real centres of learning in Germany were monasteries.

Since it directly concerns Charles the Fat we may take Notker's *Gesta*[6] out of the St Gallen context and see it in relation to the king. The great Alemannic house of St Gallen, perched in the mountains above Lake Constance, was very much a Carolingian monastery and never more so than under Charles the Fat with his Alemannic preferences. He trusted the community and drew on it for the staffing of his *Hofkapelle*. Notker had friends at court who supplied him with information on contemporary events and Frankish history; and history was important to him in a way that it had not been to Einhard. He meant to see Carolingian history as a continuum: hope for the present lay in correct interpretation of the past, which meant showing how earlier Carolingians had dealt with the problems that faced their successors. If Notker makes the past heroic it is because the present is not, but should be. Charles the Fat's predecessors had ridiculed their magnates' oriental dress, condemned the extravagance of bishops and criticized the idleness of youth. Charles by implication should do likewise. The heroic age was an age of iron, not of indulgence. Such at least is Notker's picture. But his criticism of Charles is never explicit; there was hope for him yet. In fact he fell before the *Gesta* could be completed. The four rulers whom Charles is invited by Notker to consider (in the shape of stories that seemed to have new relevance in the context of Charles's own experience) were Pippin III, Charlemagne, Louis the Pious and Louis the German; but Charlemagne pre-

---

[6] Ed. H. F. Haefele, MGH SRG, n.s. xii (Berlin, 1959).

dominantly, though the others make significant appearances. To take an example of his method: Notker's account of the troubles following the death of Louis the Pious has more to do with what looked like happening when Charles died, as he soon did, than with the actual situation in 840. The House of David was threatened by outsiders, ambitious giants – Notker is thinking of Wido, Berengar and the Welf Rudolf – who should be rejected in favour of the rising professional families to which Notker himself belonged. But it was too late. Notker was a considerable poet and a learned man. At the same time he was an acute political observer who also knew how to manipulate history for his own ends. His *Gesta* are no simple monkish anecdotes rescued from the past but a carefully executed series of Carolingian *exempla*. We do not have to ask what basis in fact these anecdotes had but only what impression of the past they were designed to make on the mind of Charles the Fat. The king is presented with an array of predecessors; grim, bold fighters well able to control magnates and bishops, a terror to pagans and wrong-doers, students of scripture and patrons of the Church, careful of the poor. In brief, men of iron, not of gold. This may have been what others were thinking in the 880s, but it was Notker who made something of it in a skilful composition. It was not less important in its way than Einhard's *Vita Karoli Magni* written in the 830s; and it was equally original.

So much can be said in outline of the literary interests and patronage of the eastern Carolingians. There had been no real sign of major activity at anything that could be called a court school. For such activity one must look further afield to bishoprics and monasteries. First and foremost one looks to Fulda in Hesse, the home of St Boniface in the mid-eighth century and heir to some of his books. Its literary tradition was therefore strongly Anglo-Saxon. Like other German houses it kept a great collection of charters though few early originals survive. Hraban as abbot ruled over a community of some 600 monks. He collected around 2,000 charters of which something can be gathered from twelfth-century copies. The charters were arranged under the fifteen *Gaue* or districts in which Fulda had possessions. These reveal widespread interest in the making of donations to St Boniface's house, apparently among converts from the Saxon nobility and others from Hesse and Thuringia. There are important royal grants of immunity and fiscal privileges. Plainly too the house was a link between Rome and the kings. Its archives were obviously well kept. Among its earliest-known scribes was Einhard, who wrote six charters for Fulda while he was a monk there in the late eighth century. In return for much royal patronage and protection – very welcome in so exposed a site – the monastery was expected to show its loyalty in practical ways. Several of its abbots saw military service for the crown or went on diplomatic missions; and their house was used as a royal prison.

Like Würzburg, whose bishop was the diocesan of Fulda, the monastery betrays its continuing Anglo-Saxon affiliations in the script of its books. Plainly there were English-trained scribes present as well as books imported from England. Its abbot Baugulf was involved in Charlemagne's reform of education. A further source of Anglo-Saxon influence was Hraban, the pupil of Alcuin; and it was under him that the school of Fulda produced a succession of big men: Otfrid, Walahfrid, Rudolf and Gottschalk. One vital aspect of the school's work, which is best considered later, lay in vernacular translation and composition. Another lay in its formidable library, the contents of which can in part be assessed from its catalogue[7] and surviving books. These last are now scattered, unlike the hundreds of Reichenau books still together at Karlsruhe, the many St Gallen books still in their old home, and the Lorsch books, many of which reached Rome. There was also a busy interchange of books between Fulda and centres fairly near, such as Mainz, Würzburg, Fritzlar, Hersfeld and Amorbach. Anglo-Saxon influence remained strong till the mid-ninth century; and there were other influences – Irish, for example, and Bavarian. There were in addition good holdings of Italian books, some probably direct from Rome and Monte Cassino, others by way of England and western Francia. A steady stream of pupils left Fulda for further instruction elsewhere: Einhard to the palace school, Hatto and Hraban to Alcuin, Modestus and others to the Irishman Clemens, Bruno to Einhard. Alcuin himself visited the monastery. But the principal transmitter of Anglo-Saxon cultural ideas in and from Fulda was certainly Hraban, abbot from 822.

The movement of books and men was both to Fulda and from it. A prime witness to the distinction of its school and library is Lupus who studied there, remembered the books he had seen and sent his own pupils there. The ramifications were wide. Fulda's influence can be detected at Corbie, Weissenburg, Lorsch, Regensburg, St Gallen, Reichenau and other houses. Interchange is a distinguishing mark of the cultural renaissance. The link between Fulda and Reichenau is notably clear and the cause of this was presumably Walahfrid, monk at one and abbot at the other. What can be said about its books by the mid-ninth century is that Fulda was rich in biblical and patristic texts; as rich as Reichenau and St Gallen. A catalogue compiled about 840 reveals forty-six volumes of the Old and New Testaments and thirty-

[7] Ed. G. Becker, *Catalogi Bibliothecarum Antiqui* (Bonn, 1885), pp. 30–1.

eight volumes of Jerome alone. The catalogue breaks off in a lost list of Augustinian texts. Hraban's own extensive commentaries were of course in the library, and also much Bede and Isidore. There were some rarities: Tertullian, for instance, and Primasius; and the three famous books that had once belonged to St Boniface. The house appears to have had no classical Greek texts but it did have Greek – Latin Bibles and glossaries. Porphyry was there together with Boethius and Origen. And it housed a very important collection of classical Latin authors, notably historians. It had its Ammianus in the early ninth century, probably based on a Lorsch text, and also Suetonius – presumably the copy that Einhard and later Lupus read. Present too were the *Historia Augusta*, Tacitus (a Mainz copy?), Columella, Pliny, Cicero, possibly Lucretius and certainly Virgil. This is a mere selection. It shows that Fulda was not content with snippets of pagan classics transmitted in teaching manuals of grammar and dialectic. It welcomed a wide selection of full texts, or texts as full as it could make them, and thought of them as part of the Christian – Latin heritage. Such texts had as much right to be in the library as the books of the Bible and the works of the Fathers. It was not an attitude that might have commended itself a century earlier to many monastic librarians; and the place where it now happens is deep in Germany, away from the old cultural centres of western Europe. There is a clear parallel with the remote home of Bede, tucked away in Northumbria; and there is a line from Bede through Boniface, and later Alcuin, to Fulda. Thus Fulda became the great home of the blending of Insular with continental learning which marks so much of the best of Carolingian culture. But in the end one is left with the fact that the secular classical holdings of Fulda, as of any other monastic library, were and remained overshadowed by texts of the Bible, the Fathers and the liturgy.

The see of Würzburg, away to the south, was closely associated with Fulda, and its library grew under much the same stimuli. What books the founder-missionary St Kilian may have brought with him in the seventh century is unknown. Its library – an episcopal library – seems to begin with the Anglo-Saxon Bishop Burghard in the 750s and the first solid evidence of its contents comes with a partial catalogue of about the year 800. There is already a copy of Charlemagne's *De litteris colendis*. The bishop of Würzburg was entrusted by the emperor with the education of Saxon nobles, the conversion of Saxony being no longer a matter of forced baptisms *en masse* but of educating key men in centres just outside Saxony. There survives an interesting exchange of letters between Bishop Hunbert and Hraban. Hunbert is deeply concerned about biblical texts and commentaries;

and these he wants from Hraban, even providing parchment for copies. However, he is a learned man and makes it clear that he does not want just anything: the Würzburg holding in patristica was already considerable. The only two surviving Würzburg books presented by Hunbert and bearing his full title in the inscription are books of the Old Testament. Hraban did what was asked of him. Würzburg became rich in copies of Fulda texts. Hunbert's successor, Bishop Gozbald, came from the monastery of Niederaltaich on the Danube, a daughter-house of Reichenau. He had also been arch-chaplain to Louis the German. And thus a personal and a literary link was established between Würzburg and Bavaria. This was the way things happened. Gozbald took every opportunity to fill gaps in his library, using Bavarian and Fulda connections to do so. But in 855 the library was badly damaged in a storm. Gozbald himself died soon afterwards. The library never regained impetus after its double loss. Up to that time its main holdings had been in biblical and patristic texts. From England it had acquired a fifth-century Jerome, and among its rarities were Boniface's grammar and some texts that seem to have arrived with Irish refugees. Its singularity lay in its interest in canon law and legal texts generally. It had no less than twelve collections of canons and a text of *Lex Salica*. But the most significant feature of the library is the evidence that it was a working and teaching library. Scribal marginalia would alone prove this. The surviving books show every sign of having been used. Thus we can see in Würzburg, far away in the east of the Carolingian world, how a succession of efficient bishops with the right connections set about equipping themselves to deal with the business of instruction and pastoral care as these were then understood.

West of Würzburg in Hesse lay the royal monastery of Lorsch. Its magnificent *Torhalle* still stands to show what kind of reception-chamber such a house was expected to provide for its royal visitor. Founded in 764, and so twenty years later than Fulda, it sat on a main north – south route. Count Cancor and his mother established it as a shrine for their family. Among its earliest patrons was Chrodegang of Metz, and it thus came about that Lorsch, Metz and Gorze (founded by Chrodegang) hung close together. But it was in fact to escape from local family claims that Lorsch came under Charlemagne's personal protection, as did some twenty other houses lying in areas sensitive for the king's protection of missions. Its closest connection seems to have been with Mainz, its metropolitical see. It is with Abbot Ricbod, from 784, that its library starts to look impressive, notably in historical and canonical texts. Ricbod had been Alcuin's pupil and therefore Anglo-Saxon influence was to be detected at Lorsch, though never so strongly as at Fulda. More significant was Lorsch's association with the palace school and court at Aachen. The prescribed texts appear in the library. When Ricbod became bishop of Trier he retained his abbacy till his death in 804. It was not only the library that had burgeoned; so too had the monastic buildings and its properties in the Lower Rhine region. And further afield. In the course of the next generation or so its possessions came to stretch from the Low Countries in the north to Switzerland in the south, with a massive concentration in what was later to become the Palatinate; indeed, something approaching half the area of the Palatinate. It is a reminder of the enormous properties of the greater ninth-century churches and monasteries. It explains the need for the kind of managerial sophistication one encounters in the polyptychs or estate surveys and in such directives as were prepared by or for Adalhard of Corbie or Ansegis of St Wandrille.

Ricbod's successor, Adalung, was equally closely attached to the court, both of Charlemagne and of Louis the Pious. In return for services rendered he was rewarded with the abbey of St Vaast in the north; and it was from there that the shorter Lorsch chronicle was disseminated in western Francia. Lorsch's famous *Codex Aureus* must have been acquired from the court at about this time. There was a gift in the other direction in the person of the monk Gerward, who became librarian to Louis the Pious and presumably played his part in the improvement of the court library. Like Walahfrid he attached himself to the circle of the Empress Judith. Twenty-seven of his books figure in the Lorsch catalogue.[8] The Palatine Virgil may have been his. A busy man, clearly. Hraban certainly knew him, as also his successor, Abbot Samuel. To Samuel Hraban sent several poems, one accompanying the gift of a diptychon in boxwood. In one of these poems he lavishes compliments on the Lorsch library and its then librarian. In fact, it brings back to his mind the library of York as he knew it from Alcuin's poem. High praise indeed. Often Lorsch turned to other libraries for improved texts or additions to its stock; as for instance to Tatto at Reichenau for some Jerome and Augustine. When the succession to Louis the Pious had been settled, Lorsch emerged as a royal monastery in the East Frankish interest. Thus in the 850s Abbot Eigilbert was in close touch with Louis the German but not to the extent of losing the support of the Lotharingian Carolingians. It was Lothar II who gave Lorsch a handsome addition to the properties it already owned near Nijmegen. Both Louis the German and Louis the Child were buried at the monastery, which at least raises the possibility that it was intended to become the burial-place of the East Frankish Carolingians. One cannot be sure. There is no information

[8] Ibid., no. 37.

about life in the monastery from near the end of Louis the German's reign. However, a ninth-century Irishman did write in his copy of Servius: 'consult the exposition of Pomponius on Horace which I saw at Lorsch'. So he, or the writer of his original text – conceivably Sedulius in the opinion of Bischoff – had visited Lorsch and there read a rare text of Late Antique school-learning that happened not to be recorded in the library catalogues. Such catalogues were never complete inventories.

In the transmission of texts Lorsch was of the first importance. Its library was a magnet. This was specially the case with patristic texts, for which it was a good deal visited – and easily so, considering its location. A comparatively new library, unlike Lyon or Verona, it yet acquired old treasures such as the Palatine Virgil, the unique copy of half of Livy's *Decades*, a great Augustine, an ancient copy of classical texts overwritten with the Old Testament and a majuscule manuscript of Ammianus. Some of these old Italian books will have travelled from England to Aachen and thus to Lorsch. There are interesting cases of parallel transmission of texts to Lorsch, Fulda and St Riquier, all of which arguably passed through Aachen. The significant fact is always the connection between Lorsch and the libraries of Charlemagne and Louis the Pious; indeed in Bischof's view Lorsch is a mirror of their lost libraries. Though important to us in a special way, we should not overestimate the presence of classical treasures at Lorsch, which in any case seem to have been fewer than those at Fulda. More significant to the house was its large holding of biblica and patristica. Its catalogues record no less than eleven otherwise unknown works in the patristic field. It further possessed what is probably the oldest extant copy of Einhard's *Vita Karoli*, written soon after 850 in the monastery of St Amand, or near it. Much is lost. Plainly, despite the debt of Lorsch to Fulda it stood somewhat outside the direct Anglo-Saxon – German link. Its contacts were good with northern Francia and even with the south. Contacts, interchange, accessibility were the life-blood of Lorsch.

To drop down, next, south-east to Bavaria, eastern bulwark of Carolingian rule and culture since 788, is to reach the frequent home of Louis the German. Archbishop Arn, friend of Alcuin and first metropolitan of the Bavarian Church, started a fine library at Salzburg; and soon after there were libraries at Freising and Regensburg, active under learned bishops. Here too is clear evidence of the collaboration of lay and clerical magnates in the collecting of texts, in learned studies, in the life of the schools, in the founding of monasteries and in the general coming and going between centres of culture. What ruined everything were the Hungarian attacks from around the year 900. For

Freising alone we have over a hundred books or parts of such that reveal, as at Würzburg, scriptorium and library catering for the educational duties of a bishop in biblical, patristic and liturgical texts. Throughout the ninth century it was the bishops who controlled the Freising scriptorium. Their appetite appears to have been almost unlimited for texts of Jerome, Augustine, Isidore, Gregory and Bede; and in this they differed not at all from their colleagues elsewhere. As was natural, given its site, the house had no trouble in acquiring books from Italy. The Regensburg library and scriptorium had started earlier, probably around 700 and in the monastery of SS Peter and Emmeram. Secure information comes about a century later when it was firmly under its Carolingian bishop. Already there was Anglo-Saxon influence stemming perhaps from Boniface's reorganization of the Bavarian Church; and because Regensburg was the Carolingian capital of Bavaria there was equally some influence from the palace school. The great bishop was Baturic (817–47). He it was who unified and reformed the scriptorium, using his own episcopal clerics and notaries as scribes in the monastery of St Emmeram. A student at Fulda and a friend of Hraban, he was clearly intimate with Louis the German, becoming his arch-chaplain in 833. Monastery and royal chancery worked in harness. The link survived Baturic, for Louis asked the next bishop for the loan of one of his monks because his handwriting was so good. But as elsewhere there is a marked decline in book-production at Regensburg after the mid-ninth century. We still have several books written at the order of Baturic; and one Regensburg text of the Lives of the Fathers contains a famous scribal note: 'this book was begun on military service against the Slavs in the year 818'. So the scribe accompanied the army. Like other houses, Regensburg had a text of the official *Laudes* for welcoming the royal family on its visits. This contains prayers for Pope Eugenius II, the Emperor Louis, Louis the German and Bishop Baturic; and this dates it to 826–7, something that can seldom be achieved for an early medieval manuscript. What better proof could one require of the unifying drive of the Carolingian reformation that so remote a library could boast so wide a selection of the literary remains common to all? At one extreme it finds room for a simple mission-catechism and vernacular material, very various; and at another, two Virgils.

Further south still but to the west, in mountainous Alemannic country, lay two vital monasteries: Reichenau on its island in Lake Constance and St Gallen in the foothills of the Santis range. Beyond them again, in Rhaetian Switzerland, was Chur, a bright pebble left stranded by the retreating Roman tide.

Pirmin, who founded Reichenau in 724, brought fifty books with him; and some, especially liturgical, were of West Frankish origin. A long succession of abbots cared for the library and sent books to other houses. From at least 800 there was a fruitful connection with Freising and Regensburg. Abbot Peter, who died in 786, brought home a Greek psalter from Rome, lent it to his diocesan of Constance and never got it back. In fact, Reichenau often complained of books not returned by Constance. In the ninth century there were books arriving from Italy and from northern Germany. Anglo-Saxon influence was slight, though two of its monks are known to have been taught by Alcuin at Tours. By 822 we know of 415 books in the library. This was largely due to a vigorous librarian named Reginbert, the teacher of Walahfrid, who built up the library under four successive abbots and catalogued it. He was personally responsible for the copying of forty-two books on a wide variety of subjects, including the Monte Cassino text of the Rule of St Benedict. We know less of the library after the mid-ninth century except that Irish refugees were still arriving with books. Indeed this late Irish influence was in some ways more significant than the Anglo-Saxon. Inevitably there was much intercourse with St Gallen, Reichenau's nearest neighbour of consequence, and some copying of its treasures. A book that went in the other direction, from Reichenau to St Gallen, was the famous copy of the Rule of St Benedict. It is still at St Gallen. Best of all, Reichenau looked after St Gallen's books during the Hungarian attacks – and returned them. The Reichenau library was never as rich in classical texts as was Fulda – or, for that matter, Fleury or Bobbio – but it showed a marked interest in the natural history, medicine and astronomy of Late Antiquity, and was well off for school grammar, metrics and rhetoric, for which the Irish may have been responsible. Among its biblical texts of the ninth century, of which fewer survive than of liturgical texts, one may note a Greek–Latin text of the Pauline epistles, probably copied from an Irish text, with vernacular glosses. The holding in patristica was very considerable. Apart from the great Fathers it included works of Cassiodorus, Isidore, Gregory of Tours, Bede, Alcuin, Hraban and Walahfrid. And there was a decided interest in history.

St Gallen, a few miles distant, is a special case because of its great achievement in the vernacular. It had however a more conventional side and other claims to importance. The house began in the seventh century as an Irish cell. The Irish element persisted, to be reinforced in the ninth century by refugees. But it was basically Alemannic in personnel. Its climb to distinction begins with the Carolingians and reaches its climax rather late, towards the beginning of the tenth century. Yet in the eighth it was already producing fine books and had a notable scribe in the person of Winithar. The real impetus came from

Abbot Gozbert (816-36). His house proved increasingly attractive to the local Alemannic nobility and from time to time accommodation had to be found for visiting Carolingians and their entourages. Hence the need for a building programme. Gozbert turned for advice to his friend Heito, abbot of Reichenau and bishop of Basel, the man most obviously interested in ecclesiastical architecture. Heito responded with a copy of an immensely detailed plan of an ideal monastery. The origin and purpose of the plan are vexed questions; but there the copy still is at St Gallen. It is entirely possible that Heito himself was responsible for it; a covering letter to Gozbert suggests as much. It is another matter to decide when and why Heito got to work. One possibility is that Gozbert's request inspired him to start, but in this case one may wonder why he did not produce something rather more suited to the site. Another is that it took its origin from the great monastic reform councils of 816 and 817, in the sense that a renovated Rule of St Benedict, generally enforceable, would lead naturally to the preparation of a monastic site-plan. There is no evidence that it did, but none need necessarily be expected. Heito at least was present at the reform councils. He might well have conceived his plan there, or soon afterwards, whether officially or unofficially. Gozbert appears to have used part of the plan, at least for his church, but much of it was unusable for the site. Yet another possibility is that behind the plan lay one for Christ Church Canterbury, devised long before by Archbishop Theodore. However, its value to St Gallen is less significant than the fact of the plan itself. Archaeologists may yet be able to tell us that it was used elsewhere, for example at Basel.

Gozbert's successor, Grimald, was a Frank and a secular priest. He was imposed on the house by Louis the German, whose chancellor he was. The king meant to keep his eye on this remote part of Alemannia with its southern links. Grimald lasted till 872, to be succeeded in turn by two equally distinguished abbots; first Hartmut and then Salomo. Under them the teaching facilities of the house made a leap forward. By the end of the ninth century we meet with library catalogues, a busy scriptorium and connections with other houses (notably Reichenau, Fulda and Bobbio). Confraternities are arranged; interchanges occur; famous teachers emerge. Grimald was trained by Alcuin, Hartmut by Hraban. The first known St Gallen-trained teacher was Iso, among whose pupils were Notker and Radpert. To Radpert the house owed the first version of the *Casus S. Galli*, a record of its history to his own time, finishing with an account of Charles the Fat's visit in 883. Charles was always generous to St Gallen, staying there on his way to and from Italy and personally presiding over the abbatial election of Salomo, his chancellor and bishop of Constance;

and Salomo, once Notker's pupil, was unquestionably St Gallen's greatest abbot.

We should expect to find, and do find, the usual run of prescribed books in the library. As at St Wandrille, some five hundred miles to the north, so at St Gallen: theology, patristica, hagiography, history, law (including the Theodosian Code), the liberal arts and much Christian poetry. The mixture varies from monastery to monastery but the ingredients are impressively the same. There is a list of some thirty considerable books copied under Hartmut alone. Classical authors are not numerous but some Virgil and Vegetius are there, and fragments of Grimald's copy of Virgil are glossed in the vernacular. From Salomo descends an encyclopaedia and glossary notably full on the *quadrivium* subjects. Harmut ordered the making of a map of the world. Thus interests at St Gallen ranged widely; geographical isolation, like political upheaval, was not always a bar to intellectual pursuits. And one special interest must be noted: music. It seems likely that this was derived from Metz, the great centre of liturgical music. Notker composed four hymns on St Stephen for the bishop of Metz. But Reichenau may have been in the field a little earlier since it was in a position to greet Charles the Bald with a special song, probably composed by Walahfrid. However this may be, St Gallen had at least four teachers of music by the mid-ninth century. One of them, Radpert, composed hymns and litanies for processions as well as a communion chant and a vernacular hymn in honour of St Gallus. On instrumental music at least one can suspect Irish influence. But Notker was the star performer of the quartet. He composed sequences for the mass and may well have been one of the elect who understood polyphonic music. While he was composing sequences, destined to have vital effect on medieval music, his colleague Tuotilo was composing tropes for further embellishment of the mass. These he is said to have presented to Charles the Fat. Somewhere within these tropes and sequences and in their spirit of mass-embellishment involving the congregation lies one of the beginnings of medieval drama. The record of St Gallen in music is both early and good, though there can be no question that the same interest was stirring in other monasteries around the same time.

As the mind pauses in this manner over the greatest, and only the greatest, of the innumerable religious houses east and south of the Rhine, the making of books stands out as their common achievement in the eighth and ninth centuries; and this for the excellent reason that books are what survive. Written, copied and disseminated as they were in impressive numbers, one asks whether Antique literature was still no more than an aid to the teaching of the liberal arts. How did it relate to the Bible and its vast subsidiary literature? Alcuin, his pupils and his heirs answer unanimously that they were teaching aids certainly – and certainly more. In them all was a deep conviction that the best of pagan literature belonged to the Christian tradition, and perhaps especially the best of pagan poetry. Gustavo Vinay has argued persuasively that the ninth century felt the need to escape into the imagery and fantasy, and even fun, provided by poetry. The ancients had shown the way. One could try one's own hand at it. Seen thus, poetry was an escape from the conceptual rigours of prose, and particularly the kind of prose in which the clerical world habitually immersed itself. If pagan mythology was a hurdle, demythologizing was not difficult; one could and did do other things with the pagan gods. Somehow the Irish had found least difficulty in mastering pagan literature and subsuming it as their own; and on the continent they found willing pupils. In continental houses the Irish flourished, for that was where safe jobs lay and many patrons, lay and clerical. Few kinds of poetry were beyond them. Even satire was welcome. Sedulius' poem on the ram was a nice parody of monastic society, and presumably it was safe to write it. All this was a welcome safety-valve for intensely serious and able men. Antique literature, both as an example and simply for itself, was a joy. Having said which, one looks again at the manuscripts. They are overwhelmingly the Bible, its commentators and the liturgy. And in the Bible lay an emotional world more startling than anything the ancients could provide; a world, moreover, out of which one attempted to construct one's own. Christian writings had an entirely practical appeal. Beyond books lay deeds. We should do the men of the ninth century a monstrous injustice if we concluded that they were mere bibliophiles.

iv. Collective Learning: the West

The religious houses of the eastern regions were largely foundations of the Carolingian age, witnesses to unceasing missionary fervour. Those of the west were older and more numerous. They show a tendency to fall into clusters, and this by no accident: founders' generosity infects neighbours with the sting of emulation. The most northerly cluster, the monasteries of the Somme, – St Riquier, St Bertin, St Omer, St Vaast and Corbie – lay near the Channel coast, admirably sited for the earliest Viking raiders; and their sufferings were to be great. St Riquier and Corbie must stand for their neighbours.

St Riquier, or Centulum, was a seventh-century foundation. Alcuin later wrote a Life of the saint[1] and in the late eleventh century the chronicler Hariulf did what he could for the early years of the house, using sources that are not all available today.[2] The value of his chronicle lies for us in its account of the relationship of the abbots with Charlemagne and Louis the Pious, and in its citation of diplomas and charters which perished in the fire of 1131. But for Hariulf we should know little of the archives of this great house. We know also something of what the church and cloister looked like around the year 800, when Abbot Angilbert, Charlemagne's son-in-law, had completed his building programme with much imperial help. Hariulf had made an excellent sketch of the buildings in their original condition in his chronicle. What survives is a copy of the sketch (highly schematic) made in 1612.[3] Clearly it was a noble complex apparently boasting no less than three churches appropriate to an elaborate liturgical ritual and fit, too, for an aristocratic and wealthy clientele of 300 monks, 100 *scholarii* and the many *milites*, *servientes* and other monastic retainers who lived outside the monastery in what has been called a holy city. In monastic terms it was the equivalent of what Charlemagne created at the same time in Aachen. The great church of the monastery had something in common with the later church of St Gallen. Angilbert himself described its rich embellishments.[4] These included stucco images in relief that would have given little pleasure to Theodulf. A cadastral plan made in the nineteenth century shows the Gothic church that supplanted Angilbert's, and the site of its triangular inner cloister. Such a house was unlikely to be short of books. Hariulf proves very informative on books for the early ninth century though he says little about the scriptorium. The great benefactor and second founder was plainly Angilbert himself, who contributed some two hundred volumes to the library. There were fifty-six more recorded in the inventory of 831. Angilbert's Gospels written in letters of gold and partly on purple vellum survive.[5] Artistically they belong to a well-known group of illuminated manuscripts of the court school, just as the monastery that owned them belonged architecturally to the convention of Charlemagne's Aachen. They were doubtless a present from Charlemagne to his abbot. But grand books like this only bear witness to prestigious connections and add nothing to our knowledge of what the monks found in their library for daily use; in other words, are no evidence of the application of educational reform. Without

---

[1] MGH SRM iv, pp. 389–401.
[2] Ed. F. Lot, *Hariulf: chronique de l'abbaye de Saint-Riquier* (Paris, 1894).
[3] Illus. in Horn and Born, *Plan of St Gall*, i, pp. 209, 250–1.
[4] MGH SS xv, i, pp. 173–9.
[5] See *Karl der Grosse, Werk und Wirkung* (catalogue), no. 414, p. 251 and plate 55.

doubt the scriptorium helped to fill the shelves. It could hardly have done otherwise under the direction of an abbot who was himself a poet and the author of an account of the restoration of the monastery and its life and buildings in his *Libellus de diversitate officiorum*;[6] who further inveigled Alcuin into visiting the house to refurbish the Life of the founder and compose hymns and responses for the saint's festival. There were distinguished men in the community; Mico, for example, author of the saint's *miracula*. When the monks fled before the Vikings in 880 they did not forget to take with them all books concerning the history of their house and the cult of their patron. Sophistication had not atrophied their vivid awareness of ghostly patronage. But one turns to Hariulf (and it is uncommon for a chronicler to provide this information) for a view of what the community was reading in the early ninth century. His book-list is incorporated in a chapter entitled 'Inventory of the treasures, possessions and vassals of St Riquier'. The list is impressive; but, as generally with catalogues, doubtless incomplete. What does it contain? First, the canonical books; a large collection of the biblical commentaries and other writings of Jerome, Augustine, Gregory, Isidore, Origen, Hilary, John Chrysostom, Cassiodorus, Fulgentius and Bede; 'books various' which include Paschasius, Primasius and Gregory Nazianzan (there were eight in this section, the librarian had recorded); then collections of canons and related literature, Lives and Passions of saints, monastic rules, homilies and letters (seventy of these). The librarian has next noted that the total of claustral books on divinity amount to 195. He goes on: grammar (an admirable selection, including Virgil's *Eclogues* glossed, and Aldhelm); books of the ancients on *gesta regum* and geography, some law, and the Lord's Passion in German and Latin; and last of all, books of the altar, liturgical books – there were thirty-five in all. The librarian wished it to be understood that he had listed volumes, not books: the latter would come to something over 500. 'Such were the claustral riches, the opulence of the heavenly life fattening the soul with sweetness, by which the monks of St Riquier fulfilled the salutary bidding to love the wisdom of the scriptures rather than vice.' A book-list of this order can only signify close attention to the principles of reformed monasticism: nothing significant was missing. The business of this wealthy house was worship. However, souls will be fattened with sweetness in proportion to the means available; and such means there were under a succession of abbots of the highest social standing; St Riquier himself, *nobilissimus*, and then over the Carolingian period, Angilbert who married Charlemagne's daughter, Nithard son of Angilbert, Ricbod cousin of Angilbert, Louis cousin of Charles the

[6] Ed. Lot, *Chronique*, appendix vi.

Bald, Rodulf brother of the Empress Judith, and Carloman son of Charles the Bald. Few indeed were the monasteries that could claim patronage of this order.

Corbie was different: a great centre of Carolingian book-production, whose surviving manuscripts are Mecca to the palaeographer. But also something more. Unlike St Riquier it was a direct Merovingian foundation. It belonged to a group of houses founded by Queen Balthildis in the mid-seventh century destined to live under the *Regula Mixta*, like Luxeuil, and to be ascetic cult-centres where the patronage of many saints might fortify the dynasty. The queen's privilege for her new house (or strictly that of her young son Chlotar III, whose regent she was) was shortly followed by one from the diocesan, Berthefrid of Amiens, the form of which belongs to a privilege-group also comprising St Denis, St Pierre-le-Vif and St Bertin (Sithiu). Corbie, always close to the crown, was to be very wealthy. From its earliest days it was the recipient of books and soon the maker and distributor of books; but of these times little certain is known. Its first identifiable scripts link it with the diploma-scripts of the royal chancery, which is not surprising, as also with Luxeuil from which its first abbot came. By the late eighth century the learned nunnery of Chelles (also founded by Balthildis) was copying texts for Corbie; but the Corbie scriptorium was already capable of copying and annotating texts for itself. One can say that by the eighth century the library had marked interests of its own: Augustinian texts certainly, but also monastic rules, law and history. Its rich endowments facilitated purchases and contacts. Predominantly the early contents of the library (no contemporary catalogue survives) were biblical and patristic; in short, reflected the general pattern of monastic libraries. By the mid-eighth century the scribes had developed a distinctive script of their own under Abbot Grimo, a trusty of Charles Martel; and it may have been through Charles that the house developed contacts with Italy that brought the library valuable accessions. Of the great Merovingian houses, Corbie was one of the earliest to accept the Carolingians.

The first Carolingian kings were happy to confirm the immense endowments of Corbie without noticeably adding to them. Only under Charles the Bald did the flow of royal donations resume its course. With Abbot Maurdramn begins the emergence of the script known as Caroline minuscule: that pleasant and regular script that so much facilitates the understanding of the literature of the Carolingian renaissance. E. A. Lowe, greatest of modern palaeographers, called it 'splendid'.[7] In effect, we still write and type and print in it. Lowe lists the Corbie books that seem most likely to have been written in the

---

[7] CLA vi, p. xxiv.

eighth century; biblical, patristic and devotional for the most part. But the library will already have had some classical treasures acquired from foreign parts. Some came from Charlemagne's own library and scriptorium, and more after his death. With them came patristic texts. Bernhard Bischoff believes that Corbie texts of the earlier ninth century prove a valuable guide to what the court-library contained under Charlemagne. The abbot under whom this great accession occurred was Maurdramn's successor Adalhard (780–826, apart from a seven-year exile at Noirmoutier, when a second Adalhard reigned), cousin of Charlemagne. But it was also under Adalhard that Corbie found itself on the brink of political convulsion, soon deeply involved, under Wala, in the troubles of Louis the Pious. Sharp divisions of loyalty within the community were to find some reflection in Radbert's lament for Wala's lost ideal of imperial unity. However, intellectual stagnation was not the outcome. Radbert and Ratramn were at the same time deeply involved in theological debate of a high order on the nature of the Eucharist. This is not the place to discuss their writings, but it should be noted that both scholars were deeply read in patristic theology. Ratramn declares that he follows the footsteps of the Fathers and particularly Augustine and Ambrose. Radbert lists his sources in his preface: Cyprian, Ambrose, Augustine, Hilary, Isidore, John Chrysostom, Gregory, Jerome, Hesychius and Bede. Where would these learned men have found their texts if not in the library at Corbie? The house was also strong enough to found a prestigious offshoot at Korvei in Saxony. The mid-century was a vital period for both scriptorium and library. Under the more generous Charles the Bald their fortunes take a turn for the better. The man most closely associated with this was Hadoard, priest and librarian. There exists a manuscript written at Corbie in his hand that has claims to be a very early, if not the earliest, handbook of Augustinian theology; in other words, a collection of excerpts designed for the use of a theologian. In the same hand we have a *florilegium* of Cicero and other classical authors. In his verse prologue Hadoard states that he first collected these excerpts on wax tablets. What he takes is Ciceronian philosophy; but he adds material from Sallust, Macrobius, Servius, Martianus Capella and Publilius Syrus. He seems to lack the scholarly equipment of Lupus. Nevertheless, he has compiled a monument to Carolingian humanism. The monastery of Rebais was to claim in its twelfth-century catalogue that it possessed a book by Hadoard on the four virtues. Clearly we are faced with a scholar of wide interests. His Cicero was not left as he found the texts: they have been retouched in a Christian sense; and what he found was already in the Corbie library. We have to bear in mind that Hadoard was not alone in his library.

Ratramn and Radbert were also at work, and along with them Rodbert who composed a sacramentary and Engelmod who wrote verses. These we know of; others we do not. There is thus no doubt that mid-century Corbie was a major centre of study, of composition and of copying. Bernhard Bischoff has compiled a list of the classical authors copied in the scriptorium around this time, and it is formidable.[8] Not many of the greater names known to the ninth century are missing. If Corbie's debt to Charlemagne was vital, its scriptorium certainly built to great effect on its acquisitions. However, it should not be thought that Corbie alone was fruitful, for several other centres could have boasted impressive collections of classical texts: Tours, Ferrières, Fleury, Auxerre, Lorsch and Fulda among them. It would be idle to suppose that such collections witnessed to no more than a resolve to get teaching of the liberal arts on a wide classical foundation. There is love for the literature itself, a willingness to share treasures and a ready acceptance of Antiquity as a major contributor to Christian knowledge. In this distinguished company Corbie was foremost.

Next to the Somme monasteries come those of the Seine. Near its mouth, St Wandrille (or Fontanella) and Jumièges, facing across the broad river to the ancient Forest of the Brotonne; and further south, the houses of the Parisian basin, notably St Denis and her not-much-loved neighbour, St Germain-des-Prés. St Wandrille is not wholly exemplary; no monastery is; but its general features and indeed its purpose are like those of its sister, Jumièges. Founded at the same time in the mid-seventh century by aristocrats who had served their time as Dagobert's officials and then turned to the monastic life, both followed the *Regula Mixta* of Luxeuil and may possibly have been intended to further missionary work in the north-eastern approaches to Brittany. Both, certainly, gave birth to monastic offspring that hint at missionary endeavour and both invited royal favour, Merovingian and Carolingian. St Wandrille soon owned properties and founded dependent houses over a wide area reaching far to the south. This owed much to royal favour bestowed on successive abbots, which in its turn encouraged aristocratic generosity; or it may have been the other way about. When the house inventoried its holdings on Charlemagne's orders in 787 they amounted to more than 4,000 *manses* – excluding, the record is careful to add, those properties wrongly released by Abbot Witlaic.[9]

[8] 'Hadoard und die Klassikerhandschriften aus Corbie', *Mittelalterliche Studien*, i, pp. 58–60.

[9] *Gesta sanctorum patrum Fontanellensis coenobii*, ed. F. Lohier and J. Laporte (Rouen–Paris, 1936), p. 82.

Among the literary interests of St Wandrille were hagiography and history (specifically, the history of the house). The Lives of Wandregesil the founder, and of Abbots Lantbert, Ansbert[10] and Hildebert, form an impressive series. The great historical achievement was the composition in stages of the *Gesta* of the abbots from the foundation to the mid-ninth century. Despite gaps and incompletion it is the most impressive of all Carolingian monastic histories and it centres upon the powerful initiatives of the abbots themselves. The greater part was written between 838 and 840 during the abbacy of Fulco. A chronicle, in effect a continuation, is valuable for the reign of Charles the Bald.

Abbot Fulco is worth pausing over, since his career is startlingly like that of other Carolingian abbots who battled through the political ups and downs of the reign of the Emperor Louis. He emerges as abbot of St Hilary at Poitiers by 827; he is arch-chaplain by 830, abbot of St Wandrille and of Jumièges in 834, and abbot of St Rémi and administrator of Reims (*vice* Ebbo) in the same year; by 838 he has lost Jumièges but acquired St Vaast at Arras; his losses increase at the death of the Emperor Louis in 840, finally losing St Wandrille in 845; and then he disappears from view. Though able, he seems to have had little capacity for political survival. The connection with St Vaast and the north explains why, after the Viking assault of 858, the monks fled thither with their relics and treasures, which included the *Gesta*.

The *Gesta*, then, were composed during the abbacy of Fulco. They record many of the books acquired under successive abbots, without stating their provenance. Nor do they state what books were already in the library at the point where their recording begins. They start with thirty-two books during the reign of Abbot Wando (747–54), but do not specify how many volumes these comprised. Chiefly doctrinal, they included works of Augustine, Jerome, Gregory, Pope Leo, Isidore, Gennadius and Arnobius; but also extracts from Rufinus, the Life of Felix of Nola, Appollonius of Tyre's History, Jordanes, the Rules of Serapion, Macharius, Augustine, Benedict and Columbanus, and a martyrology. This suggests choice rather than haphazard acquisition. The next abbot, the wicked Witlaic, gave a Tours antiphonary, the Miracles of St Andrew, the Pauline epistles and a Life of St Martin. From Abbot Gervold came a Pentateuch, the minor prophets, Augustine's *Enchiridion* and his commentary on St John, and a volume of sermons. Under him there also flourished a priest named Harduin, who lived in a near-by cell and taught the *alumni* to write, being himself a very skilled scribe. No doubt the work of the scriptorium under the next abbot benefited from his teaching. More than this: he left or gave to the library a set of Gospels, the Pauline epistles,

---

[10] All in MGH SRM v.

Gregory's homilies, part of the *De Civitate Dei*, Bede's *De natura rerum*, some Lives, three sacramentaries, a lectionary, an evangeliary, a psalter with hymns and canticles, a Roman antiphonary and an arithmetical treatise. Clearly a remorseless scribe. By far the most important abbot was Ansegis (822-33), restorer of Benedictine observance, author of a famous set of monastic constitutions[11] and in himself striking evidence of what monastic reform entailed under the Emperor Louis. Once again, the *Gesta* record his gifts to his library. He ordered the preparation of a set of Gospels in gold on purple vellum, incomplete at his death, and a lectionary and antiphonary also on purple, and bound in ivory. He added to this munificence a luxury Bible, thirteen volumes of Augustine, four of Jerome, the letters of Jerome and of St Sixtus, Taius' *Sententiae*, extracts of Gregory (part of the *Moralia*) and Augustine, the works of Fulgentius and Ferrandus, Bede on Genesis, Bede's computus, Josephus, and collections of collects and canons. The total of abbatial gifts between 747 and 833 amounted to at least seventy volumes and the writer of that section of the *Gesta* admits that his list is incomplete. He stops just when the scriptorium was becoming most active. Little indeed now survives, or probably survived the attacks of the Vikings. It is clear enough from this record of gifts (and of course it tells us nothing of the gifts of others) that St Wandrille did not share Corbie's interest in Antiquity. A wealthy abbot shook the superflux in the appropriate direction: the Bible and its commentators, doctrine, liturgy and hagiography. And this was precisely what Charlemagne had intended.

The reconstruction of the monastery by Ansegis is reasonably clear from the description in the *Gesta*. It was a noble complex but quite unlike the more or less simultaneous building at St Riquier and St Gallen. If there ever was a Carolingian master-plan, this was not it. What is of interest here is the presence of a separate library building. It stood in a very large cloister yard facing a charter-house of similar construction.[12] St Gallen too had a separate library, beneath which was the scriptorium. Thus Carolingian abbots made special and permanent provision for the accommodation of their books and records, by this time too important to the life of the community to be stored anywhere. Learning has become a major preoccupation.

Perhaps less prestigious and certainly smaller was the monastery of St Germain-des-Prés, lying outside the enceinte of Paris to the West. St Germanus (his Life was composed by Venantius)[13] became bishop

---

[11] Ed. J. Semmler, *Consuetudines Corbienses, Corpus Consuet. Mon.* i (Siegburg, 1963), pp. 355–422; trans. C. W. Jones in Horn and Born, *Plan of St Gall*, iii, appendix 2.

[12] Plan in Horn and Born, ii, pp. 278–9.

[13] AA iv, ii, pp. 11–27.

of Paris in 565 and was clearly very influential at the court of Childebert I. He was buried in the basilica founded by the king and dedicated to the Holy Cross and St Vincent. Under this double patronage the community flourished until, in the seventh century, the name of Germanus was added, soon indeed to supplant the original patrons. No Merovingian house had a more obviously spiritual purport: the great Spanish saint, Vincent, and Germanus himself were patrons second to none; but upon the Merovingians it relied for succour in running battles with bishops of Paris who were jealous of the prosperity and freedom enjoyed by a house dedicated to their own predecessor. Local dedications or re-dedications of houses to St Germanus were sometimes the work of the monastery but sometimes of the bishops; and this makes it difficult to assess the extent of the monastery's grip on the Parisis till well into the ninth century. It seems to have housed something over one hundred monks in Carolingian times, which makes it considerably smaller than St Riquier, St Wandrille and Corbie, but around the same size as St Denis. By about the year 800 it appears to have owned some 33,000 hectares, on which lived about 13,000 persons. From this handsome reservoir the monks provided the crown with military service and also provisions and carts as required. This we know from the survival of the earliest and best Carolingian polypytch or estate-survey, put together during the abbacy of Irmino.[14] A polypytch is not literature but it is evidence of administrative efficiency; of the ability of a scriptorium to put together a mass of detailed information in usable form. It can have been no coincidence that Irmino himself, like so many of his predecessors and successors, was close to the court and thus directly influenced by Carolingian example in surveying its own estates with remarkable exactitude. Furthermore, some of the monastery's largest estates lay within the region of royal fiscal lands round Compiègne and Soissons. There could be no better example of royal and monastic estate-policy marching hand in hand.

St Germain suffered, as did all Parisian houses, from the Viking assaults on Paris. Like St Denis, it paid a large ransom in 856 to escape destruction; and in 858 the community (or the greater part of it) anticipated further trouble by fleeing to an outlying property with its relics, treasures – and library. No ancient catalogue of St Germain's books survives. Delisle, surveying the great collection still housed in the library on the eve of the French Revolution, pointed out that much of it may have been added in comparatively recent times. It is not easy to assess its acquisitions and losses at any time, but particularly in the ninth century. Few very early books can be assigned with certainty to St Germain. One such was a sixth-century uncial psalter presented by

[14] Ed. A. Longnon (Paris, 1886–95); B. Guérard (Paris, 1844).

Childebert I, and another may have been a Bible sent by Justinian to Childebert. Of around a hundred books known to have been there before the twelfth century, about one half were of the ninth. Mostly these were patristic and it would be tedious to repeat the familiar list. It was none the less the heart of what interested the monastic reader. But also there were canonical collections and history: Eusebius and Orosius were represented. There was much hagiography, fifteen texts of the liberal arts, pagan and Christian poets, some natural science and medicine. A few books can be dated by scribal notes; for example, a *Dionysio-Hadriana* of 805, a Bible of 822 and another Bible of approximately 860; but these may not have been written in the scriptorium. Émile Lesne concluded that the library may have housed about a thousand books of the ninth century or earlier. This sounds generous. Certainly one cannot imagine that so many were moved to safety in 858. One notes the quantity of assorted hagiography. Saints, their Lives, relics and associated treasures, were so very basic to monastic life that a mere threat to them, especially by pagans, explains the horror with which one monastery after another left its account of the impact of the Viking raids upon western Europe. It was not easy to burn stone buildings, though it happened: it was pathetically easy to desecrate a shrine.

The Viking assault on Paris is vividly recounted as a piece of contemporary history by a St Germain monk, who was an eyewitness.[15] Abbo's endless hexameters are not great poetry and he did not suppose they were when he offered them to his monastic teacher, Aimoin. They were rather in the nature of an exercise by a student. His master was unimpressed, as indeed have been others who think that a youthful connoisseur of Virgil might have scanned better and been less repetitive. None the less, he created an epic of the historic present. His two books (a third, moralizing, may have been added as a tribute to the Trinity) are a true epic to the glory of the resistance of Paris and especially of Odo, king since 888. The poem must have been written towards the close of the ninth century. Abbo was certainly alive in 922, by then a learned priest honoured outside his own monastery and even importuned to publish a collection of his sermons. He says that his poem was based mainly on his own recollections and he hoped that it might inspire others to fight for their cities. He does not shirk criticism of those who might have done better. Obviously his account is of political and military value. As a source, it may rank with Ermold's verses; as a monk's tribute to his people in distress, much higher. The *Siege of Paris* is a distinct facet of the literary preoccupations of Carolingian monasticism.

Yet one more St Germain production merits notice. A martyrology,

[15] Ed. H. Waquet (Paris, 1942).

it represents a class of literature with which every Carolingian church and monastery was acquainted. The martyrs (loosely interpreted) and their commemorations brood over the liturgy with their daily summons to remember Christian heroism and to hope for heavenly intercession. But Usuard, monk and grammarian, produced a specially memorable martyrology.[16] Based on established exemplars – Jerome and Bede, but particularly the more recent Florus and Ado – it collected vast material, abridging it and arranging it succinctly. Usuard plainly had access to an admirable monastic library, not simply for older martyrologies but for saints' calenders, hagiography and patristic sources; and he could add material personally collected, especially for France, Italy and Spain. His colleague Aimoin left an account of Usuard's journey to Spain, to acquire relics of St Vincent to protect the monastery. He found none in Barcelona but went on to Córdoba for more up-to-date relics of those who had suffered in the Arab persecutions of 850–9. Indeed he there met Eulogius, who was to suffer martyrdom one year later. His haul of relics was not great, though it included the body of Aurelius (without the head) and the head of Natalia (without the body). More important was the Spanish literary material he was able to incorporate in his martyrology. His letter-preface, written about 865 and addressed to Charles the Bald, attributes the composition to the king's command.[17] This can hardly have been so; the work was certainly begun long before 865 and bears the marks of slow and careful construction. But this is no reason to question that the king was personally interested in it and played his part in its rapid dissemination. Within its genre, the martyrology was a notable feat of research, of winnowing and arrangement, fit to become, as it did, the basis of the Roman martyrology. It witnesses to the state of the cultus of saints in Francia on the eve of the Viking upheavals and once again takes our eyes away from the bureaucratic splendours of estate-management to things that mattered more. In a word, it was a significant achievement in the process of renaissance.

Hermits prefer hills, monks valleys. The Loire valley of the early middle ages was studded with monasteries: among them, St Martin's at Tours, St Aignan at Orléans, Fleury and Micy. St Martin's was in many ways the greatest in wealth, in book-production and in prestige of patronage. Its Carolingian fortunes could occupy many pages. Fleury, if slightly less distinguished, was on that account more typical, even in the one respect that marks it out for special consideration. It housed the bones of

16 Ed. J. Dubois, *Subsidia hagiographica*, xl (Brussels, 1945).
17 MGH Epist. iv, p. 193.

St Benedict. It was founded in 651 by Abbot Leodebod of Orléans and stood, it was said, on an old druidical site. Certainly it attracted royal donations from an early date. From it the monk Aigulf went, some ten years later, to be abbot of Lérins, and proceeded to reform that ancient house according to Columbanic-Benedictine principles; or at least he meant to, but met with sturdy opposition. The move tells us something of the practices of the youthful Fleury. It is certain that Fleury's connections with Italy were very old. By the eighth century its library contained Italian treasures; as, for example, a Sallust (now a fragment) of the fifth century, a sixth-century copy of the minor prophets, a fifth-century fragment of Eusebius-Jerome and Origen's homilies of the sixth century; 'noble rags', Lowe calls them.[18] But it contained much else. No clearly distinguishable script emerges from its scriptorium before about the year 800, when Paterius' biblical exposition, or part of it, was written at the order of Abbot Dodo. Its fame as a writing-centre came much later. Its library, meanwhile, grew great with acquisitions. The difficulty, as always, is to determine when a book reached the library; there is so much that may have come to Fleury at any time between the seventh and the ninth century. True, there survive catalogues, one probably of the late ninth century that lists over one hundred books including liturgy, saints' Lives, civil and canon law, much theology or patristics and an impressive list of pagan classical texts. The fact that no biblical texts are listed (in which Fleury was undoubtedly rich) warns us that the catalogue was no more all-embracing than catalogues normally were. Indeed, most of the surviving pre-twelfth-century books figure in no catalogue at all. Traube considered that Fleury possessed the completest collection of classical texts in ninth-century Francia.[19] It was then that the scribe Herbert dedicated his copy of Horace to St Benedict, while his colleague Ildemar furnished his Virgil with the same dedication. But there was almost no intellectual field in which Fleury showed no interest. To all other religious houses it remained bound by its passion for patristic collections. We may well suspect that these interests lost nothing by lying within the intellectual orbit of Orléans, ruled by such bishops as Theodulf and Jonas.

The Italian connection will have owed much to the celebrated transfer of St Benedict's bones, together with those of his sister St Scholastica, from Monte Cassino to Fleury; a deliciously medieval tale of confusion, misunderstanding and forgery involving not only Monte Cassino and Fleury but also the see of Le Mans. Briefly, the story must start with the reading at Fleury of St Benedict's Life in Pope Gregory's *Dialogues*.

[18] CLA vi, p. xviii.
[19] *Vorlesungen und Abhandlungen*, iii (repr. Munich, 1965), p. 5.

There the monks learnt that the saint had been buried in an oratory built by himself on the summit of Monte Cassino, and in a tomb where he had already laid his sister's bones. As usually happened, the saint's tomb was the significant factor in any question involving relics. Monte Cassino was a ruin by the seventh century. Fleury therefore decided to send a delegation to bring what remained of the two saints to Fleury, no doubt inspired by Gregory's observation that 'where the bodies of holy martyrs rest it is certain that wonders occur, as innumerable miracles bear witness'. This may have happened as late as 703, but a tradition reinforced by an early catalogue of the abbots puts it as early as 660. By the ninth century Le Mans was claiming that the Fleury delegation had included some Le Mans representatives, who took St Scholastica home with them. All that is certain is that Fleury's claim to the bones of St Benedict was undisputed except by the revived house of Monte Cassino, which held that they had never left their original site. Perhaps they had not; who shall say whose bones the Fleury monks actually removed? What mattered was the immense prestige accruing to Fleury from this claim: it brought it wealth and a steady flood of pilgrims from at least the end of the eighth century, when the Rule dominated all monastic reform.

The effect of St Benedict on writing at Fleury was very marked. Contributions came from a series of distinguished monks; most notably Adrevald, who entered the house about 826 and died there some fifty years later. Four considerable works came from his pen: a Life of Aigulf (the leader, he held, of the expedition to Monte Cassino),[20] an attack on Eriugena, Book I of the Miracles of St Benedict and a history of the translation of the relics.[21] These last two are our principal sources for the history of Fleury before the tenth century. The Miracles contain much information, above all for the ninth century, and an appendix covering the later years of Charles the Bald and his sons includes an account of the Vikings at work in the Loire valley. The history of the translation, fuller if not more accurate than earlier accounts, was to become the accepted account; over thirty manuscripts earlier than the twelfth century still survive. On it the monks based the text of their feast of the translation. There can be no doubt that they were saved from a Viking attack in 855 by a large ransom paid by Orléans; but they were less lucky in 865. The monks fled with their relics to a temporary refuge. It is unclear whether on return they found Fleury literally burnt to the ground or whether they simply found their fine decorations, including allegories painted on the walls of the refectory, destroyed beyond repair. The Vikings paid a further

[20] Vita 1, AA SS Sept. 1, pp. 743–7; Vita 2, AA SS OSB ii, pp. 628–36.
[21] Ed. E. de Certain, *Les Miracles de saint Benoît* (Paris, 1858).

visit in 878. But the community survived to become a centre of intellectual distinction in the tenth century and later. And always St Benedict dominated its literary endeavour: 'misfortunes', said the saint speaking through Adrevald, 'will become triumphs and your enemies friends if you will observe my Rule'. Abbot Abbo, in the tenth century, was a busy correcter of Fleury texts. According to Aimoin, he held that, after prayer and fasting, study and composition best checked the passions of the flesh, and to these occupations he devoted every spare moment. Indeed, he had his wax tablets with him when he died. Behind all this activity lay not only the inspiration of a saint's bones but also a magnificent library. Juvenal was there, in company with Horace, Sallust and a host of Antique writers, great and small. But what were they beside the mass of patristics and hagiography, beside twenty manuscripts of Augustine, ten of Jerome, twelve of Gregory and seven each of Ambrose and Bede? Fleury fell nicely into line with so many other communities who had not forgotten the directives of Charlemagne.

Further still to the south and east lay the ancient see of Lyon; yet not only the see but also the religious communities associated with it that clustered in the environs of the city. The cluster was more than a chance agglomeration; and it is this that makes it of special interest. The oldest Gallo–Roman metropolis, the see had felt the influence of Lérins in the fifth century and for long continued to resist the pressure of the Martinian cultus from the West. It stood indeed for a distinctive form of Burgundian monasticism common to the whole region of the Rhône. Politics were its downfall – understandably so, when one considers its position on a vital artery to Provence. Merovingian kings might endow its communities but always it lay open to reverses in political fortune; thus Aunemund was one of the nine southern bishops executed by Balthildis. Yet it was, and remained, a centre of intellectual distinction and a place of books. Bishop Wilfrid stayed to be taught there, in a most troubled period, for three years.[22] The earlier eighth century proved to be a terrible time. Desolation followed the campaigns of the first Carolingians and the Arabs in the Rhône valley. The see was left vacant for several years by Charles Martel and thereafter royal visits became rare. But not royal interest. The break came with Charlemagne's appointment of the Bavarian Leidrad to the see. Educated at Freising, he had served his time at the Palace School under Alcuin and had already worked as a *missus* in Septimania and

[22] *The Life of Bishop Wilfrid by Eddius Stephanus*, ed. B. Colgrave (Cambridge, 1927), ch. vi, p. 12.

Provence before his elevation in 797. He thus looks like a safe man. But he was more. He would never have been entrusted with a *missaticum*, in conjunction with Theodulf, to deal with the heresy of Adoptionism if he had not understood the theology of the issue. In short, he was a scholar and a spiritual man. There survives his famous letter to Charlemagne,[23] reporting on the situation at Lyon after a decade of reforming efforts. It is no mere progress-report but an earnest supplication to his 'constans et sacer imperator' to forgive the little he had been able to achieve and to beg for continued and practical support for Lyon when he himself had gone.

What had Leidrad achieved? Reorganization and rebuilding figure largely in his letter; not only the cathedral clergy but neighbouring communities of canons, monks and nuns had required much attention, and required more. And all this activity was centred on spiritual renewal; in particular, on liturgical renewal and study. Leidrad had established schools: *scholae cantorum* (run by experts from Metz) and *scholae lectorum*, doubtless for teaching biblical exegesis and meditation. These in their turn presupposed an efficient library and scriptorium. Attached to his letter was a *Breve* or schedule,[24] now fragmentary but of a familiar pattern, listing the members of the communities under the archbishop's immediate control and their means of support. In his labours he was assisted by Agobard, who succeeded him and plainly shared his hopes. Agobard and his clergy ran into political trouble through their support of the Emperor Lothar against Louis the Pious. Indeed, he did more than any other cleric to bring Louis to his knees, and paid for it. But this should not dim his achievement as a reformer. He showed as much awareness as his predecessor that only episcopal supervision would ensure uniform liturgical practice throughout all his dependent communities. The great monastic and canonical reform movement that had originated with Charlemagne, at least from 802, and had been carried further by Louis in the councils of 816, had their effect on Lyon; but it would be wrong to attribute too much to the latter, at least so far as Lyon was concerned. Reform was already well under way there (as also elsewhere) before the appearance of Benedict of Aniane on the scene. It seems likely enough that if we sought for the mainspring of reform at Lyon we should find it in Chrodegang of Metz; excavations show that the building-plans of Leidrad, carried on by Agobard, were modelled on those of Chrodegang at Metz. After Agobard came Amolo, and finally Remigius; all deeply concerned in reform and its objectives: a

---

[23] Ed. A. Coville, *Recherches sur l'histoire de Lyon* (Paris, 1928), pp. 283–7.
[24] Ibid., pp. 287–8.

wonderful quartet of Carolingian bishops at their best, reigning in succession from 797 to 875.

Such was the background to a period of remarkable intellectual activity. No Lyon books survive that were certainly written there before 800, though some may have been. What is certain is that the library, however built up, was much older. It must already have been rich in patristic writings and in law before Leidrad's accession. Books presented by Leidrad himself were very probably local products; as for example a copy of Gregory of Nazianzen and an Origen collated by the archbishop. Not only the cathedral scriptorium but those of dependent communities were now kept busy, among them probably the nunnery of St Peter's; and this ranks St Peter's with Chelles as an example of houses of learned women which could be entrusted with copying texts. The four great archbishops kept their scriptoria constantly at work. Their personal activity is instanced in the writings and letters of Leidrad, the polemic of Agobard and the doctrinal treatises of Amolo and Remigius. But more striking even than these were the writings of Amalar, temporary administrator of Lyon during Agobard's disgrace, and of his opponent, Florus. Amalar's *Offices* (the content of which is considered elsewhere) were ordered to be copied and read at Lyon during his administration, and also his antiphonary and 'a new book' which he had bound and decorated with silk. Florus said that Amalar had spread his errors through many books. A contemporary manuscript of the *Offices* is rich in glosses refuting his errors with striking vigour. Florus certainly made heavy demands on the scriptorium for his treatises, poems and letters. He directed the work of the scribes, correcting and annotating as necessary. A Theodosian Code is marked by him for excerpting for his collection of canon law, and the same marks appear in some twenty other Lyon books. A letter from him to Eldred recommends the correct procedure for composition; and he had, he said, consulted the Septuagint and the Hebrew books and corrected the psalter in use at Lyon. The tradition of learning persisted, and attracted outside pupils, as for example Lupus' pupil Ado, who retired to Lyon in 860 and there composed the martyrology of which Usuard was to make good use. Later still, in the tenth century, Magilo, future abbot of Cluny, could seek instruction at Lyon, praised by his biographer as a place famous for the study of the liberal arts, and mother of philosophy.

What was written at Lyon from the late eighth century, together with what books it acquired, are some indication of the resources of its libraries. Florus lists the patristic texts available and in his Pauline commentary cites no less than 165 of the writings of Augustine. Amolo's treatise on predestination contains excerpts from five

Augustinian works. In fact, Augustine was a Lyon speciality. It was often to Lyon that others turned for advice on the great Father, and much misunderstanding ensued from divergences between northern and southern texts of the same writing. Lyon housed some unusual patristic texts – Tertullian for example – as well as the common ones. But the Fathers were not all. The legal collection included the Theodosian Code, two copies of Alaric's Breviary and two of the *Lex Romana Visigothorum*, an epitome of the *Hispana* and a collection of Gallic councils. The liberal arts and especially grammarians were well represented; Martianus Capella was present, along with Cicero's *De officiis*, Plato's *Timaeus* translated by Chalcidius, and a collection of logic. In a word, there was no more impressive library in the Carolingian world and it served the needs of its times. Building on ancient foundations and turning to its daughter-houses for assistance, it was a powerhouse for any who looked beyond the simple tools of instruction to the materials on which theological debate could fasten: What was the nature of Scripture? How should one understand the Trinity? How did one reconcile Pauline theology with patristic and canonical teaching? Independent by tradition and irascible when challenged, Lyon owed its flowering to Carolingian inspiration.

St Riquier and Corbie, St Wandrille and St Germain, Fleury and Lyon form an exemplary group in a certain sense. Their histories differ and their special interests do not always coincide. What they had in common was that they were all successful. It would be possible to take six other western centres and reach much the same conclusions. All reveal the working of the same Carolingian yeast. Ignorance meant heresy. As in East Francia so in the West, books were for teaching and meditation. They provided the common basis for reformation and renaissance.

v. Deviation and Exploration

The forward drive of the Carolingians, implemented at so many levels, leaves the impression that the Church, whatever its weaknesses, knew what it wanted and how to set about it if allowed to do so. Its achievement, however astonishing, must still be seen against a background of running battles on issues that lay at the heart of the faith. One such was clearly the debate on Adoptionism: what more likely to rock the boat than doubt about the nature of Christ himself? Another was iconoclasm, essentially a dispute between East and West but still a matter for grave thought within Francia itself. Differences in interpretation between East and West on the nature of the Trinity proved rather more divisive, though to begin with they failed to distort Frankish unity of doctrine. The case against the Greeks was best put by the Corbie monk Ratramn in a fierce and detailed examination of their errors.[1]

Ratramn also appears in a controversy with his brother-monk Paschasius Radbert on the nature of the Real Presence in the eucharist. Both wrote treatises entitled *De corpore et sanguine Domini*.[2] Their problem was the liturgical significance of the mass and its sacrifice, and nothing could have touched the Carolingian Church more keenly. Both turned to Augustine, as so often happened in the theological disputes of the century. Augustine is not only a difficult writer but also very voluminous; and the rediscovery and re-examination of what he wrote, often a matter of chance, points to a vital advance in sophistication from the early Carolingian scholars to those of the mid-ninth century. Radbert and Ratramn looked at the same texts to reach different conclusions. Radbert's was the more orthodox; and this was understandable since he was writing between 831 and 833 at the request of an old pupil, abbot of Corbie's daughter-house of Korvei, for the instruction of monks and Saxon converts. It was still a remarkable treatise. Radbert concluded that the consecrated elements were indeed and always the body and blood of Christ even if this could only be perceived by faith. He distinguished between appearance and reality, the first physical and the second spiritual. Ratramn on the other hand concluded that though faith revealed the reality of the eucharist, there remained a distinction between Christ's physical and spiritual bodies. The elements of the eucharist were symbolic only, and therefore the mass was a memorial of what had once happened but did not happen again. The dispute seems to have made no general impact at the time, though it had a future. Radbert produced a second edition of his treatise and dedicated it afresh to Charles the Bald. What is significant is that so central an issue could be raised and argued at a high intellectual level in a Frankish monastery, and that different interpretations could be placed on the teaching of Augustine and on the nature of the central rite of the Church.

More wide-reaching in its effects was a dispute – surely the dispute of the century – on the problem of predestination. It was an accident, but a characteristic accident, that the issue should have been raised at all: it was due to the thinking of one man. In another sense one can see why, once raised, it should have seemed vital to the whole outlook of the reformed Church. The man was Gottschalk, son of a Saxon count

---

[1] *Contra Graecorum opposita libri quatuor*. PL 121, cols. 225–346.
[2] Ratramn, ed. J. N. Bakhuizen van den Brink, 2nd edn. (Amsterdam–London, 1974); Radbert, ed. Beda Paulus, CC xvi, 1969.

named Bern, clearly a member of an influential family. The fact that he was a Saxon is significant: someone from what had so recently been the periphery of the Frankish world could fail to get the message of conformity and proceed to speak for himself, sharply and persistently. He had been born around 803 and sent as an oblate to Fulda. What else is known is that he was sent for further instruction to Reichenau, where he struck up a friendship with Walahfrid. Reaching the age when he should have taken deacon's orders, he took the uncommon step of asking to be freed from his monastic vows, arguing that vows taken on his behalf by his parents were invalid. He further demanded the return of family-property oblated in his name. His archbishop allowed him to leave Fulda but did not return the property. His abbot, Hraban Maur, countered the archbishop's decision with an appeal to the emperor - *De oblatione puerorum*.[3] But tempers remained high. We next find him studying at Corbie under Ratramn and at Orbais in the diocese of Soissons. It is difficult to tell in what sense he now was, or was not, a monk. Certainly he received ordination (irregularly, however, at the hands of a *chorepiscopus*) and apparently preached in Italy – to the great Eberhard of Friuli among others – and further afield in Croatia. Hraban was incensed, not only by the unorthodoxy of Gottschalk's preaching but also by his leaving his original monastery and being irregularly ordained. So Gottschalk came home, was condemned at the synod of Mainz in 848 and finally sent to Hincmar of Reims for imprisonment. Hincmar reopened the case by arraigning him before a synod at Quierzy in 849. He was then deprived of his orders, beaten and condemned to life imprisonment in the monastery of Hautvillers (where, by coincidence, the great Utrecht Psalter was being written and illustrated at about the same time). Gottschalk, unshaken, continued to teach and write, and chiefly on predestination. Hincmar next consulted a wide range of scholars on what he considered Gottschalk's heresy, which seems to have been gaining the ear of clergy in Hincmar's own province. The answers were surprising and varied. Only in 859 was a satisfactory formula of compromise arrived at, though Gottschalk himself remained obdurate to the end, clearly hoping that Hincmar's enemy, Nicholas I, would intervene on his behalf. But Nicholas died too soon and Gottschalk himself died unreconciled two years later, in 869. One can see at once that he had been a prickly and independent man who, simply on grounds of discipline, woud have run foul of the authorities. His writings, like those opposing him, breathe rancour and personal abuse. His sufferings, which were great and not entirely merited, earned him extensive coverage at the time. Everyone knew about Gottschalk.

[3] PL 107, cols. 419–40.

However, what lay at the heart of the rumpus was not discipline but theology. The issue, an old one, was this: does God predestine certain men to salvation? If he does, does he predestine the rest to damnation? In either case, is predestination more than divine prescience? What happens to man's free will and to his ability to escape from Adam's curse by free acceptance of salvation through Christ's sacrifice? Augustine had been clear that predestination was more than mere prescience and that men were indeed predestined by God to salvation or damnation. But as always there were nuances in his thinking: good works and Christ's sacrifice were in no way rendered unnecessary by what God had predestined; and what Augustine said, and what he meant, were not widely understood in the West. The Frankish position, a compromise, had been determined long ago in 529 at the council of Orange.[4] It was a compromise that still reflected something of the Pelagian position against which Augustine had reacted – namely, that man has responsibility for choosing his own salvation or damnation; if he has not, what is the use of trying? The fathers at Orange had concluded that man was clearly responsible for his own damnation by refusing to mend his ways and accept Christ's sacrifice, but that his eventual salvation rested with God alone. In other words, they sidestepped the problem of double predestination, the implicit 'either . . . or'. Orange became accepted doctrine and the matter was allowed to rest. Isidore indeed, in his *Sententiae*, did use the phrase *gemina predestinatio*, and Bede was strongly against anything that smelt of Pelagianism. But the Carolingian Church remained unruffled. Until Gottschalk came along.

A quite small triangle of Francia, the sides of which are not longer than ninety miles, covers the area most critical to the Carolingian Church in the mid-ninth century. It runs from Paris in the south to Reims in the north-east, then across north-west to Corbie, and so down south to Paris. Within this triangle lie St Denis, Laon, Quierzy, Soissons and Compiègne in addition to Reims and Corbie. It was the stamping-ground of Hilduin, Hincmar, the younger Hincmar, Prudentius for a time, Ratramn, Radbert, Eriugena and his circle, Gottschalk and Charles the Bald himself. It was here, at Corbie and at Orbais, that Gottschalk made his first serious acquaintance with Augustine, a writer on the whole better known in the south than in the north. He came to Augustine as a trained grammarian. He was already equipped to face Augustine's theological positions with the weapons of dialectic and rhetoric as understood by the school of Alcuin. Up to a point, he grasped the significance of what Augustine had written in his attack on the Pelagians: if God is omnipotent, eternal and the creator of

[4] MGH Conc. i, pp. 46–54.

all, he must inevitably do more than foresee the fate of all men; he must determine it. A crucial but separate problem was how predestination was to be reconciled with the facts of Adam's fall and Christ's sacrifice. This also Augustine faced. He did not believe that good works were unnecessary. Gottschalk was greatly struck by Augustine's first proposition: that God must predestine all, both salvation and damnation. Eriugena was, as we shall see, equally struck by Augustine's arguments but reached rather different conclusions. Both men, however, learnt from Augustine that one must try to imagine things from God's point of view, whatever the consequences. And the consequences were in fact very serious. The orthodox Carolingian position was clear as inherited from Alcuin and taught by the pupils of the honoured master, Hraban Maur included. The newly-converted of the ninth century were thus taught to believe in the efficacy of faith through baptism, and in good works. This was clearly set out by the council of Paris in 829 and at other times. Faith without works was useless; you worked for your salvation and could attain it. Thus the issue of predestination had its setting in a troubled society. Hraban had not fully understood what Gottschalk was at, but his report to Hincmar remained the basis of the latter's views till he had had time to assemble and consider the texts.

Up to this point, the only considerable men who seem to have known the full-fledged Gottschalk personally were Ratramn and Lupus. But his main opponent, both on theological and disciplinary grounds, was Hincmar; and from Hincmar's two large treatises or assemblages of texts bearing on predestination (a third is lost) we learn most about him.[5] More than many, Hincmar had reason to appreciate the significance of the mid-century's political collapse: what was it but moral collapse? The only hope lay in the re-establishment of order and discipline in society; and it was up to the bishops to protect their flocks from public discussion of deep issues that they could not understand. His clergy must cast forth Gottschalk's writings, if they had them; and not only clergy but monks, who were perhaps more liable than clergy to harbour heterodox views and discuss them. As Hincmar saw him, Gottschalk was a-social, the enemy of social responsibility; he wanted to go his own way as an individual vessel of inspiration and to reduce society to a collection of individuals. He was a social leper, having and feeling no pastoral responsibility. It is true that Hincmar feared for himself; issues of debate tended to end up in the matter of his own election and the deposition of Ebbo. Yet he was much more than a bureaucrat who feared the rocking of the Church's boat. The good Carolingian bishop believed passionately and primarily in God's crea-

[5] PL 125, cols. 49–474; MGH Epist. vi, 1, i, no. 99, pp. 44–9.

tion of a Christian society. He went on to warn his clergy and monks against what he saw as a related heresy of Gottschalk on the subject of the Trinity. Gottschalk's enquiring mind had found material for speculation in his reading of Boethius' theological writings, the effect of which on ninth-century thinking was far from negligible. To speculate on the Trinity was bound to cause ripples. Thus we find what looks like a ripple in the cartulary of the distant monastery of Weissenburg; the invocation, namely, 'in nomine trini et uni Dei salvatoris'.[6]

Charles the Bald personally felt involved in the stir caused by Gottschalk. It was his duty as king to ensure that peace in society without which no man could work for his salvation. Repeatedly he urged bishops and councils to reach a firm decision and have done with doubt. He sought advice and received it; for example, in the form of a massive dossier of texts from Ratramn,[7] who felt much sympathy for Gottschalk's arguments. But Gottschalk was not to be silenced. He thought well to let Hincmar know directly what his views were; and these he set out in a *Confessio Brevis*,[8] where he put the case for predestination to salvation or to damnation – but not to sin, which was another matter. Whether a man were damned or not was God's concern; whether he sinned was his own. He soon elaborated this argument in a *Confessio Prolixior*, where his points were better buttressed from the Fathers. It is a very ardent and direct appeal to God, not to the Church. Hincmar was busily assembling texts and meanwhile turned for advice to others he respected; for he was beginning to grasp the profundities of the issue. Prudentius of Troyes replied, no doubt to Hincmar's discomfiture, in a sense favourable to double predestination, while Lupus also leant rather towards Gottschalk. Hraban, always outside the real theological debate, replied that there was nothing to argue about: it must be morally wrong to make God responsible for our sins. Nobody had said that he was. In brief, he had no solid support to offer. Eriugena, on the other hand, seemed to understand what worried the heretic. His reply was bitterly hostile to Gottschalk but was based on a rationalizing approach that confused many. His argument, logically developed, was that God cannot predestine to evil since evil is nothing and hell is simply the absence of eternal bliss. At least he may have alerted Hincmar to the existence of the range of Greek Fathers. Though Gottschalk and Eriugena reached widely different conclusions, the first proceeding intuitively and the

---

[6] *Traditiones Wizenburgenses: Die Urkunden des Klosters Weissenburg*, ed. A. Doll (Darmstadt, 1979), p. 373.

[7] PL 121, cols. 14–80.

[8] C. Lambot, ed. *Œuvres théologiques et grammaticales de Godescalc d'Orbais* (Louvain, 1945).

second logically, both saw the problem of predestination from God's point of view. The ripples of the debate spread out beyond those immediately concerned; probably there was no matter that engaged the attention of so many bishops. Gottschalk did not drop out of the debate, but it could now be carried on without direct reference to him.

Both sides (if they may be called that) decided to appeal to the southern Church of Lyon, rich as it was in Augustinian texts. Gottschalk had raised two bogies for consideration. One was pre-destination and the other was his use of the innocuously-intended phrase *trina deitas*, which he claimed to be common usage in hymns. Hincmar thought out a long rejoinder to the second: *De una et non de trina deitate*.[9] There is no question that Gottschalk had used violent language about Hincmar, as about authority generally; but he got as good as he gave. Each was ready to accuse the other of falsifying texts, the explanation of which is often that they consulted variant versions of the same texts. What Hincmar hated about *trina deitas* was the possibility that the simple would interpret it as meaning three Gods instead of three persons in one God. Gottschalk meant nothing of the sort; but then, he took no account of the pastoral problems of a bishop. Hincmar knew what to say about the Trinity, as about predestination, for he had by now assembled a mighty collection of texts at Reims. Alcuin's *De Trinitate* was to hand to help him: an excellent guide, which the archbishop did not hesitate to emend. But still it seemed wise to consult the textual experts at Lyon. Hincmar turned to Arch-bishop Amolo, who did his best to be accommodating; while Prudentius turned to the formidable Florus. The two Lyon experts received different texts for comment. Florus found that he agreed with Gottschalk about predestination though not on the subject of free will; and in agreement with his archbishop he was deeply worried at the raising of such issues at the present time. But the king was pressing for a solution. The consequent synod at Quierzy provided a fair summary of Hincmar's arguments, though, as Lyon was to point out, the North was still short on Augustine. At least it safeguarded men's liberty to choose grace or sin for themselves, in accordance with the orthodoxies of Rome and the Anglo-Saxons. But if Lyon was stronger on Augustinian texts and the early Fathers it was less strong on Gregory the Great, Bede, Alcuin and Prosper than was the North. However, the North could show several centres where Augustine was seriously studied, as at Corbie, Troyes and St Riquier. The fact remained that for purposes of debate on predestination Hincmar and his advisers seemed to choose the Augustinian texts they liked and could under-stand.

[9] PL 125, cols. 473–618; MGH Epist, vi, 1, i, no. 141, pp. 108–15.

A southern council at Valence, attended by the Churches of Lyon, Vienne and Arles, drew up a series of *capitula* that in effect supported Gottschalk and Prudentius, but without dealing with Hincmar's objections. This drew from Hincmar a further treatise on predestination that ignored the arguments of Valence as Valence had ignored his own. He seemed to be more concerned with the personal unfairness of the Valence *capitula* than with the meaning of texts. Again pressed by Charles – and Hincmar always complained that he was being hurried – he compiled a dossier for yet another treatise that should form a basis for full discussion; and this treatise, a massive collection of texts defending Quierzy, shows that he had indeed been doing his homework. It came to this: God cannot predestine men to damnation; all he has is prescience, foreknowledge, of damnation. Otherwise he is responsible for evil. He can only predestine to good. Hincmar further attempts to put the issue in a historical setting by arguing that predestination to damnation was an old heresy already condemned; and of this, Gottschalk, Prudentius and Ratramn were merely modern revivers. This was untrue, but it gave Hincmar a canonical basis where he felt at home. Lyon admitted that he was right to say that the words 'predestined to damnation' did not occur in texts of authority. However, this did not remove the fact of predestination, which must logically emerge from God's nature as eternal and immutable.

Gottschalk could have made things easier for himself by allowing that faith and good works were likely signs that a man was predestined to salvation. But his concern was with God, not man; and he did not say so. His integrity was absolute. On the other hand, Hincmar's humanity and pastoral care were equally admirable in their way. At Douzy, in 860, an exhausted compromise was arrived at, rather in Hincmar's favour. Gottschalk was soon largely forgotten. He had committed the sin of thinking for himself, and one sees why it was a sin in the eyes of responsible churchmen. Certainly the debate had brought intellectual gains; it was fought by a surprising number of learned men at a level that would have been unthinkable not many years earlier; it brought the learned centres of North and South into contact with one another; and it disseminated texts very remarkably.

There remains another side to Gottschalk. He was a poet. Whatever his views of the establishment, he was a thinker of deep piety within the Christian tradition of hymn-writing. Some of his best hymns are lyrical poems invoking Christ: for example, 'Christe mearum lux tenebrarum' and 'Spes mea Christe rex benedicte'. They were his contribution to the liturgy. Like his contemporaries he saw religious poetry as an act of praise in itself. And there were poems of a different sort; a long set of verses to Ratramn, and a very moving poem of which the first line is 'O mi custos, o mi heros, mi pater misericors'.[10] This last in a way synthesizes the heart of Gottschalk's thought about theology and grammar. In form it is a *confessio*, an act of praise and a gift to God, and an elaborate construction built round a system of symmetries and oppositions, balances and correspondences. The theology is clear enough; predestination is there; but behind this lies a grammatical and arithmetical aesthetic. We are left with a highly personal confession and prayer, bewailing sin and importuning the blessing of tears. The same compunction can be felt in ninth-century collections of confessions, prayers and *orationes* that may go no further back in time than Alcuin and the Irish masters. It was part of the ninth century's obsessive moral introspection. Liturgically, the high feast of compunction and penitence was Lent and, often associated with it, the invocation of the Trinity (or sometimes of the Holy Spirit alone). Gottschalk's poem was a powerful invocation of what he called the 'deus unus et trius'. He may have foreseen its use by others. Walahfrid certainly approved of the inclusion of hymns of this kind in the liturgy. So it may have been composed as a lyrical contribution to public devotion.

But the two sides of Gottschalk are really one. He could fearlessly isolate God from the working of the Church and cause a great deal more trouble than he may have intended. He could also appeal with passion to the God he envisaged. However he saw his own pre-destiny, he felt more keenly than most the urge to bewail his sin, and offered his penance to the Trinity in a poem of oblation and praise. Somehow it fitted better into the Carolingian moral outlook than investigations of Augustine.

Gottschalk was a big man. But there was a bigger. John Scottus Eriugena was, as his name insists, an Irishman: literally, John the Irishman, native of Ireland; and Eriugena appears to have been the name he himself used. Irishmen were continuing to reach the con-tinental centres as refugees, pilgrims and teachers, no doubt urged on by the plight of Irish monasteries under Viking attack. They were scattered far and wide over the Frankish world but with some con-centration in northern Francia. Liège, the refuge of Sedulius Scottus, was one favoured centre. Others were St Amand, Reims and, further south, Auxerre. Nothing is known of Eriugena's life in Ireland except that he was the product of an Irish monastic school and a trained grammarian with some knowledge of Greek. How much more he picked up on the continent is equally unknown. He must have left

[10] MGH Poet, vi, i, no. 1, pp. 86–97.

Ireland before 847 and fairly soon made his way to the court of Charles the Bald at Quierzy or Compiègne. There he made learned friends, among them Prudentius of Troyes and Wulfad of Bourges. The centre with which his name is associated was the cathedral-city of Laon, not far from the royal court though certainly distinct from it for teaching purposes. It seems probable that Eriugena's links were always closer to the court than to Laon; but his association with Laon was sufficiently real to necessitate some consideration of the city's role in ninth-century teaching.

If only for its proximity to the royal court, Laon was a city directly under the Carolingian eye. Its bishops, notably Pardulus and the younger Hincmar, were exceptional men and scholars in their own right. Its cathedral school under their care was among the greatest of the century. We know of a succession of Laon masters, covering three generations: first, the Irishman Martin, friend and contemporary of Eriugena, then Manno and Bernard, and finally Adelelm who died as bishop of Laon in 930. Well over one hundred books are known as having been in use there over this period, many given by the bishops or well-wishers further afield. They were meant for teaching. Hundreds more books that no longer survive are known to have been in the library, or can be inferred to have been. Certainly Laon had its scriptorium in the ninth century; even the neighbouring royal nunnery of Nôtre Dame la Profonde may have been busy copying, like the greater nunnery of Chelles; but Laon was never a well-known writing-centre. Teaching was its forte. So, for all its patristic wealth, eastern and western, the book that best stands for Laon's achievement is Martin's own Greek–Latin glossary, to which he added a grammar and some more personal matter.[11] Bernhard Bischoff called it 'a true *Thesaurus linguae Graecae* for its century'. The influence of these learned masters was felt far outside Laon; at Reims notably, and also by Hucbald at St Amand, at Auxerre, the home of Haimo and Heiric, and at Soissons, where the learned Wulfad was abbot of St Médard before Charles the Bald jobbed him into the see of Bourges. Indeed, it is the interchange of men, books and ideas between these centres that is most striking. But the Greek of the masters should not lead us to think that they were primarily experts in eastern sources, let alone philosophy. They were teachers of grammar and computus and students of biblical commentary in general. Martin's own compendium of doctrine, with its marked interest in the Trinity, is the wide and conventional teaching-manual of a typical Carolingian master; so also his copy of Jerome's guide to Hebrew words and his heavy annotation of

[11] Ed. E. Miller, 'Glossaire grec-latin de la bibliothèque de Laon', *Notices et Extraits*, 29, 2 (1880), pp. 1–230.

Bede's computistical works. No heresy here. A medieval school depended largely for its survival on the reputation of its master and its luck in finding a successor to him. Laon did exceptionally well; and through it more than through any other school the idea of Carolingian teaching was to survive.

Eriugena's strange treatise on predestination is his earliest known work, written probably in 851 or 852.[12] It betrays a close knowledge of Augustine and not of the Greek Fathers in whom he later specialized; and since it was commissioned it is clear that he already enjoyed some reputation as a scholar. But he was now set on a fresh course by Charles the Bald, the initiator of much in the field of Greek–Latin translation. It was not for nothing that Eriugena and Heiric praised their king for his Greek interests. In 827 the Emperor Michael the Stammerer had presented Louis the Pious with a copy of the works of the Greek theologian known as Pseudo-Dionysius. The manuscript (which still exists) will have been housed at St Denis, where it was translated into Latin by the Abbot Hilduin. It was an astonishing achievement that opened up at least some western minds to the wealth of what is called Greek negative-theology. Hilduin was a good, if too literal, translator, and the nuances of Dionysius' thought sometimes escaped him. How or by whom this was detected is unknown though in itself of great interest. Charles at least was determined to secure a better translation and turned to Eriugena. No doubt he looked upon the Greek theologian as identical with the first bishop of Paris, and thus a founding father of the *patria*. This proved a turning-point for Eriugena. He now had to apply his mind to Greek theology and its Neoplatonist armoury. His direct knowledge of the pagan Neoplatonists, to say nothing of Plato and Aristotle, was and remained minimal and indirect. His knowledge of them came only through the Greek Fathers and such Latins as Boethius, Cassiodorus, Augustine and Ambrose. He was never a philosopher in our sense but a theologian who used the weapons of philosophy, and above all of dialectic. Already his treatise on predestination rested on the argument that the truths of scripture could only be revealed by the methods of dialectic; and this remained his view. Apart from the Greek scriptures, he had direct knowledge of the writings (or some of them) of eight Greek Fathers: Origen, Basil, Gregory of Nazianzen, Gregory of Nyssa, Maximus the Confessor, Chrysostom, Epiphanius and Dionysius. Those of them that he was to translate into Latin were inevitably the ones that most influenced his own thinking. But the thinking was his own. Its characteristic was a blend of the Latin and the Greek to produce a new philosophical theology.

[12] PL 122, cols. 355–440.

When Eriugena turned to translate the four treatises of Dionysius he had before him the translation of Hilduin. This proved a valuable basis. Nevertheless, the new translation showed a much clearer interpretative skill.[13] Eriugena understood the theology where Hilduin understood the grammar. There can be no question that 'understanding' Dionysius did sometimes mean that Eriugena modified the text to lend support to his own, more Augustinian, views. But he approached his task with reverence for the man he believed to provide a direct echo of apostolic teaching, and particularly that of St Paul. For one of the four treatises, on the celestial hierarchy, he also provided a commentary from which it appears that he made not one but two translations of the text.

His appetite whetted by Dionysius, Eriugena then provided the king with a translation of Maximus the Confessor's *First Ambigua*;[14] and he then went on, apparently without royal urging though surely with royal knowledge, to translate at least three more Greek works: the *Quaestiones ad Thalassium* of Maximus,[15] the *De hominis opificio* of Gregory of Nyssa and the *Ancoratus* of Epiphanius. (The Epiphanius translation is now lost, as also a translation of Basil.) This mass of translations, some of them of texts very long as well as difficult, has understandably been called 'a gigantic enterprise'. The Franks were indeed robbing the Greeks with the assistance of Irishmen, Greek residents and even some natives (for example, Hilduin, Wulfad, the younger Hincmar, Ratramn, Aeneas of Paris and, though not competing for honours, Lupus). It is a most marked difference between the earlier and the later phases of the Carolingian renaissance. It is reasonable to suppose that Eriugena's translations must have been begun around 850 – that is, immediately after the treatise on predestination. All were completed by about 866. It is hard to believe that so huge an undertaking could have been completed, as is often stated, between 860 and 866. Moreover within this period of translations must be fitted other writings. One of them is a commentary on St John's Gospel,[16] a highly individual performance, notably in its treatment of the difference between mysteries and symbols. It is prefaced by a homily splendidly mystical, informed by the image of flight: the upward flight of the eagle among the evangelists who with one beat of his wings reaches the bosom of the Trinity and the hidden mystery of the principle of all things. The image of ascent and descent, dear to Eriugena, no doubt exploits the patristic tradition of the flight of the soul. It owes something to Dionysius, as also to the *De nuptiis Philologiae et Mercurii* of Martianus Capella, a favourite text for Carolingian

---

13 Ibid., cols. 1029–1194.   14 Ibid., cols. 1193–1222.
15 Unedited.   16 Ed. E. Jeauneau, SC 180 (1972).

commentators, including Eriugena himself. But the result is special to Eriugena. Jeauneau rightly calls the homily 'the jewel of Latin rhetoric and philosophy of the early middle ages'.

Within this same period of marvellous productiveness there must also be placed Eriugena's greatest and most original work: what he called his *Periphyseon* or, in Latin, *De divisione naturae*.[17] Begun around 864, it developed through several stages to what we now have. The present Book I seems to constitute the first stage. It rests on Latin sources: Augustine (influential throughout), Boethius and Martianus Capella. It was particularly in the field of cosmology that Martianus helped him. He seems to have kept a separate collection of teaching notes on Martianus; perhaps a text complete with observations, of which epitomes were soon made. His colleague Martin did much the same, and it is difficult to tell which of the two was responsible for the material on Martianus later used in the school of Auxerre, notably by Remigius, pupil of Heiric. At all events, faulty conflations of Eriugena on Martianus were what good scholars were using within fifty years of the time when Eriugena was glossing his text. It is a salutary reminder that Eriugena, like Martin, was a teacher. He had pupils (whether at the palace, Laon or elsewhere) who themselves kept notes and glossed texts. It is even possible that the revised versions of the *Periphyseon* were themselves the work of pupils. We are faced with a large movement of interest, if not with overmuch understanding. Glossing in the ninth and tenth centuries, and not only of Martianus and Boethius, was widely indebted to Eriugena, the glosses varying according to teaching requirements.

Book I of the *Periphyseon* rises from a foundation of Latin reading, the remaining four from a reading of Greek texts. Augustine does not fade away, either in structure or in spirit. He lies solidly behind Eriugena's view of the Trinity, his distinction between *sapientia* (knowledge of eternal things, which is true theology and philosophy) and *scientia* (knowledge of temporal things), his insistence that faith is the essential preliminary to understanding by the exercise of reason, and above all his assertion of the central role of Christ, the tree of life. But where they differ the Greeks have come to the fore. The whole work is arranged as a dialogue between the teacher (*nutritor*) and the pupil (*alumnus*) and of course is not original in this respect. In fact, the dialogue is within the mind of the author. Its structure is hard to grasp, partly because of frequent digressions and long quotations. Basically it is a structure of a fourfold division in Nature, as Eriugena conceives of

---

[17] PL 122, cols. 439–1022; ed. I. P. Sheldon-Williams, bk. 1 (Dublin, 1968), bk. 2 (Dublin, 1972), bk. 3 (Dublin, 1981). The remaining two books are to be edited by Professor J. J. O'Meara.

Nature: first, that which is not created but creates, namely God; second, that which is created and creates, the Primordial Causes emanating from God, corresponding to the Platonic Forms; third, that which is created but does not create, the material universe; and fourth, that which is not created and does not create, and this is God as Final Cause. This structure controls the five Books. But an inner structure may well lie in the first three chapters of Genesis, to comment on which Eriugena constantly reverts from his digressions. These three chapters tell the story of God's creation of heaven and earth and of all things in them, and finally man; of Adam's disobedience and of the banishment of Adam and Eve from Eden. Like his contemporaries, Eriugena regarded Moses as the author of Genesis, which gave it authority of a special kind. The *Periphyseon* seems to orbit round the opening words: 'In the beginning God created the heaven and the earth'. Book I rests upon *creavit Deus*, Book II upon *in principio* and the remaining Books upon *coelum et terram*. This at least is one pattern that gives the whole work structural coherence. But Book I is the foundation of the author's theology: God is creator, and he and his creation are one. He is both generally the maker of all and specifically the maker of man in his own image. Thus when we ask how we can know God, the answer must be only through what he himself has created: he is, in other words, only discernible to man through what Eriugena calls his theophanies or manifestations. These will never tell us what God is – God is not a 'what' – but only that he is. Moreover, man must describe what he discerns in words, which can never be the realities they seek to represent. In any case we cannot describe what we cannot know. Here is one ground of what is called Eriugena's negative theology; namely, whatever we assert of God, God is different and beyond it and more.

Book II considers the Primordial Causes of Nature, which are in God; then Christ, the realized type of divine and human unity; and finally the road back to God. Always Eriugena sees a creative progression down from God, and then a return to him. Some thought they discerned in this a smack of pantheism but clearly Eriugena saw nothing of the sort. Book III is concerned with the first five days of creation and Book IV with the sixth day, when God created man in his own image, and with the nature of Adam's fall. In Book V, from Adam's fall to Christ, man moves towards his perfection on the seventh day; for God promises the return of all Nature *ad Unum*. The question then arises, how can man achieve this promised reintegration with God, his natural goal? The answer is, through virtuous living, submission to God, and contemplation. There are steps in the re-ascent, as there had long been for those following monastic rules. In short, the destiny of universal Nature is resurrection and reunion with God, its creator. Which is not to deny the realities of the consequences of failure: the demons and tortures of hell.

In ways such as these one attempts to see patterns in the *Periphyseon* though the fact is that, despite its remorseless logic, it defies categorization. However little we may understand it – and its nuances are extremely subtle – this at least can be said: unlike his contemporaries, whose concern was with religion as a social phenomenon, Eriugena rises to the consideration of God himself, both religiously and suprareligiously (though he would not have accepted the distinction). He was in a region where few could follow him. Yet the *Periphyseon*, as well as the Greek and Latin writings that lay behind it, and his translations, were certainly read; and equally certainly he taught and had friends in more than one place who could appreciate something of his exposition. In short, he cannot be divorced from the Carolingian world that sheltered him. His orthodoxy was inevitably challenged, then and later. Pope Nicholas had heard rumours about his heterodoxy and complained to Charles the Bald that he had received no copy of the translations of Dionysius. Suspicion must always centre round a very clever man. Hence William of Malmesbury's story that when Eriugena was teaching in England (which, however implausible, cannot be disproved) he was stabbed to death with the pens of his pupils. A Dublin gloss adds to this: they did it because he forced them to think. Apocryphal no doubt; but a true reflection of suspicion.

Eriugena's way to God was through the exercise of reason. We have, he considered, to use everything we have been given to approach God's reality. We do it through Nature and we do it through scripture. But though reason is a faculty of the soul, it will not by itself take us far on the road. God will remain unknowable, and there is nothing true or real that we can say of him except that he is, and is eternally. Whatever we can guess about him through his manifestations and creations is not the truth but a human image of the truth. A passage in Book I makes this plain:

God is *anarchos*, that is, without beginning, because nothing precedes him or makes him to be; nor does he have an end, because he is infinite; for it is understood that there is nothing after him since he is the limit of all things beyond which nothing proceeds. Therefore he does not admit any motion. For he has nowhere to move himself since he is the fullness and the place and the perfection and the station and the whole of all things, or rather he is more than fullness and perfection, more than place and station, more than the whole of all things. For he is more than that which is said or understood of him, in whatever way anything is either said of him or understood.

To which summary the pupil in the *Periphyseon* answers, 'these things are quite clear to me – I think'. *Ut opinor*. Perhaps. But what Eriugena has said is in effect that nothing he has said is or could be true. God is *anarchos*; he is he who is more than Being and more than creator. There is even more than this to the great book, for it is the subsuming and transformation of the essential theologies of the Eastern and Western Fathers, to whom Eriugena frequently and reverently refers.

Eriugena belonged to a circle, however much he might tower within it. Within a few years of the completion of the *Periphyseon* it was being emended and glossed by others and studied at Corbie, Auxerre and other centres, which may have included the palace. Heiric of Auxerre dedicated his *Collectanea* to Bishop Hildebold of Soissons, a learned man and a friend of Charles the Bald, and his Life of St Germanus direct to the king. The circle turns round the king. Eriugena was above the heads of most people but never an anachronism. The background to his development from grammarian to translator and theologian was surely the stimulation of discussion at Charles's court. His interests were wide. The *vir barbarus*, as Anastasius called him from the safety of Rome, was alive to the beauty of music, art and architecture; they demanded intellectual effort. He may even have affected the iconography of Charles's artistic circle, for it seems as if his difficult poem on a church dedication[18] refers to the round church dedicated to the Virgin and founded by Charles at Compiègne shortly before his death. A modified version of the sixth verse of the poem appears in a famous manuscript of the time, the *Codex Aureus* of St Emmeram at Regensburg, and appears in association with its most famous illustration: Christ throned in majesty, surrounded by the four major prophets and the symbols of the evangelists. There is, then, this slim but plausible connection between Eriugena and artistic production influenced by the court.

Eriugena thus went far beyond the workaday minds of the Carolingian reformers. Gottschalk would have understood his aims, and no doubt also Wulfad, to whom the *Periphyseon* was dedicated. The speculations of such men were no part of Charlemagne's original programme. Indeed they disturbed it in one way or another. Yet they were part of a movement of thought. Much depended on the arrival and appraisal of Greek patristic writings and also upon a deepening appreciation of Augustine and his Latin successors. The foundation of all was still instruction in the liberal arts. The teaching of Alcuin and his many pupils was alive. Eriugena shared a common background in the liberal arts with Wulfad, Heiric, Hildebold, Hincmar, Lupus and many others, and never questioned their majesty and mystery. Much gratitude was ultimately due to Alcuin.

[18] PL 122, cols. 1235–8.

A twelfth-century manuscript of the *Clavis physicae* of Honorius of Autun contains an illustration of two sages in grave debate.[19] One is Theodore of Tarsus, archbishop of Canterbury, closely resembling a conventional St Paul and clearly symbolizing the learning of the Greeks. The other is Eriugena, arrayed as a Roman philosopher and symbolizing the learning of the West. Thus the twelfth century could see him: as a philosopher, which he was not, and as the type of the westerner, which equally he was not. But to have seen him as a great western master and teacher was right. His influence on thought came slowly, for his writings were not widely appreciated at once or soon after. But even in his strangeness and foreignness and unique distinction he could have belonged nowhere else but the Carolingian ninth century.

vi. The Vernaculars

Vernacular literature is part of the Carolingian renaissance. Behind it lay long traditions of oral transmission of songs and stories. But oral transmission is not literature: it only safeguards some of the material for literature and some of the linguistic skills required for its presentation. This sounds as if our earliest extant Germanic literature ought to be secular, not to say heroic. But in fact it is not. Why this is so can be explained by the needs of Carolingian religious education from the later eighth century onwards.

A start can be made with St Boniface and the Anglo-Saxon missionaries in Hesse and Thuringia. It was probably not difficult for them to make themselves understood. Certainly they brought with them a tradition of expounding the faith in the vernacular. They also knew how to write it; for Old English was already a literary language. Bede himself had been translating St John's Gospel into Northumbrian on his death-bed. The tradition remained firmly rooted in the continental houses of Anglo-Saxon foundation. The vernacular was a weapon of exposition and thus of conversion; and more particularly of exposition to the early generations of local clergy. As for the people, it was enough that they should be made to understand the nature of baptism and the elements of the faith. Boniface's *statuta*[1] (collected if not composed by him) insist on priests explaining the renunciation of the Devil and the need for confession in the vernacular, since otherwise baptism would be meaningless. The rite of baptism, however, had to be in Latin – and correct Latin.

---

[19] Illus. in Sheldon-Williams, i.

[1] See de Clercq, *Légis. Relig.*, pp. 285 ff.

Einhard records that Charlemagne intended to introduce some order into the two main legal codes of the Franks – presumably the vernacular Salian and Ripuarian Laws – but lacked the time to get far with it. Alcuin confirms this. But Einhard goes on to say that the emperor actually did cause *barbara et antiquissima carmina* to be written down and thus saved.[2] These were the songs that recorded the deeds and wars of former kings; whether of his own family or of the Merovingians is not stated. Moreover, he started a grammar of the vernacular, perhaps of the Rhenish–Franconian that he himself spoke. This would naturally have followed a Latin grammatical model, such as the grammar of Donatus. But none of this survives. One may feel confident that the *barbara carmina* at any rate would not have appealed to Alcuin; they certainly did not appeal to Louis the Pious, if Thegan is right. There was a large secularity about Charlemagne's mind. It may have been from the Anglo-Saxon mission-field as much as from his Anglo-Saxon confidants at court that he learnt the literary possibilities of vernacular. The impetus to write vernacular still came from the mission-field and to it the emperor had something to say. There can be no doubt that to him, as to all his contemporaries, the language of Christianity in the liturgical sense remained Latin, one of the three sacred languages. It was the language of the liturgy, the mass and the Bible. There was no question of changing it. But the Anglo-Saxons like the Goths had shown that the language of religious exposition could be vernacular; and this was to be encouraged. It was a limited objective. If the same did not apply to his western kingdom it was because Latin of a kind was still sufficiently understood as late as the eighth century, so that there was no pressing need for Romance vernacular to supplant it. Such at least is the inference drawn from the absence of evidence to the contrary. There is no specifically West-Frankish vernacular heritage in Romance. We have to wait till the end of the ninth century for the Sequence of St Eulalia, the first extant piece of literature in Romance. The Strassburg Oaths are rather earlier,[3] but they are not literature. It is significant that the young Frankish noble-man, Gregory of Utrecht, appeared to know insufficient Frankish to be able to expound scripture in the vernacular. Boniface had to help him.

What Charlemagne wanted, and what his directives required, was that not only clergy but also people should in the end understand the Latin of the Church. A proper use of vernacular was a way to this. He needed *boni interpretes*, good expositors, and was certainly not the conscious begetter of Old High German as a literary language. When

---

[2] *Vita Karoli Magni*, ch. 29.
[3] Recorded by Nithard, *Histoire des fils de Louis le Pieux*, ed. P. Lauer (Paris, 1926), bk. 3, ch. 5.

it came to the crunch, the sword was the quickest converter of all. After the sword came tithes, to which Alcuin objected on one occasion; and after tithes some glimmering of Christianity in Germanic guise and a hint of a new social morality. It was a slow business. There is even no clear chronological connection between Carolingian pronouncements on conversion and vernacular conversion-literature, though sometimes it can be suspected. It looks, in fact, as if the literature that we must now consider developed more or less independently of any central directives; which is not to say that the Carolingians were uninterested in the results.

Two early specimens of pagan Germanic verse do survive, copied in the tenth century in a manuscript that is now at Merseburg, near Halle.[4] The same manuscript contains an earlier Frankish baptismal vow, and other liturgical material. There is good reason to connect these Merseburg Charms, as they are called, with Fulda. The first charm is for binding and loosing prisoners; and the second, more elaborate, concerns the curing of an injury to the horse of Baldr by Woden and other gods. One recalls the same motif on the gold bracteates of Sievern that circulated among the Saxons of northern Germany at an earlier date. In fact, it is a charm for curing injuries; and the conjecture is very likely right that some monk interested in medicine, and therefore magic, copied down these two ancient recipes in a convenient manuscript. The same sort of interest is well attested elsewhere and for a long time.

We next come, also at Fulda, to a vernacular heroic lay (or a large part of one) that is unique of its kind: the *Hildebrandslied*, or 'Lay of Hildebrand and Hadubrand'.[5] What is now lacking is the denouement of the duel between what appear to be the champions of two opposing armies, namely Hildebrand and his son. It is a familiar Germanic moral dilemma wrapped up in allusions that cannot satisfactorily be unravelled and recorded in language that is hard to do justice to. If the philologists are right, the original lay may have come from the Lombards in the seventh century and then achieved literary form in Bavaria. At Fulda, it seems, an attempt was made to render the lay into Old Saxon, at least orthographically. It has further been guessed that the intended recipient was one of the Saxon nobles who frequented Fulda and endowed it; but there may have been none outside Fulda. Two scribes copied the text, around the middle of the ninth century, on the first and last leaves of a manuscript that is largely Old Testament;

[4] Text and trans. in J. Knight Bostock, *A Handbook on Old High German Literature*, 2nd edn. revised K. C. King and D. R. McLintock (Oxford, 1976), p. 26 ff. I restrict references to major texts to Bostock's texts and translations, where further reference to other editions and commentaries will be found.

[5] Bostock, pp. 45 ff.

and they copied it as if it were prose, though their punctuation suggests that they recognized alliterative verse when they saw it. Here, then, at Fulda, is something very revealing. Monks copy out a lay that illustrates the mercilessness of Fate and the duty, in the face of it, to do the right thing bravely and regardless of the consequences. Heroic virtue had not been discarded with pagan ritual. A Christian Saxon warrior would need it as much as Hildebrand did, and Fulda monks can appreciate the niceties of the drama and copy it in a scriptural book – unofficially, no doubt, yet without any sense of incongruity. That is what Christianity was like. But the lay is unique, at least to us. Its focus was in the past, not the future.

More significant, if less exciting, are the very large number of vernacular glosses, sermons, hymns and confessions that survive, often in fragments. They can seldom be tied down to particular places on palaeographical or any other ground even when they can be assigned to particular regions. This wide-ranging reach of written vernacular for religious and educational purposes throughout the Carolingian world is of the first significance. As to the glosses and glossaries, their purpose no doubt was to assist the literate to a better understanding of Latin. We identify the greater glossaries by the first word glossed, and thus what is probably the oldest of them is known as the *Abrogans* glossary.[6] In its original form it was probably compiled in southern Germany in the later eighth century, and a possible compiler would be Arbeo, bishop of Freising, who died in 784. His purpose was less to explain meanings than to provide a list of alternatives, Latin and vernacular. Thus his first entry reads 'Abrogans, humilis, aotmoat, samftmoati'. He rather enriched literary vocabulary than provided a dictionary; and he made mistakes. There were special glossaries; for example, a partial glossary of Isidore made by Walahfrid Strabo and apparently based on his notes taken at the lectures of Hraban Maur at Fulda and written up later at Reichenau, where he also did some glossing of the Old Testament. A poet and Latinist as sophisticated as Walahfrid thus turned his attention to the vernacular. Reichenau, like Fulda, was obviously an important glossing centre. There were patristic glossaries and glosses on classical Latin, notably Virgil. One well-known glossary, arranged under subjects and therefore rather personal, is the word-list or *Vocabularius* of St Gallen.[7] Late eighth century, it has been ascribed to the monastery of Murbach, though as is so often the case it is rather the general area than the house that seems clear. Behind it may lie an Anglo-Saxon original belonging to

---

[6] Ibid., pp. 92–7. The glosses are edited by E. Steinmeyer and E. Sievers, *Die althochdeutschen Glossen*, 5 vols. (Berlin, 1879–1922).
[7] Bostock, p. 100.

missionaries, and behind that again an *Interpretatio* much older. This glossing of glossaries was an old game. The practitioners belong anywhere within a wide spectrum of Old High German dialects. Thus we find glosses in Alemannic, Bavarian, East Franconian and Rhenish–Franconian and mixtures of these, sometimes alarming. There can be no question that the great corpus of glosses, when it is eventually explored, will be found to contain matter of the first importance to historians.

Vernacular glossing starts in the late eighth century at St Gallen with the New Testament and Jerome, going on in the ninth to Prudentius, Bede, Caesarius, Hraban, Juvencus, Sedulius and Donatus. Meanwhile Reichenau was glossing St Paul and St Luke. Such activity arose naturally from monastic teaching and developed independently of Anglo-Saxon influences. Perhaps the Irish counted here. The Rule of St Benedict was a natural subject for glosses and several copies containing glosses, complete or not, survive. One famous interlinear gloss-translation of the non-administrative parts of the Rule was made in the earlier ninth century at St Gallen or Reichenau. The dialect was therefore Alemannic. Probably it was intended as an aid for the instruction of monks and was certainly copied in other houses. Alemannic Reichenau also translated a collection of twenty-six Ambrosian hymns, now known as the Murbach Hymns,[8] presumably for the lay congregation to sing. These two were interlinear translations; one does not move too far from the Latin. Reichenau catalogues of the ninth century record *carmina theodiscae linguae* and the like; but liturgical hymns are not *carmina*. What is significant is this clear evidence of the willingness of the reformed Church to encourage the laity to take an active part in worship, and to do so with understanding. That people should understand underlies a large part of all surviving vernacular translation of the period. As with hymns so with baptismal confessions, the creed and the Lord's Prayer, One text, an *Exhortatio ad plebem Christianum*, is a vernacular address to a congregation that needs reminding about the articles of faith, prayer and the instruction of children. South-German in origin, one copy was preserved at Fulda. Instructional matter of this kind may stem from Charlemagne's *Admonitio* or equally well from the personal initiative of bishops. Men like Theodulf, or later Baturic, did not need to be told what to do. The *Admonitio* was never slavishly followed. This is clear in the collection of five texts known as the Catechism of Weissenburg in Alsace:[9] namely, Latin texts with translations or explanations of the Lord's Prayer, the deadly sins, the Apostles' Creed, the Athanasian Creed, and the *Gloria in Excelsis* (not the *Gloria Patri* as ordered by

[8] Ibid., pp. 106–7.   [9] Ibid., pp. 112–13.

Charlemagne). It is a useful compendium, not a literary exercise, whether for teaching backward congregations or for more explicit missionary work. A mission-training centre, possibly a monastery connected with the court, seems to be the source of a fine translation of Isidore's *De fide catholica contra Judaeos*. To its Old Testament evidence for Christ's divinity was added a translation of St Matthew on Christ's life and teaching, and other matter tending to demonstrate Christ's headship of the Church. Composed about the year 800, it appears to belong to West Francia and then to move south. The translator will have had a didactic purpose though his linguistic skill suggests that language itself interested him.

Most of what has so far been considered has little claim to literary merit. This is in part because what survives is so scrappy. It also has the disadvantage of being often enough transmitted as one dialect version of another dialect version. But this is not to say that Germanic dialects were incapable of literary sophistication. Mostly they were being employed, either orally or in writing, for purposes of elementary religious instruction of newly-converted laymen or ignorant clergy. But now and again they faced stiffer tasks. One of these is the Wessobrunn Prayer, entitled *De Poeta* in the manuscript.[10] Wherever it originated, it survives in Bavarian, perhaps from the diocese of Augsburg or near by. Its theme, common enough since at least the time of Virgil but specially momentous in Christian thinking, is the Creation. The manuscript as a whole is a compendium of useful information on the liberal arts, and the Prayer is inserted under arithmetic for the good reason that the Creation affects the calendar and the calendar is an arithmetical subject. The compiler knew what he was doing and the original author of the Prayer was a well-educated man. To be precise, his theme was not so much the Creation as the Creator, whom he invokes. He begins thus, in prose: 'This I heard tell among marvels of men the greatest, that earth was not, nor sky above, nor tree . . . nor hill was. Then was the one almighty God, the most generous of men, and there were also many with him, glorious spirits.' Then comes the Prayer itself in alliterative verse, asking God for faith, goodwill, knowledge, understanding and the power to resist devils. The work could be thought of as a contribution to missionary instruction, for the background to the Creation is couched in terms that pagans would have understood and the whole would fit in with the kind of approach that Bishop Daniel of Winchester recommended to St Boniface.[11] On the other hand, it could be a personal outpouring without reference to wider use. The mind turns, without justification, to the Bavarian Sturmi at Fulda.

[10] Ibid., pp. 127–35.　　　　　　[11] Tangl, no. 23.

With the Prayer may be taken the *Muspilli*,[12] another original vernacular composition that deals with great issues. What remains of it was copied in the ninth century on three blank pages and the margins of a handsome text of the Pseudo-Augustinian *Sermo de symbolis contra Judaeos* and was so copied because of the relevance of one to the other. Since the text was presented by Bishop Adalram of Salzburg to Louis the German it can certainly be associated with Louis's court at Regensburg. The poem has even been written over the dedication. Some think that only the king would have disfigured his book in such a way. Anyone might have done so. The title of the poem is derived by modern scholars from line 57: 'there no kinsman may aid another in the face of the Muspilli'. Nobody knows who or what the Muspilli was. He might have been a personification of the Day of Judgement or Atonement, if indeed he is a person at all. At least the poem's themes are plain enough: the fate of the soul after death, judgement and the cataclysm of the world. These are arranged in the order (1) the soul faces heaven or hell, (2) the unavoidableness of the Last Judgement, (3) phenomena heralding the end of the world, (4) the advantages of doing right and especially of avoiding corrupt judgements, (5) the eternal Judge proceeds to judgement in court. Only fasting and almsgiving count as amends. The Cross and Wounds of Christ will finally be exhibited as proof of what he suffered for love of man. The poem, like its themes, is obviously Christian; and yet it has a flavour that hints at something more basic to the German mentality, now subsumed into its Christianity. The very concept of Muspilli is a case in point. So also is a famous passage recording, uniquely, a battle between Elias and Antichrist, where the outcome is not clear in the text as we have it. 'Yet many men of God believe that Elias will be wounded (or slain?) in the battle. When the blood of Elias drips into the ground the mountains will take fire . . .'. The concept could come quite simply from the Book of Revelation which, with Old Testament apocalyptic material and biblical commentaries, underlies much of the poem. It may also suggest the sort of *Götterdämmerung* that one meets with in later Norse poetry. It certainly has no known single source and is the creation, from whatever materials, of the poet himself. If we call it a Christian didactic poem we have to be careful about what we think a ninth-century German understood by Christianity. He saw redemption and salvation in terms of judgement and battle. To whom, further, is the poet addressing his remarks on just and unjust judgement in the world? He might have been thinking of all judges, or of Carolingian *missi*, or of the king himself. At least we can see that the poem is a major event. A Germanic dialect is well up to coping with a series of

[12] Bostock, pp. 135–54.

difficult theological concepts and giving them dramatic edge. It would not disgrace a king's book.

In the second century AD Tatian had composed a Gospel Harmony or conflated Gospel-narrative in Greek or Syriac. Around 830 the monks of Fulda (Hraban being abbot) translated the Harmony into the vernacular.[13] They used a Latin version though not apparently any Latin version at present known. The only surviving complete copy, probably written in the Mainz area, reached St Gallen. There was something official about this project. It was the work of six skilled scribes, one of whom corrected the whole with much care. Though Tatian was a useful introduction to the Gospel narratives he was not specially popular in the ninth century. Perhaps his chief attraction to Hraban lay in the fact that the founder himself, St Boniface, had provided Fulda with a copy of Victor of Capua's Latin version: a book deserving of some veneration that, with two other books of St Boniface, was still – and still is – at Fulda. Thus there was more than one Latin version of Tatian at Fulda in Hraban's time, and it may be that the vernacular translation was rather a work of piety than of utility.

However, Tatian was one source of another, but different, vernacular venture and at about the same time. This was a poem in Old Saxon called the *Heliand*, or Saviour,[14] though it was not so called by the poet. In fact it is uncertain where the two extant Old Saxon copies were written; Fulda is a possibility for one but so too Korvei and Werden. There are a number of other fragments, including one recently found in Straubing. There survive some 6000 lines; not quite the complete poem but still a formidable epic version of the Gospel narratives. More than most other religious pieces it betrays the poet's resolve to use vernacular words in a Christian context that his hearers would already be familiar with in a secular context: secular, not pagan. An example is *drohtin* or *truhtin* – lord. Nothing suggests that he was stealing words with specific pagan content and applying them to Christ and his followers. He makes no attempt to recast the story of Christ in terms of the Germanic *comitatus*. The military terms of Germanic institutions had already been subsumed in Christian contexts and could be applied to Christianity without affecting the traditional doctrines of the Church. Christ can be called 'the ring-giver' and his disciples 'ring-friends'; the shepherds can turn into horse-herds and the feast of Cana into a splendid Saxon carousal – all without disturbing the narrative. Indeed, St Paul had long since shown the way by seeing the faithful as soldiers of Christ. The poet, then, does not germanize the Gospel story. What he does is to accommodate it to a Germanic public, somewhat as St Luke accommodated it for another

[13] Ibid., pp. 157–68.   [14] Ibid., pp. 168–83.

public when he hellenized it. He can stress the lessons that would appeal to the ninth century – for example, the lesson of loyalty – and minimize what would not appeal. He obviously does not believe that Christ entered Jerusalem on an ass. Neither did Hraban believe it. St Peter in particular appealed to the poet, who sees him as a soldier caught in a web of disloyalty that he bitterly regretted. One scholar concludes that the most that can be urged against the poet's orthodoxy is that he emphasizes the conception of Christ as king and teacher rather than as sacrifice and judge. But even this was not unorthodox in the ninth century. We must accept the fact that those responsible for teaching Christianity to the Germanic world succeeded just in so far as they could make the Gospels dramatically viable. Their weapon was the vernacular. The *Heliand* marks something of a climax in its employment, and it is a very splendid literary achievement. All that can be said of the poet is that he was a cleric and a widely-read one. Apart from Tatian he could use the commentaries of Hraban on Matthew, Bede on Luke and Alcuin on John; and of course the Gospels direct. It is possible, but no more, that Louis the Pious himself may have taken some initiative in causing the poem to be written. There was certainly a ninth-century belief that he had ordered a Saxon to write poems dealing with the Old and New Testaments. The *Heliand* might be part of the response; and another part might be what remains of a long epic built on Genesis, which survives largely in an Old English version and only partially in Old Saxon.[15] If this is so, the *Heliand* poet produced an enormous epic. Possibly the whole of it reached England – it has been suggested, as a gift on the marriage of Charles the Bald's daughter Judith to King Aethelwulf in 856. It does not follow that the *Heliand* itself was translated into Old English. More interesting is the demonstration of the flow-back of teaching in literary vernacular from the continent to England. The *Heliand* remains one of the major achievements of the Carolingian renaissance.

Another glory is the Gospelbook of Fulda-trained Otfrid of Weissenburg,[16] under whom the monastery's scriptorium flourished in the mid-ninth century, possessing a large library of its own. Of the poem of over 7,000 rhyming lines on Christ's life we still have four contemporary or near-contemporary copies, each with a separate dedication. One of them, written by five scribes, may have been corrected by Otfrid himself. He adds his name to the poem, which is something new for the vernacular and reveals his pride in his achievement. The dedications are to Louis the German, Bishop Salomo of Constance, and two of his St Gallen friends, Hartmut and Werinbert. He also inserts an explanatory letter to his metropolitan, Liutbert of

---

[15] Ibid., p. 184.   [16] Ibid., pp. 190–212.

Mainz; but this, very properly, is in Latin. He points out that his poem is not a Gospel Harmony. Then he gives the archbishop a synopsis: the five books deal with Christ's beginnings, the significance of the coming of Christ, Christ's miracles and teaching, the Passion, and finally the Resurrection and Day of Judgement. He has, he adds, selected his material with care and has had to ómit much. His chapters (or some of them) are headed *spiritaliter, mystice* or *moraliter*. In other words his interpretation is orthodox. So too is the reading that lies behind it. There is nothing innovatory about his theology. How should one expect it from Fulda? What is new is his shaping of Gospel material as vernacular narrative and his use of direct speech. It is a vivid performance. Whatever the practical use of his work, he meant it to be literature. Indeed, the heading of his opening chapter explains this: 'why the writer of this book has employed vernacular'. He wants to give his folk a worthy piece of Christian literature in their own language, such as others had. Why have the Franks alone failed to praise God in their own tongue? They are a wonderful people (how many times had they been told that?) but yet had failed to develop their language for literary purposes: all they could manage was obscene songs. And now Otfrid has been encouraged to remedy the defect. He writes for educated men who know how to think and who can be encouraged through the vernacular to read more for themselves. Moreover, he combines learning with piety with great technical skill; something which no one had hitherto attempted in German on such a scale.

Like the *Heliand* poet, Otfrid moved within the Germanic thought-world of warrior–ethos, loyalty and obedience, the lord–man relationship. Obedience was not characteristic of the reciprocal association proper to a chieftain and his followers in the classical *comitatus*; but it was indeed characteristic of the settled society of the ninth century, and of the Church itself. None of this affects Otfrid's treatment of doctrine. It only affects the way he looked at the obligations of men to God, which were not unlike those of the same men to their earthly king. Otfrid's God claimed obedience; that is clear. So equally did Christ, also a king, though unlike other kings he chose to die for his subjects. However, the Last Judgement would not be like the judgement of an ordinary king. Earthly bonds, like earthly possessions, will have disappeared; and above all, there will be no kindred or powerful friends to assist. Each man must stand or fall on his own merits. This had been said before, but never in a virtuoso performance in the vernacular. In the end, one's impression is that Otfrid's poem would have been too stiff a dose for ordinary teaching, let alone conversion. It looks much more like a glorious attempt to recast the Gospels and their lessons into contemporary thought-patterns for which the vernacular was best suited. It offered a conceptual framework in which further reading of the Gospels might be attempted: a bold literary experiment, and dedicated (at least in one copy) to a king.

Round these solid monuments cluster the penthouses of the vernacular; numerous and in the aggregate weighty. There are many minor religious poems; among them, and typically, a hymn in Bavarian to St Peter entered in a Freising copy of Hraban's commentary on Genesis; a hymn to St George, honoured at Reichenau; and a St Gallen hymn to their founder, which survives only in a Latin translation. The inference must be that the Church, especially in the south German monasteries, now accepted the vernacular as much more than an aid to conversion or instruction. It could enrich the whole liturgy.

One curious survivor that does not belong to this class is the *Ludwigslied*,[17] a poem of fifty-nine lines of rhyming verse celebrating the victory of Louis III over the Vikings at Saucourt in 881. Royal victories of this magnitude were rare and a comfort when they did occur. Saucourt seemed a great matter to the annalist of the neighbouring monastery of St Vaast of Arras.[18] The poet held the view common to many clergy that the Vikings were the tool of the Almighty: 'he let heathen men journey across the sea to remind the Frankish people of their sins'. God addresses the king thus: 'Louis my king, help my people. The Northmen have them hard pressed.' Then the king rides forth and addresses his army: 'whoever does God's will here with courage, if he comes out of it alive, I will reward him for it, and if he does not survive I will reward his family'. So 'the king rode bravely forth and sang a holy song, and all together they sang *Kyrie eleison*. The song was sung, the battle begun, blood shone in cheeks, the Franks romped there. There every warrior fought, but none like Louis: swift and brave, that was in his blood. This one he hewed through, that one he ran through. He at once poured out bitter drink for his enemies; so woe to them for ever!' In fact, it was by no means for ever. The poet must have been writing immediately after the victory; and the king himself died the following year. The poem ends: 'praised be the power of God. Louis was victorious. Thanks to all the saints. His was the triumph. Hail again to Louis, our fortune-blessed king' (*salig* is the word used). 'As ready as he has always been wherever there has been need of it, may the Lord in his mercy save him!' Bostock, whose translation this is, goes on to comment that 'the poem

[17] Ibid., pp. 239–48.

[18] *Annales Vedastini*, s.a. 881 (ed. R. Rau, *Quellen zur karolingischen Reichsgeschichte*, ii, Berlin, n.d.), p. 300.

is a glorification of the Church Militant, and of the king its servant'. But in fact the poet is seeing the king as God's direct instrument, not the Church's. There is a difference. The poet is a cleric, living in a threatened world where kings all too seldom come to grips with the pagan Vikings who ravish the Frankish Church. This is God's punishment for the moral shortcomings of a whole people, for which the only expiation is penance. Kings should lead their people in penance and then go forth with God's blessing to slaughter the enemy. This is what Louis does. He may indeed be doing the work of the Church but primarily he is leading an army of warriors in defence of his realm. It is an entirely secular matter; the Church does not come into it; but God does. The role of the king as God's direct instrument was never blurred in the ninth century by the fact that he had been consecrated by, and was in some sense answerable to, bishops. It is possible that the poem was recited at court. Built round a new heroic theme, it glorified the victory of yesterday, not of some far-off Germanic past. The language of the poem is not Old French (which happens to be the language of the St Eulalia sequence preserved in the same northern French manuscript and written by the same scribe) but Rhenish-Franconian. The poet could presumably have written his song in Latin. There would have been precedents for this, as for example the poems celebrating Pippin's Avar victory in 796 and Louis II's adventure at Benevento in 871. Even more relevant might be the Old Testament. But the poet chose Rhenish-Frankish. It was the right vernacular for his heroic tale, and one must suppose that Louis III's court would have followed it with relish. What it highlights is the value of the vernacular as a literary vehicle. The victory of a Christian king, so much hoped for, is best celebrated in a Germanic dialect.

One last poem is, as it happens, in Latin and may in its extant form be no more than an exercise, even though it comprises 1,456 hexameters. Unlike the *Ludwigslied* it tells a heroic story of Germanic tradition, known also in England, Scandinavia and even Poland. It is the story of the journey home from the land of the Huns of Walter and Hildegunde, and particularly of the attempt of a band led by Gunther and Hagen to rob them.[19] In the end the pair reach their destination, which is Worms. They marry, and Walter succeeds his father as king. Several traditional motifs of Germanic epic crop up: the return from exile, the exercise of valour and guile, the problem of divided loyalties. It is in fact an old tale told with some up-to-date Christian moralizing by a monk who is not very conversant with his material, though fairly well read in some of the classical and Christian Latin poets. Quite possibly a vernacular epic about Walter was the back-

[19] Bostock, pp. 259–70.

ground to the poem; something like the Old English *Waldere*, which is incomplete.[20] The poem we have could have been written at any time in the later ninth or earlier tenth century, and the writer was certainly a German, apparently with St Gallen contacts. He takes a Germanic lay or lays, perhaps only known to him orally, adds some Christian colouring and writes in the language of his Church and of educated men familiar with Virgil. It reminds us that the vernacular was not supplanting Latin but supplementing it. There remains the possibility that he had a complete Walter-epic in front of him and did little more than translate it into Latin. It deserved translation, if only as an exercise. One could move from Latin into vernacular but also from vernacular into Latin.

By the close of the ninth century literary vernacular was still in its infancy. A splendid period lay just ahead; at St Gallen, for instance, with Notker Labeo, translator of the Psalter, the Book of Job, Boethius and much else. Beyond that lay the age of the *chansons de geste* in France. There is no evidence for the employment of written vernacular in the early stages of the conversion of Scandinavia; that is, the period beginning with the mission of Archbishop Ebbo of Reims, sponsored by Rome and by Louis the Pious in 822, and going on to that of Anskar of Hamburg-Bremen, organized by Wala of Corbie and recorded by Rimbert in an admirable biography; but in Latin. The conversion of Scandinavia had not got far by the early tenth century, and this probably explains why there were no Scandinavian clergy capable of using their vernacular as a literary aid in the mission-field.

Looking at the overall achievement of Germanic vernacular in the ninth century, one is equally struck by the speed of its development and the variety of uses to which it could be put. It is astonishing that it could produce work of high sophistication in so many genres so quickly. It fast becomes so much more than a mere aid to conversion and to instruction of ignorant clergy and monks. It becomes literature, both poetry and prose, and those who write it are proud of what they are doing. Always, even in the eyes of those who wrote the best vernacular, Latin remained the true language of religion and civilization; but vernacular was now another literary language of Christians, not pagans, and was to remain so.

[20]   Ed. B. Dickins, *Runic and Heroic Poems of the Old Teutonic Peoples* (Cambridge, 1916), pp. 56 ff.

XVI

THE CHURCH AND SOME
UNSOLVED PROBLEMS

i. The Jews and Their Religion

MORE than paganism or any heresy, the Jews worried the conscience of medieval Christians and quite painfully so in Carolingian Europe, with its high sense of the Church's destiny. The reason for this was neither social nor moral, and certainly not racial: it was religious. Jews on the whole lived peaceably in their communities among Christians. They were industrious, adaptable, orderly and intelligent. The trouble was that Judaism met Christianity half-way; they shared the Old Testament. It was not uncommon for Christian commentators on the Old Testament to turn to the rabbis for expert advice. St Jerome had done so, and Hraban Maur frequently acknowledged help from a 'Hebraicus moderni temporis'. But then the Jews rejected what to Christians was the whole purpose of the Old Testament: to witness to the coming of the Messiah. Despite this rejection, Christians could not wash their hands of Judaism. The people of the beloved Old Testament had been Jews. St Augustine had advanced an additional argument why God tolerated the continued existence of Jews – why, in fact, most of them were destined never to be converted to Christianity: they were permanent witnesses to the historical beginnings of the Faith, blind men holding a lantern for others; that is, for the New Israel that fulfilled the mission which they had rejected. Augustine therefore looked upon the Jews with a mixture of sorrow and respect. This, the patristic attitude, lasted among Christian thinkers for several centuries. The days of vilification and persecution lay a long way ahead, and in fact are scarcely noticeable before the ninth century; and even then bear no comparison with the ferocious anti-Jewish polemic from the time of the crusades. No doubt the heretical problems of the ninth century formed a general religious solvent that made the Jewish faith seem menacing in a new way.

We must be clear about what did not distinguish the early medieval Jew from his neighbours. In the first place, language did not. The Jew spoke the language of those he lived among and used Hebrew in his synagogue. Before at least the eleventh century he did not necessarily bear a distinctively Jewish name. Neither did he wear distinguishing clothing before about the same time. In an early eleventh-century manuscript of the Pentateuch he appears wearing a peculiar round hat, and this looks like the start of a local tradition perhaps confined to England and Flanders. Later, he was to acquire a pointed hat. Above all, the Jew had no distinguishing occupation. Clearly there were Jewish merchants in the early middle ages, no doubt handling large amounts of money; but there were also Jewish physicians and farmers and craftsmen and sailors; and it is impossible to know whether any one occupation predominated at any one time or place. French cartularies from the ninth century contain good evidence of small Jewish farmers working their own land. One suspects that farming had for long been an entirely characteristic occupation. In the towns the Jews carried out the normal duties of citizens, taking up arms to defend their walls irrespective of the identity of the assailants. Thus they played a big part in the defence of Naples against the Byzantine mercenaries of Belisarius, as also of Arles against the Burgundians. At Arles indeed they were allotted a special section of the wall to defend, which may argue that they lived together in a quarter abutting on that section. But if they did so live, it was voluntarily; the earliest known Jewish ghetto was at Speyer, where in the year 1084 the bishop allotted them a separate quarter so that, as he put it, they could escape the insolence of the people. He built a wall round their quarter, and that made it a ghetto. Popes agreed with bishops that Jews should not be physically attacked. So, in 599, Gregory the Great pointed out to a zealous convert to Christianity that when the enemy is at the gates it is no time for attacking Jews.

Nor was there any doubt about the legal position of Jews under Roman Law. Forty-nine laws affecting Jews directly were included in the Theodosian Code, all enacted after the State had become officially Christian. Jewish religion was to be tolerated though the building of synagogues was restricted and proselytism forbidden; if a man were not born a Jew he could not become one. Conversion from Judaism to Christianity was of course encouraged. In all other respects Jews and Christians were on an equal footing in the eyes of the law. Further, Roman Law recognized Jewish Law: that is, the code of cult-regulations proper to Jews and based on the Old Testament, the Talmud and rabbinical decisions over the centuries. Thus it was never seen as personal law in the same way as Frankish or any other Germanic law. In brief, the Jew was a full Roman citizen; everyone knew, as the *Interpretatio* of the Theodosian Code boldly put it, that Jews were Romans. It is significant that it was thought necessary to say so. The legal standing of Jews and their right to practise their religion thus seemed secure in Roman eyes; and indeed their legal position was to remain an imperial concern, and this the papacy acknowledged. Their business dealings with Christians were not interfered with and it does not appear that they were regarded as outsiders or foreigners on account of their religion in the Germanic successor-states. However, the good times were unlikely to survive the disintegration of Roman Law. The mood changed.

The position of Frankish Jewry in the sixth century is deftly sketched in by Gregory of Tours, himself a bishop. He relates how on Ascension Day the citizens of Clermont had been over-stimulated by their bishop's attempts to convert the local Jews and rushed upon the synagogue, which they destroyed. The Jews cannot have been greatly comforted by the bishop's reassurance – 'I do not drive you by force to confess the Son of God.'[1] Again, when King Guntramn entered the city of Orléans he took exception to the loyal shouts of the Jews, observing that they only did it in the hope that he might order the rebuilding of their synagogue, destroyed some time since by the citizens.[2] Such outbreaks of local violence might easily be whipped up, no doubt partly inspired by jealousy of the Jews' success as survivors and by their maddeningly dogged community of belief. Jews lived and prospered within walls that stood under the protection of saints whom they would by no means propitiate. They at once belonged and did not belong; ordinary men and women who, unlike heretics and schismatics, could rouse other ordinary men and women to frenzy. This atmosphere made it possible for one Merovingian king to take active anti-Jewish measures. The chronicler Fredegar reports that Dagobert I was persuaded by the Eastern Emperor Heraclius to have all Jews in his kingdom baptized, which he proceeded to do.[3] This sounds implausible. It might be no more than a generalization from the known fact of a forced conversion of Jews by Bishop Sulpicius of Bourges between 631 and 639. But Fredegar was not always wrong; his story seems to have what looks like independent confirmation from the later *Gesta Dagoberti*.[4] At any rate, Frankish Jewish communities in the seventh century were not immune from attention, nor in the sixth. Gregory has a long story of how the Jewish merchant Priscus, with whom King Chilperic had dealings, was on one occasion in danger of forced baptism.[5] Certainly Chilperic believed in forced conversion and indeed stood godfather to many so converted. It may not have been easy to draw the line between forced and willing conversion, particularly when the converted could pay formal respect to Christianity but privately continue to observe the Sabbath. It was a problem not confined to Francia. It was in towns that the Merovingian Jew had

---

[1] Hist. v, ch. 11.
[2] Ibid., viii, ch. 1.
[3] Chron. iv, ch. 65.
[4] MGH SRM ii, p. 409.
[5] Hist. vi, ch. 5.

most to fear from over-zealous bishops and citizens quickly stirred up to synagogue-smashing.

Things went from bad to worse under the Carolingian Church with its passion for uniformity. One might as well have expected Calvin to show restraint. Yet the Jews remained useful to kings. Louis the Pious, of all people, legislated to protect them, though the legislation has not survived. We only know of it because it is referred to in one of his letters of protection for Jews.[6] In fact the Carolingians were prepared to do a good deal for Jews, to the dismay of the Church and particularly in the South, where Jewish communities were strongest. The bishops of Lyon tried their hand at some anti-Jewish measures of their own which the crown refused to sanction. These continued to enjoy some publicity under the bogus title of 'Charlemagne's *capitula* against the Jews'. But other bishops with less of a Jewish problem in their cities kept quiet; and it is significant that some of the most important canonical collections of the ninth century have little to say about Jews. None of them has a special section devoted to Jews such as might suggest that they were a pressing problem within the reach of legislation. Yet individually they plainly were a problem. Hence the steps taken by Louis the Pious to make sure that when local justice worked unfairly towards them, such cases should be brought to his notice and settled 'in our presence'.[7] There was even an official called the *Magister Judaeorum* whose business it was to see that this was done. Kings continued to act thus. The Emperor Henry IV ratified the establishment of the bishop of Speyer's ghetto but added that he personally reserved the right to take particular Jews under his direct protection. The bishop was acting by delegated authority.

At no time was the Roman principle denied that Jews had a right to practise their own religion and to observe their own law in so far as it regulated their religious life. That is to say, they could in principle keep their sabbath and the appointed feasts and fasts, and stick to their own dietary regime. And they could teach in their own schools, which they did with marked effect. The only Jewish religious ceremony that was at all likely to impinge on the Christian populace at large was their burial service, with its processions and chanting. Almost everything else happened within the synagogue; and this could give no offence so long as the synagogue were not too near a church. Indeed there is little to suggest (except in Spain) that Jewish religious practice was seriously interfered with in the early middle ages. It did happen once at Naples; and this brought down on the bishop a sharp rebuke from Gregory the Great, who reminded him that Jews had the legal right to observe the

---

[6] MGH Legum Formulae, no. 32, p. 311.
[7] Ibid., p. 310.

solemnities handed down to them by their ancestors, and that interference with their services was no way to win converts. Synagogues
were licensed by public authority and to some extent protected; necessarily, since they were the first target of any local Christian rioting and
were not always repaired. But if Jewish cultus interfered hardly at all
with Christian life, the converse was not true. Jewish masters were
strictly bound to see that their Christian employees were free to
observe Sundays and the feasts of the Christian year, and were sometimes even required to do so themselves in the interests of civic unity.
In practice the Jewish minority of citizens who took no part, or an
unwilling part, in Christian celebrations were automatically marked
off from the majority and to that extent isolated.

These were some of the ways in which law and custom defined or
protected or restricted the lives of Jews, and basically they had been
inherited from the Romans. They betray a keener interest in the
practical relationships of Jews and Christians living together in urban
communities than in the theoretical position of Judaism versus
Christianity. The practical difficulties seemed to increase; the presence
of Jewish enclaves became more and not less of a problem, and not
only in the old centres. As towns grew up in ninth- and tenth-century
Germany to become centres of trade and defence, Jews moved in and
were invited to do so. Thus old problems persisted in new settings.
But when we leave regulations behind and seek to find out how in
practice Jewish–Christian relationships worked, we have to turn to
southern France and Spain, where Jewish communities were strong
enough in numbers, and probably in wealth, to make themselves felt.

In southern France the Jews had gathered round trade centres since
Roman times. Not all were in business but all, whatever they did,
tended to congregate for protection and to practise their religion in
cities like Lyon, Narbonne and Bordeaux, with a preference for the
Mediterranean coast. Judging from the decrees of church councils it
looks as if their communities were prosperous. Their members did
occasionally marry into Christian families while remaining deeply
attached to their religion. There was as much likelihood of conversion
from Christianity to Judaism as the other way about, and this despite
every barrier the Church could devise. Often they were landowners
and thus employers of labour, free and unfree, Christian and non-
Christian. Some of their tombstones survive, as for instance from
seventh-century Narbonne, with Latin inscriptions followed by an
invocation in Hebrew, such as 'Peace upon Israel'. Till Carolingian
times south-eastern France north of the Pyrenees (i.e. Septimania) was
in Visigothic hands, and thus the Jews of the region lived under
Visigothic control exercised ultimately from Toledo. But Toledo was

a long way south and Septimania had a tradition of independence, not to say unrest. In 673 the Septimanians rose in revolt against the Visigoths, under the leadership of a Duke Paul. King Wamba marched north and dealt with the trouble. The campaign is vividly described by a contemporary, Archbishop Julian of Toledo.[8] He was as bitterly anti-Jewish as a child of parents converted from Judaism was likely to be. What is interesting is that he describes the rebel Paul as a Judaizer and attributes Wamba's difficulties in Septimania to Jewish activity. One cannot be sure whether the Septimanians favoured Frankish control as an alternative to Visigothic but the Frankish seemed rather less hostile to Jews than did the Visigothic. Once the Carolingians had conquered Septimania in the eighth century they showed a certain degree of understanding of Jewish problems. There are charters of protection to prove this, both for individuals and for groups of Jews.

There is a further important aspect of the life of western Jews particularly noticeable in southern France. It is that the Jews cherished in one form or another their messianic tradition. They looked to an eventual triumph, and they looked abroad. The ancient Jewish patriarchate of Jerusalem, once recognized by Rome, had not been forgotten. There were in addition various forms of local Jewish leadership, especially in the East, which together demonstrated that Jews considered themselves to be dispersed nuclei of a people inspired by a single purpose. Ultimately this purpose might take political shape though immediately it did not affect their loyalty to the overlords among whom they lived. For practical purposes their *patria* was where they happened to have settled. The Septimanian Jews had their local hierarchies and dynasties of chief men who transmitted royal commands to their communities and represented their interests to the overlord, whether Visigothic, Frankish or Arabic. They had a yet deeper significance for the faithful. They encapsulated the sense of Jewish unity, of a group isolated within a larger and hostile group; and to this larger group they could speak, while keeping in touch with Jewish leaders in the East. The greatest of these last was the Jewish exilarch who lived under the protection of the caliphs of Baghdad. From the mid-eighth century the Baghdad caliphs were of the Abbasid dynasty, whereas the Arab rulers of Spain belonged to the older Umayyad house. Their mutual antagonism led to a *rapprochement* between the Abbasids and the Carolingians. The Frankish Jews fell in with this. They too had something to gain from an Abbasid connection since the Jewish rulers in Baghdad lived under Abbasid protection. Thus far the Carolingians and their Jews shared common

[8] MGH SRM v, pp. 500–35.

ground. It would not of course follow that Carolingian rites of unction and coronation, with their Old Testament parallels, owed anything to Jewish influence; they stemmed solely from the Church and not from any imagined rabbinic pressure. Charlemagne or Louis the Pious could see himself as a second David leading a new Chosen People without for a moment supposing that he was a new kind of Jew. Augustine had long ago pointed out the danger involved when a good Christian thought it only logical to call himself *Judaeus* or *Israelita*, as the true heir to the Children of Israel. Even so, rites of Old Testament lineage betrayed no hostility towards Jews.

Umayyad Narbonne fell to the Franks in 759, so bringing the Carolingians into direct contact with the largest and most articulate group of Jews in Septimania. It is a question whether the Jews actually helped in the surrender of the city to the Franks. One view, expressed in contemporary sources, is that the Visigoths in the city brought about its surrender in return for a promise of self-government. Another, chiefly found in later sources, is that the Jews caused the surrender, also in return for a promise of self-government under the local Jewish leader or Nasi. It is likely enough that the Visigoths did indeed play the principal part, perhaps with Jewish support. The outcome was that the Septimanian Jews enjoyed a more privileged status after the surrender than before; and not only them but also the Jews of northern Spain who fell under Carolingian control. This in its turn inevitably caused agitation among Catholic clergy. It further distressed Pope Stephen III who wrote a letter to the archbishop of Narbonne, making the point that Jews were now getting favourable cessions of land, some of it ecclesiastical. It is not very likely that these new proprietors had a military role as defenders of the Spanish March. Certainly there were Jews in the armed forces but the higher military echelons remained solidly Frankish. A twelfth-century Jewish writer claimed that after the fall of Narbonne the Carolingians recognized a new Jewish ruler there, of the House of David. This ruler was named Makhir and he had been sent to the West by the caliph of Baghdad. There is said to be more evidence to the same effect in late Arabic and Jewish sources. However, there is no hint that Jews were ever politically, let alone militarily, predominant in Septimania. The Franks, firmly in control, had some interest in mollifying local Jewish sentiment: it is not impossible that they did allow a Jewish potentate to come from Baghdad to Narbonne. What title he bore is neither here nor there. Plainly he was no autonomous king. At best, he and his family were a dynasty of high-born eastern Jews acceptable to Septimanian Jews and equally to the Franks. The mainstream of Septimanian-Jewish cultural and spiritual life still led back to Abbasid Baghdad, not to Umayyad Córdoba; and there is evidence that the Jews of Narbonne were alert to the implications of that life.

They were alert to the messianic tradition; namely, that a Jewish king would continue to reign somewhere until the coming of the Messiah. This entailed that the Christian claim for the messianic role of Christ could be denied so long as a Jewish king was believed to rule. Their exegesis rested on Genesis 49: 10: 'the sceptre (sc. of royal power) shall not depart from Judah nor the ruler's staff from between his feet until Shiloh cometh'. Whether or not the Septimanian Jews thought of their local chieftain as such a king, there were other candidates for the title in the East, of whom they may have been aware. A possibility was the Jewish kingdom of the Khazars on the Black Sea coast. One can thus appreciate that the Church had matters for consideration apart from Jewish landholding and possession of Christian slaves. There was something active in the spirit of early medieval Judaism. Christian apologists took this seriously. Isidore of Seville and Julian of Toledo were equally alarmed at the implications of the Jewish Messiah argument; it had been a firm ground of Christian teaching that the native kings of Judah had disappeared with the coming of Christ. In the ninth century the matter was further pursued by Paschasius Radbert, who wanted to know what evidence there was of the existence of a Jewish king anywhere. The question would not have been asked if there had been no ground for worry. Later still, Peter the Venerable persisted in being worried: 'as for myself, I do not accept that king whom some of you claim to have in Narbonne, others in Rouen; and I will not accept a Jew as king of the Jews except one residing in and ruling over the kingdom of the Jews'[9] – by which he meant Palestine. There will have been something behind this. Medieval Christendom was not nearly so sure of itself as is sometimes thought. So far as the earlier middle ages were concerned, Jews could have been forgiven for holding that the coming of their Messiah might not be far distant.

Military control of the Spanish March was entrusted by the Carolingians to their kinsmen, the family of William of Toulouse. There is no case whatever for the recent claim that this great clan married into the leading family of the Narbonne Jews. It is enough that the ninth-century viceroys of the March made use of local Jews both as merchants and soldiers, and observed the terms of Carolingian protections issued in their favour. We do not know the extent of Jewish landholdings in the March or the number of Jews in relation to the total population. Perhaps they overstepped the mark and obtained too many favours from the viceroys. For whatever reason, there was a

[9] PL 189, col. 560.

strong reaction against all Frankish Jews from the 840s. This can be seen both in conciliar legislation and in polemical writings, of which the most notorious were Agobard's five books,[10] which included an attack on the Talmud, and Amolo's *Liber contra Judaeos*.[11] Amolo's contribution was a collation of anti-Jewish legislation together with a consideration of the Messiah controversy. What chiefly worried him seemed to be the publicity given to a recent debate in Spain between Albar of Córdoba, son of two Jewish converts to Christianity, and a Christian convert to Judaism named Bodo, formerly a deacon in the service of Louis the Pious. Bodo had left court with the emperor's blessing and a good retinue, ostensibly bound for a pilgrimage to Rome. Instead, he crossed the Pyrenees to Saragossa and became openly what he had long been by conviction, a Jew. He then changed his name to Eleazar. Presumably he had been converted by Jews at or near the imperial court. The Arabs tolerated him to the extent of permitting him to try his hand at conversion among the Spanish Christians. His technique was successful enough to cause them to appeal to Louis's successor, Charles the Bald. They needed support of some kind though we cannot tell what came of their appeal. We should know little about Bodo's arguments if they had not been quoted in Albar's rejoinder; and this only survives in one mutilated manuscript.[12] As Amolo took up the argument at Lyon, one begins to see why the Albar–Bodo debate could have repercussions far beyond Spain. The bishop mistrusted the Jews at two levels. First, they had now so infiltrated the city-populations of Francia that the distinction between them was in practice hardly observable; and secondly, their polemical skill was such that they were winning converts, including important people. Despite this, the Carolingians were still protecting Jews, though in fact the Spanish March and southern France were the only regions where they seemed to have prospered under royal protection. These naturally were the regions that most felt the weight of anti-Jewish polemic by Christian apologists anxious to protect their flocks. These very flocks had been the ones most exposed to the impact of heresy. They were an emotionally unstable people. Yet there was also some anti-Jewish feeling in the north; it is clear enough in the St Bertin Annals under Prudentius, himself a Spaniard. There had even been signs of the same feeling as far west as Vannes in Brittany and as long ago as the fifth century.

One is left with the impression of spasmodic outbreaks against Jews throughout the Carolingian world, sometimes intense, as in the Rhône valley and Septimania, but never enjoying royal approval.

---

[10] PL 104, cols. 69–114, 173–8.   [11] PL 116, cols. 141–84.
[12] Ed. J. Madoz, *Epistolario de Alvaro de Córdoba* (Madrid, 1947); PL 121, cols. 478–514.

Many bishops would have been easier in their minds if they could have roused Carolingian interest in the matter. The situation was very different in Spain, of which passing notice must be taken if only to point the contrast with the Frankish north. Here the Jewish enclaves were even stronger than in Septimania; but their lot was no mere endurance of pinpricks, with church councils periodically reaffirming prohibitions as to mixed marriages, slave-owning and conversion. The Visigothic kings went much further. With the seventh century came royal orders for the baptism of all Jews under pain of banishment and confiscation, rather to the surprise of a Church that had no experience of forced baptism and foresaw what would happen. A Jew then was no longer one who openly practised his faith but a formal Christian of Jewish antecedents who observed the Sabbath in secret. There was no looking back. Anti-Jewish measures became increasingly draconian, especially as they affected children. The religion of the Jews went underground. It was a tragedy for the Church as well as for the Jews, for it was compelled to administer its rites to those it knew were revolted by them. The sacred magic of baptism was cheapened. Even worse, this was known to happen nowhere else. The popes raised objections. Some Jewish refugees reached Rome, where they were allowed to practise their religion, while more escaped to Frankish territory or crossed from Gibraltar to Islam. King after king added to the corpus of anti-Jewish Visigoth legislation, always savager and always failing. Their threats were even directed at bishops who aided or protected or concealed Jews suspected of apostasy. Wherever the Spanish Jew went he was under surveillance. The more he professed to be a Christian the more he was suspected of being no such thing. Finally in 694 they were deprived of all their possessions, reduced to slavery and dispersed over Spain to masters designated by the king. They had nothing more to hope for, and twenty years later were understandably tempted to fight by the side of the Arabs against the Christian Visigoths. One asks why a succession of kings should have legislated as they did against Jews when their own Church would have favoured a more traditional approach to conversion. The answer is that the kings feared Judaism in an intensely personal way. Apart from their numbers and wealth, Spanish Jews enjoyed contacts with foreign parts, as to which the Visigoth kings were more sensitive than were their Frankish contemporaries, perhaps with some reason. But beyond this, every Visigoth king was horrified that he should rule over people who denied the New Testament, and expressed this feeling with extraordinary vehemence. It was not for nothing that the Visigoths had abandoned Arianism and accepted Catholicism in 589. Jews stood ideologically apart. Kings and councils repeatedly expressed dismay that their benevolent intentions met with no response. The Jews did not want to be done good to. It was unforgivable. Who can tell what pogroms would have resulted if the Arabs had not intervened? Certainly the Arabs must have seemed kind masters to all Spanish Jews after the Visigoths. Active supporters of the advancing Arab armies, Jews were permitted to practise their religion freely, only paying the taxes that fell on all tributary peoples. Some were converted to Islam; many more contented themselves with learning to speak Arabic. There is no discernible trace of anti-Jewish feeling among the Arabs of Spain before the eleventh century and no persecution till an even later date. Christians on the other hand faced greater difficulties, as witness the fate of the martyrs of Córdoba in the mid-ninth century. This was still fresh in men's minds when the monk Usuard visited Spain. Meanwhile the Jews flourished, comparatively speaking, in commerce, finance, diplomacy and administration; and they were certainly active in the international slave trade, though not to the exclusion of Christians who could break into the market. This much makes plain how different was the fate of the Jews of Spain from that of their brethren living under the Franks.

However impressed one is by the enormous endurance of Jews under this particular form of persecution, it would be wrong to think that they were merely passive. There is another side to the story that may in part explain the Christian reaction to them. Jews, like Christians, had a mission. In the *Collations* of John Cassian, written in the fifth century, is the following strange story:[13] a Mesopotamian monk, in the course of a severe fast, had a dream in which he saw Jewish and Christian armies locked in combat. The Jews won. As a result, he had himself circumcised next day and became a Jew. Cassian's book was widely read in the middle ages. The story bore witness to the fact that Judaism was always on the march and always had its attractions. It could win converts piecemeal but also on a big scale, as among the Berbers of Africa. In the West it sought to win over not regions or classes but groups or individuals, as chance afforded. The obvious candidates were the slaves who worked for Jewish masters. These were consistently subjected to pressure. A slave so converted bettered his condition under Mosaic Law, indeed rather to his master's detriment. The attractions of Judaism were more than a chance of social improvement for a pagan slave; they equally affected Christians – and Christian clergy. The risk of such apostasy was not negligible, which was why the deacon Bodo fled to Spain, preferring life under the Arabs to what Louis the Pious might have done to him. Another convert, Archbishop Andrew of Bari, fled to Egypt. Yet another,

---

[13] PL 49, cols. 535–6.

John of Oppido, was imprisoned but escaped to Islam under the name of Obadiah. Moreover, Jewish teachers were quite willing to debate with Catholics, and even to provoke them to debate. For this reason the Church prepared its own manuals of answers to difficult questions about the veneration of saints, the cult of images, belief in miracles and the failure of the Church's universal mission of peace. One trouble was that the Church already met the Jews half-way by attaching so much importance to the Old Testament: if the Jews of the Old Testament were indeed the People of God in Christian eyes, why not the modern Jews, too? Agobard of Lyon fastened on this point and admitted that the Jews of his city were more successful at winning converts among the Catholics than the other way about. His successor, Amolo, added a further reason for this: the Jewish rabbis preached so much better than the Catholic priests.

But preaching of an elementary kind was not going to win over educated Catholics. To get at them the rabbis equipped themselves by mastering Catholic theology and apologetic, and learnt to present their arguments with a degree of irony and raillery that infuriated their opponents. Not much of the written polemic survives; Jewish books were for ever being hunted out and burnt, at least from the seventh century. Gregory the Great on the other hand had ordered the authorities at Palermo to restore to the Jews any books seized from synagogues and not to worry themselves about the contents. The only remaining way of assessing the importance of Jewish polemic is through the large quantity of anti-Jewish polemic that does survive. Julian of Toledo's treatise against the Jews was compiled, he says, because not to say anything might result in the loss of Christian souls.[14] He thought he might not succeed in convincing the Jews but at least he might assist Christians. But there also survive fragments of the anti-Christian polemic of two converts to Judaism. One of them was Bodo, to whom we must turn again. The most interesting point he makes concerns the diversity of Christian practice. He alleges that he had witnessed no less than fourteen distinct Christian observances at Aachen. Perhaps Louis the Pious experimented, as Charles the Bald certainly did. Bodo argues from experience that Christians behave more or less as they wish and believe what they wish to believe. They know nothing of the simplicity and certainty and unity of orthodox Judaism. How would Charlemagne have reacted to such a judgement on a half-century of reform? To this Bodo adds a tremendous messianic perspective, firmly based on Ezekiel, to demonstrate that the best guarantee for a bright future is the darkness of the present; and part of

---

[14] Ed. J. N. Hillgarth, *Sancti Iuliani Toletanae sedis episcopi opera*, i (CC cxv, 1976), pp. 143–212, with important introduction; PL 96, cols. 537–86.

the brightness will properly consist in divine vengeance on Christians. A second piece of polemic came from the pen of a Jewish physician in the suite of the Emperor Conrad II. His line was to attack the doctrines of the Trinity and of the saints.[15]

Yet another polemical venture of more durable influence, and circulating at least by the ninth century, was the *Toledoth Yeshu*, a Gospel parody designed to show that Christ was a normal man who suffered a conventional execution; though in fact it burgeons with interesting extraneous detail. In brief, the writer's aim was to defuse the story of the Passion, and this at a time when the Passion was moving to the forefront of Christian teaching. It was a story so vividly told by the Evangelists that it was said to move even Jews to compassion. To make it prosaic by representing Christ as a misguided Jew of no special importance shook people.

Apart from polemic, Judaic liturgy and practice could be made to seem more attractive than their Christian counterparts. For example, instead of a morsel of bread parsimoniously distributed at mass by the priest, the Jew got what by comparison amounted to a banquet every Friday evening, which all the family attended; not a symbol but a reality. Then again, presents were distributed on feast days and a genuine rest imposed on the Sabbath. No wonder Christians were forbidden to join in Jewish feasts, especially in Francia where relations were easiest. When the poor Bulgars were converted to Christianity in 866 they naturally assumed from a first reading of the Old Testament that they could expect a good time on the Sabbath and were pained to learn from Pope Nicholas that they were in for no such treat:[16] Sundays and Sabbaths were quite different. Somehow the Sabbath seemed more attractive. How necessary it was to keep simple Christians uninfected by so much jollity.

But there was yet more to it. Given the chance, Jews were not above persecuting. Bodo himself begged the Arabs to offer Spanish Christians the alternative of conversion to Judaism or Islam, or death. His own nephew was forced to become a Jew. Much pressure could also be exerted by Jewish masters and officials on those under them; and it was exerted. This was one reason why the Church objected to Jews holding office under the crown. We think of the Church as an all-powerful organization efficiently deployed over the countryside. It was no such thing. Parish clergy in the ninth century were desperately thin on the ground and wonderfully ignorant. Hence the anxiety of the Carolingians to increase the number of clergy and improve their education. Thus a Jewish landlord who meant to convert his depend-

---

[15] Anselm of Liège, *Gesta epis. Leod.* 44 (PL 142, col. 735; SS vii, 216; xiv, 112).
[16] MGH Epist. vi, no. 99, 568–600.

ants might encounter little or no opposition, especially where his slaves were in question. In the end, the surest proof of the success of Jewish efforts at conversion is the weight of Christian legislation and polemic directed against it. The Christian case is put more directly and urgently than the calm denunciations of the patristic age. The general arguments of the Fathers are subsumed by the ninth-century Church and at the same time particularized. The Jewish mission worked quite well.

It must be repeated that the Jew's distinctiveness rested in his religion. Christian writers of the early middle ages did not distinguish him on grounds of appearance. It is true that Jews grew their beards, but so too did many Christians. It is also true that under Islam Jews wore a distinguishing kind of belt, and in ninth-century Arabic Sicily they wore a white badge with an ape on it. But this was not within Christendom. Nobody describes a Jew as being physically unlike a Christian. There remained the Jewish religion; a religion that was not simply un-Christian but shared uncomfortably much with Christianity. It was the cruellest of all rejections. The Church was far from being in a position to meet the challenge effectively in every town and village where there happened to be Jews. This was why it seemed vital to the survival of the Christian polity in the ninth century to expose Judaism, to isolate it and crush it whenever possible. It is only when we grasp how frail was the hold of organized Christianity and how various its practices that the reaction to Judaism makes sense.

ii. *The Church and the Marriage Bond*

There is a fundamental issue, already referred to in passing, that demands further consideration: what did the Frankish Church make of the relationship of men with women within marriage and outside it? The answer cannot be found in the legislation of the Church, though the guide-lines were there. If it could be, there would be no problem. As it is, one must look also at the opinions of those whose duty it was to implement legislation at the diocesan level; and these opinions differed. In brief, there was something here that defeated uniform application of the decisions of the Church; and hence the responses of churchmen to a large range of human problems fit uneasily into the application of the Carolingian programme of reform.

When it came to the relationship of men with women the Church was heir to the fast-held traditions, often expressed in legislation, of Roman and Germanic society; traditions that it was either unable or unwilling to modify to any great extent. This was inevitable. The lot of men and women was to marry. Roman Law had been perfectly clear about the civil contract involved, the nature of the marriage bond and the position of children born in wedlock. It was an association freely entered upon, marking the transference of the woman from the *potestas* of her father's family to that of her husband's, and its principal object was the procreation of children. There was nothing here that the Church could object to. Whatever the form that marriage solemnities might take, they were and remained secular or, in legal terms, civil. Moreover, they applied exclusively to those who were free. The unfree did not marry: they merely achieved the hazardous condition of living in *contubernium* at the pleasure of their masters. On this the Church was to have other thoughts. It was equally to have other thoughts on the matter of dowry, which to the Romans meant the dowry brought by the woman to her husband and not, as in Germanic practice, what the husband provided for his wife. All at least agreed that dowry was a constituent part of marriage.

Germanic, and specifically Frankish, tradition differed from the Roman in some important respects. In the first place, the woman herself seemed to present certain problems. A foretaste of this emerges in Tacitus. He says[1] (what Caesar confirms) that the Germans believed their women to possess a spiritual power denied to men; they had a divine spark of foreknowledge and thus their advice was not to be overlooked, even on military questions. Aside from her natural gifts and abilities, the Germanic woman was a prophetess. So, too, were Celtic women; and the two came together in western Europe to fuse into a formidable female instrument for plumbing the unseen. Moreover, she was a healer. For good or ill she was associated with magic. What seemed true to Tacitus was certainly true in the centuries that followed. Married, the Frankish woman held the honour of two kindreds in her keeping: her husband's and her father's. In this respect the wife's responsibility was the greater and the risks she ran if she dishonoured either kindred correspondingly greater. Thus burdened, she was no mere chattel. She could hold and administer land, defend herself in the courts, act as compurgator, make donations and free her slaves if she wished. The higher her social rank the likelier it was that she would carry many other responsibilities than care for her household. In short, a queen was an honorary man. Germanic law even as late as Charlemagne remained concerned about the connection of women with magic. Thus, *Lex Salica* did what it could to protect women from unjustified charges:

if somebody calls someone else a follower of witches, that is, one who helps them (e.g. carries the cauldron in which they brew) and cannot make good

---

[1] *Germania*, ch. 8.

the allegation, let him be fined 2500 *denarii*; and if a charge of witchcraft is brought against a free woman and is disproved the fine is tripled; and if a witch is proved to have eaten a man the fine is 8000 *denarii*.[2]

It is fair to say that men as well as women could be sorcerers and magicians but they were never the real experts and had a more limited range. They lacked enterprise. One could trace this suspicion of women through the pages of Gregory of Tours to the time of that unhappy emissary of Satan, the Empress Judith. Specialists in the occult, moral degradation dogged their steps. It can at least be said for their accusers that the stability of the family, its good name and the purity of its blood, appeared to rest upon the woman, not the man. She it was who was required to be watched over at every stage of her life. The sexual *mores* of the man, married or single, were a matter of small account, while those of the woman were vitally important.

The Church was thus heir to a body of secular legislation and at the same time to a highly-charged atmospheric condition. The Fathers of the Church can scarcely be said to have made matters easier. Tertullian in the early third century had written of woman as the gateway of the Devil, the unsealer of the forbidden tree and the first rebel against the divine law. He was thinking of Eve, but the Bible also provided unsavoury examples in Jezebel and other notorious women. The good ones were really only good despite themselves. Augustine, most widely read of the Fathers, had no doubt that women were by the fact of their sex more depraved than men, though he had sensible things to say about marriage. Unlike his contemporary, Jerome, he did not rail against sex and at the same time keep on intimate terms with well-born and highly intellectual nuns. Jerome's *Vita Malchi*, a *historiam castitatis*, was as powerful a plea to women to retain their virginity as could well be imagined. The Fathers were thus in an awkward position: the function of sex was unavoidable, and within the Church women could be useful and even holy; but women's sex was the Devil's favoured instrument. The Penitentials could insist that no menstruating women should enter a church; nor might women enter a church for forty days after childbirth. They had to be purified from natural functions they could not avoid. But behind the Church's misogyny lay something else: the medical profession was equally troubled about women, even in Antiquity. It seemed to physicians that male domination was Nature's intention, to the extent that the birth of a girl pointed to some defect in her parents. In the second century Galen, a brilliant practical anatomist, gave much thought to the problem of female inferiority and traced it to a physiological

[2] *Lex Salica* 64.

difference; namely, that a woman, sexually considered, was neither more nor less than a man turned inside out. In this way classical medicine and patristic teaching reached much the same general conclusion; and in any case God was a man, not a woman. Everyone knew that.

However, there was a more positive aspect of the Church's approach to the dangers and snares inherent in womanhood. Virginity was a good in itself. Indeed, it applied to men as well as to women. A virgin could save others from temptation but at the same time do something for herself and for society. It was much more than a lucky escape. Augustine was clear about this in his *Soliloquies*. If it was meritorious for a man to escape the snares of woman by remaining virgin, it was more meritorious for a woman to spring her own trap and withdraw from the hunt; for she saved not only herself but men as well. Naturally more lustful than the man (so ran the argument), the woman made the greater sacrifice. The ascetic woman had her ideal in the Virgin Mary, whose cult had its beginnings in the Early Church but was not to reach its climax till the eleventh and twelfth centuries. In the fourth century there were signs of liturgical interest in the Virgin, and in the fifth appeared panegyrics on the Mother of God and her essential virginity, often preached at Christmas. By the sixth century particular occasions in the Church year were allotted to her praise: the nativity, the purification, the annunciation and the assumption. The Emperor Marcian, anxious for relics of the Virgin for Constantinople, applied to the bishop of Jerusalem for her body. Much surprised, the bishop replied that her body was in heaven; and the emperor had to content himself with relics from the tomb. Along with this went elaboration of legends about the Virgin, much of it orally transmitted. One apocryphal work, the *De Transitu Mariae*, was banned by Pope Gelasius; but the feast of the nativity was part of the Roman liturgy by the seventh century, when an inscription on an altar-table from Ham, near Coutances, records the dedication of a church 'in mid-August, in honour of the blessed Mary'. The Virgin was thenceforth the object of widespread cultus and elaborate manifestations of veneration; churches were dedicated to her, her feasts regularly observed and her relics sought after. To venerate the Mother of God as the greatest of the saints was indeed to venerate virginity, but also motherhood. Hence the importuning by Charles the Bald of Maria Genetrix as 'the most prolific Virgin'.

The Early Church had accepted that a woman could take a vow, privately or publicly, to remain a virgin; and if publicly she submitted to ecclesiastical discipline. Virgins were soon to live together in communities. The parable of the ten virgins could suggest that there was safety in numbers if you wished to be wise. Moreover, not to be married to a man was in a sense to be married to Christ; and this mystical union could be expressed somewhat after the normal terminology of marriage. The nun's *velatio*, or initiation, was a kind of marriage ceremony that made her relationship to Christ quite unlike that of man's relationship. It took account of her sex. Virginity was thus a vital step for a woman in a long spiritual adventure: she joined an aristocracy that had a role to play for society in general. None of this was lost upon the thinkers of the early middle ages. The Church was as proud of its virgins as it was concerned about its married members.

For the Church, the problems raised by marriage never centred upon the rites of marriage. From the fifth century certainly, and perhaps earlier, a ceremony of blessing of nuptials was known and available. Paulinus of Nola described such an occasion in a long set of verses.[3] He did not speak of a nuptial mass, though one existed, but of a blessing; a blessing that was clearly a privilege and no constitutive part of a contract that was essentially civil. In 866 Pope Nicholas went so far as to inform the Bulgars that *consensus* alone made a marriage: no other usage, religious or civil, was inescapably necessary.[4] No canonical collection of the early middle ages insists on benediction. Nevertheless, such benedictions were sought and obtained in Francia, though they do not seem to have been bestowed according to any generally-recognized liturgical formula and were in theory reserved for couples that could prove pre-marital continence. It is true that a nuptial *ordo* was designed in 856 for the marriage of the Anglo-Saxon Aethelwulf with Judith, daughter of Charles the Bald;[5] but this was an altogether exceptional occasion involving a coronation as well as a marriage. It was no precedent for common folk. At the same time, however, it constituted one of several indications that the Frankish Church felt an increasing obligation to participate in marriages. All that the synod of Verneuil had asked in 755 was that marriages should be publicly celebrated to give better opportunity for the avoidance of marriages within the prohibited degrees.[6] The Church was still a long way from insisting on nuptial benediction of any kind. It was far more anxious to ensure that the civil forms had been complied with. If any of them had not – for example, if a couple were subsequently shown to have married within the prohibited degrees – then there had been no marriage. No question of divorce (always difficult) arose. Certainly the Carolingians agreed with the Church that a marriage legitimately entered upon was effectively indissoluble. No liturgical provision existed for divorce: it merely had to be recognized in certain rare cases.

[3] *Carmen* 25 (CSEL 30). [4] MGH Epist. iv, pp. 568–600.
[5] MGH Capit. ii, ii, no. 296, pp. 425–7. [6] MGH Capit. i, no. 14, p. 36.

Thus no liturgical provision existed for marriage itself, let alone divorce. The Church recognized that two persons claimed, by reason of free assent, to be married: its further judgement, a moral one, was confined to the question whether they should continue to live together, and whether sanctions in the shape of penance or excommunication should be invoked to force them to separate. Frankish conciliar legislation as affecting marriage was in consequence much taken up with problems of separation; a couple, namely, should or must live apart because their marriage had been vitiated from the start and was null. Whether persons so separated could marry again was an even more difficult question. Adultery in particular could cover not merely the immoral relationship of one of a married couple with a third party but equally the proof of incest or of union with a person consecrated to God. The uncertain use of terms (e.g. *separari, solvere, dimittere*) is proof enough that Carolingian clergy were as hesitant as their Merovingian predecessors about what exactly was involved in their decisions. At least they seemed clearer that careful examination before marriage, and prohibition if necessary, was a wiser step than dealing with trouble afterwards. It was not easy even to determine the prohibited degrees of consanguinity since this turned on whether one were reckoning in Roman, Germanic or canonical degrees. This mattered less often in preventing unions than in assessing what should happen once consanguinity had been acknowledged; for upon the degree of relationship would depend whether separation after penance could be followed by remarriage. It was a minefield, and could not be otherwise in a society where civil and Germanic usages continued to exist in what often looks like total confusion. Abduction, for example, was very differently viewed according to civil or Germanic tradition. In the latter it was regarded as one possible step towards a marriage which both kindreds could be brought to accept. But it was a step less easily accepted by Carolingian clergy than by Merovingian. Slowly and under many pressures the Frankish clergy examined cases involving marriage as they cropped up and, using what canonical precedents they had, reached and recorded their decisions. As a result, the Church can be said to have extended its interest in and control over many aspects of marriage. It did so willingly.

Where the Church in council moved with caution, individual clergy called upon for opinions moved much more so; indeed, with little appearance of certainty. This one can find reflected in their *specula conjugatorum* or mirrors of marriage composed privately to meet particular needs. At least they agreed, as good Carolingian clergy, that society was or should be conceived as grouped into *ordines*, each with its own specific function. One function of the lay order was to marry.

Marriage was therefore a basic consideration for clergy who aimed to display their characteristic virtues and vices to the laity, much in the manner in which they held up appropriate mirrors to monks and kings. Those most likely to attract advice of this kind were naturally aristocrats; hence Paulinus of Aquileia's *Liber Exhortationis* for Heiric of Friuli,[7] Alcuin's *De virtutibus et vitiis* for Wido of Brittany,[8] and Jonas of Orléans's *De institutione laicali* for Matfrid of Orléans.[9] Responsible public men such as these might all benefit from specially structured essays on family morality among other topics; but they might not all receive the same advice, and their advisers might take different views of the patristic heritage on which they drew. Public men would be liable to the vices of pride, cruelty and violence: where better to seek a remedy than in the sage conduct of married life? Here lay the *remedium luxuriae*; a *remedium* that, so far from urging the recipient to abandon the machismo of his order, accepted the moral hazards involved and presented an attractive counterpoise in his family life. It called for heroism of a kind, a battle against the flesh with spiritual rewards. The winner would be the man who schooled himself to practise temperance in sexual intercourse and take seriously his responsibilities to his family. Such a man would have learnt *castitas* – but not the *castitas* of a monk. He would have found in marriage less an incitement to sex than a damper on it which, even at the lowest level, would bear fruit in added robustness and healthier heirs. It was all very practical.

When churchmen ventured to offer more positive advice than had their predecessors on marriage and its consequences it followed that they had also to pay more attention to the role of women. St Jerome's diatribes on the weaker sex would no longer do; women were something more than daughters of Eve, *auctor culpae*; they were the equal partners of their husbands. Of course they had their special sins, as temptresses; but so did men, liable as they were to make off with women without anyone's leave. Jonas of Orléans was particularly insistent on equality within marriage,[10] and for this he could find much support in conciliar legislation from the mid-eighth century onward. And the fruit of free and equal partnership was children to bring up as members of a Christian society. Too often the Church had had to fulminate against abortion, contraception and infanticide. It could now define a role for child-bearing that went beyond the mundane business of projecting the family into the future. In such a

---

[7] PL 99, cols. 197–282.
[8] PL 101, cols. 613–38. Cf. L. Wallach, 'Alcuin on virtues and vices', *Harvard Theol. Rev.* 48 (1955), pp. 175–95, or ch. xii of *Alcuin and Charlemagne* (Ithaca, 1959).
[9] PL 106, cols. 121–80.   [10] Ibid., cols. 170 ff.

context the irksome business of foreseeing impediments to marriage before it was too late, and then ensuring that marriage was effectively indissoluble, made even more sense than in the past. Yet the fact remains that this heightened concern resulted in nothing that could be called a sacrament of marriage. The eucharist, penance and above all baptism could excite constant liturgical attention among Carolingian clergy; these were sacraments that were understood, and understood to need careful theological examination and much exposition. Marriage was otherwise. One looks in vain for any reference to it in, for example, Amalar's *De ecclesiasticis officiis* or Walahfrid's *Libellus*; both of them books in which one might expect to find notice taken of the sacrament of marriage if there were one. On the contrary, bishops had no formal instruction to offer their clergy, beyond the warning that marriage festivities were occasions of regrettable licence.[11] One can only conclude that they found themselves faced with an insurmountable barrier of secular tradition. It was enough to indicate the duties of the married state and hope for the best. Hincmar clearly defined the Christian view of marriage, as understood by Carolingian clergy, in his admirable *Epistula de nuptiis Stephani*,[12] a report to his colleagues on the case of a young man who had had second thoughts about his marriage to the daughter of the powerful Count Raymond when he discovered that his former mistress was related to the bride. The archbishop goes into the case with all the thoroughness he devoted to the divorce of Lothar II but reaches a different conclusion. Beyond the social aspect of marriage he sees a Christian mystery that reflects the Incarnation and Christ's marriage with his Church; and he sees it much as Augustine had seen it. Marriage, in a word, was a *signum* of the great and true mystery of Christ's incorporation in the Church, a promise of salvation, a unique and irreversible gift. He is thinking of it in a way that suggests how close he was moving to a sacramental definition, without quite getting there. His contemporaries would not have found this surprising; for they too came up against the moral barrier of secular usage. All things considered, they had got remarkably far from their patristic heritage towards the full medieval concept of the role of marriage in society.

Saints' Lives yield a respectable crop of evidence on the trials of the virgin, the anxieties of her parents, the lot of the married woman and the sad condition of widowhood. The case of St Rictrudis is of special interest. The Life of this Merovingian lady was written in the first years of the tenth century by Hucbald of St Amand.[13] He describes the

---

[11] e.g. Hincmar, PL 125, col. 776.

[12] PL 126, esp. cols. 137–8. A better text in MGH Epist. vi, i, pp. 88 ff.

[13] PL 132, cols. 829–48; also AA SS May 3, 81–9, and the dedication letter in MGH SRM vi, pp. 91–4.

stages of her marriage to Adalbald, a Frank in the service of Dagobert: her *desponsatio*, endowment and acceptance by her husband after due enquiries had been made, as custom required. His suitability is attributed to his *virtus*, blood, good looks and wisdom; and hers is much the same, except that she also has wealth. All this added up to an honourable marriage and an immaculate bed; and thus they became one flesh; they had achieved *unanimitas in domo*. Hucbald is describing very much what Hincmar saw as the exemplary Christian marriage. They had four children before the husband's assassination caused Rictrudis to take the veil, which Dagobert clearly considered a waste of a very desirable candidate for a second marriage. For forty years she remained in the abbey of Marchiennes, where she died and was buried in 687. Her marriage as described had been a thoroughly secular affair, conducted on approved principles; but widowhood led to the cloister, not a second marriage. Hucbald does not suppose that the couple had received a nuptial benediction but he does see their marriage as conforming to the Christian requirements of his own day.

In its groping towards some moral control over the society it ministered to, the Carolingian Church did not overlook marriage. Without discarding the ideal of virginity it faced facts as they were and attempted to see beyond the secular roots of marriage a Christian dimension that was a good in itself.

iii. *Exterae Gentes*

The Church's sense of mission is as old as the Church itself. As it grappled with domestic problems – the definition of orthodoxy, the search for the seat of authority, the protection of property – and at the same time with heresies within its borders and opaque amalgams of Christianity and paganism beyond them, it never lost sight of its true goal: the conversion of real pagans. This sounds, and was, aggressive. Often combined with requirements of military and political security, it was yet distinct from them. Father Serra, bravely pushing up his mission into eighteenth-century California, would have understood eighth-century missionaries better than we can. It was so much the quickening spirit of the Frankish Church that it demands separate consideration and must come to the fore at the last.

The Merovingian Church was alive to its missionary duties even when least able to fulfil them. Mostly it looks like private enterprise, the appearance of right men at right times, occasionally with royal support. Some of these have already been touched on. The regions obviously inviting missionary intervention lay to the north and the east of the Frankish realm; and they continued so to lie, far beyond the

days of the Merovingians. One recalls the efforts of Aquitanian and
other missionaries on the Lower Rhine and the approaches to Frisia; of
men like Eligius of Noyon, Kunibert of Cologne, Bavo of Ghent and
St Amand, bishop with a general mission; and at the same time of the
largely-unchronicled advance of the Franks east of the Rhine and up
the courses of the Main and the Neckar. A Frankish settlement meant a
church. Not much later came the better-known missions of the Anglo-
Saxons and Irish, of *peregrini* as devoted as Wilfrid, Willibrord,
Boniface and Pirmin. None of these could have moved without
Frankish support and Frankish sympathy for their aims. Rome under-
stood this. If missions to the pagans were conducted by others than
Franks, the Frankish Church was the beneficiary. Now and again one
glimpses more active Frankish collaboration. A case in point to which
Levison drew attention was the possible collaboration of the Anglo-
Saxon missionaries in Frisia with the monastery of St Wandrille. The
Life of Bishop Wulfram of Sens (written about 800, that is, a century
after his death at St Wandrille) hints at the connection.[1] The bishop
himself may have been a missionary; more certainly he urged on the
community of St Wandrille to take active measures. The Life alleges
that they had some success, and it has further information about
Frisians living in the monastery, 'for among you to this day dwells the
venerable priest Ovo, native of Frisia, who relates how the holy
bishop wrought miracles through Christ's power among his people'.
The Frisian connection seemed so significant to the author of the Life
that it would be as foolish to doubt it as to accept much else that he
writes. On the other hand, a Frankish sortie without ecclesiastical
backing need not result in conversion of the subjugated. When the
Frankish merchant Samo established his principality among the
Wends it appears that his Christianity lapsed, if credence may be
placed in Fredegar's dramatic account of the buccaneer's interview
with Dagobert's representative.[2] Samo was no missionary, and
wanted none. When all is said, missionary work under the Merovingians
lacked finish.

The story is quite otherwise under the Carolingians. Certainly they
faced greater threats from the pagan world and possibly were better
attuned to them since their homelands lay nearer the threats. It is thus
tempting to see Charlemagne's campaigns in pagan territory as a
simple military response to Saxon and other threats to outlying
Frankish settlements, and even to the Rhineland itself. In part they
certainly were. Einhard, however, having been brought up at Fulda,
saw things rather differently, as did also the Royal Annals: 'the
Saxons, like most Germanic peoples, were naturally ferocious and

practised the cult of demons, always hostile to our religion and seeing nothing dishonourable in violating and transgressing human and divine laws'.[3] The Saxons inevitably identified Frankish aggression with Frankish religion; the two went hand in hand. But Saxon ferocity was at least equalled by Frankish. Charlemagne's measures to extirpate paganism and substitute safe Christian enclaves left nothing to chance except the possibility of instant results. Saxon patriotism was long to be associated with memories and remnants of the paganism of its golden age. The language of Charlemagne's two Saxon capitularies is quite unlike that of the later crusader cutting his way through pagans to the rescue of Holy Places. He is interested in the pagans themselves and intends to use his sword to compel them to be Christians. This is abundantly clear from certain clauses of the first capitulary, no doubt promulgated after the baptism of the Saxon chieftain Widukind in 785. They run thus:[4]

1. It is pleasing to all that the churches of Christ now built in Saxony and consecrated to God shall be honoured not less but more than have been the temples of idols.
3. Whoever makes violent entry into a church and forcibly or secretly steals any object or burns the building shall die.
4. Whoever despises Christianity by slighting the Lenten fast and eating flesh shall die, though the priest shall take into consideration whether it was done through necessity.
5. Whoever kills a bishop, priest or deacon shall die.
6. Whoever, deceived by the Devil, follows pagan practice by believing a man or woman to be a witch and eats human flesh and cooks it . . . shall die.
7. Whoever cremates a dead person following pagan ritual and reduces the bones to ashes shall die.
8. Henceforth, any unbaptized Saxon who conceals himself among his people and refuses to seek baptism but rather chooses to remain a pagan shall die.
17. According to God's commands we further order that all shall give a tenth part of their substance and income to the churches and priests – nobles, free and unfree shall return in part to God what God has given to every Christian.
18. There shall be no public meetings or *placita* on Sundays except in cases of grave necessity or attack, but all shall go to church to hear the word of God and give themselves to prayer and good works. So also on the great festivals . . .
19. All children shall be baptized within their first year. Whoever refuses to have a child so baptized, without the knowledge or dispensation of a

---

[3] *Vita Karoli Magni*, ch. 7.
[4] MGH Capit. i, no. 26. A second capitulary, ibid., no. 27, was milder.

priest, shall pay a fine of 120 *solidi* if he is of noble birth, 60 if a freeman, 30 if unfree.

21. Whoever invokes springs or trees or groves and makes offerings to them like the pagans, or holds a feast in honour of demons, will be fined . . . If such people can genuinely not pay at once, they shall work for the church until the fine is fully paid.

22. We order that the bodies of Christian Saxons shall be taken to church cemeteries for burial and not to pagan *tumuli*.

Measures like these were ill-advised because they were practical. When it is specified not merely how a man shall worship and not worship but how he shall deal with his children, spend his money and bury his kindred, one is reaching to the roots of society. They are the measures of a king who intended to add a whole new people to the *Regnum Christianum*. There was nothing haphazard about it. No reverses, no number of assassinations and burnt churches, deflected the Carolingians. Slowly their ecclesiastical organization penetrated the whole of Saxony in the shape of a series of missionary zones controlled by Frankish bishops and abbots, and this at a time when the Frankish Church itself was dangerously short of trained clergy. Sees with Saxon responsibilities included Mainz, Utrecht, Würzburg, Liège and Metz certainly; Reims and Châlons possibly. To these must be added monasteries: Fulda, Hersfeld, Corbie and Ferrières among them, and particularly Corbie's Saxon daughter-house of Korvei. Sees within Saxon territory emerged painfully enough from 777, when Charlemagne laid the foundations of an ecclesiastical organization for the Saxons, till well into the ninth century: Hamburg, Hildesheim, Halberstadt, Osnabrück, Münster, Verden, Minden, Paderborn and especially Bremen. The missionary clergy of these latter days lacked the heroic aura of the generation of Willibrord and Boniface, but they were formidable men, whose attraction to the mission-field cannot be explained in terms of colonial expedience. It was dangerous work. However, the missionary-clergy of the ninth century in Saxon territory had at least the comfort of feeling that their settlements were 'twinned' with well-established centres in safer places.

Hamburg–Bremen constituted a particularly sensitive missionary complex because of the nearness of the Danes. One can see the entire region between the Elbe and the Eider as a Frankish March designed to hold a frontier; but it was more than that. Representatives of Danish kings, first Godric and then Harald, arrived in Francia to seek Charlemagne's support. It was not to be conceded except in return for permission to pursue missionary work in Denmark; but what one Danish faction could allow might be nullified by the other. A remarkable attempt at penetration was organized in 822 by Ebbo of Reims, assisted by Halitgar of Cambrai. Their plans had the support of both the Frankish and papal courts. Pope Pascal I enjoined them to keep him fully informed and to refer back to him any matter requiring special consideration. Bishop Willeric of Bremen joined them. They had moderate success *ad terminos Danorum*, at least to the extent of baptizing some Danes; but nothing more could be done among warring factions. Ebbo came home. No doubt to forestall his rival, Harald decided to seek baptism from Louis the Pious, and at Mainz the ceremony was performed with much splendour.[5] Ermold describes the scene at length, attributing both to Harald and to Louis speeches that they perhaps did not make. Harald prefaces his surrender of the demons with a neat summary of Trinitarian doctrine, concluding 'such, most loving Caesar, is the religion that the holy bishop Ebbo said was yours. Relying on him and enlightened by his teaching I now believe in the true God and renounce my idols. Hence am I come to your kingdom in my ships, to become one with you in faith.' The emperor then stands godfather to the Dane, Lothar to his son, and Judith to his queen. 'O noble Louis, how many are the faithful you have brought to God! How sweet the savour that your action wafts to Christ! You have seized a whole people from the wolf's jaws, to give them to God!' The description of the celebrations and exchange of gifts goes on. But Harald left a hostage behind him on leaving. A whole people was far from converted, or even likely to become so. But to the Franks it seemed a great occasion and one need not doubt that Ermold captured the flavour of it.

A missionary was dispatched north with Harald, the monk of Anskar of Corbie, and then of Korvei. The year was 826. A remarkable account of Anskar's mission into Scandinavian territory was later written by Rimbert,[6] who succeeded him as bishop of Hamburg–Bremen and was himself to be the subject of a workmanlike biography. Better here than anywhere else one can sense the perils facing Frankish missionaries on their own, insecurely supported both by local kings and by the court at home. The continuing interest of Ebbo, Wala and a few others near the emperor was no substitute for a settled base and guaranteed protection on the spot. So we find the indomitable Anskar pushing on with a series of brief missions both in Denmark and in Sweden, winning a few converts, bringing comfort to and perhaps ransom money for Frankish captives, and enduring reverses. If the chances of permanent success were no better than they had been more than a century earlier, when the Anglo-Saxons entered Frisia, the evidence of royal interest is more striking. It mattered

[5] *Ermold le Noir, poème sur Louis le Pieux et épitres au roi Pépin*, ed. E. Faral (Paris, 1932), pp. 170 ff.

[6] Ed. G. Waitz, MGH SRG in usum schol. (1884).

greatly to Louis the Pious that a Christian mission should gain a footing in the far north. The dominant sentiment of Rimbert's Life of Anskar is pride. Here was a man who could trust his life to Harald, recruit young Danes for future instruction, accept the leadership of a still more perilous mission to Birka in Sweden, win over a Swedish courtier who was even able to build a church, and finally return to found at Hamburg a provincial see on the northern frontier of the empire expressly equipped to watch over missionary work in Sweden, Denmark and the neighbouring Slavs of the western Baltic coast. Thus, consecrated by Drogo of Metz and commissioned by the pope, he faced his task with no military backing and no suffragans. This was no state-directed enterprise in any sense remotely modern. In its way it was a braver venture than that of Boniface. Hraban Maur, safe in Fulda, watched with interest the progress of Gauzbert, Anskar's first appointment to a bishopric in Sweden; it was a credit to everybody at home. But it could not survive; neither Gauzbert nor Anskar himself could make progress against pagan reaction and the social instability that now accompanied Viking ventures. Hamburg was sacked, the church lost and a library destroyed. The first northern mission was at an end. Scandinavian liturgies made no room for Ebbo, Anskar and Gauzbert before the late middle ages. Behind much fuss had trembled the beginnings of a small-scale enterprise. But it pointed the way to how matters might be tackled in a more favourable climate.

The second major area of Carolingian missionary endeavour lay to the east and had Bavaria for its starting-point. Fully Christian since at least the beginning of the eighth century, Bavaria had been the home of Irish and Frankish missionaries working from Freising, Salzburg, Regensburg and Passau. St Boniface had been concerned here with organization, not conversion. The work had been achieved with the support of the Bavarian dukes and of a succession of popes. However we view the contribution of Boniface (and opinions differ as to its extent) there can be no question that a clear Bavarian diocesan organization functioned after his visit in 739 and not before. The days of wandering Irish clerics were past. The process was completed by the appointment of Arn as archbishop of Salzburg and first Bavarian metropolitan in 797; that is, after Charlemagne's subjugation of Bavaria and removal of the ducal dynasty. The extraordinary activity of the Bavarian *scriptoria* is proof enough of the intellectual vigour of the whole region in the eighth and ninth centuries. Arn himself laid the foundations of a noble library at Salzburg. His colleagues at Freising and Regensburg soon followed his example. The initiative was thus episcopal. It was also monastic. Bavarian monasteries, for example Benediktbeuern, seemed moved by a new spirit to accumulate biblical, liturgical and ascetic texts and to explore, as we have seen, the possibilities of the vernacular. To this extent the Bavarian Church was singularly well equipped to undertake missionary work.

A vast missionary objective lay to hand in the Slavs, whose ill-recorded migrations into central Europe had been completed in the seventh century. It is at once obvious that their settlements, stretching from the Baltic to the Balkans and lying astride the Danube, cut off land communications between the Frankish world and the Byzantine. Nor were they particularly placid. They had been followed by the non-Slavic and warlike Avars, who oppressed them and provoked their further movement but were beginning to be seen as paper tigers before their final defeat by Charlemagne. The immediate Frankish–Bavarian response to a threat of this order on the eastern frontier could only be military; and it is the military rather than the missionary aspect of this response that affected the record of the Fulda Annals, our best western literary source.[7] What is astonishing is the reach of the Frankish arm eastward into Balkan regions where Byzantine interests would naturally predominate; not so much as a systematically conquering force as one perpetually stemming revolt, supporting one Slav chieftain against another and founding ecclesiastical establishments as and when possible. Tassilo III, last Bavarian duke, certainly planned a mission to the Slavs after a visit to Rome. It was he who halted the Slav advance into the eastern Bavarian Alps. In 769 he founded the monastery of Innichen in the wastes between the rivers Inn and Drau, presenting it to the abbot of Scharnitz 'in order to lead the unbelieving Slavs into the way of truth'. He followed this up in 777 by founding the more important house of Kremsmünster in the Traungau for the conversion of the Carinthian Slavs. Missionary activity within the first great loop of the Danube on its way to Vienna and Budapest was henceforth to be largely the responsibility of Salzburg. A natural division of labour developed. While Salzburg concentrated on the Slavs of the Danube loop, Passau (standing at the junction of the Inn with the Danube) struck along the north bank to the territory of the Slovaks, and Regensburg took a still more northerly route to the Czechs. The germanization of the future Ostmark was the work of Bavarian mission-settlements. By 805 it is clear that much of Bohemia was within the mission-area of Passau and Regensburg. The Fulda annalist records that in 845 Louis the German (most active of the Carolingians on the eastern front) received fourteen

[8] Ed. F. Kurze, MGH SRG in usum schol. (1891) and with trans. by R. Rau, *Quellen zur karolingischen Reichsgeschichte*, iii (Berlin, 1960).

Bohemian chieftains with their followings and at their request caused them to be baptized at Epiphany. This would have taken place at Regensburg, his eastern capital, and Bishop Baturic would have baptized them. But the Regensburg mission, with support from Salzburg, went much further afield. It entered Pannonia and Bulgaria. At the request of the Bulgar Boris, Louis the German in 847 sent Bishop Ermanric of Passau into this new mission-area, only to find that it had been forestalled by a Roman mission dispatched by Nicholas I; and so, says the annalist, 'with the king's permission they came home'.

One now enters a tangled period when Frankish, Roman and Byzantine missions and interest collide. The great Nicholas was quite ready to extend traditional papal interest in Illyria further east in the Balkans, where he was bound to meet with Byzantine competition. The Bulgars in particular were too near Byzantium to be neglected when it came to the matter of conversion. But it was John VIII who authorized the work of the Byzantines Cyril and Methodius, the most successful missionaries of the period, in Pannonia. It is not clear whether he also authorized Methodius' most radical step: the use of Slavic vernacular as a liturgical language. The consecration of Methodius to the see of Sirmium would effectively close the middle Danube to further Frankish missions. This was at once realized. The Frankish reaction was sharp. Methodius was summoned to Regensburg where he had a furious meeting with the Bavarian bishops. Ermanric of Passau had to be restrained from laying about the Greeks with a horsewhip. Methodius was in fact imprisoned by them for over two years. The Bavarians embodied their claims in a document called the *Conversio Baiuvariorum et Carantanorum*[8] that is in effect a neat historical rehearsal of the missionary claims of the Church of Salzburg that ignores the labours of many others, and notably of Aquileia. But the pope did not yield. Within a generation much, but not all, of the missionaries' labours in the Danube area was to be undone by the first wave of the Hungarian invaders. The mission to Bohemia-Moravia was to last rather longer under the guidance of Regensburg. The bishopric of Nitra in Moravia remained under the patronage of St Emmeram of Regensburg. One appreciates that Slav, and still more Avar, pressure on and over the borders of eastern Francia called for immediate military response. Neither the Bavarian dukes nor their Frankish successors failed to respond. But it was not only military requirements that drew the Franks into central Europe. The duty to convert was never more strongly felt. If it had not been, the future of central Europe would have been very different.

[8] Ed. H. Wolfram (Vienna–Cologne–Graz, 1979).

In the Slav mission-field, as in the Scandinavian, the urgings of the Carolingian churchmen find their practical application. Their message was clear and persistent. Their kings had, as they had always had, a duty to defend the faithful from attack, external as well as internal. That duty seemed greatly accentuated as the attacks of non-Christian Vikings and Arabs multiplied within and around Frankish territory. There still remained a second duty: to extend the boundaries of Christianity and to meet paganism on its own ground. Scholars would not forget the prayer of the Merovingian *Vetus Gallica* liturgy: 'let us pray for the most Christian kings, that our Lord God shall subject all barbarous peoples to our perpetual peace'. Alcuin praises Charlemagne as a missionary preacher; he has and fulfils his role as *praedicator* to the heathen. Paulinus too sees him as a successful propagator of the faith in the missionary sense, and this finds an echo in the great Frankfurt synod of 794.[9] 'May God in His infinite power bring under the king's subjection the barbarian peoples, so that they may thus come to a knowledge of the truth and recognize their true creator, the living God.' Victory over heathen enemies should be followed by their conversion. Louis the German had well understood this. Sedulius, eulogizing him for all he was worth, did not miss the point; he not only subdued Germans and Vikings, the *barbara lingua* now learns to sing songs of praise, *alleluiatica carmina*. Finally two archbishops: Hincmar pleads for the turning of Carolingian swords away from fratricidal strife to the *exteras gentes*, so that, they submitting to the faith, the frontiers of the kingdom of the faithful shall be extended; and Agobard in his *Liber Apologeticus* is equally insistent on the duty of extending the frontiers of Christianity and cites the Roman Passion-tide prayer that the emperor shall subdue the barbarian peoples. So thoughtful men viewed the duty to convert the heathen over a Carolingian half-century. They served different kings and expressed in different circumstances their duty to push forward the frontiers of Christianity. But it was one voice.

[9] MGH Conc. i, i, no. 19.

BIBLIOGRAPHY

ALL I attempt here is to record those books and articles to which I am conscious that I am immediately indebted, and which I believe to be accessible. Full bibliographies are available in many of the books to which I draw attention.

GENERAL

1. *General Works*: Valuable and sometimes fundamental studies of persons, places and themes will be found in the great dictionaries, e.g.: *Dictionnaire de droit canonique* (Paris, 1924–); *Dictionnaire d'histoire et de géographie ecclésiastiques* (Paris, 1922–); *Dictionnaire de théologie catholique* (Paris, 1930–72); *Dictionnaire de spiritualité, ascétique et mystique* (Paris, 1923–). Reliable general guides are: Hubert Jedin (ed.), *Handbuch der Kirchengeschichte*, vol. 3, i (Freiburg, 1966); A. Fliche and V. Martin (eds.), *Histoire de l'église*, vols 4, 5 and 6; F. Lot, C. Pfister and F. L. Ganshof, *Les Destinées de l'empire en occident* (Paris, 1940); Wattenbach-Levison, *Deutschlands Geschichtsquellen im Mittelalter*, 5 vols. (Weimar, 1952–); R. Folz, A. Guillou, L. Musset and D. Sourdel, *De l'antiquité au monde mediéval* (Peuples et Civilisations series, Paris, 1972). More particular studies that reach through the period are: E. Lesne, *La Propriété ecclésiastique en France*, 6 vols. (Lille–Paris, 1910–); L. Duchesne, *Fastes épiscopaux de l'ancienne Gaule*, 3 vols. (Paris, 1907–15); E. de Moreau, *Histoire de l'église en Belgique des origines au XIIᵉ siècle* (Vienna–Leipzig, 1945); A. Hauck, *Kirchengeschichte Deutschlands,* vols. 1 and 2 (Leipzig, 1904–); K. Voigt, *Staat und Kirche* (Stuttgart, 1936); Y. Congar, *L'Ecclésiologie du haut moyen âge* (Paris, 1968); B. Smalley, *The Study of the Bible in the Middle Ages* (2nd edn., Oxford, 1952); W. Lange, *Texte zur germanischen Bekehrungsgeschichte* (Tübingen, 1962); R. Folz, *L'Idée d'empire en occident* (Paris, 1953). The following volumes of the Settimane di Spoleto contain important studies: 4(*Il monachesimo nell'alto medioevo*); 7(*Le chiese nei regni dell'Europa occidentale e i loro rapporti con Roma*); 10 (*La Bibbia nell'alto medioevo*); 14 (*La conversione al cristianesimo nell'alto medioevo*); 19 (*La scuola nell'occidente latino*); 22 (*La cultura antica nell'occidente latino*); 23 (*Simboli e simbologia*); 24 (*Il matrimonio nella società altomedievale*). By no means all the contributions are in Italian.

2. *Studies on the Merovingian Church or affecting its background include*: P. Courcelle, *Histoire littéraire des grandes invasions germaniques* (3rd edn, Paris, 1964); E. Griffe, *La Gaule chrétienne à l'époque romaine* (3 vols., Paris, 1947–); G. Kurth, *Études franques* (2 vols., Paris, 1919); E. Zöllner, *Geschichte der Franken* (Munich, 1970); E. Salin, *La Civilisation mérovingienne* (4 vols., Paris, 1950–); R. Macaigne, *L'Église mérovingienne et l'état pontifical* (Paris, 1929); G. Tessier, *Le Baptême de Clovis* (Paris, 1964); P. Goubert, *Byzance avant l'Islam,* vol. 2, i, *Byzance et les Francs* (Paris, 1956): P. Riché, *Éducation et culture dans l'occident barbare* (Paris, 1962); J. M. Wallace-Hadrill, *The Long-Haired Kings* (London, 1962).

3. *On the Carolingian Church and its background*: H. Fichtenau, *Das karolingische Imperium* (Zürich, 1949; Engl. trans, 1957); K. Bosl, *Franken um 800* (Munich, 1959); L. Halphen, *Charlemagne et l'empire carolingien* (Paris, 1947); D. Bullough, *The Age of Charlemagne* (London, 1965); J. M. Wallace-Hadrill, *Early Germanic Kingship in England and on the Continent* (Oxford, 1971); D. H. Green, *The Carolingian Lord* (Cambridge, 1965 – a vital semantic study); E. S. Duckett, *Carolingian portraits* (Ann Arbor, 1962); F. L. Ganshof, *The Carolingians and the Frankish Monarchy* (London, 1971); *Frankish Institutions under Charlemagne* (Providence, Rhode Island, 1968); P. Riché, *Écoles et enseignement dans le haut moyen âge* (Paris, 1979); J. Hubert, J. Porcher and W. F Volbach, *Carolingian Art* (London, 1970); F. Mütherich and J. E. Gaehde, *Carolingian Painting* (London, 1977); *Karl der Grosse, Lebenswerk und Nachleben* (4 vols., Düsseldorf, 1965–; a series of fundamental studies on all aspects of the Carolingian age); *Karl der Grosse, Werk und Wirkung* (Aachen, 1965; a richly illustrated catalogue of the commemorative exhibition on Charlemagne and his times held at Aachen in 1965).

CHAPTER I: GALLO-ROMAN PRELUDE

Essential for the background of Late Roman Gaul are: J. Gaudemet, *L'Église dans l'empire romain* (Paris, 1958); E. Griffe, *La Gaule chrétienne à l'époque romaine* (3 vols., Paris, 1947–); K. F. Stroheker, *Der senatorische Adel im spätantiken Gallien* (Tübingen, 1948); A. Loyen, *Recherches sur les panégyriques de Sidoine Apollinaire* (Paris, 1942); C. E. Stevens, *Sidonius Apollinaris and his age* (Oxford, 1933); N. K. Chadwick, *Poetry and Letters in early Christian Gaul* (London, 1955); O. Brogan, *Roman Gaul* (London, 1953); T. J. Haarhoff, *Schools of Gaul* (Johannesburg, 1958); E. Stein, *Histoire du Bas-Empire* (2 vols., Paris, 1949–); J. Matthews, *Western Aristocracies and Imperial Court* (Oxford, 1975); W. Goffart, *Barbarians and Romans* (Princeton, 1980); P. Courcelle, *Histoire littéraire des grandes invasions germaniques* (3rd edn., Paris, 1964); and the concluding vols. of C. Jullian's great *Histoire de la Gaule* (8 vols., Paris, 1920).

For Gallo-Roman Christianity: E. Mâle, *La Fin du paganisme en Gaule* (Paris, 1950); Owen Chadwick, *John Cassian* (2nd edn., Cambridge, 1968); P. de Labriolle, *La Réaction paienne* (Paris, 1942); H. Delehaye, *Sanctus* (Brussels, 1927), and *Les Origines du culte des martyrs* (Brussels, 1933); P. Brown, *The Cult of the Saints* (Chicago, 1981), and *Society and the Holy in Late Antiquity* (London, 1982) – both with a wealth of fresh insights; P. Rousseau, *Ascetics, Authority and the Church* (Oxford, 1978); C. E. Stancliffe, *St Martin and his hagiographer* (forthcoming); M. Heinzelmann, *Bischofsherrschaft in Gallien* (Zürich, 1976). D. J. Chitty, *The Desert a City* (Oxford, 1966) is a noble introduction to the eastern contribution to Gallic monasticism; Henry Chadwick, *Priscillian of Avila* (Oxford, 1976) explores the role of the occult and the charismatic in the early Church; and M. Roblin, *Le Terroir de Paris* (Paris, 1971) is a major study of the development of a great *civitas*. J. Gaudemet, *L'Église d'occident et la Rhénanie* (Variorum Reprints, London, 1980) is important for developments up to the fifth century. Articles on particular aspects (e.g. inscriptions) will be found in the periodicals *Francia* (vols. 1, 2, 4, 5, 8) and especially on archaeological matters in *Gallia*; also in *Reallexikon für Antike und Christentum*, esp. vol. 8, cols. 801–1268 (1971).

CHAPTER II: FROM PAGANISM TO CHRISTIANITY

A basic general study is Jan de Vries, *Altgermanische Religionsgeschichte* (3rd edn., Berlin, 1970, 2 vols.), and also valuable is E. Gamillscheg, *Romania Germanica*, vol. 1 (2nd revised edn., Berlin, 1970) for linguistic problems of the Frankish settlement. The role of magic is considered by P. Riché, 'La magie à l'époque carolingienne', *Comptes rendus des séances de l'Académie des Inscriptions et Belles-Lettres* (1973), pp. 127–38, and in an introductory way in R. W. V. Elliott, *Runes* (Manchester, 1959). The fundamental study of gold bracteates is K. Hauck, *Goldbrakteaten aus Sievern* (Munich, 1970) with subsequent revisions. I draw heavily on E. Salin, *La Civilisation mérovingienne* (4 vols., Paris, 1950–) and on the same writer's *Les Tombes Gallo-Romaines et mérovingiennes de la basilique de Saint-Denis* (Paris, 1958). Also on tombs see J. Werner, 'Frankish royal tombs in the cathedrals of Cologne and Saint-Denis', *Antiquity*, 38 (1964) and K. H. Krüger, *Königsgrabkirchen* (Munich, 1971); and an excellent specialist study is the Marquise de Maillé, *Les Cryptes de Jouarre* (Paris, 1971). E. Wig, 'La prière pour le roi et le royaume dans les privilèges épiscopaux de l'époque mérovingienne', *Mélanges Jean Dauvillier* (Toulouse, 1979), shows one way in which the Church helped kings.

Among the first to recognize that Frankish paganism drew strength from the remains of Gallo-Roman paganism was F. Ozanam, *La Civilisation chrétienne chez les Francs*, iv (1855), p. 80, a point not lost on O. Höfler, 'Der Sakralcharakter des germanischen Königtums', *Das Königtum* (Lindau and Konstanz, 1956). Relevant material and discussion will be found in R. Weiss, *Chlodwigs Taufe* (Bern, 1971), K. Schmid, 'Über das Verhältnis von Person und Gemeinschaft im früheren Mittelalter' (FMSt. i, 1967) and in my *Long-Haired Kings* (London, 1962). F. J. Dölger, 'Christliche Grundbesitzer und heidnische Landarbeiter', *Antike und Christentum*, 6 (Münster, 1950) is important for the role of landowners in converting peasants, and W. H. te Brake, 'Ecology and economy in early medieval Frisia', *Viator*, 9 (1978) for the fierce pagan reaction to the Franks in the Tournai–Arras–Tongres area in the late sixth century.

CHAPTER III: THE CONTRIBUTION OF HISTORY

The best book on Gregory known to me is G. Vinay, *San Gregorio di Tours* (Turin, 1940). There is valuable material on Gregory in both volumes of G. Kurth, *Études franques* (Paris, 1919) and a famous if grudging assessment by L. Halphen, 'Grégoire de Tours, historien de Clovis' in *Mélanges d'histoire du moyen âge offerts à M. Ferdinand Lot* (Paris, 1925). E. Zöllner, *Geschichte der Franken* (Munich, 1970) is sound on Gregory's chronology. On Gregory's literary skill see M. Bonnet, *Le Latin de Grégoire de Tours* (Paris, 1890);

E. Löfstedt, *Syntactica*, 2 (Lund, 1933); H. Beumann, 'Gregor von Tours und der sermo rusticus', *Spiegel der Geschichte, Festgabe für Max Braubach* (Münster, 1964); and E. Auerbach, *Literary Language and its Public in Late Latin Antiquity and in the Middle Ages* (London, 1965). On Gregory and St Martin see E. Ewig, 'Le culte de Saint Martin à l'époque franque', *Spätantikes und fränkisches Gallien, Gesammelte Schriften,* 2 (Munich, 1979) and J. Leclercq, 'S. Martin dans l'hagiographie monastique du moyen âge', in *Saint Martin et son temps, Studia Anselmiana,* 46 (1961).

P. Brown, 'Relics and social status in the age of Gregory of Tours', *Society and the Holy in Late Antiquity* (London, 1982) is illuminating, and so too P. Riché, *Éducation et culture dans l'occident barbare* (Paris, 1962). P. A. Arcari, *Idee e sentimenti politici dell'alto medioevo* (Milan, 1968) is interesting on Gregory's view of providence; R. A. Meunier, *Grégoire de Tours et l'histoire morale du centre-ouest de la France* (Poitiers, 1946) studies regional connections; M. Heinzelmann, *Bischofsherrschaft in Gallien* (Munich, 1976) is useful on Gregory's family-sees; and Giselle de Nie, 'Roses in January', *Journal of Medieval History*, 5 (1979) considers Gregory's approach to natural phenomena.

Sir Francis Oppenheimer's *Frankish Themes and Problems* (London, 1952) and *The Legend of the Ste Ampoule* (London, 1953) must be used with caution.

CHAPTER IV: THE MEROVINGIAN CLOISTER

The best general guide to Frankish monasticism is F. Prinz, *Frühes Mönchtum im Frankenreich* (Munich, 1965), and a shorter summary is C. Courtois, 'L'évolution du monachisme en Gaule de St Martin à St Colomban', Spoleto, iv (1957). L. van der Essen, *Le Siécle des saints, 625–739* (Brussels, 1948) is an excellent guide to Christian beginnings in northern Francia. *Études Mérovingiennes*, actes des journées de Poitiers (Paris, 1953) contains several useful papers. Important for the social setting are: A. Bergengruen, *Adel und Grundherrschaft im Merowingerreich* (Wiesbaden, 1958); F. Irsigler, 'Untersuchungen zur Geschichte des frühfrankischen Adels', *Rheinisches Archiv*, 70 (Bonn, 1969); and R. Sprandel, 'Der merovingische Adel und die Gebiete östlich des Rheins', *Forschungen zur oberrheinischen Landesgeschichte*, v (Freiburg, 1957). P. Schmitz, *Histoire de l'ordre de Saint Bênoit*, i, 2nd edn., (Maredsous, 1948) is a clear guide for Francia, and E. John. 'Saeculum Prioratus and the rule of St Benedict', *Revue Bénédictine*, lxxv (1965) discusses the origins of the mixed rule. E. Ewig, *Spätantikes und fränkisches Gallien,* ii (Munich, 1979) is devoted to the Frankish Church and contains fundamental studies of individual sees and of monastic privileges though 'L'Aquitaine et les pays Rhénans', invaluable for ecclesiastical connections, appears in vol. i. F. L. Ganshof, 'L'Étranger dans la monarchie franque', Les Éditions de la Librairie Encyclopédique (Brussels, 1958) emphasizes the dangers facing foreign missionaries on the continent.

More particular studies include the following: G. Moyse, 'Les origines du monachisme dans le diocèse de Besançon', *Bibliothèque de l'école des chartes*, 131, i and ii (1973), important for the early use of St Benedict's Rule in

Francia; G. Scheibelreiter, 'Königstöchter im Kloster', *Mitteilungen des Instituts für österreichische Geschichtsforschung*, 87 (1979), effectively on Radegundis; C. Brunel, 'Les actes mérovingiens pour l'abbaye de Saint-Médard de Soissons', *Mélanges d'histoire du moyen âge pour Louis Halphen* (Paris, 1951); L. Levillain, *Examen critique des chartes mérovingiennes et carolingiennes de l'abbaye de Corbie* (Paris, 1902); F. Lot, *Études critique sur l'abbaye de Saint Wandrille*, Bibliothèque de l'école des hautes études, 204 (Paris, 1913); J. M. Theurillat, *L'Abbaye de Saint Maurice d'Agaune* (Sion, 1954); E. Vacandard, *Vie de Saint Ouen* (Paris, 1902); W. H. Fritze, 'Universalis gentium confessio', FMSt 3 (1969) for St Amand; *Sainte Fare et Faremoutiers* (Abbaye de Faremoutiers, 1956); *Mélanges Colombaniennes* (Paris, 1950), particularly the contributions of Gaudemet, Cousin, Mitchell and Coolen; E. Ewig, 'Das Privileg des Bischofs Berthefrid von Amiens für Corbie von 664 und die Klosterpolitik der Königin Balthild', *Francia*, i (1973); A. Dierkens, 'Un aspect de la christianisation de la Gaule du Nord à l'époque mérovingienne', *Francia*, viii (1980) on the Vita Hadelini and archaeological discoveries; *Columbanus and Merovingian Monasticism*, ed. H. B. Clarke and M. Brennan (BAR International Series 113, 1981); and H. Löwe, 'Columbanus und Fidolius', DA 37, i (1981) – a defence of the authenticity of some of Columbanus' poems. I have been unable to take account of *Die Iren und Europa im früheren Mittelalter*, ii, ed. H. Löwe (Stuttgart, 1982).

CHAPTER V: THE MEROVINGIAN SAINTS

A. Marignan, *Le culte des saints sous les mérovingiens*, in Études sur la civilisation française (Paris, 1899) is still a useful introduction, though there are greater insights in F. Graus, *Volk, Herrscher und Heiliger im Reich der Merowinger* (Prague, 1965), and in P. Riché, *Éducation et culture dans l'occident barbare* (Paris, 1962). R. R. Bezzola, *Les Origines et la formation de la littérature courtoise en occident*, i (Paris, 1944) and E. R. Curtius, *European Literature and the Latin Middle Ages* (London, 1953) should not be neglected. L. van der Essen, *Étude critique et littéraire sur les Vitae des saints mérovingiens* (Louvain–Paris, 1907) is confined to saints of Belgium, and W. Pohlkamp, 'Hagiographische Texte als Zeugnisse einer "histoire de la sainteté"', FMSt 11 (1977) to those of Aquitaine. O. G. Oexle, 'Die Karolinger und die Stadt des heiligen Arnulf', FMSt 1 (1967) casts light on St Arnulf's background. The value of monastic necrologies for the study of holy men is exemplified by the *Liber Memorialis* of Remiremont (MGH Libri Memoriales, i, 1970). P. Brown's innovative 'Relics and social status in the age of Gregory of Tours' is reprinted in his *Society and the Holy in Late Antiquity* (London, 1982), and see R. A. Markus, 'The cult of icons in sixth-century Gaul', *Journ. of Theol. Studies*, xxix, i (1978), pp. 151–7. Still the best summary of Gregory's hagiography is C. A. Bernouilli, *Die Heiliger der Merowinger* (Tübingen, 1900). The selection of translations in W. C. McDermott, *Gregory of Tours, Selections from the Minor Works* (Philadelphia, 1949) is generally sound, so far as it goes. There are relevant contributions, especially on Venantius, in *Études Mérovingiennes*;

but the principal studies of Venantius are D. Tardi, *Fortunat, étude sur un dernier représentant de la poésie latine dans la Gaule mérovingienne* (Paris , 1927) and better, R. Koebner, *Venantius Fortunatus* (Leipzig–Berlin, 1915). J. Leclercq, 'L'Écriture sainte dans l'hagiographie monastique du haut moyen âge' is in Spoleto, x (1963), and B. de Gaiffier, 'Hagiographie et historiographie' in Spoleto, xvii, i (1970). On the Assumption of the Virgin see A. Cameron, 'The Theotokos in sixth-century Constantinople'. *Journ. of Theol. Studies*, xxix, i 1978). The picture of Ezra-Cassiodorus is reproduced by R. L. S. Bruce-Mitford, 'The art of the Codex Amiatinus' (Jarrow Lecture, 1967, reprinted from *Journ. of the Archaeol. Assoc.* xxxii, 1969) and in colour in K. Weitzmann, *Late Antique and Early Christian Book Illumination* (London, 1977), plate 48.

CHAPTER VI: THE CHURCH IN COUNCIL

In addition to Hefele-Leclerq, constant reference should be made to P. Fournier and G. Le Bras, *Histoire des collections canoniques en occident* (Paris, 1931) who look back to the past when considering Carolingian councils. The basic study, to which I am chiefly indebted, is C. de Clercq, *La Législation religieuse franque de Clovis à Charlemagne*, i (Louvain–Paris, 1936). Also valuable are: É. Griffe, *La Gaule chrétienne à l'époque romaine*, iii (Paris, 1965); H. E. Feine, *Kirchliche Rechtsgeschichte*, 3rd edn., i (Weimar, 1955); E. Loening, *Geschichte des deutschen Kirchenrechts* (Strassburg, 1878); U. Stutz, *Geschichte des kirchlichen Benefizialwesens*, i (Berlin, 1895); L. Duchesne, *L'Église au viᵉ siècle* (Paris, 1925); and, by the same, *Fastes épiscopaux de l'ancienne Gaule*, 3 vols. (Paris, 1907–15), the essential guide to episcopal succession; and H. J. Sieben, *Die Konzilsidee der alten Kirche* (Paderborn, 1979), the first vol. in a new Konziliengeschichte. E. Lesne, *Histoire de la propriété écclesiastique* continues, as always, to be helpful.

Among studies devoted to particular regions or aspects may be noted: G. Constable, *Monastic tithes* (Cambridge, 1964); F. L. Ganshof, 'L'Immunité dans la monarchie franque', Éditions de la librairie encyclopédique (Brussels, 1958); O. K. Binding, *Das burgundisch-romanische Königreich* (Leipzig, 1868, repr. 1969); M. Chaume, *Les Origines du duché de Bourgogne* (Dijon, 1925–); and by the same, *Recherches historiques* (Dijon, 1947); P. E. Martin, *Études critiques sur la Suisse à l'époque mérovingienne* (Geneva-Paris, 1910); M. Rouche, *L'Aquitaine des Wisigoths aux Arabes* (Paris, 1979); and E de Moreau, *Histoire de l'église en Belgique*, i (Brussels, 1947). Spoleto vii (1960) contains important contributions.

CHAPTER VII: THE MEROVINGIANS AND THE PAPACY

The general position of the papacy *vis-à-vis* the western kingdoms is discussed by W. Ullmann. *The growth of Papal Government in the Middle Ages* (London, 2nd edn. 1962); E. Ewig, 'Zum christlichen Königsgedanken im Frühmittelalter', *Das Königtum* (Lindau–Konstanz, 1956); E. Pfeil, *Die fränkische und deutsche Romidee des frühen Mittelalters* (Munich, 1929);

R. Macaigne, *L'Église mérovingienne et l'état pontifical* (Paris, 1929); K. Hallinger, 'Römische Voraussetzungen der bonifatianischen Wirksamkeit im Frankenreich', *Sankt Bonifatius Gedenkgabe* (Fulda, 2nd edn. 1954). E. Caspar's great *Geschichte des Papsttums*, ii (1933) is fundamental for papal-Frankish relations to the mid-eighth century.

On Gregory the Great and Francia: F. Homes Dudden, *Gregory the Great: his place in history and thought* (London, 1905 and repr.); R. A. Markus, 'Gregory the Great and a papal missionary strategy', *Studies in Church History*, 6 (Cambridge, 1970); P. Meyvaert, papers in *Benedict, Bede and Others* (London, 1977); C. Dagens, *Saint Grégoire le Grand: culture et expérience chrétiennes* (Paris, 1977); and P. Grierson, 'The Patrimonium Petri in illis Partibus and the pseudo-imperial coinage in Frankish Gaul', *Rev. belge de numismatique*, 150 (1959).

On liturgical relations: G. Dix, *The Shape of the Liturgy* (London, 1945); L. Duchesne, *Les Origines du culte chrétien* (Paris, 1925); C. Vogel, *La Discipline pénitentielle en Gaule des origines à la fin du viiᵉ siècle* (Paris, 1952); M. Andrieu, 'La liturgie romaine en pays franc et les ordines romani', *Les Ordines Romani du haut moyen âge*, ii (Louvain, 1948); W. S. Porter and F. L. Cross, *The Gallican Rite* (London, 1958); A. Chavasse, *Le Sacramentaire gélasien* (Tournai, 1958); B. Moreton, *The Eighth-Century Gelasian Sacramentary* (Oxford, 1976); and D. Sicard, *La Liturgie de la mort dans l'église latine des origines à la réforme carolingienne* (Münster, 1978). E. Bishop, *Liturgica Historica* (Oxford, 1918) should always be raided for its treasures. *Spoleto*, vii contains the following relevant papers: E. Delaruelle 'L'Église romaine et ses relations avec l'église franque jusqu'en 800'; C. Vogel, 'Les échanges liturgiques entre Rome et les pays francs jusqu'à l'époque de Charlemagne'; and, at great length, M. Maccarrone, 'La dottrina del primato papale dal iv all' viii secolo nelle relazioni con le chiese occidentali'.

CHAPTER VIII: THE BURDEN OF PROPERTY

E. Lesne, *Hist. de la propriété éccles.* i, ii and vi is indispensable, and there are important studies in D. Herlihy. *The Social History of Italy and Western Europe* (London, 1978), notably ch. v ('Church property on the European continent'). For monastic cartularies see ibid., pp. 100–1. The best example of a monastic estate-survey is B. Guérard, *Polyptyque de l'abbé Irminon* (Paris, 1844), illustrating the great wealth of the Church. P. Roth, *Geschichte des Beneficialwesens* (Erlangen, 1850) is still valuable; and so too A. Pöschl, *Bischofsgut und Mensa Episcopalis* (Bonn, 1912). F. Prinz, *Frühes Mönchtum im Frankenreich*, has much useful material and an excellent bibliography. See also W. Metz, 'Zu Wesen und Struktur der geistlichen Grundherrschaft', Spoleto, xxvii (1981). Consideration of particular themes will be found in: F. J. Felten, *Äbte und Laienäbte im Frankenreich* (Stuttgart, 1980), who also contributes to a notable collection of papers gathered together in *Mönchtum, Episkopat und Adel zur Grundungszeit des Klosters Reichenau* (Sigmaringen, 1974); G. Constable, *Monastic Tithes;* M. Rouche, *L'Aquitaine*; A. H. M. Jones, P. Grierson and J. A. Crook, 'The authenticity of the Testamentum

S. Remigii', *Revue belge de philol. et d'histoire*, 35 (1957); W. Levison, 'Das Testament des Diakons Adalgisel-Grimo vom Jahre 634', repr. in *Aus rheinischer und fränkischer Frühzeit* (Düsseldorf, 1948), also valuable for Merovingian wills in general; M. Roblin, *Le Terroir de Paris*; K. H. Krüger, *Königsgrabkirchen* (Munich, 1971); K. H. Debus, *Studien zu merowingischen Urkunden*; U. Nonn, 'Das Bild Karl Martells in den lateinischen Quellen vornehmlich des 8 und 9 Jahrhunderts', FMSt 4 (1970); I. Heidrich, 'Titulatur und Urkunden der arnulfingischen Hausmeier', *Archiv für Diplomatik*, 11 (1965); E. Ewig, 'Die fränkischen Teilungen und Teilreiche, 511–613' and 'Die fränkischen Teilreiche im 7 Jahrhundert, 613–714' both repr. in *Spätantikes und fränkisches Gallien* i, and 'Milo et eiusmodi similes', ibid. ii.

On St Denis, valuable early studies are J. Doublet, *Histoire de l'abbaye de S-Denys* (1625) and M. Félibien, *Histoire de l'abbaye royale de Saint-Denis* (1706). Much of their work is summed up, with important archaeological matter, in S. M. Crosby, *The Abbey of St Denis*, i (New Haven, 1942). But the basic modern study is that of L. Levillain, 'Études sur l'abbaye de Saint-Denis à l'époque mérovingienne', BEC 82(1921), 86(1925), 87(1926) and 91(1930). See also G. Tessier, 'Les travaux de M. Levillain sur Saint Denis', *Le Moyen Âge*, 30(1929).

CHAPTER IX: THE MAKING OF THE GERMAN CHURCH

The starting-point for any study of the Anglo-Saxon missions on the continent must be W. Levison, *England and the Continent in the Eighth Century* (Oxford, 1946). Equally important are the contributions of T. Schieffer: *Winfrid-Bonifatius und die christliche Grundlegung Europas* (2nd edn. Darmstadt, 1972); *Angelsachsen und Franken* (Akad. der Wissenschaften . . . no. 20, Mainz, 1950); and 'La chiesa nazionale di osservanza romana – l'opera di Willibrord e di Bonifacio', Spoleto vii, i (1960). Two large and valuable collections of papers are: *Willibrordus, Echternacher Festschrift* (Luxemburg, 1940) and *Sankt Bonifatius Gedenkgabe* (Fulda, 1954). I have attempted a summary in 'A background to St Boniface's mission', repr. in *Early medieval history* (Oxford, 1975).

Short but useful are: S. J. Crawford, *Anglo-Saxon Influence on Western Christendom* (Oxford, 1933) and G. W. Greenaway, *Saint Boniface* (London, 1955). The basic study of Willibrord's monastery is C. Wampach, *Geschichte der Grundherrschaft Echternach* (2 vols., Luxemburg, 1929–30). Among much else may be noted: R. Sprandel, 'Der merovingische Adel und die Gebiete östlich des Rheins', *Forschungen zur oberrheinischen Landesgeschichte*, 5 (Freiburg, 1957); M. Coens, 'S. Boniface et sa mission historique d'après quelques auteurs récents', *Analecta Bollandiana*, 73(1955); T. Zwölfer, *St Peter, Apostelfürst und Himmelspförtner* (Stuttgart, 1929); A. Bergengruen, *Adel und Grundherrschaft im Merowingerreich* (Wiesbaden, 1958); K. F. Werner, 'Les principautés périphériques dans le monde franc du viiie siècle', Spoleto, 20, ii (1973); H. Löwe, *Ein literarischer Widersacher des Bonifatius – Virgil von Salzburg und die Kosmographie des Aethicus Ister* (Akad. d. Wissen., Mainz, 1951); F. Prinz, 'Salzburg zwischen Antike und Mittelalter', FMSt 5 (1971);

and E. Delaruelle, 'En relisant le De Institutione Regia de Jonas d'Orléans – l'entrée en scène de l'épiscopat carolingien', *Mélanges Louis Halphen* (Paris, 1951).

CHAPTER X: PIPPIN III AND THE PULL OF ROME

No one book covers this difficult transitional period. There are however several significant studies. I. Haselbach, *Aufstieg und Herrschaft der Karlinger in der Darstellung der sogenannten Annales Mettenses priores* (Lübeck–Hamburg, 1970) outlines Pippin's continuing political difficulties. On relations with Rome see L. Levillain, 'L'Avénement de la dynastie carolingienne et les origines de l'état pontifical', BEC 94(1933) and W. H. Fritze, *Papst und Frankenkönig* (Sigmaringen, 1973). M. Rouche, *L'Aquitaine,* covers Frankish relations with the South up to 781, and thereafter L. Auzias, *L'Aquitaine carolingienne, 778–987* (Toulouse–Paris, 1937). Felten, *Äbte und Laienäbte,* discusses Pippin's dealings with monasteries, and H. Frank, *Die Klosterbischöfe des Frankenreichs, Beiträge zur Geschichte des alten Mönchtums,* 17 (Münster, 1932), his dealings with a class of bishop. P. Riché, *Éducation et culture,* remains invaluable and more particularly his 'Le renouveau culturel à la cour de Pépin III', *Francia,* 2 (1974) in which see also J. Hubert,' Les prémisses de la renaissance carolingienne au temps de Pépin III'. Another aspect is treated by F. Prinz, 'King, clergy and war at the time of the Carolingians', in *Saints, Scholars and Heroes – studies in honour of C. W. Jones,* 2 (Ann Arbor, 1979). There is ecclesiastical matter in J. Hubert, 'Évolution de la topographie et de l'aspect des villes de Gaule du ve au xe siècle', Spoleto 6 (1959). Studies on somewhat narrower fronts are: E. Ewig, 'Saint Chrodegang et la réforme de l'église franque', *Spätankikes und fränkisches Gallien,* 2 (1979), J. Formigé, *L'Abbaye royale de Saint-Denis, recherches nouvelles* (Paris, 1960); E. Morhain, *Origines et histoire de la Regula Canonicorum de S. Chrodegang* (Miscellanea Pio Paschini, Rome, 1948); T. Klauser, 'Die liturgischen Austauschbeziehungen zwischen der römischen und fränkisch-deutschen Kirche vom 8 bis 11 Jahrh.', *Hist. Jahrb.* 53 (1933): G. Jecker, 'St Pirmins Erden- und Ordensheimat, *Archiv für mittelrhein. Kirchengeschichte,* 5 (1953); E. Delaruelle. 'L'Église romaine et ses relations avec l'église franque jusqu'en 800', Spoleto, 7, ii (1960) and C. Vogel, 'Les échanges liturgiques entre Rome et les pays francs jusqu'à l'époque de Charlemagne' (ibid.); E. H. Kantorowicz, *Laudes Regiae* (Berkeley–Los Angeles, 1946) is the vital study of liturgical acclamations. C. de Clercq, *Légis. Relig.* and Hubert, Porcher and Volbach, *Carolingian Art,* should always be at hand for reference. F. Prinz, 'Der fränkischer Episkopat zwischen Merowinger- und Karolingerzeit', Spoleto, xxvii (1981) covers a difficult transition. See also H. Fuhrmann, 'Das Papsttum und das kirchliche Leben im Frankenreich' (ibid).

CHAPTER XI: CHARLEMAGNE

i. The Metropolitan Line

The study of Frankish expansion under Charlemagne must now start with the relevant chapters of *Karl der Grosse*, i, *Persönlichkeit und Geschichte* (Düsseldorf, 1965): E. Ewig, 'Descriptio Franciae'; P. Classen, 'Karl der Grosse, das Papsttum und Byzanz' (of which a revised text was published in 1968); H. Jankuhn, 'Karl der Grosse und der Norden'; J. Deér, 'Karl der Grosse und der Untergang des Awarenreiches'; M. Hellmann, Karl und die slawische Welt zwischen Ostsee und Böhmerwald'; and W. Schlesinger, 'Die Auflösung des Karlsreiches'. Also valuable are: D. Bullough, *The Age of Charlemagne* (London, 1965) and the same scholar's summary of recent work, 'Europae Pater', *Engl. Hist. Rev.* 85(1970); and L. Halphen, *Études critiques sur l'histoire de Charlemagne* (Paris, 1921), particularly for the Saxon wars. K. Leyser's *Rule and Conflict in an early Medieval Society* (London, 1979), though primarily concerned with Ottonian Saxony, has interesting observations on Carolingian Saxony. General studies that repay reading are: A. Kleinclausz, *Charlemagne* (Paris, 1934); J. Calmette, *Charlemagne, sa vie et son œuvre* (Paris, 1945); and H. Fichtenau, *Das karolingische Imperium* (Zürich, 1949) of which there is an English translation by P. Munz (Oxford, 1957). Fichtenau refines his ideas in *Karl der Grosse und das Kaisertum* (Darmstadt, 1971). A useful collection of texts with translations is W. Lange, *Texte zur germanischen Bekehrungsgeschichte* (Tübingen, 1962). Studies of particular aspects include: W. Ullmann, *The Growth of Papal Government in the Middle Ages* (London, 2nd end. 1962); C. Brühl, *Fodrum, Gistum, Servitium Regis* (2 vols., Cologne–Graz, 1968) for the movements and sustenance of Carolingian kings; F. L. Ganshof, *Recherches sur les capitulaires* (Paris, 1958); and E. Pfeil, *Die fränkische und deutsche Romidee des frühen Mittelalters* (Munich, 1929).

ii. The Inner Circle

Karl der Grosse, Lebenswerk und Nachleben, ii and iii, contains many important studies. Attention should particularly be drawn to the following: in i – F. Brunhölzl, 'Der Bildungsauftrag der Hofschule'; B. Bischoff, 'Die Hofbibliothek Karls des Grossen' and 'Panorama der Handschriftenüberlieferung aus der Zeit Karls des Grossen'; W. von den Steinen, 'Karl und die Dichter'; B. Fischer, 'Bibeltext und Bibelreform unter Karl dem Grossen'; and in ii – F. Mütherich, 'Die Buchmalerei am Hofe Karls des Grossen'; W. Braunfels, 'Karls des Grossen Bronzewerkstatt'; J. Beckwith, 'Byzantine influence on art at the court of Charlemagne'; M. Vieillard-Troiekouroff, 'L'architecture en France du temps de Charlemagne'; F. Kreusch, 'Kirche, Atrium und Portikus der Aachener Pfalz'; and L. Hugot, 'Die Pfalz Karls des Grossen in Aachen'. In B. Bischoff's collected papers, *Mittelalterliche Studien* (Stuttgart, 1966–7) see in vol. i, 'Biblioteche, Schuole e Letteratura nelle Città dell'alto medioevo' and 'Wendepunkte in der Geschichte der lateinischen Exegese im Frühmittelalter', and in vol. ii, 'Die mittellateinische Literatur',

'Caritas-Lieder', 'Das griechische Element in der abendländischen Bildung des Mittelalters', and 'Scriptoria e Manoscritti mediatori di civiltà dal sesto secolo alla riforma di Carlo Magno'. *Festschrift Bernhard Bischoff* (Stuttgart, 1971) contains D. Schaller, 'Der junge "Rabe" am Hof Karls des Grossen'. P. Riché, *Écoles et enseignement dans le haut moyen âge* (Paris, 1979) throws light on dark places. D. A. Bullough, 'Roman books and Carolingian Renovatio', *Studies in Church History*, 14(1977) contrasts the disparate materials reaching Francia under Charlemagne with associated texts, pagan and Christian, reaching the next generation. The same writer's 'The educational tradition in England from Alfred to Aelfric – teaching utriusque linguae', Spoleto, xix (1972) is valuable for comparison with the Frankish tradition. F. J. E. Raby, *A History of Christian–Latin poetry* (Oxford, 1927) and *A History of Secular Latin Poetry* (2 vols., Oxford, 1934) are a mine of information. W. Edelstein, *Eruditio und Sapientia, Weltbild und Erziehung in der Karolingerzeit* (Freiburg im Breisgau, 1965) considers the Carolingian sense of two evocative words. R. P. H. Green, *Seven versions of Carolingian Pastoral* (Reading, 1980) provides useful texts of pastoral verse by Alcuin, Angilbert, Modoin and others.

The best book on Einhard is A. Kleinclausz, *Éginhard* (Paris, 1942) especially if read in association with H. Beumann's brilliant *Ideengeschichtliche Studien zu Einhard* (Darmstadt, 1962). J. Fleckenstein, *Die Hofkapelle der deutschen Könige*, i (Stuttgart, 1959) is essential reading for Charlemagne's chapel and its officers, but is supplemented by S. Haider, 'Zum Verhältnis von Kapellanat und Geschichtsschreibung im Mittelalter', in *Festschrift für Heinz Löwe – Geschichtsschreibung und geistiges Leben im Mittelalter* (Cologne–Vienna, 1978) and in another way by H. Wolfram, *Intitulatio* (Graz–Vienna, 1967) who studies royal and the other titles to the end of the eighth century. L. Falkenstein, *Der Lateran der karolingischen Pfalz zu Aachen* (Cologne–Graz, 1966) unravels the meaning of the Aachen Lateran. P. J. Geary, *Furta Sacra* (Princeton, 1978) discusses Einhard's connection with relic-dealers.

CHAPTER XII: RECEIVED WISDOM

i. Alcuin

Good general studies of Alcuin include: A. Kleinclausz, *Alcuin* (Paris, 1948); E. S. Duckett, *Alcuin, Friend of Charlemagne* (New York, 1951); W. Levison, *England and the Continent*, ch. 6; and still best of all, C. J. B. Gaskoin, *Alcuin, his Life and his Work* (London, 1904). F. J. Felten, "Abte und Laienäbte, pp. 229 ff., emphasizes Alcuin's wealth and political importance.

On Alcuin, the Bible and liturgy: *Cambridge History of the Bible,* 2 (1969) contains contributions by R. Loewe on the history of the Vulgate and by Dom J. Leclercq on exposition and exegesis; Spoleto, x (1963), *La Bibbia*, includes Dom B. Fischer on early medieval biblical editions and B. Smalley on exegesis; Fischer continues his study of biblical texts and reform in *Karl der Grosse*, 2, and in the same volume W. Heil writes on Adoptionism and C. Vogel on Charlemagne's liturgical reforms. F. L. Ganshof, 'La révision de la Bible par Alcuin', *Bibliothèque d'humanisme et renaissance*, ix (Geneva, 1947) is a model of clarity. G. Ellard, *Master Alcuin, Liturgist* (Chicago, 1956) should be read in conjunction with the critical review by C. Hohler in *Journ. Eccl. Hist.* viii, ii (1957). Dom G. Dix, *The Shape of the Liturgy* (London, 1945) places Carolingian liturgical reform in a general context, and so too B. Smalley, *The Study of the Bible in the Middle Ages.*

Among other specialized studies: J. Marenbon, *From the circle of Alcuin to the school of Auxerre* (Cambridge, 1981) examines in a fresh way the use of logic by Alcuin and his disciples; H. Meyer, 'Die allegorische Deutung der Zahlenkomposition des Psalters', FMSt 6, studies Alcuin's numerology; B. Bischoff, 'Aus Alkuins Erdentagen', *Mittelalterliche Studien*, ii, examines Paris MS BN lat. 1572 containing Alcuin's hand; L. Wallach, *Alcuin and Charlemagne* (Ithaca, 1959) is a rigorous analysis of some of Alcuin's major works; G. B. Blumenshine, *Liber Alcuini contra haeresim Felicis* (Vatican, 1980) is an edition with a valuable introduction on the Adoptionist heresy.

To two scholars I am grateful for access to unpublished writings: Professor D. A. Bullough and Dr Peter Godman. The former's Ford Lectures on Alcuin will be essential reading when published. Meanwhile, his 'Hagiography as patriotism – Alcuin's York poem and early Northumbrian vitae sanctorum' (*Hagiographie, cultures et sociétés, ive – xiie siècles,* Études Augustiennes, Paris, 1981) gives a foretaste. See P. Godman, 'The textual tradition of Alcuin's poem on York', *Mittellateinisches Jahrbuch*, 15 (1980); and 'Alcuin's poetic style and the authenticity of O Mea Cella', *Studi Medievali*, 3rd series xx, ii, Spoleto, 1979). We await his book on Carolingian political poetry, and his forthcoming edition of the York poem.

ii. Theodulf

The study of Theodulf has been given fresh impetus and a new direction by Ann Freeman in three distinguished articles: 'Theodulf of Orleans and the Libri Carolini', *Speculum*, xxxii, 4 (1957); 'Further studies in the Libri Carolini', ibid. xl, 2 (1965); and 'Further studies in the Libri Carolini, iii, ibid. xlvi, 4 (1971). She has not convinced L. Wallach that Alcuin was not the author of the Libri: see his *Alcuin and Charlemagne* (Ithaca, 1959) and *Diplomatic Studies in Latin and Greek Documents from the Carolingian Age* (Ithaca, 1977) – both argued with curious acerbity. P. Meyvaert has convincingly disposed of Wallach's arguments in 'The authorship of the Libri Carolini', *Rev. Bén.* lxxxix (1979). However, D. A. Bullough made a good case in his Ford Lectures for Alcuin as the author of Bk. iv, chs. 14–17, if with Theodulf's authority. See also P. Bloch, 'Das Apsismosaik von Germigny-des-Prés – Karl und der alte Bund', *Karl der Grosse* iii (Karolingische Kunst).

On the Bible, exegesis and liturgy: L. Delisle, *Les Bibles de Théodulfe* (Paris, 1879); S. Berger, Histoire de la Vulgate (Paris, 1893); Dom F. Cabrol, *Les Origines liturgiques* (Paris, 1906) for the Visigothic rite; E. Dahlhaus-Berg, *Nova antiquitas et antiqua novitas* (Cologne–Vienna, 1975) for Theodulf's debt to Isidore, though not entirely convincing; and E. A. Lowe, CLA vi, intro., on Theodulf's Bibles.

H. Liebeschütz, 'Theodulf of Orleans and the problem of the Carolingian Renaissance', in *F. Saxl, A Volume of Memorial Essays*, ed. D. J. Gordon (London, 1957) is perceptive; *Zum Kaisertum Karls des Grossen*, ed. G. Wolf (Darmstadt, 1972) summarizes views on contributions to Charlemagne's imperial coronation; and E. Lévi-Provençal, *Histoire de l'Espagne musulmane* i (Paris–Leiden, 1950) provides Spanish background for Theodulf.

CHAPTER XIII: THE NEW ISRAEL AND ITS RULERS

i. Louis the Pious

The fundamental study of court learning under Louis the Pious is B. Bischoff, 'Die Hofbibliothek unter Ludwig dem Frommen' in *Medieval Learning and Literature, Essays Presented to R. W. Hunt* (Oxford, 1976). Also useful: P. E. Schramm and F. Mütherich, *Denkmäle der deutschen Könige und Kaiser* (Munich, 1962); Fleckenstein, *Hofkapelle*, i, for continuity at court after 814; and R. Bezzola, *Les Origines et la formation de la littérature courtoise en occident* (Paris, 1944). For political background, W. Schlesinger, 'Die Auflösung des Karlsreiches', *Karl der Grosse*, i. On Louis's Aquitanian career, L. Auzias, *L'Aquitaine carolingienne* (Toulouse–Paris, 1937). On historical writing: W. Wehlen, *Geschichtsschreibung und Staatsauffassung im Zeitalter Ludwigs des Frommen* (Lübeck–Hamburg, 1970); H. Hoffmann, *Untersuchungen zur karolingischen Annalistik* (Bonn, 1958); and J. L. Nelson, 'The annals of St Bertin' in *Charles the Bald, Court and Kingdom*, ed. M. Gibson and J. L. Nelson (BAR, 1981).

On individuals: P. Schmitz, 'L'influence de S. Benoît d'Aniane' in Spoleto, iv (1957), and on his wealth and political muscle, Felten, *Äbte und Laienäbte*; L. Weinrich, *Wala, Graf, Mönch und Rebell* (Lübeck–Hamburg, 1963); J. Reviron, *Jonas d'Orléans et son De Institutione Regia* (Paris, 1930) and E. Delaruelle, 'En relisant le *De Institutione Regia* de Jonas d'Orléans' in *Mélanges d'histoire du moyen âge, Louis Halphen* (Paris, 1951); O. Eberhardt, *Via Regia*, for Smaragdus; E. Boshof, *Erzbischof Agobard von Lyon* (Cologne, 1969).

ii. Charles the Bald

This chapter is a revised version of my Raleigh Lecture, 'A Carolingian renaissance prince: the Emperor Charles the Bald' (Proc. Brit. Acad., lxiv, 1978), where fuller references will be found. For background see my *Early Germanic Kingship in England and on the Continent* (Oxford, 1971), ch. 6; F. Lot and L. Halphen, *Le Régne de Charles le Chauve* (Paris, 1909, part i only, 840–51); J. Calmette, *La Diplomatie carolingienne* (Paris, 1901); J. Dhondt, *Études sur la naissance des principautés territoriales en France* (Bruges, 1948); C. Brühl, *Fodrum, Gistum, Servitium Regis* (Cologne–Graz, 1948); and J. Devisse, *Hincmar, archevêque de Reims*, 3 vols. (Geneva, 1975). Much that is good will be found in *Charles the Bald: Court and kingdom*, ed. M. Gibson and J. Nelson (BAR, 1981), most relevantly here: P. Godman, 'Latin poetry under Charles the Bald and Carolingian poetry', and R. McKitterick. 'The palace school of Charles the Bald'.

On art: D. Bullough, 'Imagines Regum and their significance in the early medieval west', in *Studies in Memory of David Talbot Rice* (Edinburgh, 1975); E. H. Kantorowicz, 'The Carolingian king in the Bible of San Paolo fuori le mura', in *Selected Studies* (New York, 1965), pp. 82–94; S. Lewis, 'A Byzantine Virgo Militans at Charlemagne's court', *Viator*, xi (1980); R. Deshman, 'The exalted servant: the ruler theology of the prayerbook of Charles the Bald', ibid.; V. Leroquais, *Les Psautiers manuscrits latins des bibliothèques publiques de France*, 3 vols. (Paris, 1940–1) ii, no. 314 for Charles' psalter; F. Mütherich and J. E. Gaehde, *Carolingian Painting* (London, 1977); conts. of Mütherich, Schramm and Weitzmann in *La cattedra lignea di S. Pietro in Vaticano* (App. iii of *Atti della Pontificia Accademia Romana di Archeologia*, series iii, Memorie, x, Vatican 1971); and D. Lohrmann, 'Trois palais royaux de la vallée de l'Oise d'après les travaux des érudits mauristes: Compiègne, Choisy-au-Bac et Quierzy', *Francia*, 4 (1976).

Dealing with special themes: J. Nelson, 'National synods, kingship as office and royal anointing: an early medieval syndrome', *Studies in Church History*, vii, *Councils and Assemblies* (Cambridge, 1971); C. A. Bouman, *Sacring and Crowning* (Groningen, 1957); U. Penndorf, *Das Problem der Reichseinheitsidee nach der Teilung von Verdun* (Munich, 1974); E. H. Kantorowicz, *Laudes Regiae* (Berkeley and Los Angeles, 1946) for Natales Caesarum; O. G. Oexle, 'Die Karolinger und die Stadt des heiligen Arnulf', FMSt, i (1967); J. Fleckenstein, *Die Hofkapelle der deutschen Könige,* i (Stuttgart, 1959); E. Ewig, 'Das Bild Constantins des Grossen in den ersten Jahrhunderten des abendländischen Mittelalters', repr. in *Spätantikes und Fränkisches Gallien*, i (Munich, 1976); and O. Eberhardt, *Via Regia* (Munich, 1977). G. Tessier, *Recueil des actes de Charles II le Chauve*, contains the king's numerous charters for churches and religious houses.

CHAPTER XIV: REFORM AND ITS APPLICATION

i. *Legislation and Exhortation*

The essential analysis of the sources used in this chapter is C. de Clercq, *La Législation religieuse franque*, i (Louvain–Paris, 1936) and ii (Antwerp, 1958). P. Fournier and G. Le Bras, *Histoire des collections canoniques en occident*, i (Paris, 1931) is important for the ninth century but is supplemented on the secular side by R. Buchner, *Die Rechtsquellen* (Beiheft to Wattenbach-Levison, Deutschlands Geschichtsquellen, Weimar, 1953) and F. L. Ganshof, *Recherches sur les capitulaires* (Paris, 1958). Reference should also be made to R. McKitterick, *The Frankish Church and the Carolingian Reforms* (London, 1977), chap. i.

On particular problems and aspects: F. L. Ganshof, 'Observations sur le synode de Francfort de 794', in *Miscellanea Historica Alberti de Meyer* (Louvain, 1946); E. Seckel, 'Studien zu Benediktus Levita', NA 26–41 (1900–16), fundamental for more than Benediktus; J. Devisse, *Hincmar*, especially for the legal aspects of Lothar II's divorce proceedings and the quarrel of the Hincmars; W. Goffart, *The Le Mans Forgeries*, for the embroglio over St Calais; H. Fuhrmann, *Einfluss und Verbreitung der pseudoisidorischen Fälschungen*, 3 vols. (Schriften der MGH, vol. 24, i, Stuttgart, 1972–4) is a masterly study, though W. Ullmann, *A History of Political Thought, the Middle Ages* (Harmondsworth, 1965) neatly summarizes the essentials of Pseudo-Isidore; and see also Ullmann's 'Public welfare and social legislation in the early medieval councils', *Studies in Church History*, 7 (Cambridge, 1971), repr. in his *The Church and the Law in the Earlier Middle Ages* (London, 1975).

ii. *The Bishops and Reform*

R. McKitterick, *The Frankish Church and the Carolingian Reforms, 789–895* (London, 1977) assesses the ways in which reform was attempted and is particularly useful on *statuta*, sermons and *florilegia*. Dom G. Dix, *The Shape of the Liturgy* (London, 1945) is valuable on the Frankish contribution to liturgical development. On penance, see C. Vogel, 'La réforme liturgique sous Charlemagne', *Karl der Grosse*, ii (Das geistige Leben) and *La discipline pénitentielle en Gaule des origines à la fin du viie siècle* (Paris, 1952); also, for sources in translation, J. T. McNeill and H. M. Gamer, *Medieval Handbooks of Penance* (Columbia, 1938, repr. 1965). G. Constable, *Monastic Tithes* (Cambridge, 1964) covers the subject. F. J. Felten, *Äbte und Laienäbte im Frankenreich*, is rich in information on Carolingian relations with abbots of any kind. W. Metz, *Das karolingische Reichsgut* (Berlin, 1960) provides the necessary background to monastic polyptychs. K. Voigt, *Die karolingische Klosterpolitik* (Stuttgart, 1917) remains a seminal study.

On more confined topics see: W. A. Eckhardt, *Die Kapitularien-sammlung Bischof Ghaerbalds von Lüttich* (Germanenrechte, Neue Folge, Deutschrechtl. Archiv 5, Göttingen, 1955); H. Barré, *Les Homéliaires carolingiens de l'école d'Auxerre* (Rome, 1962); E. Bishop, *Liturgica Historica*, pt. i, ch. 2, for the history of the altar; R. Kottje, *Die Bussbücher Halitgars von Cambrai und des Hrabanus Maurus* (Berlin, 1980); L. Genicot, 'Sur le domaine de St Bertin à l'époque carolingienne', *Rev. d'Hist. Ecclés.* lxxi, 1976 for an assessment of Ganshof's edn. of the polyptych; P. le Maître, 'L'œuvre d'Aldric du Mans et sa signification, 832–857', *Francia*, viii (1980) on Aldric as a reforming diocesan; J. Devisse, *Hincmar*, on episcopal control of the parishes of Reims; and *Mönchtum, Episkopat und Adel zur Gründungszeit des Klosters Reichenau*, ed. A. Borst (Sigmaringen, 1974), which is not confined to Reichenau.

iii. *An Exemplary Bishop: Hincmar*

All aspects of Hincmar's career are discussed exhaustively by J. Devisse, *Hincmar, archevêque de Reims*, 3 vols. (Geneva, 1977) and the legal side in *Hincmar et la loi* (Dakar, 1962). H. Schrörs, *Hinkmar, Erzbischof von Reims* (Freiburg, 1884) remains valuable. Particular aspects are treated by the following: J. Fleckenstein, 'Die Struktur des Hofes Karls des Grossen im Spiegel von Hinkmars De ordine palatii', *Zeitschr. des Aachener Geschicht-*

svereins, 83 (1976); Janet L. Nelson, 'Kingship, law and liturgy in the political thought of Hincmar of Rheims', *Engl. Hist. Rev.* 92 (1977); E. S. Duckett, ch. vii of *Carolingian Portraits* (Ann Arbor, 1962); H. Fuhrmann, *Einfluss und Verbreitung*, for Hincmar's use of Pseudo-Isidore; Y. Congar, *L'Ecclésiologie du haut moyen âge* (Paris, 1968) pp. 164 ff. for Hincmar's ecclesiology; C. Brühl, 'Hinkmariana', *Deutsches Archiv*, 20 (1964); M. Jacquin, 'Hincmar et Saint Augustin', *Mélanges C. Moeller* (Louvain, 1914); M. David, *La Souveraineté et les limites juridiques du pouvoir monarchique du ixe au xve siècles* (Paris, 1954); C. A. Bouman, *Sacring and crowning* (Groningen, 1957) on Hincmar's liturgical work; H. G. J. Beck, 'Canonical election to suffragan bishoprics according to Hincmar of Rheims', *Cath. Hist. Rev.* 43 (1957), and 'The selection of bishops suffragan to Hincmar of Rheims', ibid. 45 (1959); E. Perels, 'Ein Denkschrift Hinkmars im Prozess Rothads von Soissons', NA 44 (1922). I have glanced at Hincmar's approach to the past in 'History in the mind of Archbishop Hincmar'. *The Writing of History in the Middle Ages, Essays presented to R. W. Southern*, edd. R. H. C. Davis and J. M. W-H. (Oxford, 1981), and reprinted 'Archbishop Hincmar and the authorship of Lex Salica' in *The Long-Haired Kings* (London, 1962).

CHAPTER XV: THE USES OF LEARNING

i. *A Classical Scholar: Lupus of Ferrières*

An excellent conspectus of Lupus' achievement is R. J. Gariépy, 'Lupus, Carolingian scribe and critic', *Med. Studies,* 30 (1968), and, in a general setting, L. D. Reynolds and N. G. Wilson, *Scribes and Scholars* (2nd edn, Oxford, 1974). C. H. Beeson, *Servatus Lupus as Scribe and Text Critic* (Med. Acad. of America, 1930) has a facsimile of Lupus' copy of *De Oratore*. P. Riché, *Écoles et enseignement*, places him in the context of Carolingian education. See also Riché's 'Les bibliothèques de trois aristocrates laics carolingiens', *Le Moyen Âge,* 1963, pp. 87–104, for Eberhard's booklist. Spoleto xxii (1975), La cultura antica nell'occidente latino dal vii all'xi secolo, includes: B. Bischoff, 'Paläeographie und frühmittelalterliche Klassikerüberlieferung'; A. Vernet, 'La transmission des textes en France'; J. Irigoin, 'La culture grecque dans l'occident latin du viie au xie siècle'; G. Vinay, 'Letteratura antica e letteratura latina altomedievale'; and C. Leonardi, 'I commenti altomedievali ai classici pagani da Severino Boezio a Remigio d'Auxerre' – all relevant to the place of Lupus among early medieval scholars. E. S. Duckett, *Carolingian Portraits*, paints an efficient picture of the man. W. Edelstein, *Eruditio und sapientia* (Freiburg im Breisgau, 1965) examines two central concepts of Carolingian learning. P. Meyvaert, 'Bede the scholar', *Famulus Christi*, ed. G. Bonner (London, 1976) reveals Bede's textual expertise as a precursor of Lupus, and on the same subject see J. Gribomont, 'Conscience philologique chez les scribes du haut moyen âge', Spoleto, x (1963). W. Levison, 'Ein Predigt des Lupus von Ferrières', repr. in *Aus rheinischer und fränkischer Frühzeit*, publishes a sermon of Lupus on St Josse. M. L. W. Laistner, *Thought and Letters*, p. 213, provides a convenient translation of Paul Albar's diatribe against the liberal arts, with not all of which Lupus would have disagreed.

ii. *Scholarship, the Bible and the Liturgy:*
Hraban Maur, Walahfrid, Amalar

General studies of importance are: B. Bischoff, 'Wendepunkte in der Geschichte der lateinischen Exegese im Frühenmittelalter', *Mittelalt. Studien* i, pp. 205–73; P. Lehmann, 'The Benedictine Order and the transmission of the literature of ancient Rome in the middle ages', *Erforschung des Mittelalters*, iii, pp. 173–83; R. Kottje, *Studien zum Einfluss des Alten Testamentes auf Recht und Liturgie des frühen Mittelalters* (Bonn, 1970); and W. Schlesinger, 'Die Auflösung des Karlsreiches', *Karl der Grosse*, i, pp. 792–857.

On Hraban: Maria Rissel, *Rezeption antiker und patristischer Wissenschaft bei Hrabanus Maurus* (Bern–Frankfurt, 1976); P. Lehmann, 'Zu Hrabans geistige Bedeutung', *Erforschung*, iii, pp. 198–212; D. Schaller, 'Der junge "Rabe" am Hof Karls des Grossen (Theodulf carmina 27)', *Festschrift Bernhard Bischoff* (Stuttgart, 1971), pp. 123–41; R. Kottje, *Die Bussbücher Halitgars von Cambrai und des Hrabanus Maurus* (Berlin–New York, 1980); J. Murphy, *Rhetoric in the Middle Ages* (California, 1974), pp. 82 ff. for Hraban.

On Walahfrid: E. S. Duckett, *Carolingian Portraits*, has chapters on Walahfrid and Amalar; D. A. Traill, *Walahfrid Strabo's Visio Wettini* (Bern, 1974); B. Bischoff, 'Eine Sammelhandschrift Walahfrid Strabos (Cod. Sangall. 878)', *Mittelalt. Studien*, ii, pp. 34–51, with plates showing Walahfrid's handwriting in his *vademecum*; G. Bernt, 'Die Quellen zu Walahfrids Mammes-Leben', *Festschr. Bischoff*, pp. 142–52; Johanne Autenrieth, 'Heitos Prosaniederschrift der Visio Wettini – von Walahfrid Strabo redigiert?', *Festschrift Heinz Löwe*, pp. 172–8 (Cologne, 1978).

The essential study of Amalar is the introduction to Hanssens's edition, in vol. i.

iii. *Collective Learning: the Eastern Courts and Centres*

The fundamental studies of ninth-century books, libraries and scriptoria are those of Bernhard Bischoff; in particular, with J. Hofmann, *Libri Sancti Kiliani* (Würzburg, 1962) for Würzburg; *Die südostdeutschen Schreibschulen und Bibliotheken in der Karolingerzeit*, i (Wiesbaden, 1960) for dioceses of Augsburg, Eichstätt, Freising, Regensburg, and vol. ii (Wiesbaden, 1980) for Passau, Salzburg and Säben-Brixen; *Lorsch im Spiegel seiner Handschriften* (Munich, 1974, repr. from vol. ii of *Die Reichsabtei Lorsch, Festschrift zum Gedenken an ihre Stiftung*, ed. F. Knöpp, 1973–7); and 'Literarisches und künstlerisches Leben in St Emmeram (Regensburg) während des frühen und hohen Mittelalters', repr. in *Mittelalt. Studien*, ii. On Fulda: *Die Klostergemeinschaft von Fulda im früheren Mittelalter*, ed. K. Schmid, 5 vols. (Munich, 1978); M. Parisse, 'La communauté monastique de Fulda', *Francia*, 7 (1979); E. E. Stengel, *Urkundenbuch des Klosters Fulda* (Marburg, 1958); and

P. Lehmann, 'Die alte Klosterbibliothek Fulda und ihre Bedeutung', *Erforschung des Mittelalters*, i (Stuttgart, 1959). On St Gallen: J. M. Clark, *The Abbey of St Gall as a Centre of Literature and Art* (Cambridge, 1926); W. Horn and E. Born, *The Plan of St Gall*, 3 vols. (California, 1979) and Paul Meyvaert's review in *University Publishing*, no. 9 (Summer, 1980), which has given rise to further discussion; and G. Noll, 'The origin of the so-called plan of St Gall', *Journ. Med. Hist.* 8 (1982). On Notker: W. von den Steinen, *Notker der Dichter und seine geistige Welt* (1948), and H. Löwe, 'Das Karlsbuch Notkers von St Gallen und seine zeitgeschichtlicher Hintergrund', *Schweizerische Zeitsch. für Geschichte*, 20, iii (1970). On Reichenau: *Die Kultur der Abtei Reichenau*, 2 vols., ed. K. Beyerle (Munich, 1925; repr. Aalen 1970), and P. Lehmann, 'Die mittelalterliche Bibliothek der Reichenau', *Erforschung*, iv (Stuttgart, 1961); *Mönchtum, Episkopat und Adel zur Gründungszeit des Klosters Reichenau*, ed. A. Borst (Sigmaringen, 1974) is a collection of papers covering south German houses.

    J. Fleckenstein, *Die Hofkapelle der deutschen Könige*, i (Stuttgart, 1959) is indispensable, and take with it W. Koehler and F. Mütherich, *Die Hofschule Kaiser Lothars, Einzelhandschriften aus Lotharingien* (Die karolingischen Miniaturen, iv, Berlin, 1971). H. H. Anton, *Fürstenspiegel und Herrscherethos in der Karolingerzeit* (Bonn, 1968), pp. 261–81 for Sedulius; Maria Rissel, *Rezeption antiker und patristischer Wissenschaft bei Hrabanus Maurus* (Bern–Frankfurt, 1976); and G. Vinay, 'Letteratura antica e latina alto-medievale', Spoleto, xxii (1975) for poetry as relief.

iv. Collective Learning: The West

St Riquier: in addition to Lot's introduction to his edition of Hariulf see his 'Nouvelles recherches sur le texte de la chronique de l'abbaye de Saint-Riquier', repr. in *Recueil des travaux historiques* (Geneva–Paris, 1968), i, pp. 608–29; J. Hubert, 'Saint-Riquier et le monachisme bénédictin en Gaule à l'époque carolingienne', Spoleto, iv (1957), pp. 293–309; F. Prinz, *Frühes Mönchtum*; B. Bischoff, 'Panorama der Handschriftenüberlieferung aus der Zeit Karls des Grossen' and J. Semmler, 'Karl der Grosse und das fränkische Mönchtum' in *Karl der Grosse*, ii (Das geistige Leben); E. Lesne, *Hist. de la propriété éccles.* iv (Les Livres), pp. 229 ff;

    St Wandrille: F. Lot, *Études critiques sur l'abbaye de Saint-Wandrille* (Paris, 1913); Lesne, iv, pp. 582 ff.; P. Grierson, 'Abbot Fulco and the date of the Gesta abbatum Fontanellensium', *Engl. Hist. Rev.* 55 (1940), pp. 275–84; W. Levison, 'Zu den Gesta abbatum Fontanellensium', repr. in *Aus rheinischer und fränkischer Frühzeit*, pp. 530–50.

    Corbie: B. Bischoff, 'Hadoard und die Klassikerhandschriften aus Corbie', repr. in *Mittelalt. Studien*, i, pp. 49–63; D. Ganz, 'The Merovingian library of Corbie', *Columbanus and Merovingian monasticism* (BAR, 1981), pp. 153–71; O. Dobias-Rozdestvenskaia, *Histoire de l'atelier graphique de Corbie de 651 à 830 reflétée dans les manuscrits de Leningrad* (Leningrad, 1934); E. Ewig, 'Das Privileg des Bischofs Berthefrid von Amiens für Corbie von 664 und die Klosterpolitik der Königen Balthild', *Francia*, i (1973); L. Levillain, *Examen critique des chartes mérovingiennes et carolingiennes de l'abbaye de Corbie* (Paris, 1902); E. Lesne, iv, pp. 217 ff.

St Germain: R. Poupardin, *Recueil des chartes de l'abbaye de Saint-Germain-des-Prés*, i (Paris, 1909); *Polyptyque de l'abbaye de Saint Germain des Prés*, ed. A. Longnon, ii (Paris, 1895); W. Metz, *Das karolingische Reichsgut* (Berlin, 1960) for background; M. Roblin, *Le Terroir de Paris* (2nd edn. Paris, 1971); F. Lot, 'La grande invasion normande de 856–82', repr. in *Recueil*, ii, pp. 713–70; intro. to Waquet's edn. of Abbo; Lesne, iv, pp. 594 ff.

Fleury: for discussion of MSS, CLA vi, pp. xviii–xxi; W. Goffart, 'Le Mans, St Scholastica and the literary tradition of the translation of St Benedict', *Rev. Bén.* lxxvii (1967), pp. 107–41; P. Meyvaert, 'Peter the Deacon and the tomb of St Benedict', ibid. lxv (1955) and 'L'invention des reliques Cassiniennes de St Benoît en 1484', ibid. lxix (1959), both repr. in *Benedict, Gregory and others* (London, 1977); Lesne, iv, pp. 131 ff.

Lyon: E. A. Lowe, *Codices Lugdunenses antiquissimi* (Lyon, 1924); CLA vi, pp. xiii–xiv; A. Coville, *Recherches sur l'histoire de Lyon* (Paris, 1928); E. Boshof, *Erzbischof Agobard von Lyon* (Cologne–Vienna, 1969); O. G. Oexle, *Forschungen zu monastischen und geistlichen Gemeinschaften im westfränkischen Bereich* (Munich, 1978), pp. 134–62; C. Brühl, *Palatium und Civitas*, i (Cologne–Vienna, 1975), no. 19; Lesne iv, pp. 108–15, 513–18; H. Mordek, *Kirchenrecht und Reform im Frankenreich* (Berlin–New York, 1975).

Valuable throughout on western centres: Lesne, *Hist. de la propriété éccles.*, all six vols; Prinz, *Frühes Mönchtum*; and P. Riché, *Écoles et enseignement dans le haut moyen âge* (Paris, 1979).

v. *Deviation and Exploration*

Essential studies of ninth-century learning are: B. Bischoff, 'Das griechische Element in der abendländischen Bildung des Mittelalters', *Mittelalt. Studien*, ii, pp. 246–75, and W. Berschin, *Griechisch-lateinisches Mittelalter* (Bern, 1980).

On Corbie's contribution: J. P. Bouhot, *Ratramne de Corbie* (Paris, 1976); D. Ganz, 'The debate on predestination', *Charles the Bald, Court and Kingdom* (BAR, 1981), pp. 353–73; and J. Devisse, *Hincmar*, on Hincmar's reaction to the debate on predestination. Further to Gottschalk: J. Jolivet, *Godescalc d'Orbais et la Trinité: la méthode de la théologie à l'époque carolingienne* (Paris, 1958); Bischoff, 'Gottschalks Lied für den Reichenauer Freund', *Mittelalt. Studien*, ii, pp. 26–34; and P. von Moos, 'Gottschalks Gedicht O mi Custos – eine confessio', i, FMSt 4, pp. 201–30, and ii, FMSt 5, pp. 317–58.

Centring on Eriugena and his circle: M. Cappuyns, *Jean Scot Érigène, sa vie, son œuvre, sa pensée* (Brussels, 1964); valuable papers in *The Mind of Eriugena*, edd. J. J. O'Meara and L. Bieler (Dublin, 1973), and in *Jean Scot Érigène et l'histoire de la philosophie* (Paris, 1977); E. Jeauneau, *Quatre thèmes érigéniens* (Montreal–Paris, 1978); J. J. Contreni, The *Cathedral School of Laon from 850 to 930, its manuscripts and masters* (Munich, 1978); J. Marenbon, *From the Circle of Alcuin to the School of Auxerre* (Cambridge, 1981), and 'Wulfad, Charles the Bald and John Scottus Eriugena', *Charles the Bald, Court and Kingdom*, pp.

375–83; I. P. Sheldon-Williams, 'The Greek Christian Platonist tradition from the Cappadocians to Maximus and Eriugena', *Cambridge Hist. of Later Greek and Early Medieval Philosophy*, pp. 425–533; P. Janin, 'Heiric d'Auxerre et les Gesta Pontificum Autissiodorensium', *Francia*, 4 (1976), pp. 89–105; and R. Quadri, *I Collectanea di Eirico di Auxerre* (Fribourg, 1966).

Margaret T. Gibson, 'Boethius in the Carolingian schools', *Trans. R. Hist. Soc.*, fifth series, 32 (1982).

vi. The Vernaculars

Though the revised edition of J. Knight Bostock's *Handbook on Old High German literature* (Oxford, 1976) is a reliable guide, especially for English students, to the very extensive literature on Germanic vernaculars, other guides cannot be neglected. In particular, B. Bischoff's fundamental study, 'Paläographische Fragen deutscher Denkmäler der Karolingerzeit', FMSt 5 (1971) faces more than palaeographical issues; and G. Baeseke, 'Die karlische Renaissance und das deutsche Schrifttum', *Kleinere Schriften zur althochdeutschen Sprache und Literatur*, ed. W. Schröder (Bern–Munich, 1966) is important. Also valuable is W. Betz, 'Karl der Grosse und die Lingua Theodisca', in *Karl der Grosse*, ii, *Das geistige Leben* (Düsseldorf, 1965). R. McKitterick, *The Frankish Church and the Carolingian Reforms* (London, 1977), ch. 6, is a useful summary.

On particular topics: L. Bieler, 'The Irish in the Carolingian empire', in *Ireland, Harbinger of the Middle Ages* (London, 1963); D. H. Green, *The Carolingian Lord* (Cambridge, 1965), a semantic study of some OHG words; J. M. Clark, *The Abbey of St Gall as a Centre of Literature and Art* (Cambridge, 1926); F. Delbono, 'La letteratura catechetica di lingua tedesca – Il problema della lingua nell'evangelizzazione', Spoleto, xiv (1967); B. Raw, 'The probable derivation of most of the illustrations in Junius 11 from an illustrated Old Saxon Genesis', *Anglo-Saxon England*, 5 (1976), which faces some problems of the OE Genesis and the Heliand; and on the relation of Latin to vernacular see F. Lot, 'A quelle époque a-t-on cessé de parler latin?', repr. in *Recueil des travaux historiques*, i (Geneva–Paris, 1968), and W. D. Elcock, *The Romance Languages* (London, 1960). The historical role of the vernacular is not overlooked by M. L. W. Laistner, *Thought and Letters in Western Europe, 500 to 900* (2nd edn. London, 1957).

CHAPTER XVI: THE CHURCH AND SOME UNSOLVED PROBLEMS

i. The Jews and Their Religion

Excellent background is provided by S. W. Baron, *A Social and Religious History of the Jews* (New York–Philadelphia, 1952–) and J. Parkes, *Judaism and Christianity* (London, 1948). The basic book is B. Blumenkranz, *Juifs et chrétiens dans le monde occidental, 430–1096* (Paris–The Hague, 1960), to which should be added his papers reprinted in *Juifs et chrétiens, patristique et moyen âge*

(Variorum, London, 1977). A. J. Zuckerman, *A Jewish Princedom in Feudal France, 768–900* (New York–London, 1972) is replete with interesting ideas but should be used with caution.

Particular issues are faced, and sometimes solved, by: Mgr A. Bressolles, 'La question juive au temps de Louis le Pieux', *Rev. hist. Égl. de France,* 28 (1942); A. Cabaniss, 'Bodo-Eleazar, a famous Jewish convert', *Jewish Quart. Rev.* n.s. 43 (1952–3); D. M. Dunlop, *A History of the Jewish Khazars* (Princeton, 1954); S. Katz, *The Jews in the Visigothic and Frankish Kingdoms of Spain and Gaul* (Cambridge, Mass, 1937), and 'Pope Gregory the Great and the Jews', *Jewish Quart. Rev.* n.s. 24 (1933); E. I. J. Rosenthal, 'The study of the Bible in medieval Judaism', *Camb. Hist. of the Bible,* 2, ch. vi (5); P. Wolff, 'L'Aquitaine et ses marges', *Karl der Grosse,* i; L. Auzias, *L'Aquitaine carolingienne, 778–987;* E. Lévi-Provençal, *Histoire de l'Espagne musulmane,* 3 vols. (Paris–Leiden, 1950–3); E. Boshof, *Erzbischof Agobard von Lyon;* F. X. Murphy, 'Julian of Toledo and the fall of the Visigothic kingdom in Spain', *Speculum,* 27 (1952); S. Runciman, 'Charlemagne and Palestine', *EHR* 50 (1935); C. M. Sage, *Paul Albar of Cordoba: studies on his life and writings* (Cath. Univ. of America studies in medieval history, n.s. 5, Washington DC, 1943).

I have not been able to take account of Spoleto, xxvi, 2 vols. (1980) – Gli Ebrei nell'alto medioevo.

ii. *The Church and the Marriage Bond*

The role of women in medieval society is attracting increasing attention; publications are numerous, if not always solidly based. Among those most relevant to the present chapter, a good start can be made with Spoleto, xxiv (1977): in vol. i, G. Duby, 'Le mariage dans la société du haut moyen âge', J. Gaudemet, 'Le legs du droit roman en matière matrimoniale', P. Toubert, 'La théorie du mariage chez les moralistes carolingiens', C. Vogel, 'Les rites de la célébration du mariage'; and in vol. ii, C. Verlinden, 'Le "mariage" des esclaves', and G. Fransen, 'La rupture du mariage'. *Women in Medieval Society,* ed. Susan M. Stuard (Pennsylvania, 1976) contains interesting papers, e.g. D. Herlihy, 'Land, family and women in continental Europe, 701–1200', and J.-A. McNamara and S. F. Wemple, 'Marriage and divorce in the Frankish kingdom'. D. Herlihy's reprinted papers, *The Social History of Italy and Western Europe, 700–1500* (London, 1978) include several affecting the role of women, and especially 'Land, family and women in continental Europe'. P. Riché's two books, *Éducation et culture* and *Écoles et enseignement,* contain illuminating observations on the education of women, and J. T. Noonan, *Contraception et mariage* (Paris, 1969) should not be overlooked. The following are all useful: F. L. Ganshof, 'Le statut de la femme dans la monarchie franque' (Les éditions de la librairie encyclopédique, Brussels, 1962); J. Anson, 'The female transvestite in early monasticism', *Viator,* v (1974); J. A. Brundage, 'Concubinage and marriage in medieval canon law', *Journ. Med. Hist.* i (1975); R. Metz, 'Les vierges chrétiennes en Gaule au IVᵉ siècle', *Studia Anselmiana,* 46 (Rome, 1961); in *Viator,* iv (1973), J. T. Noonan, 'Power to choose', and V. L. Bullough, 'Medieval medical and scientific views of women'; Devisse, *Hincmar*, on the archbishop's views on divorce.

iii. *Exterae Gentes*

On missions to the North: much ground is covered by L. Musset, *Les Peuples scandinaves au moyen âge* (Paris, 1951); *Les Invasions, le second assaut contre l'Europe chrétienne* (Paris, 1965); and 'La pénétration chrétienne dans l'Europe du nord et son influence sur la civilisation scandinave', Spoleto, xiv (1967). W. Lange, *Texte zur germanischen Bekehrungsgeschichte*, edits what is relevant on conversion from Rimbert and Adam of Bremen. Two papers by W. Levison on Anskar are reprinted in his *Aus rheinischer und fränkischer Frühzeit*. C. Reuter, 'Ebbo von Reims und Ansgar', *Hist. Zeitschr.* 105, is useful though polemical.

On missions to the East and South-east: E. Dümmler, *Geschichte des ostfränkischen Reiches*, 2nd edn. (Leipzig, 1887) remains the standard treatment. J. Deér, 'Karl der Grosse und der Untergang des Awarenreiches', *Karl der Grosse*, i (Personlichkeit und Geschichte) is valuable, and so too H. Büttner, 'Christentum und Kirche zwischen Neckar und Main im 7 und frühen 8 Jhdt.', *Sankt Bonifatius Gedenkgabe*. B. Bischoff, *Die südostdeutschen Schreibschulen und Bibliotheken in der Karolingerzeit* (Wiesbaden, 2 vols., 1960, 1980) is much more than a study of MSS. Equally significant is H. Löwe, *Die karolingische Reichsgründung und der Südosten* (Stuttgart, 1937). Specifically on Bavaria: B. Romuald, *Kirchengeschichte Bayerns* i (St Ottilien, 1949); I. Zibermayr, *Noricum, Baiern und Österreich*, 2nd edn. (Horn, 1956) discusses conversion from the monastery of Lorch (not Lorsch); K. Reindel, 'Das Zeitalter der Agilolfinger', *Handbuch der bayerischen Geschichte*, 3, (1975) outlines Agilolfing missionary enterprise; and Wolfram's edition of the *Conversio Bagoariorum* contains valuable commentary. On the Moravian missions see F. Dvornik, *Byzantine Missions among the Slavs* (Rutgers, NJ, 1970) and P. F. Barton, 'Die Frühzeit des Christentums in Österreich und Südostmitteleuropa bis 788', *Studien und Texte zur Kirchengeschichte und Geschichte* 1, i (1975).

Generally, both O. Eberhardt, *Via Regia* (Munich, 1977) and H. H. Anton, *Fürstenspiegel und Herrscherethos in der Karolingerzeit* (Bonn, 1968) refer to ethical problems in Christian expansion. R. Schieffer, *Die Entstehung von Domkapiteln in Deutschland* (Bonn, 1976) is important for episcopal penetration of Saxony.

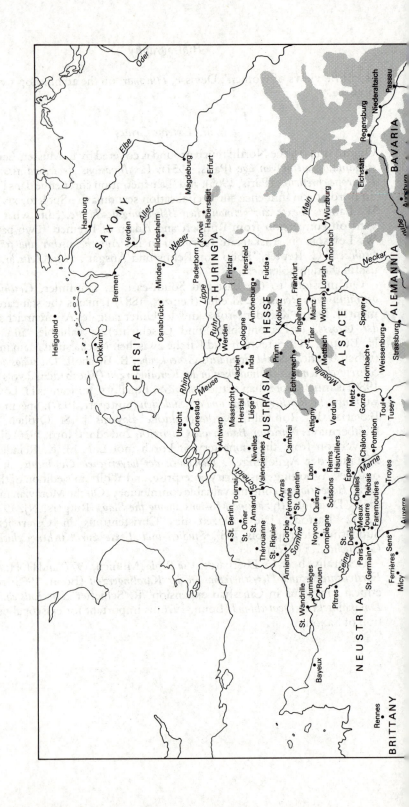

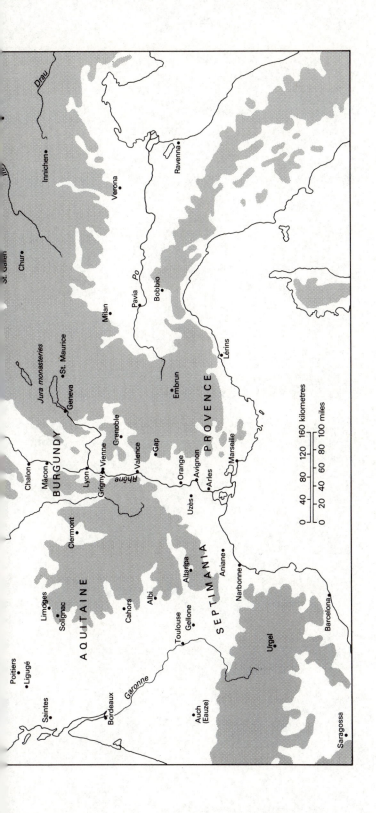

INDEX

DATE DUE

NOV 2 0 1989